# Third Edition

# PSYCHOTROPIC DRUGS FAST FACTS

D0395391

A NORTON PROFESSIONAL BOOK

# Third Edition

# PSYCHOTROPIC DRUGS FAST FACTS

**Jerrold S. Maxmen, M.D.**
**Nicholas G. Ward, M.D.**
**Special Advisor to**
**Third Edition,**
**Steven L. Dubovsky, M.D.**

W. W. Norton & Company · New York · London

NOTICE
We have made every attempt to summarize accurately and concisely a multitude of references. However, the reader is reminded that times and medical knowledge change, transcription or understanding error is always possible, and crucial details are omitted whenever such a comprehensive distillation as this is attempted in limited space. We cannot, therefore, guarantee that every bit of information is absolutely accurate or complete. The reader should affirm that cited recommendations are still appropriate by reading the original articles and checking other sources including local consultants and recent literature.

DRUG DOSAGE
The authors and publisher have exerted every effort to ensure that drug selection and dosage set forth in this text are in accord with current recommendations and practice at the time of publication. However, in view of ongoing research, changes in government regulations, and the constant flow of information relating to drug therapy and drug reactions, the reader is urged to check the package insert for each drug for any change in indications and dosage and for added warnings and precautions. This is particularly important when the recommended agent is a new and/or infrequently used drug.

**Library of Congress Cataloging-in-Publication Data**
Maxmen, Jerrold S.
    Psychotropic drugs : fast facts / Jerrold S. Maxmen, Nicholas G. Ward. — 3rd ed. / special advisor, Steven L. Dubovsky.
        p. ; cm.
    "A Norton professional book."
    Includes bibliographical references and index.
    **ISBN 0-393-70301-0 (pbk.)**
    1. Psychotropic drugs—Handbooks, manuals, etc.   I. Ward, Nicholas G.   II. Dubovsky, Steven L.   III. Title.
    [DNLM: 1. Psychotropic Drugs—Handbooks.   QV 39 M464p 2002]
RM315.M355   2002
615'.788—dc21        2002016688

W. W. Norton & Company, Inc., 500 Fifth Avenue, New York, N.Y. 10110
www.wwnorton.com

W. W. Norton & Company Ltd., Castle House, 75/76 Wells Street,
London W1T 3QT

1   2   3   4   5   6   7   8   9   0

*To those who have gone before:*

Jere, whose spirit lives on in those whom he knew, and whose words and thoughts live on in his books.

My brother Jeff and my father, who were my first guides and teachers.

*To those who are present:*

My mother, Eleanor, and my brothers Ned, Corry, and Dick; Jean, Galen, and Joanna for their love, support, and patience even when the "book" became a four-letter word; Mimi, Jere's wife; and my patients who taught me so much about being human.

*And to those to come . . .*

Nicholas G. Ward

To Anne Dubovsky.

Steven L. Dubovsky

"The village doctor was a great success. His success was due to his sympathy with his patients, each of whom he treated as an individual with an idiosyncracy of his own and worthy of special and separate consideration. It was as if, instead of giving everyone mass-produced medicine, he had molded the portrait of each on his pill."

—Oliver St. John Gogarty

# Introduction
# to the First Edition

Wisdom arrived one afternoon. Drs. Donald F. Klein and John M. Davis' brand-new 1969 *Diagnosis and Drug Treatment of Psychiatric Disorders* came by mail. The book was splendid. Yet what electrified were pages 96 and 97, which listed the percentage of side effects of ten antipsychotics. Granted, four neuroleptics were now obsolete, and a fifth was for vomiting. Nevertheless, I was the only psychiatric resident to possess these cherished numbers.

Cherished? Well, although they were not exactly psychoanalytic theory or pharmacologic conjecture, they did reveal that chlorpromazine disturbed menstruation 16.3% of the time, thioridazine induced akathisia 8.9% of the time, and perphenazine blurred vision 17.8% of the time. When I met a patient who feared a dry mouth on neuroleptics, page 96 told me whether trifluoperazine, fluphenazine, or perphenazine caused it the least.[1]

Were these two pages number-crunching? Definitely. Were the data skewed, outmoded, or dead wrong? Occasionally. Did these figures cover vast territory? Absolutely. (Klein's second edition of the book jokes that chlorpromazine sedates 9–92% of the time.) Nonetheless, patients *do* want to know which medications cause more weight

---

[1] It's trifluoperazine at 2.3%

By the way, there was also page 229, but it was less cherished. Although affording side-effect percentages for antidepressants, it displayed *broad* numbers—imipramine gave dry mouth 10–30% of the time, tranylcypromine triggered dizziness 5–20% of the time. Broad figures were common sense, but that fluphenazine on page 96 induced hypotension precisely 0.79% of the time—that was enlightenment

gain and which ones reduce libido; and clinicians *should* know the answers. With Klein and Davis, I finally had some informed answers.

For 16 years, Klein and Davis stuck to me. When I wrote a textbook in 1985, I wanted it stuffed with pages 96 and 97. Yet I quickly discovered that this was exasperating: Data diverged, disagreed, and didn't exist. Instead, I wrote a "normal" textbook.

Even still, this idea of a "dictionary of details" continued. For routine clinical work, I wanted *one* place to get the *facts*. I was tired of hunting through a dozen books to unearth a mere fact: the half-life of protriptyline versus nortriptyline, the dose of amoxapine versus bupropion, or the cost of triazolam versus quazepam. What's more, new drugs kept arising; *Newsweek* announced them; so would patients. I heard too often, "I want Prozac." But aside from what pharmaceutical houses told me, or the *PDR* (written by the drug companies) told me, or even what Ted Koppel told me, I did not know whether Prozac sedated more or less than doxepin, amitriptyline, or clomipramine. I needed one source with all this information. What I wanted was not a textbook that explains everything, but a single reference. I wanted *Fast Facts*.

Norton obliged.

*Fast Facts* simply presents the facts of clinical psychopharmacology. It describes nine categories of medications: antipsychotics, anticholinergics, antidepressants, MAOIs, lithium, anticonvulsants, antianxiety agents, hypnotics, and stimulants. Every chapter details the drugs' names, forms, pharmacologies, dosages, indications, predictors, clinical applications, therapeutic levels, outcomes, alternatives, side effects (and their percentages), pregnancy and lactation data, drug/food interactions, adverse response in children, the elderly, and the sick, medication alterations of laboratory studies, withdrawal hazards, overdoses (and remedies), toxicities, suicide potentials, precautions, contraindications, nurses' information, patients' concerns, and costs. And yet, with all this information, this drug almanac still posed problems.

*Fast Facts* is a Book Without Verbs (BWV). (I do not consider "increase" and "decrease" to be verbs, but attitudes. Excoriate, guffaw, swoon, and sashay—these are verbs.) Good writing, "good-writing" manuals tell me, highlights good verbs. If so, a BWV could be very dull. I hope it will inform and stimulate.

A bigger dilemma was the same number problem faced by Klein and Davis. The literature bursts with scientific "facts"; numbers conflict, contradict, and confuse; they measure similar, but different, parameters; they lie. Correct numbers can be "incorrect," as when the "correct" dose can be incorrect for a particular patient. Definitions baffle. If I write that a drug generates weight gain, how much weight has to be gained? The criteria depend on the pounds increased, the period's duration, the person's size, etc. Aside from how carefully a scientist defined dizziness, how could I reconcile dissimilar "truths," as when researcher A found dizziness in 47 of 100 patients while researcher B uncovered it in 5 out of 1,000 patients? These problems are endless. Ultimately, I did what most authors do: I reviewed the printed material, averaged the findings, factored in personal experience, and compromised on the best clinical information. For the errors, I alone bear responsibility. Nevertheless, some people really helped. Drs. Greg Dalack, Brian Fallon, Laurence Greenhill, David Kahn, Neil Kavey, Ron Rieder, Holly Schneier, Michael Sheehy, and David Strauss made suggestions that greatly improved the book.

The enclosed data are generalizations: they do not, or could not, suit every patient under all circumstances. Patients are allergic to drugs, react atypically to the same agents, and respond paradoxically to others. Moreover, the doses, neurotransmitter actions, and other specifications must be altered to the newest scientific developments and tapered to specific patient's requirements.

Although *Fast Facts* focuses on drugs, this does not mean that only drugs are effective. Medications function best to alleviate specific *symptoms* (e.g., delusions, panic attacks). Psychotherapy, in contrast, functions best to resolve specific *issues* (e.g., marital fights); issues may accompany, cause, or result from symptoms. Psychotherapy addresses the content of symptoms (e.g., "the homeless spy on me"). Psychotherapy clarifies how medications reduce symptoms (e.g., "I understand why I'm taking this drug"). Psychotherapy puts life into perspective (e.g., "My elevator phobia is fearsome, but my wife is fantastic!"). Psychotherapy explores how to behave with a mental disorder (e.g., to tell one's husband, not one's boss, about hallucinating). If one had diabetes, a medication, insulin, would reduce blood sugar; a self-help group, a psychotherapy, would discuss the stresses of living with diabetes. Insulin and a self-help group do not conflict, but serve different, albeit complementary, purposes. The same applies for psychotropic drugs and psychotherapy. To compare the two is akin to asking whether the length *or* the width of a football field determines its size.

In short, *Psychotropic Drugs: Fast Facts* is an up-to-date reference with tables and charts for psychiatrists, psychologists, nurses, social workers, activities therapists, internists, psychotherapists, and anyone I forgot. It is *not* a beginner's manual or a "how to prescribe" book, but a comprehensive guide for experienced clinicians. Enjoy this BWV.

Jerrold S. Maxmen, M.D.
New York, January 1991

# Introduction
# to the Second Edition

*Fast Facts* continues to be a work in progress, even four years after the publication of the first edition. Fortunately, this second edition was revised just following the FDA's approval of a wave of new drugs. Important changes were being incorporated even as the book was being typeset. One area, drug interactions (especially the P450 enzyme system), is expanding so quickly and complexly that a new appendix was created to keep them straight. As you read this, remember the pharmacology maxim, "All drugs have at least 2 effects: those that we know about (a short list) and those that we don't know about (a long list)."

Many people were very helpful. Donald Klein provided a 17-page letter to Jere that was passed on to me containing page-by-page critiques of the first edition. It proved to be invaluable. Gary Tucker took the initiative to be the matchmaker for me with Norton Professional Books. David Dunner, Daniel Casey, Alan Unis, Arifulla Khan, Phil Hantsen, Nelda Murri, and Karen Hansen generously provided valuable critiques and information. Leslie McEwen tirelessly typed seemingly endless revisions of chapters. She did a superb job and is even better at singing opera professionally. I am also thankful to my editor at Norton, Susan Munro, the editor's editor. She also put me in touch with Margaret Ryan, who undauntingly waded through the tables, lists, and phrases without verbs looking for flaws and potential improvements, and Christi Albouy, who got the manuscript ready for the printers.

Nicholas G. Ward, M.D.
Seattle, June 1995

# Introduction to the Third Edition

With the continuing development of psychopharmacology, *Psychotropic Drugs: Fast Facts* continues to grow. New areas, such as cholinesterase inhibitors, contribute to the valuable expansion of treatments. It is my hope that the information presented here is easily understood and assessed.

Many people have been helpful in this endeavor. Many thanks to Shawn Zeimet, who has been invaluable in getting this edition together, and Dick Miyoshi, our pharmacologist, who continues to be a walking computer giving valuable information quickly and accurately. Then thanks to Carl Brandt, who is unfailingly helpful and supportive, and to Margaret Ryan, who continues to undauntingly wade through each chapter to insure accuracy.

Nicholas G. Ward, M.D.
July, 2001

As information in psychopharmacology explodes, clinicians must master increasingly complex information about new medications, new applications of existing medications, and the growing potential for adverse effects and interactions. This book organizes and presents data the clinician needs to choose the right treatment for common psychiatric problems and to anticipate and deal with problems that arise in treatment. Published material deemed by the authors to be relevant to clinical practice is summarized concisely so that the reader can have the latest material available. Details of individual medications are summarized in convenient charts and tables.

The authors have tried to ensure that all the information in this book is up-to-date and is presented to maximize its clinical utility. However, in any field as complex and fluid as modern psychopharmacology, the reader must evaluate the information critically and remain aware of new developments. We are confident that *Psychotropic Drugs: Fast Facts, Third Edition* will prove to be a useful starting point in guiding current treatment and future study for clinicians at any level of experience and expertise.

Steven L. Dubovsky, M.D.
November, 2001

# Organization

Each chapter contains 16 sections—give or take a few depending on the circumstances. Here are some details:

## INTRODUCTION

This section presents the general category of medications, their broad indications, the disorders they treat in this and other chapters. It's a traffic guide.

## NAMES, CLASSES, MANUFACTURERS, DOSE FORMS, AND COLORS

Only drugs currently sold in the United States are listed.

## PHARMACOLOGY

This part sketches a medicine's basic clinical pharmacology: its absorption, distribution, metabolism, and elimination. Several terms are often employed:

- *Bioavailability* is the percentage of an oral dose that can act pharmacologically.
- *Plasma Binding* is the percentage of drug bound clinically to plasma proteins.
- *Volume of Distribution* (liters/kg) is the total body volume of distribution at the steady-state level in the plasma.
- *Half-life*, usually expressed in hours, is when 50% of the drug has been eliminated. The book's figures usually represent the drug's major active fractions, including metabolites; the broader numbers in parentheses are ranges.

- *Excretion* is typically the percent of drug unchanged in the urine.

## DOSES

Described here are the standard doses, ranges, initial dosages, therapeutic serum levels, drug amounts for different age groups, and so on.

## CLINICAL INDICATIONS AND USE

This section conveys when a drug is specifically indicated. It addresses what can predict a drug's clinical potential, how to employ these medications practically, when (and how) to use different forms of the drug, what to do when problems arise, how to maintain and terminate these agents, and how to apply these drugs for other conditions.

## SIDE EFFECTS

This section affords a reasonably comprehensive, but not complete, description of side effects and what to do about them. Although these agents are presented under organ categories, this does not suggest that each side effect belongs exclusively to a single system. Weight gain of any cause was placed under "Gastrointestinal." Categories are for convenience.

## PERCENTAGES OF SIDE EFFECTS

This section offers the incidence of specific drug side effects. The first number is the best average we could determine from the literature, whereas the parenthesized number is the range of these side effects. We have only included ranges that we thought might clarify a side effect's frequency. For instance, if the average is 18%, but the range is 10–90%, this suggests that most of the side effects are usually closer to 10%.

For uniformity's sake, and also because most studies don't display placebo comparisons, these percentages include placebo findings. The sign "—" occurs throughout these tables and refers to the nonexistence of information and not to the nonexistence of the side effect. If, under vomiting, three drugs are —, —, and 5.5, this does not mean that only the third drug causes vomiting. The other two might, or might not, but there are no data to decide. If a study has demonstrated that a drug does not create a problem, the chart reads "0.0." The enclosed numbers reflect both exact percentages (e.g., 13.7%) and broad ranges (e.g., 10–30%).

The chief aim here is to compare the frequency of adverse reactions. People will have no trouble finding exceptions to these figures. If you find some, please send them along.

## PREGNANCY AND LACTATION

This section summarizes these agents' adverse effects in utero, on newborns, and from breast milk.

The *Milk/Plasma Ratio* underscores that milk and plasma drug concentrations are not parallel throughout breast-feeding.

The *Time of Peak Concentration in Milk* is the hours between the medication's ingestion until it peaks in the milk. It is generally safest to feed the infant at the trough of maternal plasma concentration—that is, just prior to the next dose—to minimize the baby's ingestion of the drug.

*Infant Dose* ($\mu$g/kilogram/day) is calculated from peak milk concentrations, unless stated otherwise. It represents the maximum likely exposure the child has to the drug.

*Maternal Dose Percentage* is the infant dose compared to the maternal dose controlled for weight.

Safety Rating conveys how relatively safe it is for a mother to consume a drug while breast-feeding during the first year.

## DRUG-DRUG INTERACTIONS

This section indicates the major drug interactions with psychotropic agents. This list is thorough, but not complete; it stresses clinical effects and interventions, not mechanisms.

## EFFECTS ON LABORATORY TESTS

This section outlines how these medications influence laboratory tests.

## WITHDRAWAL

If problems emerge on withdrawal of the drug, this section depicts what happens and what to do about them.

ORGANIZATION

## OVERDOSE: TOXICITY, SUICIDE, AND TREATMENT

This section portrays clinical overdose symptoms, gives toxic and suicide blood levels, signifies how many days' supply can be lethal, outlines drug-abuse signs and how to remedy intoxications and overdoses.

## PRECAUTIONS

When should a drug *not* be taken? That's addressed here—the contraindications and dangers clinicians should exercise when prescribing these medications.

## NURSES' DATA

Much of what has already been written will be of great assistance to all staff, including nurses, but this section informs staff about observing patients on medication, showing them how to handle side effects, and using the various dose forms of the drug.

## PATIENT AND FAMILY NOTES

This book is written for professionals, not laymen. This section affords the key information staff should insure patients receive: whether to consume medications in relation to meals, how to deal with forgetting a dose, how to cope with immediate side effects, when to call a doctor regarding a crisis, etc.

If one member of a family is affected by a mental disorder, all members are affected. Some of these concerns, therefore, are for the entire family.

## APPENDICES

*Two drug identification guides,* describing the major action of all drugs mentioned in the book and "translations" between generic and brand names.

*A symptom checklist,* to be given to patients before and during their drug-taking to see which symptoms arose before or after the drug was begun.

*P450 enzyme system drug interactions*

*The bibliography* of this book provides these data.

# ABBREVIATIONS

| | |
|---|---|
| ACA | Anticholinergic agents |
| Ach | Acetylcholine |
| AD | Antidepressant |
| ADR | Adverse drug reaction |
| AV | atioventricular |
| bid | Twice a day |
| CBC | Complete blood count |
| d | Days |
| D/S | Dextrose and saline |
| D/W | Dextrose and water |
| DST | Dexamethasone suppression test |
| ECG | Electrocardiogram |
| ECT | Electroconvulsive therapy |
| EEG | Electroencephalogram |
| EPS | Extrapyramidal side effects |
| EUCD | Emotionally unstable character disorder |
| g | Gram |
| GABA | Gamma-aminobutyric acid |
| GAD | Generalized anxiety disorder |
| h | Hours |
| Hg | mercury |
| h/o | History of |
| HCAs | Heterocyclic antidepressants (includes TCAs, maprotiline, and amoxapine) |
| hs | At sleep |
| IM | Intramuscular injection |
| IV | Intravenous injection |
| kg | Kilogram |
| LFT | Liver function tests (SGOT, SGPT, LDH, bilirubin, alkaline phosphotase) |
| MAOI | Monoamine-oxidase inhibitor |
| mEq/l | milliequivalents/liter |
| $\mu$g | Microgram ($10^{-6}$ grams) |
| mg | Milligrams ($10^{-3}$ grams) |
| MI | myocardial infarction |
| NDI | Nephrogenic diabetes insipidus |
| ng | Nanograms ($10^{-9}$ grams) |
| NIMH | National Institute of Mental Health |
| NMS | Neuroleptic malignant syndrome |
| NSAID | Nonsteroidal anti-inflammatory drug |
| OCD | Obsessive-compulsive disorder |
| PTSD | Posttraumatic stress disorder |

ORGANIZATION

| | |
|---|---|
| po | Oral dose |
| prn | as needed (pro re nata) |
| q | every |
| qd | Once a day; daily |
| qhs | each night at bedtime |
| qid | Four times a day |
| qod | Every other day |
| r/o | Rule out |
| SC | Subcutaneous |
| SGOT/AST | Aspartate aminotransferase |
| SGPT/ALT | Alanine aminotransferase |
| SSRI | Selective serotonin reuptake inhibitor |
| $T_3$ | Triiodothyronine |
| $T_4$ | Thyroxine |
| TCAs | Tricyclic antidepressants |
| TD | Tardive dyskinesia |
| tid | Three times a day |
| TSH | Thyroid-stimulating hormone |

# Contents

C
O
N
T
E
N
T
S

CONTENTS

CONTENTS

# 1. Antipsychotic Agents

## INTRODUCTION

Antipsychotics block psychosis, whereas anxiolytics do not.

Both antipsychotics and hypnoanxiolytics can sedate, which accounts for the outmoded terms "major" and "minor" tranquilizers, respectively. To avoid confusion, this book does not use the term *tranquilizer*.

Neuroleptics are antipsychotic drugs that cause neurological side effects. Atypical antipsychotic drugs are equally effective treatments for psychosis but have fewer neurological side effects. All antipsychotic medications treat psychotic disorders of any cause.

This chapter focuses on

- Schizophrenia (pages 8–14)
- Brief psychotic disorder (page 22)
- Delusional disorder (page 22)
- Depressive symptoms in schizophrenia (pages 22–23)
- HIV/AIDS-related psychotic disorders (page 23)
- Autism/pervasive developmental disorder (page 23)
- Schizotypal personality disorder (page 24)
- Extrapyramidal symptoms, NMS and TD (pages 28–29)

Other chapters discuss the use of antipsychotics for

- Aggression (Anticonvulsants, pages 281–87)
- Anorexia nervosa (Antidepressants, page 131)
- Anxiety (Antianxiety, page 324)
- Atypical psychosis (Anticonvulsants, page 288)
- Borderline personality disorder (Lithium, page 232)
- Depression (Antidepressants, pages 122–23)
- Hallucinogen-induced psychosis (Anticonvulsants, page 289)
- Mania (Lithium, pages 223–24)

# NAMES, CLASSES, MANUFACTURERS, DOSE FORMS, COLORS

| Generic Names | Brand Names | Manufacturers | Dose Forms (mg)[1] | Colors |
|---|---|---|---|---|
| | | **PHENOTHIAZINES** | | |
| *Aliphatics* | | | | |
| Chlorpromazine | Thorazine | SmithKline Beecham | t: 10/25/50/ 100/200 <br> sr: 30/75/150/ 200/300 <br> o: 10/30/100 <br> p: 25 mg/ml <br> s: 10 mg/5 ml <br> sp: 25/100 mg/ml | t: all orange |
| *Piperidines* | | | | |
| Mesoridazine | Serentil | Boehringer Ingelheim | t: 10/25/50/ 100 <br> o: 25 mg/ml <br> p: 25 mg/ml | t: all red |
| Thioridazine | Mellaril | Sandoz | t: 10/15/25/50/ 100/150/200 <br> o: 30/100 mg/ml | t: chartreuse/ pink/tan/white green/yellow/pink <br> o: straw yellows/ light yellow |
| | Mellaril-S | Sandoz | su: 25/100 mg/5 ml | |
| *Piperazines* | | | | |
| Fluphenazine | Permitil | Schering | t: 2.5/5/10 <br> o: 5 mg/ml | t: light orange/ purple-pink/light red |
| | Prolixin | Apothecon | t: 1/2.5/5/10 <br> e: 0.5 mg/ml <br> o: 5 mg/ml <br> p: 2.5 mg/ml | t: pink/yellow/ green/red |
| Fluphenazine decanoate | Prolixin decanoate | Apothecon | p: 25 mg/ml | —— |
| Fluphenazine enanthate | Prolixin enanthate | Apothecon | p: 25 mg/ml | —— |
| Perphenazine | Trilafon | Schering | t: 2/4/8/16 <br> o: 3.2 mg/ml <br> p: 5 mg/ml | t: all gray |
| Trifluoperazine | Stelazine | SmithKline Beecham | t: 1/2/5/10 <br> o: 10 mg/ml <br> p: 2 mg/ml | t: all blue |
| | | **BUTYROPHENONES** | | |
| Haloperidol | Haldol | McNeil | t: 0.5/1/2/5/ 10/20 <br> o: 2 mg/ml <br> p: 5 mg/ml | t: white/yellow/ pink/green/ aqua/salmon |
| Haloperidol decanoate | Haldol decanoate | McNeil | p: 50/100 mg/ml | —— |

| Generic Names | Brand Names | Manufacturers | Dose Forms (mg)[1] | Colors |
|---|---|---|---|---|
| **THIOXANTHENES** | | | | |
| Thiothixene | Navane | Roerig | c: 1/2/5/10/20<br>o: 5 mg/ml<br>p: 2/5 mg/ml | c: orange-yellow/<br>blue-yellow/<br>orange-white/<br>blue-white/dark<br>blue-light blue |
| **DIPHENYLBUTYLPIPERDINES** | | | | |
| Pimozide | Orap | Lemmon/Gate | t: 2 mg | t: white |
| **DIBENZAZEPINE** | | | | |
| Loxapine | Loxitane | Lederle | c: 5/10/25/50 | t: dark green/<br>yellow-green/<br>light green-dark<br>green/blue-dark<br>green |
| | Loxitane-C | Lederle | o: 25 mg/ml | —— |
| | Loxitane-IM | Lederle | p: 50 mg/ml | —— |
| **DIHYDROINDOLONE** | | | | |
| Molindone | Moban | Lemmon/Gate | t: 5/10/25/50/<br>100<br>o: 20 mg/ml | t: orange/lavender/<br>light green/blue/<br>tan<br>o: cherry |
| **THIENOBENZODIAZEPINE** | | | | |
| Olanzapine | Zyprexa | Lilly | t: 2.5/5/7.5/10/15<br>t: 5/10 | t: white (2.5–10<br>mg)/blue (15 mg)<br>t: yellow (orally<br>disintegrating) |
| **DIBENZODIAZEPINE** | | | | |
| Clozapine | Clozaril | Sandoz[2] | t: 25/100 | t: all yellow |
| **DIBENZOTHIAZEPINE** | | | | |
| Quetiapine | Seroquel | AstraZeneca | t: 25/100/200/300 | t: peach/yellow/<br>white round/white<br>capsule |
| Ziprasidone | Geodon | Pfizer | c: 20/40/60/80 | c: blue/white-<br>blue/blue-<br>white/white-<br>blue white |
| **BENZISOXAZOLE** | | | | |
| Risperidone | Risperdal | Janssen/<br>SmithKline<br>Beecham | t: 1/2/3/4 | t: white/orange/<br>yellow/green |

[1] c = capsules; e = elixir; o = oral concentrate; p = parenteral concentrate; s = syrup; sp = suppository; sr = sustained-release spansules; su = suspension; t = tablets.
[2] Prescribing clozapine through Sandoz has greater specificity than some generic formulations but generic formulations much less expensive.

## PHARMACOLOGY

Antipsychotics are dopamine antagonists; some can also elevate prolactin and are antiemetics. All typical neuroleptics are probably equally effective for psychosis and differ mainly in side effects. Typical neuroleptics are mainly effective for positive symptoms but significantly less effective for negative symptoms and cognitive functions.

In general, the atypical antipsychotics are preferred over the typical neuroleptics. The atypical antipsychotics—risperidone, clozapine, olanzapine, ziprasidone, and quetiapine—are at least as effective as typical neuroleptics for positive symptoms, more effective for negative and cognitive symptoms, and sometimes effective in psychosis not responsive to typical neuroleptics. Clozapine is less likely than the neuroleptics to cause dystonic reactions, tardive dyskinesia (TD), or increased prolactin levels. Quetiapine has an average half-life of 6 hours. This could result in subtherapeutic dosing even at high doses, e.g., 600–800 mg. Divided dosing, e.g., bid-tid, may result in more uniform blood levels. When steady state is achieved, qd or bid dosing may be appropriate. Risperidone and olanzapine differ from typical neuroleptics because at usual therapeutic doses, under 6 mg qd for risperidone and 20 mg for olanzapine:

- They cause extrapyramidal symptoms (EPS) and TD less frequently than typical antipsychotics (0.4–0.5% per year for TD) (*see also* Chapter 2 for further details).
  √ Risperidone generally remains "atypical" at doses 5 mg qd or less.
    □ During treatment with risperidone, schizophrenic patients had significant improvement on Brief Psychiatric Rating Scale (BPRS), Positive and Negative Symptoms Scale (PANSS), and performance level on tests of alertness and both sustained and selective attention.
  √ Olanzapine dose generally needs to be at least 10 mg qd, and 15 or 20 mg may be needed for optimal outcome.
- When switching a responder from clozapine to risperidone or olanzapine, do it very gradually or relapse risk is increased.
- Risperidone also risks hyperprolactinemia, with prolactin levels frequently over 100 ng/ml in premenopausal women.
  √ In a study of 1,000 patients with schizophrenia or schizoaffective disorder, patients more likely to continue on risperidone if they had a higher maximum dose (5.7 vs. 4.7 mg/day), a longer number of days to maximum dose (5.7 vs. 3.9 days), and a maximum rise in dose of 0.5–2 mg/day.
- Quetiapine (Seroquel), N = 361, was both superior to placebo

and comparable to haloperidol in reducing positive symptoms at doses ranging from 150 to 750 mg/day.
- √ Reduces negative symptoms at a dose of 300 mg/day and probably higher doses.
- √ Equal to placebo across the dose range regarding incidence of extrapyramidal symptoms or changes in prolactin concentrations.
- √ Superior to placebo and haloperidol in improvement of affective/mood symptoms.
  - □ Used BPRS factor 1 score (mean of depressed mood, guilt feelings, somatic concern, anxiety) and a BPRS mood cluster score (mean of depressed mood, guilt feelings, anxiety, tension).
  - □ At doses of 600 mg/day, was superior to placebo in decreasing aggression and hostility.
- Clozapine treatment yielded significant results in refractory schizophrenia.
  - √ When plasma clozapine concentrations above 400 ng/ml, all patients responded.
  - √ High positive response rate continued over a 3-year period with average plasma clozapine concentration 652 ng/ml after 1 year, 436 ng/ml after 2 years, and 394 ng/ml after 3 years.
  - √ Only 17.6% of patients showed any treatment-emergent extrapyramidal symptoms.
- When all atypical antipsychotics were compared in a meta-analysis, only risperidone, olanzapine, and clozapine were superior to conventional neuroleptics at p < .00001 level; quetiapine and ziprasidone were not.

The antidopaminergic antiemetics—metoclopramide (Reglan), thiethylperazine (Torecan), and promethazine (Phenergan)—have all the side effects of neuroleptics, including EPS and TD, but their antipsychotic properties are weak.

- Triflupromazine (Vesprin) and prochlorperazine (Compazine) are the only 2 with an antipsychotic indication.
  - √ Not generally used or recommended for this indication.
- Promazine (Sparine) is a very low-potency neuroleptic that is not recommended because of probable low efficacy.

Most patients respond to 300–500 mg chlorpromazine equivalents. Higher doses are seldom needed for schizophrenia and may be less effective.

Most neuroleptic metabolites are inactive, but a few retain antipsychotic actions (e.g., mesoridazine's 7-hydroxychlorpromazine).

*Oral form*

- Antipsychotics' peak concentrations usually occur around 2–4 h.
  √ Pimozide peaks at 6–8 h, with range of 4–12 h.
- Neuroleptics are highly lipophilic.
- They accumulate in the brain, which typically permits once-a-day doses for psychosis.
  √ Aside from antipsychotic actions, oral neuroleptics have side effects that can arise quickly (e.g., dry mouth in 30 minutes) or slowly (e.g., tardive dyskinesia in 2+ years).
  √ Tardive dyskinesia was 3 times greater for patients with more than two neuroleptic interruptions than for patients with two or fewer interruptions.
    ▫ Long-term neuroleptic treatment much better than targeted or intermittent neuroleptic treatment.
- Generally avoid prescribing 2 neuroleptics concurrently.
  √ Some experts combine a neuroleptic and an atypical antipsychotic drug for refractory schizophrenia.

*IM (not depot) form*

- Peak concentrations occur 15–30 minutes after injection.
- Expect 2–4-fold greater potency of IM over po doses.

The different neuroleptic groups have different side-effect profiles (*see* Side Effects, pages 24–25).

## Pharmacology of Neuroleptics

| Generic Names | Bioavailability (%) | Plasma Binding (%) | Half-Life (hours) | Excretion (%)* |
|---|---|---|---|---|
| Chlorpromazine | 32 ± 19 | 95–98 | 30 ± 7 | 25 ± 15 R/70–80 F |
| Clozapine | 50–60 | 95 | 8 ± 4 (12 (4–66)) | 50 R/30 F |
| Fluphenazine | ? | 80–90 | 14.7–15.3 (16–24) | R/F |
| Haloperidol | 70 ± 18 | 91 ± 1.4 | 17.9 ± 6.6 | 40 R |
| Loxapine | ? | 90 | 3.4 (1–19) | 61 R/22 F |
| Mesoridazine | ? | 70 | 24–84 | R/F |
| Molindone | ? | 98 | 1.5 (4–12) | R/F |
| Olanzapine | 60 | 93 | 30 ± 17 | 57 R/30 F |
| Perphenazine | low | high | 9.5 (8–21) | R/F |
| Pimozide | > 50 | 99 | 55 | 38–45 R |
| Quetiapine | 90 ± 9 | 83 | 6 | 73 R/20 F |
| Risperidone | 70 | 90 | 20 | 70 R/15 F |
| Thioridazine | 30 | 70–99 | 16 (7–42) | ? |
| Thiothixene | ? | ? | 34 | ? |
| Trifluoperazine | ? | > 80 | 9.3 | R/F |
| Ziprasidone | 60 | 99 | 7 | 20 R/66 F |

* B = bile; F = fecal; R = renal; ? = unavailable or inconsistent.

# DOSES

## General Neuroleptic Doses

| Generic Names | Chlorpromazine Equivalent Doses (100 mg) | Acute Doses (mg/day) | Ranges (mg/day) | P.R.N. (mg/po) | P.R.N. (mg/IM) |
|---|---|---|---|---|---|
| Chlorpromazine | 100 | 200–1600 | 25–2000 | 25–100 | 25–50 |
| Clozapine | 75 | 150–500 | 75–700 | N/A | N/A |
| Fluphenazine | 2 | 2.5–20 | 1–60 | 0.5–10 | 1–5 |
| Haloperidol | 2 | 2–40 | 1–100 | 0.5–5 | 2–5 |
| Loxapine | 15 | 60–100 | 30–250 | 10–60 | 12.5–50 |
| Mesoridazine | 50 | 75–300 | 30–400 | 10–100 | 25 |
| Molindone | 20 | 50–100 | 15–25 | 5–75 | N/A |
| Olanzapine | 4 | 5–20 | 3–30 | N/A | N/A |
| Perphenazine | 10 | 16–32 | 4–64 | 4–8 | 5–10 |
| Pimozide | 0.5 | 10–12 | 1–20 | N/A | 1–3 |
| Quetiapine | 100 | 200–800 | 100–1000 | N/A | N/A |
| Risperidone* | 1 | 2–8 | 1–16 | N/A | N/A |
| Thioridazine | 100 | 200–600 | 40–800 | 20–200 | N/A |
| Thiothixene | 0.5 | 6–30 | 6–60 | 2–20 | 2–4 |
| Trifluoperazine | 5 | 6–50 | 2–80 | 5–10 | 1–2 |
| Ziprasidone | 15 | 40–200 | 20–160 | 2–25 | N/A |

* Doses over 6 mg yield less improvement and more side effects than 6 mg.

## Specific Neuroleptic Doses

| Generic Names | First Oral Dose (mg) | First Day Total Dose (mg/day) | Therapeutic Plasma Levels (mg/ml) |
|---|---|---|---|
| Chlorpromazine | 50–100 | 300–400 | 30–100 |
| Clozapine | 25 | 50 | 141–204* |
| Fluphenazine | 1–2 | 2.5–10 | 0.2–3 |
| Fluphenazine decanoate** | 12.5 | 12.5 | 0.15–2.7 |
| Haloperidol | 1–5 | 3–20 | —— |
| Loxapine | 10–25 | 20–50 | —— |
| Mesoridazine | 50 | 150 | —— |
| Molindone | 10–25 | 50–75 | —— |
| Olanzapine | 5–10 | 10 | —— |
| Perphenazine | 4–8 | 16–32 | 0.8–12.0 |
| Pimozide | 1–2 | 2 | —— |
| Quetiapine | 25 | 50 | —— |
| Risperidone | 0.5–1 | 1–2 | —— |
| Thioridazine | 50–100 | 150–300 | 1–1.5 |
| Thiothixene | 5 | 4–13 | 2–20* |
| Trifluoperazine | 2–5 | 4–20 | 1–2.3 |
| Ziprasidone | 20 | 20–40 | —— |

* Women statistically higher than men.
** Not given orally.

## Age-Related Doses

| Generic Names | Childhood | | Geriatric Dose Range (mg/day) |
| | Weight (mg/kg/day) | Dose Range (mg/day)* | |
| --- | --- | --- | --- |
| Chlorpromazine | 3–6 | 45–430 (196) | 25–200 |
| Clozapine | —— | —— | 100–400 |
| Fluphenazine | 0.05–0.1 | 4.9–50 (10) | 2–10 |
| Haloperidol | 0.05 | 1–4.5 | 0.5–6** |
| Loxapine | 0.5–1 | 25–60 | —— |
| Mesoridazine | | | 75–200 |
| Molindone | 0.5–1 | 25–50 | 50–150 |
| Olanzapine | —— | 4–10 (5) | 3–15 |
| Perphenazine | 0.05–0.1 | 4–24 | 4–48 |
| Pimozide† | —— | —— | 10–50 |
| Quetiapine | —— | 50–150 | 50–300 |
| Risperidone | —— | —— | 0.5–4 |
| Thioridazine | 2–5 | 160–500 (282) | 25–200 |
| Thiothixene | 0.5–1 | 2–24 (16) | 2–15 |
| Trifluoperazine | 0.5 | 6–10 (0.5–15) | 2–15 |
| Ziprasidone | —— | —— | 20–80 |

\* Mean in parentheses.
\*\* 0.03–0.05 mg/kg often enough.
† Not officially recommended for psychiatric disorders; used for Tourette's.

## CLINICAL INDICATIONS AND USE

As mentioned, typical and atypical antipsychotics generally relieve schizophrenia's "positive" symptoms (e.g., hallucinations), but atypicals are better at treating "negative" symptoms (e.g., blunted affect) and improving cognitive function. A majority of patients taking atypical neuroleptics are likely to have

- Positive symptom improvement that tends to plateau at 3–6 months
- Negative symptoms improve most rapidly in 2–3 months, with continued gradual improvement
- Improved neuropsychological function with examples of improvement
  - √ Verbal memory: remembering instructions and names
  - √ Recognition of affect: ability to sense how somebody feels
  - √ Executive functioning: ability to make plans
  - √ Reaction time: safety operating equipment
  - √ Attention: ability to stay on task or listen to somebody else
  - √ Visuospatial memory: ability to remember how something appeared or where something should go

Atypical antipsychotic side effects ≥ 10% (based on PDR)

- Caveat: Methods for obtaining and counting side effects differed between drugs.

√ Frequency of a side effect depends on whether investigators ask about it.

- Risperidone (Risperdal)
  - √ Insomnia (26%)
  - √ Weight gain (18%)
  - √ Nasal stuffiness (10%)
- Olanzapine (Zyprexa)
  - √ Drowsiness (34%)
  - √ Agitation, restlessness (23%)
  - √ Insomnia (20%)
  - √ Headache (17%)
  - √ Parkinsonism (17%)
  - √ Dizziness (11%)
  - √ Akathisia (10%)
- Quetiapine (Seroquel)
  - √ Weight gain (23%)
  - √ Headache (19%)
  - √ Drowsiness (18%)
  - √ Dizziness (10%)
- Clozapine (Clozaril)
  - √ Weight gain (67%)
  - √ Drowsiness, fatigue (39%)
  - √ Salivation (32%)
  - √ Tachycardia (22%)
  - √ Obsessions, emergence or increase (21%)
    - □ Other antipsychotic drugs (1%)
  - √ Dizziness, lightheadedness (19%)
- Ziprasidone (Geodon)
  - √ Somnolence (14%)
  - √ Nausea (10%)
  - √ Respiratory disorder (8%)
  - √ Extrapyramidal syndrome (5%)

## Target Symptoms for Antipsychotic Agents*

| Positive Symptoms | Negative Symptoms |
| --- | --- |
| Agitation | Alogia |
| Assaultive behavior | Anorexia |
| Bizarrre ideation | Blunted affect |
| Confusion, disorientation | Cognitive dysfunction |
| Delusions, paranoia | Inattention |
| Hallucinations | Social withdrawal |
| Insomnia | |
| Mania | |

* Applicable only if they are a result of a psychotic process.

## Initiating Therapy

Start with high enough dose to squelch symptoms but low enough to minimize side effects. The equivalent of 300–600 mg chlorpromazine is a reasonable target dose for a majority of schizophrenic patients, then wait two weeks. Exceeding a patient's own antipsychotic threshold doesn't speed recovery. Generally less sedating, more potent neuroleptics are preferred because they have fewer side effects during the maintenance phase than the highly sedating ones (e.g., chlorpromazine or thioridazine).

- The use of neuroleptic threshold (NT) is sometimes used.
  - ✓ Not expected to work with risperidone, clozapine, olanzapine, ziprasidone, or quetiapine.
  - ✓ May work best with high-potency neuroleptics.
    - ▫ Low-potency neuroleptics with intrinsic anticholinergic effects may mask threshold EPS.
- The neuroleptic threshold (NT) guides initial dosing.
  - ✓ The neuroleptic threshold is defined as a slight increase in cogwheel rigidity after starting the neuroleptic.
    - ▫ This can be tested by flexing and extending the patient's arms at the elbow and the wrist.
    - ▫ If patient is unable to relax the tested arm, have patient perform and concentrate on rapid, alternating movements with the other arm.
  - ✓ Others have argued that the fine motor signs of micrographia or decreased arm swing while walking are more sensitive indicators of threshold.
- To establish baseline rigidity
  - ✓ The patient should be evaluated for 1–3 days before medications are started.
  - ✓ Initially haloperidol 2 mg qd (or its equivalent) is given, and if no increase in rigidity occurs, this is increased by 2 mg every other day.
  - ✓ If rigidity is equivocal, wait 1 or 2 days to see if it increases, and if not, increase by one more 2 mg dose.
- Effective antipsychotic dosing in the 3–5 mg range of haloperidol can sometimes be achieved.
  - ✓ However, sickness, missing one or more doses, and other risks can result in a quick return of psychotic symptoms.
- 86 inpatients with chronic schizophrenia with maximum doses fixed at 6 mg/day of risperidone and 300 mg/day of clozapine at endpoint (8 weeks) were clinically improved:
  - ✓ 67% of the risperidone group and 65% of the clozapine group

showed reduction of 20% or more in total Positive and Negative Symptom Scale scores.
- √ Risperidone had faster onset than clozapine.
- This approach may be particularly helpful in certain problematic populations, including
  - √ Adolescents
  - √ Geriatrics (use 0.5 or 1 mg equivalents of haloperidol)
  - √ Patients who have never been on neuroleptics.

## Outcome Predictors for Schizophrenia

| Good Outcome | Poor Outcome |
|---|---|
| Later age of onset | Earlier age of onset |
| Short duration of illness | Long duration of illness |
| Acute onset | Slow onset |
| Good premorbid functioning and social competence | Poor premorbid functioning and social competence |
| Anxiety, tension, or other affective symptoms | Emotional blunting |
| Highly systematized and focused delusions with clear symbolism | Unsystematized and unfocused delusions |
| Confusion and disorientation | Clear sensorium |
| Precipitating factors | No precipitating factors |
| Married | Single |
| Family h/o affective disorder | No family h/o affective disorder |
| Family without h/o schizophrenia | Family with h/o schizophrenia |

Since the efficacy among typical antipsychotics is roughly equivalent, choosing the "right" antipsychotic can be elusive. Atypical antipsychotics have much lower EPS risks and are more potent in reducing negative symptoms. In general, the atypical antipsychotics are a first choice. Best to

- Select an agent that has previously helped the patient, but if none exists:
  - √ If the first dose seems to be tolerated by the patient, continue it.
  - √ If not (e.g., patient is dangerously woozy), try a much lower dose or consider another antipsychotic.

Olanzapine vs. haloperidol vs. risperidone

- N = 83 patients.
- Clinical response with 67% (N = 39) of olanzapine patients and 30% (N = 7) of haloperidol patients.
- No patients who received clozapine (N = 49) and remained discharged for more than 10 months were readmitted, while readmission rate for risperidone-treated patients continued up to 24 months.

√ 87% of clozapine patients and 66% of the risperidone-treated patients remained in the community.
- If patient is not agitated, give a less sedative antipsychotic (e.g., risperidone or fluphenazine) in a single dose 30 minutes before bedtime.
  √ Risperidone usually effective in 3–5 mg range for healthy adults.
  √ For elderly or patients with significant medical problems, 0.5–2 mg qd is often useful.
  √ After 4 weeks treatment, greater overall improvement in patients receiving risperidone than haloperidol.
    □ Far more risperidone than haloperidol patients had 30%, 40%, or 50% improvement rates on the Positive and Negative Symptom Scale.
    □ Antiparkinsonian drugs were required by 61% of the haloperidol patients vs. only 21% of risperidone (this last number is probably lower still, now that most doses of risperidone are less than 6 mg qd).
    □ When patient is switched from clozapine to risperidone or olanzapine, will need prolonged cross-titration > 1 month.
- Bedtime doses lessen the experience of side effects, since peak levels occur only during sleep.
- If the patient is agitated and requires sedation
  √ Choose a more sedating neuroleptic (e.g., olanzapine or perphenazine).
    □ Olanzapine 15 mg is superior to 10 mg on most negative symptoms.
  √ Rapidly increase to target antipsychotic dosage.
    □ 8 patients with chronic refractory schizophrenia received high dose (30 or 40 mg/day for ≥ 12 days).
    □ EPS side effects were found in 5 of 8 patients, with akathisia in 1, parkinsonism in 2, and both side effects in another 2.
    □ Symptoms were usually mild, with 1 patient requiring benztropine and propranolol, and a sixth patient had possible parkinsonism.
  √ Take advantage of sedating effects by using tid or qid doses.
  √ Make sure patient is getting medication: Give IM neuroleptic (e.g., haloperidol 5 mg) if rapid effect is needed, or give liquid form and observe patient taking it.
  √ If at target dose, to avoid unnecessary further risks of EPS, add benzodiazepines (e.g., lorazepam 1–2 mg/po or IM, diazepam 5 mg IM).
    □ Beware of disinhibition at low and intermediate benzodiazepine doses.

- Special precautions with clozapine
  √ Do not rapidly increase clozapine; increases seizure risk.
  √ Monitor clozapine for sedation and hypotension and beware of rare (1:3,000) respiratory or cardiac arrest.
  √ Start at 12.5 mg qd or bid and increase by 25–50 mg qd every 2 days.
  √ In the responders (N = 18, 16 males, 2 females), after 1 week of treatment there was a significant reduction from baseline on BPRS, psychosis, and tension.
  √ In another study with treatment-refractory schizophrenic inpatients (N = 50), it took an average of 60 days for subjects to reach the dose at which clozapine response was achieved.
  √ At baseline (N = 331), 31% of patients on clozapine showed overt physical aggression.
    □ After an average of 47 weeks of treatment with clozapine, rate of aggression had fallen to 1%.
  √ Once this dose was reached, the average response time was 17 days (range = 2–56).
  √ Little clinical gain in prolonging exposure to clozapine beyond 8 weeks at any dose, if no response is seen.
  √ 55% of 73 patients on clozapine demonstrated initial improvement within 6 months.
    □ A majority had significant response at 3 months.
    □ However, 18 of 73 patients demonstrated improvement by 11 months.
  √ In another study, 50% of patients with treatment-refractory illness and 76% of the treatment-intolerant patients responded to clozapine in up to 52 weeks.
    □ Optimal trial of clozapine appeared to be 12–24 weeks.
- In cases of severe refractory psychotic agitation, IM droperidol 2.5–15 mg (1–6 ml) can be considered.
  √ 0.15–0.25 mg/kg can be started in physically healthy adults (< 65 y.o.).
  √ Duration of action usually under 5 h but can be as high as 12 h.
  √ Shows rapid onset (3–10 minutes) and peak action (20–30 minutes).
  √ Can be very sedating/tranquilizing.
  √ Low risk of prolonged oversedation.
  √ Occasionally doses up to 50 mg required.
  √ Less hypotensive than low-potency sedating phenothiazines.
  √ Increases EPS risk of other drugs.
  √ Prolongs QTc interval.

ANTIPSYCHOTIC AGENTS

## Choosing a Neuroleptic

| Problem | Choice |
| --- | --- |
| High dystonia risk (under 30-y.o. male; under 25-y.o. female) | High-potency atypical antipsychotics are a first choice, e.g., risperidone or olanzapine. Mid-potency neuroleptic somewhat decreases dystonia risk but may still need ACA. |
| Geriatric (high anticholinergic, orthostatic, sedation) risks, cognitive impairment, or delirium | Risperidone or haloperidol; olanzapine acceptable if without sedation risk. |
| Predominant or severe negative symptoms | Risperidone, ziprasidone, olanzapine, or clozapine; quetiapine may be effective but optimal dosage can be difficult or impossible to find. |
| Treatment resistant | Risperidone, olanzapine, or clozapine (*see* Augmentations on pages 16–18) |
| TD or Parkinson's disease | Clozapine, olanzapine, or risperidone; first consider reducing L-dopa, which may be causing or exacerbating psychosis. Increased EPS with risperidone at doses of 5 mg or more and in geriatric patients at 2 mg or more. |
| Seizure risk | High-potency neuroleptics, risperidone, olanzapine, or quetiapine: low risks. Clozapine risks up to 5% seizures with 600+ mg qd. Molindone and fluphenazine have some increased risk but not as much as clozapine. |
| Obesity | Molindone: advise patient to lose weight. Avoid low-potency neuroleptics, e.g., clozapine (67% gain weight), chlorpromazine, chlorprothixine, thioridazine, or mesoridazine. Weight gain also with quetiapine and somewhat less for risperidone. Ziprasidone does not cause weight gain. |
| Cardiac arrhythmia | High potency (possibly medium potency). Avoid pimozide, thioridazine, and clozapine. |
| Extreme unresponsive agitation | Droperidol prn as adjunctive agent |
| Minimal compliance with medications | Haloperidol or prolixin decanoate, rarely pimozide orally. Haloperidol decanoate often only needs injection once a month. |
| Mental retardation | Haloperidol or an atypical antipsychotic that does not increase confusion and memory loss. However, an atypical antipsychotic drug that is effective for nonpyschotic agitation and does not impair cognition would be more appropriate for this group. |

# Treatment Resistance

What happens if patient does not improve sufficiently?

- Psychotic symptoms may resolve in days, but many require 2–12 weeks (or more) to disappear.
- If all symptoms remain unchanged after initial 2 weeks, consider:
  √ Is patient taking the medication?
    □ If patient does not have a common side effect (e.g., dry mouth), probably is *not* ingesting the medication.
  √ To be certain, obtain a plasma level by drawing blood 12 h after an oral dose.
    □ Too high levels may interfere with antipsychotic effect.
    □ Too low levels suggest noncompliance or rapid metabolism of drug.
  √ Liquid medication is more readily swallowed than pills, which are graciously "cheeked."
- If patient is taking pills but without a good response, then:
  √ Reconsider diagnosis and make sure there are clear target symptoms.
    □ Raise (or lower) the dose of the same neuroleptic.
    □ Try an IM form.
    □ Switch to depot medication (see below); this may particularly help patients with extensive first-pass metabolism.
    □ BPRS at 4 weeks was significantly better for risperidone (24%) than haloperidol (11%) but very little improvement after the first 4 weeks of treatment.
    □ If on high doses (e.g., 50 mg/qd haloperidol), gradual reduction to 30–50% of this dose may help.
- Older patients (mean age/77) taking typical agents may have a 3–5 times greater risk of TD.
  √ In spite of low doses, cumulative TD rates were 25%, 34%, and 53% after 1, 2, and 3 years, with moderate severity in the majority of patients affected.
  √ Atypical antipsychotic agents should be considered first choices in this older population.
  √ Clozapine-treated patients had 17% rehospitalization compared to patients taking typicals, who had 31% readmission.
- If there is inadequate response after 3–4 weeks on neuroleptic, consider measuring prolactin level.
  √ On haloperidol, 16–30 ng/ml prolactin may be optimal range.
    □ Adjust dose up or down if outside this range.
  √ On risperidone, 20 premenopausal women had significantly higher average prolactin levels of 102 ng/ml, while typical neuroleptics had an average of 48 ng/ml.

        □ 8 (40%) of the risperidone-treated patients were symptomatic, 6 with amenorrhea and 2 with galactorrhea.

    ✓ Prolactinemia aggravates depression more than psychosis.

- If prominent negative symptoms remain, consider risperidone, olanzapine, ziprasidone, clozapine, or possibly quetiapine.
  - ✓ Effects of clozapine usually seen within 12 weeks.
    - □ At 100 mg/day of clozapine, tapering of conventional neuroleptic can be started as dose of clozapine is increased.
  - ✓ Fluvoxamine, fluoxetine, desipramine, and probably other ADs can augment clozapine-resistant schizophrenia.
    - □ Maprotiline did not significantly improve negative symptoms.
  - ✓ If patient is on high-potency neuroleptic with only partial response, clozapine can be added safely, with an eventual goal to just take clozapine.
  - ✓ With lack of response to two antipsychotic drugs, 30% of 126 patients treated with clozapine had significant improvement over a 6-week period.
  - ✓ Of 141 patients, only 5% treated with chlorpromazine had significant improvement.
  - ✓ In a group of 1,847 patients with chronic schizophrenia, dropouts due to lack of efficacy were less frequent with risperidone (7%) compared to placebo (80%), haloperidol (18%), or other typical antipsychotics (17%).
    - □ Except for clozapine, other atypical antipsychotic agents were not available.
- If prominent positive symptoms remain, consider a different class of neuroleptic.
- If patient is treatment-resistant to 2 or more typical neuroleptics, consider risperidone, olanzapine, ziprasidone, or clozapine.
- If partial response observed, consider augmentations.
- Depressive symptoms with schizophrenia improve in a larger percentage of patients and to greater extent with olanzapine than with haloperidol.
- If negative symptoms are worse, consider neuroleptic akinesia and lower dose and/or add anticholinergic agent.

## Augmentations

- Benzodiazepines can improve positive and negative symptoms.
  - ✓ 50% response rate.
  - ✓ 2–3 mg qd alprazolam typical dose.
  - ✓ Clonazepam may diminish agitation and possibly psychosis, although findings are unclear.

  □ For instance, 31% improvement shown in 4 studies.
  □ Decreased paranoid thinking and hallucinations when combined with neuroleptic.
  □ Helped 4 patients with atypical psychosis who were unresponsive to neuroleptics.
  □ Dose:
  □ Start at 0.5 mg bid-tid.
  □ Increase 0.5–1.0 mg every 3 days until stabilization occurs.
  □ Dose may reach 3 mg/day.
- Adding lithium can help "good prognosis" schizophrenics as well as schizoaffective bipolars.
- Anticonvulsants may help
  √ If "atypical" features, seizure-like, organic symptoms (e.g., olfactory, tactile, or kinesthetic hallucinations).
  √ With prominent negative symptoms (e.g., affective flattening).
  √ If bipolar symptoms observed.
- Bromocriptine 2.5 mg/qd
  √ Case reports positive in treatment-resistant psychosis.
- Propranolol in doses > 800 mg qd
  √ May function as anticonvulsant at this dose.
  √ May also aggravate or cause psychosis.
- Eicosapentaenoic acid (EPA) can sustain remission of positive and negative symptoms of schizophrenia.
  √ In study of 20 schizophrenic patients, reduction of both positive symptoms and tardive dyskinesia occurred.
  √ All were on their regular antipsychotic medication.
  √ Average symptom response about 25%.
- Clozapine augmentation with ondansetton 8 mg q 8 hr
  √ Decreased delusions and hallucinations.

**Augmentation with Negative Symptoms**

- Glycine, a potentiator of NMDA neurotransmission for negative symptoms of schizophrenia, dissolved in water and given orally tid, was titrated to 0.8 mg/kg/day (mean dosage 60 gm/day).
  √ 19 patients on glycine showed a decrease of negative symptoms as measured on PANSS, a significant improvement ($30\% \pm 18\%$, $p < .001$) in the BPRS total scores, and a 50% reduction in scores on Simpson-Angus Scale for Extrapyramidal Symptoms.
  √ 15 (79%) subjects showed a 20% or greater improvement in PANSS scores.
  √ Total BPRS scores decreased by 30% during glycine treatment.

- D-serine treatment, 30 mg/kg/day, added to stable antipsychotic regimen, resulted in significant improvement in positive, negative, and cognitive symptoms.
  - √ These results support the hypothesis of NMDA receptor hypofunction in schizophrenia because D-serine is an NMDA receptor complex co-agonist.
- D-cycloserine given 50 mg/day resulted in 61% of D-cycloserine–treated patients responding and 26% of the placebo group.
  - √ Gains were greatest in the area of blunted affect, with improvements also in anhedonia and associativeness, but no differences in apathy, attention, or alogia.
  - √ Mean improvement on Alzheimer's Disease Assessment Scale, cognitive subscale, with 100 mg of D-cycloserine, was 3 points.
- Trazodone 100–500 mg (mixed results; used for negative symptoms)
  - √ Essentially no positive effects.
- Famotidine (Pepcid), a potent lipophylic histamine-2 blocker, 20 mg bid, improved negative symptoms in small (N = 18) open trial.
  - √ Patients experienced reduction of 14% in BPRS, 18% in SANS scores, and improvement in CGI.
- Anticholinergic agents may worsen positive symptoms and improve negative symptoms.
  - √ Might be useful adjunct in patients with mostly negative symptoms.
- Pimozide 4–20 mg qd may have more effect on refractory negative symptoms and refractory delusional disorder.
  - √ In 7 cases, 5 with schizophrenia and 2 with schizoaffective disorder
    - ▫ Pimozide's average dose was 4 mg (range 2–8 mg).
    - ▫ All patients had consistent clinical improvement while on pimozide (mean baseline BPRS = 51; after pimozide use BPRS = 27.
- Selegiline 5 mg po bid taken for 1 month in an open trial significantly reduced negative symptoms, e.g., affective flattening, alogia, avolition/apathy, and anhedonia/asociality.
  - √ No effect on positive symptoms.
  - √ Negative symptoms continued to improve over several months.
- Antidepressants may help negative symptoms/depression.
  - √ Risk of exacerbating positive symptoms of psychosis has been overestimated.
- Amantadine 50 mg 3 times daily resulted in 23% responders who had negative symptoms without exacerbation of positive symptoms.

## Maintenance

After the initial schizophrenic break:

- Qd dosing for most patients; divided dosing only if side-effect problem (e.g., orthostatic hypotension) or if short half-life (e.g., 5–8 hrs) of antipsychotic requires dosing 2 or 3 times a day.
  - √ At beginning of treatment risperidone is recommended in bid dosing, but if there is no hypotension, it can be given qd.
- From 6–9 months after discharge (or point of maximum improvement), consider tapering to 20–50% of the highest dosage.
  - √ If symptoms begin to recur, increase dose.
- If patient will be under high stress (e.g., new job), do not alter medication until stressor has past.
- Some studies suggest that serum prolactin predicts relapse risk.
  - √ In fluphenazine decanoate study
    - □ ≥ 16 ng/ml level was protective.
    - □ ≤ 6 ng/ml level was high relapse risk.
- In patients who unilaterally stop medication, 15% can be expected to relapse per month.

*Depot neuroleptics*, which are IM antipsychotics lasting 2–4 weeks, are employed for maintenance therapy, particularly for patients with poor or inconsistent compliance.

- They are effective treatment for chronic psychoses.
- Their advantages are:
  - √ Patient does not have to remember to take pills every day.
  - √ Certainty that drug is in the patient.
  - √ Less staff work.
  - √ Lower relapse rates than with oral meds.
- Their disadvantages are:
  - √ Once injected, the patient must deal with any adverse consequences, such as an EPS.
  - √ They are not very effective for negative symptoms.
- Be aware of the following precautions.
  - √ Do not start any treatment with depot neuroleptics unless usual medications have already been tried, without good results.
  - √ Suddenly switching from oral to depot forms can radically alter serum level.
    - □ For instance, 4 weeks of fluphenazine 10 mg/day po was stopped, replaced by fluphenazine decanoate 12.5 mg IM; 2 weeks later the serum level dropped from 0.51 ng/ml to 0.08 ng/ml and symptoms reappeared.
    - □ Oral neuroleptics can reach steady state in 3–7 days.

- Safety factors
  √ *Gradually* shift from oral to depot forms, and
  √ Test dose.
- Method
  √ No depot form is clearly better than another in controlling psychosis.
    □ Fluphenazine enanthate has significantly higher side effects, especially EPS, and is not recommended.
  √ First, stabilize the patient on a dose of oral fluphenazine or haloperidol; ensure adequate blood-level and side-effect tolerance.
  √ To detect rare sensitivity to vehicle (sesame oil) or side effects, inject 6.25 mg (by insulin syringe for accurate measurement) of fluphenazine decanoate (or any depot form).
  √ Dose schedules include:
    □ Fluphenazine decanoate (FD), with a 7–10-day half-life, allowing depot injections about every 2 weeks, and fluphenazine enanthate (see tables that follow) not generally recommended due to high EPS risk.
    □ Haloperidol decanoate (HD) dose should equal 10–20 times the daily dose of haloperidol orally. If not on any neuroleptic, the initial dose is usually 20 times oral dose; the next dose, approximately 1 month later, 15 times oral dose; and the final maintenance dose 1 month later, closer to 10 times the oral dose.
  √ Maintain stable blood level.
    □ If needed, continue oral medication.
    □ Gradually taper oral medication as depot levels increase.
    □ Example schedule: Give full po dose on first day of IM; decrease po dose 20% of original dose each day; add more po medication if clinically indicated; po medication may accompany IM for 1 or 2 months until proper IM dose is determined.
- After being stabilized on fluphenazine decanoate 25 mg, some patients continue to do well with much lower doses (as low as 5–10 mg).
- Depot neuroleptics have not been approved for children under 12.

**Approximate Equivalents of Oral and Depot Fluphenazine**

| Dosage | PO | IM* |
|---|---|---|
| Low dose | 1–8 mg | 6.25–12.5 |
| Medium dose | 8–20 mg | 12.5–37.5 |
| High dose | 20–40 mg | 37.5–100 |

* One study suggested 12.5 mg decanoate = 10 mg po.

## The Use of Depot Neuroleptics*

| Profile | Fluphenazine Decanoate | Fluphenazine Enanthate** | Haloperidol Decanoate |
|---|---|---|---|
| Usual dose (mg) | 25 (6.25–100) | 25–75 (12.5–100) | 50–100 (50–300) |
| Usual frequency of injections (weeks) | 3 (2–6) | 2 (1–3) | 4 (2–5) |
| Antipsychotic action begins (days) | 1–3 | 1–3 | 6–7 |
| Peak plasma level (days) | 1–2 | 2–4 | 3–9 |
| Protein binding | 80 | 80 | 92 |
| Half-life (days) | 6.8–9.6 (one injection) 14.3 (many doses) | 3.5–4 (one injection) | 21 (one injection) 12 (many doses) |
| Maximum dose recorded | 400 mg/week | 1250 mg/week | 1200 mg/injection |

* Ranges in parentheses.
** Not generally recommended because of high EPS risk (> 40%) compared to decanoates.

Pimozide as an alternative to depot neuroleptics in low-compliance patients:

- Frequently patients refuse depot neuroleptics because they do not want IM.
  √ Check with patient to see if it is the site of administration and not IM that is reason for refusal.
  √ Some patients resist buttocks IM but tolerate thigh or shoulder.
- If patient refuses IM medication and is part of a program that cannot monitor daily oral meds but can oversee 3–5 doses a week, then consider pimozide.
  √ Pimozide's 55-h half-life allows dosing every 2–3 days.
  √ However, pimozide is rarely, if ever, administered in this way.

Indications for long-term antipsychotic therapy:

- After 2 schizophrenic episodes, probably need neuroleptics for years (if not for life), always weighing the risks of psychosis against those of tardive dyskinesia and other side effects.
  √ Consider risperidone, olanzapine, or quetiapine (but beware of its 6-h average half-life).
  √ If minimal or no response to these, try clozapine.
- Maintenance antipsychotic therapy over 2 years is superior to placebo.
  √ Averts schizophrenic relapses in 40–70% of patients.

# Brief Psychotic Disorder

- Lower doses (2–5 mg haloperidol) are often effective.
- Improvement frequently seen in days, not weeks.
  √ May be a result of high spontaneous remission rate.
- Benzodiazepines may be valuable for sleep and agitation if psychosis with marked stressors.
- Lithium or an anticonvulsant may be helpful for patients with bipolar II history or strong family h/o disorder.
- Antidepressants should be considered for patients who have h/o major depression.

# Delusional Disorder

Many case reports but no controlled studies suggest that pimozide is effective for

- Somatic type
  √ Case reports suggest that some somatic types may have severe body dysmorphic disorders and should be treated with serotonergic antidepressants, then OCD medications.
- Jealous type

Other antipsychotic trials are recommended first for erotomanic, grandiose, and persecutory types.

- Low (< 30%) response rate usually reported.

# Depressive Symptoms in Schizophrenia

Depressive mood, insomnia, and poor concentration are frequently the earliest prodromal symptoms before a psychotic relapse.

- These often occur before hallucinations, delusions, or thought disorders appear.
- Symptoms may have regularly preceded prior psychotic episodes.
- A temporary increase in antipsychotic medication, along with benzodiazepines for sleep and agitation, may prevent the full relapse.
- Depressive symptoms, including anhedonia, low energy, and poor concentration that occur 3–4 weeks after treatment begins, may be symptoms of akinesia.
  √ If akinesia is diagnosed, reduction of antipsychotic dose may relieve this depression-like syndrome.
- If a true major depression occurs, antidepressants should be considered (*see* Antidepressants).
- Sometimes depressive symptoms are grief reactions that may not be amenable to medications. Clues to this include

✓ Symptoms occur after psychosis is nearly or completely gone, and

✓ Content of depressive thoughts is completely centered on what has been lost or not accomplished because of the psychotic illness.

✓ Open trials of antidepressants indicate that these can help if given along with grief therapy.

## HIV/AIDS-Related Psychotic Disorders

• 21 HIV and/or AIDS patients with psychotic disorder: Most responded to low doses of risperidone (mean maximum dose 3.3 mg) with treatment for a mean of 6.4 weeks.

✓ 13 of 21 patients became symptom-free, 7 were substantially improved, and 1 was nonresponsive.

✓ 12 of these patients were manic and 9 became symptom-free.
  ▫ The mean Young Mania Rating Scale fell from 28 to 4.

✓ 3 patients complained of drowsiness and 2 had drooling that remitted with dosage reduction or by end of treatment.

## Autism/Pervasive Developmental Disorders

Risperidone (Risperdal) over 12 weeks with average dose 3 mg shows efficacy with 8 (57%) of 14 patients taking risperidone vs. none of 16 in the placebo group ($p < .002$).

• Risperidone was superior to placebo in reducing repetitive behavior, aggression, anxiety, depression, irritability, and the overall behavioral symptoms of autism.

Haloperidol (0.5–4.0 mg/day) may decrease uncooperative behavior, emotional lability, and irritability.

• Avoid sedating antipsychotics.
• Carefully monitor target symptoms to be treated.

Serotonergic antidepressants (SSRIs), clomipramine, and divalproex sodium decreased autistic symptoms in open trials.

• May best help decrease repetitive behaviors and
• Increase interaction with others.

### Fluvoxamine (Luvox)

• Over 12 weeks, with the last 9 weeks at maximum dosage of 300 mg/day, yielded efficacy with 8 of the patients rated as "much improved" or "very much improved." None of the placebo patients had significant improvement.

√ Reductions in repetitive thoughts and behavior, maladaptive behavior, and aggression.

√ Increased communicative use of language, more initiation and response to verbal communication, more appropriate speech, and less echolalia.

- Fluvoxamine, fluoxetine, sertraline, and clomipramine are effective for the treatment of selected symptoms of autism.
    √ Paroxetine at 10 mg/day results in a marked reduction of various symptoms.

### Divalproex Sodium (Depakote)

- Open trial of divalproex involving 10 children and 4 adults with autism spectrum disorders:
    √ 10 had autism, 2 had Asperger's disorder, and 2 had pervasive developmental disorder (NOS).
    √ One-fifth of autistic patients had epilepsy, and half had abnormal EEGs.
- After a mean of 10.7 months of treatment, 10 of the 14 were classified as "much improved" or "very much improved" on the clinical global improvement scale (CGIS).
    √ There were fewer mood cycles, less manifestation of aggression, and less impulsivity.
    √ 4 patients showed social gains (more social relations, greater awareness and listening).
    √ 4 patients showed reduced obsessive-compulsive symptoms and increased flexibility.
    √ 1 showed improvement in communication.

## Schizotypal Personality Disorder

Ideas of reference, odd communication, social isolation, and transient psychosis respond to neuroleptics.

- Haloperidol 2–6 mg often effective range.
- Positive results often seen in 2 weeks.
- Higher drop-out rate from side effects (as much as 50%) seen when compared to schizophrenic patients.

## SIDE EFFECTS

The 3 phenothiazine groups have different side-effect profiles.

- Aliphatic—chlorpramazine (Thorazine) causes more hypotension, sedation, dermatitis, and convulsions, but less EPS.
- Piperidines—thioridazine (Mellaril) and mesoridazine (Serentil) cause more ECG effects, retinal toxicity, and ejaculatory problems, but least EPS.

- Piperazines—perphenazine (Trilafon), fluphenazine (Prolixin), and trifluoperazine (Stelazine) cause more EPS but less sedation, hypotension, and lens opacities.

### Comparison of Antipsychotic Side Effects

| | Sedation | Anticholinergic Effects | Orthostatic Hypotension | Extrapyramidal Symptoms |
|---|---|---|---|---|
| Chlorpromazine | + + + + | + + + | + + + + | + + |
| Clozapine* | + + + + | + + + + | + + + + | +/0 |
| Fluphenazine | + | + | + | + + + + |
| Haloperidol | + | + | + | + + + + |
| Loxapine | + + | + + | + + + | + + + |
| Mesoridazine | + + + | + + + + | + + + | + |
| Molindone | + + | + + | + | + + + |
| Olanzapine | + + + | + + + | + + | +/0 |
| Perphenazine | + + | + + | + + | + + + |
| Pimozide | + + + | + + + | + + | + + + + |
| Quetiapine | + + | + + + | + + | +/0 |
| Risperidone* | + | + + | + | + |
| Thioridazine | + + + | + + + + | + + + + | + |
| Thiothixene | + | + | + | + + + + |
| Trifluoperazine | + | + | + | + + + |
| Ziprasidone | + + + | + | + | + + |

+ + + + = most; + = least; * Dystonia not usually seen with risperidone (≤ 5 mg qd), clozapine, olanzapine, or quetiapine.

## Anticholinergic Effects

Anticholinergic actions affect many systems and produce a variety of symptoms:

- Hypotension
- Dry mouth
- Constipation
- Paralytic ileus
- Urinary hesitancy or retention
- Blurred near vision
- Dry eyes
- Narrow-angle glaucoma
- Photophobia
- Nasal congestion
- Confusion and decreased memory

Most anticholinergic symptoms decrease in 1–4 weeks but don't completely remit. (These anticholinergic effects are discussed with their respective organ systems.) Bethanechol 10–50 mg po tid or qid can reverse peripheral but not central effects. Duration of action is 2–8 h. Switching to a less anticholinergic neuroleptic and/or switching to a non-anticholinergic extrapyramidal drug (e.g., amantadine) can reduce or eliminate anticholinergic side effects.

## Cardiovascular Effects

*Nonspecific ECG changes and arrythymia*

- Especially with thioridazine, clozapine, and pimozide.
  - √ Usually quinidine-like effects (prolonged QT and PR interval and wave).
- Get baseline ECG before using higher-risk agents.
  - √ Do not use high-risk agents if congenital long QT syndrome seen
    - □ Or if taking other drugs that delay cardiac conduction (including some nonsedating antihistamines).
  - √ ECG is periodically recommended with pimozide during dose adjustment.
- *Torsade de Pointes* seen with high-dose IV haloperidol and pimozide (also a calcium channel-blocker) usually begins with QT interval lengthening.
  - √ Mean increase in QTc from baseline ranged from 9 to 14 msec greater than 4 comparison drugs (risperidone, olanzapine, quetiapine, and haloperidol).
  - √ Ziprasidone increased the QTc interval by a mean of 10 msec at the 160 mg daily dosage.
    - □ Ziprasidone should be avoided in patients with QT prolongation, recent acute MI, uncompensated heart failure or cardiac arrhythmia, or if persistent QTc measurements > 500 msec.
    - □ Ziprasidone and neuroleptic patients with symptoms that could indicate the occurrence of *Torsade de Pointes*—e.g., dizziness, palpitations, or syncope—should receive further medical evaluation.
  - √ Other agents that can increase risk
    - □ Phenothiazines
    - □ Heterocyclic antidepressants
    - □ Ia and III antiarrhythmics
  - √ Conditions that increase risk
    - □ Electrolyte or metabolic abnormalities
    - □ Hypokalemia and/or hypomagnesemia may risk QT prolongation and arrhythmia.
    - □ Hypokalemia can result from diuretic therapy, diarrhea, and other causes.
    - □ Low serum potassium and/or magnesium should be corrected before proceeding with treatment.
    - □ CNS disease

◻ Cardiac disease
◻ Toxins
◻ Congenital long QT syndromes

*Orthostatic hypotension*

See table on page 25 for drug comparisons.

- Dizziness, lightheadedness, weakness, fainting, and syncope on standing up; worse at times of peak blood levels.
  - √ Highest risk with low-potency phenothiazines, including clozapine, and moderate risk with mid-potency and atypical antipsychotics.
- Syncope reported in 0.6% of patients treated with ziprasidone.
- Management
  - √ Hypotension is more frequent with low salt intake, low fluid intake, antihypertensive agents, hypothyroidism, or stimulant withdrawal.
    - ◻ Correct these first.
    - ◻ Use least hypotensive antipsychotic drugs in these high-risk patients.
  - √ Suggest that patient stand up slowly over 15–60 seconds.
  - √ If more severe hypotension, lower head and elevate legs.
  - √ Use support hose (since middle of the night is highest risk time, patient needs to wear hose day and night).
  - √ Use divided doses to avoid high blood levels.
  - √ Try dihydroergotamine.
  - √ If medically serious, employ volume expanders and, if necessary,
    - ◻ Alpha-adrenergic pressor agents, such as metaraminol, phenylephrine, or norepinephrine.
    - ◻ *Do not use epinephrine or isoproteronol.*
  - √ Fludrocortisone 0.1—0.2 mg/daily
    - ◻ *Check electrolytes and BP regularly.*

*Tachycardia* (> 100 beats/minute)

- More often seen as isolated symptom without hypotension in young adults.
  - √ Stronger heart adequately compensates for BP drop.
- Especially common on clozapine and frequent on low-potency antipsychotics.
  - √ Manage by lowering antipsychotic dose or changing antipsychotic.
  - √ If persists, treat with peripheral beta-blocker or propafenone (antiarrhythmic).

## Central Nervous System Effects

- Low serum iron has been reported to be common in patients (particularly females) with akathisia, dystonic reactions, and neuroleptic malignant syndrome.
  - √ Anecdotal evidence suggests that measuring serum iron and, if needed, correcting with supplemental iron, may improve EPS.
- Atypical neuroleptics
  - √ Clozapine infrequently causes EPS and extremely rarely TD.
  - √ Changing to clozapine in neuroleptic-resistant patients with coexisting TD, parkinsonism, or akathisia can improve EPS side effects.
    - ▫ At mean final dose of 200 mg after 18 weeks, improvement rate was 50–74% for TD, 69% for parkinsonism, and 78% for chronic akathisia.
  - √ Risperidone causes EPS in doses ≥ 6 mg, but even at 16 mg qd, is significantly lower than haloperidol.
  - √ Risperidone can cause EPS at lower doses in high-risk patients, including
    - ▫ Geriatric patients
    - ▫ Parkinson's patients
    - ▫ Adolescent patients
    - ▫ Bipolar patients on lithium
    - ▫ Patients on SSRIs
  - √ Olanzapine can cause EPS in doses over 20 mg, but symptoms usually mild.
- Tardive dyskinesia has been observed following risperidone and olanzapine treatment (~0.4–0.5% per year on med).
  - √ However, schizophrenic patients who have never been on a neuroleptic have a lifetime 15% TD risk.

### Types of Extrapyramidal Symptoms

| Syndrome | Onset | Risk Groups | Clinical Course |
|---|---|---|---|
| Dystonia* | 8 h–5 days | Young males (under 30 y.o.) and females (under 25 y.o.) | Acute, spasmodic, painful; usually remits spontaneously in 10 days; can be prevented with ACA. |
| Parkinsonism | 5 h–30 days | 12–45% of patients; elderly, particularly women | Occurs throughout treatment. |
| Akathisia* | 2 h–60 days | 20–50% of patients, 35–50 y.o. | Persists during treatment; propranolol and amantadine may be more effective than ACA. |

| Syndrome | Onset | Risk Groups | Clinical Course |
|---|---|---|---|
| Neuroleptic malignant syndrome (NMS)* | Weeks | 0.5–1% of patients; 80% are under 40; affects 2X men as women; high-potency neuroleptics | Mortality rate is 20–30%; symptoms typically persist 5–10 days on oral forms and 20–30 days after depot injections. |
| "Rabbit" syndrome | Months–years | 4% of patients untreated with ACAs | Usually reversible with ACAs. |
| Tardive dyskinesia (TD) | Months–years | 20–30% of patients, with range of 0.5–60%; women, the elderly, and patients with mood or CNS disorders | Treat best with prevention; 50% irreversible; vitamin E 400 mg tid or qid may help (~1600 IU per day). ACAs usually hurt. |
| Tardive dystonia | Months–years (avg. 2–5 yrs.) | < 2% of patients; men < 40 y.o. | May start with blepharospasm; seldom remits; may partially respond to ACAs. |

\* Risk is substantially increased by rapid dosage increase of neuroleptic.

*Akathisia*

- The least obvious but the most prevalent EPS.
- The most common side effect that causes patients to stop neuroleptics.
    √ Erupts between 6 hours and 2 weeks after starting antipsychotic.
- Haloperidol-treated patients had higher treatment-emergent akathisia (8 of 21, 38%) vs. olanzapine (6 of 53, 11%).
- Symptoms include
    √ Subjective restlessness
    √ "Jitters," fidgety
    √ Tapping feet incessantly, "restless legs"
    √ Rocking forward and backward in chair
    √ Shifting weight from side to side when standing or sitting
- May present as a muscular discomfort in an agitated, frightened, dysphoric, pacing, hand-wringing, and weeping individual.
- Patients might not notice, or be bothered by, their regular, rhythmic leg-jiggling.
- Akathisia can be misdiagnosed as anxiety, psychotic agitation, attention-deficit/hyperactivity disorder, or stimulant abuse.
    √ Important to know patient's presentation before medication is started.
    √ If diagnosis is unclear, ask patient if restlessness is a "muscle" feeling or a "head" feeling; the muscle feeling often experienced in the limbs suggests akathisia; the head feeling, anxiety.
    √ Myoclonic jerks sometimes accompany akathisia.
    √ May see voluntary movements to reduce symptoms.
    √ May only be a subjective state with no observable behaviors.

- Treat with propranolol, amantadine, or benzodiazepine (*see* Chapter 2).
  - √ Anticholinergic agents are less effective.
- Differs from restless legs syndrome (RLS); frequent features of RLS, rarely seen in akathisia, include
  - √ Restricted to legs
  - √ Unpleasant sensory symptoms in calves
  - √ Myoclonic jerks
  - √ Insomnia
  - √ Worse, or only occurs, in evenings
  - √ Worse lying down, relief with walking
  - √ Responds best to benzodiazepines, L-dopa, or bromocriptine

*Parkinsonism*

- In parkinsonism (EPS) tremor, the fingers, hands, and wrists move faster and as a unit; micrographia also appears (but not in lithium tremor).
  - √ In Parkinson's disease, the tremor is slow and rhythmic, with prominent rotational and flexing movements (pill-rolling).
  - √ In anxiety, the tremor is fine, rapid, and rhythmic, with side-to-side movements.
- Symptoms include:
  - √ Decreased arm swing
    - □ Often the first sign and easiest to detect.
  - √ Stiffness, stooped posture
  - √ Masklike face, bradykinesia
  - √ Shuffling, festinating gait (with small steps)
  - √ Cogwheel rigidity
  - √ Drooling, seborrhea
  - √ Tremor
  - √ Coarse pill-rolling of thumb and fingers at rest
  - √ Micrographia
- In elderly, check for signs of parkinsonism *before* treatment with neuroleptic.
  - √ Shuffling gait, stooped posture, bradykinesia, increased extremity tone, and decreased facial mobility are not rare baseline signs in this population.
- Parkinsonism contributes to inactivity (which can be misdiagnosed as catatonia), withdrawn and negative symptoms, schizophrenia, and depression.
- Case reports suggest that pyridoxine 50 mg bid may help drug-induced parkinsonism.
- Treat by
  - √ Lowering dose
  - √ Switching to lower-risk EPS drug (e.g., atypicals)
    - □ Risperidone, even at 16 mg qd, has lower EPS than haloperidol.

√ Adding anticholinergic agent.
√ Adding amantadine.

*Akinesia*

- Symptoms include
  √ A paucity of spontaneous gestures or voluntary useful movements
  √ Apathy
  √ Rigid posture
  √ Diminished, or total lack of, conversation
  √ Arm swing decreased
  √ Walk with a shorter stride
- May or may not be associated with parkinsonism.
  √ Sedation 12 h after last dose suggests akinesia.
  √ Absence of leg-crossing also indicates akinesia.
- First approach to akinesia is to lower neuroleptic dose.
  √ Then add ACAs or amantadine, if needed.

*Neuroleptic malignant syndrome* (NMS)

- Uncommon yet hardly rare disorder; potentially fatal unless recognized and treated early.
- NMS affects 0.2–0.5% of patients treated with antipsychotics.
- Typically erupts in 24–72 h.
- Manifestations include hyperpyrexia, muscle rigidity, altered mental status, and evidence of autonomic instability (e.g., irregular pulse or blood pressure, tachycardia, diaphoresis, and/or dysrhythmia).
  √ Other signs may include elevated MB isoform of creatinine, myoglobinuria (rhabdomyolysis), and/or acute renal failure.
- Deaths, which usually result in 3–30 days, occur in 11–18% of NMS patients.
  √ Prior NMS episodes are a significant risk factor for future episodes.
    □ About 17% of NMS patients have experienced a similar episode.
  √ Estimated 1,000–4,000 NMS fatalities in the U.S. every year.
- Recurrence of NMS drops to 15% when low-potency neuroleptics are used and probably lower than that with atypical neuroleptics.

*DSM-IV* Research Criteria for NMS*

A. The development of severe muscle rigidity and elevated temperature (both labeled *A* below) associated with the use of neuroleptic medication.

---

* (A)—in criteria A *DSM-IV*.
  (B)—in criteria B *DSM-IV*.

B. Two or more of the items labeled *B* below. NMS symptoms are not accounted for, or due to, another substance, general medical condition, or mental disorder.

- NMS displays
  - √ Severe parkinsonism with
    - □ Muscle rigidity, catatonic appearance (A)
    - □ Tremors (B), dyskinesias
    - □ Akinesias, "lead-pipe" muscle tone
    - □ Flexor-extensor posturing
    - □ Festinating gait
  - √ Hyperpyrexia (101° F→107° F) (A)
  - √ Altered consciousness, which may present first, can be
    - □ Alert
    - □ Dazed mutism (B)
    - □ Agitated, confused, or comatose (B)
    - □ Obtunded (B), incontinent (B)
  - √ Autonomic dysfunction with
    - □ Tachycardia (> 130 beats/minute) (B)
    - □ Labile or increased BP (> 20 points diastolic) (B)
    - □ Profuse sweating (B)
    - □ Increased salivation
    - □ Tachypnea (> 25 respirations/minute)
    - □ Pallor
    - □ Dysphagia (B)
  - √ Severe abnormalities on laboratory tests
    - □ Evidence of severe muscle damage with high creatine kinase (C K 347 → 4286 U/ml) or myoglobinuria (B)
    - □ Renal decline or failure
    - □ Raised WBCs (15,000–30,000/mm$^3$) (B), and/or
    - □ Elevated LFTs

Each of the following has hyperthermia but with different symptoms than NMS hyperthermia.

*Anticholinergic syndrome* symptoms not seen in NMS (*see also* pages 138–39 in Antidepressants for further anticholinergic side effects).

- Dry skin
- Pupil dilation
- Hyperreflexia
- Muscle relaxation

*Hyperthermia* from drugs (e.g., lidocaine, meperidine, NSAID toxicity) or endocrinopathy (e.g., hyperthyroidism)

- No muscle effects

*Autonomic hyperreflexia* from CNS stimulants (e.g., amphetamine) not seen in NMS

- Hyperreflexia

NMS more commonly associated with

- Patients under 20 and over 60 y.o. have higher mortality rates from NMS.
- Patients with CNS syndromes, mental retardation, and drug addiction have greater mortality rates from NMS.
- Five factors were associated with risk of neuroleptic malignant syndrome.
    √ History of ECT
    √ High agitation and dehydration
    √ High neuroleptic doses, e.g., > 600 mg on chlorpromazine, another reason to generally avoid them.
        ▫ However, several reported risperidone NMS with doses < 6 mg.
    √ Maximum neuroleptic dose on any one day
    √ More days in restraint or seclusion
- Rapid neuroleptization, another reason not to use this approach.
- Depot antipsychotic agents generate more symptoms of NMS, but same number of deaths.
- Higher- rather than lower-potency antipsychotics, although greater use of high-potency drugs may inflate the frequency.
    √ If NMS with low-potency drug, generally higher fatality.
    √ One-third of NMS patients develop it again if placed on any antipsychotic.
- On lithium
    √ Risk factor may be bipolar mood disorder and not lithium itself.
- Low serum iron
    √ Cause vs. effect of NMS not resolved.
- High ambient temperatures
    √ More often in summer.
- Dehydration
- Taking 2 or more neuroleptics.

Fatalities from NMS, in percentage of patients who developed NMS on a specific antipsychotic, are

- Trifluoperazine (43%)
- Chlorpromazine (40%)
- Thiothixene (40%)
- Fluphenazine (depot) (33.3%)
- Fluphenazine (8.3%)

- Haloperidol (5.5%)
- Thioridazine (0%)

Supportive measures must be instituted immediately.

- Stop neuroleptics and anticholinergic agents.
- Maintain hydration by oral or IV routes.
- Correct electrolyte abnormalities.
- Use antipyretic agents.
- Cool body to reduce fever.
- Diagnose and treat pneumonia or pulmonary emboli.
- No drug treatment has been proven to be more effective than intensive supportive measures.
- One study compared supportive care with supportive care plus dantrolene alone, bromocriptine alone, or dantrolene/bromocriptine combined.
  - √ All treatments showed improvement within 2–4 days after neuroleptic was stopped.
  - √ Duration of NMS with supportive treatment was 5–14 days.
  - √ Duration of NMS with drug treatments was longer, averaging 14 days.
    - □ 20% lasted 4 weeks or more.
    - □ 30% of bromocriptine-treated patients had recurrence of NMS signs when bromocriptine reduced.
- For patients not markedly better after a few days of intensive supportive treatment, consider drug treatments, including
  - √ Bromocriptine
    - □ Safest drug treatment for NMS.
    - □ Rigidity quickly disappears.
    - □ Temperature, BP instability, and creatine kinase levels normalize after a few days.
    - □ Failing bromocritpine, consider amantadine.
  - √ Dantrolene
    - □ Lowers hyperthermia and creatine kinase, while increasing muscle relaxation, often in hours.
    - □ Initial dose may be 2–3 mg/kg/day.
    - □ Hepatic toxicity occurs with doses > 10 mg/kg/day.
  - √ Carbamazepine
    - □ Reported effective within 8 h after first dose of 600 mg followed by 200 mg tid.
    - □ Dose later titrated to establish therapeutic CBZ level.
  - √ ECT has been successful, especially in the post–NMS patient.
- ACAs usually do not help and risk hyperthermia.
- Failing reasonable trial(s), consider plasmapheresis for NMS.
  - √ When patient has recently had a decanoate preparation, special case to consider plasmapheresis.

Neuroleptic rechallenge after prior NMS

- High (> 80%) success rates reported.
- Best chances of success (no NMS) with
  √ 2 or more week wait after the last clinical sign of NMS.
  √ Start with low doses and very gradual dose increases.
    □ Low-potency antipsychotics may be safer, but this is unproven.
    □ Atypical antipsychotics, e.g., olanzapine (10–20 mg) or risperidone (2–5 mg), and especially clozapine (25–250 mg) have significantly lower NMS rates and are therefore first choices for patients with h/o NMS.
  √ Plentiful hydration.
  √ Cool room temperatures.
  √ Monitor temperature and other vital signs frequently.
  √ Check WBC and CPK regularly.

### Drugs Used to Treat NMS

| Generic Name | Dose |
|---|---|
| Anticholinergic agents | —— |
| Bromocriptine | 7.5–60 mg/day po |
| Dantrolene | 0.8–10 mg/kg/IV; 50 mg qd–qid po |
| Levodopa | 100 mg bid po |
| Carbidopa-levodopa | 25 mg tid–200 qid po |
| Amantadine | 100 mg bid or tid po |
| Lorazepam | 1.5–2 mg IV, then po |

*Paresthesia*

- Burning paresthesia reported with risperidone
  √ Seen most often on hands and feet
  √ Severity dose-related
  √ Incidence ~2%

*"Rabbit syndrome" (a.k.a. perioral tremor)*

- Arises late during neuroleptic treatment.
  √ Consists of rapid lip (typically a 5 Hz tremor) and buccal masticatory movements that mimic a rabbit.
  √ Sometimes mistaken for TD but unlike TD.
    □ Does not involve tongue.
    □ Continues during sleep.
- Responds well to ACAs.
- Stops when neuroleptic is stopped.

*Sedation*

- See table (page 25) for drug sedation comparisons.
- Sedation declines during first 2 weeks of therapy.

- Management
  - √ Prescribe full dose at bedtime.
  - √ Diminish daytime doses.
  - √ Switch to less sedating neuroleptic.
- Some impairment may be related to dopamine blockade.
  - √ Increasing cognitive impairment seen.
    - □ In one study nicotine transdermal patches reversed impairment.

## Seizures

- Uncommon.
- Occur when antipsychotics raised or lowered (especially abruptly).
- More common with clozapine.
  - √ Dose related:
    - □ 1–2% with < 300 mg qd
    - □ 3–4% with 300–500 mg qd
    - □ 5% with 600–900 mg qd
  - √ In patients on > 300 mg clozapine, 65% have abnormal EEGs.
  - √ Increased risk with large single doses and/or rapid dose titration.
    - □ Lower risk with tid or qid dosing.
    - □ Lower risk with increases of 12.5–25 mg every 2–4 days.
  - √ Increased risk with high plasma levels ($\geq 450$ $\mu$g/ml).
    - □ Obtain plasma levels in patients with high seizure-risk.
- Interventions if seizure occurs include:
  - √ Reduce dose by half if possible.
  - √ Get neurology consult.
  - √ Get EEG.
  - √ Begin valproate or other appropriate anticonvulsant.
    - □ Do not use carbamazepine with clozapine.
- After blood level stabilized, increase clozapine 25 mg/day to desired dose.
- After 6 months wean anticonvulsant.
- Much lower risk with molindone and fluphenazine.
- Seizures common in epileptics, although epileptics can usually tolerate neuroleptics without seizures.

## Tardive dyskinesia (TD)

- Consists of involuntary face, trunk, and/or limb movements.
- Presents with 3 major types of symptoms.
  - √ *Facial-lingual-oral involuntary hyperkinesis* (most common type):
    - □ Frowning, blinking, smiling, grimacing, puckering, pouting, blowing, smacking, licking, chewing, clenching, mouth

opening, rolling and protruding ("fly catcher's") tongue, and spastic facial distortions.

√ *Limb choreoathetoid movements:*
  ▫ Choreiform movements that are rapid, purposeless, irregular, and spontaneous.
  ▫ Athetoid movements that are slow, irregular, complex, and serpentine.
  ▫ Tremors that are repetitive, regular, and rhythmic.
  ▫ Lateral knee movements.
  ▫ Foot tapping, squirming, inversion, and eversion.

√ *Trunk movements:*
  ▫ Movements of neck, shoulders, dramatic hip jerks.
  ▫ Rocking, twisting, squirming, pelvic gyrations, and thrusts.

- TD patients
  √ May grunt,
  √ Suppress symptoms temporarily by intense voluntary effort and concentration,
  √ Have TD symptoms disappear while asleep,
  √ Experience exacerbation under stress.
- TD typically arises after 6–36 months of neuroleptic treatment.
  √ Rarely occurs before 3 months, but
  √ Symptoms may emerge in weeks.
  √ Initially appears milder in people on larger neuroleptic doses, which mask TD.
  √ Typically appears or worsens when antipsychotics are lowered or stopped, but often seen while still on full antipsychotic dose.
  √ Severity often reaches a plateau in 3–8 years and may not worsen further.

TD in elderly (N = 261)

- 60 patients (23%) developed TD.
- Severity of TD rated severe in 8 patients (13%), moderate in 24 patients (40%), and mild in 28 patients (47%).
- Persistent (at least 3 months) TD developed in 46 (77%), and 39 (85%) had movements during the entire follow-up period.

Drug-induced TD

- All antipsychotics can cause TD.
- Atypical neuroleptics have much lower TD risk.
  √ Typical neuroleptics with 5–10% per year risk.
  √ Risperidone's lower risk in < 6 mg qd doses with 0.34–0.5% per year risk.
    ▫ One study of 3,298 patients yielded only 4 cases of TD.
  √ Olanzapine has similar risk, 0.52% per year.

√ 129 patients with presumptive TD treated up to 52 weeks showed a 55% reduction of TD symptoms at 6 weeks and a 71% reduction at 30 weeks using Abnormal Involuntary Movement Scale.
- Other drugs may cause TD, such as
  √ Amoxapine, an antidepressant with significant neuroleptic properties.
  √ Dopamine-blocking antiemetics, e.g., prochlorperazine (Compazine), metoclopramide (Reglan), promethazine (Phenergan), trimethobenzamide (Tigan), thiethylperazine (Torecan), triflupromazine (Vesprin).
- Drug-induced rate may be lower than suspected because spontaneous dyskinesias occur in 15–20% of chronic never-treated schizophrenics and in 24+% of schizotypal (and not in paranoid or schizoid) personality disorder.
  √ Risk factors for spontaneous dyskinesia include
    □ Prominent negative symptoms, deficit form of schizophrenia,
    □ Lower premorbid IQ,
    □ Hebephrenic subtype (46% prevalence).
- Frequency varies enormously among studies.
  √ Probably closest to 15% (over spontaneous dyskinesia rate) in patients treated with antipsychotics for over 2 years.
    □ About 50% of these are reversible.
  √ Most cases mild.
  √ 2–5% of patients get severe symptoms.
  √ Once TD syndrome manifests, it doesn't usually progress.
  √ Dyskinesia affects 1–5% of nonschizophrenics *never* exposed to neuroleptics.
    □ Particularly the elderly.
- Antipsychotic-induced TD risk factors include:
  √ More interruptions in neuroleptic treatment
  √ Longer use and higher dose equivalents of neuroleptics
  √ Female patients over 40 y.o.
  √ Male patients under 30 y.o.
  √ Mood disorder
    □ May be due to intermittent neuroleptic use
  √ African ethnicity
  √ Older age
  √ Brain impairment/mental retardation
  √ Diabetes ($2 \times$ higher)
  √ Prior EPS symptoms
    □ However, TD can occur when EPS has never occurred.
- Make sure "TD" does not stem from ill-fitting dentures!
- Prevention of TD:

√ Regularly monitor patients on antipsychotics with a standardized TD assessment scale, such as the Abnormal Involuntary Movement Scale (AIMS).

√ Neuroleptics should not be used longer than 6 continuous months in *non*schizophrenic patients who do not have chronic psychotic symptoms or significant risk of relapse.

√ Assess long-treated patients at least every 6 months to see if neuroleptics can be reduced or stopped.

    ▫ Reduction is usually the most likely alternative, since long-treated patients rarely do well off of neuroleptics.

√ If antipsychotic discontinued and TD emerges, allow at least 3–7 months for symptoms to disappear or lessen on their own.

    ▫ Spontaneous remission rate in 6 months about 50%.

    ▫ After 6 months spontaneous remission rate for 10 yrs. about 2.5–5% a year.

    ▫ After 18 months, abnormal movements diminish by mean of 50%.

√ ACAs do not usually alleviate TD and often aggravate it.

√ Neuroleptics can temporarily mask TD, but symptoms eventually reemerge, frequently worse.

- 2 drugs effective in controlled trials:

  √ Vitamin E 1200–1600 mg qd

    ▫ Strongest evidence of efficacy particularly in cases with TD under 5 yrs.

    ▫ Approximately 50% have clinically significant improvement.

    ▫ Not curative—symptoms may return within 12 weeks after Vitamin E discontinued.

    ▫ Minimal efficacy in TD > 5 yrs. duration.

  √ Acetazolamide 1.5–2.0 g qd with tid dosing for 2 months (double-blind crossover with placebo)

    ▫ 41–46% improvement in TD.

    ▫ 40% improvement in EPS.

    ▫ Thiamine 1.5 g in tid dosing given to prevent kidney stones and 8 oz. orange juice to maintain K+.

    ▫ May be effective for patients with TD > 5 yrs.

- Odansetron may reduce TD.

  √ 30 schizophrenic inpatients (mean age 69) with mild or worse TD that persisted 3–45 yrs.

    ▫ Patients treated with 4–8 mg of odansetron daily for 4 weeks.

    ▫ Mean reduction in total AIMS was 45%, and 4 patients showed a reduction of 50% or more.

    ▫ Significant improvement in the Positive and Negative Symptom Scale.

    ▫ Another study with 6-week duration and 12 mg/day of odansetron had "solid" results.

- Lacking convincing evidence, other drugs that might inhibit TD include:
  - √ Amantadine (100 mg bid–tid)—15% average improvement in very chronic (most > 5 yrs.) population, some with 25% improvement.
  - √ Baclofen (5–20 mg tid)
  - √ Benzodiazepines (e.g., diazepam, clonazepam)
  - √ Bromocriptine (2.5 mg/day) helped in placebo-controlled trial
    - □ Perhaps by preferentially stimulating autoreceptors.
  - √ Buspirone (45–120 mg/day)
  - √ Calcium channel-blockers
    - □ Verapamil (160–320 mg qd), diltiazem (120–240 mg qd)
  - √ Carbamazepine (100–800 mg/day)
  - √ Choline (2–8 g/day)
  - √ Clonidine (0.3–0.7 mg/day)
  - √ Lecithin (10–40 g/day)
  - √ Levodopa (100–2000 mg/day)
  - √ Lithium (300 mg tid–qid)
  - √ Reserpine (1–6 mg/day)
  - √ Valproic acid (1000–1500 mg/day)

*Tardive dystonia*

- Tardive dystonia is characterized by sustained involuntary muscular contractions frequently causing twisting and repetitive movements or abnormal postures.
  - √ Like tardive dyskinesia, occurs after prolonged neuroleptic exposure.
    - □ Appears while on medication or after withdrawal.
- Tardive dystonia develops faster and is more painful, distressing, and disabling than tardive dyskinesia.
  - √ Neuroleptic exposure is most significant etiologic factor.
  - √ Tardive dystonia is also a known complication of cerebral injury, with a range of 7–48%.
- Acute contractions typically affect tongue, face, neck, jaw, and/or back.
  - √ Spasms of tongue, jaw, and neck are the first to erupt, typically within a few hours or days.
  - √ Patient may describe stiff tongue as "thick."
  - √ Neck involvement (retrocollis, torticollis) most common.
- Other dystonic symptoms include
  - √ *Opisthotonos*, a tetanic tightening of the entire body, with torso and head extended
  - √ *Oculogyric crisis* with eyes locked upward
  - √ *Laryngospasm* with respiratory difficulties
  - √ *Torticollis*, a twisting of cervical muscles with an unnatural head position

- When less severe, patient has some voluntary control, as with normal eye blinking.
  - √ Voluntary control does not mean patient faking.
- More common with manics (26%) than with schizophrenics (6%).
- So common (> 70%) with high-potency typical neuroleptics in males under 30 and females under 25 that prophylactic treatment with anticholinergic advised for first 10 days of treatment.
  - √ Consider atypical neuroleptic instead.
- Generally self-limited duration 10–14 days.
- Risk factors include male gender, youth, mental retardation.
- Tardive dystonia differs from tardive dyskinesia:
  - √ Occurs more often in men.
  - √ Twice as often in bipolars.
  - √ Occurs after a relatively short history of exposure.
    - □ Average < 2.5 years
  - √ Often causes significant disability.
  - √ Rarely remits.
  - √ May partially respond to anticholinergic agents.
  - √ May first present with blepharospasm.
- Treatments of tardive dystonia include:
  - √ Benzodiazepines (e.g., clonazepam)
  - √ Atypical neuroleptics
    - □ Clozapine, risperidone, olanzapine, ziprasidone, and quetiapine
    - □ Much lower EPS risk with olanzapine and risperidone, minimal with ziprasidone or quetiapine, and nearly no EPS with clozapine.
  - √ Reserpine—depletes dopamine.
  - √ Baclofen and other muscle relaxants.
  - √ Anticholinergics
  - √ Antiemetics—e.g., odansetron (Zofran), trimethobenzamide (Tigan), and many others
  - √ Tetrabenazine—depletes and blocks dopamine.
  - √ Botulinum toxin type A injected into affected muscle group (duration of effect weeks to months) (N = 34).
    - □ Of 38 affected body regions among the 34 patients, 29 were moderately to markedly improved.
    - □ Mean duration of improvement was $12.5 \pm 3.6$ weeks.
    - □ Five patients showed no improvement; none worsened.
    - □ Adverse effects lasted for less than 3 weeks.
- Alternatively, patients may experience
  - √ Tardive akathisia (with persistent restless feelings),
  - √ Tardive tics.

ANTIPSYCHOTIC AGENTS

## Side Effects from Depot Neuroleptics

| Side Effects | Fluphenazine Decanoate (FD) | Fluphenazine Enanthate (FE) (Not Preferred) | Haloperidol Decanoate (HD) |
|---|---|---|---|
| Anticholinergic | Occasional | More anticholinergic than FD | Occasional |
| Cardiovascular | Hypotension occasionally; some hypertension reported | Hypotension and some hypertension reported at start of therapy | Occasional hypotension; no severe hypertension reported |
| CNS | Drowsiness and insomnia | Same as FD | Same as FD |
| Endocrine effects | Menstrual disturbances (galactorrhea and amenorrhea) | Same as FD | Same as FD |
| EPS | EPS frequent, FD > HD; 25% have dystonias; NMS more common than with po forms | EPS more frequent (30–50%) than with FD, but 11.7% have dystonias; more NMS than po forms | EPS common, but equal to po form; TD in HD > FD; more NMS than with po form |
| Eye changes | 17% (11/63) of patients displayed lens and/or corneal opacities after 5 years | None reported | None reported |
| Laboratory changes | One case of jaundice; ECG changes noted; QT prolongation possible | No account of jaundice; some ECG changes; QT prolongation can occur | Within normal variation |
| Mood | May increase depression in vulnerable patients | Same as FD | No data |
| Skin and local reactions | One case of induration at high doses; skin reactions arise | No indurations reported; skin reactions occur | Inflammation at injection site; one case of photosensitivity; needle "tracks" observed |
| Weight gain | 11% of patients had a 10% weight increase; 4 times more patients gain weight than on oral fluphenazine | Similar to FD | Weight gain more common than weight loss |

# Endocrine and Sexual Effects

Increased blood prolactin can occur with all antipsychotics except clozapine and maybe quetiapine.

- Olanzapine can cause a modest, often transient, increase in prolactin.
- SSRIs, particularly paroxetine, may increase prolactin and exacerbate neuroleptic-induced prolactinemia.

- Get prolactin levels if
  √ Any of the prior symptoms occur.
  √ Postmenopausal woman not on estrogen.

Elevated prolactin may produce

- *Amenorrhea, menstrual irregularities, delayed ovulation*
  √ Risperidone may have the highest risk, with prolactin levels routinely as high as, or higher than, in patients on haloperidol.
    ▫ > 100 ng in many premenopausal women
- *Breast enlargement and tenderness, in women and men (gynecomastia)*
- *Breast cancer growth increased*
  √ In approximately 1/3 of breast cancers, increased prolactin increases growth rate.
  √ Change to a lower-risk neuroleptic, i.e., clozapine, olanzapine, or quetiapine.
  √ In patients with these tumors, clozapine may be safest.
- *Galactorrhea*
  √ Neuroleptics studied included phenothiazines, butyrophenones, and atypical agents.
  √ 28 women (19%) reported galactorrhea, most during the first 3 weeks of treatment.
  √ Prolactin levels were assayed in 24 of these patients.
    ▫ 16 were elevated, 4 were borderline, and 4 were in normal range.
    ▫ Initial average daily doses of neuroleptics were significantly ($p < .001$) higher in patients with galactorrhea.
    ▫ Women who had been previously pregnant were more than twice as likely to develop galactorrhea during antipsychotic drug treatment than women who had never been pregnant.
- *Diminished libido*
  √ Changed quality of orgasm for men and women.
  √ Diminished ability to reach orgasm.
  √ Decreased erectile and/or ejaculatory function in men.
- *Osteoporosis*
  √ Correlates with the magnitude and duration of hyperprolactinemia.
  √ Cigarette smoking also causes worse, and/or worsens, osteoporosis in women by interfering with the protective effect of estrogen.
  √ Polydipsia through increased calcium loss in the urine also causes/worsens osteoporosis.

Management of elevated prolactin

- Bromocriptine, which inhibits prolactin secretion, exists as 2.5 mg tablets or as 5 mg capsules.

√  Start at 1.25–2.5 mg/day.
√  Add 2.5 mg every 3–7 days as tolerated,
√  Until optimal dose of 5–7.5 mg/day is reached, or
√  The therapeutic range of 2.5–15 mg/day is satisfied.
- Bromocriptine occasionally worsens psychoses.
   √  Amantadine sometimes can substitute.

*Hyperglycemia, glycosuria, high or prolonged glucose tolerance tests*

- 52 patients (42 males) were followed for up to 1 year while taking a mean of 23.7 mg/day of olanzapine.
   √  5 (10%) of the patients had blood glucose levels above 140 mg/dL at the beginning of the study, but that number went up to 16 (31%) by the end of the study.
   √  7 (44%) of the patients developed hyperglycemia at follow-up but had no history of diabetes or blood glucose at baseline.
- Elevated blood glucose level of 290 mg/dL six weeks after starting olanzapine in 3 (22%) patients. After 13 weeks the drug was stopped, and within 12 weeks blood glucose was normal.
   √  All 3 were obese males, and 2 of 3 were African-Americans.
   √  Many of the reported cases of clozapine-induced hyperglycemia have been in African-Americans.

*Hypothyroidism*

- Slight decrease of total T-3, total T-4, free T-4 without increase of TSH.

*Insulin, leptin, and blood lipids in olanzapine-treated patients* (N = 14)

- 12 (85%) reported weight gain between 1 and 10 kg over 5 months.
- 8 (57%) had BMI above the normal limit.
- 10 (71%) had insulin levels above the normal limit.
- 8 (57%) had hyperleptinemia.
- 8 (62%) had triglyceridemia.
- 11 (85%) had hypercholesterolemia.
- 3 (22%) patients were diagnosed as having diabetes mellitus.

*Priapism*

- Occurs most often with alpha$_1$ adrenergic blockade (e.g., low-potency antipsychotics).

*Retrograde ejaculation/erectile dysfunction*

- May be physically painful.
- Occurs with patients on all neuroleptics, but especially common with thioridazine.

√ 44% had difficulties achieving an erection.
√ 35% had trouble maintaining an erection.
√ 49% had "changes" in erections.

*Sexual dysfunction*

- Reported in 25+% of patients taking neuroleptics.
- Affects 60% of patients on thioridazine.
- Management
  √ Cyproheptadine 2–8 mg po prn 2 hours before intercourse or tid to allow spontaneous sex.
  √ Yohimbine 2.7–8.1 mg prn 2 hours before intercourse or tid to allow spontaneous sex.
    □ Yohimbine (5 mg tid) or bethanechol (10 mg tid) may reduce impotence.
    □ May aggravate psychosis
  √ Amantadine 100–400 mg qd.
  √ Bupropion 75–225 mg a day, in divided doses.
    □ May aggravate psychosis

## Eyes, Ears, Nose, and Throat Effects

*Blurred vision*

- Difficulty in vision close up, not far away.
  √ Most often an anticholinergic side effect.
- Management
  √ Pilocarpine 1% eye drops, or
  √ Bethanechol 5–30 mg po effective for 2–8 h.
  √ Eye glasses can be used temporarily, but they need frequent changing.

*Cataracts*

- Seen with quetiapine in beagle dogs (a breed with increased risk of cataracts without quetiapine); not yet seen in primates, including humans.
  √ Regular 6-months ophthalmologic screening still recommended by manufacturer.

*Dry bronchial secretions and strained breathing*

- Aggravate patients with respiratory patients.

*Dry eyes*

- This anticholinergic disturbance particularly bothers the elderly or those wearing contact lenses.
- Management

√ Artificial tears
  ▫ Employ cautiously with soft contact lenses, or
  ▫ Apply patient's usual wetting solution or comfort drops.
√ Bethanechol 5–30 mg po.

*Narrow-angle glaucoma*

- Highly anticholinergic neuroleptics can trigger narrow-angle glaucoma.
- A h/o eye or facial pain, blurred vision, or halos circling outside lights suggest acute narrow-angle glaucoma.
  √ When shining a penlight across the eye's anterior chamber, if the entire eye does not illuminate, suspect narrow-angle glaucoma.

*Nasal congestion, dry throat*

*Photophobia*

- Pupils dilated by anticholinergic effects.

*Pigmentation*

- Long-term neuroleptic use, especially chlorpromazine, places granular deposits chiefly in the back of the cornea and the front of the lens.
  √ Star-shaped opacities in front of the lens indicate a more advanced case.
- Pigmentation probably dose-dependent.
- Vision usually unimpaired.
  √ Eye pigmentation often coexists with neuroleptic-induced skin pigmentation or photosensitivity reactions.
- Eye pigmentation does not require slit-lamp examination,
  √ But if shining a light into the eye displays an opaque pupil, patient should consult ophthalmologist.

*Pigmentary retinopathy*

- Caused almost always by chronic use of > 800 mg/day of thioridazine.
- Reduced visual acuity and blindness.
- Management
  √ Stop thioridazine.
  √ Symptoms may disappear, if caught early.
  √ *Never* prescribe > 800 mg/day of thioridazine.

*Hallucinations*

- Visual
- Auditory

## Gastrointestinal Effects

*Allergic obstructive hepatitis*
- √ This cholestatic jaundice is much less common now than when chlorpromazine (and its impurities) was introduced.
- √ Occurred in < 0.1% of patients in first month of treatment.
- √ Rarely leads to hepatic necrosis or permanent damage.
- √ Reversible if drug stopped.
- √ Routine LFT do not predict.
- √ Lower risk with higher-potency neuroleptics.

*Anorexia, nausea, vomiting, dyspepsia*

*Constipation*

- Management
  - √ Increase bulk (e.g., bran, salads) and fluids (water, milk).
  - √ Improve diet (e.g., prunes).
  - √ Add stool softener (e.g., docusate), fiber (e.g., psyllium), or
  - √ Bethanechol 10–50 mg tid–qid.

*Dry mouth*

- Management
  - √ Sugar-free gum and sugarless candy to reduce dental cavities, thrush, and weight gain
  - √ Cool drinks (minimal sugar, e.g., Gatorade, or drinks with sugar substitutes)
  - √ Biotène—sugar-free cool mints
  - √ Ice chips
  - √ Frequent brushing
  - √ Wash mouth with
    - ▫ Pilocarpine 1% solution, or
    - ▫ Gradually dissolve cholinergic agonist bethanechol 5–10 mg tablets.

*Diabetes*

- Type 2 diabetes frequency was
  - √ 15.5% treated with clozapine
  - √ 11% treated with olanzapine
  - √ 6.6% treated with haloperidol
  - √ 6% treated with risperidone
  - √ 4.5% treated with fluphenazine

*Diarrhea (occasionally)*

*Excessive salivation*

- Seen most often with clozapine (32%).
  - √ Can be treated with
    - ▫ Anticholinergic agents
    - ▫ Clonidine patch
    - ▫ Pirenzepine 25–100 mg qd

*Hepatic transaminase enzymes*

- Mild transient increase seen with atypicals and many typical antipsychotics.
- Two boys with probable steatohepatitis due to long-term risperidone and resultant weight gain.

*Paralytic ileus*

*Weight gain*

- Usually due to increased appetite and decreased activity.
- Meta-analysis of 73 trials
  - √ Mean weight increases after 10 weeks were 9.8 lbs. with clozapine, 9.1 with olanzapine, 4.6 with risperidone, 2.3 with haloperidol, and 1.9 with ziprasidone.
- 25 inpatients (21 men, 4 women) were treated with olanzapine.
  - √ Mean weight increased 12 lbs. over 12 weeks.
  - √ Fasting glycerides increased a mean of 60 mg/dL
    - ▫ Range 162–222 mg/dL.
  - √ No change seen in cholesterol.
- More common with clozapine, chlorpromazine, chlorprothixene, thioridazine, mesoridazine.
  - √ Most common with clozapine.
    - ▫ About 70% gain an average of 14–17 lbs. in 4–6 months.
  - √ Quite common with the atypical antipsychotics other than ziprasidone, probably due to postsynaptic H1 blockade.
    - ▫ Olanzapine and quetiapine have higher weight gain than high- and mid-potency typical neuroleptics.
    - ▫ With chronic use (238 median days) 56% of olanzapine patients gained more than 7% of their baseline weight; average long-term weight gain was 5.4 kg.
    - ▫ Risperidone has less weight gain, more comparable to other high-potency neuroleptics.

*Weight loss*

- Molindone does not cause significant weight gain.
  - √ Molindone average weight loss at 100 mg dose is 4.8 lbs. in 2 months.

# Hematologic Effects

*Agranulocytosis* (Schultz syndrome)

- Agranulocytosis is a granulocyte count (polys 4 bands) < 500/mm$^3$.
- Occurs suddenly, often within hours, usually in the first month of treatment, but can erupt any time during the initial 12 weeks of therapy.
- Arises in < 0.02% of patients on neuroleptics.
- Results most frequently with clozapine (0.85–1.3%) and chlorpromazine (0.7%).
  - √ < 1% with frequent monitoring.
  - √ Extremely rare with high-potency neuroleptics and atypical antidepressants.
- Statistically more frequent in white females over 40 y.o.
- Common signs and symptoms are
  - √ Acute sore throat
  - √ High fever
  - √ Mouth sores and ulcers
- Also possible are
  - √ Upset stomach
  - √ Weakness, lethargy, malaise
  - √ Lymphadenopathy
  - √ Asthma
  - √ Skin ulcerations
  - √ Laryngeal, angioneurotic, or peripheral edema
  - √ Anaphylactic reactions
- Management
  - √ Do not start any patient on low-potency neuroleptic if WBC is < 3000–3500/mm$^3$.
  - √ With onset of sore throat and fever, *stop* all non–life-sustaining drugs (e.g., neuroleptics).
  - √ Routine or frequent CBCs do not help, except with clozapine.
- Mortality high if drug not ceased and treatment initiated.

Clozapine-induced agranulocytosis—special considerations:

- High-risk groups/factors include:
  - √ Women twice as often as men
  - √ Lower baseline WBC counts
  - √ Over 40 y.o. but may be under 21 y.o.
  - √ Ashkenazi Jews with specific HLA haplotype
  - √ Coadministration of drugs at risk for agranulocytosis
- Cumulative incidence over time of 73 patients who developed agranulocytosis
  - √ 2 months—31%; 3 months—84%; 6 months—96%

- Incidence on clozapine
  - √ 0.75% first 6 months, 0.05% second 6 months, 0.06% third 6 months.
  - √ Should get labs, including agranulocytosis, weekly for 6 months and then decrease to biweekly if stable.

Agranulocytosis prodrome (time from first WBC drop to agranulocytosis):

- Mean of 28 days
- However, 28% dropped abruptly in 8 days or less.

May be 2 types of clozapine-induced neutropenia:

- $500–1500/m^2$ neutrophils ↓
  - √ May be due to destruction in blood or spleen.
  - √ Usually asymptomatic in 3–7 days after clozapine discontinued.
  - √ Lithium increases granulocyte-macrophage colony stimulating factor.
  - √ May be preventable by starting lithium 3 weeks prior to clozapine reexposure and maintaining lithium level at 0.8–1.1 mEq/l.
- $< 500/m^3$ neutrophils
  - √ Neutrophil precursor production stopped.
  - √ Recovery in 14–22 days (mean = 16 days).
    - ▫ Risks neutropenic sepsis.
    - ▫ Count may initially fall further after clozapine discontinued.

Treatment of agranulocytosis

- Hematopoietic growth factors, i.e., granulocyte colony stimulating factor and granulocyte-macrophage colony stimulating factor (GM CSF), given 48 h after onset.
  - √ Both accelerate recovery in mean of 8 days.

Starting clozapine contraindicated if

- WBC $< 3500/m^3$ or neutrophils $< 1500/m^3$.
- These limitations include those with benign neutropenia, cancer chemotherapy, or HIV infection.

Clozapine WBC monitoring:

- Initial 6 months, weekly while on drug and for 4 weeks after discontinued.
- After 6 months, monitor every other week if patient has acceptable WBC counts.
- Patient must report any sign of infection (e.g., lethargy, weakness, fever, sore throat).

- Sandoz controls protocol, e.g., when to increase monitoring and when to stop medication.
  - √ Generic clozapine now available.
    - ▫ Has wider range of blood levels.
    - ▫ May risk too low or too high blood levels.

*Eosinophilia* (clozapine-induced)

- Occurs at 3–5 weeks after clozapine administration and usually disappears after another 4 weeks.
  - √ 10–60% of patients experience this.
  - √ Eosinophil may reach as high as 55% of total WBC count.
  - √ Clozapine should be stopped if eosinophils reach $1400/\mu$l–$3000/\mu$l.
- Do not immediately change to olanzapine, due to reports of prolonged (mean/21 days) granulocytopenia in some patients.

*Leukopenia*

- WBC 2000–3500/mm$^3$
- Usually gradual and without symptoms, and
- More common than agranulocytosis.
  - √ Usually transient.

Management

- Symptoms may be similar to agranulocytosis.
- If no symptoms and not severe, wait and repeat labs.
- May be prevented with lithium addition if mainly neutropenia.
- If more severe, reduce or stop antipsychotic.

## Renal Effects

*Polydipsia and hyponatremia*

- Polydipsia (compulsive water drinking) frequently occurs in chronic schizophrenia, particularly during psychotic exacerbations.
  - √ 25–50% of patients with polydipsia develop hyponatremia.
  - √ 3–5% of chronic schizophrenics are hyponatremic and may experience episodes of life-threatening water intoxication accompanied by impaired water excretion usually related to inappropriate antidiuretic hormone secretion.
  - √ Signs and symptoms of acute water intoxication include lethargy, nausea, confusion, blurred vision, vomiting, ataxia, myoclonus, cramps, large diurnal weight gain, and seizures.

√ Water intoxication can cause delirium, seizures, coma, irreversible neurological deficits, and death.
  ▫ Usually seen with acute water intoxication and < 120 nmol sodium.
  ▫ Chronic cases may experience headache, constant thirst, anorexia, and excretional dyspnea.
√ Detection of self-induced water intoxication includes
  ▫ Consumption of water > 3–4 liters qd
  ▫ Greater than a 3–5% weight gain from A.M. to P.M.
  ▫ Urine specific gravity < 1.01
√ Treatments for hyponatremia include
  ▫ Fluid restriction—usually too difficult to enforce
  ▫ Furosemide, a loop diuretic, decreases urinary osmolality and enhances renal water excretion. With salt tablets, allows for ↑ sodium and ↑ urine excretion, best pharmacologic alternative. Goal is serum sodium concentration rapidly increased by 5–6 mmol/L and then restrict water intake.
  ▫ Clozapine appears to correct hyponatremia and may prevent water intoxication.
  ▫ Demeclocycline 600–1200 mg qd reduces severity and frequency of hyponatremic episodes but carries low risk of nephrotoxicity.
  ▫ Lithium can be effective but risks ↓ renal function and other problem side effects.
  ▫ Phenytoin is rarely used.

## Urinary hesitancy or retention

• Urinary retention increases risk of urinary tract infections, which require periodic urinalyses and cultures. Urinary retention
  √ Occurs equally often in males and females.
  √ Usually caused by anticholinergic effects.
• Management
  √ Reduce anticholinergic exposure by moving to less anticholinergic neuroleptic and switching to amantadine or propanolol if on an anticholinergic for EPS.
  √ Bethanechol 10–25 mg tid–qid or 5–10 mg qd until symptom abates.
  √ May prescribe IM/SC bethanechol 5–10 mg for more serious cases.

## Urinary incontinence

• Incontinence develops in > 20% of patients 2 weeks to 7 months after starting clozapine.

√ Associated with female gender and treatment with typical antipsychotic drugs.
√ A majority of cases spontaneously resolve.
√ Alpha-adrenergic blockage probable cause.
√ Rare with other antipsychotics.

- Management
  √ Ephedrine 25–150 mg/day stops incontinence in > 70% of patients.
    □ 17 of 57 patients had urinary incontinence while started on clozapine.
    □ 15 of 16 patients showed improvement in 24 h after reaching maximum ephedrine dose.
    □ 12 of 16 patients had a complete remission.
    □ Of remaining 4, 3 had reduction of incontinence and 1 showed no response.
  √ On clozapine 5 of 12 patients had documented enuresis.
    □ One reported 5 days after starting 300 mg qd clozapine.
    □ Four episodes that began within 3 months of initiating therapy.
  √ All incontinence resolved spontaneously early in treatment and did not recur.
  √ Oxybutynin (Ditropan) less successful.

## Skin, Allergies, and Temperature Effects

*Hypothermia more common than hyperthermia.*

Management

- Warn patients in advance so they can protect themselves.
- Proper heated (or cooled) environment.
- Avoid overexercising or working in hot places.
- Ensure adequate hydration.

*Decreased sweating*

- May cause a secondary, and sometimes fatal, hyperthermia.
- Be careful with patients who
  √ Work in hot weather.
  √ Take neuroleptics with high anticholinergic effects.
  √ Drink excessive alcohol.
  √ Suffer from CNS disease.
  √

*Photosensitivity*

- Chlorpromazine and other neuroleptics foster severe sunburn after 30–60 minutes of direct sunlight.

- Management
  - √ Cautious exposure to the sun
  - √ Apply PABA sunscreens with high UV blocking.

*Skin rashes*

- Seborrheic dermatitis highly associated with parkinsonian signs.
  - √ As high as 60% in this group.
  - √ Treat with appropriate soaps, lotions, and shampoos.
- Check nature and distribution to exclude contact dermatitis.
  - √ If mainly on neck or wrists, probably need new laundry detergent.
- Stop neuroleptic if not contact dermatitis.

## PERCENTAGES OF SIDE EFFECTS

## Part I

| Side Effects | Chlorpromazine | Clozapine | Fluphenazine | Haloperidol | Loxapine |
|---|---|---|---|---|---|
| **CARDIOVASCULAR EFFECTS** | | | | | |
| Cardiac arrhythmias | 6 | — | — | < 2 | — |
| Dizziness, light-headedness | 10 (6–14) | 19 (1.7–22) | 7 | 14 (10–30) | 20 |
| ECG abnormalities | 20 | 1.0 (0.17–1) | 2 | < 2 | < 2 |
| Fainting, syncope | 3 | 6 (0.62–7) | — | 2 | — |
| Hypertension | 0 | 3.5 | — | 1 | — |
| Hypotension | 6 | 9 (0.55–13) | 0.79 | 1 | 20 |
| Sweating | 9 | 7.3 | — | 15 | — |
| Tachycardia | 11 (10–30) | 22 | 2 (5.3–25) | 1 | 20 |
| **CENTRAL NERVOUS SYSTEM EFFECTS** | | | | | |
| Akathisia | 8.4 (6–12.1) | 3.5 | 21.6 | 29 | 24 (17–30) |
| Akinesia | 10 | 4 (0.36–5.0) | — | 16 | — |
| Anxiety, nervousness (mental) | 10 | 2 | — | 24 | — |
| Confusion, disorientation | 6.8 (5–6.8) | 2.4 (0.74–4) | — | 4 | — |
| Depression | 13.9 | 1 | — | — | — |
| Drowsiness, fatigue | 39.8 (23.4–50) | 39 (9–44) | 16.2 (13–19.5) | 21.8 (2–39) | 24 (16–30) |
| Dystonia | 3 | 0 | 5 (2.5–8) | 30 (16–65) | 14 (8–30) |
| Excitement | 0.5 | 2 | — | 12 | — |

| Side Effects | Chlorpromazine | Clozapine | Fluphenazine | Haloperidol | Loxapine |
|---|---|---|---|---|---|
| Headache | 8 | 5.9 (0.86–7) | —— | 6 | —— |
| Insomnia | 22 | 3 (0.19–6) | —— | 36 | —— |
| NMS | 0.6 | —— | 0.5 | 0.9 | —— |
| Parkinsonism | 12.5 | 6 | 15.4 | > 30 | 23 |
| Restlessness, agitation (motoric) | 8 | 5 | —— | 24 | —— |
| Rigidity | 6 | 3 | —— | 30 | —— |
| Seizures | 1 (0.5–1.5) | 2.3* (0.36–5) | 0 | 1 | 1.8 |
| Speech, slurred | 1 | 1 | —— | 0 | —— |
| Tremor | 12 | 7 | —— | 25 | —— |
| Weakness | 1 | 1 | —— | 1 | —— |
| **ENDOCRINE AND SEXUAL EFFECTS** | | | | | |
| Breast swelling | 1.1 | —— | 2.2 | —— | —— |
| Ejaculation, inhibited | 6 | 1 | 2 | < 2 | 6 |
| Lactation | 0.72 | —— | 3.3 | —— | —— |
| Menstrual changes | 16.3 | —— | 4.4 | —— | —— |
| Sexual function, disturbed | —— | 0.19 | —— | —— | —— |
| **EYES, EARS, NOSE, AND THROAT EFFECTS** | | | | | |
| Lenticular pigmentation | 6 | —— | < 2 | < 2 | < 2 |
| Nasal stuffiness | 2.5 | 1 | 9.2 | 15 | 20 |
| Pigmentary retinopathy | 6 | 0 | < 2 | 0 | —— |
| Vision, blurred | 14.4 | 5 | 4.3 | 6.8 | 15 |
| **GASTROINTESTINAL EFFECTS** | | | | | |
| Anorexia, lower appetite | 2 (0.5–0.29) | 0.6 | —— | 0 | —— |
| Constipation | 13 | 14 (1.9–16) | 9.6 | 6 | —— |
| Diarrhea | 1.1 | 1.1 | 1.1 | —— | —— |
| Edema | 2.8 | 1–3 | 0 | —— | —— |
| Jaundice | 0.64 | 1 | 0 | < 2 | < 2 |
| Mouth and throat, dry | 23 (10–30) | 6.6 | 8 | 13 (10–30) | 20 |
| Nausea, vomiting | 6 | 4.4 (1.1–11) | 4.3 | 6 | —— |
| Salivation | 11 | 32 | —— | 16 | —— |
| Weight gain | 13.3 (0–30) | 67 | 16.0 | 3 | 2 |
| **HEMATOLOGIC EFFECTS** | | | | | |
| Agranulocytosis | 0.67 (0.32–1.1) | 0.9 (0.004–3.0) | —— | —— | —— |
| Leukopenia | 3 (1–10) | 2.7 (0.63–3.0) | 1 | —— | < 2 |
| **RENAL EFFECTS** | | | | | |
| Enuresis | —— | 1 | —— | —— | —— |
| Urinary hesitancy or retention | 3 | 2 | 1.3 | 1.5 | 15 |

| Side Effects | Chlorpromazine | Clozapine | Fluphenazine | Haloperidol | Loxapine |
|---|---|---|---|---|---|
| **SKIN, ALLERGIES, AND TEMPERATURE EFFECTS** | | | | | |
| Allergies | 6.6 | 0.1 | 2.6 | 0 | —— |
| Fever, hyperthermia | 1 | 5.3 (1–13) | —— | 1 | —— |
| Photosensitivity | 6 | —— | < 2 | < 2 | < 2 |
| Rashes | 4 | 1.5 | < 2 | 1.2 | 5.5 |
| Skin pigment, abnormal | 15 | —— | < 2 | < 2 | —— |

\* Significantly increased risk of seizure with plasma levels ≥ 350 $\mu$g/ml.

# Part II

| Side Effect | Mesoridazine | Molindone | Olanzapine | Perphenazine | Pimozide |
|---|---|---|---|---|---|
| **CARDIOVASCULAR AND RESPIRATORY EFFECTS** | | | | | |
| Cardiac arrhythmias | —— | —— | —— | —— | < 2 |
| Dizziness | 8 (1–10.2) | 20 | 11 | 12 | 12 (0–30) |
| ECG abnormalities | 20 | < 2 | —— | —— | 6 |
| Hypotension | 8.4 (9–11.7) | 6 | 5 | 4 | 7 |
| Tachycardia | 1.8 | < 2 | 4 | —— | 6 |
| **CENTRAL NERVOUS SYSTEM EFFECTS** | | | | | |
| Agitation, restlessness (motoric) | 1.5 | —— | 23 | —— | 5 |
| Akathisia | 0.8 | > 30 | 0.5 | 27.3 | 19.9 (7.3–40) |
| Akinesia | —— | | —— | —— | 26.3 |
| Depression | —— | —— | —— | 6.2 | 10 |
| Drowsiness, fatigue | 15.7 (6–25) | > 30 | 34 (20–39) | 16.3 | 36.3 (10–70) |
| Dystonia | 3.4 (1.7–5) | > 30 | 2–3 (2.8–5.6) | 4.2 | 16.3 (10–30) |
| Headache | —— | —— | 17 | —— | 5 |
| Insomnia | —— | —— | 20 | —— | 10 |
| Muscle cramps | —— | —— | 2 | —— | 15 |
| NMS | —— | —— | —— | 0.5 | —— |
| Parkinsonism | 5.5 | > 30 | 14–20 | 21.1 | 16.3 |
| Rigidity | 1.4 | —— | 4 | —— | 10 |
| Seizures | —— | < 2 | 0.9 | 0.7 | 6 |

| Side Effect | Mesoridazine | Molindone | Olanzapine | Perphenazine | Pimozide |
|---|---|---|---|---|---|
| Speech, slurred | 1.4 | —— | 4 | —— | 10 |
| Tremors | 4 | —— | 6 | —— | —— |
| Weakness | 9.5 | —— | 4 | —— | —— |

### ENDOCRINE AND SEXUAL EFFECTS

| Side Effect | Mesoridazine | Molindone | Olanzapine | Perphenazine | Pimozide |
|---|---|---|---|---|---|
| Breast swelling | 5 | —— | < 1 | —— | 0 |
| Ejaculation, inhibited | —— | —— | < 1 | —— | —— |
| Lactation | —— | —— | < 1 | 0.9 | 15 |
| Menstrual changes | 5 | —— | 2 | —— | 0 |
| Sexual function, disturbed | 5.5 | —— | < 1 | —— | 15 |

### EYES, EARS, NOSE, AND THROAT EFFECTS

| Side Effect | Mesoridazine | Molindone | Olanzapine | Perphenazine | Pimozide |
|---|---|---|---|---|---|
| Increased light sensitivity | —— | —— | —— | —— | 5 |
| Lenticular pigmentation | —— | —— | < 1 | —— | < 2 |
| Nasal stuffiness | 20 | 20 | 10 | 18 | 20 |
| Vision, blurred | 8.9 (2.8–20) | 15 | < 0.1 | 17.8 | 20 |

### GASTROINTESTINAL EFFECTS

| Side Effect | Mesoridazine | Molindone | Olanzapine | Perphenazine | Pimozide |
|---|---|---|---|---|---|
| Anorexia, lower appetite | —— | —— | < 2 | 4.2 | —— |
| Appetite, increased | —— | —— | 2 | —— | 5 |
| Constipation | 10 (1–20) | | 9 | 4.2 | 20 |
| Diarrhea | —— | —— | —— | —— | 5 |
| Edema | —— | —— | 2 | 0.8 | —— |
| Jaundice | < 1 | < 2 | 0 | 0 | —— |
| Mouth and throat, dry | 13.7 | 20 (7.4–30) | 7 (5–13) | 18.8 | 22.5 |
| Nausea, vomiting | 2.3 | —— | 5 (2–9) | 0.9 | 0 |
| Taste changes | —— | —— | < 2 | —— | 5 |
| Thirst | —— | —— | —— | —— | 5 |
| Weight gain | 20 | < 2 | 6 | 5.9 | 4 |

### HEMATOLOGIC EFFECTS

| Side Effect | Mesoridazine | Molindone | Olanzapine | Perphenazine | Pimozide |
|---|---|---|---|---|---|
| Agranulocytosis | —— | —— | —— | 0 | —— |
| Leukopenia | —— | —— | —— | —— | —— |

### RENAL EFFECTS

| Side Effect | Mesoridazine | Molindone | Olanzapine | Perphenazine | Pimozide |
|---|---|---|---|---|---|
| Urinary hesitancy or retention | 5 | 15 | < 1 | —— | 15 |

### SKIN, ALLERGIES, AND TEMPERATURE EFFECTS

| Side Effect | Mesoridazine | Molindone | Olanzapine | Perphenazine | Pimozide |
|---|---|---|---|---|---|
| Allergies | —— | —— | —— | 0.8 | —— |
| Itch, subjective | 0.9 | < 2 | —— | —— | —— |
| Photosensitivity | —— | —— | —— | < 2 | < 2 |
| Rashes | 6 | 4 | —— | —— | 6 |

# Part III

| Side Effects | Quetiapine | Risperidone | Thioridazine | Thiothixene | Trifluoperazine | Ziprasidone |
|---|---|---|---|---|---|---|
| **CARDIOVASCULAR EFFECTS** | | | | | | |
| Cardiac arrhythmias | < 1 | < 1 | 15 | < 2 | —— | < 1 |
| Dizziness | 10 | 42.3 | 23.3 | 18 (21.2–35) | 28.1 | 8 |
| ECG abnormalities | < 1 | 2.1 | 15 | < 2 | 6 | |
| Hypertension | | | | | | > 1 |
| Hypotension | 7 | 16 | > 30 | 11.2 | 2.4 (0.8–4) | 1 |
| Tachycardia | 7 | 3 | 6 | 6 | —— | 2 |
| **CENTRAL NERVOUS SYSTEM EFFECTS** | | | | | | |
| Akathisia | * | * | 8.9 | > 30 | 15.9 (4.8–27) | 8 |
| Confusion, disorientation | —— | < 1 | 5.2 | —— | —— | > 1 |
| Drowsiness, fatigue | 18 | 3 (21–36.2) | 28.6 (10–30) | 19.5 (3–61) | 24.5 | 14 |
| Dystonia | * | 0 | 0.7 | 14.2 (8.3–30) | 5.1 (3–8.2) | 4 |
| Headache | 19 | —— | —— | —— | —— | —— |
| Insomnia | —— | 26 | 0 | —— | 4.3 | > 1 |
| NMS | —— | * | < 0.1 | 0.6 | 0.7 | < 0.1 |
| Parkinsonism | * | * | 11.8 | 30 | 35.9 (23.7–48) | 5 |
| Seizures | 0.8 | 0.3 | 1.2 | 6 | 1.3 | .4 |
| Weakness | 4 | —— | —— | —— | 40 | > 1 |
| **ENDOCRINE AND SEXUAL EFFECTS** | | | | | | |
| Breast swelling | < 1 | < 1 | 0.6 | —— | —— | < 1 |
| Ejaculation, inhibited | < 1 | < 1 | 37 (10–44) | < 2 | —— | < 1 |
| Lactation | < 1 | < 1 | 3.1 | | —— | < 1 |
| Menstrual changes | < 1 | > 1 | 3.3 | —— | 4.4 | < 1 |
| Sexual function, disturbed | < 1 | > 1 | —— | —— | 3.4 | < .1 |
| **EYES, EARS, NOSE, AND THROAT EFFECTS** | | | | | | |
| Ear pain | 1 | —— | —— | —— | —— | —— |
| Lenticular pigmentation | < 1 | 0 | 0 | 6 | —— | —— |
| Nasal stuffiness | 3 | 10 | 20 | 20 | 3 | 4 |
| Vision, blurred | < 1 | 2 | 18.1 | 5 | 4 | 3 |
| **GASTROINTESTINAL EFFECTS** | | | | | | |
| Anorexia, lower appetite | > 1 | > 1 | 0 | —— | 27.7 (12.3–43) | 2 |
| Constipation | 9 | 7 | 16.8 | —— | 1.1 | 9 |
| Diarrhea | < 0.1 | > 1 | 3.3 | —— | 1.1 | 5 |
| Edema | > 1 | < 1 | 2.3 | —— | 1.4 | > 1 |
| Jaundice | < 0.1 | —— | < 2 | < 2 | 0 | < 0.1 |
| Mouth and throat, dry | 7 | > 1 | 28.1 | 12 | 2.3 | 4 |

| Side Effects | Quetiapine | Risper- idone | Thiorid- azine | Thiothixene | Trifluoper- azine | Ziprasidone |
|---|---|---|---|---|---|---|
| Nausea, vomiting | 6 | 6 | 9.3 | —— | 2.4 | 10 |
| Weight gain | 23 | 18 | 15 | 20 | 5.6 | 10 |
| **HEMATOLOGIC EFFECTS** | | | | | | |
| Agranulocytosis | 0 | 0 | 0 | —— | —— | < 0.1 |
| Leukopenia | > 1 | < 1 | —— | < 2 | —— | < 1 |
| **RENAL EFFECTS** | | | | | | |
| Urinary hesitancy or retention | < 1 | < 0.1 | 22 (5.5–30) | 12 | 0.6 | < 1 |
| **SKIN, ALLERGIES, AND TEMPERATURE EFFECTS** | | | | | | |
| Allergies | < 1 | < 0.1 | 3.2 | —— | 4.2 | 2 |
| Photosensitivity | —— | > 1 | 6 | < 2 | 6 | 3 |
| Rashes | 4 | 2 | 15 | 20 | 14 | 4 |
| Skin pigment, abnormal | < 1 | > 1 | 6 | < 2 | < 2 | —— |

\* EPS risks not available separately. Risperidone total EPS risk 16% (not significantly different from placebo) at 6 mg qd, 13% with placebo. Most of these were Parkinson-type side effects. Quetiapine EPS risk 4–8% throughout 75–750 mg dose range (below placebo rate of 16%).

\*\* Highest mean weight gain and highest incidence of clinically significant weight gain (> 7% of body weight) in patients with low BMI (< 23). Normal and overweight patients as a group had no weight gain. —— No data available.

## PREGNANCY AND LACTATION

| | |
|---|---|
| Teratogenicity (Ist trimester) | • No proven risk of increased anomalies.<br><br>• Low-potency phenothiazines may increase malformations if administered during weeks 4–10. |
| Direct Effect on Newborn (3rd trimester) | • EPS (may last 6 months), excessive crying, hyper-reflexia, hypertonicity, vasomotor instability can occur.<br><br>• Neonatal jaundice.<br><br>• Up to 18% of patients on chlorpromazine have had a marked fall in BP during last 10 days of pregnancy; this can harm both mother and newborn. |

- Although chlorpromazine is usually safe during pregnancy, other neuroleptics are preferred.

Lactation
- Present in breast milk in concentrations equal to plasma.

## Drug Dosage in Mother's Milk*

| Generic Names | Milk/Plasma Ratio | Time of Peak Concentration in Milk (hours) | Infant Dose ($\mu$g/kg/day) | Maternal Dose (%) | Safety Rating** |
|---|---|---|---|---|---|
| Chlorpromazine | ? | 2 | 44 | 0.2 | A |
| Chlorprothixene | ? | 4–4.5 | 4.7 | 0.14 | A |
| Haloperidol | ? | ? | 0.75–3.2 | 0.15–2 | B |

* Significant levels of clozapine have been reported in breast milk, e.g., 60–110 ng/ml. Breast-feeding not advised for clozapine.

** A: Safe throughout infancy, but unsafe for infants suspected of a glucose-6-dehydrogenase deficiency; B: Reasonably unsafe before 34 weeks, but safe after 34 weeks.

## DRUG–DRUG INTERACTIONS

| Drugs (X) Interact with: | Anti-Psychotics (A) | Comments |
|---|---|---|
| Acetaminophen | X↓ | May overuse acetaminophen. |
| *Alcohol | X↑ A↑ | CNS depression; haloperidol increases alcohol effect. |
| Alpha-methyldopa | X↑ | Increases hypotension and confusion. |
| Alprazolam | A↑ | Increases sedation, haloperidol and fluphenazine levels. |
| Aluminum hydroxide | A↓ | Give aluminum hydroxide at least one hour before, or 2 h after, antipsychotic agents. (*See also* calcium carbonate.) |
| Amphetamines (*see* dextroamphetamine) | | |
| Anesthetics (general) | X↑ | CNS depression, hypotension. |
| *Anticholinergics | X↑ A↓? | Added anticholinergic effect. Consider amantadine; may decrease antipsychotic effect. |
| Anticonvulsants | X↓? | Carbamazepine level unchanged. Clozapine could interfere with anticonvulsant. |
| Antihistamines | X↑ A↑ | CNS depression. Added anticholinergic effect. |
| Antihypertensives | X↑ | Increased hypotension, particularly with low-potency neuroleptics. |
| Bromocriptine | X↓ A↓ | All neuroleptics except clozapine can reduce effectiveness for reducing prolactin. Increased psychosis. |
| Caffeine | A↓ | Increased psychosis in high doses, 600–1000 mg. |
| Calcium carbonate | | No effect, unlike aluminum and magnesium hydroxides. |
| Citalopram (*see* SSRIs) | | |

| Drugs (X)<br>Interact with: | Anti-<br>Psychotics<br>(A) | Comments |
|---|---|---|
| Clonidine | X↑ | Hypotension. |
| *Dextroamphetamine | X↓ A↑ | Chlorpromazine treats dextroamphetamine overdose, but amphetamines should never treat neuroleptic overdose. |
| Dichloralphenazone | A↓ | Hastens neuroleptic metabolism. |
| Digoxin | X↑ A↑ | Each may increase unbound fraction of the other. |
| Diuretics (thiazides) | X↑ | Increased orthostatic hypotension, hypotension, risk of shock. |
| †Epinephrine | X↓ | Hypotensive phenothiazine-treated patients might do better on levarterenol or phenylephrine. |
| Estrogen | A↑ | May increase phenothiazine level. |
| *Fluoxetine (see SSRIs) | | |
| Griseofulvin | A↓ | Speeds neuroleptic metabolism. |
| *Guanethidine | X↓ | Hypotensive action inhibited by phenothiazines, haloperidol, and possibly thioxanthines. |
| Hypnoanxiolytics | X↑ A↑ | CNS depression. |
| *Isoproterenol | X↓ | Marked hypotension |
| *Levodopa | X↓ | Antagonizes effects of dopamine agonists; try clozapine or possibly risperidone. |
| *Lithium | X↑ A? | May cause EPS; extremely rare. Acute neurotoxicity at normal serum levels, especially with haloperidol or thioridazine. Chronic combination a smaller problem. Lithium and chlorpromazine may *lower* levels in both. Increases molindone levels. |
| Magnesium hydroxide | A↓ | Give magnesium hydroxide at least one hour before, or 2 h after, antipsychotic agents. (See also calcium carbonate.) |
| MAOIs | X↓ A? | Hypotension may result; MAOIs may trigger EPS. |
| Methyldopa | X↑ | Hypotension, rarely delirium. |
| Methylphenidate (see dextroamphetamine) | | |
| Nicotine | A↓ | Decreased blood levels. |
| Norepinephrine | X↓ | Hypotension. |
| *Opiates | X↑ A↑ | CNS depression. |
| *Orphenadrine | X↓ A↓ | Lowers neuroleptic levels; with CPZ may cause hypoglycemia; increases anticholinergic effects. |
| Paroxetine (see SSRIs) | | |
| Phenylbutazone | X↑ A↑ | More drowsiness. |
| Phenytoin | X? A↓? | Toxicity may occur. Obtain phenytoin level and adjust; can reduce clozapine and other levels. |
| *Propranolol | X↑ A↑ | Hypotension, toxicity, and seizures. Monitor serum levels; decrease dose. |
| Quinidine | X↑ A↑ | Increased quinidine-like effects with dysrhythmias, especially phenothiazines. Increases risperidone levels. |
| Rifampin | A↓ | Speeds neuroleptic metabolism. |
| SSRIs (citalopram, fluoxetine, fluvoxamine, paroxetine, sertraline) | A↑ | May increase EPS and plasma levels. Fluvoxamine least likely to increase antipsychotic levels. Haloperidol, perphenazine, thioridazine most likely to be increased. |
| Stimulants (see dextroamphetamine) | | |
| Succinylcholine | X↑ | May have prolonged paralysis. |
| *TCAs | X↑ A↑ | Possible toxicity or hypotension; TCAs may diminish EPS. TCA levels increased by phenothiazine and haloperidol. |
| Trazodone | X↑ A↑ | Additive hypotensive effects. |
| Tobacco (see nicotine) | | |
| Valproic acid | A↑ | Potentially increases levels; reported with risperidone and clozapine. |
| Warfarin | X↑ A↑ | Increased bleeding time by increasing warfarin. May increase unbound antipsychotic. |

| Drugs (X) Interact with: | Chlorpromazine (C) | Comments |
|---|---|---|
| Antimalarial agents (amodiaquine, chloroquine, pyrimethamine, sulfadoxine) | C↑ | Chlorpromazine 2–4 times higher levels. |
| Anorectic agents | X↓ | Inhibits anorectic effect. |
| Antidiabetics | X↑↓ | Loss of glucose control possible; change neuroleptics. |
| *Barbiturates | X↑ C↓ | CNS depression acute; antipsychotic effects lowered. |
| Captopril | X↑ | Hypotension. |
| Cimetidine | C↓ | Avoid cimetidine; try ranitidine or nizatidine. |
| Enalapril | X↑ | Hypotension. |
| *Insulin (see antidiabetics) | | |
| Meperidine | X↑ C↓ | Hypotension, lethargy, CNS depression; switch one drug. |
| *Phenmetrazine (see anorectic agents) | | |
| Sulfonylureas | X↑ | Change neuroleptic. |
| Valproic acid | X↑ C↑ | Toxicity; switch to haloperidol. |

| Drugs (X) Interact with: | Clozapine (C) | Comments |
|---|---|---|
| *Carbamazepine | X↑ C↑ | Increases agranulocytosis risk. |
| Cimetidine | C↑ | Increases clozapine levels; consider ranitidine as alternative. |
| Diltiazem | C↑ | Increases clozapine levels. |
| Fluvoxamine | C↑ | Increases clozapine levels. |
| *Hypnoanxiolytic benzodiazepines | H↑ C↑ | Increased risk of respiratory arrest. |
| †Phenytoin | C↑ | Increases agranulocytosis risk. |
| *Risperidone (see risperidone below) | | |
| Verapamil | C↑ | Increases clozapine levels. |

| Drugs (X) Interact with: | Haloperidol** (H) | Comments |
|---|---|---|
| *Carbamazepine | H↓ | Psychosis; 50% lower serum level. |
| Indomethacin | H↑ | Drowsiness, tiredness, and confusion; change one agent. |
| Buspirone | H↑ | About 26% increase in haloperidol level. |

| Drugs (X) Interact with: | Loxapine (L) | Comments |
|---|---|---|
| Lorazepam | X↑ | Rare respiratory depression, stupor, and hypotension. Switch one drug. No other benzodiazepine apparently interacts with loxapine. |

| Drugs (X) Interact with: | Thioridazine** (T) | Comments |
|---|---|---|
| *Phenylpropanolamine | X↑ | One sudden death. Tell patients to avoid common over-the-counter drugs with PPA (e.g., Dexatrim, Allerest, Dimetapp); causal effect not proven. |

| Drugs (X) Interact with: | Risperidone** (T) | Comments |
|---|---|---|
| Carbamazepine | R↓ | Decreased level with chronic carbamazepine. |
| Clozapine | R↑ | Increased level with chronic clozapine. |
| SSRIs | R↑? | Probable increase in risperidone levels. |
| P4502D6 metabolized drugs** | X↑ | Increased levels possible. |
| Haloperidol | | |
| Thioridazine | | |
| Perphenazine | | |
| Dextromethor- phan | | |
| Bufaralol | | |
| Propranolol | | |
| Tricyclic antidepressants | | |
| Timolol | | |

* Moderately important; † Extremely important; ↑ Increases; ↓ Decreases; O = No effect; ? Unsure or increases and decreases.
** *See* 2D6 table in appendix.

## EFFECTS ON LABORATORY TESTS†

| Generic Names | Blood/Serum Tests | Results* | Urine Tests | Results* |
|---|---|---|---|---|
| Chlorpromazine | LFT** | ↑ | VMA | ↓ |
| | Glucose | ↑↓ | Urobilinogen | ↑ |
| Clozapine | WBC | ↓ | ? | |
| | LFT | ↑ | | |
| Fluphenazine | LFT | ↑ | VMA | ↓ |
| | Cephaline flocculation | ↑ | Urobilinogen | ↑ |
| Haloperidol | Only prolactin | | None | |
| Loxapine | LFT | ↑ | None | |
| Molindone | LFT | ↑ | ? | |
| | Eosinophils | ↑ | | |
| | Leukocytes | ↓ | | |
| | Fatty acids | ↑ | | |
| Perphenazine | Glucose, PBI | ↑↑ | Pregnancy tests | False↓ |
| Risperidone | Only prolactin | ↑ | Pregnancy tests | False↑ |
| Thioridazine | None | | | |
| Thiothixene | LFT | ↑ | None | |
| | Uric acid | ↓ | | |
| Trifluoperazine | LFT | ↑ | VMA | ↓ |
| | Glucose | ↑↓ | Urobilinogen | ↑ |

* ↑Increases; ↓ Decreases; ↑↓ Increases and decreases; ? Undetermined or unclear.
** LFT = liver function tests refer to AST/SGOT, ALT/SGPT, alkaline phosphatase, bilirubin, and LDH.
† All except clozapine can elevate prolactin.

## WITHDRAWAL

Neuroleptics do not cause

- Dependence
- Tolerance
- Addiction

*Antipsychotic discontinuation syndrome(s)*

Suddenly stopping high antipsychotic doses may produce

- Flu-like symptoms without a fever
- Insomnia and nightmares
- Gastritis, nausea, vomiting, diarrhea
- Headaches
- Diaphoresis, increased sebaceous secretion, restlessness, and general physical complaints
  - √ May see EPS but probably related to abrupt withdrawal of antiparkinson agents.
  - √ May be more prevalent with low-potency/high anticholinergic antipsychotics.
    - □ Low-potency agents are highly anticholinergic, and sudden withdrawal is more likely to cause diarrhea, drooling, insomnia, and/or nightmares (due to REM rebound).
  - √ Psychotic symptoms not part of withdrawal syndrome

These symptoms

- Begin 2–4 (up to 7) days after discontinuing antipsychotics.
  - √ Symptoms worse when patients are on antipsychotics *and* ACAs or TCAs and both are stopped.
- Can persist 2 weeks.
- Can cease by more gradually withdrawing neuroleptics over 1–2 weeks.
- Less often, sudden discontinuation causes
  - √ Sweating
  - √ Rhinorrhea
  - √ Increased appetite
  - √ Giddiness
  - √ Dizziness
  - √ Warmth or cold sensations
  - √ Tremors
  - √ Tachycardia

Clozapine abrupt withdrawal syndrome can differ.

- Symptoms include delirium, psychosis, severe agitation, and abnormal movements.

- Clozapine may need to be tapered over 2+ months to avoid a withdrawal syndrome.

Maintain ACAs a week after terminating antipsychotics to prevent EPS; this allows for full clearing of antipsychotic. When long-term neuroleptics are rapidly stopped or quickly lowered, TD may emerge, as discussed above. Also, a *transient withdrawal dyskinesia* (probably caused by dopaminergic rebound) can arise occasionally if antipsychotics are quickly halted.

- Withdrawal dyskinesia resembles a tardive dyskinesia with abnormal movements of the neck, face, and mouth.
- Antiparkinsonian drugs do not relieve it.
- Withdrawal dyskinesia stops with
  √ Reestablishing maintenance neuroleptic dose, and
  √ Reducing neuroleptics more gradually (1–3 months).

## OVERDOSE: TOXICITY, SUICIDE, AND TREATMENT

Even if consumed all at once, antipsychotics are relatively nonlethal drugs.

- A 30–60-day supply of antipsychotics can be fatal.
  √ This amount is 10 times less dangerous than TCAs or MAOIs.
- Neuroleptics can still create serious problems.
  √ 2 reports of risperidone overdose with doses of 240 mg and 230 mg with only EKG abnormalities (e.g., QRS = 112 msec, QT = 565 msec).

Suicide more common with less potent antipsychotics (e.g., chlorpromazine).

- The therapeutic index—the ratio of lethal to effective dose—ranges from
  √ 25–200 for low-potency phenothiazines, to
  √ > 1000 for high-potency piperazines and haloperidol.

More serious symptoms emerge when antipsychotics are consumed with another drug, particularly one that increases or exaggerates antipsychotic CNS effects. In one series of studies,

- A chlorpromazine overdose induced coma in 4%, whereas
- A combined chlorpromazine and TCA overdose produced coma in 13%.

The general management of neuroleptic overdoses includes:

- Stop all neuroleptics and ACAs.
  √ Be alert for dystonias.

- Hospitalize, if needed.
- Obtain ECG, temperature, vital signs, and if needed, establish an airway.
- Arousal may not occur for 48 h.
- Observe awake patient for 8–12 h after ingestion.
- Ascertain other drugs ingested during past 2–10 days.
- Speak soon with family or friends who might afford life-saving information.
- Begin gastric lavage as soon as possible.
  - √ Before initiating gastric lavage, employ cuffed endotracheal intubation to prevent aspiration and pulmonary complications.
    - ▫ Stop convulsions before passing stomach tube.
- Avoid emetic because an acute dystonic reaction of the head or neck could cause aspiration.
- Lavage best if overdose transpired within 4 h, yet it can remove drugs consumed 24–36 h earlier.
- *After* lavage, supply activated charcoal (40–50 g in adults, 20–25 g in children) by mouth or through lavage tube to prevent further absorption.
- Loss of consciousness can be reversed with stimulants.
  - √ Use amphetamine, dextroamphetamine, or caffeine with sodium benzoate.
  - √ Avoid drugs that can cause convulsions, e.g., picrotoxin or pentylene tetrazol.
- If slow-release pills ingested, follow with a saline cathartic to speed evacuation.

Most overdoses accentuate side effects, so their treatment is akin to treating side effects. These treatments include:

- Hypotension, dizziness
  - √ May appear in 2–3 days.
  - √ May evolve into shock, coma, cardiovascular insufficiency, myocardial infarction, or arrhythmias.
  - √ First treatment is fluids.
  - √ Second treatment is sympathomimetics, such as levarterenol (norepinephrine), metaraminol, phenylephrine.
  - √ *Do not use epinephrine;* may result in lower blood pressure.
- Severe urinary retention
  - √ Catheterize patient if no recent voiding.
  - √ Hemodialysis is relatively useless because of low drug concentrations.
  - √ Hematuria, which arises later, often occurs with chlorprothixene and loxapine.
- Seizures
  - √ Common in children.

√ Manage with standard interventions.
  □ IV diazepam is first choice.
  □ Avoid barbiturates due to risk of respiratory depression.
  □ Avoid pentylenetrazol, picrotoxin, and bemegride.

**Toxicity and Suicide Data**

| Generic Name | Toxicity Doses Average (Highest) (g) | Mortality Doses Average (Lowest) (g) |
|---|---|---|
| Chlorpromazine | 25.0 (30.0) | (1.250) |
| Chlorprothixene | (8.0) | —— |
| Clozapine | (4.0) | 2.50 |
| Fluphenazine | —— | —— |
| Haloperidol | —— | —— |
| Loxapine | —— | 1.5–3 |
| Mesoridazine | —— | —— |
| Molindone | —— | —— |
| Perphenazine | —— | —— |
| Pimozide | —— | —— |
| Thioridazine | 2.0 (20.0) | 5–10 |
| Thiothixene | 20.0 | (0.736) |
| Trifluoperazine | —— | —— |

## PRECAUTIONS

Hypotension occurs most with parenteral use and high doses, and especially > 50 mg of IM chlorpromazine.

Use antipsychotics cautiously with

- Narrow-angle glaucoma
- Prostatic hypertrophy
- CNS depressive agents
- Breast cancer
- Bone marrow depression, blood dyscrasias
- Parkinson's disease
- Neuroleptic hypersensitivity
- Extreme hypotension or hypertension
- Acutely ill children (e.g., chickenpox, measles, Reye's syndrome, gastroenteritis, dehydration)
  √ Increased EPS, particularly dystonias and akathisias
  √ Increased hepatotoxicity risk
- Elderly who have
  √ Hepatic disease
  √ Cardiovascular illness (especially low-potency)
  √ Chronic respiratory disease

√ Hypoglycemic conditions
√ Seizures (especially low-potency)

Avoid pimozide in patients with

- Tics other than Tourette's disorder,
- Medications stimulating tics (e.g., methylphenidate, dextroamphetamine), or
- Prolonged QT interval.

Sudden death has occurred with patients on neuroleptics.

- Most freqeuntly with thioridazine
  √ No recent reports
- Sudden death has also occurred in seemingly healthy adults for no obvious reason.
  √ Ventricular fibrillation, aspiration from food or vomit, and grand mal seizures may be culpable.

## NURSES' DATA

Discuss with the patient the myths about, and the reasons for, taking medications.

### Oral Medication

- Take with milk, orange juice, or semi-solid food to reduce bitter taste.
  √ Haloperidol is a tasteless and colorless elixir, unlike chlorpromazine and thioridazine.
- Protect oral liquids from the light.
- Discard markedly discolored solutions (slight yellowing does not alter potency).

### Injections

- Do not hold drug in syringe for > 15 minutes, as plastic may absorb drug.
- Administer IM injections very slowly.
- To avoid contact dermatitis, keep antipsychotic solution off patient's skin and clothing.
- Give IM injections into upper outer quadrant of buttocks, deltoid, or thigh.
  √ Deltoid speeds absorption because of faster blood perfusion.
  √ Tell patient injection may sting.
  √ Massage slowly after injection to prevent formation of sterile abscesses.
  √ Alternate sites.

- Watch for orthostatic hypotension, especially with parenteral administration.
  - √ Show patients how to stand up slowly over 15–60 seconds when dizzy (*see* page 27).

### Depot Injections

- Use dry needle (at least 21-gauge).
- Give deep IM injection into a large muscle using Z-track method.
- Rotate sites and specify in charting.
- Can inject SC.
- Do not let drug remain in syringe for > 15 minutes.
- Do *not* massage injection sites.

## PATIENT AND FAMILY NOTES

Patient and family should notify doctor if

- Patient has a sore throat during first several months of treatment.
- NMS appears.
- Patient is having general or dental surgery.

Tell patients and families:

- Antipsychotics treat psychotic symptoms, including hallucinations, delusions, confused thinking, paranoia, and oversensitivity to stimuli.
  - √ Many patients who deny that their symptoms are psychotic will try antipsychotic medication to treat insomnia, poor concentration, over-worrying (paranoia), and/or short temper.
- Particularly if on low-potency antipsychotic, patients may have
  - √ Anticholinergic side effects (e.g., dry mouth, constipation, blurred vision, fuzzy thinking),
  - √ Sedation that should wear off and can help with sleep and anxiety,
  - √ Low blood pressure with dizziness when standing up.
  - √ May see similar symptoms on high- or mid-potency antipsychotics.
- The 3 main forms of EPS are
  - √ Dystonia, a sudden and often sustained pull of any muscle group;
  - √ Akathisia, a feeling of physical (not necessarily mental) restlessness; and
  - √ Parkinsonism, involving stiff muscles, slowed movements, tremor, and drooling.
- TD not necessarily discussed during acute treatment phase while patient actively psychotic.

√ TD won't occur in that phase and there is no assurance that drug will be taken chronically.
- Discuss TD *before* 3 months of neuroleptic treatment elapse.
    √ Best to do it when patient and physician are beginning a chronic course of treatment.
- When starting neuroleptics, carefully drive cars, work around machines, and cross streets.

Patients initially should check for psychomotor impairments.

- May drink alcohol with antipsychotics, but "one drink often feels like two drinks."
- Avoid overexposure to sun; use sunscreens.
- Do not keep medication at bedside to avoid accidental ingestion.
    √ Keep safely away from children.
- If forget a dose, patient can take up to 3–4 h late, but
    √ If more than 3–4 h late, wait for next scheduled dose.
    √ Do not double the dose unless this has already been tried successfully.
- Do not suddenly stop medication.
    √ Even if there is no immediate return of symptoms, there is a very high risk of relapse in the weeks and months after medication has been stopped.

# 2. Neuropsychiatric Disorders

Neuroleptic-induced extrapyramidal side effects (EPS) are diminished by anticholinergic agents (ACAs), including most antihistamines, and by $\beta$-blockers (BB), benzodiazepines (BZ), and dopaminergic agonists (DA).

Some extrapyramidal drugs (EPD) (e.g., benztropine) are prescribed almost exclusively for EPS, while others (e.g., propranolol) are given for both nonEPS and EPS. One ACA, ethopropazine (Parsidol), a phenothiazine derivation, will not be discussed; it is mainly used in Parkinson's disease and is less effective than other ACAs for drug-induced EPS.

This chapter focuses on:

- Pharmacology and treatment of extrapyramidal symptoms with anticholinergic drugs, amantadine, and antiparkinsonian drugs.

Other diagnoses and their treatments include:

## NAMES, MANUFACTURERS, DOSE FORMS, COLORS

| Generic Names | Brand Names | Manufacturers | Dose Forms (mg)* | Colors |
|---|---|---|---|---|
| Amantadine | Symmetrel | Du Pont | c: 100<br>s: 50 mg/5 ml | c: red |
| Benztropine | Cogentin | Merck Sharp & Dohme | t: 0.5/1/2<br>p: 1 mg/ml | t: all white |
| Biperiden | Akineton | Knoll | t: 2<br>p: 5 mg/ml | t: white |
| Bromocriptine | Parlodel | Sandoz | t: 2.5<br>c: 5 | t: white<br>c: caramel-white |
| Diazepam | Valium | Roche | t: 2/5/10<br>p: 5 mg/ml | t: white/yellow/blue |
| Diphenhydramine† | Benadryl | Parke-Davis | c: 25/50<br>p: 10/50 mg/ml | c: all pink-white |
| Lorazepam | Ativan | Wyeth-Ayerst | t: 0.5/1/2 | t: all white |
| Procyclidine | Kemadrin | Burroughs Wellcome | t: 5 | t: white |
| Propranolol | Inderal | Wyeth-Ayerst | t: 10/20/40/80<br>p: 1 mg/ml | t: orange/blue/green/pink/yellow |
| Trihexyphenidyl | Artane | Lederle | t: 2/5<br>sr: 5 mg<br>e: 2 mg/5 ml | t: all white<br>sr: blue |

\* c = capsules; e = elixir; p = parenteral; s = syrup; sr = sustained-release sequels; t = tablets.
† Can be purchased over the counter only in 25 mg.

## PHARMACOLOGY

## Theoretical Mechanisms for EPS

The basal ganglia, which mediate involuntary movements, have a critical ratio of

$$\frac{Dopamine}{Acetylcholine}$$

When neuroleptics block these dopamine receptors, they lower this ratio and generate EPS.

By reducing acetylcholine, ACAs help to restore this balance. By releasing dopamine in the basal ganglia system, amantadine also helps restore this balance.

For akathisia there may be a critical ratio of

$$\frac{Dopamine}{Norepinephrine}$$

By reducing norepinephrine, $\beta$-blockers may restore this balance. For EPS there may also be a critical ratio of

$$\frac{Dopamine}{Serotonin}$$

Because serotonin $5HT_2$ receptors mediate psychosis and reduce dopamine release in basal ganglia, atypical antipsychotic drugs, which block these receptors, ameliorate psychosis and decrease abnormal movements caused by dopamine receptor antagonists; SSRIs, which increase serotonin stimulation of $5HT_2$ receptors, further reduce dopamine release, which can cause EPS.

## Pharmacology of Anticholinergic Drugs and Amantadine

| | Time to Peak Concentration (hrs)* | Half-Life (hrs)* | Oral Bioavailability** (%) |
|---|---|---|---|
| Amantadine | 1–6 | 16 | 60–95 |
| Benztropine | —— | 12–24 | —— |
| Biperiden | 1–1.5 | 18–24 | 29 |
| Procyclidine | 1–2 | 12 | 52–97 |
| Trihexyphenidyl | 1.2 | 6–10 | 100 |

\* Higher numbers generally in elderly.
\*\* Lower numbers generally in elderly.

## DOSES

| Generic Names | Oral Doses (mg) | IM/IV Doses (mg) | Major Chemical Group |
|---|---|---|---|
| Amantadine | 100 bid–tid* | —— | Dopaminergic agonist |
| Benztropine | 1–3 bid | 1–2 | ACA |
| Biperiden | 2 tid–qid | 2 | ACA |
| Diazepam | 5 tid | 5–10 | Benzodiazepine |
| Diphenhydramine | 25–50 tid–qid | 25–50 | Antihistamine and ACA |
| Lorazepam | 1–2 tid | —— | Benzodiazepine |
| Procyclidine | 2.5–5 tid | —— | ACA |
| Propranolol | 10–20 tid; up to 40 qid | —— | $\beta$-blocker |
| Trihexyphenidyl** | 2–5 tid | —— | ACA |

\* Amantadine can often be given 200 mg qd instead of 100 mg bid. In geriatrics, 100 mg qd is usually enough.
\*\* Start with trihexyphenidyl tablets or elixir; only later transfer to sustained-released sequels (capsules). Use sequels as a single dose after breakfast or one dose q12 h. For akathisia, give trihexyphenidyl 6–10 mg qd; other EPS, provide 2–6 mg qd.

## CLINICAL INDICATIONS AND USE

### Influence on Extrapyramidal Symptom*

| Generic Names | Akathisia | Akinesia | Dystonia | Rabbit | Rigidity | Tremor |
|---|---|---|---|---|---|---|
| Amantadine | 3 | 3 | 2 | 2 | 3 | 2 |
| Benztropine | 2 | 2 | 3 | 3 | 3 | 3 |
| Biperiden | 1 | 2 | 3 | 3 | 3 | 3 |
| Diazepam | 2 | 0 | 1–2 | 1 | 1–2 | 0–1 |
| Diphenhydramine | 2 | 1 | 2–3 | 3 | 1 | 2 |
| Lorazepam | 2 | 0 | 1–2 | 1 | 1–2 | 0–1 |
| Procyclidine | 1 | 2 | 3 | 3 | 3 | 3 |
| Propranolol | 3 | 0 | 0 | 1 | 0 | 1–2 |
| Trihexyphenidyl | 2 | 2 | 3 | 3 | 3 | 3 |

\* 0 = no effect; 1 = some effect (20% response); 2 = moderate effect (20–40% response); 3 = good effect (> 40% response).

ACAs' effects depend on the symptom. Therefore, when should one use ACAs or other EPDs?

- The *pro* arguments include:
  √ EPS are uncomfortable.
  √ EPS can induce patients to stop taking neuroleptics.
  √ High-potency neuroleptics cause EPS.
  √ ACAs especially help patients under 45 y.o.
  √ ACAs clearly relieve some EPS (a.k.a. dystonia, akinesia, pseudoparkinsonism).

- The *con* arguments include:
  √ Low-potency neuroleptics less frequently produce EPS.
  √ Patients without EPS initially can receive EPDs if EPS arise later.
  √ ACAs have side effects, which may compound neuroleptic side effects (e.g., dry mouth, confusion).
  √ ACAs are not very effective for other EPS (e.g., akathisias).
  √ Avoid ACAs in children under 3 y.o.

- In general, prophylactic ACAs are indicated for
  √ Males under 30 y.o. and females under 25 y.o. starting high-potency neuroleptics (e.g., haloperidol) (dystonia rate without ACA over 70%) or
  √ Patients with dystonia (or have h/o dystonia).
    ▫ Tolerance to dystonia usually develops in 1–3 weeks.
    ▫ Doses can then be increased to usual levels.
  √ Patients with a past history of EPS with neuroleptics.

- When depot antipsychotics peak after 2–14 days, patient may need ACAs.

- Whether to use ACAs in other circumstances depends on the seriousness of symptoms and the preferences of patients.

## Starting Oral Doses of Antiparkinsonian Drugs

| Symptom | Medication |
|---|---|
| Akathisia | Propranolol or other lipophilic β-blocker (e.g., metoprolol, pindolol, or nadolol, but not atenolol) are first choices if akathisia is an isolated symptom. |
| | Amantadine or benzodiazepines (lorazepam or diazepam) are second choices. |
| | ACAs are third choices. If other EPS also occur, which are better treated with ACA, use ACA first. |
| | Clonidine (0.15–2 mg/qd) also reported to help. |
| | If patient has not improved, double-check the diagnosis. May help in chronic or "tardive" akathisia. |
| Dystonia | Diphenhydramine 25–50 mg IV/IM as first choice; often provides complete relief in minutes and reduces patient anxiety. Hydroxyzine alternative. |
| | Benztropine 1–2 mg IV/IM is the second choice, and always works quickly. |
| | If patient does not respond to the above, question the diagnosis. |
| | Prevent future dystonias with any ACA. |
| Parkinsonism | Reduce neuroleptics to lowest effective dose. |
| | Try any ACA. |
| | Prescribe amantadine if troublesome anticholinergic symptoms already exist. |
| | Consider amantadine in geriatrics and to preserve new memory acquisition in any age group. |
| Rabbit syndrome | Responds well to any ACA. |

# General Considerations of Extrapyramidal Drugs (EPDs)

- β-blockers, clonidine, and benzodiazepines (e.g., clonazepam 1 mg q A.M.) mostly limited for use in akathisia and perhaps tremor.
  √ Clonidine's effect may be secondary to sedation and not a specific effect.
  √ β-blockers are first choice for akathisia alone.
- Amantadine is well-tolerated, broadly effective (including on akathisia), does not effect memory, protects from type-A influenza, is expensive, and occasionally may worsen psychosis.
- Anticholinergics are broadly effective (except on akathisia), have highest side effects, including on memory, and probably don't cause psychosis unless in toxic range.
- Buspirone 5–10 mg tid may help akathisia.
  √ Only a few case reports but no controlled studies.

# Speed of Response

- Only dystonia routinely responds in minutes to hours.
- Other symptoms (including akathisia) may take 3–10 days to respond significantly, although responses after 1–2 doses are not rare.

- Do not keep increasing daily dose just because effect is not yet visible.
- Pick a target dose and stay with it for 3–4 days.

## ACA Dosage Adjustment

- Benztropine drug levels can vary 100-fold with comparable dosing.
  √ Both under- and over-dosing is common.
  √ This may also be true of other ACAs.
- Some patients can become toxic at very low doses.
- Poor correlation between ACA dosage and control of EPS.
- High correlation between ACA blood levels (greater than 7 pmol of atropine equivalents) and control of EPS.
- 25% of patients on normal doses of ACA (usually 4 mg/qd benztropine) have very low blood levels.
  √ In these patients, most responded when dose was increased to 6–12 mg/day.
  √ If this is done, carefully monitor patient for ACA effects (e.g., dry mouth, constipation, memory impairments).
- Dry mouth often early sign of clinically significant ACA activity.
  √ If patient has poor control of EPS and no dry mouth, might try increasing ACA dose.
  √ If patient has good control of EPS but with severe ACA symptoms, try lowering ACA dose.
- Once a day dosing is often possible with long half-life ACAs (i.e., benztropine, biperiden).
  √ This should be tried only after optimal dose for patient has been established.

After 1–6 months of antipsychotic therapy, ACAs often can be withdrawn.

- About 15% of patients reexperience clear neurological side effects, whereas about 30% will feel "better"—less anxious, depressed, sleepy—on continued ACAs.
- Because antipsychotics have longer half-lives than ACAs, prescribe ACAs for several days *after* stopping neuroleptics.

## Delirium

Delirium is a syndrome of clouding of consciousness that produces disorientation, disturbed concentration, confusion, and loss of recent memory.

- It usually lasts no more than several days or, in some cases, weeks.
  √ Patients either improve or die.
- Ensure that medications are not causing the delirium.

✓ Anticholinergic toxicity is the most common medication cause.
  ▫ In addition to many psychotropic medications, many routine nonpsychiatric medications have significant anticholinergic activity (*see* pages 89–90).
- Indicators of *anticholinergic toxicity* include
  ✓ Dilated pupils
  ✓ Hot, dry skin
  ✓ Dry mucous membranes
  ✓ Tachycardia
  ✓ Absent bowel sounds
- Sedative medications (e.g., benzodiazepines, opiates, meprobamate), sedating and anticholinergic antidepressants, and neuroleptics are the next most common cause.
- Toxicity occurs more often in high doses of low-potency antipsychotics, in patients already on a drug with anticholinergic effects, and in the elderly.
- Other medications associated with delirium include:
  ✓ Amantadine
  ✓ Aspirin
  ✓ Cimetidine
  ✓ Hydrochlorthiazide
  ✓ Insulin
  ✓ Methyldopa
  ✓ Propranolol
  ✓ Reserpine
- Memory impairment alone can occur without other signs of toxicity.
- Anticholinergic toxicity can constitute a medical emergency.
- Management
  ✓ Stop all neuroleptic and antiparkinsonian agents.
  ✓ If medical emergency, IM/IV physostigmine can diagnose and treat this toxicity.
  ✓ Physostigmine's (cholinergic) risks include
    ▫ Increased salivation, vomiting, sweating, bradycardia, abdominal cramps, desire to urinate or defecate, seizures;
    ▫ Transient sinus arrest in cardiac patients;
    ▫ Bronchospasm in asthmatics.
  ✓ Before and after injecting physostigmine, obtain BP and pulse rate.
  ✓ Give 1–2 mg IM/IV physostigmine no faster than 1 mg/minute.
  ✓ Anticholinergic delirium clears in 15–20 minutes after injection.
    ▫ Physostigmine's effect lasts 30–60 minutes.
    ▫ If patient does not improve with 1 mg of physostigmine, may repeat 1 mg dose in 30–40 minutes.
    ▫ May inject up to 4 mg IV of physostigmine in one day.

NEUROPSYCHIATRIC DISORDERS

√ Switch to less anticholinergic neuroleptic.
√ Change ACA to amantadine.
√ If patient agitated during anticholinergic delirium, may use lorazepam to calm, since it is shorter-acting benzodiazepine without significant anticholinergic activity.

To manage combative, disorganized, or confused behavior, haloperidol is useful.

- Haloperidol has limited anticholinergic and hypotensive effects.
- Avoid toxicity by avoiding standing regular orders.
- Haloperidol 1–5 mg po or IM:
  √ Wait 1 h and
  √ Titrate repeat doses q 2–8 h.
- Delirious patients rarely need >10 mg of haloperidol.
  √ 2–4 mg/day typically suffices.
- Avoid adding ACAs, since
  √ Increased anticholinergic actions can worsen delirium, and
  √ Only 20% of delirious patients develop dystonia.

Benzodiazepines are an alternative to antipsychotic agents.

- Example: lorazepam 1–2 mg po or 2–4 mg IM.
  √ May risk increased confusion secondary to sedative effects.

Carbamazepine with buspirone reported effective in early posttraumatic delirium.

- Combine controlled-release carbamazepine 400 mg qd with buspirone 10 mg tid.
  √ Quieting effect noted in 12 h.
  √ Well tolerated.
  √ No comparison made with carbamazepine alone.

## Dementia—Alzheimer's

In Alzheimers's dementia there is a loss of intellectual abilities, e.g., judgment, memory, abstract thinking, control over impulses, and/or language.

- Unlike delirium, in dementia there usually is no or very little clouding of consciousness.
  √ Demented patients have increased risk of superimposed delirium.
- Dementias are usually chronic.
- Behavioral disturbances in dementia include delusions, hallucinations, dysphoria, anxiety, agitation/aggression, euphoria, disinhibition, irritability/lability, apathy, and aberrant motor activity.

- Deterioration of cognitive abilities is related to reduction in cholinergic function in the basal forebrain and the appearance of neurofibrillatory tangles and plaques containing $\beta$-amyloid ($\beta$A).
  √ Some plaques are neurotoxic and contain acetylcholinesterase (AchE) and butyrylcholinesterase (BuChE).
  √ Reduction of Ach synthesis in the cortex and hippocampus
- Research on Alzheimer's disease in 625 elderly patients:
  √ Each patient was assigned to placebo or risperidone, 0.5 mg/day, 1 or 2 mg/day.
    □ 1 mg/day usually was effective.
  √ Most common dose-related adverse events were
    □ Extrapyramidal symptoms
    □ Somnolence
    □ Mild peripheral edema
  √ On 1 mg/day, extrapyramidal symptoms were equal to placebo.

### Antidementia Drugs

Acetylcholinesterase inhibitors

- Increase acetylcholine levels
- May temporarily reduce, and later delay, cognitive and behavioral symptoms of dementia but not ongoing neural destruction.

### Tacrine

Advantages:

- A variety of proven measurements (e.g., Neuropsychiatric Inventory, NPI) generally yield the greatest positive change with moderate dementia.
- A 63% reduction occurred in 10 behavioral symptoms at high (100–140 mg) dosages of tacrine.
- Most improvement seen in apathy, disinhibition, anxiety, aberrant motor behaviors, and visual hallucinations.

Drawbacks:

- 40% of patients had elevated liver enzymes.
- Tacrine requires slow titration taking several months before effective therapeutic dosage is reached.
- Tacrine has a short half-life requiring 4 dosages daily.
- GI adverse events include nausea, vomiting, diarrhea, dyspepsia, anorexia, and abdominal pain.
  √ These effects are largely dose-dependent.
- Tacrine is now prescribed for < 0.5% of Alzheimer's patients.

NEUROPSYCHIATRIC DISORDERS

**Donepezil (Aricept)**

- In a group of 40 patients there was significant reduction in total NPI scores.
- Another behavioral study demonstrated that patients treated with donepezil for their cognitive impairment were less likely to need other psychotropic medications than patients receiving placebo.
- In a 60-patient study with mild to moderate dementia, scores on the Alzheimer's Disease Assessment Scale cognitive subscale significantly improved in 44% of patients on donepezil and 19% on placebo.
- ADAS scores deteriorate when donepezil is withdrawn.

**Rivastigmine (Exelon)**

- Selectively targets the cortex and hippocampus.
- In one study a reduction in psychotic symptoms, as assessed by the NPI, was observed.
- Inhibits butyrylcholinesterase as well as acetylcholinesterase.
- Improvement in cognition and functioning.

**Galantamine (Reminyl)**

- Cholinergic agonist as well as cholinesterase inhibitor
- Multicenter trials demonstrate statistically significant improvements on measures of cognition.

Similarities and differences in new AchE inhibitors in Alzheimer's disease.

- Goal is to inhibit central AchE in order to boost the action of Ach long enough to enhance cognition and probably reduce disruptive behavior.
  - √ All 4 of the presently available AchE inhibitors have this ability.
- Donepezil is a highly selective and potent AchE inhibitor.
- Rivastigmine is a dual inhibitor of both AchE and butyrylcholinesterase.
  - √ Uniquely more selective for the form of AchE in hippocampal neurons where cognition is important.
  - √ BuChE also breaks down Ach.
  - √ Only rivastigmine inhibits both AchE and BuChE.
    - ◻ May be cause of higher incidence of GI side effects.
- Galantamine is both an AchE inhibitor and a selective agaonist of nicotinic cholinergic receptors and causes the release of many other neurotransmitters (e.g., dopamine, serotonin, $\gamma$-aminobutyric acid (GABA), glutamate, and norepinephrine).

## Adverse Effects of Acetylcholinesterase Inhibitors in Alzheimer's Disease

| | Nausea | Vomiting | Diarrhea | Dizziness | Headache | Abdominal Pain |
|---|---|---|---|---|---|---|
| Donepezil | +++ | ++ | ++ | + | − | − |
| Galantamine | ++ | ++ | + | + | − | − |
| Rivastigmine | +++ | ++ | ++ | ++ | + | + |
| Tacrine | +++ | ++ | ++ | ++ | + | + |

| | Anorexia | Fatigue | Muscle Cramps | Agitation | Heparotoxicity |
|---|---|---|---|---|---|
| Donepezil | + | − | − | ++ | − |
| Galantamine | − | + | + | − | − |
| Rivastigmine | + | + | − | − | − |
| Tacrine | ++ | + | − | + | +++ |

Patients showing symptoms: − = 0 or less than 5%; + = 5–10%; ++ = 10–20%; +++ = 20–50%.

## Pharmacologic Characteristics of Approved Cholinesterase Inhibitors

| Drug | Class | Types of Cholinesterase Inhibition | $t^{1}/_{2}$(serum) (h) | Dosage (mg/day) |
|---|---|---|---|---|
| Donepezil | Piperidine | Reversible; mixed competitive/ noncompetitive | 70–80 | 5–10 (qd) |
| Galantamine | Phenentrine alkaloid | Reversible; competitive | 5–7 | 20–50 (tid) |
| Rivastigmine | Carbamate | Pseudoreversible | 1.5** | 6–12 (bid) |
| Tacrine* | Acridine | Reversible; noncompetitive | 1.3–2 | 80–160 (qid) |

\* Only tacrine has hepatotoxicity.
\*\* Brain $t^{1}/_{2}$ = 8–10 hrs.

# Other Treatments

Vitamin $B_{12}$ and folate

- Healthy elderly adults (90–101 y.o.) with lower folic acid levels (< 13 ng/ml) showed impairment in both word recall and object recall. Subjects with normal folate levels did not show impairment.
- $B_{12}$ had minimal improvement.

Vitamin E

- Early in disease, course appears to slow down or prevent much of the neural destruction and decline of dementia but does not directly reduce cognitive and behavioral symptoms.
- At least 2 studies suggest that 50% of people regularly using neuroleptics and vitamin E will have full remission from tardive dyskinesia.

√ In patients with over 5 yrs. of tardive dyskinesia, very few remit while taking vitamin E.

- Does not easily penetrate blood–brain barrier, so higher doses are needed, e.g., ≥ 1000 mg.
- Vitamin E may slow rate of motor decline.

Estrogen replacement

- Slows cognitive decline in postmenopausal women.
- Higher doses appear to be better than lower.
- Lower AD risk in women on hormone replacement therapy.
- Estrogen has cholinergic agonist properties and enhanced tacrine's effects in one study.
- Donepezil plus estrogen yielded a 75% greater increase in cognitive performance than donepezil (Aricept) alone.

Selegiline (selective MAO-B inhibitor) (basic pharmacology in Chapter 4)

- May be as effective as vitamin E in preventing neural destruction.
- However, some studies could not demonstrate efficacy after 3 months of treatment.
- In one study, adding selegiline to vitamin E did not enhance outcome.

Anti-inflammatory agents, e.g., NSAIDs (e.g., aspirin, ibuprofen)

- May decrease rate of cognitive decline but are only recommended for those who must take them for other conditions, e.g., arthritis.

Calcium channel-blockers

- Most promising indication for nimodipine is with dementia caused or complicated by multi-infarcts, but mechanism of action of nimodipine may not be limited to prevention of infarcts.
- Large multicenter trial showed nimodipine no better than placebo for AD.

Zidovudine (antiviral), 1000–2000 mg qd

- Has been shown to reduce dementia symptoms and/or prevent cognitive decline in patients with HIV infection.
- Response lasts 6–12 months.
- Higher doses give more optimal response.

Thyroid replacement may help geriatric patients with cognitive impairment accompanied by elevated TSH levels.

- 3.8 times higher dementia rate in > 65 y.o. patients with elevated TSH levels.

- Thyroid replacement may not reverse preexisting dementia but may slow its progress.

Glycine (bioglycin, a biologically active form of the amino acid glycine) affects memory and attention in normal young (mean age 20.7 yrs.) and middle-aged (mean age 58.9 yrs) men:

- Bioglycin given in 100 mg qd.
- Compared to the young group, the middle-aged group had significantly poorer verbal episodic memory and poorer focused, divided, and sustained attention.
- Bioglycin significantly improved retrieval of episodic memory for both young and middle-aged groups.
  - √ Did not affect focused or divided attention.
  - √ Middle-aged men significantly benefited from improved sustained attention.

## Ancillary Agents for Dementia

Antipsychotic agents may reduce agitation and confusion in dementia, although they are not a first choice for these symptoms.

- Haloperidol 0.5–2 mg po or IM q 4–6 h
  - √ Bedtime dosing might help regulate sleep cycle.
  - √ Low-potency neuroleptics (e.g., chlorpromazine) risk further cognitive impairment, hypotension, and possible seizure.
  - √ Avoid adding an ACA, since it may augment toxicity.
  - √ For agitation with psychosis, 1–3 mg qd is usually optimal.
- Thioridazine (mean 92 mg) and fluoxetine (mean 36 mg) every other day dropped Alzheimer's Disease Assessment Scale after 32 weeks from
  - √ 16 to 11 on thioridazine
  - √ 14 to 9.5 on fluoxetine
  - √ 14.5 to 13.1 on haloperidol (no significant change)
  - √ Thioridazine is a poor choice because its anticholinergic side effects aggravate dementia.

Atypical antipsychotic agent—risperidone (800–1000 mg bid)

- 64 nursing home patients with primary diagnosis of dementia (55% with Alzheimer's and 20% with multi-infarcts) were treated with 0.25 to 0.5 mg of risperidone twice daily.
- After 6 months, risperidone was very helpful in 41% of patients, moderately helpful in 26%, slightly helpful in 16%, and not helpful in 17%.

- Areas of greatest improvement included decreases in physical agitation, verbal outbursts, physical aggression, depressed mood, anxiety, abnormal movements, and eating problems.
- Similar findings with olazapine 2.5–5 mg/day.

Short-acting hypnoanxiolytics (lorazepam 0.5 mg po) have less drug accumulation and therefore induce less confusion than longer-acting hypnoanxiolytics (chlordiazepoxide).

Trazodone in daily total doses between 25 and 500 mg, and buspirone in daily total doses between 10 and 60 mg, can decrease agitation and aggression without decreasing cognitive performance. (For further discussion of agents that treat agitation and aggression, *see* pages 281–87.)

## Frontotemporal Dementia (FTD)

- Frontotemporal dementia caused by selective degeneration of frontal and/or anterior temporal cortical regions.
- Decreased serotonin receptor binding reported in the frontal lobes, temporal lobes, and hypothalamus.
  √ Patients have frontal and/or anterior temporal lobe atrophy.
- Behavioral symptoms of FTD include disinhibition, labile affect, depressive symptoms, carbohydrate craving, and compulsions.
- With SSRI treatment, all of the above symptoms showed improvement in at least half of the 11 patients.
  √ Disinhibition was present in 9 (82%) and improved in 6 (67%).
  √ Depressive symptoms were present in 6 (55%) and improved in 4 (67%).
  √ Carbohydrate craving was present in 9 (87%) and improved in 5 (56%).
  √ Compulsions were present in 7 (64%) and improved in 4 (57%).

## SIDE EFFECTS

Side effects of ACAs and amantadine are listed below. $\beta$-blocker and clonidine side effects are listed in Chapter 7 (pages 354–56).

In order of frequency, the most common (> 3%) side effects of

- ACAs include
  √ Memory impairment
  √ Dry mouth, nose, and throat
  √ Blurred vision
  √ Light sensitivity

√ Urinary hesitancy
√ Constipation
√ Appetite loss/nausea
√ Listlessness
√ Excitement
- Amantadine
√ Blurred vision
√ Dry mouth
√ Urinary hesitancy
√ Nausea
√ Insomnia
√ Depression
√ Psychosis

Amantadine's side-effect frequencies are only slightly more than placebo. In experimental trials in healthy volunteers, ACAs interfered with learning new material in adults of all ages and caused ratings of fatigue-inertia, tension-anxiety, and depression-dejection. Amantadine had none of these effects.

The side effects of diazepam, lorazepam, and propranolol are listed in Chapter 7 (*see* pages 354–56).

Since the side effects of ACAs are anticholinergic, deal with them by

- Eliminating or reducing the ACA.
- Changing to a less anticholinergic antipsychotic (*see* page 25).
- Substituting the non-anticholinergic amantadine for the ACA.

## Cardiovascular Effects

*Palpitations, tachycardia*

*Dizziness*

## Central Nervous System Effects

*Confusion, delirium, disturbed concentration, disorientation*

*Restlessness, tremors, ataxia*

*Weakness, lethargy*

*Numb fingers, inability to move particular muscles, slurred speech, incoherence*

- More common in the elderly and in high doses.

*Stimulation, nervous excitement, insomnia, depression*

- All may be more common with trihexyphenidyl (*see* Precautions).

*Psychosis*

- This occurs especially with amantadine (0.5% psychosis, 3% hallucinations). Rate for ACA is lower in the absence of overdose. Before changing a neuroleptic in a "treatment resistant" psychotic patient, first try taking the patient off amantadine.

## Endocrine and Sexual Effects

Amantadine may reduce galactorrhea provoked by neuroleptic-induced increased prolactin.

## Eyes, Ears, Nose, and Throat Effects

*Vision, blurred* (*see* page 45).

*Photophobia*

- From dilated pupils

*Eyes, dry* (*see* pages 45–46).

*Narrow-angle glaucoma*

- ACAs can trigger narrow-angle glaucoma.
- If patient has a h/o glaucoma, test intraocular pressure before giving ACAs, TCAs, or neuroleptics (*see* page XX).
- If narrow-angle glaucoma becomes a problem, stop all ACAs and neuroleptics.

*Nasal congestion, dry throat*

*Dry bronchial secretions and strained breathing*

- Aggravate respiratory ailments.

## Gastrointestinal Effects

*Mouth, dry*

- Management (*see* page 47).

*Nausea, vomiting*

- Reduce ACA.

*Constipation*

- Management (*see* page 47).

*Paralytic ileus*

# Renal Effects

*Urinary hesitancy or retention* (*see* pages 52–53).

# Skin, Allergies, and Temperature Effects

*Diminished sweating* (*see* page 53)

*Skin flushing*

*Skin rashes*

- Stop ACA.
- Check nature and distribution
  √ To exclude contact dermatitis.
  √ If only on neck or wrists, probably need new soap.
  √ Stop neuroleptic if not contact dermatitis.

*Fever*

- Apply ice bags.

## PERCENTAGES OF SIDE EFFECTS

| Side Effects | Anticholinergics | Amantadine | Diphenhydramine |
|---|---|---|---|
| **CARDIOVASCULAR EFFECTS*** | | | |
| Congestive heart failure | —— | < 1 | —— |
| Dizziness | < 1 | 2 | 20 |
| Hypotension | < 0.1 | 1 | —— |
| Tachycardia | < 0.1 | 1 | < 1 |
| **CENTRAL NERVOUS SYSTEM EFFECTS** | | | |
| Agitation | 2 | 0 | < 1 |
| Anxiety | 4 | 2 | —— |
| Ataxia | —— | 3 | —— |
| Confusion | 2 | 0.7 | —— |
| Depression | < 1 | 0.7 | —— |
| Drowsiness | 2.8 | 2 | 20 |
| Fatigue | —— | 0.5 | 19 |
| Hallucinations | —— | 3 | —— |
| Headache | 0 | 2 | —— |
| Insomnia | 0 | 3.1 | —— |
| Irritability | —— | 3 | —— |
| Limbs, weakness in | 2.7 | 1.4 | < 1 |
| Muscle cramps | < 1 | —— | —— |
| Nightmares | —— | —— | < 1 |
| Numbness | < 1 | —— | —— |
| Psychosis | —— | 0.5 | —— |
| Seizures | —— | < 0.1 | —— |
| Speech, slurred | —— | 0.5 | —— |

| Side Effects | Anticholinergics | Amantadine | Diphenhydramine |
|---|---|---|---|
| **EYES, EARS, NOSE, AND THROAT EFFECTS** | | | |
| Contact lenses, less tolerance for | —— | —— | 5.5 |
| Dyspnea | —— | 0.5 | —— |
| Light sensitivity | 20 | —— | —— |
| Narrow-angle glaucoma | < 1 | —— | —— |
| Nose and throat, dry | 20 | —— | 20 |
| Oculogyric episode | —— | < 0.1 | —— |
| Throat, sore | —— | —— | < 1 |
| Vision, blurred | 26 | 10 | —— |
| Visual disturbance | —— | 0.5 | 5.5 |
| **GASTROINTESTINAL EFFECTS** | | | |
| Anorexia | 4.7 | 0.7 | 5.5 |
| Constipation | 15 | 1.4 | —— |
| Edema | —— | 3 | —— |
| Mouth, dry | 33 | 9 | 20 |
| Mouth, sore | < 1 | —— | —— |
| Nausea | 15 | 7.5 | 20 |
| Vomiting | 3 | 1.4 (0.1–1) | —— |
| **HEMATOLOGIC EFFECTS** | | | |
| Bruising, easy | —— | —— | < 1 |
| **RENAL EFFECTS** | | | |
| Urinary hesitancy | 15 | 3 | —— |
| Urination, painful or difficult | —— | —— | —— |
| **SKIN, ALLERGIES, AND TEMPERATURE EFFECTS** | | | |
| Dermatitis, eczematoid | —— | < 0.1 | —— |
| Fever | —— | —— | < 1 |
| Rash | 1.4 | 0.5 | —— |
| Sweating, decreased | 2.0 | < 0.1 | 3.0 |

\* —No report

## PREGNANCY AND LACTATION

Teratogenicity (1st trimester)
- No apparent fetal risk from trihexyphenidyl.
- No reports on biperiden.
- A few cases of amantadine-induced cardiovascular anomalies may exist, but relationship to drug unknown.

Direct effect on newborn (3rd trimester)
- A few cases of paralytic ileus with mother on chlorpromazine and benztropine.

Lactation
- No data.

- Amantadine secreted in breast milk.
  - √ Amantadine blood levels are useful to determine if a safe and low enough level has been reached to avoid potentially problematic effects on the baby.

## DRUG–DRUG INTERACTIONS

Drugs with significant anticholinergic effects all interact with each other, causing increased anticholinergic effects (toxicity and/or better control of EPS). These include

- Psychiatric drugs (e.g., tertiary amine tricyclic antidepressants),
- Nonpsychiatric medical drugs that are commonly prescribed, and
- Antihistamines.

### Anticholinergic Drugs

| Commonly Prescribed Medications | Nonpsychiatric Anticholinergic Agents | Antihistamines |
|---|---|---|
| Codeine | Anisotropine (Valpin) | Brompheniramine (Dimetane) |
| Coumadin | Atropine | Chlorpheniramine (Chlor-Trimeton) |
| Digoxin | Belladonna alkaloids | Clemastine (Tavist) |
| Dipyridamole | Clidinium (Quarzan) | Cyproheptadine (Periactin) |
| Disopyramide | Dicyclomine (Bentyl) | Dexchlorpheniramine (Polaramine) |
| Isosorbide | Ethopropazine (Parsidol) | Diphenhydramine (Benadryl) |
| Meperidine | Glycopyrrolate (Robinul) | Hydroxyzine (Atarax, Vistaril) |
| Nifedipine | Hexocyclium (Tral) | Methdilazine (Tacaryl) |
| Prednisone | Homatropine | Promethazine (Phenergan) |
| Procainamide | Hyoscyamine | Trimeprazine (Temaril) |
| Quinidine | Ipratropium | Triprolidine (Actidil) |
| Ranitidine | Isopropamide (Darbid) | |
| | Mepenzolate (Cantil) | |
| | Methantheline (Banthine) | |
| | Methscopolamine (Pamine) | |
| | Orphenadrine (Disipal) | |
| | Oxyphencyclimine (Daricon) | |
| | Propantheline (Pro-Banthine) | |
| | Scopolamine | |
| | Tridihexethyl (Pathilon) | |

| Drugs (X) Interact with: | Anticholinergics (A)** | Comments |
|---|---|---|
| Acetaminophen | X↓ | May increase acetaminophen use. |
| Amantadine | X↑A↑ | Increased amantadine and ACA effects. |
| *Antihistamines | X↑A↓ | Increased anticholinergic effects. |
| *Antipsychotics | X↓A↑ | ACAs may slow antipsychotic actions. ACAs enhance anticholinergic effects of antipsychotics, particularly low-potency phenothiazines. |

| Drugs (X) Interact with: | Anticholinergics (A)** | Comments |
|---|---|---|
| Atenolol | X↑ | May increase atenolol's concentration. |
| *Cocaine | A↓ | Decreased anticholinergic effects. |
| Digoxin | X↑ | Increases level, more slowly dissolved digoxin tablet. |
| Levodopa (L-dopa) | X↓ | May reduce L-dopa's availability; when ACAs stopped, L-dopa's toxicity may erupt. |
| *Methotrimeparazine | A↓ | Combination may increase EPS. |
| MAOIs | A↑ | May increase anticholinergic effects. |
| Nitrofurantoin | X↑ | ACA may increase nitrofurantoin effects. |
| Primidone | X↑ | Excessive sedation. |
| Procainamide | X↑ | Increased procainamide effect. |
| Propranolol | X↓ | ACAs can block β-blocker's bradycardia. |
| *TCAs | A↑X↑ | May diminish EPS; increased risk of anticholinergic toxicity. |
| Tacrine | X↓A↓ | Interfere with each other's effects. |

| Drugs (X) Interact with: | Amantadine (A) | Comments |
|---|---|---|
| Alcohol | X↑ | Increased alcohol effect; possible fainting. |
| Anticholinergics | X↑A↑ | Increased amantadine and ACA effects. |
| Anti-emetics | X↓ | Possible decreased efficacy. |
| Antipsychotics | X↓ | May interfere with antipsychotic effect. |
| *Cocaine | X↑ | Major overstimulation. |
| *Sympathomimetics | X↑ | Increased stimulation and agitation. |
| Trimethoprim, sulfamethoxazole (Bactrim, Septa) | X↑A↑ | May increase each other's levels; CNS toxicity possible. |
| Quinidine† | A↑ | Modest increase in amantadine levels. |
| Quinine† | A↑ | Modest increase in amantadine levels. |
| Triamterene (in Dyazide)† | A↑ | Modest increase in amantadine levels. |

* Moderately important reaction; ↑ Increases; ↓ Decreases.
** See also preceding lists of other drugs with anticholinergic effects.
† Decreases renal clearance of amantadine.

## EFFECTS ON LABORATORY TESTS

| Generic Names | Blood/Serum Tests | Results* | Urine Tests | Results* |
|---|---|---|---|---|
| Amantadine | WBC Leukocytes | ↓↓ | ? | |
| Benztropine | None | | None | |
| Biperiden | ? | | ? | |
| Diphenhydramine | WBC, RBC, platelets | ↓↓ ↓ | ? | |
| Procyclidine | ? | | ? | |
| Trihexyphenidyl | None | | None | |

* ↑ Increases; ↓ Decreases; ? = Undetermined.

## WITHDRAWAL

ACAs do not cause

- Dependence (but abuse is possible)
- Tolerance
  √ Some tolerance with amantadine occurs after 8 weeks.
- Addiction

## ACA Withdrawal

Yet, even more than with antipsychotic agents, abruptly stopping ACAs can induce, in 2–4 (up to 7) days, a flu-like syndrome without a fever.

- Nausea, vomiting, diarrhea
- Hypersalivation
- Headaches
- Insomnia
- Nightmares

Less often develop

- Rhinorrhea
- Increased appetite
- Giddiness
- Dizziness
- Tremors
- Warm or cold sensations

These symptoms

- Represent cholinergic rebound,
- May persist 2 weeks,
- Are not life-threatening,
- Can diminish substantially by more gradually tapering off neuroleptics and ACAs.
- This approach also decreases risk of rebound EPS.

## Amantadine Withdrawal

Stopping amantadine abruptly can result in rebound EPS with "parkinsonian crisis" in patients with Parkinson's disease and a severe worsening of neuroleptic-induced EPS.

## OVERDOSE: TOXICITY, SUICIDE, AND TREATMENT

ACAs' side effects are more severe in overdoses.

Treatments as listed above.

NEUROPSYCHIATRIC DISORDERS

For general management of overdoses, *see* pages 65–67.

If overdosage (OD) is with ACA or amantadine alone, emetics are okay, in contrast to antipsychotics. Physostigmine 1–2 mg IV q 1–2 h may decrease CNS toxicity for both ACA and amantadine.

For amantadine OD, acidifying the urine may speed elimination; specifically, watch out for hyperactivity, convulsions, arrhythmias, and hypotension.

## PRECAUTIONS

Be alert to growing reports of ACA abuse.

- Arises in 0–17.5% of patients taking ACAs.
- Occurs with all ACAs.
- Most common with trihexyphenidyl, due far less to alleviating EPS, and far more to side effects:
  √ Energizing
  √ Inducing euphoria
  √ Sedating
  √ Enhancing socializing
  √ Affording psychedelic and psychotogenic experiences

ACAs contraindicated in patients with

- Urinary retention, prostatic hypertrophy
- Paralytic ileus, bowel obstruction, megacolon
- Hyperthermia, heat stroke
- Congestive heart failure
- Narrow-angle (i.e., acute angle-closure) glaucoma
- Hypersensitivity to ACAs
- Dry bronchial secretions (especially in the elderly)
- Delirium and dementia
- Cardiac patients with hypertension

Use ACAs with extreme caution in patients with

- Cardiac arrhythmias
- Hypotension
- Liver or kidney disorders
- Geriatric conditions
- Peripheral edema

## NURSES' DATA

EPS are tough. These tips might help.

- Teach patients to explain to others about EPS, especially TD.

√ Have patients role-play explanations; it is good practice for real life and ensures that patients have accurate information.

- Patients should wear loose, lightweight clothing, with garments closing in front and fastening with velcro instead of buttons or zippers.
  √ If one side of the body is stiffer, recommend that patient put on or remove clothes from the other side first.
  √ Shoes—slip-on or those that fasten with elastic laces or velcro—are preferable to standard laced or zipped shoes.
  □ Long-handled shoehorn might assist.
  □ Avoid high-heeled shoes or other styles that make walking difficult.
- Prevent bathing accidents.
  √ Use of no-slip rubber mat.
  √ Insertion of grab-bars.
  √ Removal of glass tub or shower doors.
  √ Installation of a shower chair.
  √ Soap attached to a rope and placed conveniently in bath or shower.
- Walking can be complicated and too fast, especially when people walk on the balls of their feet and with raised heels.
  √ To discourage shuffling, teach patients the following routine.
  □ Stop their usual walking.
  □ Place their feet at least 8 inches apart.
  □ Correct their posture.
  □ Take a large step.
  □ Bring their foot higher in a "marching fashion."
- Because patients may fall on turns, show them how to walk (not pivot or swing) into turns.
- For patients with problems getting out of bed at night because of stiffness or rigidity, show them how to
  √ First lie (and then sit) on the side of the bed.
  √ Slowly drop one leg over the edge while pushing down with elbow on the bed with the opposite hand.

Dentures can rub and ulcerate gums as well as provoke mouth movements that imitate TD.

Apply elastic stockings to reduce swelling from orthostatic hypotension.

Make referrals for physical, occupational, or speech therapy as TD or other EPS problems arise.

## PATIENT AND FAMILY NOTES

### General Information

If blurred vision occurs or alertness is lowered, do not drive or work in situations needing close-up focusing or quick reflexes.

For dry mouth, avoid calorie-laden beverages and candy; they foster caries and weight gain. Increase sugar-free fluid intake and try sugar-free candy.

To avoid accidental ingestion, do not keep medication at bedside; keep safely away from children.

To prevent or relieve constipation, increase bulk-forming foods, water (2500–3000 ml/day), and exercise. Stool softeners are okay, but laxatives should be avoided if possible.

### ACA Information

Most common side effects of ACAs are dry mouth and throat, blurred vision, light sensitivity, urinary hesitancy, constipation, depression, and less memory.

Take ACAs with meals to reduce dry mouth and gastric irritation.

Although one may consume alcohol on ACAs, "one drink often feels like 2 drinks" and confusion is much more likely.

Use extra caution in hot weather; heat stroke more likely.

May take oral dose up to 2 h late.

- If dose is more than 2 h late, skip it; do not double the dose.
- Benztropine's and biperiden's relatively long action may allow for a single bedtime dose.

Do not stop ACAs or amantadine until a week after antipsychotic agents have been stopped.

### Amantadine Information

Side effects reported include blurred vision, dry mouth, urinary hesitancy, nausea, and insomnia.

- Most people don't get these side effects.

Take it once a day (up to 200 mg), but if side effects become a problem, divide the dosage into a twice-a-day regimen. Sometimes taking it on a full stomach reduces nausea.

May consume alcohol on amantadine.

# 3. Antidepressants

## INTRODUCTION

Antidepressants (ADs) are of 4 types:

- Multicyclic, often called heterocyclic, antidepressants (HCAs)
    - √ All of these except maprotiline and amoxapine have 3 rings and are called *tricyclic* antidepressants (TCAs).
    - √ The abbreviation TCA will be used if data is only available for TCAs but not for the larger group of HCAs (which include tetracyclics, maprotiline, amoxapine).
- Selective serotonin reuptake inhibitors (SSRIs)
- Atypical (bupropion, mirtazapine, nefazodone, trazodone, venlafaxine)
- Monoamine-oxidase inhibitors (MAOIs)

This chapter discusses HCAs, SSRIs, and atypicals; the next chapter, MAOIs.

This chapter focuses on

- Major depression (pages 102–18, 130–31)
- Treatment-resistant depression (pages 118–25)
- Electroconvulsive therapy (ECT) and medications (pages 125–30)
- Seasonal affective disorder (mood disorder with seasonal pattern) (page 135)
- Bereavement (page 132)
- Chronic pain disorders (pages 133–34)
- Anorexia nervosa (page 131)
- Bulimia nervosa (page 132)
- Premenstrual syndrome (premenstrual phase dysphoric disorder) (pages 134–35)

- Pseudodementia (page 135)
- Pseudobulbar affect (page 135)
- Adult physical disorders (pages 131–38)
  √ Allergies
  √ Cardiac conduction problems
  √ Cataplexy
  √ Congestive heart failure
  √ Constipation (chronic)
  √ Dementia, delirium, cognitive disorder
  √ Diabetes, type II
  √ Diarrhea (chronic)
  √ Epilepsy
  √ Impotence (partial) (organic)
  √ Irritable bowel syndrome
  √ Migraine headache
  √ Narrow-angle glaucoma
  √ Neurogenic bladder
  √ Parkinson's disease
  √ Peptic ulcers
  √ Sleep apnea
  √ Tardive dyskinesia
- Childhood stage-4 sleep disorders (pages 137–38)
  √ Enuresis
  √ Night terrors
  √ Sleepwalking

As detailed elsewhere, ADs treat

- Agoraphobia (Antianxiety, page 335)
- Attention-deficit/hyperactivity disorder (Stimulants, pages 427–31)
- Atypical depression (MAOIs, pages 183–84)
- Borderline personality disorder (Lithium, page 232)
- Dysthymic disorder (MAOIs, pages 184–85)
- Hypochondriasis (Antianxiety, page 345)
- Narcolepsy (Stimulants, pages 435–36)
- Obsessive-compulsive disorder (Antianxiety, pages 338–344)
- Panic disorders (Antianxiety, pages 329–334)
- Schizoaffective disorders (Lithium, page 233)
- Social phobia (Antianxiety, pages 335–37)
- Treatment-resistant depression (Stimulants, page 434)

## NAMES, CLASSES, MANUFACTURERS, DOSE FORMS, COLORS

| Generic Names | Brand Names | Manufacturers | Dose Forms (mg)[1] | Colors |
|---|---|---|---|---|
| | | **HETEROCYCLICS** | | |
| *Tertiary Amine* | | | | |
| Amitriptyline | Elavil | Stuart | t: 10/25/50/75/ 100/150 p: 10 mg/ml | t: blue/yellow/ beige/orange mauve/blue |
| | Endepryl | Roche | t: 10/25/50/75/ 100/150 | t: orange/orange/ orange/yellow/ peach/salmon |
| Clomipramine | Anafranil | CIBA/Basel | c: 25/50/75 | c: ivory-melon- yellow/ivory- aqua-blue/ ivory-yellow |
| Doxepin | Sinequan | Roerig | c: 10/25/50/ 75/100/150 o: 10 mg/ml | c: red-pink/blue- pink/peach-off- white/pale pink- light pink/blue- white/blue |
| Imipramine | Tofranil | Geigy | t: 10/25/50 p: 25 mg/2 ml | t: triangular coral/ round biconvex coral/round biconvex coral |
| | Janimine | Abbott | t: 10/25/50 | t: orange/yellow/ peach |
| Imipramine pamoate | Tofranil-PM (sustained- release) | Geigy | c: 75/100/125/ 150 | c: coral/dark yellow- coral/light yellow- coral/coral |
| Trimipramine | Surmontil | Wyeth-Ayerst | c: 25/50/100 | c: blue-yellow/blue- orange/blue- white |
| *Secondary Amine* | | | | |
| Desipramine | Norpramin | Marion Merrell Dow | t: 10/25/50/75/ 100/150 | t: blue/yellow/ green/orange/ peach/white |
| Nortriptyline | Pamelor | Sandoz | c: 10/25/50/75 o: 10 mg/5 ml | c: orange-white/ orange-white/ white/orange |
| Protriptyline | Aventyl | Lilly | c: 10/25 | c: cream/gold |
| | Vivactil | Merck, Sharp & Dohme | t: 5/10 | t: orange/yellow |
| | | **TETRACYCLICS** | | |
| Amoxapine | Asendin | Lederle | t: 25/50/100/150 | t: white/orange/ blue/peach |
| Maprotiline | Ludiomil | CIBA | t: 25/50/75 | t: oval orange/ round orange/ oval white |

| Generic Names | Brand Names | Manufacturers | Dose Forms (mg) | Colors |
|---|---|---|---|---|
| **SELECTIVE SEROTONIN REUPTAKE INHIBITORS** | | | | |
| Citalopram | Celexa | Forest | t: 20/40 | t: pink/white |
| Fluoxetine | Prozac | Dista/Lilly | c: 10/20 o: 5 mg/ml | c: green-gray/ off-white |
| Fluvoxamine | Luvox | Solvay | t: 50/100 | t: yellow/beige |
| Paroxetine | Paxil | Smith Kline Beecham | t: 20/30 | t: pink/blue |
| Sertraline | Zoloft | Roerig/Pfizer | t: 50/100 | t: light blue/ light yellow |
| **ATYPICALS** | | | | |
| Bupropion | Wellbutrin SR | Glaxo Wellcome | t: 100/150 | t: blue/purple |
| Mirtazapine | Remeron | Organon | t: 15/30/45 | t: yellow/red-brown/white |
| Nefazodone | Serzone | Bristol Myers Squibb | t: 100/150/ 200/250 | t: white/peach/ light yellow/white |
| Trazodone | Desyrel | Apothecon (Bristol Meyers Squibb) | t: 50/100/150/ 300 | t: orange/white/ orange/yellow |
| Venlafaxine | Effexor | Wyeth-Ayerst | t: 25/37.5/50/ 75/100 | t: all peach |
| | Effexor XR | Wyeth-Ayerst | t: 37.5/45/100 | t: grey/pink pink/red |

[1] c = capsules; e = elixir; o = oral concentrate; p = parenteral concentrate; s = syrup; sp = suppository; sr = sustained-release spansules; su = suspension; t = tablets.

# PHARMACOLOGY

TCAs are divided into tertiary and secondary amines.

- Tertiary TCAs have 2 $CH_3$ groups on a side chain, whereas secondary TCAs have one $CH_3$ on a side chain.
- Tertiary TCAs are more potent blockers of serotonin reuptake, whereas secondary TCAs are more potent blockers of norepinephrine reuptake.
- Tertiary TCAs tend to be more anticholinergic, antihistaminic, and antialpha-adrenergic than secondary TCAs.
- SSRIs tend to be mainly serotoninergic; only sertraline has significant dopaminergic reuptake inhibition.
  √ Paroxetine inhibits serotonin reuptake at high doses (~50 mg).

Sedative effects of TCAs are attributed to antihistaminic ($H_1$ receptor) actions and somewhat anticholinergic actions.

# Antidepressant Reuptake and Postsynaptic Receptor Blockade of Neurotransmitters

| Receptor: | POSTSYNAPTIC RECEPTOR BLOCKADE* | | | | | REUPTAKE BLOCKADE* | |
|---|---|---|---|---|---|---|---|
| | Histaminic-1 | Dopaminergic | Cholinergic (Muscarinic) | α₁-Adrenergic | α₂-Adrenergic | Norepinephrine | Serotonin |
| Potential results from blockade: | • Sedation<br>• Weight gain<br>• Hypotension | • EPS<br>• Prolactin elevation | • Vision, blurred<br>• Mouth, dry<br>• Memory loss | • Postural hypotension<br>• Dizziness<br>• Tachycardia | • Block clonidine's antihypertensive effects | • Sweating<br>• Anxiety | • Diarrhea<br>• Nausea |
| Generic Names | $H_1$ | DA | ACH | $\alpha_1$ | $\alpha_2$ | NE | 5HT |
| Amitriptyline | 3 | 1 | 4 | 4 | 3 | 2 | 2 |
| Amoxapine | 2 | 2 | 1 | 3 | 2 | 3 | +/− |
| Bupropion | +/− | +/− | 0 | +/− | 0 | +/− | 0 |
| Citalopram | 2 | 1 | 3 | 1 | 0 | 2 | 3 |
| Clomipramine | 3 | 1 | 3 | 4 | 2 | 2 | 3 |
| Desipramine | 1 | 1 | 2 | 2 | 1 | 4 | +/− |
| Doxepin | 4 | 1 | 3 | 4 | 3 | 2 | 1 |
| Fluoxetine | +/− | 0 | +/− | +/− | 0 | 1 | 3 |
| Fluvoxamine | 0 | 1 | 0 | +/− | 0 | 1 | 4 |
| Imipramine | 2 | 1 | 3 | 3 | 2 | 2 | 2 |
| Maprotiline | 3 | 1 | 1 | 3 | 1 | 3 | 0 |
| Mirtazapine | 4 | 2 | 3 | 2 | 0 | 1 | 1 |
| Nefazodone | +/− | 0 | 1 | 2 | 0 | 1 | 2 |
| Nortriptyline | 2 | 1 | 2 | 3 | 2 | 3 | +/− |
| Paroxetine | 0 | 1 | 2 | +/− | 1 | +/− | 4 |
| Protriptyline | 2 | 1 | 4 | 2 | 0 | 4 | +/− |
| Sertraline | 0 | 3** | +/− | 1 | 0 | 1 | 4 |
| Trazodone | 1 | 1 | 0 | 4 | 4 | +/− | 1 |
| Trimipramine | 4 | 2 | 3 | 4 | 4 | +/− | 0 |
| Venlafaxine | 0 | +/− | 0 | 0 | 0 | 1 | 2/3 |

* 4 = most potent; +/− = weak affect; 0 = no effect.
** This primarily represents *pre*synaptic uptake blockade rather than *post*synaptic blockade.

99

Antidepressants are completely absorbed from the gastrointestinal tract and largely metabolized by first-pass metabolism.

- These highly lipophilic compounds are concentrated in the heart and brain.

Peak concentrations are reached at 2–8 h but may extend to 10–12 h. Trazodone peaks in ½–2 h.

## Pharmacology of Antidepressants

| Generic Names | Bio-Availability (%) | Plasma-Bound (%) | Half-Life (hours)* Mean | Half-Life (hours)* Range | Excretion** (%) |
|---|---|---|---|---|---|
| Amitriptyline | 48 ± 11 | 94.8–0.8 | 21 | 6–44 | 98 R |
| Amoxapine | — | 90 | 8 | 8–30 | 69 R 18 F |
| Bupropion | — | > 80 | 9.8 | 3.9–24 | 87 R 10 F |
| Citalopram | — | 80 | 35 | 4–48 | 85 R 10 F |
| Clomipramine | — | 97 | 32 | 19–77 | 51–60 R 24–32 F |
| Desipramine | 33–51 | 87 ± 3 | 22 | 12–36 | 70 R |
| Doxepin | 27 ± 10 | 90 | 17 | 8–68 | 98 R |
| Fluoxetine | — | 94 ± 1 | 60 | 48–216 | 60 R 30 F |
| Fluvoxamine | 53 | 80 | 15.6 | — | 90 + R |
| Imipramine | 50 | 93 ± 1.5 | 25 | 15–34 | 98 R 2 B/F |
| Maprotiline | — | 88 | 40 | 27–58 | 60 R 30 F |
| Mirtazapine | 50 | 85 | 31 | 20–40 | 75 R 15 F |
| Nefazodone | 20 | > 99† | 4 | 3–6 | 55R |
| Nortriptyline | 51 ± 5 | 92 ± 2 | 32 | 18–93 | 67 R 10 F |
| Paroxetine | 100 | 94 ± 1 | 26 | — | 64 R 36 F |
| Protripyline | — | 92 | 78 | 55–127 | 50 R ? F |
| Sertraline | — | 98 | 26 | 15–95 | 45 R 45 F |
| Trazodone | — | 93 ± 2 | 5 | 3–9 | 70–75 R 20–25 F |
| Trimipramine | — | 95 | 10 | 9–30 | 80 R 10 F |
| Venlafaxine | 92 | 30 ± 2 | 5 ± 1 | 4–24 | 87 R |

* Half-lives of parent compound; active metabolites have different half-lives and are reflected in range.
** B = bile; F = fecal; R = renal; ? = unavailable or inconsistent.
† Despite high % binding, it is loosely bound and has not yet been shown to displace other drugs to any clinically significant degree.

Children and adolescents:

- TCAs act differently in children and adolescents.
  - √ Children have less fat/muscle ratio
  - √ Decreased volume distribution

√ Faster metabolism resulting in shorter half-lives
√ Quicker absorption
√ Lower protein-binding
- Therefore, some children and adolescents are
  √ Likely to have higher, faster peak levels and sooner, lower trough levels.
  √ Not as protected from large doses as adults.
- Ineffectiveness and toxicity of TCAs may stem from the increased fluctuation of serum TCAs in children and adolescents; more frequent doses (e.g., bid rather than qd) provide more stable therapy.

## DOSES

### General Doses

| Generic Names | Equivalent Doses (mg) | Usual Therapeutic Doses (mg/day) | Extreme Doses* (mg/day) | Geriatric Doses** (mg/day) |
|---|---|---|---|---|
| Amitriptyline | 100 | 100–300 | 25–450 | 25–100 |
| Amoxapine | 100 | 200–400 | 50–600 | 100–150 |
| Bupropion | 150 | 225–450 | 100–450 | 75–150 |
| Citalopram | 20 | 20–40 | 10–80 | 10–20 |
| Clomipramine | 100 | 125–300 | 25–500 | 50–150 |
| Desipramine | 150 | 150–300 | 25–400 | 20–100 |
| Doxepin | 150 | 150–300 | 25–350 | 30–150 |
| Fluoxetine | 20 | 20–40 | 20–80 | 5–40 |
| Fluvoxamine | 100 | 100–300 | 50–400 | 50–200 |
| Imipramine | 150 | 150–300 | 25–450 | 30–100 |
| Maprotiline | 75 | 150–225 | 25–225 | 50–75 |
| Mirtazapine | 30 | 15–45 | 10–90 | 7.5–30 |
| Nefazodone | 150 | 300–600 | 100–600 | 200–600 |
| Nortriptyline | 50 | 75–150 | 20–200 | 10–75 |
| Paroxetine | 20 | 20–40 | 10–50 | 10–40 |
| Protripyline | 20 | 30–60 | 10–80 | 10–30 |
| Sertraline | 50 | 50–150 | 25–200 | 25–150 |
| Trazodone | 150 | 200–600 | 50–600 | 50–200 |
| Trimipramine | 100 | 150–300 | 25–350 | 25–150 |
| Venlafaxine | 100 | 75–225 | 25–350 | 25–225 |

* The low doses are used for children and sometimes geriatric.
** These doses apply to 50–70% of geriatric patients; 30–50% still require usual adult doses.

### Specific Antidepressant Doses

| Generic Names | Starting Dose (mg/day) | Days to Reach Steady-State Levels | Therapeutic Plasma Levels$^\Psi$ (ng/ml) | Active Metabolite | Reliability of Plasma Level |
|---|---|---|---|---|---|
| Amitriptyline | 25–75 | 4–10 | > 95–160* | Nortriptyline | Maybe |
| Amoxapine | 50–150 | 2–7 | 150–500* | 8-hydroxyamoxapine | No |
| Bupropion | 200–225 | 4–15 | 10–29** | — | Maybe |
| Citalopram | 20 | 4–10 | 10–80 | Desmethylcitalopram | Maybe |
| Clomipramine | 75–225 | 7–14 | 72–300* | Desmethylclomipramine | No |

## Specific Antidepressant Doses (*Cont.*)

| Generic Names | Starting Dose (mg/day) | Days to Reach Steady-State Levels | Therapeutic Plasma Levels$^\Psi$ (ng/ml) | Active Metabolite | Reliability of Plasma Level |
|---|---|---|---|---|---|
| Desipramine | 25–75 | 2–11 | > 115 | — | Maybe |
| Doxepin | 25–75 | 2–8 | 100–200 | Desmethyldoxepin | Maybe |
| Fluoxetine | 20 | 21–35 | 72–300* | Norfluoxetine | No |
| Fluvoxamine | 100 | 3–8 | — | — | Maybe |
| Imipramine | 25–75 | 2–5 | > 175–350* | Desipramine | Yes |
| Maprotiline | 25–75 | 6–10 | 200–300 | Desmethylmaprotiline | No |
| Mirtazapine | 15–30 | 3–9 | — | 8-hydroxymirtazapine N-desmethylmirtazapine N-oxidemirtazapine | Maybe |
| Nefazodone | 100 | 4 | — | Hydroxynefazodone | No |
| Nortriptyline† | 20–40 | 4–19 | 50–150 | — | Yes |
| Paroxetine | 20 | 5–10 | — | — | No |
| Protripyline | 10–20 | 10 | 100–240 | — | No |
| Sertraline | 50 | 4–21 | — | Desmethylsertaline*** | No |
| Trazodone | 50–100 | 7–14 | 650–1600 | Oxotriazolo-pyridin-propionic acid | Maybe |
| Trimipramine | 25–75 | 2–6 | 200–300 | — | No |
| Venlafaxine | 50–75 | 3 | 100–500 | O-desmethylvenlafaxine | No |

\* Parent compound plus active metabolite.
† Only TCA with a definite therapeutic window.
$^\Psi$ With drugs that have no plasma level reliability, these numbers represent population norms.
\*\* Therapeutic window possible.
\*\*\* Serotonin syndrome not seen with MAOI/desmethylsertaline together; significant clinical activity questionable.

# CLINICAL INDICATIONS AND USE

## General Information

Antidepressants typically require 10–30 days on a therapeutic dose to start working. Their full effect may take 6 weeks and, in many cases, improvement continues over several months.

Two major mistakes in prescribing TCAs are inadequate dose and inadequate time.

One major mistake in prescribing SSRIs is inadequate time.

Some symptoms on TCAs may improve before 10–14 days.

- Insomnia abates after 3–4 days, secondary to side effects.
- Appetite returns after 5–7 days, secondary to side effects.

Different symptoms on SSRIs improve before 10–14 days.

- Energy better in 4–7 days.
- Mood, concentration, and interest begin to improve in 7–10 days.

Symptoms of TCAs or SSRIs that improve before 9–16 days include:

- Diurnal mood variation (worse in A.M., better in P.M.) recedes around 8 days.
- Libido revives in 9–10 days.
- Anhedonia, hopelessness, and helplessness fade after 10–14 days.
- Dysthymia, excessive guilt, and suicidal thoughts dwindle by 12–16 days.

Antidepressants have efficacy for major depressions with or without major stressors.

- However, if the major stressor is continuing when antidepressant treatment first begins, then the antidepressant will be less effective.
- When the stressor resolves, the antidepressant returns to its usual level of efficacy.

For a "typical" depression, all antidepressants have equal efficacy if the patient can tolerate a full therapeutic dose.

- Bupropion SR 150 mg administered once daily had efficacy comparable to bupropion 75 mg administered twice daily. However, some patients need a higher dose and may need to take 100 mg bid or 150 mg bid using the SR version of bupropion.

Relative predictors of a *good* AD response are:

- Acute onset
- Anorexia
- Middle or late insomnia
- Psychomotor retardation
- Emotional withdrawal
- Anhedonia
- Past success with ADs
- Guilt

Relative predictors of a *poor* TCA response are:

- "Atypical" symptoms (hypersomnia, hyperphagia, rejection sensitivity, profound anergy)
  - √ Just one of these symptoms lowers response to TCAs to under 50%.
- Hypochondriasis (under 50% response).
- Childhood depression
  - √ No proven effectiveness over placebo.
  - √ Fluoxetine and sertraline superior to placebo.
  - √ Other SSRIs probably also effective.

- Anxiety, agitation, panic attacks with depression.

MAOIs, SSRIs, and atypical ADs do not lose effectiveness with atypical symptoms and/or hypochondriasis.

- Lowest drop-out rates are bupropion 9% and venlafaxine 11%.
- Medium drop-out rates (~15%) occur with fluoxetine, sertraline, mirtazapine, and nefazodone.
- Higher drop-out rates (20–32%) seen with TCAs and paroxetine (21%).
- Usually starting dose for SSRI is the therapeutic dose.
- Very low lethality in OD.
- Strongly consider SSRI as first treatment.

### Severe Inpatient, Melancholic, or Geriatric Depression

- TCAs, venlafaxine, nefazodone, and mirtazapine may be more effective than SSRIs for geriatric melancholic depression and, perhaps, for nongeriatric melancholic depression.
- In 3 studies, TCAs performed better than fluoxetine.
- In 1 study, paroxetine not as good as amitriptyline at 4 weeks of treatment, but equal at 6 weeks.
- In other studies in patients with Hamilton's depression scores over 25, SSRIs and TCAs had same outcome.
  - √ Patients had been maintained on full dose nortriptyline (N = 19) for 2 years.
    - ▫ 58% of new episodes occurred within 6 months,
    - ▫ 92% within one year.
- Published data comparing SSRIs with TCAs' very severe Hamilton scores ≥ 30 suggest equivalent efficacy.
- Venlafaxine's and mirtazapine's effects on serotonin and norepinephrine are very complex.
  - √ Venlafaxine and mirtazapine probably have TCAs' advantage in severely depressed populations, with much lower frequency of significant side effects.
    - ▫ One study suggests superiority over SSRIs.
  - √ For patients requiring > 300 mg/day of venlafaxine, there is a significant risk of elevated supine diastolic blood pressure during acute-phase therapy.
    - ▫ Need to evaluate diastolic blood pressure until it routinely stabilizes or discontinue medication.
- Folate levels and melancholic depression
  - √ Melancholic depression but not any other subtype was associated with lower folate levels ($p = .01$).
  - √ Consider getting folate levels in depressed (especially melancholic) patients who do not respond to antidepressant treatment.

√ Full response of normal folate level ($> 2.5$ ng/ml) was 65%, of low (1.5–2.5 ng/ml) 50%, and deficient ($< 15$ ng) 40%.
√ Vitamin $B_{12}$ and homocysteine did not correlate with folate.

### Mild to Mild-Moderate Depression (Hamilton $\leq 15$)

- Placebo and antidepressants have same outcome.
  √ High placebo response rate makes it difficult to establish superiority of active drug.
- Psychotherapy has same outcome as antidepressants.
- Several studies suggest that nonsuppressors on the dexamethasone suppression test respond poorly to psychotherapy alone.

A trial of antidepressants not recommended initially in mild depression if patient will accept a psychotherapeutic approach.

### Bipolar Depression: Mania Induction Risk

In known bipolar patients

- TCAs induce mania or hypomania in about 15% of patients.
- Paroxetine and sertraline (and probably other SSRIs) induce mania less often (2–3%) than TCAs.
- Bupropion SR might have a lower risk of incuding mania.

### Childhood Depression

- TCAs not better than placebo.
- SSRI safest and most effective option.
- Get baseline 12-lead EKG when using TCAs.
  √ In $< 10$ y.o. incomplete right intraventricular conduction defect is normal, and if without other cardiac disease, benign.
  √ Sinus tachycardia ($> 100$ 6 pm) is common in younger children.
  √ Escalate q 4 d by 1 mg/kg/day to a maximum of 5 mg/kg/day.
- At target dose, get repeat EKG at maximum plasma level, preferably 2–4 h after ingestion of medicine.
  √ PR interval should be $< 0.2$ sec.
  √ QRS duration $< 0.12$ sec.
  √ Qtc $\leq 0.45$ sec.
  √ Avoid $> 250$ ng/ml imipramine plus desipramine level.
    ▫ Risks delayed cardiac conduction and increased HR and BP.
    ▫ HR $> 130$ should be evaluated further.
  √ Increase dose further, if needed,
    ▫ Using plasma level and not mg/kg as guide.
    ▫ Up to 5 mg/kg may be possible.
- Because of anticholinergic effects of TCAs, there is increased risk of dental cavities.

√ Children on long-term TCA need increased frequency of dental evaluation.
- Sudden death in 5–14 y.o. may be 8 per million on desipramine compared to baseline rate of 4 per million.
  √ Desipramine may have higher lethality risk in overdose.
- Start SSRI st 10 mg fluoxetine equivalent and gradually increase dose to 50% adult doses. If no response and no side effects, increase to usual adult doses.
- Use bupropion for depression with ADD.

**Delusional Depression**

Antidepressants benefit about 65–80% of patients with nondelusional unipolar depressions but

- About 25% of psychotically depressed patients improve with TCA alone.

Treat delusional-depressed patients with

- ECT—1st choice if patient is suicidal with a plan or extremely impaired.
  √ 80–85% effective
- TCAs with neuroleptics—1st choice if patient safe and can wait 4–6 weeks.
  √ Can have > 70% response if maintained on this combination.
  √ TCA can then be continued to prevent relapse.
- Neuroleptic alone—2nd choice; 40–50% response.
- Antidepressant alone–3rd choice.

Combining antidepressants and antipsychotics

- Amoxapine, a dopaminergic blocker, may diminish the need for a neuroleptic, but locks in a neuroleptic effect during maintenance phase.
- Amitriptyline with perphenazine found superior to amoxapine, but latter had fewer EPS.
- Avoid low-potency neuroleptics (e.g., chlorpromazine) because they aggravate the high anticholinergic action of TCAs.
- SSRI plus neuroleptic also effective.

**Postpartum Depression**

- Affects 10% of new mothers of newborns.
- Can respond to antidepressants.
- If patient has had prior postpartum depression or mania, added estrogen reduces risk of postpartum depression.
  √ At delivery, start mother on high dose estrogen about 3 mg qd for 1 week, then taper by about 50% of original dose 2nd week, and 25% of original dose 3rd week.

- Predictors of treatment response in postpartum onset major depression:
  - √ Of the 53 women being evaluated, 34 (64%) demonstrated a therapeutic response within 4 weeks, 13 (24.5%) responded within 4–8 weeks, and 6 (11%) after 8 weeks.
  - √ With early onset of illness, response occurs in 64% of early responders, 46% of middle responders, and only 17% of late responders.
- Venlafaxine (75 to 225 mg)
  - √ 12 (80%) of the 15 women remitted after only 4 weeks of treatment.
    - ▫ Improvement began as early as 2 weeks into treatment.
    - ▫ A rapid and substantial response to antidepressant treatment when intervention is early in the course of an episode, even in women with severe postpartum depression.
  - √ Venlafaxine has anxiolytic properties that enable it to treat both depression and anxiety at the same time.

### Late-Life Depression

- AD efficacy is 70%.
- SSRIs, bupropion, venlafaxine, mirtazapine, nefazodone, or secondary amine TCAs (e.g., nortriptyline, desipramine) best tolerated by the elderly.
- Initiate about one half (or less) the starting dose in adults, but for people weighing < 70 kg, 10 mg/day of nortriptyline might suffice.
  - √ Adjust dose of nortriptyline or desipramine by trough serum level.
- If TCA used, get baseline EKG.
- Increase dose slowly until
  - √ Clinical response noted,
  - √ Sufficient plasma levels attained, or
  - √ Intolerable side effects arise.
- Tertiary amines tend to show twice the plasma levels of younger patients on the same dose.
- Venlafaxine dosing about 25% less in geriatric than in younger patients.
- Nefazodone initiate at 50 mg in geriatrics, but go to same final dose (300–600 mg) as in younger patients.
- In many studies there is a subgroup of depressed men (particularly older men) who have reduced testosterone levels while depressed.
  - √ In hypogonadal men, exogenous androgen treatment consistently elevates mood, libido, appetite, and energy and may be an effective antidepressant.

√ HIV positive, hypogonadal, or SSRI-refractory patients may benefit with added testosterone.
- Nortriptyline or sertraline 208 patients, age ≥ 60 years.
- Clinical response (≥ 50% reduction in HDRS) occurred in 60–70% of patients.
  - √ Patients age ≥ 70 years receiving nortriptyline showed improvement for the first 6 weeks but not thereafter.
  - √ Improvement continued until week 12 in patients age < 70 receiving nortriptyline and all ages receiving sertraline.
  - √ Patients treated with sertraline had better cognitive status, vigor, and overall physical and psychological health.

### Dexamethasone Suppression Test

The dexamethasone suppression test (DST) might have limited usefulness in determining treatment plans.

- When a healthy person receives dexamethasone, blood cortisol is usually suppressed for over 24 h.
  - √ However, about 40% of depressed patients do not suppress cortisol the day after dexamethasone administration.
- A nonsuppressed DST predicts
  - √ Failure in psychotherapy.
  - √ High risk of relapse if ADs are withdrawn.
- An abnormal response does not adequately help
  - √ Make a diagnosis of depression.
  - √ Predict response to antidepressants.
- DST protocol
  - √ On day 1, give 1 mg dexamethasone po at 11 P.M.
  - √ On day 2, draw venous blood for a cortisol assay at 4 P.M.
  - √ DST is positive if either value is equal to, or above, 5 $\mu$ g/dl.
    - ▫ The greater the value, the greater the certainty of an abnormal response.

## Comparison of Antidepressants

There are significant differences between the classes of antidepressants. Venlafaxine's therapeutic profile (effects on NE + 5HT at doses > 150 mg) resembles that of TCAs, particularly clomipramine, but low side-effect profile resembles SSRIs. The atypicals and SSRIs are better tolerated and less toxic.

### Side Effects and Compliance

Drop-outs due to side effects, based on premarketing clinical research studies:

## Drop-Out Rate (4–6 Weeks)

| | |
|---|---|
| High sedation TCAs | > 30% |
| Low sedation TCAs and trazodone | > 25% |
| Paroxetine | 21% |
| Nefazodone | 16% |
| Mirtazapine | 16% |
| Citalopram | 15% |
| Fluoxetine | 15% |
| Sertraline | 15% |
| Venlafaxine | 11% |
| Bupropion | 9% |

Drop-outs due to side effects during the maintenance stage of treatment are also higher with TCAs.

### Expense

Generic HCAs cost less. There are no generic forms for SSRIs (with the exception of fluoxetine), bupropion, venlafaxine, mirtazapine, or nefazodone, but many for HCAs.

- Cutting SSRI costs
    - √ Generic fluoxetine is now available.
        - □ Generic prices are only slightly lower than brand name.
        - □ Fluoxetine brands released for PMDD (Serafem) and weekly dosing cost about as much as Prozac.
    - √ Sertraline 100 mg costs nearly the same as 50 mg.
        - □ Prescribing sertraline at 100 mg and dividing the scored tablet in half can make it nearly as affordable as many TCAs.
    - √ Paroxetine has a free medication program for low-income patients.

### Suicide Risk

- HCAs have a very high risk of death with overdose.
    - √ Often a 1-week supply is lethal.
- SSRIs and all atypical antidepressants have a very low lethality risk.
    - √ Usually a 2–3 month supply is not lethal, but
        - □ If a 4–6 month supply is available, successful suicides can occur.
    - √ Fewer than 50 deaths strictly from an SSRI have been reported in U.S.

## Selecting an Antidepressant

If a particular antidepressant previously aided the patient or a close blood relative (without significant side effects), use it first with the patient. SSRIs, bupropion, and venlafaxine are recommended as first choices in most depressions, except severe inpatient or melancholic depression and mild outpatient depressions. At doses of 450 mg/day or less, bupropion SR now has only a 0.4% rate of seizure, which is similar to other ADs.

- SSRIs and bupropion have low lethality and side effects and higher compliance and chance of getting a therapeutic level.
- The total cost of the drug is usually significantly less than the total costs of inadequately treated depression or treatments with multiple side effects.

A panel of international experts on the pharmacologic treatment of depression, convened at the NIMH, unanimously made the above recommendations. Now with more experience with venlafaxine, mirtazapine, and nefazodone, these too appear to be safe.

Side effects as clinical considerations:

- SSRIs are far more alike than different.
- SSRI differences include:
  - √ Fluoxetine has slightly higher agitation (in mild form) and slightly lower somnolence rate.
  - √ Paroxetine has slightly higher somnolence (23%) in mild form, antianxiety and constipation (13%), and slightly lower diarrhea (11%) rate.
    - ▫ Paroxetine is only SSRI with significant anticholinergic effects.
  - √ Fluvoxamine has higher rate for nausea (40%) and insomnia (21%).
  - √ Sertraline tends to be "neutral" or average, having no side effect particularly more or less than average SSRIs.
  - √ Fluoxetine has a much longer half-life (> 3 days) than other SSRIs (25 h) and its active metabolite, norfluoxetine, has an even longer half-life of > 9 days.
  - √ Citalopram is less activating and has no active metabolites.

Antidepressants can be chosen for a potentially positive side effect, e.g., activation or sedation, to treat a particular symptom. This choice should be made with caution.

- Make this choice only if side effect would still be an advantage 4 weeks later.
- If the symptom to be treated is a symptom of depression, then any successful antidepressant trial will improve it.
- May be better to add specific temporary treatment for a symptom.
  - √ Hypnotic for sleep.
  - √ Antianxiety agent for anxiety and agitation.
- Patients should be warned to *avoid taking St. John's wort* with other psychoactive agents. Discontinue the herbal remedy several weeks before starting an SSRI.

- Using an adjunctive agent for sleep and anxiety is especially preferred over using sedating TCAs that have many other significant side effects (orthostatic BP, anticholinergic).

Comorbid conditions or depression subtypes may help determine best choice. (*See* depression subtypes, pages 104–8).

Choosing TCAs

Desipramine and nortriptyline are lowest in side effects on average and are first choices if TCA is selected.

- Anticholinergic: desipramine < nortriptyline.
- Orthostatic hypertension: nortriptyline < desipramine.
- Sedation: desipramine < nortriptyline.
- Weight gain: desipramine > nortriptyline.

Choosing non-TCAs

*Note: Only characteristics that differentiate these drugs are listed.*

SSRIs produce discontinuation symptoms, including dizziness, lightheadedness, insomnia, fatigue, anxiety/agitation, nausea, headache, and sensory disturbance. Symptoms may last up to 3 weeks and may be improved by restarting antidepressant or starting an antidepressant with a similar profile, e.g., another SSRI.

If patient on SSRI with antidepressant effectiveness but with sexual dysfunction, adding bupropion SR or nefazodone often significantly improves sexual desire and frequency.

*Bupropion*

- Pros
  - √ Low overall side effects make it lowest in drop-outs (9%).
  - √ Dopamine reuptake inhibition produces early activation in lethargic patients.
  - √ Has no anticholinergic, antihistaminic, antiserotonergic, cardiovascular, or sedating side effects.
  - √ Low mania induction.
  - √ Short half-life avoids build-up in geriatric and medically compromised patients.
  - √ Low sexual side effects
    - □ Case reports suggest sexual increase in some.
  - √ For smokers, begin bupropion SR (150–150 mg bid) for 10–30 days, or nortriptyline for 5 weeks, and then attempt to stop smoking.
- Cons
  - √ Seizure risk significantly higher in "at risk" individuals.
    - □ Bulimics, head injury, seizure history (4% at higher doses).

✓ In low-risk patients, risk is about the same as other antidepressants as long as daily doses are 300 mg SR or less.
  ▫ To avoid peak plasma levels, divided dosing preferred; however, once-a-day medication is often sufficient with bupropion SR.
  ▫ Need to build up dose gradually over 5–10 days.
✓ May have therapeutic window, with high levels not therapeutic.
  ▫ Makes adequate dosing trickier since therapeutic level has
  not been demonstrated.

*Citalopram*

- Pros
  ✓ Half-life 35 h
    ▫ Not likely to accumulate excessively at initial dose.
  ✓ Sedation and drowsiness about 18%.
    ▫ May help insomnia and anxiety.
  ✓ 650 adult outpatients with moderate to severe major depres-
  sion were treated with citalopram or placebo.
    ▫ Patients randomly assigned to 40 mg/day or 60 mg/day
    showed significantly greater improvement on all efficacy
    measures.
    ▫ Outcomes were not as robust with citalopram at doses of
    10 mg, 20 mg, or placebo.
  ✓ Has modest or no effect on P450 enzymes.
  ✓ Anxiety and nervousness only occur in about 4%.
- Cons
  ✓ Significant weight gain in about 10%.
  ✓ Nausea and vomiting in 21%.
  ✓ Insomnia occurs in about 15%.
    ▫ May interfere with functioning.
  ✓ Both constipation at 7% frequency and diarrhea at 8%.
  ✓ At least 35% incidence of sexual side effects (similar to other
  SSRIs).

*Fluoxetine*

- Pros
  ✓ Long half-life
    ▫ Missed doses less of a problem.
    ▫ Children can take once a day.
  ✓ Slow-release capsules
    ▫ Patients treated with fluoxetine, 10–60 mg/day for 2–14
    weeks, then switched to once-weekly administration using
    slow-release capsules and, for most, 90 mg weekly.
    ▫ Increase of dose if symptoms occurred between weekly sup-
    plements.

□ 6 patients were maintained on their initial weekly fluoxetine dose, and 4 required a dosage increase.

□ 8 patients had a CGI score of 1, and 2 patients had a CGI score of 2.

√ Activating

□ Patient experiences more energy quickly.

√ Decreased appetite in a minority of patients.

□ May help hyperphagic or overweight patients.

□ May be a problem in 25% of low-weight geriatric patients.

√ Somnolence and lethargy very uncommon.

- Cons

√ Long half-life

□ High levels could accumulate in geriatric and liver-impaired patients.

√ Agitation

□ May cause immediate worsening of depression.

√ Decreased appetite

□ May be a problem in 25% of low-weight geriatric patients.

√ Potent inhibitor of CYP450 II D6 enzyme

□ Regularly increases levels of TCAs, and other drugs metabolized by this pathway, by 200+%.

*Mirtazapine*

- Pros

√ Mirtazapine affects the serotonin and norepinephrine systems in the brain.

□ Beginning on day 21, mirtazapine ranged from 3.7 to 4.2 points more improvement than fluoxetine on HRSD.

√ Low mania induction.

√ Low to no sexual side effects.

√ 19 fluoxetine-treated patients in remission from major depression, with treatment-emergent sexual dysfunction, were switched to mirtazapine.

□ All patients (N = 19) maintained their antidepressant response and 11, mostly men, returned to normal sexual functioning while on mirtazapine.

- Cons

√ Somnolence common at 54%

□ May interfere with functioning.

□ Somnolence worse at 15 mg/day and low at 45 mg (~ 5%).

√ Anticholinergic effects more frequent

□ Dry mouth (25%) and constipation (13%) more frequent.

√ Increased appetite (17%) and weight gain (12%) also seen.

*Nefazodone*

- Pros
    - √ Little anxiety, nervousness, or insomnia side effects
    - √ Few sexual side effects
    - √ Low mania induction
    - √ Less likely than other ADs to disrupt sleep architecture.
    - √ Low risk of excessive build-up in geriatrics or medically com-promised.
        - □ Relatively short half-life
        - □ Okay in renal and liver diseases
- Cons
    - √ Usual dose is bid, but several reports indicate that some pa-tients respond well to once-a-day dosing (half-life about 20 h).
    - √ Significant somnolence, dry mouth, nausea, and dizziness
        - □ ~10–12% more than placebo
    - √ Bradycardia risk ~1.5% more than placebo
    - √ Potent CYP3A inhibitor
        - □ Increases triazolobenzodiazepine levels (alprazolam, triazo-lam, estazolam).
        - □ Increases certain $H_2$ blockers (terfenadine, asternizole).
        - □ Increases levels of carbamazepine, calcium channel-blockers, and triazolobenzodiazepine.

*Paroxetine*

- Pros
    - √ Somnolence more common
        - □ May reduce insomnia and anxiety.
    - √ Half-life 26 h
        - □ Is a potent and specific SSRI that causes down-regulation of $5\text{-}HT_2$ receptors but not $\beta$-receptors.
        - □ Not likely to accumulate excessively at initial dose.
        - □ No active metabolite.
    - √ Diarrhea less common
    - √ Low mania induction in bipolars (~2.2%).
- Cons
    - √ Somnolence more common
        - □ May interfere with functioning.
    - √ Anticholinergic effects more common
        - □ Constipation definitely more common
        - □ Other anticholinergic effects (e.g., decreased memory could be risk in geriatric patients).
    - √ Significantly inhibits CYP2D6 enzyme.

□ More potent 2D6 inhibitor than fluoxetine.
□ Withdrawal syndromes more severe than other SSRIs.

*Sertraline*

- Pros
  - √ Generally low in side effects
  - √ Low in nervousness
  - √ Lowest in anorexia
  - √ Half-life 26 h
    - □ Not likely to accumulate excessively.
    - □ Main metabolite, N desmethylsertraline, has 62–104-h half-life, significantly less active.
  - √ Weaker inhibitor of II D6 enzyme system.
    - □ At 50 mg dose, expect < 30% increase of TCA level.
  - √ Low mania induction in bipolars (< 3%).
- Cons
  - √ Maximum absorption requires full stomach.
    - □ 25% higher levels this way.
  - √ Slightly higher dry mouth than other SSRIs.
  - √ Can cause somnolence.
  - √ Nausea, diarrhea, somnolence, and/or sweating relatively frequent.

*Venlafaxine*

- Pros
  - √ Affects NE and 5HT systems in similar way as TCAs but with fewer side effects. 5HT reuptake inhibition significant only at doses > 150 mg.
  - √ Has minimal drug interaction risk.
    - □ 30% protein-bound
    - □ Minimal effect on P450 enzyme.
  - √ Short half-life and 87% renal excretion avoids build-up in geriatric patients.
  - √ Effective in severe geriatric and inpatient melancholic depression.
    - □ First choice for this indication
  - √ Geriatric dosing is similar to nongeriatric.
  - √ Low sexual side effects under 300 mg dosing
  - √ Extended release form (Effexor XR) well tolerated and can be given once a day at doses < 200 mg.
- Cons
  - √ Increased diastolic (10–15 mHg ↑) blood pressure risk
    - □ Ranges from 3% (75 mg) to 13% (375 mg).
    - □ Tolerance does not usually develop.

√ Nausea risk 26% more than placebo
  ▫ Dose-related, and tolerance develops in most over 2–6 weeks.
√ Immediate-release form requires bid–tid dosing.
√ Final dose quite variable.
√ Somnolence, dry mouth, and dizziness can be problematic.

**Preexisting Conditions**

With depression *and* preexisting

- Panic disorder—avoid trazodone and bupropion because they are relatively ineffective for panic.
- Bipolar disorder—avoid TCAs, consider lower mania risk, such as paroxetine or bupropion.
- Obsessive-compulsive disorder—pick an SSRI or clomipramine.
- Physical disorders—*see* chronic pain disorder (pages 133–34) and other physical disorders (pages 136–37).
  √ If patient has longstanding symptom (e.g., constipation, diarrhea), choose antidepressant that does not risk worsening it.

## Dosage

- For imipramine, desipramine, or doxepin, therapeutic dose is about 3–3.5 mg/kg (e.g., 200–225 mg for a 70 kg person).
  √ Therapeutic trough levels are 50–140 ng/ml for nortriptyline, 125–200 ng/ml for desipramine, > 225 ng/ml for imipramine.
- With SSRIs, the first dose is usually a therapeutic dose.
  √ Paroxetine more often increased from 20 to 40 mg/day in many patients.
- Venlafaxine, mirtazapine, nefazodone, and bupropion typically require higher doses than starting ones.

When starting SSRIs, begin at 20 mg for fluoxetine and paroxetine, 50–100 mg for sertraline, and wait 3–6 weeks for response before increasing dose.

- Sertraline and paroxetine are not predictably activating or sedating. Patient may try test dose in middle of day to find out.
- Sertraline has better (25%) absorption on a full stomach.

When starting TCA (e.g., desipramine), begin at 25 mg on day 1 and increase around 25 mg/day to reach a therapeutic dose by days 6–10.

- Because of low side effects, nortriptyline and desipramine are recommended as first choice TCAs.
  √ However, desipramine is the most lethal of the antidepressants, requiring as little as a 2-week supply.

- Maprotiline, because of seizure risk at dose > 225 mg, and amoxapine, because of EPS and potential TD, are not generally recommended for routine use.
- Body size has some effect on target dose.
  - √ Doxepin, desipramine, and imipramine often need 3.0–3.5 mg/kg.
  - √ Amitriptyline needs 2.5–3.0 mg/kg (*see* table on page XX).
- If patient has no improvement after one week, escalate by 25 mg/day until reaching high side of usual therapeutic dose.
- If patient is not better by 6th week, obtain plasma level from a trusted laboratory.
- If plasma level suggests changing the dose, do so by 25–50 mg q 2–3 days.

## Prescribing Antidepressants

Prescribe antidepressants in the following ways:

- Except for nefazadone, bupropion, trazodone, and fluvoxamine, the new atypicals, dispense in a single easy-to-remember (usually bedtime) dose to minimize side effects experienced during the day.
- Fluoxetine, desipramine, and protriptyline are often activating and need A.M. dosing.
  - √ Fluoxetine had an initial response to 20 mg/day, but 85% of patients relapsed, and increasing dosage to 40 mg/day gave at least a temporary benefit.
  - √ Sertraline and paroxetine can be activating, but not typically.
- Bupropion SR can be given once a day or in divided doses.
  - √ Seizure risk with bupropion SR is only 0.1–0.2% at recommended doses.
  - √ When 2 doses per day, increase total daily dose no faster than 75–100 mg/3 days, and do not exceed 450 mg/day.
  - √ Usual goal is 150–300 mg/day.
- To reduce seizure risk with maprotiline, do not exceed 225 mg/day.
- Venlafaxine and nefazodone have a short half-life (~ 20 h) and sometimes require multiple dosing.
- Trazodone also has a short half-life and may perform better with multiple dosing.
  - √ If given in daytime, take on a full stomach to increase absorption and decrease peak side-effect level.

Explain most common side effects to patient.

- For tertiary TCAs (amitriptyline, doxepin, imipramine), sedation, dry mouth, urinary hesitancy, constipation, and lightheadedness on standing up are common.

- For secondary TCAs, all of the above can occur, but most patients do not get any one of these side effects.
  √ With desipramine and protriptyline, activation is more common than sedation and therefore an A.M. trial might be considered first.
- For SSRIs, nausea, diarrhea, overactivation, insomnia, dizziness, dry mouth, tremor, and drowsiness are most common.
  √ 5% drop-out on fluoxetine because of insomnia and/or overactivation/agitation.

## Treatment-Resistant Patients

Before changing treatment, assess:

- Is diagnosis accurate?
  √ Is there a hidden psychosis?
- Is dosing adequate?
- Is the patient on other drugs that could cause or exacerbate the depression?
  √ Common ones are
    □ $\beta$-blockers
    □ High-dose benzodiazepines (> 3 mg alprazolam)
    □ Corticosteroids
- Are there untreated illnesses (e.g., hypothyroidism, Cushing's, hypogonadal) causing or exacerbating depression?

### Plasma Levels

Most patients do *not* need AD *plasma levels.*

- Therapeutic plasma levels for many antidepressants are based on average blood levels sent to the labs (i.e., population norms) and not based on efficacy.

Plasma levels are useful for patients who

- Have not responded to adequate 4–6 week-trials of nortriptyline, desipramine, imipramine, or amitriptyline.
- Are at high risk from age or medical illness.
- Are prone to overdose.
- Display medication noncompliance.
- Require documentation of TCA plasma levels for future treatment.
  √ Example: Patients attain therapeutic plasma level on small TCA doses (e.g., imipramine 50 mg/day).
- Are expected to have raised or lowered TCA levels because of drug interactions (e.g., SSRI also being used).

Measured plasma levels may be of

- The parent drug only (e.g., desipramine), or
- The drug and its chief metabolites (e.g., imipramine → imipramine + desipramine).

There may be a 30-fold difference in TCA levels after a single fixed dose.

- Slow metabolizers (e.g., elderly) are at higher risk for toxicity.
- Fast metabolizers may have trouble reaching adequate levels.

The menstrual cycle may affect AD blood levels.

- Desipramine and trazodone case reports suggest
  - √ Plasma level 5 days before menses can be 50% lower than 7 days after cessation of menses.

Patients have 1 of 2 types of plasma-level response curves.

- Linear
  - √ A direct, straight-line (linear) relationship exists between plasma level and clinical response; a specific plasma level yields a favorable response.
  - √ An example is imipramine (with metabolite desipramine), which collectively must equal 200–250 ng/ml to be maximally effective.
  - √ If the patient's plasma level is low, raise the dose. If very high with significant side effects, lower the dose to avoid toxicity.
- Curvilinear
  - √ A curvilinear response appears as a ∩ curve.
  - √ This curve shows an unfavorable response on the 2 vertical axes, but a therapeutic action on the horizontal plane.
  - √ Nortriptyline may have a curvilinear response, also known as a "therapeutic window," which is 50–150 ng/ml.
    - □ Nonresponding nortriptyline patients with plasma levels of above 150 ng/ml often improve by *lowering* the dose into the therapeutic window. A few do better with raising the dose.
  - √ Bupropion may also have a therapeutic window.
    - □ Several studies suggest 300 mg dose is better than 400–450 mg.
  - √ Some patients on fluoxetine (total half-life over 3 weeks) may respond quickly in 5–14 days and then lose this effect at 3–4 weeks.
    - □ Case reports suggest that lowering dose might return response because 3-week level was too high.

To obtain plasma levels

- Wait until TCA has reached a steady-state level, which is usually 5–7 days
- Draw blood 10–14 h after last dose.
- Make sure tube is free of the contaminant tris-butoxyethyl.
  - √ Can use Venoject vacutainer or glass syringes.
  - √ Do not use rubber stoppers.
  - √ Promptly centrifuge.

**Increasing Dose**

If patient shows partial response, higher doses should be tried if tolerated.

If patient is partially responsive at 3 to 4 weeks

- Raising fluoxetine dose increases responsiveness at 6 weeks.
- Raising citalopram dose to 40 mg was significantly better than staying at 20 mg.

If patient has had aggressive dosing and adequate plasma levels and is definitely not responsive at 6 weeks

- Change to a different drug, or
- Add an augmenting agent.
  - √ For example, 17% of 700 elderly women had a metabolically significant vitamin $B_{12}$ deficiency and were at twice the risk of depression as those without this deficiency.
- The comparative outcomes of these 2 alternatives have not been researched.

**Changing Antidepressants**

- If patient could not get an adequate trial on one class of AD drug because of side effects, a trial of another drug in the same class may not have the same side effects and might work.
  - √ About 70% of patients who could not tolerate fluoxetine tolerated sertraline.
- If patient had an adequate trial but drug was ineffective
  - √ Moving to another drug in the same class (e.g., fluoxetine to paroxetine or fluoxetine to fluvoxamine) may be effective, or
  - √ Change to a drug in a different class with a different mechanism of action.
- The distinctly different classes of antidepressant treatments, based on similarity of neurotransmitters affected (trazodone does not easily fit in), include:
  - √ TCAs, venlafaxine, and mirtazapine: serotonin and norepinephrine

A
N
T
I
D
E
P
R
E
S
S
A
N
T
S

√ SSRIs: primarily serotonin
   ◻ Fluoxetine, sertraline, paroxetine, and citalopram are relatively pure serotonergic medications.
   ◻ Trazodone and nefazodone have mixed serotonergic effects (both inhibiting and increasing).
√ Bupropion: mechanism of action probably
   ◻ Dopamine, norepinephrine
√ MAOIs: norepinephrine, serotonin, dopamine, phenylalanine
√ ECT: most neurotransmitters

- AD treatments except ECT eventually down-regulate beta-adrenergic receptors.
- When switching from SSRI, if
  √ Typical depression, consider venlafaxine, mirtazapine, or TCA trial.
  √ Atypical depression, consider bupropion or MAOI.
  √ If severely impaired or suicidal, consider ECT.
- MAOIs often effective alone when other medications have failed.
  √ Do *not add* a TCA to ongoing MAOI! (*see* page 187).
  √ May start MAOI and TCA together, both in low doses initially; or
  √ Safer to add MAOI to amitriptyline, doxepin, or trimipramine.
  √ Avoid adding MAOI to imipramine, clomipramine, venlafaxine, bupropion, nefazodone, mirtazepine, or SSRIs.
  √ Before starting MAOI, must stop fluoxetine 5–6 weeks and sertraline and paroxetine for 2 weeks.

### Augmentations: Lithium, $T_3$, TCA/SSRI, Neuroleptics

If patient has no or minimal response at 3–4 weeks, lithium or $T_3$ augmentation may increase responsiveness by 6 weeks.

- Probably better than dose increase if
  √ Reasonable dose has been used with certain TCAs.
  √ Therapeutic plasma levels were achieved.

Some will need to stay on augmentation, while others can stop in one month without relapse.

- In one study, about 30% of lithium-augmented patients (300 mg tid) improved markedly; 25% improved partially.
  √ Most patients recovered in 19–24 days; 3.6%, in 2 days.
  √ Clinical response did not correlate with serum lithium levels (usual levels = 0.5–0.7 mEq/l).
  √ Melancholic patients reacted better than nonmelancholic patients.

- After remission of depression, 29 patients were randomly assigned to receive lithium or placebo with antidepressant.
  √ All relapses occurred in the 7 of 15 placebo-treated patients and none of the 14 patients in the lithium group had a relapse.
  √ Successful lithium augmentation probably should be continued for at least 6 months.
- Another approach is to *add* $T_3$ to the AD.
  √ Triiodothyronine ($T_3$) 25–50 $\mu$g/day lifts mood after 3–21 days in about 50–55% of patients in controlled and uncontrolled reports. 25 $\mu$g/day has had several negative trials.
    ▫ Benefits euthyroid patients. Not usually enough to suppress normal thyroid function or cause hypermetabolic state, but can suppress TSH.
  √ Thyroxine (150 $\mu$g), when started with AD in euthyroid patients, blocked antidepressant effect.
    ▫ Average outcome on this combination was worse than placebo.
  √ Patients with subclinical hypothyroidism or with hypothyroidism treated with $T_4$ may benefit from increasing $T_4$.
    ▫ Many patients already being treated with $T_4$ are determined to be "euthyroid" but are at the low end of the normal range.
    ▫ Correcting $T_4$ to the high end of the normal range may make depression less treatment-resistant.
    ▫ $T_3$ in these hypothyroid patients also reported to help (in the brain there are only $T_3$ receptors, and not $T_4$).
    ▫ May help females more than males.

TCA and SSRI can augment each other.

- If failed on either, cautiously add other.
  √ Response often < 1 week.
- Paroxetine and fluoxetine can increase TCA plasma levels several times; sertraline, less so (average 30%).
- If TCA failed, reduce dose to about 10–25% of final dose and add paroxetine or fluoxetine; reduce to 50% of previous dose when adding sertraline. Because the amount of plasma level change is unpredictable, best to check level after 3–5 days and/or carefully monitor side effects.
- If SSRI failed, add 10–25 mg of TCA and very slowly increase, if needed.

Neuroleptics

- Trifluoperazine 4–20 mg/day or perphenazine 16–32 mg/day can be added for delusional or severely agitated patients.

- Patients who are "softly" delusional (e.g., nihilistic or overvalued negative ideas) may respond to added neuroleptic.
  √ Use briefly to avoid tardive dyskinesia.

### Stimulants (*see also* page 434)

Stimulants are better than placebo in treatment-resistant depression, geriatric depression, and medically-induced depressions.

- Hidden comorbidity of stimulant responsive syndromes (e.g., sleep apnea, ADHD) might account for some of the response in these groups.
- Usual doses
  √ Methylphenidate 10–40 mg/day
  √ Dextroamphetamine 5–30 mg/day
  √ Pemoline 37.5–75 mg/day
- A predominantly dysphoric response to dextroamphetamine has been reported in
  √ Postmenopausal women, but not in men or premenopausal women.
  √ Patients with borderline personality disorder.
  √ Patients with atypical depression.

### Sleep Deprivation

- By itself, a single night of sleep deprivation has transient positive effects in 50% of patients.
- With antidepressant or lithium, positive effect is usually maintained.
- All-night, or just second half of night, deprivation equally effective, but any nap until next night can cancel effect.
  √ REM deprivation may be the mechanism.
  √ Second half of night deprivation preferred because it is less disruptive than total sleep deprivation.
  √ Patients with melancholia respond 75% of the time, but those with atypical symptoms or mood reactivity only 48%.
- If single night positive, can add booster nights every 3–6 days.
  √ Some evidence suggests that bipolar depressed patients respond more often than recurrent unipolars.
- Substances causing insomnia: alcohol, CNS stimulation, beta-blockers, bronchodilators, corticosteroids, caffeine, decongestants, dilantin, stimulating antidepressants, thyroid hormone, nicotine.

### Less Proven Approaches to Treatment-Resistant Depression

- Carbamazepine (300–1200 mg/day) may relieve unipolar depression.

√ Valproic acid not shown to be effective.
√ Both carbamazepine and valproic acid may augment antidepressant.
√ Buspirone
  ▫ 40–60 mg: > 60% response in case series.
  ▫ Buspirone reported to be effective alone in 45–90 mg/day dose range.
√ Dehydroepiandrosterone (DHEA) for midlife onset dysthymia
  ▫ 17 patients (13 men, 4 women)
  ▫ Men had to be 40 or older with midlife onset dysthymia.
  ▫ Women had to have amenorrhea or a ≥ 6-month menstrual irregularity.
  ▫ Treatment was DHEA 90 mg/day for 3 weeks and then 450 mg/day for 3 more weeks.
  ▫ 9 responded to DHEA and 3 responded to placebo.
  ▫ Significant decreases on the Hamilton depression scale and the Beck depression instrument.
  ▫ Improvement observed in 7 of 13 symptoms: low energy, anhedonia, lack of motivation, emotional flattening, sadness, excessive worry, and inability to cope.
  ▫ 60% response rate and onset of most responses by 3 weeks suggests that 90 mg/day DHEA is probably as effective as the higher dosage.
  ▫ Probably best used adjunctively for patients with an incomplete response to an established AD.
√ Dopamine agonists (bromocriptine, pergolide, amantadine)
√ Estrogen replacement therapy (ERT) in pre- and postmenopausal women and augmentation of sertraline (and other SSRIs)
  ▫ R/o breast and endometrial carcinoma.
  ▫ 34 sertraline-treated depressed women outpatients also received ERT vs. 93 sertraline-treated women who did not.
  ▫ 79% of women on ERT were "much improved" or "very much improved" vs. 58% of women not on estrogen.
  ▫ Gradually increase dose from 1.25 mg/day conjugated estrogen to 3.75–4.375 mg/day during the first 21 days of menstrual cycle.
  ▫ Then progesterone 5 mg/day for 5 days to permit menstruation and reduce endometrial cancer risk.
  ▫ Supplement with pyridoxine 25–50 mg bid and prenatal vitamins to prevent estrogen-induced reductions.
√ Folic acid 500 mg/day or placebo for 10 weeks (N = 69 women)
  ▫ All on fluoxetine 20 mg/day
  ▫ Those on folic acid had decreases of HDRS from 27 to 7

points and 27 to 12 points in the fluoxetine plus placebo group (p < .001).

□ 73% of women receiving folic acid and 47% of women in the placebo group responded.

□ Supplementation with folate did not affect male response rates.

√ 5,000–10,000 lux light from 6–7 A.M. daily for 2 weeks

□ 7 of 10 substantially improved.

□ With response to daily use of light, patients often did not have seasonal affective disorder (SAD) but may have winter worsening of depression.

√ Phenylalanine 500–2000 mg given in A.M. in single or divided dose.

□ Expect responder to have stimulant effect with risk of small BP rise and insomnia.

□ Research outcomes mixed; favors highly treatment-resistant women but not patients newly starting on ADs.

√ Pindolol 2.5 mg tid added to SSRI, MAOI

□ When started with AD, may speed time to response (< 1 week), but typically works better with family medicine patients than with psychiatric patients.

□ When added in treatment resistance, may facilitate response.

□ A significantly greater response rate scores (HDRS) at p = .00003 showed after 1 and 2 weeks of treatment with paroxetine 20 mg and pindolol 7.5 mg.

□ Paroxetine with metoprolol was not more effective than paroxetine alone.

□ Results of other studies of pindolol augmentation are contradictory.

√ Captopril (50–100 mg/day) alone or with other ADs

□ Can induce mania; need to carefully watch for hypomania or mania.

• Ineffective treatments for depression, when compared with placebo, include:

√ Tyrosine 900 mg/kg/day

√ Baclofen

√ Reserpine

## Electroconvulsive Therapy (ECT) and Medications

• Most effective treatment for depression

√ 75–85% efficacy

□ Does best with melancholic and psychotic depressions.

□ Atypical depressions respond less well.

√ Also effective in stopping mania with only 2–3 treatments.

ECT concerns

- Need adequate seizure length to be effective, but avoid status epilepticus.
  - √ 30–40 sec duration desirable.
  - √ Motor seizure >120 sec or EEG seizure >180 sec undesirable.
    - □ Treat with IV benzodiazepine.
- Minimize cardiovascular risk during ECT.
  - √ Death from ECT has not occurred in past 15 years.
  - √ Hypertension and tachycardia pose MI and stroke risk.
    - □ Post-seizure bradycardia, asystole, and arrhythmias pose further cardiac risk.
    - □ Do not administer ECT for six months post-MI.
- Minimize motor component of seizure.
- Minimize post-ECT confusion.

To get adequate seizure length, minimize use of the following drugs that decrease seizure activity.

- Anticonvulsants
- Benzodiazepines
- Barbiturate anesthesia
- Propofol
- Lidocaine and related antiarrhythmics (e.g., procainamide)
  - √ Also can enhance succinylcholine's neuromuscular blockade.
- Dextromethorphan
- High doses of propranolol and perhaps other beta-blockers

Drugs that increase seizure length and may enhance, but also overly prolong, a seizure include:

- Theophylline
- Caffeine
- Lithium
- Bupropion
- Clozapine
- Fluoxetine and perhaps other SSRIs
- HCAs (e.g., maprotiline, amoxapine)
- Neuroleptics, especially low-potency phenothiazines
- Possibly trazodone

Anesthesia agents affect seizure duration and extent of spread in the brain.

- Ketamine
  - √ Prolongs seizure.
  - √ Prolongs full recovery time ~1 h longer.

- Etomidate
  - √ May slightly prolong seizure.
  - √ Reports of adrenal shutdown with prolonged (hours to days) use.
- Methohexital
  - √ Somewhat shortens seizure duration, depending on dose.
    - □ 1.2 mg/kg definitely shortens seizure and increases number of seizures needed.
    - □ 0.67 mg/kg reasonable dose for most, except those with tolerance to hypnoanxiolytics (alcohol, benzodiazepines, barbiturates).
- Thiopental
  - √ Definitely shortens seizure length.

Choice of sleeping medication is more limited prior to ECT.

- Avoid agents that shorten seizures (e.g., benzodiazepines, barbiturates)
- Consider agents that have no, or positive, effects on seizures.
  - √ Trazodone
  - √ Chloral hydrate
  - √ Zolpidem
  - √ Sedative antihistamines

Drugs that minimize cardiac and aspiration risks include beta-blockers and anticholinergics.

### Beta-Blockers

- Short-acting beta-blockers decrease hypertension and tachycardia.
  - √ labetolol: 4-min serum half-life
  - √ esmolol: 9-min serum half-life
- Decrease heart rate more than blood pressure.
- Shorten seizures in doses
  - √ > 20 mg labetolol.
  - √ > 200 mg esmolol.
- No data to support routine use, but recommended with cardiac risk.
  - √ Has risk of bradycardia and hypotension.
    - □ May increase effects of post-stimulus vagal hyperactivity and cause profound bradycardia or asystole.
- If hypertension more significant risk than tachycardia, then
  - √ IV nitroglycerine more effective than beta-blocker.
- Avoid mixing potent hypotensive agents (e.g., nitroglycerine with beta-blocker).

**Anticholinergics**

- Brain stimulation results in vagal hyperactivity which can cause
  - √ Arrhythmias
  - √ Bradycardia
  - √ Asystole
  - √ Excessive saliva
- Without atropine, "vagal" arrhythmias, bradycardia or asystole, occurred in 30–70% of ECT treatments.
- Anticholinergic agents (i.e., atropine and glycopyrrolate) can reverse all of these effects.
  - √ Glycopyrrolate superior for excessive saliva.
  - √ Atropine superior for reducing cardiac vagal effects, but no significant effect on saliva.

High-risk groups in which atropine should be considered include:

- High seizure threshold
  - √ Vagal hyperactivity proportional to electrical stimulus
- Failed seizure
  - √ Absence of seizure's catecholamine flood increases vagal effects.
- Beta-blockers used
  - √ Will accentuate cardiac vagal effects.
- Cardiovascular risk in patient
  - √ Reserpine can lead to cardiovascular collapse or respiratory depression during ECT.

Excessive salivation/secretion not a serious problem, but when it is

- Glycopyrrolate recommended.

Atropine side effects include

- Tachycardia
- Relaxed lower esophageal sphincter
  - √ Increases risk of gastroesophageal reflux/aspiration.
- Confusion
  - √ Atropine but not glycopyrrolate crosses blood–brain barrier.

*Administering anticholinergics*

- IV route preferred.
  - √ More reliable and faster
  - √ Should always have IV established in case of emergency.
- Doses given 2–3 min before treatment.
  - √ Atropine 0.4–1.0 mg IV
  - √ Glycopyrrolate 0.2–0.4 mg IV

Minimizing motor component of seizure

- Musculoskeletal injury common prior to use of muscle paralytic agents.
- Succinylcholine, a depolarizing agent, generally preferred.
  √ 0.4–0.7 mg/kg dosage
  √ Doses of 1 mg/kg may be used to
    □ Avoid any muscle movement in patients with significant musculoskeletal problems.
    □ Possibly reduce postanesthesia agitation.
  √ Use low-end dose for high % adipose tissue and high-end for high % muscle mass.
  √ There is no medical need to routinely get spine films prior to ECT because succinylcholine prevents damage.
    □ However, some still get spine films for medico-legal reasons.
    □ Advisable if back has significant injury in which any abrupt movement is dangerous or if patient has h/o significant back pain and no films were obtained.
  √ To ablate motor component of seizure, give ECT 1–2 min after succinylcholine.
    □ Use absence of fasciculations as guide.
    □ Expect longer wait in geriatrics and those with compromised circulation.
  √ Inflating BP cuff or tourniquet on lower half of one leg or arm prior to succinylcholine administration allows observation of motor seizure.
    □ EEG more accurate and usually longer than motor seizure.
- Avoid succinylcholine if patient
  √ Has recent large mass of damaged muscle tissue (e.g., stroke, burns, muscle injury).
    □ Risks hyperkalemia.
    □ Use mivacurium, a short-acting non-depolarizing agent, instead.
  √ Is hypocalemic or hyperkalemic.
    □ Diuretics increase this risk factor.

## Augmenting ECT

- For short or failed seizures, use agents that lower seizure threshold.
  √ Caffeine IV 500–2000 mg
    □ Decreases seizure threshold but probably does not increase duration.
  √ Sustained-release theophylline 200 mg given night before ECT.
    □ Longer seizures and fewer ECTs needed.

      ▫ Less immediate confusion and fewer long-term memory deficits.
   ✓ Hyperventilation
      ▫ Patient is hyperventilated for 2–3 min before ECT.
      ▫ Modest decrease in seizure threshold and increase in duration.
      ▫ Still see "tolerance" to stimulus requiring increased energy for later treatments.

*Psychotropic agents*

- Neuroleptics may augment ECT for manic and schizophrenic psychosis.
   ✓ High-potency may be safer.
- TCAs, SSRIs, and MAOIs have questionable positive effects with possible increased complications.
   ✓ TCAs risk cardiac and other risks.
   ✓ MAOIs have unproven hypertension risks.
   ✓ To speed getting started with ECT, antidepressants probably don't need to be completely withdrawn and can be tapered during ECT.
- Lithium risks increased cognitive side effects.
   ✓ Confusion, disorientation, encephalopathy reported.

## Maintaining Therapy

Major depressive episodes usually persist for 6–12 months.

- If drug stopped earlier than 6 months, > 50% relapse rate.

After 1–3 months of treating acute depression, maintenance therapy can begin.

- Lowest relapse rate if acute dosage is maintained.
   ✓ If the patient is symptom-free, continue the same dose.
- If the patient has annoying side effects, slowly lower the dose.
   ✓ Beware of higher relapse rate.
   ✓ To lower side effects, benign substitutions could be desipramine for imipramine and nortriptyline for amitriptyline.

After the initial 6 months, if there have been at least 4 consecutive symptom-free months, may taper TCA dose no faster than 25 mg q 2–3 days. Both TCAs and SSRIs (except fluoxetine and sertraline) have withdrawal symptoms to be avoided. It is safest to taper antidepressants by about 25% q 3–4 weeks. This avoids most withdrawal symptoms and provides opportunity to catch a relapse early while it is still mild.

If symptoms flicker (with or without stress), maintain acute dose.

Can adjust above schedules as follows:

- If this is the patient's first depression and the family's first depression, slowly discontinue TCA or SSRI at 4–6 months after maximum improvement.
- If the patient has had repeated depressions, or the family has a h/o depression, do not lower TCAs, SSRIs, or atypical ADs until 9–12 months.
  - √ If frequency of depression is more often than once a year, patient may need to stay on antidepressant indefinitely.
    - ▫ Unless seasonal and then may need treatment only annually.
  - √ Interpersonal or cognitive-behavioral therapy is highly recommended in frequent relapse to optimize response and as potential prophylactic measure.
- Patients with full recovery are much less likely to relapse upon withdrawal than patients who have had only partial recovery.
- Patients who remain nonsuppressors on the dexamethasone suppression test are likely to relapse when antidepressants are withdrawn.
- Approximately 10–15% of patients with depression will have chronic depressions and will need to stay on antidepressants for years and perhaps for life.

## Physical and Other Conditions/Disorders

### Anorexia Nervosa

No single drug has been proven effective by itself or as an adjunct for treating anorexia nervosa. Nevertheless,

- Cyproheptadine, an antihistamine and serotonin $5HT_2$ antagonist, may help patients gain weight.
  - √ Dose 12–32 mg/day.
  - √ Free of TCAs' cardiovascular effects.
  - √ Do not use in anorectics with bulimic characteristics.
    - ▫ Can increase binge-purge cycle.
- Amitriptyline and doxepin may help anorectics gain weight, but the drugs have significant side-effect risks in this population (e.g., orthostatic BP and severe constipation).
- If severely obsessional, high-dose SSRI (e.g., fluoxetine 60 mg/day) might help with
  - √ Weight gain
  - √ Decreased eating and exercise rituals
  - √ Less distorted body image
- If patient is depressed, SSRI safer in this group.

**Bereavement**

- Mild to moderate uncomplicated bereavement responds well to social support.
- Severe acute (< 4 months) or moderate to severe chronic bereavement may benefit from ADs.
  √ TCAs and SSRIs reported to be effective in controlled trials.
    □ Usual AD doses.
  √ Vegetative symptoms most responsive.
    □ "Normal" fluctuation of intense depressed mood characteristic of grief is usually less responsive.

**Bulimia Nervosa**

Recommendations for treating bulimia include:

- Fluoxetine (60 mg/day superior to 20 mg/day) or other SSRI.
- Prior to treatment with fluoxetine, women with bulimia nervosa reported elevated cardiac vagal tone.
  √ Fluoxetine reduced cardiac vagal tone among bulimics (N = 25) to a level similar to the healthy volunteer women (N = 41).
  √ Vomiting decreased 56% at 60 mg, 29% at 20 mg, and 5% on placebo.
  √ Failure on one AD does not predict failure on another.
- Imipramine or desipramine 25 mg qhs.
  √ Escalate dose by 25 mg q 2 d up to 200 mg/day for normal-weight bulimics.
- ADs may jump-start treatment with faster initial results, but when used alone are no better than, and often worse than, psychotherapy at 6 months.
- If these trials do not work, consider
  √ Lithium, or
  √ MAOI (preferably phenelzine), or
  √ Opiate antagonist (e.g., naltrexone)
- Avoid amitriptyline and doxepin, since they may stimulate appetite.
- Bupropion SR has a seizure risk that is extremely low 0.1%.
  √ 0.1% is the same as placebo.
  √ Higher risk in vomiters with electrolyte abnormalities.
  √ Risk increases at doses > 450 mg/day.

Cyproheptadine does *not* help bulimics.

**Cardiac and Ischemic Conditions**

- SSRIs appear to ameliorate the adverse effects of depression on cardiovascular disease and inhibit platelet aggregation, which may have positive effects on the heart.

- Paroxetine vs. nortriptyline in ischemic disease
  - √ Both medications had similar efficacy, e.g., 60% of both paroxetine and nortriptyline groups achieved a 50% ischemic reduction in baseline Hamilton and final Hamilton $\geq 8$.
    - □ Paroxetine did not affect heart rate, blood pressure, cardiac conduction, or heart rate variability.
    - □ Nortriptyline had a significant increase in heart rate and orthostatic drop, and a significant decrease in R to L variability. Serious cardiovascular events occurred in the nortriptyline group compared with paroxetine.

### Chronic Fatigue Syndrome and Depression

- Chronic fatigue syndrome (CFS) treatment with venlafaxine ($N = 2$)
  - √ Patient A had NK-cell activity of 3.6%, did not respond to sertraline 100 mg/day, and her Beck Depression Inventory (BDI) increased to 19.
    - □ Sertraline and bupropion were stopped and venlafaxine started with goal dose of 75 mg tid.
    - □ After 6 weeks at 75 mg tid her BDI dropped to 12 and her NK-cell activity increased to 9.4%. Eleven months later, she continued to show improvement in overall functioning.
  - √ Patient B had a 7-month h/o CFS, with NK-cell activity 8.1%, and BDI 19.
    - □ After 3 months BDI decreased to 9, but
    - □ Paroxetine 30 mg/day at first was helpful but after 3 months caused incapacitation, fatigue.
    - □ Adding bupropion 200 mg/day and increasing paroxetine to 40 mg/day worsened depression.

### Chronic Pain Disorders

ADs may alleviate chronic but not acute pain.

- TCAs are effective by themselves and also augment narcotic efficacy.
  - √ No evidence that one TCA is more effective than another.
  - √ In patients with chronic pains, expect 50% or more improvement in pain 50% of the time.
  - √ Equal efficacy in depressed and nondepressed patients.
  - √ In patients with neuropathy and/or migraine, improvement rate often > 60%.
  - √ Presence of physical findings does not decrease response rate.
- If patients depressed, use the same TCA dose as in treating depression. If not depressed, can use lower (25–75 mg) TCA dose.
- Most studied TCAs are amitriptyline, desipramine, and doxepin.

- SSRIs not reliably effective for chronic pain.
  - √ Fluoxetine reduced migraine recurrence in 2 small studies.
    - □ Serotonergic action sometimes aggravates migraine.
- Trazodone marginally effective.
- Bupropion ineffective.
- Nefazodone effective in fibromyalgia.
- Venlafaxine reduced neuropathic pain in a laboratory model.

TCAs have also been shown to augment opiate analgesics by

- Slowing development of tolerance and
- Increasing analgesic effect.
  - √ Low doses usually effective.

### HIV

When treating depression and fatigue in HIV patients, consider

- Nefazodone, N = 15
  - √ 8 (73%) were classified as full responders.
  - √ 3 were classified as partial responders (only 50% reduction in HDRS scores).
  - √ Potential drug interactions, with protease inhibitors, indicate that it is essential to evaluate for appropriate dosing to avoid adverse effects.
- Dextroamphetamine, N = 22
  - √ 73% (8/11) randomly assigned to dextroamphetamine reported significant improvement in mood and energy.
  - √ Only 25% (3/12) among placebo patients had improved mood and energy.

### Premenstrual Dysphoric Disorder

Serotonergic antidepressants reduce behavioral and physical symptoms.

- Fluoxetine 20 mg/day—first choice — > 80% response.
  - √ Similar positive results with sertraline at 80 mg for ½ cycle were seen for premenstrual syndrome, particularly mood (∼ 66% response).
  - √ Studies report positive results when used for 5–10 days premenstrually or throughout the month.
- Other SSRI (paroxetine, sertraline) or clomipramine (more side effects)—2nd choice.
- Lithium may augment response and, used alone, has modest positive effects, particularly on mood.
- Women on ADs who are euthymic except premenstrually can have lower blood levels premenstrually.

√ Check pre- and postmenstrual levels and, if needed, increase antidepressant dose premenstrually.
- Premenstrual alprazolam effective in one study.

**Pseudobulbar Affect**

- Usually caused by subcortical brain damage.
- Patient bursts out crying or laughing without cause.
- Low-dose AD can effectively treat in a few days.

**"Pseudodementia"**

- A depression in the elderly that mimics dementia.
- Treat as regular depression. Choose ADs with very low anticholinergic activity.

**Seasonal Affective Disorder (Mood Disorder with Seasonal Pattern)**

- Treatments superior to placebo include:
  √ 2,500 lux light 0.5–2 h in early A.M. (5–8 A.M.).
    □ 60–75% response
  √ 10,000 lux light 0.5–2 h in early A.M. (5–8 A.M.).
    □ > 70% response
    □ 0.5 h usually enough.
    □ Always use non-UV light to avoid eye damage.
  √ Light treatment most effective in depression with hypersomnia or phase-delayed sleep (sleeping in later).
  √ 20–60 mg propranolol at 5:30–6 A.M. qd
    □ Shuts down nocturnal melatonin and resynchronizes body clock.
- Treatments with positive outcomes (> 60% response) but not yet proven superior to placebo include:
  √ Fluoxetine 20–40 mg/day
  √ Visor lights
  √ Melatonin 0.5–2 mg qhs
    □ Starts nocturnal melatonin cycle.
    □ Patients can be treated effectively by melatonin if it is taken 2 or 3 h before or after peak melatonin level (e.g., 11:00 P.M.).
  √ High placebo response rates seen in some, but not most, trials may be caused by temporary increases in sunny winter days.

**Other Adult Physical Disorders**

Major depression coexisting with the following physical disorders can be treated as follows:

## Treatment of Depression with Comorbid Conditions

| Disorder[1] | Preferred | Avoid |
|---|---|---|
| Allergies (MH) | Doxepin*<br>Mirtzapine<br>Trimipramine* | |
| Cardiac conduction problem (WH)[2] | Bupropion<br>Citalopram<br>Fluoxetine<br>Fluvoxamine<br>Paroxetine<br>Sertraline | TCAs[2] |
| Cataplexy (MH) | Desipramine*<br>Fluoxetine<br>Imipramine<br>Protriptyline*<br>Tranylcypromine* | |
| Congestive heart failure (WH) | Bupropion<br>SSRIs | Trazodone<br>Nefazodone[3]<br>TCAs or venlafaxine? |
| Constipation (chronic) (MH) | Fluoxetine<br>Fluvoxamine<br>Sertraline<br>Trazodone<br>Venlafaxine | Amitriptyline<br>Doxepin<br>Protriptyline<br>Trimipramine |
| Dementia, delirium, cognitive disorder (MH) | Bupropion<br>Fluoxetine<br>Fluvoxamine<br>Nefazodone<br>Paroxetine<br>Sertraline<br>Trazodone<br>Venlafaxine | Amitriptyline<br>Clomipramine<br>Doxepin<br>Imipramine<br>Protriptyline<br>Trimipramine |
| Diabetes, type II | Fluoxetine | Amitriptyline<br>Doxepin |
| Diarrhea (chronic) (MH) | Amitriptyline<br>Doxepin<br>Protriptyline<br>Trimipramine | Bupropion<br>SSRIs (except paroxetine)<br>Venlafaxine |
| Epilepsy (WH) | Desipramine<br>Doxepin<br>Phenelzine<br>SSRIs | Amoxapine<br>Bupropion<br>Maprotiline<br>Trimipramine |
| Impotence (partial) (organic) (WH) | Bupropion (MH)<br>Serzone (MH)<br>Trazodone | Fluoxetine<br>Fluvoxamine<br>Paroxetine<br>Sertraline<br>Phenelzine |
| Irritable bowel syndrome (MH) | Amitriptyline<br>Desipramine<br>Doxepin<br>Nortriptyline<br>Phenelzine<br>Trazodone | |
| Migraine headache (MH) | Amitriptyline*<br>Doxepin*<br>Fluoxetine<br>Imipramine*<br>Mirtzapine<br>Paroxetine | |

A
N
T
I
D
E
P
R
E
S
S
A
N
T
S

| Disorder[1] | Preferred | Avoid |
|---|---|---|
| | Phenelzine* | |
| | Sertraline | |
| | Tranylcypromine | |
| | Trimipramine | |
| Narrow-angle glaucoma (WH) | Bupropion | Amitriptyline |
| | Fluoxetine | Clomipramine |
| | Fluvoxamine | Doxepin |
| | Nefazodone | Imipramine |
| | Sertraline | Paroxetine |
| | Trazodone | Trimipramine |
| | Venlafaxine | |
| Neurogenic bladder (WH) | Bupropion | |
| | Fluoxetine | |
| | Sertraline | |
| | Venlafaxine | |
| Parkinson's disease (MH) | Amitriptyline | Amoxapine |
| | Bupropion | SSRIs? |
| | Doxepin | |
| | Imipramine | |
| | Protriptyline | |
| | Selegiline | |
| | Trimipramine | |
| Peptic ulcers (MH) | Doxepin* | |
| | Trimipramine* | |
| Sleep apnea (MH) | Protriptyline* | |
| | Tranylcypromine* | |
| Tardive dyskinesia (WH) | Desipramine | Amoxapine |
| | Imipramine | |
| | Nefazodone | |
| | Trazodone | |
| | Trimipramine | |
| | Venlafaxine | |

[1] MH = might help; WH = won't hurt.
[2] Although TCAs have quinidine-like Type 1-A antiarrhythmic effects, new studies suggest that Type 1-A has increased mortality in MI patients.
[3] Beware of rare bradycardias.
* Efficacy established.

## Childhood Stage-4 Sleep Disorders

In children, common difficulties in stage-4 sleep include:

- Enuresis
- Night terrors
- Sleepwalking

For childhood enuresis, the following TCAs seem equally effective:

- Imipramine
- Desipramine
- Amitriptyline
- Nortriptyline

Often require smaller doses than in treating depression in childhood. For instance,

- Start imipramine at 10–25 mg hs.
  √ If without response, increase each week by increments of 10–25 mg.
  √ Until reaching 50–75 mg/day.
- If necessary, maximum dose is 2.5 mg/kg/day.

Eighty percent of children reduce bedwetting in less than one week with TCAs.

- Yet total remission is < 50%.

Wetting often returns when drug is stopped.

TCAs are especially useful for short-term treatment, as during summer camp.

TCAs might assist children with:

- Sleepwalking
- Severe night terrors
  √ Adults with night terrors might also be helped by diazepam 5–20 mg or other shorter-acting benzodiazepines.

## SIDE EFFECTS

### Anticholinergic Effects

Clinicians should select an AD considering its anticholinergic side effects (*see* page 99 for comparison of ADs).

TCAs are generally more anticholinergic than neuroleptics.

- Enormous anticholinergic differences among ADs themselves, such as amitriptyline being >18,000 times more anticholinergic than trazodone.

Anticholinergic actions occur frequently, especially in the elderly.

Most anticholinergic symptoms taper off in 1–2 weeks.

Anticholinergic actions arise in many systems and include symptoms of

- Confusion
- Memory poor
- Hypotension
- Mouth dry
- Constipation
- Paralytic ileus
- Urinary hesitancy or retention
- Vision blurred

- Eyes dry
- Narrow-angle glaucoma
- Photophobia
- Nasal congestion

These anticholinergic effects are discussed with their respective organ systems.

## Cardiovascular/Hematologic Effects

### Bleeding

Abnormal bleeding in 5 patients, aged 8–15 years, within 1 week to 3 months after starting on 25–100 mg/day sertraline.

- 4 patients experienced frequent episodes of nosebleed and another had bruising on the lower extremities.
- In adults, bleeding complications have been reported with use of all SSRIs and have included melena, rectal bleeding, menorrhagia, nosebleeding, and bruising.
- In children (and probably adults) scheduled for surgery who have had presumed SSRI-related bleeding, it may be wise to discontinue SSRI therapy.
- Caused by blockage of serotonin uptake by platelets.

### Cardiac Problems

Patients should be carefully checked for TCA-cardiac interactions.

Cardiac problems with ADs are of 4 general types:

- Blood pressure
- Heart rate fluctuation
- Cardiac conduction
- Heart failure

### Blood Pressure

- *Hypertension*
  - √ Venlafaxine only AD with significant hypertensive risk.
    - □ Treatment-emergent hypertension:
      375 mg, 4.5%
      225 mg, 2.2%
      75 mg, 1.1%
      Placebo, 1.1%
    - □ Sustained (3 consecutive visits) hypertension (supine diastolic BP: > 90 mm and > 10 mm above baseline):
      300 mg, 13%
      201–300 mg/day, 7%

101–200 mg/day, 5%
< 100 mg/day, 3%
Placebo, 2%

- *Hypotension with dizziness*
  √ Most common form is orthostatic hypotension.
  √ MAOIs cause the most hypotension.
  √ TCAs generate considerable hypotension (with nortriptyline least).
  √ SSRIs cause almost no hypotension.
  √ Hypotension more common in
    ▫ Cardiac patients (14–24%) than in medically well patients (0–7%).
    ▫ The elderly report a 4% injury rate (e.g., fractures, lacerations).
  √ Measure BPs reclining, sitting, and standing, before and during the first few days of TCA, trazodone, or nefazodone treatment.
  √ Tell patient to deal with hypotension by
    ▫ Sitting a full 60 seconds—or longer—if at all lightheaded.
    ▫ Standing slowly while holding onto stable object (e.g., bed).
    ▫ Waiting at least 30 seconds before walking.
    ▫ Consider support stockings or corsets even at night.
    ▫ Highest risk time is getting out of bed in middle of night.
  √ Other management
    ▫ Check if patient is on low-sodium diet, antihypertensives. If so, increase sodium or reduce antihypertensive dose.
    ▫ Increase dose more slowly, even though hypotension may not be dose-dependent.
    ▫ Try less hypotensive AD.
    ▫ If BP problems threaten continued use in patients without a cardiac illness or edema, may add sodium chloride (500–650 mg bid–tid) or yohimbine (5 mg tid).
    ▫ Hydrate with about 8 glasses of fluid a day. Patient must also have adequate sodium intake for this to work.
    ▫ Add methylphenidate or D-amphetamine.
    ▫ Greater BP drops may be treated with fludrocortisone (0.1 mg qd–bid), but this should be considered only if AD is the only acceptable alternative.

## Heart Rate Fluctuations

- TCAs elevate heart rate and reduce heart rate variability, both of which can raise cardiac risk.
- *Arrhythmias*
  √ After several weeks of TCAs (especially imipramine), a quinidine-like action may ensue, which can cut down premature beats but may increase mortality in MI patients.

- √ TCAs at toxic plasma levels (e.g., > 500 ng/ml imipramine and desipramine) can induce new arrhythmias.
- √ At therapeutic doses, trazodone in cardiac patients can induce new arrythmias.
  - □ Of most concern is ventricular fibrillation.
- Sudden death
  - √ Of 1,650 users of TCAs, there were 16 (0.97%) MIs,
  - √ 2 (0.31%) among 655 SSRI users,
  - √ None of 279 users of "other antidepressants."
    - □ TCAs are a type 1 antiarrhythmic drug, a class that has been associated with increased chance of sudden death.
- *Bradycardia*
  - √ Nefazodone has 1.5% risk of bradycardia.
  - √ Occasional reports of significant bradycardia with fluoxetine.
    - □ May occur with other SSRIs.
- *Tachycardia*
  - √ Seen with TCAs and venlafaxine.
  - √ May occur with mirtazapine.
  - √ Patients may be frightened or distracted by tachycardia and benefit from reassurance.
  - √ More common with more anticholinergic TCAs.
  - √ Occasionally seen with noradrenergic TCAs (e.g., desipramine, protriptyline).

**Cardiac Conduction**

- *ECG changes* with TCAs include:
  - √ Nonspecific ST and T wave changes
  - √ Prolongation of PR interval
  - √ Widening QRS complex
  - √ Prolongation of QTc interval
- TCA doses, and not cardiac disease, incite these ECG alterations.
- TCAs can increase cardiac risk with certain types of heart block.
  - √ Some risk with bundle-branch or bifasicular block.
  - √ Little risk in first-degree atrioventricular or hemiblock.
  - √ Can produce fatalities in patients with second- and third-degree heart block.
- If TCA is used in patient with cardiac conduction disease,
  - √ Monitor serial ECGs.
  - √ Monitor TCA level.
- Causing fewer cardiac-conduction problems are probably
  - √ Bupropion
  - √ Citalopram
  - √ Fluoxetine
  - √ Fluvoxamine
  - √ Mirtazapine
  - √ Nefazodone

√ Paroxetine
√ Sertraline
√ Trazodone (but may create ventricular arrhythmias)
√ Venlafaxine

**Heart Failure**

- *Myocardial depression, decreased cardiac output, congestive heart failure*
- *Pedal edema* frequently induced by
  √ Amitriptyline
  √ Trazodone

*Sudden death* occurs unexpectedly; supposedly due to cardiac arrhythmias.

- About 0.4%, more common after TCA overdose.
  √ Desipramine may be most likely to cause this fatality in O.D.

# Central Nervous System Effects

*Ataxia*

*Confusion, disturbed concentration, disorientation, delirium, memory impairment*

**Effect of Increasing Age on Risk of Confusional States with TCAs**

| Age (years) | Risk Rate (%) |
|---|---|
| 10–29 | 0 |
| 30–39 | 4 |
| 40–49 | 25 |
| 50–59 | 33 |
| 60–69 | 43 |
| 70–79 | 50 |
| Overall risk | 13 |

- Switch to a less or non-anticholinergic AD, in particular, citalopram, fluoxetine, sertraline, bupropion, trazodone, or nefazodone.
  √ Start with these if > 40 y.o.
  √ If TCA needed, consider nortriptyline; if there is no suicide risk, desipramine also effective.
- *Delirium*
  √ Dose-dependent; in 6% of tertiary TCA-treated patients.
  √ Occurs with plasma levels of > 450 ng/ml.
  √ May begin with greater depression or psychosis.
    □ Increased TCA dose or adding neuroleptics may worsen toxicity.

ANTIDEPRESSANTS

- *Memory impairment*
  - √ Especially in the elderly.
  - √ Determine cause carefully. May be
    - □ Depression
    - □ CNS illness
    - □ Endocrine or other medical problem (e.g., pneumonia)
    - □ Medication-induced toxicity.
- Difficulties in word finding and name recall have been reported on all antidepressants, including lithium and MAOIs.
  - √ Frequency and mechanism of this side effect is unknown.

*Delusions, visual or auditory hallucinations, "serotonin syndrome"* (*see* MAOIs, page 185, for more details)

- With SSRIs and clomipramine
  - √ Usually doesn't occur with sole use of drug in normal doses.
  - √ Occasionally seen in mild forms with very high doses.
    - □ "Mild forms" means to see color trails behind moving objects (sometimes called "tracers" by LSD users).
- Occurs with dangerous combinations:
  - √ SSRI or clomipramine with MAOI (not with selegiline)
  - √ Tryptophan, dextromethorphan, or meperidine with MAOIs (and possibly SSRIs)
- Must wait 5 weeks after fluoxetine 20 mg stopped, 6–9 weeks after fluoxetine 40 mg stopped, and 2 weeks after sertraline and paroxetine stopped before starting MAOI.
- Patients may experience one, several, or all of these symptoms.
  - √ Restlessness
  - √ Diaphoresis
  - √ Hyperreflexia
  - √ Myoclonus
  - √ Nausea, abdominal cramps
  - √ Diarrhea
  - √ Insomnia
- Management
  - √ Serotonin antagonist cyproheptadine 4–12 mg can alleviate the serotonin syndrome.
  - √ Hospitalize; can be fatal.
  - √ Select less serotonergic antidepressant.

*Excitement, restlessness, or precipitation of*

- *Hypomania, mania*
  - √ With no h/o bipolar disorder
    - □ 2% with TCA

> □ 1% with SSRIs, bupropion, venlafaxine, nefazodone, and probably mirtazapine
- With h/o of bipolar disorder
  - □ 12% with TCA
  - □ ~ 2% with paroxetine, nefazodone, and sertraline
  - □ Reported low with other SSRIs and bupropion.
  - √ In a known bipolar disorder, use full-dose anticycling agent first before antidepressant.

*Extrapyramidal side effects*

- Most often seen with amoxapine.
  - √ Parkinsonian reactions
  - √ Dyskinesia
    - □ Uncommon.
    - □ Arises with reduced dose.
    - □ Disappears quickly.
  - √ Tardive dyskinesia
- Rarely seen with other HCAs.
- Sometimes seen with SSRIs.
- *Agitation/akathisia*
  - √ Extremely difficult to separate agitation from akathisia—physical components strong in both.
  - √ Most common with bupropion and SSRIs, especially fluoxetine.
  - √ Occasionally with protriptyline and desipramine.
  - √ May respond to benzodiazepines, propranolol, or clonidine.
  - √ Patients may have a remission of agitation in 2–4 weeks.
- *Neuroleptic malignant syndrome (see pages 33–35).*
  - √ Amoxapine is the only antidepressant to cause this syndrome.

*Headache*

- Frequently occurs spontaneously in depression; "tension" headache most common.
  - √ Increased incidence of migraine in depression.
- In SSRI trials, significant headache reported on placebo in 16–19%.
  - √ Same or slightly less than on active drug.
- Determine headache frequency in patient before starting medication; otherwise it may be reported as a "side effect."

*Insomnia*

- Most common with SSRIs, bupropion, venlafaxine, and protriptyline.

√ Then with desipramine and amoxapine.
- Use A.M. dosing.
- Add trazodone 25–100 mg qhs, Ambien 10–20 mg po qhs, or standard hypnotic.

*Muscle tremors, twitches, jitters* (occasional)

*Nightmares, weird dreams, hypnagogic hallucinations, vivid dreams*

- Can occur on any AD.
- Usually emerge when AD consumed all hs.
- May reduce by
  √ Changing AD.
  √ Moving part of dose to dinnertime.
  √ Spreading dose throughout day.

*Panic attacks or anxiety*

- If h/o panic disorder, start with very low dose.
  √ Imipramine 10 mg or fluoxetine 5 mg.
- Without h/o panic disorder, try another antidepressant.
  √ Reaction may have been idiosyncratic to drug used.
  √ Less activating drug should be considered (e.g., stop fluoxetine and try paroxetine).

*Paresthesias* (infrequent)

*Sedation, drowsiness*

Except for trazodone (quite sedating) and paroxetine (low-medium sedation), sedation is directly related to $H_1$ blockade (*see* page 108 for comparison of ADs).

| Most Sedative | Medium Sedative | Least (or not) Sedative |
|---|---|---|
| Amitriptyline | Amoxapine | Bupropion (not) |
| Clomipramine | Citalopram | Desipramine |
| Doxepin | Imipramine | Fluoxetine (not) |
| Mirtazapine | Maprotiline | Fluvoxamine |
| Trazodone | Nefazodone | Protriptyline |
| Trimipramine | Nortriptyline | Sertraline |
| | Paroxetine | |
| | Venlafaxine | |

- Sedation, especially fatigue, during first 2 weeks of therapy.
  √ Infrequently seen at lower doses of fluoxetine and venlaflaxine, but more often seen at higher doses (fluoxetine > 45 mg venlaflaxine > 250 mg).

- Management
  - √ Give all ADs in single hs dose except those requiring divided dosing, including:
    - □ Bupropion (but Wellbutrin SR can often be fully effective with one dose a day)
    - □ Fluvoxamine
    - □ Nefazodone
    - □ Venlafaxine
  - √ Switch to less sedating AD, in particular fluoxetine, sertraline, bupropion, trazodone, or nefazodone.

*Seizures*

- Overall incidence of first seizure without drug is 0.08%.
- Afflicts 0.1% of SSRI patients.
- Afflicts 0.2% of patients on TCA or venlafaxine.
  - √ 2–3% for clomipramine, bupropion (2.3% risk at 600 mg), maprotiline, and amoxapine in high doses.
- More recent reports of seizures with
  - √ Maprotiline when
    - □ Given in high doses (> 225 mg/day),
    - □ Rapidly escalated to 150 mg/day in 7 days, and
    - □ Patients have preexisting seizures.
  - √ Bupropion given > 450 mg/day or > 150 mg single doses.
    - □ Patients with seizure history or risks, including family h/o seizures, sedative withdrawal, bulimia, multiple concomitant medications, head injury, abnormal EEG, are higher risk.
    - □ Patients with liver disease and resulting increased bupropion levels are higher risk.
    - □ Seizures much lower risk with Wellbutrin SR (0.1–0.2 risk)
- With HCAs, seizures erupt with
  - √ Overdose
    - □ 8.4% rate
    - □ Most with blood level > 1000 ng/ml
    - □ QRS lengthening not a good predictor of seizure.
  - √ Preexisting seizures (including alcohol withdrawal).
  - √ Preexisting neurologic disorder.
- Higher TCA plasma levels (> 450 ng/ml) increase risk of, but are insufficient to cause, seizures.
  - √ Weeks of high TCA plasma levels may occur before seizures.
  - √ High chronic levels typically have no prodromal phase; they generate a single, tonic-clonic, sometimes fatal, grand mal seizure.
- Acute HCA overdose triggers multiple seizures and status epilepticus.

- Fluoxetine's anticonvulsant effects
  - √ Added a 20 mg/day dose to the anticonvulsant regimen of 17 patients (9 men, 8 women) with partial complex seizures.
  - √ Prior to fluoxetine treatment, 14 of the 17 patients had daily seizures; none was seizure-free.
  - √ After fluoxetine was added, no patient had daily seizures and 6 were completely seizure-free.
  - √ Fluoxetine raises serum levels of many anticonvulsants.

*"Spaciness," depersonalization*

- Mainly seen with HCAs, trazodone, and nefazodone.
- Management
  - √ Escalate dose more slowly.
  - √ If side effect persists, switch to another AD.

*Speech blockage, stuttering*

*Suicidal ideation (S.I.)*

- New S.I. rate in first week on HCA about same as placebo (3–3.5%).
- New S.I. rate in first week on fluoxetine, and possibly other SSRIs, slightly lower than placebo (2.5–3.0%).
  - √ In majority of reports of sudden, severe increase in S.I. while on fluoxetine, akathisia/agitation may have contributed.
    - ▫ Tell patient to call immediately if akathisia/agitation develops with SSRI.
    - ▫ Discontinue SSRI or attempt to treat with benzodiazepine, propranolol, or clonidine.

*Tremor*

- High-frequency tremor commonly seen, especially with noradrenergic TCAs, lithium (> 300 mg), and venlafaxine.
- Occasionally seen with SSRIs.
- Management of persistent tremor can involve
  - √ Lower TCA doses,
  - √ Propranolol 10–20 mg bid-qid, or
  - √ Low doses of benzodiazepines (e.g., alprazolam 0.25 mg bid).

*Weakness, lethargy, fatigue*

*Yawning without sedation*

- Occasionally seen with serotonergic drugs (SSRIs and clomipramine).

## Endocrine and Sexual Effects

Distinguish effects caused by

- Depression
- Medication
- Other causes

*Breast engorgement* (males and females)

*Decreased libido, impotence, diminished sexual arousal, impaired orgasms*

- Probably highest with SSRIs, clomipramine, and high doses of venlafaxine (> 250 mg/day).
  - √ Postmarketing data suggest at least 35% experience decrease in libido, arousal, or orgasm in males and females.
- Impotence seen more with TCAs.
  - √ Often secondary to Ach effects.

SSRIs often delay orgasm.

- This "problem" side effect can help many males with premature ejaculation.
- In males averaging less than 60 sec intravaginally to ejaculation, paroxetine 40 mg increased this to 15 minutes.
  - √ Full effect seen within 3 weeks (too "good" a response?).
- Bupropion only AD with reported increases in libido and sexual activity.
  - √ Nefazodone and trazodone can keep libido and sexual activity continuing but have a 10–20% risk of decreasing sexual functioning,
  - √ Mirtazapine at doses of 30–45 mg usually has minimal or no sexual problems.

Antidepressant-induced sexual dysfunction

- Paroxetine, sertraline, and venlafaxine
  - √ Levels of arousal/orgasm impairment were not statistically significant between men and women.
    - □ Drive/desire impairment items for men ranged from 38–50% and for women, 26–32%.
  - √ No differences were found across the 3 antidepressants in men's sexual functioning.
  - √ In women, rates of sexual dysfunction were, in general, modestly higher with sertraline and paroxetine.
    - □ Venlafaxine tended to have lower sexual dysfunction than SSRIs.

□ Venlafaxine therapy was started with final goal of 75 mg tid. After 5 weeks, scores on the BDI fell to 6, energy level increased, and NK-cell activity increased to 15.1%.

Management

- Lower dose may bring marked improvement.
- Sexual function and satisfaction improved in chronically depressed (N = 681)
  √ 3 groups were randomized to 12 weeks of nefazodone, Cognitive Behavioral Analysis System of Psychotherapy (CBASP), or combined nefazodone/CBASP (COMB).
    □ From baseline to week 12 significant improvement in sexual functioning across all groups was seen.
    □ COMB produced greater improvement in sexual interest/ satisfaction than nefazodone (p = .05) or CBASP alone (p < .03).
    □ For women, COMB produced significantly (p < .002) greater improvement in ratings of overall sexual satisfaction than CBASP alone.
    □ Men improved significantly (all p's < .002) more than women on total sexual interest/satisfaction as well as specific measures of increased frequency of pleasurable sexual thoughts, ability to become sexually excited, and frequency of initiation of sexual activity.
- Bupropion can be an antidote for serotonergic-reuptake-inhibitor-induced sexual dysfunction.
  √ 47 psychiatric outpatients complained of SRI-induced sexual dysfunction and received prn or as a fixed dose schedule.
  √ Patients received 75 or 150 mg of bupropion 1 to 2 hours before sexual activity.
    □ If needed, dose was increased gradually to 75 mg tid and sustained for 2 weeks.
  √ Bupropion reversed a variety of sexual dysfunctions caused by SSRIs in 31 (66%) of 47 patients.
  √ 52 (69%) of 75 sexual complaints improved with bupropion treatment.
  √ 18 (35%) of 47 patients used bupropion prn.
  √ Anxiety and tremor led to a discontinuation of bupropion in 7 (15%) of 47 patients.
- Buspirone (Buspar) 20–60 mg/day *improved* sexual functioning.
  √ 47 out of 117 patients (40%) reported at least one symptom of sexual dysfunction.
  √ 58% of subjects treated with buspirone and 30% in the placebo

group reported significant improvement in sexual function in the first week, but little or no further improvement after.

- Mirtazapine for depression and sexual side effects in sexually active male and female outpatients
  - √ 52% decrease in depression on HDRS
  - √ Each stage of sexual functioning (desire, arousal, and orgasm) increased an average of 33% over baseline.
- For decreased sexual arousal or anorgasmia
  - √ Sildenafil 50 or 100 mg helped women reverse symptoms such as anorgasmia, decreased libido, and poor lubrication (often with first dose).
    - □ 66% of women showed a full response to a 50 mg dose of sildenafil, 66% of patients had a full response, and 33% had a partial response when at 100 mg/day.
  - √ Several studies with men indicated that sexual dysfunction occurring in 35–45% treated with routine antidepressants (e.g., SSRIs, TCAs) responded well to sildenafil.
  - √ Men and women most often use 4–6 doses of sildenafil per month instead of taking it daily to keep expenses down and possibly because the doses are sufficient.
    - □ Ginkgo biloba 140–180 mg/day may be helpful for improved sexual desire, arousal, lubrication (in females), time to orgasm, and genital sensitivity.
    - □ Cyproheptadine 2–6 mg prn 2 h before intercourse or tid (beware of sedation).
    - □ Yohimbine 2.7–7.1 mg prn 2 h before intercourse or tid (beware of anxiety and insomnia).
    - □ Amantadine 100–400 mg/day (not used prn).
    - □ Bupropion 75–225 mg/day, in divided doses.
  - √ Yohimbine (5 mg tid) or bethanechol (10 mg tid) may reduce impotence.
  - √ Cyproheptadine can occasionally interfere with SSRI antidepressant effect.

*Priapism*

- A rare condition of persistent, painful erection related to alpha-adrenergic effects.
  - √ Highest when not opposed by anticholinergic effects (e.g., with trazodone, clonidine, risperidone).
  - √ Most common with trazodone (about 1 in 6,000), and may occur at any dose.
  - √ Occurs primarily during 1st month of treatment, but can occur anywhere from 3 days to 18 months after drug initiated.
  - √ Chlorpromazine, thioridazine, and other alpha-adrenergic antihypertensives cause other cases.

- If sexual ability is to be retained, intervention within 4–6 h is mandatory. If treated too late, condition will be irreversible, resulting in permanent impotence.
- All males on trazodone must be warned in advance about priapism (risk about 1/6,000).
- Management
  - √ Medications and ice packs provide inconsistent results.
  - √ Medications include alpha-adrenergic stimulants.
    - □ Neosynephrine (10 mg/30cc) injected intracorporally 6cc (2 mg) every 10–15 min until response is seen or maximum of 3 doses (total 6 mg) is reached.
    - □ Metaraminol 10 mg intracavernosal injection into penis.
    - □ Epinephrine if pharmacologic treatment not obtained within 6 h.
  - √ May require surgery.
  - √ In emergencies, clinicians can call Bristol-Myers Squibb at 800/321–1335.
- *Clitoral priapism* has been reported.
  - √ No apparent long-term risk related to this side effect.

*Spontaneous orgasm*

- Rare; usually associated with yawning.
- Reported with clomipramine, trazadone, and SSRIs.
- More reports in females.
- Seldom spontaneously reported; usually elicited by MD when patient insists on staying on drug when having only minimal antidepressant effect.

*Testicular swelling* (rare)

- Reported from desipramine.
  - √ Stop drug.

## Eyes, Ears, Nose, and Throat

All side effects (except nasal congestion) due to anticholinergic blockade (*see* page 99).

- All rare with fluoxetine and sertraline.

*Bronchial secretions dry and strained breathing* for patients with respiratory difficulty.

*Eyes, dry* (*see* pages 45–46)

*Narrow-angle glaucoma*

- Virtually all TCAs, but especially the most anticholinergic, can precipitate a painful narrow-angle glaucoma.

- If patient might have this type of glaucoma, postpone all anticholinergic agents, including TCAs, until diagnosis is clear (*see* page 46).

*Nasal congestion*

- Seen most with trazodone.
  √ May be alpha-adrenergic effect.

*Photophobia*

- From dilated pupils.

*Vision, blurred* (*see* page 45)

## Gastrointestinal Effects

*Anorexia, nausea, vomiting, dyspepsia*

- Common (21–35%) with SSRIs, bupropion, and venlafaxine.
- Tolerance usually develops over 10–14 days.
- If due to TCA, reduce dose.
- If SSRI or atypical, take on full stomach.
  √ Might add bismuth salicylate (Pepto-Bismol)
  √ Antacid
    □ Calcium versions offer least drug interaction problems
  √ Antireflux agent (e.g., cisapride 5 mg bid)

*Constipation*

- Generally correlated with cholinergic blockade (*see* page 47).
- Lowest with bupropion, citalopram, fluoxetine, fluvoxamine, sertraline, and desipramine.

*Diarrhea*

- Common (11–16%) with SSRIs.
  √ Tolerance may develop.
  √ If without tolerance, loperamide (Imodium) usually works.

*Mouth dry* (*see* page 47).

*Paralytic ileus*

- Rare but potentially fatal.
- Stop TCAs.

*Syndrome of inappropriate antidiuretic hormone (SIADH)*

- Induced by venlafaxine (N = 4, all female, 65–79 y.o.).
- Hyponatremia was detected, on average, 5 days following venlafaxine start or an increase in its dose.
- Sodium levels fell to between 119 and 125 mmol/l.
- Venlafaxine was stopped.

A
N
T
I
D
E
P
R
E
S
S
A
N
T

- Reversal of hyponatremia took about 9 days.

*Peculiar taste, "black tongue" glossitis*

*Weight gain, appetite stimulation, carbohydrate craving*

- Weight gain develops over time in a significant minority with SSRIs paroxetine, fluoxetine, and fluvoxamine.
- Not usually seen with venlafaxine, bupropion, desipramine, or trazodone.
- TCAs increase appetite and food intake; correlated with $H_1$ blockade (*see* page 99).
- Most common with
  √ Amitriptyline
  √ Clomipramine
  √ Doxepin
  √ Mirtazapine
  √ Trimipramine
- Doxepin is one of the most powerful $H_1$ blockers available.
  √ Many times stronger than diphenhydramine (Benadryl) or hydroxyzine (Vistaril)
  √ 25–50 mg provides nearly complete blockade.

*Weight loss*

- Sometimes seen with
  √ Bupropion
  √ Desipramine
  √ Fluoxetine
  √ Fluvoxamine
  √ Paroxetine
  √ Sertraline
  √ Venlafaxine
- Is usually minimal.
- In geriatrics on fluoxetine, can be problematic in about 25%.

## Renal Effects

*Urinary hesitancy or retention (see page 52).*

Correlated with cholinergic blockade (*see* page 99).

## Skin, Allergies, and Temperature

*Skin flushing*

Allergies rare, and display:

- *Rashes*
  √ Most often reported with desipramine.
  √ Also seen more often when tartrazine is used as a yellow coloring.

  √ Reactions developed within 2–3 weeks of starting bupropion.
    □ Symptoms include rash, arthralgia, fever, and lip swelling.
    □ Pruritis occurs 2.2% and rash about 8%.
- *Jaundice, hepatitis*
- *Photosensitivity*
- *Urticaria, pruritus*

In all cases, medication should be stopped and an unrelated antidepressant tried.

*Sweating increased, and occasionally decreased*

SSRIs, venlafaxine, and bupropion increase sweating (7–12%).

- Management
  √ Daily showering
  √ Talcum powder

## PERCENTAGES OF SIDE EFFECTS

**Part I**

| Side Effects | Amitrip-tyline | Amoxa-pine | Bupro-pion SR | Citalo-pram | Clomi-pramine | Desipra-mine |
|---|---|---|---|---|---|---|
| **CARDIOVASCULAR EFFECTS** | | | | | | |
| Cardiac arrhythmias | 6 | < 2 | 3.7 | 3 | 6 | 6 |
| Dizziness, lightheadedness | 42.5 (10–65) | > 30 | 7 | > 1 | 37 (10–54) | 6 |
| ECG abnormalities | 20 | < 2 | < 2 | < 2 | 20 | 6 |
| Edema | 1 | — | < 2 | < 2 | — | 2 |
| Fainting, syncope | — | — | 1.2 | < 1 | 0 | — |
| Hypertension | — | — | 1.6 | > 1 | — | — |
| Hypotension (postural) | 32 (10–44) | 36 (32–42) | 4.3 (2.5–10) | 2 | 13 (6–30) | 6 |
| Palpitations | 5 | — | 2 | 2 | 4 | — |
| Tachycardia | 20 | 20 | > 1 | > 1 | 14.7 (4–30) | 6 |
| **CENTRAL NERVOUS SYSTEM EFFECTS** | | | | | | |
| Agitation, restlessness, akathisia (motoric) | — | — | 3 | > 1 | 3 | — |
| Anxiety, nervousness (mental) | — | — | 3.1 | 4 | 15.5 (9–18) | — |
| Confusion, disorientation | 11.3 (0–30) | 6 | 8.4 | > 1 | 4.5 (2–10) | — |
| Drowsiness, sedation | 39.6 (30–58.8) | 16 (14–30) | 2 | 18 | 30 (2–54) | 6 |
| Excitement, hypomania | 5.7 (< 2–15) | 6 | 1.2 | > 1 | < 2 | 6 |
| Headache | 10.5 (2–15) | 6 | 25.7 | > 2 | 6 | 0.2 |

| Side Effects | Amitriptyline | Amoxapine | Bupropion SR | Citalopram | Clomipramine | Desipramine |
|---|---|---|---|---|---|---|
| Insomnia | 10.5 (2–15) | 20 | 11 | 15 | 8.5 (1.5–30) | 6 |
| Muscle cramps | 5 | — | 1.9 | | 13 | — |
| Seizures | 0.2 | 0.2 | 0.1–.2 (0.3–2.2) | 0.2–.3 | 2.1 (0.5–3) | < 0.2 |
| Speech, slurred | — | — | — | — | 3 | — |
| Tremor | 25 (5–40) | 9 (2–12) | 6 | 8 | 16.3 (6–33) | 6 |
| Weakness, fatigue | 20 | 5.5 (2–10) | 5 | 6 | 30 (2–54) | 6 |
| **ENDOCRINE AND SEXUAL EFFECTS** | | | | | | |
| Breast swelling | — | — | — | — | 2 | — |
| Lactation | — | — | — | — | 4 | — |
| Menstrual changes | — | — | 4.7 | 5 | 12 | — |
| Priapism | 0 | 0 | 0 | 0 | 0 | 0 |
| Sexual function, disturbed | 4.3 (0–10) | — | 3.2 | 4 | 16.3 (8–30) | 7 (2–10) |
| **EYES, EARS, NOSE, AND THROAT EFFECTS** | | | | | | |
| Throat, sore, flu | — | — | 5 | 5 | 10 | — |
| Tinnitus | 10 | — | — | < 1 | — | — |
| Vision, blurred | 35.2 (10–55.7) | 6.5 (2–10) | 14.6 | > 2 | 20 | 6 |
| **GASTROINTESTINAL EFFECTS** | | | | | | |
| Anorexia, lower appetite | 0 | — | 5 | 4 | 12 | — |
| Appetite, increased | 5 | — | 3.7 | 4 | 11 | — |
| Constipation | 29.4 (10–38.2) | 27 (12–> 30) | 10 | 7 | 33.5 (10–47) | 6 |
| Diarrhea | — | — | 5 | 8 | 13 | — |
| Dyspepsia, upset stomach | 5 | — | 3.1 | 5 | 16 6–14 | — |
| Mouth and throat, dry | 58.5 (30–90) | 29 (14–30) | 17 (10–24) | 1 | 43 (> 30–84) | 20 |
| Nausea, vomiting | 5.5 | — | 13 | 21 | 19.5 (2–33) | 6 |
| Taste changes | — | — | 3.1 | — | — | — |
| Weight gain | > 30 | < 2 | 13.6 | 10 | 19 (10–30) | 6 |
| Weight loss | — | — | 5 | 4 | — | — |
| **RENAL EFFECTS** | | | | | | |
| Urinary hesitancy or retention | 10.5 (2–15) | 20 | 3.9 (1.9–10) | > 1 | 11 (2–30) | — |
| **SKIN, ALLERGIES, AND TEMPERATURE EFFECTS** | | | | | | |
| Fever, hyperthermia | — | 0.5 | 1 | > 1 | 4 | — |
| Rashes | 6 | 11.5 (3–30) | < 1 — | > 1 | 7 (2–10) | 12 |
| Skin pigment, abnormal | — | — | 2.2 | < 1 | 4 | — |
| Sweating | 22.5 (10–30) | 6 | 6 | < .1 | 21 (10–30) | |

# Part II

| Side Effects | Doxepin | Fluoxetine | Fluvoxamine | Imipramine | Maprotiline | Mirtazapine | Nefazodone |
|---|---|---|---|---|---|---|---|
| **CARDIOVASCULAR EFFECTS** | | | | | | | |
| Cardiac arrhythmias | 6 | 1.5 | — | 6 | < 2 | < 1 | < 1 |
| Dizziness, lightheadedness | 20 | 5.7 | 11 | 26.3 (15–30) | 7 (2–10) | 7 | 17 |
| ECG abnormalities | 6 | < 2 | — | 20 | < 2 | < 1 | < 1 |
| Edema | — | < 1 | — | — | — | 2 | 3 |
| Hypotension (postural) | 20 | < 1 | < 1 | 37 (> 30–40) | 6 | > 1 | 4 |
| Hypertension | — | < 1 | — | — | — | > 1 | < 1 |
| Palpitations | — | 1.3 | 3 | 5 | — | < 1 | < 1 |
| Tachycardia | 20 | 1.2 | — | 20 | 6 | 5 | < 1 |
| **CENTRAL NERVOUS SYSTEM EFFECTS** | | | | | | | |
| Anxiety, nervousness (mental) | — | 10.9 (9.4–15) | 12 | — | 4.5 | > 1 | < 1 |
| Disorientation, confusion | < 2 | 1.5 | — | 4.3 | 6 | 2 | 7 |
| Drowsiness, sedation | 34.5 (30–39) | 11.8 (10–30) | 22 | 26 (20–32) | 18 (10–30) | 54 | 25 |
| Excitement, hypomania | < 2 | 7.3 (1–30) | 2 | 15 (5–30) | 6 | < 1 | 1 |
| Headache | < 2 | 20.1 (10–30) | 4.8 | 20 | 3 | < 2 | 36 |
| Insomnia | 6 | 16.9 (10–30) | 21 | 20 | 2 | 0 | 11 |
| Muscle cramps | — | 1.4 | ** | — | — | > 2 | < 1 |
| Restlessness, agitation, akathisia | — | 15 | 2 | — | 2 | > 1 | < 1 |

# Part II (Cont.)

| Side Effects | Doxepin | Fluoxetine | Fluvoxamine | Imipramine | Maprotiline | Mirtazapine | Nefazodone |
|---|---|---|---|---|---|---|---|
| Rigidity | — | <1 | ** | — | — | — | 1 |
| Seizures | < 0.2 | 0.2 (0.2–< 2) | 0.005 | > 3 (0.6–> 3) | > 3 (0.2–> 3) | < .01 | < 0.1 |
| Speech, slurred | — | — | — | — | — | — | — |
| Tremor | 6 | 13.9 | 5 | 6 | (3–30) | 2 | 2 |
| Weakness, fatigue | 6 | 4.2 | 5.1 | 20 | 4 | 8 | 8 |
| **ENDOCRINE AND SEXUAL EFFECTS** | | | | | | | |
| Breast swelling | — | < 1 | — | — | — | — | < 0.1 |
| Hypothyroidism | — | < 1 | — | — | — | 0 | 0 |
| Menstrual changes | — | 1.7 | — | — | — | — | < 0.1 |
| Priapism | 0 | 0 | 0 | 0 | 0 | 0 | — |
| Sexual function, disturbed | 6 | 15 | 8 | 2.5 | — | 35 | 1 |
| **EYES, EARS, NOSE, AND THROAT EFFECTS** | | | | | | | |
| Nasal stuffiness | — | 2.3 | ** | — | — | — | < 1 |
| Throat, sore, flu | — | 7.8 | 9 | — | — | — | 6 |
| Vision, blurred | 20 | 2.8 (2–10) | 3 | 16.7 (10–30) | 12 (4–30) | < 1 | — |
| **GASTROINTESTINAL EFFECTS** | | | | | | | |
| Anorexia, lower appetite | — | 9.0 | 18 | — | — | > 1 | — |
| Appetite, increased | — | 1 | ** | — | — | 13 | 5 |
| Constipation | 31.5 (10–43) | 5 | 10 | 20 | 13 (6–30) | 13 | 4 |
| Diarrhea | — | 12.2 | 11 | — | — | 2 | 8 |
| Dyspepsia, upset stomach | — | 6.2 | 10 | — | — | 4 | 9 |
| Jaundice | — | < 1 | — | — | — | — | < 0.1 |

**Part II (Cont.)**

| Side Effects | Doxepin | Fluoxetine | Fluvoxamine | Imipramine | Maprotiline | Mirtazapine | Nefazodone |
|---|---|---|---|---|---|---|---|
| Mouth and throat, dry | 43 (> 30–56) | 9.5 | 14 | 30 | 26 (22–> 30) | 25 | 25 |
| Nausea, vomiting | < 2 | 20.7 | 40 | 5 | 4 | 1.5 | 2 |
| Taste changes | — | 2.2 (1.8–3) | 3 | — | — | < 1 | 2 |
| Weight gain | 26 | < 1 | 1 | 20 | 20 | 7.5* | — |
| Weight loss | — | 13 | — | — | — | < 1 | < 1 |
| **HEMATOLOGIC EFFECTS** | | | | | | | |
| Blood dyscrasias | — | < 1 | — | — | — | — | < 0.1 |
| **RENAL EFFECTS** | | | | | | | |
| Urinary hesitancy or retention | 4.5 (< 2–10) | 1.5 | 1 | 20 | 6 | 2 | 2 |
| **SKIN, ALLERGIES, AND TEMPERATURE EFFECTS** | | | | | | | |
| Allergies | — | 1.1 | — | — | — | — | < 1 |
| Fever, hyperthermia | — | < 0.1 | 3 | — | — | — | < 0.1 |
| Rashes | < 2 | 2.7 | — | 6 | 20 | < 2 | < 1 |
| Skin pigment, abnormal | — | 2 | — | — | — | — | < 0.1 |
| Sweating | 20 | 7.5 (2–8.4) | 0.7 | 20 | 6 | < 2 | 0 |

**Part III**

| Side Effects | Nortriptyline | Paroxetine | Proptriptyline | Sertraline | Trazodone | Trimipramine | Venlafaxine |
|---|---|---|---|---|---|---|---|
| **CARDIOVASCULAR EFFECTS** | | | | | | | |
| Breath, short | — | < 1 | — | < 1 | 1.2 | — | > 1 |
| Cardiac arrhythmias | 6 | < 1 | 6 | — | < 2 | 6 | < 0.1 |
| Dizziness, light-headedness | 5.5 | 13 | 20 | 11.7 | 21.9 (10–30) | 20 | 20 |
| ECG abnormalities | 6 | < 1 | 20 | — | < 2 | 20 | < 0.1 |
| Edema | — | < 1 | — | < 1 | 4.9 | — | < 1 |
| Fainting, syncope | — | > 1 | — | < 1 | 3.7 (2.8–4.5) | — | < 1 |
| Hypertension | — | > 1 | — | < 1 | 1.7 | — | 2 |
| Hypotension (postural) | 6 | 1.2 | 20 | < 1 | 10.1 (3.8–30) | 20 | 1 |
| Palpitations | — | 2.9 | — | 3.5 | 0–0.7 | — | — |
| Tachycardia | 6 | > 1 | 6 | < 1 | 3.2 (0–10) | 6 | 3 |
| **CENTRAL NERVOUS SYSTEM EFFECTS** | | | | | | | |
| Agitation | — | 2.1 | — | 5.6 | — | — | 2 |
| Anxiety, nervousness (mental) | — | 5 | — | 5.6 | 10.6 (6.4–14.8) | — | 12 |
| Disorientation, confusion | 11.3 (0–30) | 1.2 | — | > 1 | 3.7 (< 20–5.7) | 20 | 2 |
| Drowsiness, sedation | 6.8 (0–15) | 23.3 (10–30) | < 2 | 13.4 | 29.1 (20–50) | > 30 | 17 |
| Excitement, hypomania | 8 (2–15) | 1 | 20 | 0.4 | 3.3 (1.4–5.1) | < 2 | 0.5 |
| Headache | < 2 | 17.6 | — | 20.3 | 10.4 (2–19.8) | 6 | 25 |

**Part III (Cont.)**

| Side Effects | Nortriptyline | Paroxetine | Proptriptyline | Sertraline | Trazodone | Trimipramine | Venlafaxine |
|---|---|---|---|---|---|---|---|
| Incoordination | — | < 0.1 | — | < 1 | 3.4 (1.9–4.9) | — | < 1 |
| Insomnia | < 2 | 13 | 20 | 16.4 (< 2–9.9) | 5.1 | 6 | 18 |
| Muscle cramps | — | 1.7 | — | 1.7 | 5.4 | — | < 1 |
| Seizures | 0.2 | — | 0.2 | 0.1 | 0.2 | 0.2 | 0.26 |
| Tremor | 11.3 (0–30) | 8 | 6 | 10.7 | 4.9 (2–10) | 20 | 5 |
| Weakness, fatigue | 20 | 15 | 20 | 8.1 | 6.6 | 6 | 12 |
| **ENDOCRINE AND SEXUAL EFFECTS** | | | | | | | |
| Priapism | 0 | 0 | 0 | 0 | 0.05 | 0 | < 0.1 |
| Sexual function, disturbed | < 2 | 15* | < 2 | 15* | 1.4 | — | 1–15* |
| **EYES, EARS, NOSE, AND THROAT EFFECTS** | | | | | | | |
| Nasal stuffiness | — | > 1 | — | 2 | 4.3 (2.8–5.7) | — | — |
| Vision, blurred | 5.5 | 3.6 | 20 | > 1 | 8.3 (2–14.7) | 6 | 6 |
| **GASTROINTESTINAL EFFECTS** | | | | | | | |
| Anorexia, lower appetite | — | 6.4 | — | 2.8 | 1.7 (0–3.5) | — | 11 |

# Part III (Cont.)

| Side Effects | Nortriptyline | Paroxetine | Proptriptyline | Sertraline | Trazodone | Trimipramine | Venlafaxine |
|---|---|---|---|---|---|---|---|
| Constipation | 8.6 | 13.8 | 20 | 8.4 | 13.6 (7–30) | 20 | 10 |
| Diarrhea | — | 11.6 | — | 17.7 | 2.2 (0–4.5) | — | 8 |
| Dyspepsia, indigestion | — | 1.9 | — | 6 | 4.6 | — | 5 |
| Mouth and throat, dry | 20 | 18.1 | 2 | 16.3 | 17.7 (2–33.8) | 20 | 22 |
| Nausea, vomiting | 2.3 | 25.7 | — | 26.1 | 15.7 (9.9–30) | < 2 | 37 |
| Taste changes | — | 2.4 | — | 1.2 | 0.7 | — | 2 |
| Weight gain | 6 | > 1 | — | < 1 | 4.5 (1.4–10) | 20 | 0 |
| Weight loss | — | > 1 | — | < 1 | 3.4 (1–5.7) | — | 3 |
| **RENAL EFFECTS** | | | | | | | |
| Urinary hesitancy or retention | < 2 | > 1 | < 2 | < 0.1 (< 2–10) | 4.8 | < 2 | 2 |
| **SKIN, ALLERGIES, AND TEMPERATURE EFFECTS** | | | | | | | |
| Rashes | < 2 | 1.7 | < 2 | 2.1 | < 2 | < 2 | 3 |
| Sweating | 2.5 | 11.2 | 20 | 8.4 | 1.2 | 6 | 12 |

* Postmarket estimates: M = F, ↓ libido ↓ arousal ↓ orgasm. Males primarily ejaculatory delays in SSRIs. Dose-dependent with venlafaxine, significantly increases at 300+ mg.

## PREGNANCY AND LACTATION

Teratogenicity
(Ist trimester)

- Little evidence of teratogenicity for TCAs.

- No evidence of increased teratogenicity with fluoxetine.

- Fluoxetine and TCAs associated with increased miscarriage rate.
  - √ 13–14% for TCA
  - ▫ Unclear if this risk is secondary to mood disorder or drugs.
  - √ 7% for controls
  - √ Difference was *not* statistically significant.

- Secondary TCAs recommended if AD needed.

Direct Effect on Newborn
(3rd trimester)

- Tachycardia, autonomic lability, respiratory distress, muscle spasm, and congestive heart failure have occurred in infants when large TCA doses taken prior to delivery.

- Clomipramine in 3 newborns caused lethargy, acidosis, hypotonia, cyanosis, jitteriness, irregular breathing, respiratory distress, and hypothermia.

- Anticholinergic effect can cause tachyarrhythmia in fetus.

- No human data on bupropion, citalopram, nefazodone, paroxetine, sertraline, and venlafaxine.

- Non-TCAs presumed safer secondary to decreased side effects.

- Imipramine and desipramine have produced neonatal withdrawal, with colic, diaphoresis, weight loss, cyanosis, rapid breathing, and irritability in newborn.

- Infants of mothers on nortriptyline developed urinary retention.

Lactation

- Sertraline and fluoxetine present in breast milk in 3 patients.
  √ All 3 breastfeeding infants showed very low levels (< 2 ng/ml) of sertraline or norsertraline and should be safe.

- Seven patients treated with citalopram had nursing infants that were estimated to receive only 3–6% of the weight-adjusted maternal dose.

## Drug Dosage in Mother's Milk

| Generic Names | Milk/Plasma Ratio | Time of Peak Concentration in Milk (hours) | Infant Dose ($\mu$g/kg/day) | Maternal Dose (%) | Safety Rating* |
|---|---|---|---|---|---|
| Amitriptyline | ? | | 16 | 0.90 | A |
| Amoxapine | ? | ? | < 3 mg | < 0.07 | A |
| Citalopram | ? | ? | ? | ? | ? |
| Desipramine | ? | ? | 18–40.2 | 0.5–1.0 | B |
| Doxepin | ? | ? | 0.25 | 0.01 | A |
| Imipramine | ? | 1 | 4.4 | 0.13 | A |
| Maprotiline | ? | ? | 39.0 | 1.60 | B |
| Mirtazapine | ? | ? | ? | ? | ? |
| Nortriptyline | ? | ? | 8.3–27.0 | 0.53–1.30 | B |
| Trazodone | 0.14 | 2 | 9 | 1.10 | B |

* A: Safe throughout infancy; B: Reasonably unsafe before 34 weeks, but safe after 34 weeks.

# DRUG-DRUG INTERACTIONS

| Drugs (X) Interact with: | Antidepressants (A)[1] | Comments |
|---|---|---|
| Acetaminophen | X↓A↑ | May overuse acetaminophen; increase HCA levels. |
| Acetazolamide | X↑ | Reduces HCAs' renal excretion; clinical importance unclear; hypotension increased. |
| *Alcohol | X↑A↑ | CNS depression with HCA and trazodone; not seen with SSRIs, bupropion, venlafaxine. |
| Aminopyrine | A↑? | Possible increase in HCA secondary to displaced protein-bound HCA. |
| Ammonium chloride | A↓ | May increase HCAs' excretion; clinical importance unclear. |
| Anticholinergics | X↑ | Increased anticholinergic actions with HCAs and paroxetine but not other SSRIs. |
| Antihistamines | X↑ | Increased drowsiness; use nonsedating antihistamine, such as asternizole. |
| *Antipsychotics (*see* *also* phenothiazines) | X↑A↑ | Potentiate each other; toxicity; more anticholinergic HCAs may diminish EPS; SSRIs may increase EPS and levels of thioridazine, perphenazine, clozapine, and risperidone. |
| Aspirin | A↑? | Possible increase in HCA secondary to displaced protein-bound HCA. |
| *Barbiturates | X↑A↑ | CNS depression; may decrease antidepressant plasma levels. |
| Benzodiazepines | X↑A↑ | CNS depression. |
| Bethanidine | A↓ | Decreases HCA effect. |
| Carbamazepine | X↓A↓ | Decreases HCA levels and effect; may lower seizure control; increased quinidine-like effect (*see* quinidine below). Monitor serum levels. SSRIs might decrease carbamazepine levels. |
| Chloramphenicol | A↑ | Increases HCA level, effect, toxicity. |
| Chlordiazepoxide (*see* benzodiazepines) | | |
| Chlorothiazide | A↑ | Thiazide diuretics increase HCA actions. |
| Cholestyramine | A↓ | Decreased absorption; decreased blood levels. |
| *Cimetidine | A↑ | Increased blood levels trigger toxicity; give patient less AD or substitute ranitidine or famotidine for cimetidine. |
| *Clonidine | X↓ | HCAs and probably venlafaxine inhibit clonidine's antihypertensive actions; trazodone, nefazodone (?), bupropion, SSRIs safer. |
| Cocaine | X↑ | Cardiac arrhythmias and increased BP with HCAs. |
| Cyclobenzaprine | A↑ | Cyclobenzaprine, which is chemically similar to HCAs, may produce cardiac problems, increased quinidine-like effects. |
| Debrisoquin | X↓ | Hypotension. |
| *Dextroamphetamine | X↑A↑ | Increase each other's effects. |
| Dicumarol | X↓ | Increased bleeding time. |
| Disopyramide (*see* quinidine) | | |
| Disulfiram | A↑ | May increase HCA level. |
| Doxycycline | A↓ | Decreased HCA level, effect. |
| †Epinephrine | X↑ | Increased arrhythmias, hypertension, and tachycardia. HCAs inhibit pressor effects of indirect-acting sympathomimetics (e.g., ephedrine). Because HCAs block the reuptake of direct-acting |

| Drugs (X) Interact with: | Antidepressants (A)[1] | Comments |
|---|---|---|
| | | sympathomimetics, their concentration increases at receptor sites. Since indirect-acting sympathomimetics require uptake into the adrenergic neuron to induce their effects, HCAs block them. The cardiovascular result from the mixed-acting sympathomimetics depends on the % of each group. Avoid HCAs with direct-acting sympatomimetics. |
| Estrogen (*see* oral contraceptives) | | |
| Fiber, psyllium | A↓ | Decreases absorption. |
| Fluconazole (*see* imidazole antifungals) | | |
| *Fluoxetine | A↑ | Increases HCA levels (300% avg.) and toxicity. |
| Griseofulvin | A↓ | Decreased HCA level, effect. |
| †Guanethidine | X↓ | Lose antihypertensive effect with NE uptake blockers; all HCAs and venlaflaxine; SSRIs, nefazodone, trazodone, bupropion safer. |
| Haloperidol | X↑A↑ | Increases HCA plasma level; EPS increase with fluoxetine and possibly sertraline and paroxetine. |
| Halothane | A↑ | Increases tachyarrythmias with anticholinergic antidepressants (HCAs and possibly paroxetine); enflurane with d-tubocurarine safer. |
| Imidazole antifungals | A↑ | Increases nortriptyline and probably other TCA levels and possibly sertraline. |
| Insulin | X↑ | HCA enhances hypoglycemia in diabetics. |
| Itraconazole (*see* imidazole antifungals) | | |
| Isoniazid | A↑ | Increases HCA level, effect, toxicity. |
| Ketoconazole (*see* imidazole antifungals) | | |
| Levodopa | X↓A↓ | Decreases absorption of HCAs; decreases effect of levodopa. |
| Lidocaine (*see* quinidine) | | |
| Liothyronine (T_3) | A↑ | Potentiates antidepressant and arrhythmic effects. |
| Lithium | A↑ | Augments antidepressant effects. |
| Meperidine | X↑A↑ | Potentiate each other; use lower doses of meperidine or another narcotic. |
| Methyldopa | X↓ | Hypotension; amitriptyline biggest problem. |
| Methylphenidate (*see* dextroamphetamine) | | |
| Miconazole (*see* imidazole antifungals) | | |
| Molindone | X↑ | Greater molindone effect. |
| †MAOIs[1] | X↑A↑ | Avoid adding HCAs to MAOIs: Risks hypertensive crisis, mania, muscular rigidity, convulsions, high fever, coma, and death. If HCAs are to be used, first taper MAOI, keep patient off MAOI for 10–14 days, maintain MAOI diet during this interval, and then slowly begin HCA. If combine HCAs and MAOIs, start both drugs together or stop HCAs for 2–3 days before adding MAOI. Best to *not* give (1) large doses, (2) IM/IV drugs, (3) imipramine with tranylcypromine, and (4) an MAOI to patients recently on SSRI or clomipramine. Trazodone only antidepressant consistently safe with MAOI, but may increase hypotension. |
| Morphine | X↑A↓ | CNS depression; may decrease HCA levels; common with amitriptyline and desipramine; HCA may augment opiate analgesia. |

*(Cont.)*

| Drugs (X) Interact with: | Antidepres- sants (A)[1] | Comments |
|---|---|---|
| Oral contraceptives (estrogen) | A↑ | Increased HCA level, effect, toxicity; inhibits HCA metabolism; higher estrogen doses may decrease HCA effect. |
| Pancuronium | A↑ | Increased tachyarrythmias with anticholinergic antidepressants; all HCAs; enflurane with d-tubocurine safer. |
| *Paroxetine | X↑A↑ | Increases HCA level (avg. 200%) and effects of both drugs. |
| Phenothiazines (see also antipsychotics) | X↑ A? | Increases neuroleptic and HCA plasma levels; increased cardiac arrythmias with thioridazine, clozapine, pimozide; increased anticholinergic and hypertensive effects but decreased EPS. |
| Phenylbutazone | X↓A↑ | HCAs may delay absorption of phenylbutazone; increases HCA due to displaced protein-bound HCA. |
| *Phenytoin | X↓A↑? | Lower seizure control; may decrease antidepressant plasma levels due to induced metabolism; may increase antidepressant plasma level due to displaced protein-bound HCA and with SSRI; venlafaxine may be safest alternative. Paroxetine levels decrease. |
| Prazosin | X↓ | Hypertension; safer to use bupropion, fluoxetine, desipramine, protriptyline. |
| Procainamide (see quinidine) | | |
| Propranolol | X↓↑A↓ | Patients may become more depressed on β-blockers; venlafaxine may reverse β-blocker effects; HCAs may exaggerate hypotension. |
| Quinidine | X↑A↑ | Because of HCAs' quinidine-like effects, possible myocardial depression, diminished contractility, and dysrhythmias, which can lead to congestive heart failure and heart block. Quinidine and HCAs may yield irregular heartbeat early on. |
| Reserpine | X↑A↑ | Patients may develop increased hypotension. |
| Scopolamine | A↑? | Possible increased antidepressant levels secondary to displaced protein-bound antidepressant. |
| *Sertraline | X↑A↑ | Increases HCA level (~30%) and effects of both drugs. |
| Sulfonylureas | X↑ | HCA enhances hypoglycemia in diabetics. |
| Thiazide diuretics | X↑A↑ | Increased hypotension with HCAs. |
| Thioridazine | A↑ | Increased HCA arrythmias. |
| Tobacco smoking | A↓ | Smoking may lower HCA plasma levels; importance unclear. |

[1] For extensive list of *potential* interactions with antidepressants, *see* Appendix P4502D6 and 3A3/4 lists.
* Moderately important reaction; †Extremely important interaction; ↑ Increases; ↓ Decreases; ↑↓ Increases and decreases; ? Unsure.

| Drugs (X) Interact with: | Amitriptyline (A) | Comments |
|---|---|---|
| Disulfiram | X↑ | Two cases of organic brain syndrome; cleared when both drugs stopped. |
| Ethchlorvynol | X↑ | Transient delirium. |
| Valproic acid | X↑A↑ | Increased plasma levels of both drugs. |

A
N
T
I
D
E
P
R
E
S
S
A
N
T
S

| Drugs (X) Interact with: | Desipramine (D) | Comments |
|---|---|---|
| Methadone | D↑ | Desipramine reported to increase by 108%; use together carefully. |

| Drugs (X) Interact with: | Doxepin (D) | Comments |
|---|---|---|
| Propoxyphene | D↑ | Propoxyphene doubles doxepin levels, inducing lethargy; five days after stopping propoxyphene, patient's mental status returns to normal. |

| Drugs (X) Interact with: | Fluoxetine (F) | Comments |
|---|---|---|
| Alprazolam | X↑ | Increased plasma level, confusion. Not seen with clonazepam or triazolam. |
| Diazepam | X↑ | Confusion. Not seen with clonazepam or triazolam. |
| Trazodone | X↑ | Increased plasma level. |
| Valproic Acid | X↑ | Increased plasma level. |

| Drugs (X) Interact with: | Fluvoxamine (F)[1] | Comments |
|---|---|---|
| Methadone | X↑ | Increased plasma level. |
| Theophylline | X↑ | Toxic plasma levels. P4501A2 inhibited by fluvoxamine but not other SSRIs. |
| Tacrine | X↑ | Fluvoxamine but not other SSRIs. |

[1] P4501A2 and 3A4 inhibitor (*see* Appendix, pages 464–66).

| Drugs (X) Interact with: | SSRI (S)[1]: Citalopram Fluoxetine Fluvoxamine[2] Paroxetine Sertraline[3] | Comments |
|---|---|---|
| β-blockers (*see* metoprolol) | | |
| Buspirone | S↑ | May augment antidepressant effect. |
| Calcium channel-blockers Nifedipine Verapamil | X↑ | Enhanced effect. |
| Dextromethorphan | X↑ S↑ | Hallucinogen-type reaction reported with fluoxetine—bright colors, distorted shapes; similar serotonergic effects possible with all SSRIs. |
| Carbamazepine (*see* P4502D6) | | |

| Drugs (X) Interact with: | SSRI (S)[1]: Citalopram Fluvoxetine Fluvoxamine[2] Paroxetine Sertraline[3] | Comments |
|---|---|---|
| Cyproheptadine (see seratonin 5HT2 receptor antagonists) | | |
| Digitoxin, digoxin | X↑ | Two cases of organic brain syndrome; cleared when both drugs stopped. SSRIs can free protein-bound digitoxin; no effect seen in healthy people. Increased plasma levels. |
| Furosemide | X↑ S↑ | Rarely SSRIs cause SIADH; additive hyponatremia result. |
| Lithium | X↑↓ | Lithium neurotoxicity may occur at normal levels. |
| L-tryptophan | X↑ | Serotonin syndrome. |
| *MAOI | X↑ S↑ | Prompt serotonin syndrome.[1] |
| Metoprolol, propranolol | X↑ | Bradycardia and heart block seen; other 2D6 metabolized include timolol and bufarol; consider atenolol as alternative. Probably increased levels of metoprolol and propranolol. |
| P4502D6 and 3A4 enzyme metabolized drugs: narrow therapeutic index—HCAs, carbamazepine, vinblastine, encainide, flecainide, dextromethorphan. | X↑ | All SSRIs inhibit 2D6 enzyme system; but fluvoxamine only 5%, and sertraline only 15–30% at starting dose. Fluvoxamine does increases imipramine, amitriptyline, and clomipramine by 1A2 path. Fluoxetine and fluvoxamine inhibit 3A4, thereby raising carbamazepine levels. |
| Neuroleptics | X↑ | Increased risk for EPS. Increased level for P4502D6 neuroleptics, haloperidol, perphenazine, thioridazine. Fluvoxamine least risk. |
| Procyclidine | X↑ | Paroxetine increases procyclidine levels (avg. ~35%); may occur with other SSRIs. |
| Serotonin 5HT2 receptor antagonists (cyproheptadine, risperidone, clozapine) | S↓ | Potentially reverses antidepressant effect. |
| Tryptophan | S↑ | Prompts agitation, restlessness, and GI distress. |
| Venlafaxine | X↑ | SSRIs potentially inhibit metabolism of venlafaxine. |
| Warfarin | X↑ | Increased bleeding time possibly due to anticoagulant effects of SSRIs. Displacement of protein-bound warfarin may sometimes occur. |

[1] See Appendix 2D6 interactions.
[2] Fluvoxamine's effects on P4502D6 are usually negligible.
[3] Sertraline's effects by 2D6 path, or P4502D6, are small at 50 mg but increase with dose.
* Moderately important reaction; †Extremely important interaction; ↑ Increases; ↓ Decreases; ↑↓ Increases and decreases; ? Unsure.

| Drugs (X) Interact with: | Maprotiline (M) | Comments |
|---|---|---|
| Propranolol | M↑ | Maprotiline toxicity. |

| Drugs (X) Interact with: | Trazodone (T) | Comments |
|---|---|---|
| *Barbiturates | T↑ | BP drops; avoid. |
| Digitalis | X↑ | Increases digitalis. |
| Clonidine, other antihypertensives | X↑ | May exaggerate hypotensive effects. Alpha drugs may increase priapism risk. |

* Moderately important reaction; †Extremely important interaction; ↑ Increases; ↓ Decreases; ↑↓ Increases and decreases; ? Unsure.

## EFFECTS ON LABORATORY TESTS

| Generic Names | Blood/Serum Tests** | Results* | Urine Tests | Results* |
|---|---|---|---|---|
| Amoxapine | WBC, LFT | ↓↑ | None | |
| Desipramine | Glucose | ↑↓ | None | |
| Doxepin | Glucose | ↑↓ | None | |
| Fluoxetine | ESR, bleeding time | ↑↑ | Albuminuria | |
| | Glucose | ↓ | | |
| | Cholesterol, lipids | ↑↑ | | |
| | Potassium, sodium | ↓↓ | | |
| | Iron | ↓ | | |
| | LFT | ↑↓ | | |
| HCAs | Glucose | ↑↓ | None | |
| Imipramine | Glucose | ↑↓ | None | |
| Maprotiline | Glucose | ↑↓ | None | |
| Nefazodone | Hematocrit (hemodilution) | ↓ | | |
| Nortriptyline | Glucose | ↑↓ | None | |
| Paroxetine | Sodium | ↓ | | |
| Sertraline | Bleeding time | | | |
| | ALT | ↑ | | |
| | Cholesterol | ↑ | | |
| | Triglycerides | ↑ | | |
| | Uric acid | ↓ | | |
| Trazodone | WBC, LFT | ↓↑ | None | |
| Venlafaxine | Cholesterol | ↑ | | |

* ↑ Increases; ↓ Decreases; ↑↓ Increases and decreases.
** LFT are liver function tests; AST (SGOT), ALT (SGPT), LDH, bilirubin, alkaline phosphatase.

## WITHDRAWAL

Antidepressants do not cause

- Dependence
- Tolerance
- Addiction, but
- HCAs and SSRIs have a withdrawal syndrome.

Probably because of cholinergic rebound (same symptoms as excessive dose of bethanechol, a cholinergic agonist; will often remit with pure anticholinergic drug), abruptly stopping HCAs can result in:

- Flu-like syndrome without fever
  - √ Anorexia, nausea, vomiting, diarrhea, queasy stomach, cramps
  - √ Increased salivation
  - √ Anxiety, agitation, irritability
  - √ Cold sweat
  - √ Tachycardia
  - √ Tension headache, neck pains
  - √ Chills, coryza, malaise, rhinorrhea, and dizziness
- Sleep disturbances
  - √ Insomnia
  - √ Hypersomnia
  - √ "Excessive" dreaming
  - √ Nightmares (due to REM rebound)
- Hypomanic or manic symptoms.

These withdrawal-like symptoms

- Begin 2–4 (and up to 7) days after suddenly stopping HCAs.
- Occasionally are seen as an interdose phenomenon while patient is still on TCA.
  - √ More likely on qd dosing.
  - √ Withdrawal symptoms seen few hours before next dose.
    - □ Treated with bid dosing.
- May persist 1–2 weeks.
- Are not life-threatening.
- Can be treated or prevented by gradually withdrawing HCAs (e.g., imipramine 25 mg q 2–3 days). Patient can titrate speed faster or slower, based on symptoms.

Studies have shown

- Somatic, GI symptoms occurred in 21–55% of adults acutely withdrawn from imipramine.
- 80% of adults developed symptoms within 2 weeks of being acutely withdrawn from amitriptyline.
- Children are more susceptible than adults.
- Amoxapine, if prescribed for a long time, can cause tardive dyskinesia (*see* pages 36–40).
  - √ May become apparent when the medication is withdrawn.

Sudden withdrawal of SSRIs, except fluoxetine (too long a half-life), can result in withdrawal syndrome with same features as HCA withdrawal, plus:

- Serotonergic "pre-migraine" features
  - √ Vertigo, often with emesis

√ Visual distortions
√ Headache, often migraine-like
√ Withdrawal from venlafzine
  □ Can occur between doses, even at correct amount
  □ Causes flu-like symptoms, dysphoria, and rebound depression

## OVERDOSE: TOXICITY, SUICIDE, AND TREATMENT

SSRIs, bupropion, mirtazapine, nefazodone, trazodone, and venlafaxine have extremely low lethality when taken alone.

- Seven fatal overdoses with fluoxetine alone.
- No fatal overdoses with others used alone.
- No predictable dose–toxicity relationship established.
- Nausea and vomiting most common with SSRI overdose.
  √ If without aspiration, may reduce risk of death.
- Seizures most common with bupropion, maprotiline, and clomipramine and seen occasionally with fluoxetine (*see* page 146).

General management of non-HCA antidepressant overdose:

- Establish and maintain airway, ensure adequate oxygenation and ventilation.
- Activated charcoal, which may be used with sorbitol, may be equally or more effective than emesis or lavage.
- Monitor cardiac vital signs.
- If seizures occur, consider IM or IV diazepam.

HCAs are prone to cause death by suicide; they are about 5–10 times more dangerous than low-potency antipsychotic agents.

- 10–20 mg/kg of HCAs result in moderate to severe toxicity.
- 30–40 mg/kg of HCAs are often fatal for adults.
  √ Often only 10–15 times daily therapeutic dose.
- Children have died from 20 mg/kg of imipramine.

There may be a latent period of 1–12 h between drug taking and toxicity.

Attempted and completed suicides seem to *decline* with *increased* (prescribed) HCA doses (and presumably, increased antidepressant effect).

| Daily Dose (mg) | Prevalence of Suicidal Behavior (%) |
|---|---|
| 0–74 | 30.4 |
| 75–149 | 10.1 |
| 150–249 | 5.1 |
| > 250 | 0.5 |

Because the antiarrythmic effects are similar for HCAs and phenothiazines, general management of overdoses is similar for both classes. See page 146.

In addition

- For cardiorespiratory problems:
  - √ Hypotension, dizziness (*see* page 140).
  - √ Cardiac arrhythmias
    - ▫ When QRS interval is <0.10, ventricular arrhythmias are less frequent.
    - ▫ Treat ventricular arrhythmias with phenytoin, lidocaine, or propranolol.
    - ▫ Phenytoin often preferred because it also treats seizures.
  - √ Supraventricular arrhythmias and
  - √ Cardiac conduction problems
    - ▫ Give IV sodium bicarbonate to achieve pH of 7.4–7.5.
    - ▫ Quinidine, procainamide, and disopyramide should be avoided in managing conduction problems and arrhythmia, since they further depress cardiac function.
  - √ Cardiac failure: Use digitalis.
- For severe urinary retention:
  - √ Acid-base problems are quite severe for TCA overdoses.
  - √ Acidosis is usually most severe.

## Toxicity and Suicide Data

| Generic Names | Toxicity Doses Average (Highest) (g) | Mortality Doses Average (Lowest) (g) | Toxic Levels ($\mu$g/ml) | Lethal Supplies (days) |
|---|---|---|---|---|
| Amitriptyline | 1.343 (2) | 2.166 (0.50) | $\geq$1 | 10 |
| Desipramine | — | — | $\geq$1 | 12 |
| Imipramine | 3.1 (5.375) | 3.619 (0.50) | $\geq$1 | 10 |
| Mirtazapine | 2.0 (8) | — | $\geq$1 | 40+ |
| Nortriptyline | — | — | $\geq$1 | 15 |
| Fluoxetine | 3 | 1.8* | 2,461 ng/ml | 90+ |

* Mixed overdose with maprotiline.

√ Dialysis is generally useless because of low drug concentrations.

√ Void patient by catheter if no recent voiding.

## PRECAUTIONS

HCAs are contraindicated in patients with h/o

- Cardiovascular problems, hypertension, and acute myocardial infarction.
  √ Hyperthyroidism might foster cardiovascular toxicity, including arrhythmias.
- Using MAOIs, or having consumed them, within past 14 days.
- Hypersensitivity to TCAs.
- Narrow-angle glaucoma.
- Increased intraocular pressure.
- Seizures
  √ Consider agent other than bupropion, maprotiline, or clomipramine in patients prone to develop seizures due to head injury, neurologic disease, active alcohol or drug abuse, h/o anorexia nervosa or bulimia.
  √ Avoid clomipramine > 250 mg/day in adults and 3 mg/kg (or 200 mg) in children and adolescents.
  √ Secondary amine TCAs do not appreciably lower the seizure threshold.

HCAs can precipitate mania in 12–50% of bipolar patients and increase the chance of rapid cycling.

- It is common for patients recovering from depression to undergo a "switch phase" into a "high" before returning to normality.
  √ This "high" might last only a day and is not worth "overtreating," yet if a true switch has uncovered a manic process, it is best to treat by
    □ Reducing or stopping TCA dose, or
    □ Adding or pretreating with lithium.
- Although HCA abuse is rare, amitriptyline abuse, with doses up to 2000 mg/day, causes intoxication, followed by prolonged sleep and retrograde amnesia. Halting amitriptyline can be difficult; active treatment is required.

Fluoxetine and paroxetine can significantly (100–1,000%) increase plasma levels of HCAs and cause toxicity.

- Occasionally fluoxetine is abused for its usually transient stimulating effects.

Venlafaxine can cause hypertension (*see* Side Effects).

- Monitor BP regularly.

Sertraline increases HCA plasma levels about 30% and occasionally much higher.

Nefazodone can cause bradycardia.

- Monitor heart rate.

## NURSES' DATA

Depressed patients may be suicidal, and therefore

- Monitor for "cheeking," hoarding, or suicidal indications.
- A sudden disappearance of a side effect (e.g., dry mouth) suggests hiding medication.

Remind patient (and family) that there is a 7–28-day lag on a full therapeutic dose before ADs fully work.

- Remind patient frequently (1–3 times a day), since depressed patients have trouble remembering or believing and need ongoing reassurance.

For constipation, have patient (especially the elderly) ingest fluids and foods with fiber.

Reassure patient on HCA that drowsiness, dizziness, and hypotension usually subside after first few weeks.

- Hypotension is more common among cardiac patients.
  √ Hypotensives often injure themselves.
- For dizzy patients, review hypotension instructions (*see* page 140).

Avoid extreme heat and humidity, as HCAs alter temperature regulation.

Reassure patient on SSRIs that nausea often disappears in 7–14 days. Ask about anxiety, agitation, sexual dysfunction, and overarousal. Too often patients do not report these symptoms, assuming it's their illness.

Help patient find right time of day to take SSRI (activated or sedated?).

- Fluoxetine is usually best in the A.M.
- Paroxetine sedation is not necessarily related to time of ingestion.

Tell male patients about trazodone's rare (1:6,000) but dangerous side effect of priapism, a painful, persistent erection that requires *immediate* treatment.

A
N
T
I
D
E
P
R
E
S
S
A
N
T
S

## PATIENT AND FAMILY NOTES

Tell patients that antidepressants are neither "uppers" nor are they addicting; indeed, they take 1–4 weeks to take effect. The most common side effects for HCAs are dry mouth, constipation, urinary hesitancy, and a lightheaded, dizzy feeling on standing. Most HCAs can also be sedating and should be taken at night to help sleep and reduce daytime sedation. Desipramine and protriptyline can be activating and first should be tried in the morning.

SSRIs (citalopram, fluoxetine, fluvoxamine, paroxetine, sertraline) have different side effects; the most common are nausea, diarrhea, overactivation, insomnia, dizziness, dry mouth, tremor, and drowsiness.

The majority of patients do not get any of these side effects. In a mild form the activating side effect can help increase energy in the morning. If drowsiness occurs, sleep might be enhanced.

In a few patients on venlafaxine, blood pressure goes up; this doesn't usually happen, but just in case, blood pressure should be monitored.

Once the AD takes full effect, patient will need to stay on it another 4–6 months.

- Depression is somewhat like a broken leg: The patient may feel better, but this doesn't mean the healing process is over.
  √ The healing process for depression is usually 6 or more months.
    □ If antidepressants are stopped sooner than this, there is a 50% chance of relapse.
    □ If there is a major emotional crisis at the planned time of stopping, delay stopping until the crisis has passed.

When starting HCAs or mirtazapine, nefazodone, or trazodone, patients should be careful driving cars, working around machines, and crossing streets. When first on HCAs, drive briefly in a safe place, since reflexes might be a tad off. This is less likely with other ADs, but same precaution should be followed.

TCAs potentiate alcohol: "One drink feels like 2 drinks."

- Although SSRIs, bupropion, and venlafaxine don't potentiate alcohol, recommend against drinking while depressed.

Patients can take most ADs at any time; food affects only trazodone and sertraline.

- Trazodone's absorption is increased by 20% with food vs. an empty stomach.

√ More is absorbed, but peak plasma levels are lowered and delayed.

√ Take trazodone with meals or all at bedtime.

√ Sertraline absorption is increased about 25% when taken after a meal.

  □ May try this before increasing, and paying, for a higher dose.

Keep ADs away from bedside or any readily accessible place, where they might be secured by "accident." Store safely away from eager children.

If possible, ingest full dose of HCAs at bedtime to reduce experience of side effects. If patient forgets at bedtime (or once-a-day dose), consume it within 3 h; otherwise

- Wait for next dose.
- Do not double the dose.

For SSRIs, patient may prefer taking once-a-day dose earlier in day. If forgotten, patient can take it within 8 h, unless side effect of insomnia prevents this.

Suddenly stopping ADs can trigger a flu-like syndrome with symptoms of nausea, bad dreams, fast heart beat, aches and chills without a fever in 2–4 days.

- If this happens, call doctor.
- If cannot reach doctor, have patient swallow one AD tablet until a physician is contacted.

# 4. Monoamine-Oxidase Inhibitors

## INTRODUCTION

This chapter discusses monoamine-oxidase inhibitor (MAOI) treatment of

Other chapters examine the MAOI treatment of

## NAMES, CLASSES, MANUFACTURERS, DOSE FORMS, COLORS

| Generic Name | Brand Name | Manufacturers | Dose Forms (mg)* | Colors |
|---|---|---|---|---|
| | | **HYDRAZINES** | | |
| Isocarboxazid | Marplan | Oxford | t: 10 | t: peach |
| Phenelzine | Nardil | Parke-Davis | t: 15 | t: orange |
| | | **NONHYDRAZINE** | | |
| Tranylcypromine | Parnate | SmithKline Beecham | t: 10 | t: rose-red |
| | | **OTHERS** | | |
| Selegiline** | Eldepryl | Somerset | t: 5 | t: white |

*t = tablets.
**Selegiline (formerly called L-deprenyl) primarily for Parkinson's disease.

## PHARMACOLOGY

MAOIs best treat depression when at least 80% of platelet MAO levels are inhibited.

- MAO-A
  - √ Preferentially oxidizes tyramine, dopamine, and phenylethylamine.
  - √ Found mainly in intestinal tract, lungs, and brain.
  - √ Generally responsible for tyramine's hypertensive effect.
- MAO-B
  - √ Preferentially oxidizes norepinephrine and serotonin.
  - √ Also capable of oxidizing tyramine and dopamine, but this is a minor pathway.
  - √ Found mainly in the brain and in platelets.
  - √ Generally associated with antidepressant effect.
- Platelets and neurons are similar partly because both have
  - √ Membrane pump that concentrates serotonin.
  - √ Vesicles containing serotonin and MAO.
  - √ However, low to no correlation between platelet MAO-B and brain MAO-B inhibition.
    - □ Phenelzine yields slightly better association than tranylcypromine, with isocarboxazid in between.
- Tranylcypromine and some of its metabolites resemble amphetamine.
  - √ Can have direct stimulating effect.
- 80% of platelet MAO levels are usually inhibited by 60 mg/day of phenelzine or 1 mg/kg.

- MAOIs interfere with hepatic metabolism of many drugs (e.g., barbiturates, atropine).

MAOIs are either hydrazines or nonhydrazines.

- Hydrazines (e.g., phenelzine, isocarboxazid) irreversibly inhibit MAO.
  √ Their actions persist after stopping the drug and stop when enzyme resynthesis occurs (about 10–20 days).
- Nonhydrazines (e.g., tranylcypromine) are also irreversible inhibitors of MAO, but this action begins and ends more rapidly.
  √ Their effects begin sooner (within 10 days) and end faster (within 3–5 days).
- Selegiline is relatively selective for MAO-B up to 10 mg/day and nonselective at 50 mg qd.
  √ Hypertensive risk and antidepressant effect increase with dosage > 20 mg/day.

Plasma half-lives in h (tissue half-lives far longer):

- Phenelzine: 2.8 (1.5–4)
- Isocarboxazid: similar to phenelzine
- Tranylcypromine: 2.4 (1.54–3.15)

## DOSES

| Generic Names | Equivalent Doses (mg) | Usual Doses (mg/day) | Extreme Range (mg/day) | Starting Doses (mg/day) | Geriatric Doses (mg/day) |
|---|---|---|---|---|---|
| Isocarboxazid | 10 | 10–30 | 10–50 | 30 | 5–15 |
| Phenelzine | 15 | 45–60 | 30–145 | 15 | 15–45 |
| Tranylcypromine | 10 | 20–40 | 10–150 | 10 | 10–30 |

## CLINICAL INDICATIONS AND USE

Studies indicate that

- Overall, HCAs, SSRIs, and MAOIs yield the same improvement rates.
- HCAs and SSRIs are equal to MAOIs in treating the nonpsychotic depressions (i.e., major depression, dysthymic disorder).
- TCAs with antipsychotics are superior to MAOIs in treating psychotic depression, although ECT may be better than either drug.
- MAOIs are probably superior to TCAs in treating atypical depression (*see* page 183), treatment-resistant depression, and depression with panic disorder.

√ SSRIs may be nearly as good as MAOIs for these diagnoses.

√ For unknown reasons, women respond significantly better to MAOIs than men.

- MAOIs successfully treat 55–70% of depressions, both typical and atypical, that fail to respond to other antidepressants.
  - √ May need higher than usual MAOI doses (75–150 mg range).
  - √ Tranylcypromine highly effective in anergic bipolar depression resistant to HCA.
    - ▫ Does not appear to have high risk for inducing mania.
    - ▫ Phenelzine may also be effective.

In elderly patients

- MAOIs may be better tolerated than TCAs because they are less anticholinergic; however, because the elderly are at greater risk for hypotension, and MAOIs may increase this risk, tranylcypromine may be preferred.
- MAOIs may alleviate depression in demented patients.
  - √ Careful supervision of diet by responsible other is essential.

### Choosing an MAOI

Sometimes MAOI side effects or differences in efficacy help in choosing an MAOI.

*When to choose phenelzine:*

- Patient has
  - √ Panic attacks (more controlled studies).
    - ▫ Superior to TCAs in depression with panic attacks.
  - √ Social phobia (more controlled studies).
  - √ Hypertension
    - ▫ MAOIs are antihypertensives in the absence of dietary indiscretions.
    - ▫ MAOIs are not contraindicated in hypertension controlled by antihypertensives; hypertensive crisis no more likely.
    - ▫ Tranylcypromine occasionally causes acute (1–3 h) transient mild hypertension after ingestion, but phenelzine rarely does.
  - √ Primary insomnia
    - ▫ Somewhat better sleep with phenelzine.

*When to choose tranylcypromine:*

- Patient has
  - √ Obesity: weight gain common (74%) with phenelzine; weight loss sometimes with tranylcypromine.

✓ Diabetes: phenelzine can decrease glucose and increase weight.

✓ Primary sexual dysfunction: phenelzine can worsen it (22%).

✓ Bipolar anergic depression: more research with tranylcypromine.

  ▫ Most patients had reverse (atypical) vegetative symptoms.

*When to choose isocarboxazid:*

- Patient has
  ✓ Not responded to one or both other MAOIs or has developed tolerance to therapeutic effects.
  ✓ Significant side effects that decrease clinical outcome.
    ▫ Isocarboxazid has lower risk of too much activation or sedation.
    ▫ Phenelzine more often causes sedation.
    ▫ Tranylcypromine more often causes excessive activation.

To start therapy

- Tell patient most common acute side effects are mild hypotension, dizziness, palpitations, dry mouth, and sedation.
- Begin with one tablet on first day.
- Boost by one tablet q 1–2 days,
- Until reach 60 mg of phenelzine, 40 mg of tranylcypromine, or 30 mg of isocarboxazid.
  ✓ 1 mg/kg may be usual best dose for phenelzine.
- May note some improvement after 2–3 days, particularly with tranylcypromine.
- If patient has insomnia with MAOIs, give the last dose before 6 P.M., or at lunch.
- Tranylcypromine is the most stimulating MAOI and usually needs to be given earlier in day.
- Phenelzine exerts a mild to moderate hypnoanxiolytic effect.
  ✓ May help with sleep.
  ✓ Can paradoxically cause insomnia at night and hypersomnia during day.

To hasten MAOI effects, may wish to *add*

- Lithium—plasma level ~ 0.6 mEq/l.
- $T_3$ 50 $\mu$g qd.
  ✓ $T_3$ 25 $\mu$g does not speed MAOI response.
- Pindolol 2.5–5 mg tid may augment MAOI.
  ✓ Monitor for hypotension.
  ✓ May increase risk of serotonin syndrome ($5HT_{1A}$ antagonist).

MONOAMINE OXIDASE INHIBITORS

- Phenylalanine 500–2000 mg qd in divided A.M. doses.
  - √ Modest elevation in BP and insomnia are main risks.
  - √ More often effective in females than males.

### General Considerations

- Negative results from early MAOI studies were partly due to low doses.
- Plasma levels are not used with MAOIs, but platelet MAO levels sometimes obtained.
  - √ Platelet MAO levels are not usually recommended.
  - √ Platelet MAOs are still very expensive and not reliable, because there is poor correlation between platelet MAO-B (what is measured) and brain MAO-B inhibition.

### Flow Chart for Treating MAOI-Resistant Patients Who Already Have Failed TCAs, SSRIs, Venlafaxine, Nefazodone, Mirtazepine

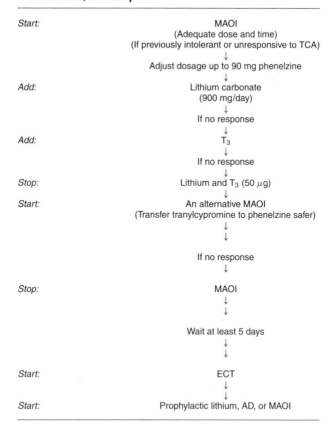

| | |
|---|---|
| *Start:* | MAOI<br>(Adequate dose and time)<br>(If previously intolerant or unresponsive to TCA)<br>↓<br>Adjust dosage up to 90 mg phenelzine<br>↓ |
| *Add:* | Lithium carbonate<br>(900 mg/day)<br>↓<br>If no response<br>↓ |
| *Add:* | $T_3$<br>↓<br>If no response<br>↓ |
| *Stop:* | Lithium and $T_3$ (50 $\mu$g)<br>↓ |
| *Start:* | An alternative MAOI<br>(Transfer tranylcypromine to phenelzine safer)<br>↓<br>↓<br><br>If no response<br>↓ |
| *Stop:* | MAOI<br>↓<br>↓<br><br>Wait at least 5 days<br>↓<br>↓ |
| *Start:* | ECT<br>↓<br>↓ |
| *Start:* | Prophylactic lithium, AD, or MAOI |

- Worthless to only measure platelet MAO after treatment.
  - √ Does not measure % of inhibition.
  - √ Need to have baseline MAO activity as reference.
- MAOIs can completely suppress REM sleep.
  - √ In many patients onset of therapeutic response may be correlated with onset of full REM suppression.
- MAOIs lose their antidepressant effects more often than other antidepressants.
  - √ Frequently this tolerance is specific to the MAOI used.
  - √ If tolerance develops, first try higher doses; if this fails
    - □ Change to another MAOI or
    - □ Add augmentation.
  - √ Later, if tolerance develops to second MAOI, patient may again respond to first MAOI.

## Atypical Depression

MAOIs, particularly phenelzine, are preferred for atypical depression, whose symptoms (as listed below) are often the opposite of melancholia. Patients with only one of the following symptoms (indicated with asterisk) may have < 50% chance of TCA response, but still have ~ 70% chance of MAOI response.

- Depressed mood reactive to environmental events and many of the following:
  - √ Overeating, increased appetite, weight gain*
  - √ Carbohydrate or sweet craving
  - √ Hypersomnia, more time in bed, or initial insomnia*
  - √ "Rejection-sensitivity"*
  - √ Profound anergia, "leaden paralysis"*
  - √ Feeling better in the morning and worse as the day proceeds (a reverse diurnal mood variation)
  - √ Phobic anxiety
  - √ Panic attacks*
  - √ Hypochondriasis/somatization
- Mood reactivity does not predict
  - √ Lowered TCA response.
- MAOIs also superior to placebo and TCAs in
  - √ Mild atypical depression (83% response).
  - √ Chronic atypical depression (70% response).
- MAOIs work equally as well on atypical depressions as on typical depressions.
- SSRIs are effective, and bupropion may also be effective in atypical depressions.

√ Adequate data on venlafaxine, mirtazepine, and nefazodone are not yet available.

## Borderline Personality Disorder

Some drugs treat borderline personality disorder traits with modest effects. If any agent is prescribed, target specific symptoms.

These agents often include

- Antipsychotics for cognitive problems ("cognitive disorganization under stress"), transient psychosis, and hostilities.
- Lithium for mood swings.
- Benzodiazepines for chronic anxiety (but disinhibition often seen).
- ADs for depression.
  √ SSRIs probably as effective as MAOIs.
  √ TCAs are less effective.
    ▫ Borderlines usually prefer MAOI over imipramine for mood swings.
- Carbamazepine or valproic acid to decrease behavioral outbursts and mood swings.

Overall, borderlines do better with MAOIs, SSRIs, or anticonvulsants (i.e., carbamazepine or valproic acid). Neuroleptics best used prn. Neuroleptics over time only decrease hostility and cognitive disorganization under stress. Benzodiazepines risk disinhibition, sedation, and withdrawal symptoms.

Always be alert to potential for overdose.

## Dysthymic Disorder

Dysthymic disorder is similar to major depression, but dysthymia

- Is chronic for at least 2 years
- Has no distinct onset
- Has fluctuating or vague neurovegetative signs

Treatment of dysthymic disorder is controversial.

- If it more closely resembles a major depression, SSRIs or TCAs are the drugs of choice.
  √ Need 6–8 weeks trial to show full effect over placebo.
  √ At 4 weeks in mild-moderate dysthymics, imipramine and placebo helped 50% of patients.
  √ At 6 weeks with imipramine, 70% were improved, but placebo was starting to slip back from 50%.

√ In a fluoxetine vs. placebo study, 63% responded by 8 weeks and only 19% responded to placebo.

Significant improvement compared to placebo didn't occur until 6 to 8 weeks.

- If it more closely resembles an atypical depression, SSRIs or MAOIs are the drug of choice.

## Serotonergic and Noradrenergic Interactions

Combining MAOIs and HCAs or venlafaxine can generate 2 major problems:

- *Serotonergic crisis (hyperthermic reaction)*
  √ Combining MAOI with SSRI, venlafaxine, mirtazepine, imipramine, clomipramine, or nefazodone risks serotonergic crisis.
- *Noradrenergic crisis (hypertensive reaction)*
  √ Combining MAOI with HCA, venlafaxine, bupropion, or possibly mirtazepine risks noradrenergic crisis.
- However, nonserotonergic TCAs have been safely combined with MAOIs if TCA not added to MAOI but both started together or MAOI added to TCA.

| Serotonergic Crisis Characterized by | Noradrenergic Crisis Characterized by |
|---|---|
| Elevated temperature, fever | Hypertension (BP increases 30–60 points) |
| Abnormal muscle movements, such as fasciculations, twitches, myoclonic jerking | Occipital headaches (often radiate frontally and can be violent) |
| Hyperreflexia | Stiff or sore neck |
| Generalized seizures (rarely) | Retroorbital pain |
| *May see* | Flushing, sweating, cold and clammy skin |
| Hypotension | Tachycardia > bradycardia |
| Anxiety, agitation | Nausea, vomiting |
| Shivering | *If severe, may see* |
| Enhanced startle response | Sudden unexplained nosebleeds |
| Insomnia | Dilated pupils, visual disturbances |
| Confusion, delirium | Photophobia |
| Seizures, shock | Constricting chest pains |
| Death | Stroke or coma |
| | Death |

MONOAMINE OXIDASE INHIBITORS

| Serotonergic Crisis Caused by<br>Adding to an MAOI | Noradrenergic Crisis Caused by<br>Adding to an MAOI |
| --- | --- |
| HCAs, mainly clomipramine and imipramine<br>SSRIs<br>Meperidine<br>Propoxyphene (1 case report)<br>Tryptophan<br>Dextromethorphan<br>Diphenoxylate?<br>Fenfluramine<br>Venlafaxine<br>Nefazodone | HCA, mainly desipramine<br>Tyramine-containing foods<br>Stimulants<br>Ephedrine<br>Isometheptine<br>Pseudoephedrine<br>Phenylephrine<br>Phenylpropanolamine<br>Venlafaxine<br>Buspirone<br>Sympathomimetics |

Drugs with tricyclic structure

- Cyclobenzaprine (Flexeril), a muscle relaxant.
  √ Can potentiate norepinephrine, hypertensive crisis.
- Carbamazepine
  √ Is a very weak norepinephrine reuptake blocker and essentially has no serotonin uptake blocking.
    □ Hypertensive or hyperthermic crisis not reported or likely.

Serotonergic and noradrenergic crises are escalated by

- Dose
- Sequence of medications
- May start MAOI and TCA together, both in low doses initially; or
- Safer to add MAOI to amitriptyline, doxepin, or trimipramine.
- Avoid adding MAOI to imipramine, desipramine, venlafaxine, mirtazepine, nefazodone, bupropion, or SSRIs.
  √ These TCAs and bupropion risk noradrenergic crisis, and SSRIs, nefazodone, and possibly high doses of venlafazine or mirtazepine risk serotonergic crisis.
- Before starting MAOI, must stop fluoxetine 5–6 weeks and paroxetine or sertraline for 2 weeks.

Sleep problems with MAOIs may be relieved by adding

- Trazodone; no dangerous interaction reported, but may potentiate hypotension.
  √ Occasional reports of subthreshold serotonin syndrome.
    □ Increased muscle twitches.
- Benzodiazepine hypnotic.
- Sedating TCAs; small potential for hypertension.
  √ On amitriptyline, 60–80% of patients have no rise in BP.

## Adding or Replacing MAOIs,* TCAs, and SSRIs

| Start With | Add/Substitute | Risks and Instructions |
|---|---|---|
| TCA | MAOI | Lower risk of reaction; reduce TCA dose by 50%, slowly add MAOI, taper TCA over 2 weeks. |
| MAOI | TCA | High risk of reaction; wait 2–4 weeks for phenelzine and 7–10 days for tranylcypromine between stopping MAOI and starting TCA. |
| MAOI + TCA together | | Lower risk of reaction; raise doses slowly. |
| SSRI/clomipramine | MAOI | High risk of hyperthermic reaction; do not start MAOI until fluoxetine stopped for 5 weeks or negative in serum; and until clomipramine, sertraline, and paroxetine stopped for 2 weeks. |
| MAOI | SSRI clomipramine | High risk of hyperthermic reaction; do not overlap; wait at least 2 weeks between stopping MAOI and starting SSRIs or clomipramine. May need to wait 4–6 weeks if on fluoxetine. |
| MAOI hydrazine (phenelzine) | MAOI nonhydrazine (tranylcypromine) | High risk of hypertensive reaction; wait 2–4 weeks before replacing with nonhydrazine. |
| MAOI nonhydrazine (tranylcypromine) | MAOI hydrazine (phenelzine) | Moderate-low risk of hypertensive reaction; wait 10–14 days before replacing with hydrazine. |
| MAOI | Surgery, dental work, ECT | Peripheral epinephrine metabolism is mainly dependent on catechol-O-methyltransferase(COMT), which is diffusely found in all extraneuronal tissues. As expected, there are no reports of hypertensive crisis with epinephrine because MAOIs do not block its metabolism. However, norepinephrine is mainly degraded by MAO localized to nerve terminals and risks hypertensive crisis. |

*Includes selegiline, used in higher doses risks hypertensive crisis or serotonin syndrome.

□ Limited research suggests that amitriptyline may even protect 50% of patients from hypertensive crisis with dietary indiscretion.

Give patients

• A wallet card describing the MAOI regimen (obtained from Parke-Davis, a division of Pfizer/Roerig, at 800/223-0432).
• MAOI diet and drug information (see below).
• Instructions on how to take their own blood pressure. Sometimes headache is described as feeling as if the top of the head were

being ripped off. Fire departments will also take BP. (However, not every bad headache is a hypertensive crisis.)

√ If diastolic BP > 120 or systolic > 175
   ▫ Risk of kidney damage highest, then
   ▫ Cardiac or brain (stroke) damage.

√ Treat with nifedipine 10 mg (give patient several for wallet, purse, glove compartment, etc.).
   ▫ For fastest actions, bite capsule open and swallow.
   ▫ Check BP in 30 minutes; if still elevated, repeat nifedipine and go to ER.
   ▫ Nifedipine has occasionally caused significant hypotension, which is treated by lying down on a slant with feet up at an angle and head down.
   ▫ Failing this, meds to raise BP should be given with volume expansion meds, which are safer than powerful pressure agents.

- If any doubts, go to ER immediately.

Emergency room interventions for hypertensive crisis include

- Nifedipine (as above) and
- Phenotolamine 5–10 mg IV slowly.
- If severe reaction, sodium nitroprusside IV slowly.

### Potentially Dangerous Over-the-Counter and Prescription Drug Products*

| Ephedrine |
| --- |
| Broncholate CS, softgels, syrup |
| Bronkaid |
| Bronkolixer |
| Marax |
| Mudrane tablets, gel, G elixer |
| Pazo hemorrhoid ointment |
| Primatene |
| Quadrinal tablets |
| Rynatuss tablets and suspension |
| Vicks Vatronel nose drops |

| Phenylephrine | Phenylpropanolamine |
|---|---|
| Atrohist suspension and plus tablets | Atrohist plus tablets |
| Cerose-DM | Alka-Seltzer plus cold and nighttime cold medicine |
| Codimal | A.R.M. allergy relief |
| Congespirin for children | Acutrim appetite pills |
| Comhist LA capsules | Allerest allergy, headache |
| D.A. chewable tablets | BC cold powder |
| Dallergy caplets, tablets | Bayer children's cough and cold remedies |
| Deconsal sprinkle capsules | Cheracol plus head cold/cough formula |
| Despec liquid | Comtrex multi-symptom cold reliever |
| Donatussin DC and drops | Contac decongestants |
| Dimetane decongestant | Coricidin "D" decongestants |
| Dristan decongestant | Coricidin maximum strength |
| Dristan nasal spray | Despec caps, liquid |
| Duo-medihaler | Dexatrim appetite pills |
| Dura-gest | Dimetane-DC cough syrup |
| Duratex | Dimetapp |
| Dura-vent | Duadacin cold and allergy |
| Endel-HD | Dura-Gest |
| Entex capsules and liquid | Duratex |
| Extendryl chewable tablets, Jr. and Sr. T.D. | Dura-Vent |
|   capsules and 4-Way fast-acting nasal | E.M.T. |
|   spray—new formula Histussin | Entex capsules and liquid |
| Hycomine compound | Entex LA capsules |
| Neo-Synephrine nasal spray and nose drops | Exgest LA tablets |
| Nostril nasal decongestant | 4-Way cold tablets |
| Novahistine elixir and DMX | Gelpirin |
| Pediacof cough syrup | Hycomine syrup |
| Phenergan | Naldecon CX, DX, EX |
| Prefrin liquifilm | Nolamine timed-release tablets |
| Protid | Nolex LA tablets |
| R-Tannate tablets and suspension | Ornade spansule caps |
| Relief eye drops | Phenylpropanolamine HCL and guaifenesin |
| Robitussin night relief | Poly-Histine |
| Ru-Tuss | Propagest tablets |
| Rynatan tablets and suspension | Robitussin-CF |
| Rynatus tablets | Ru-Tuss II caps |
| St. Joseph's nasal congestant | Ru-Tuss with hydrocodone |
| Triotann suspension and tablets | Sinarest |
| Vanex forte and HD | Sine-off sinus |
| Vicks sinex decongestant nasal | Simulin tablets |
|   spray and ultra fine mist | Snaplets-DM, EX St. Joseph's cold tablets |
| | Triaminic |
| | Triaminicin |
| | Triaminicol |
| | Tylenol cold medication |
| | Vanex-forte |

| Pseudoephedrine | | Dextromethorphan (also any drug name with *DM* or *Tuss* in it) |
|---|---|---|
| Actifed | Ornex | Anatuss DM syrup and tablets |
| AllerAct | P.V. Tussin syrup | Bromarest DM |
| Allerest no drowsy formula | Pediacare | Bromarest DX |
| Anatuss LA tablets |   Pediacare cold- | Bromfed DM |
| Anatuss DM |   allergy chewable | Cerose DM |
| |   tablets | |

M
O
N
O
A
M
I
N
E

O
X
I
D
A
S
E

I
N
H
I
B
I
T
O
R
S

| Pseudoephedrine | | Dextromethorphan (also any drug name with *DM* or *Tuss* in it) |
|---|---|---|
| Atrohist sprinkle capsules | Pediacare cold-allergy chewable tablets | Cheracol |
| Benadryl combinations | | Cheracol plus |
| Bomarest DX cough syrup | Pediacare Infants decongestant drops | Codimal DM |
| Brexin LA capsules | | Comtrex multi-symptom cold reliever |
| Bromfed capsules (timed release) | Pediacare nightrest | Comtrex day and night |
| Bromfed DM cough syrup | Pseudoephedrine hydrochloride tablets | Comtrex non-drowsy |
| Bromfed tablets | Robitussin DAC syrup | Dimetane DX cough syrup |
| Bromfed-PD capsules | Robitussin PE | Dristan cold and flu |
| CoAdvil | Rondec | Dristan juice mix-in |
| Codimal LA capsules | Ru-Tuss DE tablets | Humibid DM sprinkle and tab |
| Comtrex allergy sinus | Ryna, C, CX | Iodur DM |
| Comtrex cough formula | Seldane D tablets | Iotuss DM |
| Comtrex multi-symptom | Sinarest no drowsiness | Par-glycerol DM |
| Congess Jr. TD capsules | Sine-aid IB caplets | Pedia care cough-cold |
| Congess Sr. TD capsules | Sine-aid maximum strength | Pedia care night rest |
| Contac cold and sinus | Sine-Off, no drowsiness | Phenergan with dextromethorphan |
| Dallergy Jr. capsules | Sinutab | Poly-histine DM |
| Deconsal II Tablets | Sudafed | Quelidine poly-histine DM |
| Dimacol | Touro LA caplets | Rescon DM |
| Dimetane DX cough syrup | Touro A&H capsules | Robitussin DM |
| Dorcol cough and decongestant | Triaminic night light | Rondec DM |
| Dristan maximum strength | Trinalin tablets | Safe tussin 30 |
| Dura-Tap/PD capsules | Tuss DA RX | Touro DM |
| Duratuss HD | Tussafed drops and syrup | Tusibron DM |
| Duratuss tablets | Tussar DM | Tuss DA |
| Entex PSE tablets | Tussar SF | Tussafed drops and syrup |
| Excedrin sinus | Tussar-2 | Tussar DM |
| Fedahist | Tylenol allergy sinus medicated gelcaps | Tussi-organidin DM |
| Guaifed capsules | | Tylenol children's cold plus cough liquid formula |
| Guaifed PD capsules | Tylenol allergy sinus nighttime caplets | Tylenol cold and flu no drowsiness and hot medic |
| Guaimax D tablets | Tylenol cold | |
| Isoclor | Tylenol cold and flu | Tylenol cold medication |
| Kronofed A Jr. | Tylenol cough | Tylenol cough medication |
| Lodrane LD capsules | Tylenol flu | Tylenol flu maximum |
| Nasabid capsules | Tylenol med | |
| Novafed A capsules | Tylenol sinus | |
| Novafed capsules | Vick's 44-D, 44-M | |
| Novahistine DMX | Vick's DAycare daytime cold | |
| Nucofed expectorant | Vick's NyQuil | |
| | Vick's Pediatric | |
| | Zehrex LA tablets | |
| | Zephrex tablets | |

* Warning: However complete these lists may appear, there are always new names and new products that might contain drugs that potentiate dangerous MAOI interactions. All cold and cough medicines are forbidden until proven safe (e.g., diphenydramine is safe).

- Prescription and street drugs to avoid or be cautious of (*see* Drug-Drug Interactions for complete list, pages 206–8).
    - √ Sympathomimetics—avoid indirect and mixed-acting agents.
        - □ Less or no effects from direct-acting agents.
    - √ Anti-asthma drugs (bronchodilators)
        - □ Avoid ephedrine.
        - □ Beclomethasone and other nonsystemic steroid inhalers are safer than inhalers containing metaproterenol, albuterol, or other $\beta$-adrenergic bronchodilators.
        - □ Asthma patients on MAOIs should have BP and HR measured in office after using their particular bronchodilating drug(s). Most have no problem, but should be carefully monitored.
    - √ Antihypertensive drugs, especially
        - □ Guanethidine
        - □ Reserpine
    - √ Meperidine and dextromethorphan (can be lethal)
    - √ Amphetamines, "pep-pills," appetite suppressants
    - √ Cocaine, crack
    - √ Dopa (dihydroxyphenylalanine), dopamine, levodopa bronchodilating
        - □ L-dopa usually can be used safely at lower doses than usual.
    - √ Buspirone (elevated BP seen)
        - □ Serotonin syndrome possible.
- Drugs with lower (or no) risk than previously thought:
    - √ Epinephrine, exogenously administered (or as excreted from adrenals), is not mainly metabolized by MAO (intracellular).
        - □ No reports in literature of epinephrine-induced hypertension while on MAOI.
        - □ Patients with severe allergic reactions can safely get epinephrine.
        - □ Some may prefer to do an in-office challenge of epinephrine first to be completely safe.
    - √ Avoid norepinephrine; it is mainly metabolized by MAO and risks hypertensive crisis.
    - √ Opiates
        - □ Meperidine proven dangerous.
        - □ Morphine and oxycodone presumed safe.
        - □ Start at 20–50% of usual dose and monitor 15–60 minutes later.
    - √ Anesthetics
        - □ May prolong expected sedative or hypotensive effects, but not contraindicated.

MONOAMINE OXIDASE INHIBITORS

□ Powerful pressor agents may cause hypertension; deamination may be slowed; use low dose or avoid; volume expansion is safer.

□ If tranylcypromine discontinued, wait only 7 days for normal MAO activity to return.

Foods containing at least 6–8 mg tyramine per serving usually needed to precipitate hypertensive crisis with phenelzine.

√ For most people, ≥ 10 mg tyramine in 4 hours is risky.

√ For people on tranylcypromine, ≥ 5 mg tyramine may be risky.

These foods fall into 4 major groups.

- Aged cheeses
- Air-dried sausages
- Fava pods
  √ Beans are okay, but pod has dopamine.
- Sauerkraut
- Foods to *definitely avoid:*
  √ Aged cheeses (English Stilton, blue cheese, old cheddar, Danish blue, brick, mozzarella, Gruyère, Swiss, etc.).
    □ Because 80% of all hypertensive crises are secondary to consuming aged cheeses, hypertensive crises are called "cheese reactions."
    □ Even some of the more moderate tyramine cheeses (e.g., brie, Emmenthaler, and Gruyère) are included because people eat more than a single slice.
    □ Some cheeses are allowed in any amount: cottage, processed slices, ricotta, and cream cheeses are safe.
    □ Cheeses are particularly risky because the amount of tyramine varies based on location (whether it is the center of a cheese wheel [higher] or on outside), amount of deliberate aging (e.g., soft brie is aged more than firm), amount aging (e.g., time sitting in store or home refrigerator).
  √ Tap and microbrewery beers are suspect because of the increased hops or wort used in the secondary fermentation and the coarseness of filters that may allow bacterial contamination and further fermentation.
  √ Fava (Italian, broad) green beans (because of dopa content in pod).
  √ Concentrated yeast extracts (especially Marmite), but
    □ Beware of powdered protein diet supplements containing yeast extracts.
    □ Brewer's yeast is safe.

□ Yeast used in baking products is safe because of small amount.

√ Pickled herring in brine should be avoided, but other fish are safe.

√ Salami, mortadella, air-dried sausage, chicken liver (by day 5) must be avoided. Bologna, pepperoni, summer sausage, fresh chicken liver, corned beef, and liverwurst are safe.

√ Sauerkraut.

√ Oriental food made with soy products, such as tofu.

√ Phenylalanine in doses ≥ 1 g can occasionally cause modest increase in BP.

□ Aspartame, the artificial sweetener, contains only 60 mg per average serving.

√ If uncertain, avoid fermented protein food.

- Foods *no longer at risk:*
  √ Chocolate (has phenylethylamine) except in very high amounts
  √ Figs, raisins, overripe fruit, avocados, bananas (don't eat the skins)
  √ Tea, coffee, cola, and other caffeine-containing beverages (some experts limit these to 3 cups/glasses a day)
  √ White and red wine (assuming wine kept under 3 ounces/day), other spirits
  √ Yogurt
    □ Unless unpasteurized or > 5 days old
  √ Caviar, snails, tinned fish
  √ Tinned and packet soup
    □ Unless made from boullion or meat extracts (which can be unsafe in large quantities)
    □ Vegetable protein extracts are okay
  √ Bottled or canned U.S. or Canadian beer (*see* page 194)
    □ Based on ≤ 4 servings.

Instructions for using the following tables:

- Read all prior cautions first.
- Most people on phenelzine need at least 6–8 mg tyramine consumed within 4 hours to precipitate a hypertensive crisis.
- Tranylcypromine may require less tyramine to cause a hypertensive reaction (~ 4 mg).
- Because each person is different, should initially experiment with totals of 1–2 mg at a sitting.
  √ Then monitor BP before trying higher amounts of tyramine.

MONOAMINE OXIDASE INHIBITORS

- Remember, the cheese contents in the table can be notoriously variable.
- Products are listed from highest tyramine content per serving to lowest.

## Tyramine Content of Beers*

| Beer | Brewer | Tyramine Concentration μg/ml | Tyramine Content (mg) per Serving** |
|------|--------|------------------------------|-------------------------------------|
| **BEERS WITH ALCOHOL** | | | |
| Amstel | Amstel | 4.52 | 1.54 |
| Export Draft | Molson | 3.79 | 1.29 |
| Blue Light | Labatts | 3.42 | 1.16 |
| Guinness Extra Stout | Labatts | 3.37 | 1.15 |
| Old Vienna | Carling | 3.32 | 1.13 |
| Canadian | Molson | 3.01 | 1.03 |
| Miller Light | Carling | 2.91 | 0.99 |
| Export | Molson | 2.78 | 0.95 |
| Heineken | Holland | 1.81 | 0.62 |
| Blue | Labatts | 1.80 | 0.61 |
| Coors Light | Molson | 1.45 | 0.49 |
| Carlsberg Light | Carling | 1.15 | 0.39 |
| Michelob | Anheuser-Busch | 0.98 | 0.33 |
| Beck's | Braueri Beck | 0.90 | 0.30 |
| Genesee Cream | Genesee | 0.86 | 0.29 |
| Stroh's | Stroh's | 0.78 | 0.27 |
| Old Milwaukee | Pacific Western | 0.34 | 0.11 |
| **DEALCOHOLIZED BEERS** | | | |
| O'Doul's Malt Beverage | Anheuser-Busch | 2.25 | 0.68 |
| Labatts | Labatts Brewing Co. | 1.18 | 0.36 |
| Buckler | Heineken | 1.08 | 0.32 |
| Special Light Swan | Special Light Swan Lager | 0.97 | 0.29 |
| Texas Select | San Antonio Beverage Co. | 0.82 | 0.25 |
| Sharp's | Miller Brewing Co. | 0.37 | 0.11 |
| Molson Exel | Molson Breweries | 0.00 | 0.00 |
| Tourtel | Kronenbourg | 0.00 | 0.00 |
| Upper Canada Point Nine | Upper Canada Brewery | 0.00 | 0.00 |
| **PARTICULARLY RISKY TAP BEERS** | | | |
| Upper Canada Lager | Sleeman | 112.91 | 37.62 |
| Kronenbourg | Kronenbourg | 37.85 | 15.94 |
| Rotterdam's Pilsner | Rotterdam | 29.47 | 9.82 |
| Rotterdam's Lager | Rotterdam | 27.05 | 9.00 |

*Generally U.S. and Canadian canned and bottled beers are safe if ≤ 4 servings consumed; all Canadian beers (Labatts, Molson, Upper Canada, Pacific Western) < 3 μg/ml.
**Based on a 341 ml serving (one bottle).

## Tyramine Content of Wines

| Wine | Color | Type | Country | Tyramine Concentration (μg/ml) | Tyramine Content (mg) per Serving* |
|------|-------|------|---------|-------------------------------|-------------------------------------|
| Rioja (Siglo) | Red | | Spain | 4.41 | 0.53 |
| Sherry | Red | | | 3.60 | 0.43 |

## Tyramine Content of Wines (*Cont.*)

| Wine | Color | Type | Country | Tyramine Concentration ($\mu$g/ml) | Tyramine Content (mg) per Serving* |
|---|---|---|---|---|---|
| Ruffino | Red | Chianti | Italy | 3.04 | 0.36 |
| Blue Nun | White | | Germany | 2.70 | 0.32 |
| Retsina | White | | Greece | 1.79 | 0.21 |
| La Colombaia | Red | Chianti | Italy | 0.63 | 0.08 |
| Riesling | | | | 0.60 | 0.07 |
| Brolio | Red | Chianti | Italy | 0.44 | 0.05 |
| Sauterne | White | | | 0.40 | 0.05 |
| Beau-Rivage | White | Bordeaux | France | 0.39 | 0.05 |
| Beau-Rivage | Red | Bordeaux | France | 0.35 | 0.04 |
| Maria Christina | Red | | Canada | 0.20 | 0.20 |
| Port | Red | | | 0.20 | 0.02 |
| Cinzano | Red | Vermouth | Italy | † | † |
| LePiazze** | Red | Chianti | Italy | † | † |

*Based on a 120 ml (4 ounce) serving.
**Other Chianti sampled also with no tyramine.
†Nil.

## Tyramine Content of Other Alcohol

| Type | Tyramine Concentration ($\mu$g/ml) | Tyramine Content (mg) per Serving |
|---|---|---|
| Ale | 8.8 | 3.0/341 ml |
| Harvey's Bristol Cream | 2.65 | 0.32 mg/4 ounces |
| Dubonnet | 1.59 | 0.19 mg/4 ounces |
| Vermouth | high | high |
| Bourbon | † | † |
| London distilled dry gin (beefeater) | † | † |
| Gin | † | † |
| Vodka | † | † |
| Rum | † | † |
| Scotch | † | † |

†Nil.

## Tyramine Content of Cheeses

| Type | Tyramine Concentration ($\mu$g/g) | Tyramine Content (mg) per Serving* |
|---|---|---|
| Liederkranz | 1454.50 | 21.8 |
| Cheddar (New York State) | 1416.00 | 21.2 |
| English Stilton | 1156.91 | 17.3 |
| Cheddar, old center (Canadian) | 1013.95 | 16.4 |
| Blue cheese | 997.79 | 15.0 |
| Swiss | 925.00 | 13.9 |
| White (3-year-old) | 779.74 | 11.7 |
| Camembert (Danish) | 681.50 | 10.2 |
| Emmentaler | 612.50 | 9.2 |

## Tyramine Content of Cheeses (*Cont.*)

| Type | Tyramine Concentration ($\mu$g/g) | Tyramine Content (mg) per Serving* |
|---|---|---|
| Extra-old | 608.19 | 9.1 |
| Gruyère (British) | 597.50 | 9.0 |
| Brick (Canadian) | 524.00 | 7.9 |
| Gruyère (American) | 516.00 | 7.7 |
| Cheddar (25 samples) | 384.00 | 5.8 |
| Gouda | 345.00 | 5.2 |
| Edam | 310.00 | 4.7 |
| Colby | 285.00 | 4.3 |
| Mozzarella | 284.04 | 4.2 |
| Roquefort (French) | 273.50 | 4.1 |
| Danish blue | 256.48 | 4.1 |
| D'Oka (imported) | 234.00 | 3.5 |
| Limberger | 204.00 | 3.1 |
| Cheddar, center cut (Canadian) | 192.00 | 2.9 |
| Argenti (imported) | 168.00 | 2.5 |
| Romano | 159.00 | 2.4 |
| Cheese spread, Handisnack | 133.81 | 2.0 |
| Gruyère (Swiss) | 125.17 | 1.9 |
| Cheddar, fresh (Canadian) | 120.00 | 1.8 |
| Muenster | 101.69 | 1.5 |
| Provolone | 94.00 | 1.4 |
| Camembert (American) | 86.00 | 1.3 |
| Parmesan, grated (Kraft) | 81.08 | 1.3 |
| Old Coloured, Canadian | 77.47 | 1.2 |
| Feta | 75.78 | 1.1 |
| Parmesan, grated (Italian) | 69.79 | 1.1 |
| Gorgonzola | 55.94 | 0.8 |
| Processed (American) | 50.00 | 0.8 |
| Blue cheese dressing | 39.20 | 0.6 |
| Mozzarella cheese | 36.32 | 0.5** |
| Medium (black Diamond) | 34.75 | 0.5 |
| Processed (Canadian) | 26.00 | 0.4 |
| Swiss Emmentaler | 23.99 | 0.4 |
| Brie (M-C) with rind | 21.19 | 0.3 |
| Cambozola Blue Vein (germ) | 18.31 | 0.3 |
| Brie (d'Oka) without rind | 14.65 | 0.2 |
| Farmers, Canadian plain | 11.05 | 0.2 |
| Cheez Whiz (Kraft) | 8.46 | 0.1 |
| Brie (d'Oka) with rind | 5.71 | 0.1 |
| Cream cheese (plain) | 9.04 | 0.1 |
| Brie (M-C) without rind | 2.82 | < 0.1 |
| Sour cream (Astro) | 1.23 | < 0.1 |
| Boursin | 0.98 | < 0.1 |
| Cottage cheese | < 0.20 | † |
| Cream cheese | < 0.20 | † |
| Cheese powder (for macaroni) | † | † |
| Havarti (Canadian) | † | † |
| Ricotta | † | † |
| Bonbel | † | † |

*Based on a 15-gram (single slice) serving.
**Range 0.15–2.4 mg/15 gm
†Nil.

## Tyramine Content in Fish

| Type | Tyramine Concentration (µg/g) | Tyramine Content (mg) per Serving* |
|---|---|---|
| Pickled herring** | Up to 3030 | —— |
| Pickled herring brine | 15.1/ml | —— |
| Lump fish roe | 4.4 | 0.2/50 g |
| Sliced schmaltz herring in oil | 4.0 | 0.2/50 g |
| Smoked carp | † | † |
| Smoked salmon | † | † |
| Smoked white fish | † | † |

**Other reports indicate that the tyramine content of pickled herring is nil.
†Nil.

## Tyramine Content in Meat and Sausage*

| Type | Tyramine Concentration (µg/g) | Tyramine Content per Serving* |
|---|---|---|
| Sausage, Belgian, dry-fermented | 803.9 | 24.1 |
| Liver, beef, spoiled | 274 | 8.2 |
| Sausage, dry-fermented | 244 | 7.3 |
| Salami | 188 | 5.6 |
| Mortadella | 184 | 5.5 |
| Air-dried sausage | 125 | 3.8** |
| Sausage, semi-dried fermented | 85.5 | 2.6 |
| Chicken liver (day 5) | 77.25 | 1.5 |
| Bologna | 33 | 1.0 |
| Aged sausage | 29 | 0.9 |
| Smoked meat | 18 | 0.5 |
| Corned beef | 11 | 0.3 |
| Kolbasa sausage | 6 | 0.2 |
| Liver, beef, fresh | 5.4 | 0.2 |
| Liverwurst | 2 | 0.1 |
| Smoked sausage | 1 | < 0.1 |
| Sweet Italian sausage | 1 | < 0.1 |
| Pepperoni sausage | † | † |
| Chicken liver (day 1) | † | † |

*Based on 30 g serving.
**2 of 10 > 6 mg, 2 of 10 4–6 mg.
†Nil.

## Tyramine Content in Paté*

| Type | Tyramine Concentration (µg/g) | Tyramine Content (mg) per Serving* |
|---|---|---|
| Salmon mousse paté | 22 | 0.7 |
| Country style paté | 3 | 0.1 |
| Peppercorn paté | 2 | 0.1 |

*Based on 30 g serving.

MONOAMINE OXIDASE INHIBITORS

## Tyramine Content in Fruits and Vegetables

| Type | Tyramine Concentration ($\mu$g/g) | Tyramine Content (mg) per Serving* |
|---|:---:|:---:|
| Banana peel* (blackened) | 81.62 | 2.58/peel |
| Banana peel* (fresh) | 58.35 | 1.424/peel |
| Raspberries | † | † |
| Raspberry jam | < 38.0 | —— |
| Avocado, fresh** | 23.0 | † |
| Orange | 10.0 | —— |
| Plum (red) | 6.0 | —— |
| Tomato | 4.0 | —— |
| Eggplant | 3.0 | —— |
| Potato | 1.0 | —— |
| Spinach | 1.0 | —— |
| Banana (fresh pulp) | † | † |
| Grapes | † | † |
| Figs, California-Blue Ribbon | † | † |
| Raisins (California seedless) | † | † |
| Fava (Italian) (broad) bean pods | † | † |

*The peel of the banana and the pod of the fava bean contain considerable dopamine; the banana pulp and the actual fava bean carry no risk.
**Some claim fresh avocado is nil.
†Nil.

## Tyramine Content in Yeast Extracts

| Type | Tyramine Concentration ($\mu$g/g) | Tyramine Content per Serving |
|---|:---:|:---:|
| Marmite concentrated yeast extract | 1184 | 6.45/10 g |
| Yeast extracts | 2156 | —— |
| Brewer's yeast tablets (Drug Trade Co.) | —— | 191.27 g/400 mg |
| Brewer's yeast tablets (Jamieson) | —— | 66.72 g/400 mg |
| Brewer's yeast flakes (Vegetrates) | —— | 9.36 g/15 g |
| Brewer's yeast debittered (Maximum Nutrition) | —— | † |

†Nil.

## Tyramine Content in Other Foods

| Type | Tyramine Concentration ($\mu$g/g) | Tyramine Content per Serving |
|---|:---:|:---:|
| Soy sauce (Japanese) | 509.30 | —— |
| Soy sauce (Tamari) | 466.00 | —— |
| Meat extracts (soup, gravy, bases) | 199.50 | —— |
| Soybean paste | 84.85 | —— |
| Beef bouillon mix (bovril) | —— | 231.25 |
| Sauerkraut (Krakus) | 56.49 | 13.87 |
| Beef bouillon (Oetker) | —— | 0.102/cube |
| Fermented soybean curd | —— | 3–11/1–2 cubes |

**Tyramine Content in Other Foods (*Cont.*)**

| Type | Tyramine Concentration (µg/g) | Tyramine Content per Serving |
|---|---|---|
| Tofu (Vita) (7 days in refrigerator) | —— | 4.8 |
| Fresh tofu (Vita) | —— | 0.2 |
| Soy sauce (Pearl River Bridge) | —— | 3.4/15 ml |
| Soy sauce (Kimlan) | —— | 0.5/15 ml |
| Soy sauce (Kikkoman) | —— | 0.4/15 ml |
| Soy sauce (generic) | 18.72 µg/ml | 0.2/10 ml |
| Soy sauce (Wing's) | —— | 0.15/15 ml |
| Soy sauce (chemically hydrolized) | 1.8 | —— |
| Worcester sauce (Lea & Perrins, Sharwood, no name) | | ≤ 0.12/15 ml |
| Veggie burger (soybean curd) (9 days in refrigerator) | 0.6/g | |
| 1/2 medium double cheese, double pepperoni Pizza Hut* | 136 g | 0.06 |
| 1/2 medium double cheese Pizza Pizza* | 133 g | 0.17 |
| 1/2 medium double cheese, double pepperoni Domino's Pizza* | 104 g | 0.38 |
| 1 deluxe or pepperoni pizza McDonald's* | 80 g | 0.04 |
| Cocoa powder | 1.45 | —— |
| Beef gravy (Franco American) | 0.858/ml | < 0.1/30 ml |
| Chicken gravy (Franco American) | 0.46/ml | < 0.1/30 ml |
| Chicken bouillon mix (Maggi) | † | † |
| Vegetable bouillon mix | † | † |
| Yogurt | < 0.2 | † |

*Large chain pizza safe, but smaller outlets or gourmet pizza may contain aged cheese; Kosher pizzas do not generally have aged cheese and are safe.
†Nil.

## SIDE EFFECTS

MAOIs are less anticholinergic than TCAs.

- Almost no clinical anticholinergic actions from tranylcypromine.
- Phenelzine can generate anticholinergic episodes over 20% of the time.

Most anticholinergic symptoms taper off in 1–2 weeks (*see* pages 138–39); they are discussed with their respective organ systems.

Common long-term (> 6 months) effects of phenelzine are weight gain (74%), ankle edema (13%), muscle twitching, and decreased sexual function (22%). All but muscle twitching are rare on tranylcypromine.

### Cardiovascular Effects

*Hypotension*

- MAOIs have antihypertensive properties.
- This is their second most important side effect.
- MAOIs produce orthostatic hypotension and basal hypotension similar to HCAs.

M
O
N
O
A
M
I
N
E

O
X
I
D
A
S
E

I
N
H
I
B
I
T
O
R
S

√ Complaints of dizziness reported by 20–50% of patients on MAOIs
  ▫ About same as for nortriptyline.
√ As many as 10% of patients on MAOIs may develop severe injuries (e.g., passing out, fractures).
  ▫ Especially frequent in the elderly.
  ▫ Common with congestive heart failure.
  ▫ Hypotension happens more in people with preexisting hypertension, although it still afflicts the normotensive.
- Symptoms include
  √ Dizziness, lightheadedness
  √ Coldness
  √ Headaches
  √ Fainting, especially with salt or fluid restriction.
- Management (*see* page 140)
- Avoid adding chlorpromazine, thioridaze, clomipramine, amitriptyline, or other hypotensive agents to MAOIs.

Except for BP problems, MAOIs have fewer cardiovascular side effects than HCAs.

- Cause less myocardial toxicity.
- Exert little effect on heart rate, cardiac conduction, and myocardial function.
  √ Phenelzine produces a modest decrease in QT interval.
  √ Still within normal range.
- May be preferable over TCAs for some cardiac patients.

*Hypertension (transient)*

- Has been reported 1–3 h after MAOI.
  √ Subsides 3–4 h after dose.
  √ Occasionally a significant rise seen (e.g., 120/80 → 178/104).
- More reports with tranylcypromine.

*Peripheral edema*

- Phenelzine and isocarboxazid produce edema more than tranylcypromine.
  √ Reported as high as 5–19% with phenelzine.
- Reduce dose; prescribe a diuretic; try support hose.
- Rarely, pericardial edema has been reported.

## Central Nervous System Effects

*Myoclonic twitches*

- MAOIs cause more often than TCAs.

- Most often nocturnal.
- Management
  √ Reduce or stop MAOIs, or
  √ Shift doses earlier or spread out doses, or
  √ Change to another MAOI, or
  √ Add clonazepam, carbamazepine, or valproic acid.
  √ Sometimes cyproheptadine works.

*Difficulty finding words*

- Lower or stop MAOI.

*Pyridoxine deficiency*

- Isocarboxazid and phenelzine can lead to a pyridoxine (vitamin $B_6$) deficiency with primarily
  √ Peripheral neuropathy or
  √ Muscle spasms, pains, and parathesias.
- Other symptoms include
  √ Stomatitis
  √ Anemia
  √ Hyperacusis (or buzzing in the ear)
  √ Hyperirritability
  √ Depression
  √ Carpal tunnel syndrome
  √ "Electric shocks" or jumping movements of the extremities
  √ Ataxia
  √ Hyperactive deep tendon reflexes, clonus (possibly)
  √ Convulsions and coma (rarely)
- Treat with pyridoxine 50 mg po bid or 100 mg sustained-release qd.
  √ Occasionally, higher dose needed.
  √ Response in 2–10 weeks.
  √ Excessive pyrodoxine dose also can cause neuropathy.

*Seizures*

- MAOIs may alter the seizure threshold of patients with epilepsy.

*Toxicity*

- "Drunk," ataxic, confused.
- Reduce dose.

*Sedation*

- Phenelzine can be directly sedating.
  √ Can be expected to occur at any time.
- Insomnia often generates daytime sleepiness.

MONOAMINE OXIDASE INHIBITORS

- Some patients on phenelzine or tranylcypromine experience severe afternoon somnolence and disrupted sleep at night.
  - √ Hypnotics can treat the insomnia, but
  - √ Afternoon somnolence may persist.
    - ▫ No effective treatment for P.M. somnolence.
    - ▫ Patient must be warned of risk of accidents, etc., should this occur.

*Decreased sleep (sometimes without fatigue), insomnia*

- If without fatigue, inform patients that they have become more "efficient" sleepers, not insomniacs.
- Tranylcypromine causes initial insomnia most often.
- Switch to phenelzine or
- Move dose(s) to earlier time in day, perhaps before noon.

*Nightmares, hypnagogic phenomena, vivid dreams*

- Occur more often if MAOIs taken at night.
- Sleep disturbances more common with MAOIs than TCAs.
- At higher doses (e.g., > 60 mg phenelzine) MAOIs often completely suppress REM sleep.
  - √ Patient may report absence of strange dreams (REM) but persistence of mundane dreams (NREM).
    - ▫ May be useful "side effect" for patients with PTSD.
    - ▫ However, if patient abruptly or rapidly discontinues MAOI, risks severe REM rebound that can last up to 6 weeks.

*Psychosis, behavioral problems*

- Stimulation
  - √ May arise day or night.
  - √ More common with tranylcypromine.
  - √ Management
    - ▫ Reduce dose or transfer to another drug.
- Paranoid outbursts, delusions
  - √ Reduce or stop MAOI.
  - √ May reflect "subclinical" psychosis.
- Manic responses
  - √ Can erupt on MAOIs, with or without TCAs.
    - ▫ Hypomania more common (7% phenelzine, 10% tranylcypromine).
  - √ Apparent manic swings may actually be a sign of overstimulation.
  - √ Management
    - ▫ Reduce, or slow down rate of increase of, MAOI dose.
    - ▫ Add lithium, carbamazepine, or valproic acid to restrain the "high."

## Endocrine and Sexual Effects

Sexual effects more common with phenelzine than with tranylcypromine, especially

- Anorgasmia—22% phenelzine vs. 2% tranylcypromine
- Impotence

Also see

- *Decreased libido*
- In men difficulties achieving and maintaining erection; slowed or impaired ability to ejaculate

Management

- *See* pages 149–50.
- Reduce dose or
- Add cyprohepatidine 2–4 mg qd bid to alleviate anorgasmia in both sexes.
  - √ Cyprohepatidine may introduce drowsiness, stimulate appetite, or increase carbohydrate craving.
- Methyltestosterone po or by monthly depot injections may improve male sexual function.
- Bethanechol 10 mg tid may facilitate erectile functioning.
- Sildenafil can be useful for female as well as male sexual dysfunction.

*Carbohydrate craving*

*Falling blood sugar*

- More frequent with phenelzine and isocarboxazid.

*Lymphadenopathy*

- Reported with phenelzine and with tranylcypromine
  - √ Complete resolution seen by 6 months after MAOI is discontinued.

## Eyes, Ears, Nose, and Throat

*Narrow-angle glaucoma* (*see* pages 46, 151)

*Vision, blurred* (*see* page 45)

*Eyes, dry* (*see* page 45)

*Nasal congestion*

*Meniere's-like syndrome*

- Vertigo, tinnitus, nystagmus seen.
  - √ Remits with discontinuation of MAOI.

MONOAMINE OXIDASE INHIBITORS

## Gastrointestinal Effects

*Mouth, dry* (*see* page 47)

*Constipation* (*see* page 47)

*Hepatotoxicity*

- Incidence between 1/3,000–1/10,000.
- Frequency: isocarboxazid > phenelzine > tranylcypromine.
- Tranylcypromine is the preferred MAOI for patients with liver disease.
- Hepatotoxicity displays
  - √ Weakness, malaise
  - √ Rash
  - √ Nausea, anorexia
  - √ Jaundice
  - √ Eosinophilia
  - √ Elevated enzymes.

*Flatus* (rare)

- Giving oral lactase may help.

*Weight gain*

- Phenelzine > tranylcypromine.
- Amitriptyline causes more immediate weight gain than phenelzine, but 70% of people eventually gain weight on phenelzine.
- Phenelzine can add > 20 pounds in one year, but typical weight gain is 5–10 pounds.

## Renal Effects

*Urinary hesitancy or retention* (*see* page 52)

## Skin, Allergies, and Temperature

*Sweating, decreased*

*Fever, chills*

### PERCENTAGES OF SIDE EFFECTS

| Side Effects | Isocarboxazid | Phenelzine | Tranylcypromine |
|---|---|---|---|
| **CARDIOVASCULAR EFFECTS** | | | |
| Cardiac arrhythmias | 4 | —— | < 2 |
| Dizziness, lightheadedness | 18.6 | 17.5 | 28.3 (5–52.4) |

| Side Effects | Isocarboxazid | Phenelzine | Tranylcypromine |
|---|---|---|---|
| Hypertensive crises | 3.5 | 3.4 | 5.8 |
|  |  | (0.8–8) | (2–9.9) |
| Hypotension | 15 | 20 | 15 |
| Palpitations | 5 | 5 | 7.3 |
|  |  |  | (0–10) |
| Tachycardia | —— | 17.5 | 20 |
| **CENTRAL NERVOUS SYSTEM EFFECTS** | | | |
| Agitation, restlessness (motoric) | 4 | —— | 5 |
| Anxiety, nervousness (mental) | —— | —— | 2 |
| Confusion, disorientation | 4.3 | 4.3 | 6.2 |
|  |  |  | (2–14.3) |
| Drowsiness, sedation | 8 | 21 | 12 |
|  | (2–20) | (0–30) | (0–47.6) |
| Excitement, hypomania | 9.3 | 13.8 | 17.1 |
|  | (2–20) | (5–30) | (10–30) |
| Headache | 20 | 6 | 14.3 |
| Insomnia | 6 | 17 | 22 |
|  |  | (15–50) | (10–23.8) |
| Myoclonic jerks | 7 | 10 | 7 |
| Parathesias | —— | —— | 4.8 |
| Seizures | —— | 1 | 0 |
| Tremor | 5.5 | 12.5 | 9.5 |
| Weakness, fatigue | 6 | < 2 | < 2 |
| **ENDOCRINE AND SEXUAL EFFECTS** | | | |
| Disturbed sexual function | 6.5 | 22 | 4 |
|  | (0–10) | (0–30) | (2–6) |
| **EYES, EARS, NOSE, AND THROAT EFFECTS** | | | |
| Vision, blurred | 10.5 | 17.5 | 8.5 |
|  |  |  | (2–10) |
| Tinnitus | —— | —— | 4.8 |
| **GASTROINTESTINAL EFFECTS** | | | |
| Anorexia | —— | —— | 4.8 |
| Appetite, increased | —— | —— | 0 |
| Constipation | 9.3 | 9.3 | 10 |
|  | (2–20) | (2–20) | (5–19) |
| Dyspepsia, upset stomach | 20 | 20 | 12.5 |
|  |  |  | (2–19) |
| Edema | 7.5 | 13 | —— |
| Hepatitis | 0.02 | < 0.01 | < 0.001 |
| Mouth and throat, dry | 20 | 30 | 25.9 |
|  |  |  | (10–47.6) |
| Nausea, vomiting | 10 | 10 | 6 |
|  |  |  | (0–10) |
| Weight gain | 20 | 74 | 6 |
| **RENAL EFFECTS** | | | |
| Urinary hesitancy or retention | 6.6 | 22 | 2.5 |
| **SKIN, ALLERGIES, AND TEMPERATURE EFFECTS** | | | |
| Rashes | 6 | < 2 | 6 |
| Sweating | 8.5 | 8 | —— |
|  | (2–20) | (2–20) |  |

## PREGNANCY AND LACTATION

| | |
|---|---|
| Teratogenicity (1st trimester) | • Some increased malformations have been found with phenelzine and tranylcypromine; fetal absorption in animals. |
| Direct Effect on Newborn (3rd trimester) | • Most severe risk is hypertensive crisis during pregnancy.<br>√ Probably unacceptable risk to fetus. |
| Lactation | • In breast milk; potential risk of interaction with soy milk or other food ingested by infant. |

## DRUG-DRUG INTERACTIONS

| Drugs (X) Interacts with: | Monoamine-Oxidase Inhibitors (M) | Comments |
|---|---|---|
| Acetabutolol (*see* β-blockers) | | |
| Albuterol | X↑ | Palpitations, tachycardia, anxiety, increased BP. |
| *Alcohol | M↑ | May trigger hypertensive crisis (*see* pages 185–87). |
| Anesthetics | X↑ | Potentiate CNS depression or excitement, muscle (general) stiffness or hyperpyrexia. |
| Anticholinergics | X↑ | Increased atropine-like effects. |
| Antihypertensives | X↑ | Hypotension. |
| Antipsychotics | X↑M↑ | Hypotension; may increase EPS, particularly in typical agents and in risperidone at higher doses (5 mg or more). |
| Atenolol (*see* beta-blockers) | | |
| *Barbiturates | X↑ | CNS depression. |
| Benzodiazepines | X↑ | Increased benzodiazepine effect; disinhibition, edema. |
| **Beta-blockers<br>acetabutolol (CS)<br>atenolol (CS)<br>betaxolol (CS)<br>labetolol (CS)<br>nadolol (CS)<br>penbutalol (NCS)<br>pindolol (NCS)<br>propranolol (NCS)<br>timolol (NCS) | X↑M↑ | Hypotension, bradycardia, and rebound BP increase if quickly stopped. |
| Betaxolol (*see* beta-blockers) | | |
| Bupropion | X↑ | Hypertension; psychosis possible. |
| Buspirone | X? | Case reports of elevated BP. Wait 10 days after stopping MAOI before starting buspirone. |
| *Caffeine | X↑ | Irregular heartbeat or high BP; reports of hypertensive crisis; avoid in high quantities. |
| Carbamazepine | X↓ | Seizures in epileptics; monitor levels. |

| Drugs (X) Interacts with: | Monoamine-Oxidase Inhibitors (M) | Comments |
|---|---|---|
| Citalopram (*see* SSRIs) | | |
| *Clomipramine | X↑ | Serotonin syndrome: Do not combine. |
| Clonidine | M↑ | May potentiate MAOIs. |
| *Cocaine | M↑ | Hypertensive crisis (*see* sympathomimetics). |
| *Cyclobenzaprine | X↑M↑ | Fever, seizures, and death reported; cyclobenzaprine is chemically similar to TCAs; avoid until more data. |
| Dextroamphetamine | M↑ | Hypertensive crisis; tranylcypromine the gravest danger (*see* sympathomimetics). |
| Dextromethorphan | M↑ | A few reports of serotonergic crisis. |
| Disulfiram | X↑ | Severe CNS reactions; unclear. |
| Diuretics (thiazides) | X↑ | BP drop. |
| Doxapram | X↑ | CNS stimulation, agitation, and hypertension; MAOI may lower doxapram's cardiovascular effect; until more evidence exists, *avoid combination.* |
| Enflurane | X↑ | *See* anesthetics (general). |
| †Ephedrine | M↑ | Hypertensive crisis (*see* sympathomimetics). |
| †Fenfluramine | M↑ | Serotonergic crisis (*see* sympathomimetics). |
| *Fluoxetine (*see* SSRIs) | | |
| Fluvoxamine (*see* SSRIs) | | |
| *Guanadrel | X↑ | Initial hypertension followed by hypotension; wait 10–14 days between drugs. |
| *Guanethidine | X↑ | Initial hypertension followed by hypotension; wait 10–14 days between drugs. |
| Halothane | X↑ | *See* anesthetics (general). |
| Hydralazine | X↑ | Tachycardia; may increase BP. |
| *Hypoglycemics (oral) | X↑ | May lower blood sugar. |
| *Insulin | X↑ | May lower blood sugar. |
| Labetolol (*see* beta-blockers) | | |
| *Levodopa (L-dopa) | X↑ M↑ | Hypertensive crisis and CNS stimulation possible. Start with very low doses L-dopa and titrate up very slowly. May also induce akinesia and tremor (*see* sympathomimetics). |
| MAOIs | M↑ | Hypertension with phenelzine to tranylcypromine; not reported in other direction. |
| †Meperidine | M↑ | Serotonergic crisis; other opiates (e.g., morphine, methadone) safer. |
| †Metaraminol | M↑ | Hypertensive crisis (*see* sympathomimetics). |
| Methyldopa | M↑ | Hypertensive reaction could occur because of increased stored norepinephrine, but not reported. |
| *Methylphenidate | M↑ | Hypertensive crisis (*see* sympathomimetics). |
| Nadolol (*see* beta-blockers) | | |
| Paroxetine (*see* SSRIs) | | |
| Phenothiazines | X↑ M↑ | Increased hypotension and anticholingeric effects. |
| †Phenylephrine | M↑ | Hypertensive crisis (*see* sympathomimetics). |
| †Phenylpropanolamine | M↑ | Hypertensive crisis (*see* sympathomimetics). |
| †Pseudoephedrine | M↑ | Hypertensive crisis (*see* sympathomimetics). |
| *Reserpine | X↑ | Initial hypertension followed by hypotension; wait 10–14 days between drugs. |
| Sertraline (*see* SSRIs) | | |
| †SSRIs | X↑ | Serotonergic crisis; some deaths; wait at least 2 weeks after stopping MAOI before starting SSRI; wait at least 5 weeks after stopping fluoxetine and 2 weeks after stopping sertraline, paroxetine, or fluvoxamine before starting MAOI. |

| Drugs (X) Interacts with: | Monoamine-Oxidase Inhibitors (M) | Comments |
|---|---|---|
| *Succinylcholine | X↑ | Prolonged muscle relaxation or paralysis only by phenelzine. |
| Sympathomimetics (indirect): Appetite suppressants †Amphetamines *Cocaine † Cyclopentamine † Ephedrine † Isoproterenol *Levodopa †Metaraminol *Methylphenidate Pemoline †Phentermine †Phenylephrine †Phenylpropanolamine †Pseudoephedrine Sumatriptan †Tyramine | M↑ | Hypertensive crisis generated with indirect-acting sympathomimetics but not by direct-acting sympathomimetics (e.g., epinephrine does not cause this reaction). Most common with more stimulating tranylcypromine. Sumatriptan may exaggerate serotonin effects. Use decreased dose. |
| Terfenadine | M↑ | Increased MAOI side effects. |
| Thiazide diuretics | X↑ M↑ | Hypotension. |
| †TCAs | M↑ | *Should not add TCAs to MAOIs;* risks noradrenergic or serotonergic crisis. Best to *not* give (1) large doses, (2) IM/IV drugs, (3) imipramine with tranylcypromine, (4) an MAOI to patients recently on SSRIs or clomipramine. Amitriptyline safer: 50–70% of patients have no rise in BP. |
| Theophylline | X↑ | Palpitations, tachycardia, anxiety. |
| *Tryptophan | X↑ | Serotonin syndrome; tryptophan off American market, but old bottles exist and is available in Canada. |
| Tubocurarine | X↑ | Prolonged muscle relaxation or paralysis. |
| †Tyramine | M↑ | Hypertensive crisis (*see* sympathomimetics). |

* Moderately important interaction; † Extremely important interaction; ↑ Increases; ↓ Decreases.
** Beta-blockers: CS = cardioselective; NCS = noncardioselective.

## EFFECTS ON LABORATORY TESTS

| Generic Names | Blood/Serum Tests** | Results* | Urine Tests | Results* |
|---|---|---|---|---|
| Isocarboxazid | LFT | ↑ | ? | —— |
| Phenelzine | Glucose | ↓ | 5-HIAA, VMA | —— |
| | LFT | ↑ | | |
| Tranylcypromine | Glucose | ↓ | 5-HIAA, VMA | —— |

* ↑ Increases; ↓ Decreases; ? Undetermined.
** LFT † SGOT, SGPT, LDH, alkaline phosphotase, bilirubin.

## WITHDRAWAL

MAOIs do not cause

- Dependence
- Tolerance
- Addiction

Abrupt withdrawal from phenelzine, tranylcypromine, and possibly from isocarboxazid may result in

- Agitation
- Nightmares
- Mania
- Psychosis
- REM rebound can be significant, because MAOIs often completely suppress REM.
  - √ Symptoms decline by reintroducing a low MAOI dose.
  - √ Gradually withdrawing MAOIs one tablet every 3–4 days is safer.
- Tranylcypromine withdrawal may also cause
  - √ Prominent insomnia, disrupted sleep, hypersomnia
  - √ Restlessness, anxiety, depression
  - √ Diarrhea
  - √ Headache
  - √ Tremulousness
  - √ Hot and cold feelings
  - √ Muscle weakness
  - √ Confusion, delirium
  - √ Hallucinations, psychosis
- These patients often have a h/o tranylcypromine abuse or high doses of MAOI.
- Patients on long-term tranylcypromine *may* have greater risk.

Withdrawal from MAOIs is not life-threatening.

MAOI diet and drug regimen should persist for at least 2 weeks after the last MAOI dose.

## OVERDOSE: TOXICITY, SUICIDE, AND TREATMENT

A 10-day supply of an MOAI can be lethal.

Overdose symptoms

- May develop in 4–12 h,
- Maximal at 24–48 h,

- Usually resolve in 3–4 days,
- May persist for 12–14 days.

Most acute MAOI overdoses exaggerate side effects.

- Early and mild symptoms include
  √ Drowsiness
  √ Dizziness (can be severe)
  √ Headache (can be severe)
  √ Insomnia
  √ Restlessness, anxiety, irritability
  √ Ataxia
- Moderate to severe symptoms include
  √ Confusion, incoherence
  √ Tachycardia, rapid and irregular pulse
  √ Hypotension
  √ Seizures
  √ Hallucinations
  √ Hyperreflexia
  √ Fever
  √ Respiratory depression
  √ Increased or decreased temperature
  √ Hyperactivity
  √ Spasm of masticatory muscles
  √ Opisthotonos
  √ Sweating
  √ Rigidity
  √ Coma

Management of MAOI overdose

- Remember that diet and drug interactions may also occur during overdose.
- Hypotension
  √ May evolve into shock, coma, cardiovascular insufficiency, myocardial infarction, and arrhythmias.
  √ Push fluids.
  √ Pressor amines (e.g., norepinephrine) may help, but the hypertensive effects of these agents may be enhanced by the MAOI.
  √ Avoid CNS stimulants and contraindicated drugs.
- Seizures (*see* pages 146–47).
- For increased temperature, apply external cooling.
- For hepatotoxicity, evaluate liver function tests about 2 weeks and again 4–6 weeks after MAOI overdose.

Carefully observe patient for at least one week after the overdose.

**Toxicity and Suicide Data**

| Generic Names | Toxicity Doses Average (Highest) (g) | Mortality Doses Average (Lowest) (g) | Lethal Supply of MAOIs (days) |
|---|---|---|---|
| Isocarboxazid | 0.5 | | 10–12 |
| Phenelzine | 0.750 | 1.012 | 6–10 |
| | | 0.375 | |
| Tranylcypromine | 0.750 | | 10–12 |

## PRECAUTIONS

MAOIs *contraindicated* in

- Cerebrovascular disease and congestive heart failure.
- Pheochromocytoma.
- Foods with large amounts of tyramine, dopamine (*see* pages 192–99).
- Medications listed before (*see* pages 188–191).
- Recurrent or severe headache unless good home BP monitoring.
- Hypersensitivity to MAOIs.
- Myelography
  - √ Stop MAOI at least 48 h before myelography.
  - √ Resume MAOI at least 24 h after myelography.
- Liver disease or abnormal liver function.
- Children under 16 y.o.

Tranylcypromine addiction has been reported in a few cases.

- Arises partly from tranylcypromine's amphetamine-like properties.
- Some cases of tolerance without addiction have occurred.
  - √ Maximum dose for each patient ranged from 120–700 mg/day with an average of 267 mg/day.
  - √ Often doses of 90–130 mg have been reported to be lower in side effects than lower doses.
- Patients typically present with delirium and agitation.
- After MAOI is stopped because of complications, patients treated best with other class of antidepressant.
  - √ If patient prefers MAOI, try a different MAOI, e.g., change from phenelzine to tranylcypromine.
    - □ May need to have patient stop problem MAOI and later start 2nd MAOI.

MAOIs may suppress anginal pain, which means that patients with coronary heart disease should be warned about overexertion.

MONOAMINE OXIDASE INHIBITORS

MAOIs may increase symptoms of Parkinson's disease, but more often decrease them, as seen with selegiline.

Use MAOIs *cautiously* in patients with

- Hyperthyroidism
- Diabetes
- Renal impairment
- Epilepsy
- Recurrent or severe headaches (requires good home BP monitoring).
- Hypertension
  √ Monitor for spontaneous BP increase (seen more with tranylcypromine).
  √ Adjust antihypertensives downward if common MAOI hypotensive effect is seen.
- Asthma
  √ Okay if patient managed well with nonsystemic steroids and/or chromalyn.
  √ Acute crisis will require epinephrine, not indirect pressors.
- Severe allergic reactions
  √ Epinephrine probably okay, but test dose with BP monitoring in office advised.

## NURSES' DATA

Monitor suicidal patients for "cheeking" or hoarding MAOIs.

Remind patients about the 4–6 week lag on a therapeutic dose before MAOIs fully work.

Tell patients about MAOI diet, stressing its importance without overemphasizing its seriousness.

- Review the patient's use of
  √ Specific favorite foods, including cooking methods with wine, soy sauce, etc.
  √ Over-the-counter medications (especially nose sprays, cold tablets, diet pills)
  √ Prescription drugs (e.g., TCAs)
  √ Recreational substances (e.g., wine, cocaine)
- Make sure patient knows differences between hypertensive crisis and hypotensive reaction (*see* pages 139–140, 199–200).
- Make sure patient has nifedipine readily available and knows when to use it.

Tell patients that MAOIs may produce insomnia and overstimulation, particularly on tranylcypromine.

- On phenelzine, lethargy or sedation is higher risk.
- Excessively caffeinated beverages (e.g., Coke, Mountain Dew) may accelerate anxiety, agitation, and confuse diagnosis.
- If patient experiences insomnia on MAOIs, doctor can change timing and/or dosage of MAOI.

## PATIENT AND FAMILY NOTES

Become familiar with MAOI diet and drugs.

May take MAOIs with regular meals.

- If forget dose, can take it within 4 h.
- Otherwise wait for next regular dose.
- Do not double dose.

Most common side effects include mild hypotension, dizziness, palpitations, dry mouth, sedation, and insomnia.

MAOIs may impair patient's performance of potentially hazardous tasks (e.g., driving a car, working near machinery, crossing streets). When a patient starts MAOIs, he or she should drive briefly in a safe place to check reflexes.

No MAOIs should be left at bedside or at any other easily accessible place.

Keep safely away from children.

For dizzy patients, review hypotension instructions (*see* page 140).

Carry a Medic Alert card to inform emergency room doctors about MAOIs.

- Inform every physician, surgeon, dentist, and pharmacist about using an MAOI.
- Before buying any over-the-counter drug, check the label, or ask the pharmacist, about the drug's compatibility with MAOIs.

To discourage patients who have h/o suicide or parasuicide attempts from overdosing with MAOIs, inform them that stroke or myocardial infarction is more likely than death.

Buy a BP cuff and learn how to use it in case of suspected hypertension.

Put nifedipine in many accessible places (e.g., wallet, purse, glove compartment, desk at work, etc.).

Must remain on MAOI dietary and drug regimen for 10–14 days after stopping MAOIs.

In restaurants always ask for ingredients of potentially harmful foods.

Do not abruptly halt MAOIs; may develop GI upset and bad dreams 1–3 days after doing so.

- Call physician instead.
- If unable to reach a physician, take one more pill until contacting him or her.

# 5. Lithium

## INTRODUCTION

Lithium salts prevent and treat manic and depressive swings in bipolar disorders.[1] Drugs modulating "highs" and "lows" are called "mood stabilizers."

- Mood stabilizers include lithium and some anticonvulsants.
- This chapter considers lithium; the next chapter covers anticonvulsants.

This chapter examines lithium as a treatment for

- Bipolar disorder (pages 220–31)
- Bipolar depression (pages 225–27)
- Postpartum psychosis (page 228)
- Cyclothymic disorder (pages 231–32)
  - √ Also emotionally unstable character disorder variant (EUCD)
- Borderline personality disorder (page 232)
- Unipolar depression (pages 232–33)
- Schizoaffective disorder (page 233)
- Medical conditions (page 234)
  - √ Cyclic neutropenia
  - √ Viral syndromes

Discussed in other chapters, lithium helps

- Aggression (Anticonvulsants, pages 284–85)
- Alcoholism prevention (Hypnotics, page 412)
- Premenstrual syndrome/PMDD (Antidepressants, page 134)

---

[1] Clinicians seeking information can call the Lithium Information Center at the Dean Foundation: 608/836-8070 (fax 608/836-8033).

# NAMES, MANUFACTURERS, DOSE FORMS, COLORS

| Generic Names | Brand Names | Manufacturers | Dose Forms (mg)* | Colors |
|---|---|---|---|---|
| Lithium carbonate | Eskalith | SmithKline Beecham | t: 300 c: 300 | t: gray c: gray-yellow |
| | Eskalith CR† | SmithKline Beecham | t: 450 | t: yellow |
| | Lithane | Miles | t: 300 | t: green |
| | Lithobid | Solvay | t: 300 | t: peach |
| Lithium citrate | Cibalith-S | CIBA | s: 8 mEq/ 5 ml | s: raspberry |

* c = capsules; s = syrup; † = sustained release; t = tablets.

# PHARMACOLOGY

At an intracellular level lithium

- Inhibits norepinephrine-sensitive adenylate cyclase.
- Normalizes calcium signaling.
- Inhibits phosphatidylinosital cycle.
- Passes through sodium channels.
- At high concentrations, passes through potassium channels.
- Diminishes sensitivity of neurotransmitter receptors.

The GI tract completely absorbs lithium in 6 h.
Lithium's bioavailability is 100%.
Cerebral concentration is 40% of plasma concentration.
Peak plasma levels typically occur in $1\frac{1}{2}$–2 h (range $\frac{1}{2}$–3 h); steady-state plasma levels at 4–5 days.

Lithium's average half-life is 20–24 h and ranges from 8–35 h.

- Lithium clearance is normally 25% of the creatinine.
- Steady state is usually achieved in 4–7 days.

Sustained-release lithium

- Has delayed GI absorption (60–90%), which may slow fluctuations in plasma lithium level.
- Peaks at $4$–$4\frac{1}{2}$ h (range $3\frac{1}{2}$–12 h).
- Releases less lithium in the stomach, which may decrease gastric side effects.
- Delivers more lithium to the small intestine, which may risk diarrhea and other lower GI symptoms.
- If divided or broken, sustained-release can become fast release.

Lithium citrate is the most rapidly absorbed, usually within ½–1 h.

- The kidneys excrete 95% of lithium.
- The feces excrete 1%.
  √ Diarrhea usually has only small effect on lithium level.
- Sweat excretes 4–5%.
  √ Hot weather and increases in exercise may lower lithium levels.
    □ Counteracted by increased lithium conservation by kidneys.
- 33–67% of lithium excreted in 6–12 h.
- The rest excreted over 10–14 days.

70–80% of lithium is reabsorbed in the proximal tubules.

- With negative sodium balance there is a compensatory increase.
- Sodium depletion significantly increases lithium retention.

## Laboratory Investigations

With lithium treatment, obtain the following tests.

| | Before Starting Lithium | Every 6 Months | Every 12 Months |
|---|---|---|---|
| ECG* | Yes | —— | Yes |
| Electrolytes* | Yes | —— | —— |
| CBC, differential** | Yes | —— | —— |
| BUN, creatinine (creatinine clearance if risk of renal impairment suspected) | Yes | Yes[1] | —— |
| Urinalysis | Yes | —— | —— |
| Fasting blood sugar (optional)*** | Yes | —— | —— |
| T$_3$RU, T$_4$RIA T$_4$I**** | Yes | —— | —— |
| TSH | Yes | Yes[2] | Yes[2] |
| Antithyroid antibodies (optional)***** | Yes | —— | —— |
| Calcium****** | Yes | —— | Yes |
| Pregnancy test (women at risk) | Yes | Optional | Optional |
| Side-effect checklist | Yes | Yes | —— |
| Physical exam and general medical history+ | —— | Yes | Yes |

* For patients over 40 or with h/o cardiac disease; these patients should also take another ECG one month after obtaining steady-state plasma level.

** Obtain new baseline WBC with expected leucocytosis 4–6 weeks after lithium begins; neutrophils most increased.

*** Helps establish baseline to determine later if lithium is significantly altering glucose tolerance. Hypoglycemia greater risk from lithium.

**** RU = resin uptake; RIA = radio immunoassay; I = free thyroxin index.

***** Can help detect those who are most likely to become hypothyroid.

****** Re-obtain serum calcium 2–6 weeks after lithium begins. Further assays should be done if clinical symptoms of hypercalcemia are seen: neuromuscular signs, ataxia, apathy, dysphoria, depression. Levels approaching 11 mg/dl should be followed closely.

+ Special emphasis on cardiac, renal, thyroid, and dermatologic systems and risk of pregnancy.

[1] Check renal function q 2–3 months during first 6 months of treatment.

[2] Many women who develop hypothyroidism do so within first 2 years. Six-month monitoring recommended. Men and women euthyroid after 2 years can be monitored yearly.

## DOSES

Lithium plasma levels usually determine the most effective dose.

- However, RBC intracellular levels may correlate best with response and toxicity.

*Always* base lithium dosage on clinical state and side effects, not solely on plasma level.

- African-Americans with similar plasma levels as Caucasians had on average 60% higher intracellular lithium levels.
  - √ Many African-Americans respond better with lower plasma lithium levels and with lower side effects.

Three methods for calculating lithium's initial dose can be informative. For methods 1 and 2 beware of supplemental drugs and conditions that significantly increase or decrease lithium levels, e.g., most NSAIDs increase lithium levels, while bronchodilators and polydipsia decrease lithium levels.

1. One generally can predict the total daily effective lithium dose by giving the patient 600 mg of lithium, checking the lithium level 24 h later, and prescribing the corresponding dose from the table.

| 24-Hour Lithium Level (mEq/l) | Total Daily Dose (mg) |
|---|---|
| 0.05–0.09 | 3600 |
| 0.10–0.14 | 2700 |
| 0.15–0.19 | 1800 |
| 0.20–0.23 | 900 |
| 0.24–0.30 | 600 |
| > 0.30 | 300 |

2. Another dose prediction method to obtain a 1.0 mEq/1 plasma level involves taking 900 mg lithium and getting a blood level 12 h later. Then use the equation:

$$d = \frac{2700}{5.61x - 0.21}$$

$d$ = predicted daily dose

$x$ = 12 h lithium plasma level

3. Another empirically derived, retrospective formula that involves no test doses:

24-h dose (mg) = 486.8 + 746.83 × (desired lithium mmol/l)

− (10.08 × age in years) + (5.95 weight in kg)

$$+ \ (92.01 \ \text{outpatient or inpatient status})$$

$$+ \ (147.8 \ \text{female or male}) - (74.73 \ \text{presence}$$

$$\text{or absence of antidepressant})$$

status: outpatient = 0, inpatient = 1
gender: female = 0, male = 1
cyclic antidepressant: absent = 0, present = 1

- This method cannot be used on patients with impaired kidney function or any medical illness or coprescribed drugs that would alter serum lithium levels.
- Up to 90% of predicted doses are within ± 0.2 mmol/l of desired dose.

Whichever method is used, patients must be carefully monitored for side effects and a lithium plasma level obtained 2–3 days after starting predicted dose to insure against toxicity. During either the 12- or 24-h test, patients must maintain their normal fluid and salt consumption or the test will be invalid.

*Never completely trust any of these tests.* Can start at full dose for acute mania to insure rapid onset of effect, but monitor levels and side effects carefully. For hypomanic inpatients and outpatients, the urgency to get to the final dose is less and the risks of GI side effects or lithium toxicity unnecessary. Can start very gradually 300 mg qd and get level and then increase 300 mg every 4–5 days until desired level is achieved. If ≤ 70% of desired dose and blood level, check lithium level ∼ 2–4 days after each dosage increase. If patient is 70% or more toward desired dose and blood level, relatively accurate steady-state lithium levels can be obtained on the third day after lithium dose has been increased.

| Condition | Usual Plasma Level (mEq/l) | Extreme Plasma Level Range (mEq/l) | Elderly Plasma Level (mEq/l) |
|---|---|---|---|
| Acute mania | 1.0–1.3 | 0.5–1.5 | 0.3–1.0 |
| Maintenance | 0.60–1.0* | 0.46–1.2 | 0.3–0.6 |

* 0.8–1.0 mEq/l has lowest relapse rate.

Saliva lithium levels can assist if drawing blood becomes difficult.

- Saliva levels are 1–3 (usually 2) times the plasma level.
- To calculate this ratio for a particular patient, determine several plasma and saliva levels and note their ratio.

Lithium is often given bid, but a single bedtime dosing usually produces less polyuria and fewer renal abnormalities (i.e., sclerotic glomeruli, necrotic tubuli, or interstitial fibrosis). With qd dosing:

- Increased risk of diarrhea.
- 12-h plasma levels will be about 10–26% higher than on bid dosing.
  - √ In Europe this is usually not recalculated to correspond to plasma levels from bid dosing.
    - □ Lower doses generally used.
  - √ Outcomes are the same with bedtime and divided doses.
- Maximum qd dose is usually 1800 mg.

Sustained release or bid or tid lithium may lower side effects related to peak levels (e.g., tremor, nausea).

- May cause more diarrhea than standard lithium.
- Less blood level fluctuation than standard lithium.
- Twice daily dosing with slow-release lithium may generate 10% higher 12-h serum levels than same dose of standard lithium.
- Modest increased risk of renal structural abnormalities.

## CLINICAL INDICATIONS AND USE

### General Information

Lithium carbonate and lithium citrate have no major clinical differences.

- Lithium citrate may have fewer GI and allergic side effects.

Predictors for a good initial lithium response include:

- H/o mania or hypomania associated with grandiosity or elation.
- Depressive episodes (past or present) with anergia, hypersomnia, increased appetite.
- Less than 4 cycles/year.
- Previous compliance with treatment.
- Sequence of mania followed by depression.
  - √ Some studies suggest that 2 or more depressive symptoms mixed with mania are enough to predict lithium nonresponse.
- First-degree relative with bipolar disorder responsive to lithium.
- Absence of mixed manic/depressive features, psychosis, neurologic disorder, or lithium nonresponsive parent(s) or siblings.

Other factors that might predict lithium response include:

- H/o "switch" to mania on TCAs or spontaneously.
- Augmented TSH response to TRH in depressed bipolar patients.
- Periodic, fully remitting psychopathology of many forms

Predictors of lithium nonresponse include:

- If 10 or more previous episodes (mania and/or depression) or 4 or more cycles/year, lithium response rate may be no better than placebo.
- Patients with dementia or extrapyramidal symptoms usually do poorly on lithium, often with substantial toxicity.
    √ Anticonvulsants such as valproate may be effective and better tolerated.
- For atypical and lithium-resistant mania *see* Anticonvulsants (pages 268–69).

Most common side effects in beginning of treatment are

- Hand tremor
- Dyspepsia
- Diarrhea
- Polyuria and/or polydipsia
    √ due to reduced renal response to vasopressin

Weight gain, polyuria, thirst, edema, hair loss, acne, benign leucocytosis, and cloudy thinking are more common later in treatment.

## Initiating Therapy

### Mania

Lithium aborts 60–80% of acute typical manic and hypomanic episodes in 10–21 days.

Response rates to lithium for typical bipolar mania:

- 65–70% full initial response
- 20% partial initial response
- 10% no initial response

Consider valproate or other mood stabilizers as first choice if mania has atypical features, frequent episodes (4 or more per year), or mixed manic/depressive symptoms.

Lithium is particularly effective in reducing affective and ideational signs and symptoms of mania, especially

- Elation, grandiosity, expansiveness
- Flight of ideas
- Irritability, manipulative behavior
- Anxiety

To a slightly lesser extent, lithium diminishes

- Pressured speech
- Paranoia

- Insomnia
- Psychomotor agitation
- Threatening or assaultive behavior
- Hypersexuality
- Distractibility

Mood stabilizers and neuroleptics or benzodiazepines can all calm acute manic symptoms (e.g., grandiosity, pressured speech). Treatment may begin with mood stabilizer

- By itself.
- Plus benzodiazepines if nonpsychotic and agitated or pressured.
  √ Beware of disinhibition or oversedation.
- Plus antipsychotics, if psychosis is present.
  √ Beware of high rates (> 70%) of acute (within 36 h) dystonia with young males < 30 y.o. and females < 25 y.o. on high-potency neuroleptics (e.g., haloperidol).
    ▫ Consider instead atypical neuroleptics and sometimes mid-potency neuroleptics to reduce EPS risk.
    ▫ Some atypical neuroleptics (olanzapine, risperidone, clozapine) may increase mood stabilization.
    ▫ Olanzapine approved by FDA for treatment of mania.
- Plus antipsychotics and, if still agitated at full antipsychotic dose, benzodiazepines.
  √ Typical antipsychotics have high risk for TD in bipolar disorder.
    ▫ In patients with h/o multiple manic episodes, alternatives to antipsychotics should be considered first.
    ▫ Some psychotic manics may respond to benzodiazepines (e.g., clonazepam, lorazepam) without an antipsychotic.
    ▫ Antipsychotics probably a low risk in patients on first or second episode who do not need antipsychotics at other times.

If *lithium alone* is started

- Obtain blood tests (*see* page 217).
- Be aware that therapeutic and toxic lithium plasma levels are close.
- Treat acutely manic patients with the lowest effective dose, which typically produces lithium levels from 1.0–1.5 mEq/l.
  √ Lithium has increasing efficacy up to 1.4 mEq/l.
- Start lithium (as predicted by tests) in divided bid or tid doses to reduce initial side effects.
- Most common initial side effect is nausea/dyspepsia caused by direct irritation of gastric mucosa by lithium.

√ Lithium citrate, slow-release lithium, or full stomach can help.
√ Divided dosing or slow-release lithium can help prevent wide fluctuations in blood levels.
- Tremor is also a common initial side effect.
√ Less frequent with slow-release form.
- If not using the earlier formulas, start lithium in a healthy adult with acute mania at 300 mg bid.
  √ Increase dose by 300 mg q 3–4 days.
    □ This divided dosing can reduce early nausea, but
    □ If nausea is posing no problem, qd dosing can be used.
  √ Raise dose until
    □ Clear therapeutic results, or
    □ Plasma level reaches 1.2 mEq/l, or
    □ Raise dose further to 1.5 mEq/l if no therapeutic effect after 10 days and no significant side effects.
- Measure initial lithium level around days 4 to 7 after starting lithium to determine plasma level.
  √ Draw lithium 12 h after the last dose.
  √ If at appropriate level, get further lithium levels in 2 weeks or 3–4 days after last lithium increase.
  √ Get further lithium levels at the same post-lithium dose time each week or 3–5 days after last lithium increase, to confirm therapeutic plasma level.
  √ Obtain levels every month for the next 6 months, and then
    □ Every 2–3 months, or
    □ If 2 or 3 consecutive lithium levels are stable, can wait 3 months and then 6 months.
- Lithium can work in 7–10 days (if therapeutic levels for acute mania are rapidly achieved) but may require up to 3–5 weeks.
- During manic episodes, patients usually need higher lithium dose.
- Reduce above doses by 50% in patients over 60 or in patients with a renal disorder.
  √ If no response and no side effects, slowly increase dose, as tolerated.
- If lithium does not induce improvement in 3 weeks, add an anti-convulsant (e.g., divalproex or carbamazepine).

If starting *lithium and antipsychotic together*

- Initially, highly manic psychotic patients are best treated with an antipsychotic (e.g., olanzapine, haloperidol, risperidone) *and* lithium.
- Prescribe lithium (as above).
- Initiate a neuroleptic if patient is psychotic and still at low risk for TD.

√ Choose maximum neuroleptic dose in advance to avoid over-dosing.

√ Atypical neuroleptics (e.g., risperidone, olanzapine) may have mood stabilizing properties and are first choice if patient is able to take medication orally.

√ If atypical neuroleptic is refused, begin with either haloperidol 5 mg po or 2.5 mg IM and, if well tolerated, increase to 10 mg po or 5 mg IM in patients over 30, since it acts rapidly and sedates minimally.

  ▫ Patients often respond well to a daily 10-mg dose of haloperidol.

  ▫ Most patients do not improve further with 15 or 20 mg haloperidol a day but are much more likely to have EPS and other side effects.

√ A mildly sedating mid-potency neuroleptic (e.g., perphenazine, particularly in young adults at risk for dystonia), can be used 12–24 mg po or 6–12 mg IM qd or bid.

√ If dystonia occurs, add anticholinergic agent.

- After controlling manic delusions, taper patient off neuroleptic.
- Initiate a benzodiazepine if patient agitated but not psychotic, or still agitated on adequate antipsychotic dose, or if TD risk makes an antipsychotic a poor choice.

  √ Begin with 1–2 mg lorazepam po or IM q 1–4 h prn until agitation is controlled and patient is mildly sedated but not ataxic or stuporous.

  √ Follow with 0.5–2 mg lorazepam po or IM tid–qid, for less variation in plasma levels.

  √ Substitute a longer-lasting benzodiazepine (e.g., clonazepam) 0.25–2 mg po qd, if required.

  √ Higher benzodiazepine dose can be given qhs to help sleep (adequate sleep may speed manic recovery).

- When patient switches out of mania, he/she may appear to be overdosed (e.g., somnolent, ataxic) on the same dose that barely controlled the mania.

  √ Defer further use of benzodiazepines until significant side effects disappear.

  √ If neuroleptic dose over 15 mg haloperidol equivalents, attempt to reduce to more usual antipsychotic range (e.g., 5–15 mg).

In treating the elderly

- Start lithium in lower doses (e.g., 300–600 mg/day).
- Monitor lithium q 3–4 days.
- Increase lithium by 150–300 mg until reach an acute therapeutic level between 0.5–0.8 mEq/l.

√ Some elderly may respond to 0.3–0.4 mEq/l.
√ 150-mg pills are available.
- Doses over 900 mg/day are often unnecessary and toxic.
- If neurotoxicity develops, may take several days to several weeks to remit, in spite of negligible lithium serum levels.
  √ Intracellular lithium levels remain high because sodium/ lithium pump (extrudes lithium from cells) is temporarily poisoned by excessive lithium.

If patient develops unresponsive EPS on antipsychotic agents, may replace neuroleptic with clonazepam, carbamazepine, or valproic acid; can also try risperidone (< 6 mg), olanzapine, quetiapine, or clozapine.

- Pure anticonvulsants do not usually increase depressions.
  √ But clonazepam can, in doses over 1.5 mg qd.
- Act as quickly as antipsychotics and possibly faster than lithium, particularly valproic acid (often within 5 days).
- Seem especially useful in rapid-cycling or dysphoric manic patients.
- Clonazepam produces sedation; carbamazepine less so, and valproic acid almost none.
- May magnify CNS toxicity of lithium (e.g., ataxia, confusion).

For lithium-resistant bipolar disorder, *see* Anticonvulsants (pages 268–69).

### Bipolar Depression

Lithium is more effective against bipolar than unipolar depressions.

- Lithium can yield a 60–75% response in bipolar depression.
  √ May need 6–8 weeks for full response.
  √ Will also quell subsyndromal depressions.
  √ In unipolar depression, response is 40%.
    □ 25–55% of patients benefit at some time from adding an AD during a unipolar depression (*see* Antidepressants for treatments of unipolar depression)
  √ TCAs usually avoided because of higher mania induction.
  √ SSRIs, buproprion, nefazodone, or MAOIs preferred.
  √ Abruptly stopping the antidepressant risks hypomania or mania.
    □ MAOI rate ~ 33%
    □ SSRI ~ 11%
    □ TCA ~ 4%
    □ Atypicals < 2%
- Anticonvulsants
  √ Carbamazepine or lithium may relieve bipolar depression.

      □ In one study (N = 27) 63% with typical features remitted on carbamazepine.

      □ Only 22% with mixed depressive mania remitted.

  √ Valproate may be no better than placebo in bipolar depression, though

      □ It may prevent or delay depressive recurrence.

  √ Valproate and carbamazepine probably superior to lithium in blocking antidepressant-induced rapid cycling.

      □ In very treatment-resistant bipolar depression, valproate for 4 weeks followed by additional lithium resulted in significant improvement ($\sim$ 40%) in depression ratings.

      □ ADs may be started sooner and used more aggressively.

  √ Gabapentin appears to have acute antidepressant effects.

      □ 53% with positive results in small case series (N = 15).

- Clonazepam may help relieve depression, but in doses of 1.5 mg/qd and more, may cause or exacerbate

  √ Depression

  √ Sedation

  √ Disinhibition

General indications:

- Where faster response is needed, lithium with antidepressants are preferred.
- For bipolar depression, first try lithium alone.

  √ At first, try levels of 0.6–1.0 mEq/ml and increase if no response (e.g., 1.0–1.5 mEq/ml).

      □ However, no data to support using lithium levels (> 1.0 mEq/ml) for acute depression.

- Antidepressants are effective but may decrease cycle length, thereby increasing manic and/or depressive episodes.

  √ In 8-week trials 43% responded to bupropion and 40% to desipramine.

      □ Switch rate to hypomania or mania over 1 year at follow-up was 43% for desipramine, 14% for bupropion (p < 0.05).

  √ In another study, patients off TCAs had bipolar periods every 150 days, whereas on TCAs, they had one every 50 days.

  √ TCAs have higher risk than SSRIs, bupropion, sertraline, paroxetine, or MAOIs.

  √ If this occurs, reduce antidepressant dosage and pretreat with lithium.

Rapid-cycling patients

- Have 4 or more recurrences in a single year.
- Anticonvulsants (i.e., valproate and carbamazepine) have superior efficacy compared to lithium in this population.

If rapid cycling occurs

- Check (and treat) for hypothyroidism.
- Multiple case studies report reduction or elimination of rapid-cycling recurrences with $T_4$.
  - √ Most with elevated TSH or other laboratory evidence of hypothyroidism.
  - √ Has also been effective in euthyroid case.
  - √ $T_4$ doses of 0.075–0.4 mg/day added to mood stabilizer and, in some cases, used alone.
    - □ Usually results in increased serum $T_4$ and decreases in TSH into the hyperthyroid range.
  - √ $T_4$ dosage increases should occur about every 3–5 weeks. It takes about 4–6 weeks for thyroid axis to equilibrate after each change in dosage.
    - □ Suprametabolic doses risk tachycardia, tremor, anxiety, agitation, congestive heart failure, osteoporosis, and atrial fibrillation.
- Prescribe 2 mood stabilizers (e.g., valproate and carbamazepine) if still cycling after 2–4 months (*see* page 269).
  - √ Lithium less effective for rapid cycling but still potentially effective as an antidepressant.
  - √ If each episode results in hospitalization, may need to start these sooner.
- Bupropion, paroxetine, sertraline, and nefazodone have lowest reported rates (1.5–3%) of manic induction in known bipolars (less than or equal to placebo).
  - √ Preferred over TCAs.
    - □ Desipramine reported to have 30% risk of switching depression into mania.
  - √ MAOIs may have lower induction risk, but only case studies reported.
- Fluoxetine may not be preferred because of very long half-life.
  - √ However, one study showed that fluoxetine induced mania no more than other ADs.

Patients with less severe bipolar illnesses, such as cyclothymia or bipolar II (hypomania and major depression), may improve on lithium alone.

### Sleep Deprivation

- One night total sleep deprivation results in 60–75% responders in bipolar depression vs. 40–50% responders in unipolar depression.

√ Efficacy can be maintained or further improved with mood stabilizers and repeat sleep deprivation (q 4–10 days).

√ Sleep deprivation for only the second half of the night probably as effective as total sleep deprivation.

√ Efficacy requires no added night or daytime naps.

√ May have some risk of mania induction.

  □ Lithium and perhaps other mood stabilizers may help maintain mood.

## Postpartum Psychosis

- Occurs in 1–2/1,000 live births.
- 70% are bipolar or unipolar.
- Lithium best preventive for bipolar psychotic depression.
- Estrogen may be best preventive in postpartum psychotic depression.
  √ If identified in first 10 days after birth, can give estrogen daily.
    □ 1st week 2.5–3.125 mg
    □ 2nd week 1.25–2.5 mg
    □ 3rd week 0.625–1.25 mg
- 60% chance of recurrence next postpartum.
  √ Immediately after birth, begin prior agent used if it was successful.

## Mood Stabilizers and Suicide

- Lithium and possibly divalproex significantly reduce the risk of suicide in bipolar, schizoaffective, and unipolar depressions.
  √ Patients not on lithium have a 5–7-fold higher risk of life-threatening or fatal suicide acts when compared to those on lithium.
  √ Patients taking lithium ≥ 8 months have significantly reduced suicide attempt completion rates comparable to the general population.
  √ Patients on divalproex also have a very low suicide attempt rate: 1.5%.
  √ Lithium is more effective than carbamazepine in preventing suicide, but good comparisons with other mood stabilizers not available.
  √ Lithium significantly reduces suicidal acts in suicidal patients without depression.
  √ Beneficial effects may be partially related to decrease of aggression and impulsivity.
  √ In patients with past or present h/o suicide attempts, lithium may be a preferred main or adjunctive treatment.
    □ Main risk is suicide attempt with lithium.

# Maintainance Therapy

Frequency of bipolar relapses in 2 years

- In 20–40% of patients on lithium,
- In 65–90% of patients without lithium.

Although lithium prevents manic and depressive episodes, < 50% achieve complete relief.

- When patients stop lithium, recurrence usually occurs in several weeks to a few months, unless episodes are seasonal or only once or twice a year.

After onset of initial manic episode, maintain bipolar patient on lithium for 9–12 months.

- If manic episode erupts
  √ Important to interview patient in detail to determine first signs of mania.
  √ Decreased need for sleep is often the first sign.
- If possibility of seasonal hypomania in history
  √ Continue past 1-year anniversary of first episode.

Some experts recommend that all first-episode bipolar patients be treated for life because each new episode may be associated with more rapid cycling. Prospective clinical trials are not yet available to confirm this approach.

- Case reports suggest that stopping lithium even after years of stable prophylaxis can result in lithium nonresponsiveness and/or more rapid cycling.

Manage a recurring manic episode by

- Increasing lithium plasma level.
- Adding clonazepam, carbamazepine, or valproic acid.
  √ If psychotic and no response to antimanic drug, add a neuroleptic.
  √ If poor response, consider lamotrigine.

If a depressive episode erupts

- Check lithium level and thyroid function.
  √ Correct, if needed.
- Can raise lithium to acute range 1.0–1.2 mEq/l.
  √ Some depressions may respond to this higher level.
    ▫ No controlled research trials available to confirm or disprove this.
- If depression is severe, add non-TCA AD that has low risk of mania induction, e.g., nefazodone, sertraline, paroxetine, bupropion, or MAOI.

√ Often augmentation effect is seen with antidepressant in less than 10 days.
√ Watch out for rapid cycling.
- MAOIs, particularly tranylcypromine, are highly effective in treating bipolar anergic depression.
  √ Consider MAOIs if treatment resistance is seen.
    ▫ Have low risk of rapid cycling.

If patient is on a combination of lithium and AD, it is probably best to discontinue the AD after 1–2 months of remission to minimize AD-induced mood cycling. (Unless depression is chronic and/or there are frequent relapses, AD not usually maintained for 6+ months, as it is in unipolar depression.)

If patient needs antidepressant but cycles on it, carbamazepine or valproic acid may be preferred maintenance drug to prevent manic episodes and rapid cycling.

"Lifelong" lithium prophylaxis is favored when

- Patient is male.
- Symptoms showed sudden onset.
- More frequent manic and depressive episodes.
- More than 2 previous (high or low) episodes.
- First episode *not* precipitated by environmental event.
- Poor family and/or social supports.
- H/o bipolar disorder in first-degree relatives.

In maintenance phase patient should be informed about risks of

- Weight gain
- Edema
- Toxicity
  √ New onset diarrhea, tremors, confused thinking
- Cognitive impairment
- Risks in pregnancy

Before stopping lithium

- Should not be considered if patient has
  √ Had 2 or more episodes in a year.
  √ Rapid onset (< 7 days) of symptoms prior to full-blown manic episode.
- Discuss pros and cons with patient and family.
- Detail the first signs of mania or depression.
- Instruct everyone about what to do if symptoms emerge.
- Taper lithium gradually rather than abruptly.
    ▫ Abrupt discontinuation carries high risk of early relapse.

L
I
T
H
I
U
M

□ Rapid discontinuation (1–14 days) of lithium risks much sooner (mean 2.5–6 months) recurrence than gradual discontinuation (15–30 days) with mean recurrence time of 14+ months.
□ Longer than 30-day discontinuation taper may be safer.
□ Over 3 years 37% of gradual discontinuers remained stable vs. 1.8% of rapid discontinuers.

If patient stops but then must return to lithium, and if he/she has previously tolerated a particular lithium dose well, restart on this full dose without titrating upwards if no side effects are noted when first starting lithium.

• Have patient report side effects immediately.
• Get lithium level in 3–4 days.

Tapering lithium by 300 mg/month may be safest approach.

• This may help "catch" a recurrence before it is out of control.
  √ The recurrence on a lower dose may be milder than on no lithium.
  √ If patient has been completely off lithium, restart lithium.
    □ Efficacy for 2nd lithium treatment is comparable to 1st treatment.
  √ Suddenly stopping may lead to "rebound" recurrence of mania.

### Cyclothymic Disorder/Emotionally Unstable Character Disorder (EUCD)

Cyclothymic disorder shows depression or hypomanic mood swings, which last from a few hours to several days and are usually not environmentally triggered.

• Often responds to lithium or anticonvulsants. A resulting disorder (not in *DSM-IV*), emotionally unstable character disorder, may develop from frequent mood swings, which interfere with emotional and personality development.

EUCD patients often show at least one of the following:

• Drug and medication abuse
• Delinquent behavior, problems with authority
• Poor school/work performance
• Sexual promiscuity
• Malingering
• Childhoods with impulsivity, low frustration tolerance, and hyperactivity

Patients are often women in their late teens to early thirties. These patients have mood swings as in cyclothymic disorder, but whereas cyclothymics tend to have responsible adult goals, EUCD patients are immature, young, hedonistic, without goals, confused, "wise-guys." EUCDs' mood swings are often missed. Lithium (dosed as in treating acute mania) appears to decrease frequency and severity of

- Depression
- Impulsivity
- Antisocial behavior

Anticonvulsants (e.g., carbamazepine or valproate) may also help.

### Borderline Personality Disorder

No drug treats borderline personality disorder effectively.
If any agent is prescribed, target specific symptoms.
These agents often include:

- Antipsychotics for cognitive problems ("cognitive disorganization under stress"), transient psychosis, and irritability.
- Lithium for mood swings.
- Benzodiazepines sometimes used for chronic anxiety (but disinhibition often seen).
- ADs for depression
  √ MAOIs most effective.
  √ SSRIs may be as effective as MAOIs.
  √ TCAs less effective.
- Carbamazepine or valproic acid to decrease behavioral outbursts and mood swings.

Overall, borderlines do better with MAOIs (or possibly SSRIs) and anticonvulsants (valproate or carbamazepine). Neuroleptics best used prn. Neuroleptics over time only decrease hostility and transient psychotic episodes. Always be alert to potential for overdose.

### Unipolar Depression

ADs treat major (unipolar) depression better than lithium.

- However, lithium may be as effective as ADs in preventing relapse.
- Lithium can augment ADs in treatment of unipolar depression

Patients unresponsive to ADs after 3–6 weeks may benefit from lithium's addition.

- Lithium is favored as a prophylactic agent over ADs in more cyclic (an episode every 6–24 months) unipolar depressions.

- A depression that emerges with "reverse biological signs"—hypersomnia, anergia, overeating—might be the first glimpse of a bipolar disorder and possibly helped by lithium.
- If a depression emerges in a patient with a strong family h/o bipolar disorder, lithium might be considered as a prophylactic agent after the second depressive episode.
- Patients who have responded to ECT for chronic depression and who have failed multiple trials of all classes of antidepressants may still get a good prophylactic effect from lithium.
    √ Lithium with TCA, venlafaxine, or mirtazepine may increase efficacy.

### Schizoaffective Disorder

Schizoaffective patients may be diagnosed as "atypical bipolar disorders" with characteristics of

- Chronic psychoses between affective episodes, or alternatively,
- Reasonably good adjustment between episodes, but with marked, mood-incongruent delusions and hallucinations during euphoric or hyperactive periods (not a *DSM-IV* criterion).

Lithium at 0.8–1.2 mEq/l combined with an antipsychotic reduces affective symptoms in schizoaffective disorders.

- Lithium might help schizoaffective patients who have not responded to other treatments.

Lithium is best for

- Hyperactivity
- Posturing, mannerisms
- Confusion
- Insomnia
- Pressured speech
- Irritability
- Episodic timing of symptoms

ADs *and* neuroleptics are best for

- Schizodepressive symptoms.
- Combination is superior to either drug alone.

Anticonvulsants, such as carbamazepine, may treat schizoaffective disorders.

- Valproic acid combined with other agents improved 42–57% of schizoaffective patients.

## Medical Conditions

Cyclic neutropenia, leukopenia

- Increases neurotrophil count.

Viral infections

- Recurrent herpes simplex
  √ Reduced infection rate on lithium.
  √ Probably related to increase in WBC.
- Equivocal effect in reducing superinfections in AIDS.

## SIDE EFFECTS

Up to 75% of patients experience some side effect, with 25% having 3 or more side effects.

Lithium's side effects arise from

- Peak blood levels or
- Steady-state levels.

Peak plasma levels

- Occur 1.5–2 h after the dose.
- Most commonly generate lethargy, transient nausea, stomach discomfort, urinary frequency, and fine tremor.
- Can reduce peak plasma level side effects by:
  √ Substituting sustained-release lithium, or
  √ Giving less lithium in morning and larger dose at hs, or
    ▫ Hopefully will be asleep during peak
  √ Starting lithium at lower doses,
  √ Spreading out dosing to tid or qid.

Steady-state levels

- Arise in 4–5 days but sometimes take up to 7 days.
- Reduce by lowering lithium dose.

Starting patient on salt-restricted diets and thiazide diuretics diminishes sodium, allowing lithium to replace sodium in the cell. In addition, lithium will be retained along with sodium at the proximal tubule and lithium level will rise so that

- May get toxic lithium plasma level.
- May induce intracellular toxicity with apparently normal plasma level.
- Better to avoid starting thiazide diuretics or salt-restricted diets.

L
I
T
H
I
U
M

- If they are required, determine the lithium dose based on the patient's clinical state and not on lithium level.
  - √ Lithium should be added slowly with careful monitoring of lithium level.
  - √ Patients already at steady state on thiazide diuretic or salt-restricted diet can have lithium added relatively safely as long as doses of their other medications are not changed.
  - √ Expect lower doses to give adequate plasma levels.
  - √ Potassium- and sodium-sparing diuretics have minimal or no effect on lithium levels.

Hypokalemia can intensify lithium side effects.

## Cardiovascular Effects

At therapeutic lithium levels, the most common ECG changes are

- *T-wave flattening or inversion* in 20% of patients (similar to changes seen in hypokalemia.
- *Widening of QRS complex.*

These changes are

- Benign.
- Poorly correlated with serum lithium level.
- Eliminated readily by discontinuing lithium.
- Should not be confused with more serious problems (e.g., hypokalemia).
- May persist or disappear spontaneously during treatment.

At toxic levels ECG changes are

- *S-T segment depression.*
- *Q-T interval prolongation.*

*Arrhythmias*

- Occur usually in patients with preexisting cardiac diseases.
- Common is sino-atrial node dysfunction with fainting, dizziness, palpitations, or without symptoms.
- Reversed by halting lithium.
- Ventricular arrhythmias rarely reported.
- Bradyarrhythmia and/or conduction defects seen in $\geq 50\%$ of bipolar patients with lithium-induced hypercalcemia and seen in $\leq 25\%$ of bipolar patients without hypercalcemia.

*Sudden deaths*

- Have occurred on lithium, usually in patients with preexisting heart disease.

- Consider obtaining a cardiologist's consultation before placing a cardiac patient on lithium or if patient has significant risk factors, e.g., severe hypertension.

## Central Nervous System Effects

*Tremor (fine, hand)*

- Dose-related tremor may affect 30–50% patients.
- More likely in those who had a preexisting tremor or a family h/o essential tremor.
- Tremors may disappear after the first 2–3 weeks of constant lithium dose.
- Lithium tremor
    - ✓ Present at rest but worsens on intentional movement or maintenance of posture.
    - ✓ Worsens with anxiety and performance.
    - ✓ Usually confined to fingers but
        - ▫ If severe, may involve hands and wrists.
    - ✓ Irregular in amplitude and rhythm.
    - ✓ Jerking fingers with flexion or extension.
    - ✓ Erupting in side thrusts.
    - ✓ Variable in its frequency and intensity throughout the day, and from day to day.
    - ✓ Produces jagged, irregular, hard-to-read handwriting when severe.
- Lithium tremor differs from others in that
    - ✓ In parkinsonism (EPS) tremor, the fingers, hands, and wrist move faster and as a unit; micrographia also appears, but not in lithium tremor.
    - ✓ In Parkinson's disease, the tremor is slow and rhythmic, with prominent rotational and flexing movements (pill-rolling).
    - ✓ In anxiety, the tremor is fine, rapid, and rhythmic with side-to-side movements.
- Lithium tremor may increase with
    - ✓ Greater serum lithium, although it may exist with normal serum levels.
    - ✓ Adding TCAs, valproate, or neuroleptics.
- Tremors may be diminished by one of the following:
    - ✓ More frequent, smaller doses or single hs dose.
    - ✓ Decreasing total lithium dose, especially if serum concentration is > 0.8 mEq/l.
    - ✓ Sustained-release lithium preparations.
    - ✓ Propranolol 10 mg qid initially.

- □ May escalate dose to 20 mg tid-qid.
- □ Before starting propranolol, r/o congestive heart failure, bronchospasm, or other contraindications to $\beta$-blockers.
- □ Alternatives to propranolol are metoprolol (25–50 mg) or nadolol (20–40 mg) bid.
- □ Atenolol debatable alternative because tremor is believed to be a CNS effect, and atenolol does not easily get into CNS.
- √ *Slowly* increasing lithium doses.
- √ Stopping TCAs.
- √ ACAs don't help.

*Seizures*

- Grand mal (rarely)
  - √ Usually in epilepsy patients, if at all.
- Lithium may be appropriate in well-controlled seizures *unless*
  - √ Carbamazepine or valproic acid would be more appropriate for the seizures (and also the bipolar disorder).

*Memory loss, "dullness of senses," reduced coordination, lethargy, ataxia, inhibited motor skills*

- Confirm lithium is the cause.
  - √ Compare with baseline function.
  - √ The absence of "highs" may account for patients describing these problems.
  - √ Hypothyroidism may be the culprit.
  - √ Subclinical depression may be the cause.
- Occur on $\geq 0.8$ mEq/l levels of lithium.
  - √ Word recall memory impaired in normal volunteers (i.e., college students).
    - □ Also complained of "cognitive blurring."
    - □ Younger patients more likely to complain of memory problems.
- Management
  - √ Reduce or stop dose.
  - √ If significant lithium problems, a switch to valproate may significantly reduce CNS side effects.
  - √ Thyroid replacement, if necessary.
  - √ Assess for antidepressants.

*Cogwheeling, mild parkinsonism*

- May increase chance of this when patient on AD or neuroleptic.
- Sometimes happens on lithium alone.
- Not very responsive to ACAs but may respond to amantadine.

*Neurotoxicity and confusion*

- Lithium at high levels can poison the cellular lithium/sodium countertransport pump.
    - Result is high intracellular lithium levels and slow elimination of lithium.
    - Can continue when plasma lithium levels are very low.
- Occurs with lithium levels ≥ 1.8 mEq/l.
- Typically lasts 5–7 days in healthy nongeriatric patients.
- May last 3–5 weeks in elderly.

*Pseudotumor cerebri*

- Rare.
- Blurred vision often first complaint.
  √ Headache not always present.
- Papilledema seen.
- Elevated lumbar puncture pressure.
- Papilledema usually resolves after a few months off lithium.
- Elevated pressure doesn't always completely resolve.
  √ Shunt sometimes needed.

## Endocrine and Sexual Effects

*Euthyroid goiter, hypothyroidism*

- Mania itself transiently increases TSH to above normal values.
- 20% of lithium patients develop thyroid abnormalities.
- Overt hypothyroidism occurs in 8–19% of inpatients taking lithium vs. 0.5–1.8% in general population.
- 5–15% have clinical signs or altered hormone levels.
  √ Symptoms often reported in subclinical and clinical hypothyroidism include: fatigue, weakness, constipation, weight gain, dry skin, cold intolerance, decreased memory, decreased concentration, slowed mentation, depressed mood, menstrual changes.
- Lithium inhibits the conversion of $T_4$ (thyroxine) to $T_3$ (triiodothyronine), which stimulates TSH (thyroid-stimulating hormone), which stimulates the thyroid gland to reestablish euthyroidism. During this compensatory process, the gland might become large (goiter) or hypothyroid or both.
- Onset typically in 6–18 months after starting lithium.
- Rapid cycling more likely with hypothyroidism and subclinical ( ↑ TSH > 5 mU/l) hypothyroidism.
- A euthyroid goiter shows
  √ Normal thyroid function tests.
  √ Increased TSH.
  √ Sometimes anergia.

- Hypothyroidism shows
  √ A goiter or no goiter.
  √ Increased TSH (the most sensitive diagnostic test).
  √ Those who have antithyroid antibodies prior to start of lithium.
- Highest risk groups
  √ Those with antithyroid antibodies prior to start of lithium
    ▫ Less common to develop hypothyroidism without antibodies prior to lithium treatment.
  √ Women
- Timing highly variable.

Management

- If patient without thyroid symptoms and TSH 5–10 mU/l, immediate thyroid replacement not needed.
  √ Monitor TSH 1 month later and then every 3 months.
  √ May try thyroxine trial to prevent exacerbation of patient's psychiatric condition.
  √ If patient with symptoms suggestive of hypothyroidism, begin thyroxine (and possibly $T_3$) before starting antidepressant.
    ▫ Thyroxine therapy alone may eliminate the depression.
    ▫ If no clinical improvement after 6–12 weeks of thyroxine treatment, begin antidepressant and/or mood stabilizer depending on clinical indication.
    ▫ If severe depression, hospitalization indicated and combining thyroid and antidepressant may be indicated.
- Can usually continue lithium with thyroid disorder.
- Add thyroxine 0.05–0.1 mg/day *or* start thyroxine 0.1 mg qd. Increase dose if necessary to suppress TSH.
- Monitor TSH.
  √ If patient is rapid-cycler, suppress TSH to low end of normal range.

*Hypothyroidism and thyroiditis with gabapentin*

- Seen with high dose: 4.8g/day.
- All symptoms reversible when gabapentin stopped.
- Restarting on lower dose.
  √ 1.5g/day does not cause hypothyroidism.

*Hyperparathyroidism*

- Serum calcium and parathyroid hormone levels enter high-to-normal range in half of patients in 1st month on lithium.
  √ Most patients eventually develop laboratory evidence of hyperparathyroidism.

- Abnormally high levels occur in 5–10% of patients.
- Rarely of clinical significance.
- Symptoms of hyperparathyroidism include
  √ Mood changes
  √ Anxiety
  √ Apathy
  √ Aggressiveness
  √ Psychosis
  √ Sleep disturbance
  √ Delirium, dementia, confusion
  √ Convulsions
- Lithium may have to be withdrawn if these consequences of hypercalcemia occur.

*Glucose tolerance, carbohydrate craving*

- Lithium may change glucose tolerance, but it is not diabetogenic.
  √ Hypoglycemia more common than hyperglycemia on lithium.
- Can accentuate diabetes mellitus.
- No reason to obtain regular glucose tests on most patients.
- Lithium can cause craving for sweets and weight gain.
- Increased sugar in fluids leads to *dental caries.*

## Gastrointestinal Effects

*Nausea, initial*

- Dose-related, but may arise on normal serum lithium levels.
- Often occurs early in treatment, especially when titrating doses and with fluctuating plasma levels.
- Accompanied by other GI symptoms.

Management

- Do one of the following:
  √ Ingest lithium with meals, snacks, milk, and if necessary, antacids (avoid sodium bicarbonate, use calcium carbonate).
  √ Spread out or diminish lithium dose.
  √ Try sustained-release preparation, which might cause diarrhea.
  √ Replace with lithium citrate syrup.
  √ Sometimes lithium carbonate doses can be increased more slowly, without causing GI symptoms.

*Nausea (chronic), anorexia, vomiting, dehydration, fever*

- Vomiting can cause more dehydration, which may elevate plasma lithium.
- Stop lithium until flu-like syndrome ends.

*Diarrhea*

- More common in toxicity, but can occur with normal serum lithium and with sustained-release, qd dosing.
- Frequency decreases with
  √ Conventional release lithium.
  √ Lithium citrate syrup.
  √ Lithium with antidiarrhea medication.
  √ Lithium with (highly anticholinergic) TCAs.

Management

- Do one of the following:
  √ Spread out dosing or reduce lithium dose.
  √ Add antidiarrheal medication (e.g., loperimides).
  √ Take lithium during meals.
  √ Switch to lithium citrate (rapidly absorbed by stomach) or conventional-release lithium if patient on sustained-release.

*Weight gain, edema*

- Common, often causes patients to stop lithium.
  √ Usually occurs in patients with preexisting weight problem.
- In those who gain weight on lithium
  √ 60% gain 15 pounds.
  √ 20% gain 25 pounds.
- Unclear why some patients gain 40–60 pounds, whereas others gain nothing.
- Likely causes:
  √ Insulin-like effects on carbohydrate metabolism,
  √ Increased caloric fluid intake, or
  √ Hypothyroidism.
- Edema may also increase weight.
  √ Shortly after initiating lithium, patients often accumulate 5–7 pounds of fluid and edema.

Management

- Do one of the following:
  √ Reduce lithium dose.
  √ Diminish by starting low-calorie diet, including fluids with normal sodium intake.
  √ If edema, cautious use of potassium-sparing diuretics.
    □ Amiloride 5–10 mg qd (don't use if K over 5.5 mEq/1).
    □ Spironolactone 50 mg qd bid.
    □ Furosemide 40 mg bid.
  √ Substitute carbamazepine for lithium, since carbamazepine does not usually increase weight.

# Hematologic Effects

*Leukocytosis*

- Mainly mature neutrophils are increased, yielding average of 35% transient increase in neutrophil count after 3–10 days of lithium.
- Normalization may take up to 6 months after lithium treatment was started.
- Reversible, benign, and not indicative of disease.
- WBC around 12,000–15,000/mm$^3$.
- Rarely need to stop lithium.
- Useful to obtain one baseline WBC while on lithium.
  √ If patient later gets sick, will be able to determine if "real" leucocytosis occurs.

# Renal Effects

*Polyuria/nephrogenic diabetes insipidus (NDI)* (3,000 ml/24 h urine and lithium-induced polydipsia)

- Caused by inhibiting renal response to antidiuretic hormone (ADH, also called vasopressin).
  √ ADH levels are increased in plasma.
- Initial polyuria is associated with
  √ Higher lithium dose,
  √ But usually not changes in urine concentration.
- After long-term lithium, polyuria is associated with
  √ Longer lithium duration and higher serum level.
  √ Decreases in urine concentration.
- Characteristics include
  √ Difficulty concentrating urine.
  √ Urine volume up to 4–8 liters/day.
  √ Difficulty maintaining serum lithium.
- NDI may exhibit
  √ Polyuria
  √ Nocturia
  √ Polydipsia
    □ Almost always secondary to polyuria.
  √ Higher sodium
  √ Lower potassium
  √ Toxicity
  √ Dehydration
- More often occurs with
  √ Sustained-release lithium or
  √ Divided dosing of lithium.

L
I
T
H
I
U
M

- Less often occurs with
  - √ Once daily dosing of regular lithium.
- Rule out diabetes mellitus, kidney disease/damage, metabolic abnormalities, or other drug effects.
- Polyuria may affect 50–70% of patients on long-term lithium.
  - √ 10% of lithium patients have renal output > 3 liters/day (clinical polyuria/nephrogenic diabetes insipidus).

Management

- Do one or more of the following:
  - √ Lithium once a day is preferred as initial approach.
    - □ If possible, avoid sustained-release lithium.
  - √ Lower or stop lithium.
    - □ Benefits seen in 1–3 weeks.
    - □ Polyuria may continue in some patients months after stopping lithium.
  - √ Increase non-caloric fluid intake to dilute lithium.
  - √ Add potassium 20–40 mEq qd.
    - □ Often effective for stopping polyuria in open trials.
  - √ Paradoxically, diuretics diminish lithium-induced polyuria.
    - □ The sodium- and potassium-sparing diuretics, i.e., amiloride, spironolactone, or furosemide, are safest because of least effect on lithium level.
  - √ Prescribe amiloride 5–10 mg bid.
    - □ Markedly decreases polyuria.
    - □ Normal diet and sodium intake.
    - □ Less or no effect on lithium level and no effect on serum potassium.
    - □ To be safe, still monitor serum lithium and electrolytes.
  - √ Nonsteroidal anti-inflammatory drugs
    - □ Indomethacin or ibuprofen can rapidly (< 24 hrs) decrease hypernatremia and nephrogenic diabetes insipidus.
    - □ Other NSAIDs probably have same effect.
    - □ Neurotoxic interactions with lithium.
  - √ Thiazides in *polyuria* are not generally recommended because they
    - □ May increase serum sodium.
    - □ May decrease serum potassium.
    - □ May increase serum lithium by 30–50%.
  - √ If thiazide is absolutely needed over other diuretic, cautiously treat with hydrochlorothiazide 50 mg/day and
    - □ Reduce lithium, and
    - □ Monitor lithium and electrolyte levels.
  - √ Can combine hydrochlorothiazide with amiloride to prevent hypokalemia.

√ Carbamazepine added to lithium can halt diabetes insipidus.
  ▫ Probably secondary to antidiuretic effect of carbamazepine.
√ Synthetic antidiuretic peptides, e.g., DDAVP (1-desamino-8-D-arginine vasopressin) not effective for NDI.

*Tubulo-interstitial nephritis/renal insufficiency*

- 10–20% of patients on long-term (≤ 10 yrs.) lithium have kidney changes.
  √ Interstitial nephrosis
  √ Tubular atrophy
  √ Sometimes glomerular atrophy
- Chronic, serious form with increasing creatinine usually reversible.
  √ Frequency very rare.
    ▫ May be > 1% with lithium > 10 years.
- More often seen with long-term lithium therapy.
- Gradual rise in serum creatinine and decline of creatinine clearance.
  √ If creatinine level ≥ 1.6 mg/100 ml, consult with a nephrologist.
    ▫ Seriously consider discontinuing lithium while problem is potentially reversible.
- Discontinue lithium.

## Skin, Allergies, and Temperature

Usually idiosyncratic rather than dose-related.
Acne and psoriasis are common.

*Acne*

- May appear or get worse during lithium treatment.
- Try antibiotics and/or retinoic acid.
  √ Tetracycline can have toxic interactions with lithium.
- May need to lower or halt lithium.

*Psoriasis*

- Aggravation of preexisting or dormant psoriasis.
- Dry noninflamed papular eruption is common.
- First try lowering lithium.
  √ If this fails, begin standard medication for psoriasis; halt lithium treatment if this fails.

*Rash, allergic*

- Patients not taking lithium in hospitals often develop allergic rashes.
  √ Soaps and detergents are the common culprits, with
    ▫ Rash often only on hands, wrist, neck where clothing rubs.
- Hospital foods are other common cause.

- Allergic rash may disappear by changing specific lithium brand/formulation.
  √ May be caused by binder, additives, dyes in pill and not lithium.
- Test patient with lithium citrate; if no rash develops, patient not allergic to lithium.

*Rash, maculopapular*

- Occurs with or without psoriasis.
- Is mildly annoying, erythematous rash.
- Relieved with 50:50 zinc ointment.

*Alopecia*

- May be due to hypothyroidism.
  √ Check TSH.
- Occurs in 12% of women; rarely in men.
- Hair may disappear anywhere on body.
- Hair can regrow on or off of lithium.
- Sometimes associated with loss of curl or wave.

Management of other skin lesions:

- Antihistamines can best treat urticarial lesions.
- Topical steroids.
- Bacitracin for localized infections.

*Mycosis fungoides*

- A rare side effect to long-term lithium use.
  √ Itchy, erythematous, hyperkeratotic lesions.
  √ Lacks systemic signs, e.g., fever, lymphadenopathy, and hepatosplenomegaly.
- Discontinue lithium.

## PERCENTAGES OF SIDE EFFECTS

| Side Effects | Lithium |
| --- | --- |
| **CARDIOVASCULAR EFFECTS** | |
| Dizziness, lightheadedness | 20 |
| ECG abnormalities | 20 |
| T-wave changes (benign) | 25 |
| **CENTRAL NERVOUS SYSTEM EFFECTS** | |
| Cogwheeling | 8 |
| | (5–75) |
| Confusion, disorientation | 22.8 |
| | (1–< 40) |

| Side Effects | Lithium |
|---|---|
| Drowsiness, sedation | 22.8 |
| | (1–< 40) |
| Headache | < 40 |
| Hypertonia | < 15 |
| Limbs, jerking | < 1 |
| Memory impairment | 32.5 |
| | (0–45) |
| Muscle cramps | 5.5 |
| Resting tremor | 37.5 |
| | (10–50) |
| Rigidity | 5.0 |
| Speech, slurred | 5.5 |
| Weakness, fatigue | 10.5 |
| | (1–30) |

### ENDOCRINE AND SEXUAL EFFECTS

| | |
|---|---|
| Goiter | 4.1 |
| | (1.7–6.1) |
| Hyperparathyroidism | 5 |
| Hypothyroidism | 12* |
| | (1–20) |
| Menstrual changes | 5.5 |
| Sexual function, disturbed | 20 |

### EYES, EARS, NOSE, AND THROAT EFFECTS

| | |
|---|---|
| Vertigo | 10 |
| Vision, blurred | < 1 |

### GASTROINTESTINAL EFFECTS

| | |
|---|---|
| Anorexia, lower appetite | 12.5 |
| Diarrhea | 14.4 |
| Dyspepsia, upset stomach | 10.3 |
| Edema | 10.2 |
| Mouth and throat, dry | 27.5 |
| | (10–50) |
| Nausea, vomiting | 15.2 |
| Polydipsia | 37.6 |
| | (10–55.3) |
| Thirst | 26.7 |
| Weight gain | 29.7 |
| | (1–60) |

### RENAL EFFECTS

| | |
|---|---|
| Kidney defect | 15 |
| | (< 10–50) |
| Polyuria | 40 |
| | (10–60) |

### SKIN, ALLERGIES, AND TEMPERATURE

| | |
|---|---|
| Abnormal skin pigment | 1 |
| Acne | 18 |
| Hair loss (mainly women) | 12 |
| Rashes | 6.3 |

* Mainly women.

## PREGNANCY AND LACTATION

Teratogenicity
(1st trimester)

- Lithium clearance increases during pregnancy.

  √ Monitor lithium levels every 2–4 weeks, particularly in 2nd half of pregnancy.

  √ Need to progressively increase lithium dose.

  √ On average, lithium dose needs to increase by 40% during pregnancy.

- Increases in non-cardiovascular abnormalities not well established.

- Slightly higher frequency of Ebstein's anomaly of the tricuspid valve (i.e., 0.1–0.2% of live births).

  √ Lower estimate considered more reliable.

  √ Tenfold increase over general population.

- In less severe bipolars with infrequent recurrences or with a gradual prodrome of manic symptoms over 2+ weeks, if pregnancy is planned, discontinue lithium before conception; or if menstrual periods are regular, at first missed period.

  √ Maternal circulation to embryo connects then and not sooner.

- During first trimester, antipsychotics, calcium channel-blockers, benzodiazepines, and ECT safest for manic episode.

  √ Avoid carbamazepine.

    ▫ Causes deformities.

  √ Avoid valproic acid.

    ▫ 1–2% neural tube defects.

- Avoid most NSAIDs because they significantly (30–60%) raise lithium levels.

√ Sulindac and aspirin don't usually increase levels, and phenylbutazone averages only 11% increase.

- In severe bipolar patient stabilized with lithium, continue lithium and follow with ultrasound.

Direct Effect on Newborn (3rd trimester)

- Goiters and hypothyroidism observed in newborns with no known permanent sequelae; follow mother's thyroid status during pregnancy.

- Lithium toxicity may develop in newborn with hypotonia, decreased sucking and Moro reflexes, hypoglycemia, cyanosis, bradykinesia, depressed thyroid, goiter, atrial flutter, hepatomegaly, ECG changes, cardiomegaly, poor myocardial contractility, GI bleeding, diabetes insipidus, or shock.
  √ Neonatal toxicity can occur even when mother's serum level is in normal therapeutic range.
  √ Polyhydramnios caused by nephrogenic diabetes insipidus in the fetus can result in the uterus becoming so enlarged that the mother's lungs have no room to expand.

- Most of these effects reverse in 1–2 weeks, which corresponds to the renal elimination of lithium in the newborn; diabetes insipidus may persist for several months.

- During second and third trimesters, lithium is acceptable. In second half of pregnancy, higher doses are needed to offset higher lithium excretion rate.

- Lithium in late pregnancy can increase risk of preterm labor.

L
I
T
H
I
U
M

- In the last 5 weeks of pregnancy, get weekly lithium levels.

- Discontinue or decrease lithium dose during week before delivery.
  √ Renal clearance drops rapidly with delivery and mother could become toxic on usual pregnancy dose.

- Discontinue lithium on or before the onset of labor.

Lactation
- Infant lithium usually ranges from 20–60% of maternal level.
  √ Check infant lithium level.
    □ Often not over 25% of maternal blood level.
    □ At levels of 25–60% of mother's, consider alternatives to breast-feeding.

### Drug Dosage in Mother's Milk

| Generic Name | Milk/ Plasma Ratio | Time of Peak Concentration in Milk (hours) | Infant Dose (mg/kg/day) | Maternal Dose (%) | Safety Rating* |
|---|---|---|---|---|---|
| Lithium | 0.42 | ? | 0.41 | 1.8† | B |

\* B: Unsafe before 34 weeks, but safer after 34 weeks (although some believe it is safe at all times).
† Calculated assuming maternal dose of 20–25 mg/kg/day.

## DRUG-DRUG INTERACTIONS

| Drugs (X) Interact with: | Lithium (L) | Comments |
|---|---|---|
| *ACE (angiotensin-converting enzyme) inhibitors:* Benazepril Captopril Enalapril Fosinopril Lisinopril Quinapril Ramipril | L↑ | Increases serum lithium. Lithium toxicity and impaired kidney function may occur; may need to stop lithium or ACE inhibitor. |
| Acetazolamide | L↓ | Reduces serum lithium and efficacy; sometimes used for detoxification in lithium overdose. |
| Alcohol | L↑ | Alcohol may increase serum lithium. |

| Drugs (X) Interact with: | Lithium (L) | Comments |
|---|---|---|
| Albuterol (see bronchodilators) | | |
| Amiloride | L↑ | Potassium-saving diuretic occasionally increases lithium concentration and toxicity. |
| Aminophylline (see bronchodilators) | | |
| Ampicillin | L↑ | Increased lithium effect and toxicity. |
| *Antipsychotics:* *Haloperidol *Thioridazine Others | X↑ L↑ | Occasionally increased neurotoxicity. Rarely not reversible. Lithium plus chlorpromazine may lower both drugs and may generate NMS. Lower lithium levels seen when liquid lithium citrate given with liquid neuroleptic (i.e., chlorpromazine or trifluoperazine) secondary to lithium precipitate being formed. |
| *Antithyroids:* Carbimazole Methimazole Radioactive iodine | X↑ | Lithium increases thyroid suppression; may be clinically useful when β-blocker contraindicated for hyperthyroidism. |
| Baclofen | X↓ | Increases hyperkinetic symptoms when lithium added. |
| *Bronchodilators:* Albuterol Aminophylline Theophylline | L↓ | Theophylline, aminophylline, and possibly albuterol increase lithium clearance and decrease lithium levels; chromolyn and nonsystemic steroids safer. |
| Caffeine | L↓↑ | Increases lithium excretion; heavy coffee drinkers have trouble reaching therapeutic levels on even 2400 mg/day. Stopping caffeine when patient has therapeutic lithium level risks too high lithium. Increases lithium tremor. |
| *Calcium Channel-Blockers:* *Diltiazem *Nifedipine *Verapamil | L↑↓ | Lithium-induced neurotoxicity, nausea, weakness, ataxia, and tinnitus. Verapamil may augment anticycling effect of lithium; lithium level may decrease; stop blocker or lower lithium. |
| Captopril (see ACE inhibitors) | | |
| *Carbamazepine | X↑ L↑ | On normal lithium, carbamazepine may induce neurotoxicity; after ceasing one agent for a few days, neurotoxicity vanishes. Also synergistic for anticycling effects. |
| *Carbonic anhydrase inhibitors | L↓ | Increases lithium clearance. |
| *Corticosteroids:* Hydrocortisone Methylprednisolone | L↓ | Increases lithium clearance; monitor lithium closely. |
| Decamethonium | X↑ | Prolonged muscle paralysis. |
| Dehydroepiandrosterone (DHEA) | L↓ | DHEA-associated mania may occur with or without lithium. |
| Dextroamphetamine | X↓ | Lithium may inhibit dextroamphetamine's euphoria. |

L
I
T
H
I
U
M

| Drugs (X) Interact with: | Lithium (L) | Comments |
|---|---|---|
| Digitalis | X↑↓ | May cause cardiac arrhythmias, particularly bradyarrhythmias; occasionally lithium reduces effects. |
| Diuretics (*see* indoline, loop, osmotic, thiazide, xanthine) | | |
| *Diltiazem (*see* calcium channel-blockers) | | |
| Enalapril (*see* ACE inhibitors) | | |
| HCAs (*see* TCAs) | | |
| Hydroxyzine | L↑ | Cardiac conduction disturbances. |
| Indoline (Indapamide) | L↑ | Increases lithium level. |
| Ketamine | L↑ | Increased lithium toxicity from sodium depletion. |
| *Loop diuretics:* Ethacrynic acid Furosemide | L↑↓ | May increase or decrease lithium slightly and safer than thiazide diuretics. Potassium-sparing diuretics safest (amiloride, spironolactone). |
| Marijuana | L↑ | Increased absorption of lithium; importance unclear. |
| Mazindol | L↑ | A few cases of lithium toxicity after 3 days of mazindol; worse with inadequate salt intake. |
| *Methyldopa | L↑ | Lithium toxicity may develop with a normal lithium level; toxicity ends 1–9 days after stopping methyldopa. |
| Metronidazole | L↑ | Increased lithium level; toxicity. |
| *NSAIDs:* *Diclofenac *Ibuprofen *Indomethacin Ketoprofen Ketorolac Mefenamic acid Naproxen *Piroxicam Phenylbutazone | L↑ | NSAIDs with asterisk increase plasma lithium 30–61% in 3–10 days. Sulindac, naproxen sodium, aspirin, and acetaminophen don't appear to change levels, and phenylbutazone averages only 11% increase. |
| Osmotic diuretics | L↑ | Decreases lithium level and efficacy. |
| Pancuronium | X↑ | Prolonged muscle paralysis. |
| Phenytoin | L↑ | A few cases of lithium toxicity. |
| Physostigmine | L↓ | May reduce efficacy of lithium. |
| *Potassium iodide | L↑ | Sometimes produces hypothyroidism and goiter, which is *no* reason to halt lithium; treat thyroid instead. |
| *Sodium bicarbonate | L↓ | Decreases lithium level. |
| *Sodium chloride | L↓↑ | High sodium decreases lithium level; low sodium intake may increase serum lithium and toxicity. |
| Spectinomycin | L↑ | Increased lithium effect and toxicity. |
| Spironolactone | L↑ | Potassium-saving diuretic may occasionally increase lithium concentration and toxicity. |
| Succinylcholine | X↑ | Prolonged neuromuscular blockade. |
| *Sympathomimetics:* Dobutamine Epinephrine Norepinephrine | X↓ | Lithium usually decreases pressor actions of norepinephrine and other direct-acting sympathomimetics. |

| Drugs (X) Interact with: | Lithium (L) | Comments |
|---|---|---|
| *Tetracyclines | L↑ | Tetracycline and doxycycline moderately increase lithium toxicity. Unclear if other tetracyclines affect lithium. |
| Theophylline (*see* bronchodilators) | | |
| †*Thiazide diuretics:* Chlorothiazide Hydrochlorothiazide | L↑ | Any diuretic that promotes sodium and potassium excretion may yield cardio-toxicity and neurotoxicity; potassium-sparing diuretics are safer but may increase lithium levels. Watch for hypercalcemia. |
| TCAs | L↑ | Increased tremor. |
| Ticarcillin | X↑ | Hypernatremia. |
| Triamterene | L↑ | Potassium-saving diuretic may increase lithium concentration and toxicity. |
| Tryptophan | L↑ | Increases lithium efficacy; tryptophan off American market. |
| Urea | L↓ | Urea may reduce lithium but no clinical evidence that this occurs. |
| Valproic acid | L↑ | Increased neurotoxicity and anticycling effect. |
| *Verapamil | L↑↓ | Lithium-induced neurotoxicity, nausea, weakness, ataxia, and tinnitus. Decreased lithium levels. |
| Xanthine diuretics | L↓ | Increased lithium excretion and decreased plasma levels. |

* Moderately important interaction; † Extremely important interaction; ↑ Increases; ↓ Decreases;
↑↓ Increases and decreases.

## EFFECTS ON LABORATORY TESTS

| Generic Names | Blood Serum Tests | Results* | Urine Tests | Results* |
|---|---|---|---|---|
| Lithium*** | $^{131}$I uptake | ↑ | Glycosuria | ↑ |
| | $T_3$ | ↓ | Albuminuria | ↑ |
| | $T_4$** | ↓ | VMA | ↑ |
| | Leukocytes | ↑ | Renal concentrating ability | ↓ |
| | Eosinophils | ↑ | Electrolytes | ↑↓ |
| | Platelets | ↑ | | |
| | Lymphocytes | ↓ | | |
| | $Na^+$, $K^+$ | ↑↓ | | |
| | $Ca^{++}$, $Mg^{++}$ | ↑↑ | | |
| | Serum phosphate | ↓ | | |
| | Parathyroid hormone | ↑ | | |
| | Glucose tolerance | ↑↓ | | |
| | Creatinine | ↑$^r$ | | |
| | Lithium*** | ↑ | | |

* ↑ Increases; ↓ Decreases; ↑↓ Increases and decreases; r = Rarely.
** Mania itself may transiently increase TSH and $T_4$.
*** Atomic absorption spectrophotometry most accurate assay for lithium. Ion-selective electrode method can give falsely higher lithium levels of 0.2–0.4 mEq/l increase probably secondary to aging electrodes.

## WITHDRAWAL

Lithium does not induce

- Dependence
- Tolerance
- Addiction
- Withdrawal

It can be stopped quickly without any apparent physiologic difficulty, but compared to gradual withdrawal, rapid withdrawal has increased risk of subsequent rebound of mood disorder.

## OVERDOSE: TOXICITY, SUICIDE, AND TREATMENT

Therapeutic indexes (i.e., toxic dose:effective dose) are

- Antipsychotics = about 100
- TCAs/MAOIs = about 10
- Lithium = about 3

Being a nonmetabolized salt, lithium toxicity results not only from the drug but also from water and sodium loss based on

- Decreased fluid or food intake (during manic or depressive swings)
- Diuretics
- Fever
- Abnormal GI conditions (e.g., nausea, diarrhea, vomiting)
- Pyelonephritis

Although no clearly defined relationship exists between serum lithium and toxicity, the serum level 12 h after the last dose roughly predicts the acute intoxication's severity. Significant diarrhea in a patient who has not had it before is often the first warning sign of toxicity.

Can occur in patients on stable doses.

- Disorders of water and electrolyte metabolism (e.g., dehydration, vomiting, diarrhea, fever, hypokalemia) usually seen at time of intoxication.
  √ Renal insufficiency usually seen at time of intoxication.
    □ Water loss due to impaired renal concentrating ability major predisposing factor.
- Most over 2.0 mEq/l.

Recovery of severe lithium toxicity patients

- 70–80% fully recover.
- 10% display persistent sequelae: dementia, ataxia, polyuria, dysarthria, spasticity, nystagmus, and tremor.
- > 10% die.

Delirium and other symptoms may continue with lithium plasma level low or nil.

- EEG slowing usually accompanies delirium.
- For 4–7 days intracellular lithium may still be high.
  √ Lithium toxicity poisons lithium "pump" in cell membrane.
    ▫ Takes time to heal.
  √ Wait until side effects stopped before restarting lithium.
- In geriatric and sometimes in other patients, delirium may continue weeks to months after lithium levels have reached zero.
  √ Mechanism unknown.

The general management of lithium overdoses includes:

- Induce emesis in the alert patient or use gastric lavage and ion exchange resin to bind lithium.
- Insure adequate hydration.
- Get a baseline ECG (to determine arrhythmia, sinus node dysfunction).
- Draw
  √ Blood lithium
    ▫ Continue to monitor for "secondary peaks" after periods of decline.
  √ Creatinine
  √ Electrolytes
  √ Urinalysis (look for albuminuria)
  √ Serum glucose (before IV fluids used)
- If patient is severely intoxicated
  √ Dialysis rapidly decreases high lithium levels.
  √ Hemodialysis is first choice for 8–12 h when one of the following:
    ▫ Serum lithium between 2–3 mEq/l and patient's condition is deteriorating.
    ▫ Fluid or electrolyte abnormalities are unresponsive to conventional supportive measures.
    ▫ Creatinine clearance or urine output decreases a lot.
    ▫ Serum lithium is not reduced at least 20% in 6 h.

# Side Effects by Levels of Lithium Carbonate

| Therapeutic Lithium Levels (0.6–1.5 mEq/l) | Mild to Moderate Toxicity (1.5–2.0 mEq/l) | Moderate to Severe Toxicity (2.0–2.5 mEq/l) | Severe Toxicity (over 2.5 mEq/l) |
|---|---|---|---|
| *Central Nervous System*<br>Hand tremor<br>Memory Impairment<br>*Endocrine*<br>Goiter<br>Hypothyroidism<br>*Gastrointestinal*<br>Diarrhea (mild)<br>Edema<br>Nausea<br>Weight gain<br>*Renal*<br>Polydipsia<br>Polyuria | *Central Nervous System*<br>Dizziness<br>Drowsiness<br>Dysarthria<br>Excitement<br>Hand tremor (coarse)<br>Lethargy<br>Muscle weakness<br>Sluggishness<br>*Eyes, Ears, Nose, Throat*<br>Vertigo<br>*Gastrointestinal*<br>Abdominal pain<br>Diarrhea<br>Dry mouth<br>Vomiting | *Cardiovascular*<br>Cardiac arrhythmia<br>Pulse irregularities<br>*Central Nervous System*<br>Choreoathetoid movements<br>Clonic limb movements<br>Coma<br>Convulsions<br>Delirium<br>EEG changes<br>Fainting<br>Hyperreflexia<br>Leg tremor<br>Muscle fasciculations<br>*Eyes, Ears, Nose, Throat*<br>Nystagmus<br>Vision blurred<br>*Gastrointestinal*<br>Anorexia<br>Nausea (chronic)<br>Vomiting (chronic) | *Central Nervous System*<br>Seizures (generalized)<br>*Renal Oliguria*<br>Renal Failure<br>Death |

- Serum lithium level often rebounds after hours of hemodialysis; this requires repeated hemodialysis.
- Goal of hemodialysis is to reduce serum lithium less than 1 mEq/l at least 8 h after hemodialysis is completed.
- For less severe intoxication
  - √ Restore fluids and electrolyte balance; correct sodium depletion.
  - √ Give 0.9% infusion of IV sodium chloride (1–2 liters in first 6 h) when lithium intoxication appears secondary to total body sodium depletion.
  - √ Rapid infusion of large volumes of IV potassium diuretic does not seem to help.
- Lithium excretion also fostered by one of the following in IV:
  - √ Sodium bicarbonate
  - √ Urea
  - √ Mannitol
  - √ Acetazolamide
  - √ Aminophylline
- Treat convulsions with short-acting barbiturates (e.g., thiopental) or benzodiazepine (e.g., lorazepam).

Lithium can be restarted 48 h after the patient is clinically normal. Clinical normality may take days or weeks and does not correlate well with serum lithium levels. This should be done very gradually and not at full therapeutic dose.

- After lithium toxicity, expect interference with cellular sodium-lithium counter transport for 4–5 days.
  - √ Intracellular lithium increases and ratio of RBC/plasma lithium goes from average 1:2 to 1:1.
  - √ Therefore, serum lithium levels can be low and toxicity still seen.
  - √ Restarting lithium too quickly or giving full dose of lithium can poison sodium lithium counter-transport pump. Healthy adults under 65 y.o. will need to wait another 4–5 days for it to heal.
  - √ In geriatric patients delirium and other signs of neurotoxicity can continue for as much as 3–10 weeks.

**Toxicity and Suicide Data**

| Generic Name | Toxicity Dose Average (g) | Mortality Dose Average (g) | Toxic Levels (mEq/l) | Fatal Levels (mEq/l) |
|---|---|---|---|---|
| Lithium Carbonate | 6 | 10–60 | 2–4 | 4–5 |

L
I
T
H
I
U
M

## PRECAUTIONS

About 33–45% of patients on lithium stop taking the drug during the first year of treatment because of

- Weight gain.
- Complaints of memory loss.
- Miss the "highs."
- GI, CNS, thyroid, and renal side effects (less frequently).
- Depressive relapse (13% stopped lithium for this reason in one study).

Close follow-up, especially during the first year, is essential.

Contraindications include

- Vomiting, diarrhea, severe disability, or dehydration.
    - √ Patients should have adequate fluids (2500–3000 ml) at start of treatment.
    - √ Infection, exercising, sweating can increase salt output.
- Hypersensitivity to lithium.
- Cardiovascular disease.
    - √ Patients with sinus node dysfunction ("sick sinus syndrome") should not receive lithium.
    - √ Carefully monitor cardiac patients with ECG.
- Renal damage.
- Pregnancy (*see* pages 247–49).

Cautionary concerns include

- Brain damage.
    - √ Follow mental status closely.
    - √ Can be well tolerated in developmentally disabled populations.
- Patients started on lithium who are already on salt-restricted diet or diuretics.
    - √ Patients may need less than expected lithium dose.
    - √ Once stabilized on lithium, there should be no changes in sodium intake or diuretics.
    - √ If sodium intake or diuretic must be changed, carefully monitor lithium level (q 3 days) and change lithium dose accordingly.
    - √ If possible, change to sodium and potassium-sparing diuretic first.
- Patients already on lithium who are started on a diuretic, salt-restricted diet, or vigorous exercise program.
    - √ Extensive sweating from running 6 or more miles a day can reduce lithium level.

√ If diuretic is used, choose sodium- and potassium-sparing.
√ Decrease lithium during sodium restriction.

- Since the ability to excrete lithium diminishes with age, use reduced doses in the elderly.

## NURSES' DATA

Remind patients and family about lithium's side effects and the need to consume stable amounts of salt and sufficient fluids.

- Avoid salt-restricted diets, diuretics, vomiting, diarrhea, excessive sweating, infection, overexercise, working heavily in hot weather.
- At least initially, patients need 2500–3000 ml/day or 10 8-oz. glasses of water/day.

Importance of monitoring lithium levels

- Describe logistics and procedures for monitoring lithium.
  √ Draw blood about 12 h after last dose.
  √ Patient should not swallow lithium on morning before blood test.

Pregnancy warnings.

Be alert to noncompliance.

Remind patients and close relatives that lithium is not an "artificial chemical" but a naturally occurring mineral in the water; some find this reassuring.

## PATIENT AND FAMILY NOTES

Carry a Medic Alert wallet card or bracelet indicating lithium's use.

Tell physicians and surgeons, especially cardiologists and GI specialists, about taking lithium.

Some of the most common side effects when starting on lithium are upset stomach, diarrhea, frequent urination.

- These side effects aren't necessarily signs of toxicity early in treatment. However, after a steady state is achieved, diarrhea or a coarse tremor may be early signs of toxicity.
  √ Confused thinking is another sign.
- Tolerance to GI and GU side effects may occur with gradual dosage adjustment.

To prevent accidents, no lithium should be at bedside or any other quickly accessible place. Keep away from children.

Ingest lithium at regular times each day, as decided with physician.

- Ingest with meals, snack, or milk to diminish GI irritation.

If dose is forgotten, can consume in 8 h.

- Otherwise, wait for next scheduled dose.
- May double dose if done on same day and patient has no side effect from higher single doses.

# 6. Anticonvulsants, Mood Stabilizers, and Antiaggression Agents

## INTRODUCTION

Carbamazepine, divalproex, clonazepam, gabapentin, and lamotrigine have anticonvulsant properties that prevent and treat bipolar disorders, especially mania. Verapamil (Calan), a calcium channel-blocker, has been shown in preliminary trials (discussed on page 272) to treat acute mania and prevent manic episodes and most resembles lithium in outcomes.

- Carbamazepine is structurally similar to the TCA imipramine.
- Divalproex is chemically akin to valproic acid; they are discussed together.
  - √ Compared to valproic acid, divalproex has significantly lower rates of anorexia, nausea, vomiting, and dyspepsia.
    - □ 15% on divalproex and 29% on valproic acid have GI side effects.
  - √ Divalproex is usually preferred because of lower side effects and lower drop-out rates.
- Clonazepam is a benzodiazepine whose mood-stabilizing operations are examined here, while its other actions are presented in Antianxiety Agents.
- Lamotrigine is effective for mania and depression but usually requires a slow build-up over 3 to 5 weeks.
- Gabapentin (Neurontin) is a very low side-effect GABAergic anticonvulsant for partial complex seizures that has only uncontrolled data in bipolar disorder, suggesting that it may treat depression and hypomania but have lower efficacy for mania.

This chapter discusses the effects of anticonvulsants and calcium channel-blockers in patients with

- Aggression (pages 281–87)
- Atypical and lithium-resistant bipolar disorder (pages 268–69)
- Bipolar depression and panic disorder (page 281)
- Atypical psychosis/partial complex seizure spectrum disorder (page 288)
- Atypical residual hallucinations (flashbacks) in chronic hallucinogen users (page 289)

Other chapters examine the effects of anticonvulsants in patients with

- Alcohol and anxiolytic withdrawal (Hypnotics, page 413)
- Unipolar depression (Antidepressants, pages 123–24)
- Schizoaffective disorders (Lithium, page 228)
- Schizophrenia (Antipsychotics, page 17)
- Panic disorders (Antianxiety, page 281)

## NAMES, MANUFACTURERS, DOSE FORMS, COLORS

| Generic Names | Brand Names | Manufacturers | Dose Forms (mg)* | Colors |
|---|---|---|---|---|
| Carbamazepine | Tegretol | Geigy | t: 100/200 | t: red-speckled/ pink |
| | | | su:100 mg/5 ml | su: yellow-orange |
| Clonazepam | Klonopin | Roche | t: 0.5/1/2 | t: orange/blue/ white |
| Divalproex | Depakote ER | Abbott | t: 500 | t: gray |
| | Depakote | | t: 125/250/500 | t: salmon-pink/ peach/lavender |
| Divalproex sodium-coated particles | Depakote Sprinkle | Abbott | c: 125 | c: white-blue |
| Gabapentin | Neurontin | Parke-Davis | c: 100/300/400 | c: white/yellow/ orange |
| Lamotrigine | Lamictal** | Glaxo Wellcome | t: 25/100/150/200 | t: white/peach/ cream/blue |
| Topiramate | Topamax | Ortho-McNeil | t: 25/100/200 | t: white/yellow/ salmon |
| Valproic acid | Depakene | Abbott | c: 250 | c: orange |
| | | | s: 250 mg/5 ml | s: red |

* c = capsules; s = syrup; su = suspension; t = tablets.
** Beware of potential dispensing error confusing Lamictal vs. Lamisil.

## PHARMACOLOGY

Carbamazepine (CBZ)

- Inhibits kindling, a process that increases behavioral and convulsive responses to a repetition of the same stimulus.
- Absorbed slowly and erratically.
- Average plasma binding is 76%.
- Since carbamazepine induces its own liver metabolism, dose may need increasing after 10 days to 5 weeks. More induction may occur with each dose increase, so that several more dose increases may be needed to establish a therapeutic level.
- Occasionally it is impossible to get a therapeutic level because induction continues to reduce blood level.
- Carbamazepine's half-life diminishes rapidly.
  - √ Initially after single dose at 30–65 h.
  - √ Three weeks later to 12–20 h.
  - √ During chronic therapy about 12 h.
- Carbamazepine produces its chief metabolite in the liver, carbamazepine 10,11-epoxide, with a half-life of 5–8 h.

Divalproex/valproic acid/ Depakote ER (extended release)

- Have antikindling, anticonvulsant, and GABAergic effects.
- Quickly and almost completely absorbed.
  - √ Depakote ER reaches maximum concentration with one dose in about 7–14 h.
  - √ Divalproex maximum absorption is delayed 3–8 (average 4) h.
  - √ Absorption more rapid with syrup, with peak levels reached in $\frac{1}{4}$ –2 h.
- Half-lives range from 6–16 h.
  - √ Shorter half-life (6–9 h) when patients take other anticonvulsants that increase hepatic metabolism (e.g., carbamazepine).
  - √ Increased half-life in children < 18 months ($\sim$ 10–67 h) and in patients with cirrhosis or acute hepatitis (up to 25 h).
- Conjugated in liver ($\sim$ 70%).
- Excreted as glucuronide mostly in urine and, to a degree, in feces and perspiration.

Gabapentin (Neurontin)

- Has anticonvulsant properties.
- Has a limited rate of absorption resulting in a limited maximum blood level.
  - √ Because of this, death by overdose does not occur.

√ However, some patients may never obtain a therapeutic blood level at any dosage.
- Half-life range is 5–7 hours.
- Is almost completely unbound (99%) and is almost entirely (99%) excreted by the kidney unchanged.
  √ Kidney impairment could result in unwanted increases in gabapentin levels.
  √ Begin with lower doses.
- Hepatic impairment does not significantly affect gabapentin because it is not metabolized by liver.

Lamotrigine (Lamictal)

- An anticonvulsant that inhibits kindling and voltage-sensitive sodium channels, which stabilizes neuronal membranes.
  √ May modulate excitatory amino acids (e.g., glutamate and aspartate).
- Absorbed rapidly, completely, and 98% bioavailable after first pass metabolism.
- Half-life ranges from 7–70 h.
  √ Mean half-life, if not on other drug, is 33 h single dose, 25 h multiple dose.
  √ Shorter half-life of 7–30 h (13-h avg.) when also taking enzyme-inducing antiepileptic(s).
  √ Longer half-life (31–110 h, 53-h avg.) when taking valproate.
- Mostly metabolized in liver by glucuronic acid conjugation.
  √ 94% recovered in urine and 2% in feces.
  √ 10% of lamotrigine found unchanged in urine.

Topiramate (Topamax)

- An anticonvulsant that increases activation of GABA$_A$ receptors.
  √ This potentiates the activity of GABA as an inhibitory neurotransmitter, and
  √ Antagonizes the ability of kainate to activate the kainate/AMPA subtype of the glutamate receptor.
- Absorbed rapidly, 80% bioavailable, peak plasma concentration in 2 h.
  √ Bioavailability not affected by food.
- Mean half-life 21 h after single or multiple doses and only 13–17% bound to plasma proteins.
- Approximately 70% eliminated unchanged in the urine.
  √ Six metabolites identified, none of which constitutes more than 5% of an administered dose.

## Pharmacology of Anticonvulsants

| | Carbamazepine | Divalproex | Gabapentin | Lamotrigine | Topiramate |
|---|---|---|---|---|---|
| Bioavailability (%) | 77 | 100 | 60 | 98 | 80 |
| Plasma-bound (%) | 65–80 | 90 | < 3 | 55 (weak) | 13–17 |
| Volume distribution (liters/kg) | $1.4 \pm 0.4$ | $4 \pm 0.9$ | $58 \pm 6$ | 0.9–1.3 | ? |
| Peak plasma level (hours) | 4–8 | 1–4 | ~1–3 | 1.4–4.8 | 2 |
| Half-life (hours) | 25–65 acutely $15 \pm 5$ (after 2–3 weeks) | 6–16 | 5–7 | 25–33 | 21 |
| Excretion unchanged (%) | 15–25 in feces | < 3 in feces and urine | 97 (urine) | 10 (urine) | 70 (urine) |

A
N
T
I
C
O
N
V
U
L
S
A
N
T
S

## Laboratory Investigations

Before starting on carbamazepine, obtain the following tests:

- A general medical history, especially focusing on blood dyscrasias and liver disease.
- CBC with differential and platelet count.
  √ ≤ 3500 WBC, consider other drug.
- LFTs, BUN, UA, creatinine
  √ Consider other drug if abnormal.
  √ Use $\frac{1}{4}$–$\frac{1}{2}$ usual dose of CBZ in hepatic disease.
- Serum sodium optional but can be valuable in elderly with high hyponatremia risk (e.g., psychogenic polydipsia).

Before starting on valproate, obtain the following tests:

- LFTs (ALT, AST)
  √ Rule out hepatic dysfunction.
  √ Establish baseline values.
- Platelet counts
- Coagulation tests
  √ Not essential, but if bruising develops, will have a comparison baseline.

Before starting on gabapentin or topiramate, obtain BUN and creatinine levels.

- Build-up of gabapentin or topiramate blood levels may occur if kidney elimination is reduced.
- Half of usual dose is recommended if renally impaired.

Before starting on lamotrigine:

- Consider monitoring lamotrigine plasma levels if on concomitant mood stabilizer.
- Plasma levels may also be indicated during dosage adjustments

## DOSES

Divalproex comes in four commercial forms:

- Depakote ER tablets are preferred because of relatively stable blood levels, lower side effects, and qd medication.
- Divalproex sodium (Depakote) is an enteric-coated stable compound with equal amounts of valproic acid and sodium valproate (also available as Depakote Sprinkle, containing coated particles of divalproex sodium).
  - √ Divalproex is preferred over valproic acid because of 50% lower GI side effects.
- Valproic acid (Depakene capsules)
- Sodium valproate (Depakene capsules and syrup) is valproic acid as the sodium salt.

### General Anticonvulsant Doses for Treating Mania

| Generic Names | Starting Doses (mg/day) | Days to Reach Steady State Level | Usual Therapeutic Doses (mg/day) | Extreme Doses Range (mg/day) | Therapeutic Plasma Levels ($\mu$g/ml) |
|---|---|---|---|---|---|
| Carbamazepine | 200–400 | 4–6 | 800–1200* | 200–2000 | 5–12 (15?) |
| Clonazepam | 1–2 | 5–8 | 4–16 | 0.5–20 | ? |
| Gabapentin | 300 tid | 1–3 | 600–1800 | 300–2700 | ? |
| Lamotrigine | 25–50 | 4–7 | 100–200** | 400–500 | ? |
| Topiramate | 50*** | 3–5 | 300–400 | 25–1000 | ? |
| Valproic acid | 500–1500 | 3–6 | 1000–1500 | 750–5000 | 50–125 (150?) |

* Need higher dose with carbamazepine due to carbamazepine-inducing enzymes.
** Need lower dose with divalproex due to VPA inhibiting lamotrigine.
*** Dose usually increased by 50 mg/week with usual maximum at 200 mg bid.

- Plasma levels should be obtained approximately 12 h after the last dose.
- In acute mania divalproex sodium has been successfully initiated in medically healthy patients at a dose of 20 mg/kg.
  - √ In less urgent situations 15mg/kg is usual and 10 mg/kg if patient has mild-moderate symptoms.
- Divalproex ER therapeutic levels represent equal amounts total free and bound valproic acid and sodium valproate.
  - √ Although free valproic acid more accurately determines what gets to the brain, its therapeutic range has not been determined.
  - √ Monitoring free valproic acid may be useful when there are changes in medication or clinical conditions that affect protein-binding.

- Protein-binding of valproic acid decreases with increased therapeutic levels.
- Carbamazepine blood levels most often sought are 7–12 $\mu$g/ml.
  √ 400–600 mg/day in divided doses is usual starting procedure.
  √ Need more frequent blood level monitoring in the first few months.
    ▫ Because it accelerates its own metabolism, a subtherapeutic level is common unless dose is increased.
    ▫ Occasionally a therapeutic dose is never obtained due to continued decreases in blood levels.

## CLINICAL INDICATIONS AND USE

### General Information

When used to treat bipolar disorder and aggression, valproate and CBZ,

- Clearly control acute mania (with or without lithium).
- May prevent mania.
- May prevent recurrences of unipolar or bipolar depression.
- Treat atypical mania, rapid-cycling, and mixed depression mania more than does lithium but have lower response rate for typical bipolar patients.
- Mean length of hospital stay is different among treatments.
  √ Divalproex alone—10 days
  √ Lithium with carbamazepine—12 days
  √ Lithium alone—18 days
  √ Carbamazepine alone—18 days
- Can relieve psychotic symptoms secondary to complex partial seizures.
- Infrequently reduce schizophrenia symptoms.
- Dampen affective swings in schizoaffective patients.
- Diminish impulsive and aggressive behavior in some nonpsychotic patients.
- Can reduce symptoms of alcohol and benzodiazepine withdrawal.
- Carbamazepine's onset of action is
  √ < 1 day: seizures
  √ 6–12 days: mania
  √ > 30 days for aggression not caused by mania.
- Carbamazepine's *full effect* is
  √ Within hours for epilepsy.
  √ 2 weeks for mania.
  √ 2–3 weeks for depression.
- Valproic acid/divalproex

√ *Starts* to relieve mania in 3–5 days, especially if full initial dose (20 mg/kg) is used.

√ *Full effect* on mania in 5–12 days.

√ May be more effective than lithium for acute mania with depressive features.

√ May also be more helpful than lithium in substance-abusing bipolars.

- Verapamil (*see* page 272)

*Promising mood-stabilizing anticonvulsants usually used adjunctively:*

Gabapentin

- Best response appears to be with bipolar II (hypomania), mixed bipolar, and nonrapid cycling and/or no psychosis.
- Poorer response seen in bipolar I and rapid cycling.
- Two studies show gabapentin no better than placebo for bipolar disorder.
- One study (N = 30) reported 82% of manic-phase patients and 55% of depressed patients were markedly improved while on gabapentin.
- Gabapentin also has significant efficacy for chronic pain.

Lamotrigine

- Has antidepressant potential and may be effective for rapid (4 or more episodes a year) cycling, as well as typical mania.

Topiramate

- May be effective as an adjunctive mood stabilizer (case reports only).
- Appears to curb bingeing and often results in significant (5%) weight loss.
- Appears to reduce PTSD and possibly borderline personality disorder.
  - √ Patients state that they are aware of the frightening act that occurred but it doesn't upset them anymore.
- Patients on topiramate show cognitive impairments during acute dosing, particularly on attention and word fluency.
  - √ Increased depression, confusion, and anger/hostility also seen.

## Atypical and Lithium-Resistant Mania

Between 20–50% of bipolar patients do not respond to, or tolerate, lithium. Frequently, combining mood stabilizers is necessary.

Carbamazepine's and valproic acid's efficacy for atypical mania is 55–76%. Other anticonvulsant mood stabilizers—gabapentin, lamotrigine, and topiramate—appear to improve atypical manias somewhat better than typical manias.

- May help up to 60% of rapid cyclers; lithium assists 10–35%.
- Valproic acid equal to lithium and superior to placebo in mania.

### Clinical Profiles: Lithium and Carbamazepine or Valproic Acid

| Clinical Profile | Lithium | Carbamazepine (CBZ) or Valproic Acid (VPA) |
|---|---|---|
| Mania | | |
| Typical | ++ | + |
| Dysphoric (mixed) | + | ++ (VPA) |
| | | −/+ (CBZ) |
| Rapid cycling | + | ++ |
| Continuous cycling | + | ++ |
| Neurological history or findings (head trauma or non-paroxysmal EEG abnormalities) | + | +/++ |
| Depression | | |
| Unipolar depression | +/++ | −/+ |
| Prophylaxis of mania and depression | ++ | −/+ (VPA)(CBZ) |

+ = effective; ++ = very effective.

If patient has one of the above varieties of atypical mania, start with an anticonvulsant. If lithium fails with acute mania, can add or substitute carbamazepine or valproate.

- The chief problem with carbamazepine plus lithium is acute confusion.
  - √ Repeat mental status testing.
  - √ If possible, lower neuroleptic doses and stop ACAs and benzodiazepines.
- Valproate with lithium less likely to cause confusion.
- On lithium and carbamazepine or valproic acid, some patients improve whereas others worsen.
- Once carbamazepine or valproic acid is stabilized, can try to taper off lithium.
- Some patients will worsen as lithium is tapered and will need to stay on both carbamazepine or valproic acid and lithium.
- The elderly are safer on carbamazepine and valproic acid without lithium.
  - √ Valproic acid may often be first choice in elderly because
    - □ Fewer CNS side effects
    - □ Wide therapeutic window

# Initiating Therapy

*Divalproex*

- Divalproex preferred over valproic acid because it has only half the incidence of GI side effects.
  - √ Divalproex extended release (ER) somewhat better tolerated than divalproex delayed release, which is usually given bid.
- 54–71% of manic patients improve when divalproex is added to other treatments.
- Divalproex's efficacy is well established for mania; minimal efficacy for depression.
- Patients improve 4–14 days after obtaining a therapeutic plasma level.
- Dose
  - √ Unlike carbamazepine, divalproex can often be started at target dose.
  - √ If severe acute mania and nongeriatric, start at 20 mg/kg in divided doses with meals. With divalproex ER, may only need medication qd.
  - √ If rapid treatment not needed, start at 10–15 mg/kg.
    - ▫ To minimize GI and neurologic toxicity, start at 250 mg tid.
    - ▫ Can increase 250–500 mg *every 3 days*, depending on response and side effects.
    - ▫ Start lower and go slower with euthymic, hypomanic, depressed, or elderly patients.
    - ▫ Give tid doses until stabilized.
    - ▫ Dosing bid is effective for maintenance treatment.
  - √ Check serum levels in 3–4 days.
    - ▫ Goal is 50–100 (possibly 125) $\mu$g/ml.
- Common early side effects include
  - √ GI symptoms (e.g., nausea, diarrhea)
  - √ Sedation
  - √ Tremor
  - √ Benign hepatic transaminase elevations.

*Carbamazepine*

- Overall response rate of 52% in acute bipolar mania.
- In treating or preventing mania, start at 200 mg qd or 100 mg bid. If mania is severe, begin at 200 mg bid or tid.
- For inpatients, increase dose every other day by 100 mg/day, or if mania is severe, 200 mg/day until the patient
  - √ Reaches 800–1000 mg/day,
    - ▫ Then slow dosage increases.
  - √ Improves sufficiently and is free of significant side effects.
    - ▫ If dose raised too quickly, common side effects are nausea,

vomiting, ataxia, drowsiness, dizziness, diplopia, blurred vision, clumsiness, and skin rashes (slightly less common).

◽ If side effects occur, lower carbamazepine dose and later raise it more slowly.

√ In outpatients, increase dose by 100 mg *every other day*.

- Serum levels should not exclusively determine dosage.
  √ Draw blood levels no sooner than 4–5 days after changing dose.
- Contraindications include bone marrow depression, narrow-angle glaucoma, and use of MAOIs within prior 2 weeks.
  √ When combined with TCAs or in those with significant cardiac disorders, can risk significantly slowed cardiac AV conduction.

## Gabapentin

- Patients (N = 21) were bipolar I with mixed episodes and resistant to at least 1 conventional mood stabilizer.
  √ 10 of the 21 were considered responders, with marked improvement in 4 and moderate improvement in 6.
  √ Marked reduction in depressive symptoms but no effect on manic symptoms.

## Lamotrigine

- Probably efficacious for both mania and depression in bipolar patients.
- Contraindicated in patients < 16 y.o.
- Improvement significant for both rapid cycling and nonrapid cycling for both depression and mania (N = 75).
  √ 12 of 41 rapid-cycling and 21 of 34 nonrapid-cycling patients completed the study.
  √ Rapid-cycling patients with severe mania had little improvement.
- Significantly improved borderline personality disorder in 3 of 8 patients without concurrent major mood disorder.
- Typically given as adjunct to other meds used for bipolar disorder.
- Has ~ 10% risk of allergic rash.
  √ With 0.1% for Stevens-Johnson syndrome and toxic epidermal necrosis.
- Dosing of lamotrigine if added to enzyme-inducing antiepileptic drugs (EIAED) without VPA
  √ Weeks 1 and 2 give 50 mg every other day.
  √ Weeks 3 and 4 give 100 mg in 2 divided doses.
  √ To achieve maintenance, increase by 100 mg/day every 1 to 2 weeks.

- Dosing of lamotrigine if added to divalproex in patients over 16 y.o.
  - √ Weeks 1 and 2 give 25 mg every other day.
  - √ Weeks 3 and 4 give 25 mg every day.
  - √ Usual maintenance dose is 100–200 mg/day.

*Topiramate*

- 9 (56%) of 16 patients with treatment-resistant bipolar disorder were considered responders.
  - √ Time to response 2 to 5 weeks.
- 10 (59%) patients with treatment-resistant PTSD achieved full remission, and 15 (88%) achieved partial or full response.
- In another open study of 30 patients with manic, mixed, or cycling symptoms, significant reduction of manic symptoms were seen after 4 weeks, 10 weeks, and at last evaluation.
  - √ Patients who were initially depressed (N = 11) or euthymic (N = 13) showed no significant changes.
- In a randomized double-blind multicenter study
  - √ 38% of patients started on topiramate 100 mg/day and titrated rapidly to 400 mg/day over 3 weeks had adverse events.
  - √ In a group titrated more slowly from 50 to 400 mg/day over 8 weeks, 25% had adverse events.
- In adult patients (N = 1,300) 22% reported a decrease in weight.
  - √ If on less than 200 mg/day, about 2% decrease in weight seen.
  - √ If on more than 1000 mg/day, about 7% decrease in body weight seen.

*Benzodiazepines*

Clonazepam, lorazepam, and perhaps others may reduce mania but

- Often need high doses (> 4 mg qd).
- Risk sedation or disinhibition.
- Rarely used as monotherapy but can facilitate other antimanic treatments.
  - √ Reduce hyperactivity.
  - √ Lower frequency of seclusion and restraints.
  - √ May not need as high antipsychotic dosing.

*Calcium Channel-Blockers*

Verapamil (Calan, Isoptin) may stop and prevent mania; other calcium channel-blockers may be effective (e.g., nimodipine), but less data available.

- Verapamil, like lithium, is most effective in classic bipolar mania.
  - √ Consider its use if lithium tried but poorly tolerated.

√ Also consider using it (and perhaps other calcium channel-blockers) if bipolar patient also has medical disorders that would be helped by calcium channel-blockers, e.g., hypertension, supraventricular tachycardias, achalasia, migraine, premature labor, tardive dyskinesia, Raynaud's disease, and/or possibly stroke.

- Optimum verapamil dosing ~ 120 mg tid or qid.
  √ As effective as lithium in two double-blind studies but not in another.
- Takes 7–14 days to work.
- Usually well tolerated, and tachyphylaxis and withdrawal do not occur.
- May increase toxicity of lithium and carbamazepine.
- Contraindicated with recent MI, 2nd and 3rd degree AV blocks, hypotension, sick sinus syndrome, or severe left ventricular dysfunction.
  √ Can cause sinus bradycardia and AV blocks.
  √ Use of short-acting CCBs, including verapamil, was associated with 1.6 times increase in the incidence of MI over 4 years in elderly patients being treated for hypertension.
    ▫ Probably due to propranolol being more efficacious in reducing MI and not verapamil in increasing MI.
    ▫ Severity of hypertension not controlled in this study.
  √ May have additive hypotensive effects with beta-blockers and other antihypertensive agents.
  √ In one placebo-controlled study, adding magnesium oxide 100 mg/day enhanced the efficacy of verapamil.
  √ Most common side effects are related to vasodilation, e.g., dizziness, skin flushing, tachycardia, nausea.

When starting a patient on verapamil

- Check BP and heart rate daily both before and after starting.
- Get an ECG before and at 1-week intervals until dose is stabilized.
- Warn patient that dizziness (3.3%), hypotension (2.5%), headache (2.2%), nausea (2.7%), and constipation (7.3%) are the most common side effects. Very rarely, extrapyramidal side effects are seen.
- Calcium channel-blockers (CCB) can have significant interactions with lithium, carbamazepine, and neuroleptics. Risks include
  √ CCB with lithium: neurotoxicity, choreoathetosis, parkinsonism, cardiac slowing
  √ CCB with carbamazepine: increased carbamazepine, neurotoxicity
  √ CCB with neuroleptics: increased parkinsonism

*Neuroleptics*

Typical antipsychotics

- More effective than lithium in quickly reducing hyperactivity but less effective in stabilizing mood.
  - √ Higher doses are usually no more effective than typical doses, e.g., higher doses than haloperidol 10 mg qd are not usually superior and risk increased side effects.

Atypical antipsychotics

- Probably effective for mania.

Clozapine

- Only evaluated in open-label studies of very refractory mania.
  - √ Averaged 70% response in these mania studies.

Olanzapine

- 139 manic or mixed-manic patients treated with 5–20 mg/day olanzapine (mean dose ~ 20 mg) or placebo for 3 weeks.
  - √ 49% of the 70 olanzapine patients had a > 50% reduction in mania compared to 24% on placebo.
    - ▫ Outcome same for psychotic and nonpsychotic patients.
    - ▫ Outcome similar to valproate or lithium studies.
- In an uncontrolled study (113 responders) improvement in mania continued up to 10 weeks after initiation of treatment.
  - √ Case studies suggest occasional olanzapine-induced mania can occur.

Risperidone

- Using risperidone up to 6 mg qd in 2 studies, about half of the patients had a 50% or greater reduction in manic symptoms.
- Another study reported reduced rapid cycling from average of 5.5 affective episodes in the prior 6 months (not on risperidone) to 2 episodes during the ensuing 6 months (mean risperidone dose 3.2 mg qd).
  - √ Affective episodes were less severe while on risperidone.
- On 2.75 mg qd, 9 of 14 patients not responding well to lithium or other mood stabilizers were rated as much improved and no longer met criteria for a mood episode.

ECT

- Highly effective in acute mania.
- Often only 1–3 treatments needed.
- Consider using it with
  - √ Pregnant women

√ Drug-resistant bipolar patients
√ Severe and dangerous manics
√ Highly suicidal mixed states

## Combination Treatments with Anticonvulsants, Mood Stabilizers, or Calcium Channel-Blockers

General principles

- Synergistic therapeutic and toxic effects are often seen.
  √ Toxic effects can be seen when each drug is in the "normal" serum level range.
- Often low-normal plasma levels of both agents (e.g., lithium 0.6–0.8 mEq/1, carbamazepine 6–8 $\mu$g/ml, valproic acid 50–70 $\mu$g/ml) are preferred to maximize synergistic therapeutic effects and minimize toxicity.
- Valproic acid can increase carbamazepine plasma levels, and carbamazepine can reduce valproic acid plasma levels.
- Verapamil (see below) can also have significant toxic interactions.
  √ Increases lithium toxicity without necessarily increasing lithium levels.
  √ Increases carbamazepine levels and toxicity.

*Combinations with anticonvulsants*

Lithium and valproate

- Often efficacious, particularly with rapid cycling or mixed episodes.
- Probably superior to lithium alone in preventing mania relapse.
  √ In one report, 5 of 7 on lithium alone relapsed vs. 0 of 5 on combination.
- No changes in pharmacokinetic and blood levels.
- Can have additive side effects, e.g., weight gain, GI complaints, sedation, tremor.

Lithium and carbamazepine

- Often efficacious in rapid cycling and in lithium nonresponders.
- Probably superior to lithium or carbamazepine alone in preventing relapse, and also superior to lithium–neuroleptic combination.
- Useful for depression.
- No changes in pharmacokinetics and blood levels.
- Risk occasional neurotoxicity and/or asterixis in CNS disorder, but more often see milder side effects, e.g., weight gain, sedation.
- Lithium may reverse CBZ-induced neutropenia but not agranulocytosis.

Lithium and calcium channel-blockers

- Lithium and verapamil may augment each other in typical bipolar disorder.
  √ Verapamil risks lower lithium level due to increased excretion.
- Risk neurotoxicity, choreoathetosis, parkinsonism, and/or cardiac slowing, particularly with verapamil or diltiazem added to lithium, but less risk with nifedipine.
  √ Severe bradycardia may occur.

Lithium and gabapentin

- May be particularly helpful for hypomania and/or bipolar depression.
- Likely safe because no P450 drug interactions or protein-binding, but can risk toxic levels if kidney function is impaired (both excreted by kidney).

Lithium and lamotrigine

- Well tolerated and may be especially helpful in bipolar depression and possibly mania.
- More data needed regarding side effects and efficacy.

Valproate and carbamazepine

- Generally effective (> 60% responded).
- Carbamazepine can significantly decrease VPA levels by inducing P450 IIIA 3/4.
- Valproate can moderately decrease CBZ levels by decreasing CBZ metabolism, or increase plasma CBZ by displacing protein-bound CBZ.
- Carbamazepine and valproate levels must be monitored regularly (q 1–2 weeks) until steady state is achieved.

Valproate and lamotrigine

- Probably effective.
- VPA inhibits glucuronidation, resulting in substantially increased levels of lamotrigine.
  √ Use low doses of lamotrigine.
  √ Increased chance of more severe skin rashes.
  √ Also increased risk for ataxia, tremor, sedation, and fatigue.
- Lamotrigine may decrease valproate levels.

Carbamazepine and lamotrigine

- Possibly effective.
- CBZ increases lamotrigine metabolism.

- Lamotrigine can increase CBZ metabolites, particularly carbamazepine-10,11-epoxide, resulting in neurotoxicity.

Carbamazepine and calcium channel-blockers

- Use with extreme caution due to risk of toxic interactions.
- Increased carbamazepine may be seen.
- Neurotoxicity seen with carbamazepine combined with diltiazem or verapamil but not reported with nifedipine.

*Mood stabilizers and neuroleptics*

Lithium and typical neuroleptics

- May speed antipsychotic response and decrease agitation.
  √ Typical dose of haloperidol 5 mg IM or 10 mg po.
- No enhanced efficacy seen in controlled studies (only 2), and lithium alone is better tolerated.
- To avoid neurotoxicity, e.g., in elderly or medically disabled, lithium level should be below 1.0 mEq/l and neuroleptic used at lowest dose.
- Increased neurotoxic side effects reported with combination in elderly bipolar patients include delirium and extrapyramidal signs, e.g., tremor, cerebellar dysfunction, and if used chronically, tardive dyskinesia.
  √ Side effects are usually mild and resolve when neuroleptic is stopped.

Lithium and atypical neuroleptics

- Atypical neuroleptics may have mood-stabilizing properties that augment lithium.
- Risperidone, olanzapine, and clozapine have all been reported effective in treatment of resistant bipolar disorder.
- Side effects are usually mild but fever, increased CPK, increased WBC, and delirium have been reported.
  √ Lithium counteracts clozapine-induced leukopenia but doesn't prevent agranulocytosis.

Valproate and typical neuroleptics

- May speed antipsychotic response and decrease agitation, but little data available.
- Four cases of encephalopathy reported.

Valproate and atypical neuroleptics

- One uncontrolled study reported > 80% efficacy with clozapine and valproate, but another open study suggested that anticonvulsants decrease the antipsychotic efficacy of clozapine.

- Valproate and risperidone may improve, and at least did not worsen, outcome.

Carbamazepine and typical neuroleptics

- Can be effective, but carbamazepine can increase neuroleptic metabolism resulting in decreased neuroleptic levels.
  √ Increased neuroleptic dose may be necessary.

Carbamazepine and clozapine

- Only data available indicate that carbamazepine with clozapine is contraindicated.
  √ Each can have additive hematologic side effects, and carbamazepine lowers clozapine levels.
  √ Asterixis and neuroleptic malignant syndrome have been reported with this combination.

*Lithium and benzodiazepines*

- Lithium and lorazepam rapidly effective and safe in acute mania (N = 4).
  √ However, another study (N = 5) reported ataxia and dysarthria (probably dose-dependent).
- Lithium and clonazepam can successfully reduce psychosis, pressured speech, hyperactivity, anxiety, agitation, violence, intrusiveness, and hypersexuality.
  √ Clonazepam dose range 0.5–16 mg/day.
- Benzodiazepines probably OK with other mood stabilizers, but published data not available.
  √ Additive sedation with anticonvulsants.

**Promising Adjunctive Treatments**

Omega 3 fatty acids—preliminary controlled study:

- May inhibit neuronal signal transduction pathways in manner similar to lithium or valproate.
- Double-blind placebo-controlled trial compared omega 3 fatty acids (9.6 g/d) (N = 14) with placebo (N = 16) in addition to usual treatment.
  √ Active capsule contained 440 mg eicosapentanoic acid and 240 mg docosahexanoic acid derived from menhaden fish body oil concentrate.
  √ Subjects took 7 capsules bid for a daily total of 6.2 g eicosapentanoic acid and 3.4 g docosahexanoic acid in the active group.

- At 120 days 82% of active group (who were also on other meds) had no relapse compared to only 40% of the placebo group.
  - √ Also significantly lower Hamilton depression score (active group decrease 4.6 vs. increase 3.1 in placebo group).

Donepezil (cholinesterase inhibitor)

- N = 8 manic patients.
- Dose 5–10 mg qd.
  - √ Maximal efficacy seen with 5 mg/day with no further improvement on 10 mg.
  - √ 6 of 8 patients showed marked improvement.
  - √ Need more studies to confirm efficacy.
    - ◻ Can risk increased extrapyramidal effects by interfering with anticholinergic treatments.

Choline bitartrate

- N = 40 treatment-resistant bipolar patients.
- ∼ 60% clinically improved with 4 g/day of choline bitartrate in open-label study.
  - √ Choline given bid.
  - √ 50 mg/kg may approximate optimal effective dose.

Inositol (a simple isomer of glucose)

- 18 bipolar I or II patients with depression.
- 10 patients on 12 g inositol daily and 8 on placebo.
- 50% of inositol patients and 25% of placebo patients significantly improved.

## Maintaining Therapy

Lithium is most effective in preventing relapse, while divalproex is rated fair and carbamazepine marginal.

Divalproex maintenance considerations include:

- Obtaining plasma level 5 days after acute dose is stabilized.
  - √ This will serve as a reference for the future.
  - √ Further routine plasma levels are not needed unless there is a change in clinical status.
- Obtain repeat LFTs at 3–4 month intervals or if symptoms of liver disease appear.
  - √ Mild SGPT elevations are usually benign but should be monitored for significant changes.
  - √ Elevations of bilirubin are clinically more important and warrant a consultation from a specialist and possible discontinuation of valproic acid.

A
N
T
I
C
O
N
V
U
L
S
A
N
T
S

- European studies argue that with severe hepatotoxicity rates of less than 1:10,000, LFT monitoring is not regularly needed.
- Patient should report increased bruising or bleeding in case thrombocytopenia develops.
- Disturbing maintenance side effects include
  - √ Hair loss (alopecia) in about 8%.
    - □ Twice or more common in females than males.
  - √ Increased appetite and weight gain.
  - √ Polycystic ovaries, amenorrhea, androgenism.
    - □ Highest risks in teenaged girls.

Carbamazepine maintenance considerations include:

- Obtaining a plasma level 5–14 days after establishing the acute dose.
  - √ Carbamazepine induces its own hepatic metabolism.
    - □ Most (∼ 90%) autoinduction occurs in the first month of stable dosing.
  - √ Check level 10 days to 3 weeks after maintenance dose established to determine if level is now subtherapeutic.
  - √ Occasionally, some patients' livers continue to autoinduce with each higher dose, and a therapeutic level cannot be obtained unless a drug that blocks autoinduction (e.g., valproic acid) is added.
  - √ Levels over 15 $\mu$g/ml in children or 20 $\mu$g/ml in adults are potentially toxic.
- Monitoring CBC and platelet counts regularly.
  - √ CBC monitoring dose not reliably detect clinically significant bone marrow suppressions.
  - √ CBC monitoring is unlikely to pick up serious blood dyscrasias (e.g., aplastic anemia) because they usually develop suddenly, and mild asymptomatic leukopenia is not related to serious idiopathic dyscrasia.
    - □ Serious bone marrow suppression usually presents with symptoms such as fever, sore throat, bruising, bleeding, or petechiae.
    - □ Instruct patient to report these immediately.
  - √ Consult hematology and consider discontinuing carbamazepine if
    - □ Leukocytes < 3500/mm$^3$ or
    - □ Neutrophils < 1500/mm$^3$ or
    - □ Platelets < 100,000/mm$^3$ or
    - □ Erythrocytes < 3.0 × 106 /mm$^3$
  - √ Frequency of CBC monitoring ranges from every 2 weeks for the first 2–3 months, and then, if normal, at 1–3-month intervals after that; use the European practice of initially monitoring

every 2 weeks for the first 6 weeks; then every 2 months, and after 6 months, every 6 months or year.

- □ There is no evidence that the European practice results in more problems, but the local "standard of care" and medicolegal considerations perpetuate higher monitoring frequency in the U.S. in psychiatry but not neurology.
- □ The reaction is most likely to occur early in treatment and very unlikely after 6 months.
- Monitor LFTs monthly for the first 2–3 months, and then every 6–12 months or if hepatitis symptoms appear.
  - √ Does not reliably detect liver failure.
  - √ Bilirubin may be best indicator of liver failure.
- Asymptomatic elevated LFTs, leukopenia, or thrombocytopenia can be managed with dose reduction.
  - √ They also can spontaneously resolve.
- Hyponatremia occurs
  - √ In 6–31% of patients on CBZ.
  - √ Most often in elderly.
  - √ Occasionally develops months after starting CBZ.

A N T I C O N V U L S A N T S

## Bipolar Depression

- Carbamazepine effective in some small, uncontrolled studies but not in others.
- Valproic acid/divalproate have limited evidence for relief of depression.
  - √ Both may "augment" antidepressants, as lithium does.
- Clonazepam may help relieve depression, but in doses of 1.5 mg qd and more may cause
  - √ Depression.
  - √ Sedation.
  - √ Disinhibition.
- Gabapentin can cause a marked reduction in depressive symptoms but without effect on manic symptoms.

## Panic Disorder

- Clonazepam stops panic disorder.
- Valproic acid might help.
- Carbamazepine does not prevent panic.

## Aggression

Because aggression stems from many sources, no single agent is clearly indicated. Medications have no or little effect in predatory aggression characterized by secrecy, planning, low autonomic activation, and no remorse. Affective aggression characterized by impulsivity, irritability, intense autonomic activation, and remorse can respond to medication. Acute aggression differs from chronic aggression, and each requires its own treatment. Substance abuse markedly reduces medication response rates. Risks and side effects of medications can be found in appropriate chapters, e.g., atypical antipsychotics and hyperprolactinemia are found in Antipsychotics chapter.

*Acute aggression*

- Atypical antipsychotics (e.g., risperidone, olanzapine) or high-potency typical neuroleptics (e.g., haloperidol) are first-line treatments for acute aggression and psychosis-induced violence.
  - √ Typical neuroleptics may risk TD, hypotension, and oversedation.
    - ▫ Effective in first several weeks for impulsiveness, physical and/or verbal aggression related to psychotic ideation.
    - ▫ Haloperidol 5–15 mg po or 2.5–7.5 mg IM and monitor for extrapyramidal side effects.
    - ▫ Start at lower dose in males < 30 y.o. and females < 25 y.o. to avoid dystonic reaction, particularly with high-potency neuroleptics.
    - ▫ No better than placebo for chronic nonpsychotic impulsive aggression.
  - √ Atypical antipsychotics preferred due to lower side effects, greater efficiency and possible efficacy, particularly with negative symptoms.
    - ▫ Most atypical antipsychotics do not have an IM form if po is refused.
    - ▫ Can be acutely sedating.
    - ▫ Useful in aggression related to psychotic ideation, brain injury, mental retardation, conduct-disordered children, adolescents ± psychiatric illness, autism, injuries to self and/or others, mania, and borderline personality disorder.
  - √ When starting an atypical antipsychotic, begin risperidone 1–2 mg po or olanzapine 5–10 mg po and then increase gradually (q 2 days) monitoring for EPS.
    - ▫ If patient is still aggressive, gradually add doses to get to typical target doses, e.g., 4 mg risperidone, 15 mg olanzapine, 10 mg haloperidol.
    - ▫ Half or quarter of these doses in the elderly or medically compromised.
    - ▫ Do not use for aggression alone for > 6 weeks.
- Antianxiety agents: benzodiazepines
  - √ Short-acting forms effective, especially in episodic dyscontrol and incipient rage episodes.

√ Can lower amount of typical neuroleptic needed to control agitation, thus lowering EPS risks.

√ Can be more effective than neuroleptics in acute aggression episodes (e.g., 1–2 mg lorazepam IM more effective than 5 mg haloperidol IM).

√ Violence, aggression, and suicidality associated with panic or anger attacks and anxiety are responsive to benzodiazepines (e.g., alprazolam 1–5 mg/day) but may require longer duration of treatment for significant results.

√ Benzodiazepines with longer half-lives may be preferred for subchronic (2–6 weeks) treatment.

√ Initially, 1–2 mg po or IM, q 1–2 h until calm (lorazepam).

  ▫ If IV dose must be given, push slowly and be sure not to inject more than 2 mg IV to prevent respiratory depression and laryngospasm.

  ▫ May repeat in ½ h.

√ Maintain dose in nonagitated person at 2 mg po or IM tid.

√ Taper at 10% a day from the highest dose to avoid withdrawal, unless on drug less than a week.

√ Do not keep patient on drug for aggression alone > 6 weeks.

√ Can risk disinhibition at lower doses and at higher doses, ataxia or severe lethargy.

- Antidepressant: trazodone
  √ Acutely lowers aggression and agitation in demented or developmentally disabled patients without impairing cognition.
    ▫ Effective dose range 75–500 mg qd successfully used.
    ▫ Can be effective chronically.

- Narcotic antagonist: naltrexone
  √ Effective for repetitive self-injurious but nonsuicidal behavior.
  √ Usual dose 50 mg po qd.
  √ Most patients have no self-injuries after 1 to 2 weeks of treatment.

*Chronic aggression,* a more common problem, may only diminish *after* a therapeutic dose level is maintained 4–8 weeks.

- Should inform patient about this time lag.

Antianxiety agents

- Benzodiazepines
  √ Consider benzodiazepines as adjuncts in chronic aggression rather than first-choice treatments.
    ▫ May risk disinhibition or trigger paradoxical rage attacks.
  √ In healthy nongeriatric adults, consider longer-acting benzodiazepines, e.g., clonazepam (18–50-h ½ life), clorazepate (30–200-h ½ life), chlordiazepoxide (50–100-h ½ life), or diazepam (30–100-h ½ life).

- Titrate dose gradually to avoid high blood levels resulting in sedation and toxicity that may last days (or weeks).
- Shorter-acting benzodiazepines somewhat therapeutic in elderly with dementia and behavioral disturbance.
- Risks tolerance and addiction.
- May impair cognition.
- Can be disinhibiting.
- Buspirone
  - √ Also helpful in chronic aggression.
  - √ Takes 3–10 weeks to be effective with daily dose range of 10–30 mg bid ( ≥ 90 mg daily total dose may be more effective for many patients, if tolerated).
  - √ Effective for decreasing aggression and anxiety in developmentally disabled, cognitively impaired, head-injured, and dementia.
  - √ Generally well tolerated and usually nonsedating and nonaddicting.

Anticonvulsants

- Anticonvulsants, especially carbamazepine, valproic acid, as well as lithium, can treat aggression and violence in bipolar disorder.

Mood stabilizers

- Give same doses for aggression as for mood stabilization and anticonvulsant effect.
  - √ Anticonvulsants and mood stabilizers can treat aggression and violence in:
    - Bipolar disorder, borderline personality disorder, conduct disorder, episodic dyscontrol, and other CNS disorders, including developmental disabilities, and partial complex seizure spectrum disorder (*see* pages 288–89).
- Check plasma levels to insure meds are in therapeutic range.
  - √ Meaningful levels available for lithium, depakote, carbamazepine.
- Lithium
  - √ Effective in controlled studies of prisoners; nonpsychotic, nonbrain-injured patients; children with intermittent explosive disorder; neurologic patients; aggression and irritability due to mania; posttraumatic stress disorder (PTSD); borderline personality disorder.
  - √ In patients with or without major depression, significantly reduces suicidal thoughts or suicide attempts from 5 to 7 times higher than, to nearly the same rate (1.2) as, the general population (1.0).
    - Maximum improvement may take up to 5 months but usually much sooner results.

√ Low to moderate efficacy for uncontrolled rage triggered by "nothing" or minor stimuli.

√ Children with intermittent explosive disorder showed decreased aggressiveness (double-blind, placebo-controlled), but no effect was noted in a 2-week trial on adolescents with conduct disorder.

√ Open trials showed effective reduction of violence in mentally retarded and other psychiatric disorders, e.g., PTSD.

- Divalproex
  √ So far, divalproex is the only medication other than lithium that has been shown to significantly decrease suicide or suicide attempts.
    □ Reduces rate to 1.4 with baseline 1.0.
  √ Intermittent explosive behavior in bipolar disorder.
  √ Chronic violent impulsive behaviors (6-month study) with dosing of 15–25 mg/kg.
  √ Adolescents with chronic violent temper outbursts and irritable mood swings.
    □ Within 5 weeks, weekly outbursts decreased from 5.8 episodes to 0.1, and mood lability decreased from 3.8 to 0.5.
  √ Behavioral disturbances (e.g., combativeness, agitation, restlessness) in geriatric dementia.
    □ At plasma levels of $60 \pm 22$ $\mu$g/ml, 9 of 17 patients much improved and 1 very much improved.

- Carbamazepine (1200–1600 mg/day in divided doses) effective for
  √ Impulsive aggression from CNS disorders, e.g., brain injuries, dementia.
  √ Intermittent explosive disorder and borderline personality disorder (BPD).
    □ Another study of BPD (N = 20) did not show efficacy over placebo after 1 month.
  √ Aggression in PTSD, mania, and schizophrenia.
  √ Monitor for bone marrow suppression and blood abnormalities.

- Lamotrigine possibly effective.
  √ Uncontrolled small number of cases suggested possible efficacy similar to divalproex.
  √ Requires relatively long time to achieve effective dosing.

Antidepressants

- SSRIs consistently show positive outcomes in a variety of aggression-related disorders, with most data coming from fluoxetine trials.
  √ Decreased impulsive aggression and irritability seen in CNS disorders (e.g., dementia), pervasive developmental disorder,

schizophrenia, PTSD, personality disorder, and anger/rage attacks (panic attack equivalent and manifests as acute, intense anger rather than panic).

▫ Efficacy seen in patients with or without major depression, bipolar disorder, or schizophrenia.

▫ Usual dose range is 20–60 mg a day (fluoxetine), 50–200 mg (sertraline), 20–40 mg (paroxetine).

▫ 60–70% of rages significantly decreased or absent with SSRI treatment.

▫ Clear improvement often seen at 6 weeks to 3 months of treatment, not usually acutely.

√ Fluoxetine 20 mg for 3+ months can reduce self-injury in demented and developmentally disabled patients.

√ 3 controlled and 4 open studies showed fluoxetine effective in treating borderline personality disorder.

▫ Decreases impulsivity, irritability, self-mutilation, and anger.

▫ 70+% of depressed patients with anger attacks did not have anger attacks after 8 weeks treatment on fluoxetine.

√ Tricyclic antidepressant reported effective for aggression in brain injury and anger attacks.

▫ All are open trials and case reports. No controlled trials have been reported.

√ Patients with profound developmental disabilities, lack of verbal ability, and aggressive behavior had decreased self-injury, agitation, emotional lability, and aggression when treated with fluoxetine or sertraline.

Antipsychotics

- Atypical agents decrease impulsivity, self-mutilation, and aggression better than typical agents.
  √ Antipsychotics most effective with aggression associated with psychosis.
  √ May take months for chronic aggression to respond.
  √ Clozapine useful for chronic violence in schizophrenia and/or brain injury.
  √ Risperidone and olanzapine useful in conduct-disordered children with or without psychiatric illness, and for symptoms of autism.
  √ Typical neuroleptics can reduce aggression in psychotic patients but risk more side effects than the atypicals.
  √ Improvement often in first several weeks.
  √ Decreases injuries to self and/or others.

Beta-Blockers

- Propranalol (lipophilic)

√ Effective in stroke, dementias (Alzheimer's, Huntington's disease), brain injury, and psychotic patients whose aggression is unrelated to psychotic thought (up to 500 mg/day).

√ Reduction of agitation and rage due to brain damage seen at 60–480 mg/day.

√ Clinical response usually seen after 4 weeks.

√ Beta-blockers may risk bradycardia and hypertension.

√ May worsen asthma, chronic obstructive pulmonary disease, diabetes mellitus, cardiac, renal, or thyroid disease.

- Pindolol (partially lipophilic)

√ Effective in aggressive organic brain syndrome at 40–60 mg/day.

√ Onset of clinical response in 2 weeks.

√ More robust response in severely damaged patients.

√ Less likely than propranolol to induce hypotension and bradycardia.

- Nadolol (hydrophilic)

√ At 120 mg/day, effective in double-blind study with chronic aggressive patients.

√ At 80–160 mg/day, decreases assaultive self-aggression and suicidal behavior in aggressive schizophrenics, central nervous system disorder, and developmentally disabled.

√ Suggests beta-blocker can treat aggressive behavior by its peripheral effects.

## Psychotropic Drug Treatment of Chronic Aggression

| Generic Groups | Appropriate Dose |
| --- | --- |
| Anti-anxiety agents | Standard doses |
| Buspirone | 10–20 mg tid |
| Carbamazepine | 1200–1600 mg/day in divided doses (serum levels at 6–12 $\mu$g/ml) |
| Lithium | 300 mg tid (serum levels at 0.6–1.2 mEq/l) |
| Nadolol | 80–160 mg/day; mean of 96 g/day |
| Neuroleptics | Standard doses for schizophrenia |
| Pindolol | 2.5–5 mg tid |
| Propranolol | 200–800 mg/day in divided doses; range is 40–1440 mg/day. |
| | Start at 20 mg tid; raise by 60 mg/day q 3 days until therapeutic effect or 800 mg/day. |
| Trazodone | 50–175 mg tid |
| Valproic acid | 750–1750 mg/day in divided doses (serum levels 50–100 $\mu$g/ml) |

## Sexual Compulsions

- SSRIs

√ Can decrease unusually high sexual drive (10+ sexual acts a week) down to "normal," low normal, or none.

▫ Often preferentially reduces unconventional sexual desires, while preserving normative sexual arousal.

□ Fluoxetine's very long half-life allows for missed doses with low risk.
- Antiandrogens
  √ Most male sexual offenders have normal serum total testosterone.
  √ Medroxyprogesterone (MPA) reduces testosterone by interfering with the binding of testosterone to a serum sex-hormone–binding globulin, resulting in increased metabolic clearance of free testosterone.
  √ MPA can help control male sexual offenders and deviant sexual behaviors.
  √ MPA most commonly prescribed to sex offenders in the IM form.
    □ Effects usually seen in 2–4 weeks.
  √ Injections for sex offenders are weekly or biweekly, in doses ranging from 100–800 mg (typically 200–500 mg).
  √ IM dosing for paraphiliacs 300–600 mg per injection every 1–2 weeks.
  √ Testosterone levels are monitored, with typical goal of 50% reduction in levels.
  √ MPA in the oral form has encouraging results in the treatment of paraphilias, with doses of 50–200 mg/day.

## Atypical Psychosis/Partial Complex Seizure Spectrum Disorder

- The term *spectrum* is used because all components of "seizure" are often not seen with each episode.
  √ May have varying symptoms.
- The term *temporal lobe* is avoided because that is not necessarily where the focus is.
- Signs and symptoms include
  √ Episodic psychosis with normal intervals.
  √ Olfactory, tactile, proprioceptive hallucinations, or sensory distortions in which objects look bigger or smaller, walls tilt.
  √ Loss of memory for time intervals during which patient may have been unresponsive to environment and/or engaged in repetitive, purposeless activities, such as buttoning and unbuttoning shirt, smacking lips, walking to door and back.
  √ Complex behaviors (e.g., robbing a bank, beating up a person) are not seen.
  √ Spontaneously occurring "out of the blue" intense emotional experiences (e.g., rage, sadness, sexual, mystical).
  √ Only 50% of patients with these symptoms have abnormal EEGs.
  √ Often history of head trauma, infection, or birth complications.

- Symptoms respond to carbamazepine or divalproex.
  - √ Usually need full anticonvulsant blood levels.
  - √ Response often within 2–5 days of achieving therapeutic level.
  - √ "Typical" psychotic symptoms (e.g., auditory or visual hallucinations) are less likely to respond to an anticonvulsant alone.
    - ▫ May need antipsychotic.

*Atypical residual hallucinations (flashbacks) in chronic hallucinogen users:*

- If impairing normal function, anecdotal evidence suggests that anticonvulsants (carbamazepine or valproic acid) are effective.
- Neuroleptics are not usually effective.

## SIDE EFFECTS

### General Information

Clonazepam's side effects are outlined in the antianxiety chapter.

40–50% of patients on carbamazepine have side effects. These side effects for carbamazepine can be minimized by

- Gradually building up dose.
  - √ Not as necessary for valproic acid.
- Using more frequent, smaller doses.

Side effects appear similar when anticonvulsants are used for

- Psychiatric and neurologic disorders.
- Adults and children
  - √ Except young children, < 2 y.o., prone to hepatotoxicity with valproate.

Most common acute side effects

- For carbamazepine:
  - √ Symptoms of being "drunk"—ataxia, incoordination, dizziness, lightheadedness, blurred vision, weakness, fatigue
  - √ Rashes
- For valproic acid:
  - √ GI side effects—nausea, dyspepsia, diarrhea
  - √ Sedation
  - √ Tremor
- For lamotrigine (at 500 mg):
  - √ Dizziness, ataxia
  - √ Diplopia, blurred vision
  - √ Nausea, vomiting

- For gabapentin:
  - √ Somnolence
  - √ Dizziness, ataxia
  - √ Nystagmus
- For topiramate:
  - √ Somnolence, psychomotor slowing
  - √ Dizziness
  - √ Cognitive impairment

## Cardiovascular Effects

Usually benign.

*Atrioventricular conduction times and nodal rhythms decreased; quinidine-like effect occasionally occurs with carbamazepine.*

- AV conduction delay and bradyarrhythmias can occur at therapeutic doses.
  - √ More common in older women.
- Get ECG in patients over 50 y.o.
- Use extreme caution when combining with TCA or other quinidine-like drugs.
- Avoid carbamazepine in patients
  - √ With heart block or at high risk for cardiac conduction abnormalities (e.g., myotonic dystrophy).
  - √ Consider divalproex as better alternative with this condition.

*Dizziness from orthostatic hypotension.*

- Frequent with topiramate.
  - √ Dizziness (28%) and ataxia (21%).

## Central Nervous System Effects

*Confusion from carbamazepine*

- May be secondary to
  - √ Being on lithium and neuroleptics,
  - √ Older age,
  - √ CNS disease,
  - √ *Hyponatremia*, or
  - √ *Water intoxication* (rarely).

*Drowsiness, sedation*

- Sedation appears to be dose-related.
- Management
  - √ Gradually increase dose from beginning.
    - □ Start carbamazepine dose as low as 100 mg/day.
    - □ Then increase every 3 days up to 400 mg/day.

□ If patient accommodates to sedation at 400 mg/day, dosage can be increased 200 mg every 3 days.
□ Can minimize sedation by administering greater proportion of carbamazepine at bedtime.
- Valproic acid is less sedating than carbamazepine, but it can cause substantial *lethargy*.
√ This usually happens only when combined with other anticonvulsants or sedating drugs.
- Gabapentin causes fatigue 11% of time (5% on placebo).
- Topiramate causes asthenia 8% of time (1% on placebo).
- Lamotrigine causes somnolence 14% of time (7% on placebo).

*Severe skin reactions* from carbamazpine suggest impending blood dyscrasia.

*Tremor* is common side effect of divalproex.

- Reduce dose.
- Add beta-blocker.

## Endocrine and Sexual Effects

*Polycystic ovaries/hyperandrogenism*

- Seen in up to 80% of women started on long-term treatment on valproic acid before age 20.
√ Case controlled study, true incidence unknown.
√ At least 30% of women > 20 y.o. are reported to have polycystic ovaries/hyperandrogenism.

*Water intoxication* can occur with hyponatremia and confusion in patients on carbamazepine.

- About 5–25% of patients develop hyponatremia.
- Demeclocycline 300 mg bid and then increased to 600 mg bid after a few days often effectively reverses hyponatremia.

## Eyes, Ears, Nose, and Throat

*Nasal congestion*

*Vision, blurred* (*see* page 45)

## Gastrointestinal Effects

*Constipation* (*see* page 47)

*Hepatitis, hepatotoxicity*

Valproic acid (15–30%) and, to a lesser extent, carbamazepine raise LFTs slightly during first 3 months of therapy.

- Valproic acid may induce hyperammonemia, often with confusion and lethargy.
- High LFTs do not predict liver damage.
  √ Bilirubin may be better indicator.

Carbamazepine causes a rare, very occasionally fatal, hypersensitivity reaction with fever and generalized rash during the first month.

Valproic acid generates (very rarely) potentially fatal hepatotoxicity, especially in patients

- Under 2 years old,
- Taking other anticonvulsants, and
- Having severe neurological disease, mental retardation, or inborn error of metabolism.
- With polytherapy
  √ Fatal hepatoxicity occurs
    ▫ 1 : 17,000 in 2–21 y.o. (1 : 500 in < 2 y.o.)
    ▫ 1 : 37,000 in 21–40 y.o.
    ▫ 1 : 38,000 in > 40 y.o.

This hepatotoxicity is rarely seen in adults on anticonvulsant monotherapy; it is preceded by malaise, weakness, lethargy, anorexia, vomiting, and seizures.

- Divalproex contraindicated in patients with liver disease.
- Hepatic impairment significantly increases half-life of lamotrigine (110 h with hepatic impairment), moderately decreases clearance of topiramate, and has no effect on gabapentin because it is not metabolized by liver.

*Mouth, dry (see page 47)*

*Nausea, vomiting, anorexia, indigestion*

- Usually transient, these GI symptoms typically occur on empty stomach or if initial dose is too high or increased too rapidly.
  √ Poor appetite and/or nausea most common GI side effects.
  √ More common with valproic acid, lamotrigine, and topiramate.
- Valproic acid (Depakene) affects 15–20% of patients but divalproex sodium (Depakote) under 10%.
- Management
  √ If started on valproic acid, switch to divalproex sodium or divalproex sodium extended-release
  √ If this fails, try divalproex sodium-coated particles (Depakote "Sprinkle").
  √ May give more protection to stomach.
    ▫ Increase dosage more slowly.
  √ Give with meals.

√ Try histamine-2 antagonist.
√ Often subsides in 1–4 weeks.
√ Lamotrigine and topiramate have lower GI effects if very gradually increased to target dose.

*Pancreatitis*

- Rare side effect of carbamazepine and valproate

*Weight change*

- Topiramate tends to decrease weight (7.1%).
- Gabapentin has modest increase of weight (2.9%).
- Valproic acid increases appetite and weight.
- Carbamazepine usually does not affect weight.

## Hematologic Effects

Do not start carbamazepine in patients with bone-marrow suppression or who already are leukopenic.

*Anemia (aplastic), agranulocytosis*

- Severe and potentially fatal.
- Carbamazepine produces aplastic anemia in < 0.002% of patients.
  √ This is 5–8 times more than the spontaneous rate (6 per million for agranulocytosis; 2 per million for aplastic anemia) in the general population.

*Anemia (mild)* happens in < 5% of patients on carbamazepine.

*Other forms of bone-marrow suppression* afflict 3% of carbamazepine users.

May also see

- *Pancytopenia*
- *Eosinophilia*
- *Purpura*

*Leukopenia*

- Carbamazepine may mildly lower WBC by as much as 25% initially, but this decrease is usually transitory and without adverse effects.
  √ Women at higher risk than men.
- In 2% of patients carbamazepine induces a persistent leukopenia.
  √ With carbamazepine-induced leukopenia 76% is moderate (3000–4000 WBC/mm$^3$) and 24% severe (< 3000 WBC/mm$^3$).
    □ 50% develop the leukopenia within 16 days.
    □ Recovery usually occurs within about 6 days of stopping CBZ.

- If WBC count drops to 4000 mm$^3$ during carbamazepine therapy
  √ Obtain another WBC count in 2 weeks.
  √ If WBC count does not return to normal in 2 weeks, reduce carbamazepine.
- Consider stopping carbamazepine immediately with any of these symptoms:
  √ WBC count below 3500–4000/mm$^3$
  √ Neutrophil count below 1500
  √ LFTs increased 3-fold or bilirubin elevated
  √ Fever
  √ Infection, sore throat
  √ Petechiae, bruising
  √ Weakness
  √ Pallor
- Captopril 12.5 mg qd effective in reversing leukopenia (case report).
- Lithium at usual therapeutic levels may protect from leukopenia.
- Valproic acid rarely induces leukopenia (0.4%).
  √ About same rate as TCAs (0.3–0.4%).

*Thrombocytopenia (< 100,000/mm$^3$ platelets)*

- *Petechiae, bruising, hemorrhage, nose bleeds, and anemia* occur occasionally on divalproex.
- More likely with ≥ 2000 mg qd divalproex.
  √ If mild thrombocytopenia, reduce valproic acid dose.

## Renal Effects

- Few renal effects, and mainly with carbamazepine (i.e., urinary frequency or urinary retention).
- Renal impairment significantly increases half-lives of gabapentin, lamotrigine, and topiramate.
- Kidney stones occur in 1.5% of patients taking topiramate.
  √ This is 2–4 times expected rate.

## Skin, Allergies, and Temperature

*Alopecia* occurs with valproic acid more than carbamazepine.

- Tends to be transient.
- Case reports tout zinc and/or selenium as effective treatment.

*Fever, chills, sweating, lymphadenopathy, muscle cramps, and joint aches* may arise from carbamazepine.

*Pulmonary hypersensitivity* arises from carbamazepine, with symptoms of hay fever, dyspnea, pneumonitis, or pneumonia.

*Rash*

- Allergic rash is the most common side effect of carbamazepine.
- Seen in 3–15% of psychiatric patients.
  - √ Usually arises between 9 and 23 days after carbamazepine begun.
  - √ Stop carbamazepine if
    - □ *Exfoliative reaction,*
    - □ *Urticaria reaction,* or
    - □ *Stevens-Johnson syndrome* (acute inflammatory skin disorder with "iris" target lesions).
  - √ Rash occurs ~ 10%.
- Management
  - √ Avoid sunlight; may be a photosensitivity reaction.
  - √ Treat minor rashes with antihistamines.
    - □ Some patients may desensitize over 1–3 weeks.
  - √ May be allergic to binder in pill, not carbamazepine.
    - □ Try different form (e.g., 100 mg chewable, different brand).
- Lamotrigine also risks serious and possibly fatal rash.
  - √ 10% risk of mild to serious rash.
  - √ 1.1% serious in pediatric population.
  - √ 0.3% serious in adult population.
  - √ Valproic acid added increases lamotrigine blood levels and significantly risks more rashes that may become serious.
  - √ Severe rashes include:
    - □ *Stevens-Johnson syndrome*
    - □ *Toxic epidermal necrolysis*
    - □ *Lennox-Gastout syndrome* (lamotrigine only approved for > 16 y.o.)
  - √ Severe skin reactions suggest impending blood dyscrasia.

*Status epilepticus*

- On gabapentin 1.5% (N = 31) had status epilepticus.
  - √ 14 of these patients had no prior history of status epilepticus.
  - √ Patients were all epileptic.

## PERCENTAGES OF SIDE EFFECTS

| Side Effects | Carbamazepine | Divalproex | Gabapentin | Lamotrigine | Topiramate |
|---|---|---|---|---|---|
| **CARDIOVASCULAR EFFECTS** | | | | | |
| Bradycardia | < 1 | — | < 0.1 | < 0.1 | — |
| Cardiac conduction/nodal rhythms decreased | < 1 | — | — | — | — |

| Side Effects | Carbamazepine | Divalproex | Gabapentin | Lamotrigine | Topiramate |
|---|---|---|---|---|---|
| Chest pain | < 1 | — | — | — | — |
| Congestive heart failure | < 0.1 | — | < 0.1 | — | — |
| Dizziness, lightheadedness, hypotension, vertigo | 11.4 (5.9–40) | > 1 | 17 | 42 | 28–33 |
| Fainting, syncope | < 1 | > 1 | — | < 1 | — |
| Hypertension | < 0.1 | > 1 | > 1 | | < 1 |
| Leucopenia | — | — | — | — | 1.5–3 |
| Palpitations | < 1 | — | < 1 | < 1 | — |
| Peripheral edema | — | — | 1.7 | < 1 | — |
| Vasodilation | — | — | 1.1 | — | — |
| **CENTRAL NERVOUS SYSTEM EFFECTS** | | | | | |
| Anxiety, nervousness | — | — | 2–3 | 4 | 15–20 |
| Ataxia, incoordination | 26.8 (10.4–≤ 50) | 12 | 8–12 | 6–22 | 17–21 |
| Body jerks | < 1 | — | 5 | — | > 1 |
| Confusion, disorientation, amnesia | 5.5 | — | 2 | — | 9–15 |
| Depression | 5.5 | 5.5 | 2 | 4 | 8–13 |
| Drowsiness, sedation, somnolence | 35.4 (10–50) | 5.5 | 19 | 14–19 | 25–30 |
| Excitement, hyperactive | — | 0–11** | — | — | — |
| Hallucinations | 5.5 | — | < 1 | — | — |
| Headache | 5.5 | 5.5 | 8 | 29 | — |
| Numbness, stupor | < 1 | — | — | — | > 1 |
| Speech, slurred | 5.3 | — | 2–3 | 3 | 13–17 |
| Switch into mania | 11.8 | — | — | — | — |
| Tremor, twitching | 0 | < 1 | 2–7 | 4 | 10–14 |
| Weakness, fatigue | 5.5 | 10 | 11 | 14 | 11–31 |
| **ENDOCRINE AND SEXUAL EFFECTS** | | | | | |
| ADH, inappropriate | 5 | — | — | — | — |
| Menstrual changes | — | 20 | — | 9 | 4–8 |
| **EYES, EARS, NOSE, AND THROAT** | | | | | |
| Nystagmus | 1 | < 1 | 8 | 2–3 | — |
| Sore throat, flu, rhinitis | 5.5 | — | 4–5 | 11–17 | — |
| Vision, blurred | 12.5 (> 5–30) | < 1 | 6 | 16 | 10–15 |
| Vision, double | 1 | < 1 | 5–6 | 22 | 6–14 |
| **GASTROINTESTINAL EFFECTS** | | | | | |
| Anorexia | — | 13 | > 1 | < 1 | 5–12 |
| Constipation | — | 5 | 1–2 | 4 | 3–5 |
| Diarrhea | 3 | 3 | — | 6 | > 1 |
| Dyspepsia, upset stomach | — | 8.5* | 2–3 | 5 | 5–8 |
| Edema | 0 | < 1 | < 1 | < 1 | 1–2 |
| Mouth, dry | < 1 | < 1 | 1–2 | < 1 | 3 |
| Mouth sores | 5.5 | — | — | < 1 | > 1 |
| Nausea, vomiting | > 5 | 11–22 | 6 | 19 | 11–14 |
| Salivation | — | 3.5 | < 1 | < 1 | — |
| Weight gain, increased appetite | | 3–6 | 1.1 | < 1 | — |
| Weight loss | — | < 1 | < 1 | < 1 | 7–13 |

| Side Effects | Carbamazepine | Divalproex | Gabapentin | Lamotrigine | Topiramate |
|---|---|---|---|---|---|
| **HEMATOLOGIC EFFECTS** | | | | | |
| Anemia (mild) | 5 | < 1 | < 1 | < .1 | > 1 |
| Blood dyscrasias (all types) | 3 | — | — | — | — |
| Bone-marrow suppression | 3 | < 1 | — | — | < 0.1 |
| Bruising easily | 5.5 | 5.5 | > 1 | — | — |
| Leukopenia (transient) | 8 (7–10) | 0 | — | < 1 | 1–3 |
| Leukopenia (permanent) | 2.5 | 0 | — | — | < 1 |
| Petechiae | (2–3.2) | 5.5 | — | — | — |
| Thrombocytopenia | 2 | < 1 | < 1 | < .1 | — |
| **SKIN, ALLERGIES, AND TEMPERATURE** | | | | | |
| Hair loss | 0 | 5.5 | — | — | — |
| Rashes | 6.6 (1–15) | 5.5 | > 1 | 5–10 | 3–5 |
| Skin pigment, abnormal | 5.5 | 0 | < 0.1 | — | < 1 |

\* Valproic acid (Depakene) > 15%; divalproex (Depakote) < 8%.
\*\* Only seen in 1 study of hyperactive children, not replicated.

A N T I C O N V U L S A N T S

# PREGNANCY AND LACTATION

Teratogenicity
(1st trimester)

- Anticonvulsants have an overall teratogenic rate as high as 4–5% when taken during the first trimester.
  - √ This risk is mainly in fetus 10 weeks old.
  - √ After 10 weeks most major physical development is accomplished and risk of teratogenic defects substantially decreases.

- Among carbamazepine's teratogenic population, 20% had developmental delay, 26% had fingernail hypoplasia, and 11% had craniofacial defects.
  - √ These percentages may be higher than usual. A well-controlled second study is needed.

- Valproic acid produces a few malformations akin to fetal hyantoin syndrome—e.g., lumbosacral meningocele, microcephaly, prolonged clotting abnormalities, cleft lip, prenatal growth deficiency.

- Valproic acid poses a 1–2% chance of spina bifida.

- Risks are unclear for gabapentin, lamotrigine, and topiramate.
  √ For these reasons these medications should not be used in first trimester.

- If a woman taking antiepileptics becomes pregnant, stopping the anticonvulsants abruptly can cause withdrawal seizures and rebound of mood disorder.

- Only add anticonvulsants during pregnancy if absolutely necessary.

- During first trimester, before 10 weeks of maturation, if a mood stabilizer is needed, lithium is probably safer than carbamazepine or valproic acid to control mania.
  √ Verapamil las low risk of teratogenicity.

- Consider ECT as a safer alternative.

Direct effect on newborn (3rd trimester)

- During 2nd and 3rd trimesters, lithium and carbamazepine seem equally safe.

- Valproic acid known to cause hepatotoxicity when serum levels exceed 60 $\mu$g/ml; keep serum concentrations < 60 $\mu$g/ml.

Lactation

- Carbamazepine present in milk at about 60% of maternal plasma concentration.

- Valproic acid excreted in small amounts into breast milk.

- Clonazepam enters breast milk. Although it does not accumulate, its long half-life may produce apnea. Infants exposed *in utero* or during breast-feeding should have clonazepam serum levels monitored and CNS depression observed.

- Lamotrigine, gabapentin, and topiramate have too little data to predict effects during pregnancy and breast-feeding.

## Drug Dosage in Mother's Milk

| Generic Names | Milk/Plasma Ratio | Time of Peak Concentration in Milk (hours) | Infant Dose (mg/kg/day) | Maternal Dose (%) | Safety Rating* |
|---|---|---|---|---|---|
| Carbamazepine | 0.36 | ? | 0.38 | 2.8 | C |
| Clonazepam | ? | ? | 2 μg † | 1.3–3.0 †† | C |
| Valproic acid | 0.01–0.07 | ? | 0.27** | 1.8 | B |

\* B: Reasonably unsafe before 34 weeks, but safer after 34 weeks; C: Reasonably unsafe before week 44, but safer after 44 weeks.
\*\* Therapeutic dose for neonates 20–40 mg/kg/day.
† Infant therapeutic dose 20–200 μg/kg/day.
†† Maternal dose not specified but assumed to be 20–200 mg/kg/day.

## DRUG-DRUG INTERACTIONS

| Drugs (X) Interact with: | Carbamazepine (C) | Comments |
|---|---|---|
| Acetazolamide | C↑ | Increases levels/toxicity. |
| Alprazolam (*see* benzodiazepines) | | |
| Antipsychotics | X↓C↓ | Decreases both neuroleptic and carbamazepine effects (*see* haloperidol). |
| Azithromycin (*see* macrolide antibiotics) | | |
| Barbiturates | C↓ | Phenobarbital raises carbamazepine's metabolism to epoxide; can lower serum level in 5 days, but without causing major clinical effects. Other barbiturates probably act similarly. |
| Benzodiazepines | X↓ | Diminishes alprazolam and clonazepam plasma levels (20–50%). Other benzodiazepines potentially affected. |
| *Birth control pills | X↓ | Diminished oral contraceptives levels, loss of effect, pregnancy. Valproate, lamotrigine, tiagabine, and gabapentin do not interact and risk contraceptive failure. |
| *Cimetidine | C↑ | Increases acutely administered carbamazepine by 30% to produce toxicity in 2 days; chronically taking both drugs poses no particular risk. When cimetidine stopped, carbamazepine toxicity dissipates in about 1 week. Ranitidine can substitute for cimetidine. |
| Citalopram (*see* SSRIs) | | |
| Clarithromycin (*see* macrolide antibiotics) | | |
| Clobazam | X↓ | Reduces plasma levels. |
| Clonazepam | X↓ | Diminishes clonazepam level. |
| Clozapine | X↑C↑ | Possible synergistic bone-marrow suppression. |
| *Corticosteroids: Dexamethasone Methylprednisone Prednisolone | X↓ | Carbamazepine may chronically reduce actions and levels of most corticosteroids; may need to increase steroid dose. |

| Drugs (X)<br>Interact with: | Carbamazepine (C) | Comments |
|---|---|---|
| Cyclosporine | X↓ | Lowers blood level. |
| *Danazol | C↑ | Danazol greatly raises carbamazepine levels, at times to toxicity. Other androgen derivatives (e.g., methyltestosterone) may act similarly. If used together, closely monitor carbamazepine level and adjust dose of one or both drugs. |
| Dexamethasone (*see* corticosteroids) | | |
| Dextropropoxyphene | C↑ | Increases levels/toxicity. |
| Digitalis, digoxin | X↑ | May worsen or cause bradycardia. |
| *Diltiazem | C↑ | On adding diltiazem, toxicity may occur in 1–4 days; halting diltiazem can ignite seizures because carbamazepine declines. Nifedipine, which does not affect carbamazepine clearance, is a safer calcium channel-blocker. Nimodipine may also be safer. |
| Diuretics | X↓ | Symptomatic hyponatremia; may need periodic electrolytes. |
| *Doxycycline | X↓ | Carbamazepine may reduce doxycycline's level as well as other tetracyclines. |
| †Erythromycin (*see* macrolide antibiotics) | | |
| Ethosuximide | X↓ | Diminishes ethosuximide. |
| Fentanyl | X↓ | Reduces plasma level and analgesia. |
| Fluoxetine (*see* SSRIs) | | |
| Fluphenazine (*see* haloperidol) | | |
| Flurithromycin (*see* macrolide antibiotics) | | |
| Fluvoxamine (*see* SSRIs) | | |
| Gemfibrozil (*see* lipid-lowering agents) | | |
| *Haloperidol | X↓ | Carbamazepine reduces haloperidol by 50–60%, which may or may not induce symptoms in 24 h (in rapid-cyclers) to 3 weeks. Serum levels of both drugs may be normal or low; monitor serum levels of both drugs closely. |
| †Isoniazid (INH) | C↑ | Carbamazepine may increase to toxicity usually in 1–2 days of INH; frequently happens on INH doses > 200 mg/day. Symptoms stop 2 days after INH is halted. INH often reduces therapeutic dose of carbamazepine; when INH is reduced or stopped, serum carbamazepine decreases. |
| Josamycin (*see* macrolide antibiotics) | | |
| *Lipid-lowering agents:*<br>  Gemfibrozil<br>  Isonicotinic acid<br>  Niacinamide<br>  Nicotinamide | C↑ | Increases carbamazepine levels and high-density lipoprotein (HDL). |

| Drugs (X) Interact with: | Carbamazepine (C) | Comments |
|---|---|---|
| *Liquid medicinal agents or diluents* | X↓C↓ | Carbamazepine suspension can result in a rubbery orange mass when given with other liquid suspensions. May result in decreased bioavailability and absorption. |
| *Lithium | X↑C↑ | Lithium and carbamazepine may increase each other's neurotoxicity and therapeutic effects. Additive effect to decrease thyroid. Lower levels of each may still be therapeutic. Lithium leucocytosis may cancel carbamazepine leucopenia. |
| *Macrolide antibiotics:* Azithromycin Clarithromycin Erythromycin Flurithromycin Josamycin Ponsinomycin Troleandomycin | C↑ | Significantly (1–2 times) increases carbamazepine levels/toxicity; may subside in 2–3 days after antiobiotics stopped. Spiramycin probably safe alternative. |
| *Mebendazole | X↓ | Carbamazepine may impair mebendazole's therapeutic effect at high doses; no special precautions needed. Valproic acid may be safer than carbamazepine. |
| *Methadone | X↓ | Carbamazepine may lower serum methadone and increase withdrawal symptoms; patients may need more methadone or should be switched to valproic acid. |
| Methylprednisone (*see* corticosteroids) | | |
| Nefazodone | C↑ | Potentially increases carbamazepine levels by inhibition of 3A4 isoenzyme. |
| Neuromuscular blocking agents (*see* pancuronium, vecuronium) | X↓ | Shortens duration of action. |
| Niacinamide (*see* lipidlowering agents) | | |
| Oral contraceptives (*see* birth control pills) | | |
| Pancuronium | X↓ | Shortened neuromuscular blockade. |
| Paroxetine (*see* SSRIs) | | |
| Phenytoin | X↑↓C↓ | Monitor both serum levels: unpredictable effects on phenytonin; lower carbamazepine levels. |
| *Phenobarbital | X↓C↓ | Monitor both serum levels. |
| Ponsinomycin (*see* macrolide antibiotics) | | |
| Prednisolone (*see* corticosteroids) | | |
| Prednisone (*see* corticosteroids) | | |
| *Primidone | X↓C↑↓ | Speeds conversion of primidone to phenobarbital. |
| *Propoxyphene | C↑ | Consistently raises carbamazepine, at times to toxicity. |

A N T I C O N V U L S A N T S

| Drugs (X) Interact with: | Carbamazepine (C) | Comments |
|---|---|---|
| Propranolol (& other β-blockers) | X↓ | Theoretically, carbamazepine could speed metabolism of propranolol and other β-blockers. Propranolol may increase anticonvulsant effects of carbamazepine. |
| Sertraline (*see* SSRIs) | | |
| SSRIs | C↑ | Plasma level increases. |
| *Tetracycline (*see* doxycycline) | | |
| Theophylline | X↓ | Decreased theophylline half-life and levels. |
| *Thyroid hormones | X↓ | Accelerates elimination of thyroid hormones and may induce hypothyroidism; add thyroid. |
| TCAs | X↓↑C↓↑ | Carbamazepine may lower imipramine serum levels and probably other HCAs; monitor serum levels and increase HCA doses. Increases shared side effects (e.g., orthostatic hypotension, decreased heart conduction). |
| Troleandomycin (*see* macrolide antibiotics) | | |
| Valproic acid | X↓C↑ | Diminished valproic acid levels; can increase carbamazepine levels. |
| Vecuronium | X↓ | Reduced level. |
| *Verapamil | C↑ | On adding verapamil, toxicity may occur in 1–4 days. Increases carbamazepine levels; monitor. Halting verapamil can ignite seizures because carbamazepine declines; nifedipine may be safer. |
| Viloxazine | C↑ | Increases levels/toxicity. |
| *Warfarin | X↓ | Impaired hypoprothrombinemic response in several days to a week; adjust anticoagulants when carbamazepine changed. |

| Drugs (X) Interact with: | Valproic Acid (V) | Comments |
|---|---|---|
| Amitriptyline (*see* TCAs) | | |
| Antacids | V↑ | Increases valproic acid absorption; give 1 h apart. |
| Aspirin (*see* salicylates) | | |
| Benzodiazepines | X↑ | Valproic acid may elevate diazepam; with clonazepam, may cause absence seizures in epileptic patients. |
| Carbamazepine | X↑V↓ | Decreases valproic acid; increases carbamazepine (in epoxide form). |
| Cimetidine | V↑ | Increases valproic acid levels; monitor levels or switch to ranitidine. |
| Chlorpromazine | V↑ | Monitor valproic acid levels or switch to alternative neuroleptic (e.g., haloperidol). |
| Ethosuximide | X↑ | Decrease ethosuximide or use alternative. |
| *Erythromycin | V↑ | Increases level/toxicity; may occur with other macrolide antibiotics. |

| Drugs (X) Interact with: | Valproic Acid (V) | Comments |
|---|---|---|
| *Felbamate | V↑ | Increases level/toxicity; monitor levels; start and withdraw felbamate slowly. |
| Lithium | X↑V↑ | Increases risk of additive neurotoxicity; consider lowering levels of each. |
| Macrolide antibiotics (see erythromycin) | | |
| Nortriptyline (see TCAs) | | |
| *Phenobarbital | X↑ | Increases serum phenobarbital; may prompt toxicity. Cut phenobarbital dose by 30–75% and monitor for decreased valproic acid. |
| Phenothiazines | V↑ | May increase valproic acid levels; monitor. |
| *Phenytoin | X↑↓ V↓ | Valproic acid initially lowers serum phenytoin by 30%, but in several weeks, phenytoin may exceed pre-valproic acid levels, with accompanying ataxia, nystagmus, mental impairment, involuntary muscular movements, and seizures. Can also increase phenytoin toxicity by displacement from binding protein. Do not increase phenytoin unless seizures occur. Phenytoin may decrease serum valproic acid with reduced thymoleptic effect. |
| *Primidone | X↑ | Valproic acid escalates serum phenobarbital, which primidone substantially produces. Valproic acid also inhibits phenobarbital metabolism, increasing risk of phenobarbital intoxication. |
| Propoxyphene | C↑ | Increases levels/toxicity. |
| *Salicylates | X↑V↑ | Salicylates may increase unbound serum valproic acid concentrations to prompt valproic acid toxicity. Symptoms resolve when salicylate stopped. Bleeding time may be prolonged; decreased thrombocytes plus salicylates may yield bleeding, bruising, and petechiae. |
| TCAs | X↑ | Increases levels of nortriptyline and amitriptyline and possibly other TCAs. |
| Thiopentone | X↑ | Lower anesthesia dose of thiopentone. |
| Warfarin | X↑ | Increases unbound warfarin. |

* Moderately important interaction; † Extremely important interaction; ↑ Increases; ↓ Decreases; ↑↓ Increases or decreases.

## EFFECTS ON LABORATORY TESTS

| Generic Names | Blood/Serum Tests | Results* | Urine Tests | Results* |
|---|---|---|---|---|
| Carbamazepine | Calcium | ↓ | | |
| | BUN | ↑ | Albuminuria | ↑ |
| | Thyroid function | ↓ | Glycosuria | ↑ |
| | **LFT | ↑ | | |
| | WBC, platelets | ↓↓ | | |
| | RBC | ↓ | | |
| | Sodium | ↓ | | |
| | ***TCA | ↑ | | |
| Clonazepam | **LFT | ↑ | | |
| Valproic acid | *LFT (mainly AST [SGOT], ALT [SGPT], LDH) | ↑ | Ketone tests | False↑ |
| | WBC, platelets | ↓ | | |
| | Thyroid function | ↓ | | |
| | Lymphocytes, macrocytes | ↑ | | |
| | Ammonia | ↑ | | |

* ↑ Increases; ↓ Decreases.
** LFT tests are AST/SGOT, ALT/SGPT, alkaline phosphatase, LDH, and bilirubin. Increases in transaminases (SGOT, SGPT, and LDH) are usually benign; increases in bilirubin and other tests suggest hepatotoxicity.
*** False positive for TCA when Abbot TCA immunoassay used.

## WITHDRAWAL

In nonepileptics, carbamazepine and valproic acid do not produce

- Psychological dependence
- Tolerance
- Addiction

When suddenly withdrawing a psychiatric patient from carbamazepine or valproic acid, no psychiatric symptoms emerge. However, since withdrawal seizures can occur in nonepileptic patients, it is safest to withdraw these drugs by 10% qod.

Clonazepam, a benzodiazepine, readily causes withdrawal.

- Hard to get patients off it.
- Withdrawal over months (*see* pages 406–7)

## OVERDOSE: TOXICITY, SUICIDE, AND TREATMENT

## Carbamazepine

Acute carbamazepine overdoses produce

- Neuromuscular disturbances in 1–3 h.

- In lower overdoses, AV block is common, cardiac monitoring is useful.
- In higher overdoses, respiratory depression, stupor, and coma are more frequent.

Other problems include

- Nausea, vomiting, dry mouth, diarrhea, constipation, glossitis, stomach pain
- Agitation, restlessness, irritability
- Irregular breathing
- Vertigo
- Mydriasis, nystagmus, blurred vision, transient diplopia
- Anuria, oliguria, urinary retention
- Inability to perform rapidly alternating movements
- Hypotension, dizziness, hypertension, tachycardia
- Flushing, cyanosis
- Tremor, twitching, involuntary movements, opisthotonos, athetoid movements, ataxia
- Visual hallucinations
- Speech disturbances
- Hypoactive or hyperactive reflexes
- Seizures (especially in children)

The general management of carbamazepine overdoses is supportive (*see* pages 65–67).

- To speed elimination, try forced diuresis.
- Dialysis is used only in renal failure.
- Hemoperfusion of questionable help.
- Treat seizures with diazepam or barbiturate, but beware of aggravating respiratory depression.

## Valproic Acid

Valproic acid usually causes less toxicity.

- Most serious action is hepatotoxicity in children under 2 y.o. (*see* pages 291–92).

Symptoms include

- Anorexia and vomiting
- Somnolence, ataxia, and tremor (all respond to reduced dose)
- Rash, alopecia, stimulated appetite
- Heart block
- Coma

A
N
T
I
C
O
N
V
U
L
S
A
N
T
S

Management

- Supportive therapy (*see* pages 65–67).
- Because valproic acid is rapidly absorbed, gastric lavage is of little value; divalproex sodium extended-release tablets are absorbed more slowly; gastric lavage or emesis may help if started early enough.
- Hemodialysis and hemoperfusion have reduced valproic acid levels.
- Naloxone may reverse a coma, but it may also trigger a seizure in epileptics by reversing anticonvulsant effects.

## Gabapentin

Overdose

- A 16 y.o. girl overdosed on 48.9 g.
  √ Six hours later only complaint was dizziness and lethargy.
- The carrier-mediated L-amino acid transport system can be saturated by a large dose of gabapentin, resulting in minimal risk of toxicity.

## Lamotrigine

Acute overdoses in the 1.3–4g range produced

- Somnolence
- Ataxia, dizziness
- Headache
- Nystagmus
- Vomiting

Overdose in 4–5.6 g range produced

- Coma 8–16 h, followed by full recovery.

### Toxicity and Suicide Data

| Generic Names | Toxicity Doses Average (Largest) (g) | Mortality Doses Average (Lowest) (g) | Toxic Levels Average (Largest) ($\mu$g/ml) | Lethal Levels (mg/l) |
|---|---|---|---|---|
| Carbamazepine | (> 30)* | (> 60) | > 14 | —— |
| Clonazepam | 0.01 (0.060) | —— | > 80 (ng/ml) | —— |
| Valproic acid | —— | —— | > 100 (2000) | 1970 |

* Largest surviving dose in child was 10 g (6-year-old boy); largest surviving dose in small child was 5 g (3-year-old girl).

## PRECAUTIONS

Carbamazepine levels vary since its hepatic metabolism changes between the 2nd and 8th week on the same dose. Follow carbamazepine maintenance considerations on pages 280–81.

Avoid or monitor anticonvulsants closely in patients with

- Cardiovascular disease
  √ Carbamazepine significant risk but valproic acid is not.
- Renal disease affecting clearance.
- Bone-marrow depression, leukopenia, thrombocytopenia.
- Hepatic disease, especially if taking valproic acid or drinking excessive alcohol.
- Hypersensitivity to drug.
- Carbamazepine's manufacturer advises stopping MAOIs 14 days before starting carbamazepine, but the reason is theoretical (e.g., carbamazepine is a tricyclic), not practical. Many patients do well on carbamazepine and a MAOI; carbamazepine does not significantly block serotonin or norepinephrine uptake.

Because of carbamazepine's moderate anticholinergic properties, cautiously prescribe for patients with increased

- Intraocular pressure
- Urinary retention
- Cognitive difficulties and advancing age

## NURSES' DATA

Ensure patients on carbamazepine and valproic acid are aware of early toxicity, especially

- GI distress with valproic acid.
- Liver function changes on valproic acid.
- Hematologic reactions, weakness, fever, failure of wound to heal, sore throat rarely on carbamazepine; bleeding on valproic acid.
- Rashes, especially on carbamazepine.
- Renal impairment and urinary retention with carbamazepine but rarely with valproic acid.
- CNS depression and sedation with carbamazepine but much less frequently with valproic acid.
- Neurotoxicity (even on normal levels) with carbamazepine.

Because of valproic acid's hepatotoxicity, patients should inform doctors if they are using, or about to use

- Other anticonvulsants
  √ Phenobarbital
  √ Phenytoin
  √ Ethosuximide
- Alcohol, or
- High doses of acetaminophen regularly.

Because of valproic acid's thrombocytopenia risk, patients should inform doctors about regular aspirin use.

## PATIENT AND FAMILY NOTES

Most common side effects with carbamazepine include

- Mild intoxicated feeling (e.g., ataxia, incoordination, dizziness, lightheadedness, blurred vision, weakness, and fatigue)
- Rashes

Most common side effects with valproic acid include

- GI side effects (e.g., nausea, dyspepsia, diarrhea)

Gabapentin has not been shown to be effective for bipolar disorder in controlled studies, but case reports suggest it may help.

Note that with

- Depakene
  √ If capsules are chewed, they irritate the mouth and throat.
  √ Swallow capsules whole.
  √ Further reduce GI irritation by taking capsules and syrup with food or by slowly raising the dose.
- Divalproex (Depakote)
  √ Sprinkle capsules may be swallowed whole.
  √ They may also be opened carefully and sprinkled on a small teaspoon of soft food, such as applesauce or pudding. The drug–food mixture should be eaten immediately (avoid chewing) and *not* stored for future use.

When starting on carbamazepine, patients should exercise care when driving cars, working around machines, and crossing streets.

- To test reflexes, drive briefly in a safe place.

Patients may be mildly to considerably confused on carbamazepine until the proper dose is found.

- Carbamazepine's metabolism may require 3–8 weeks to stabilize, prompting several dosage increases during treatment.

If on valproic acid, avoid aspirin unless approved by physician.

- Bleeding, bruises, and petechiae may arise.

Avoid during pregnancy, but if pregnancy suspected

- Do *not* immediately stop drug.
- Consult with doctor.

Take valproic acid with meals.

- Food slightly delays absorption of valproic acid, but does not change its bioavailability.

Place anticonvulsants away from bedside or any readily accessible area, where they might be taken by "accident." Keep safely from children.

Have a Medic Alert wallet-card or bracelet signifying anticonvulsant use. Also indicate that the patient is taking the agent for a psychiatric, not an epileptic, disorder.

Take anticonvulsants when doctor prescribes them.

- If forget dose, can consume within 4 h.
- Otherwise wait for next regular dose.
- Do *not* take a double dose.

Do not suddenly cease anticonvulsants without first discussing with physician; sudden withdrawal of drug can cause a seizure.

ANTICONVULSANTS

# 7. Antianxiety Agents

Antianxiety agents and hypnotics share many characteristics. Because antianxiety medications primarily treat anxiety (and are not necessarily sedating), whereas hypnotics relieve insomnia, and because some newer agents' effectiveness is limited solely to anxiety or insomnia, they are discussed separately.

This chapter addresses:

- Benzodiazepines
- Buspirone
- Clomipramine
- Clonidine
- Hydroxyzine
- Meprobamate
- Propranolol

Barbiturates are presented in the next chapter.

This chapter focuses on

ANTIANXIETY AGENTS

- Obsessive-compulsive disorder[1] (pages 338–44)
- Obsessive-compulsive spectrum disorders (pages 344–46)
  - √ Anorexia nervosa
  - √ Body dysmorphic disorder
  - √ Bulimia
  - √ Hypochondriasis
  - √ Paraphilias
  - √ Pathological gambling
  - √ Pathological jealousy
  - √ Sexual "addictions"
  - √ Trichotillomania
- Panic disorders (pages 329–34)
- Posttraumatic stress disorder (pages 346–49)
- Selective mutism (page 338)
- Separation anxiety disorder (page 338)
- Social phobia (pages 335–37)

Antianxiety agents for disorders explored in other chapters include

- Aggression (Anticonvulsants, pages 282–84)
- Akathisia and dystonia (Neuropsychiatric Disorders, pages 74–75)
- Alcohol and antianxiety withdrawal (Hypnotics, pages 406–7)
- Delirium (Antipsychotics, pages 77–78)
- Dementia, (Antipsychotics, page 84)
- Mania (Lithium, pages 222, 224)
- Restless legs syndrome (Hypnotics, page 392)
- Schizophrenia (Antipsychotics, pages 16–17)

## NAMES, CLASSES, MANUFACTURERS, DOSE FORMS, COLORS

| Generic Names | Brand Names | Manufacturer | Dose Forms (mg)* | Colors |
|---|---|---|---|---|
| | | **BENZODIAZEPINES** | | |
| Alprazolam | Xanax | Upjohn | t: 0.25/0.5/1/1 | t: white (oval)/peach/ blue/white (oblong) |
| Chlordiazepoxide | Librium | Roche | c: 5/10/25 p: 20 mg/ml | c: green-yellow/ green-black/green- white |
| Clonazepam | Klonopin | Roche | t: 0.5/1/2 | t: orange/blue/blue |

[1] Clinicians seeking information on obsessive-compulsive disorder can call the OCD Information Line at the Dean Foundation 608/836-8070, Fax 608/836-8033.

| Generic Names | Brand Names | Manufacturer | Dose Forms (mg)[*] | Colors |
|---|---|---|---|---|
| Clorazepate | Tranxene | Abbott | t: 3.75/7.5/15 | t: blue/peach/lavender |
| | Tranxene-SD | Abbott | t:11.25/22.5 | t: blue/tan |
| Diazepam | Valium | Roche | t: 2/5/10<br>p: 5 mg/ml | t: white/yellow/blue |
| Halazepam | Paxipam | Schering | t: 20/40 | t: orange/white |
| Lorazepam | Ativan | Wyeth-Ayerst | t: 0.5/1/2<br>p: 2/4 mg/ml | t: all white |
| Oxazepam | Serax | Wyeth-Ayerst | t: 15<br>c: 10/15/30 | t: yellow<br>c: white-pink/white-red/white-maroon |
| Prazepam | Discontinued | All generic | c: 5/10 | c: ivory-white/green-white |
| **AZAPIRONES** |
| Azaspirodecane-dione<br>Buspirone | BuSpar | Mead Johnson | t: 5/10 | t: all white |
| **ADRENERGIC DRUGS** |
| Beta-Blocker<br>Propranolol | Inderal | Wyeth-Ayerst | t: 10/20/40/60/80 | t: orange/blue green/pink/yellow |
| α2-adrenergic agonist<br>Clonidine | Catapres | Boehringer Ingelheim | t: 0.1/0.2/0.3 | t: tan/orange/peach |
| **ANTIHISTAMINES** |
| Hydroxyzine | Atarax | Roerig | t:10/25/50/100<br>s: 10 mg/5 ml | t: orange/green/yellow/red |
| | Vistaril | Pfizer | c: 25/50/100<br>su: 25 mg/ml | c: green/green-white/green-gray |

[*]c = capsules; p = parenteral; s = syrup; su = suspension; t = tables.

## PHARMACOLOGY

Benzodiazepines enhance the actions of GABA, the brain's major inhibitory neurotransmitter.

- GABA inhibits the firing of neurons by opening chloride channels in a GABA/benzodiazepine receptor complex located on the neuronal membrane.
- This causes a hyperpolarization that requires a greater depolarization to trigger an action potential.

Benzodiazepines are of 4 chemical types:

- 2-keto compounds (clorazepate, chlordiazepoxide, diazepam, halazepam, flurazepam)
  - √ Are prodrugs, which means they can be inactive themselves (i.e., clorazepate) but have active metabolites (all go to desmethyldiazepam).
    - □ Clorazepate is rapidly hydrolyzed in the stomach and absorbed; fast onset of action.
  - √ Are slowly oxidized in the liver.

- √ Have very long half-lives.
  - □ Desmethyldiazepam, a shared metabolite, has 30–200-h half-life.
- 3-hydroxy compounds (lorazepam, oxazepam, temazepam)
  - √ Are active compounds.
  - √ Have shorter half-lives.
  - √ Are metabolized rapidly via direct conjugation with a glucuronide radical.
  - √ Do not generate active metabolites.
- Triazolo compounds (alprazolam, triazolam, estazolam)
  - √ Are active.
  - √ Do not have active metabolites.
  - √ Have short half-lives.
  - √ Are oxidized.
- 7-nitro compounds (clonazepam)
  - √ Are active.
  - √ Have long half-lives.
  - √ Have no active metabolites.
  - √ Are metabolized by nitroreduction (some by oxidation).

Any agent or disease that interferes with liver oxidating enzymes (e.g., cimetidine) can block the oxidative metabolism of 2-keto and triazolo compounds.

### Pathways of Most Benzodiazepine Anxiolytics

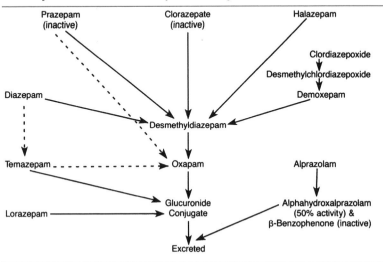

—Major pathway
---Minor pathway

**Half-Lives**

- The longer the antianxiety agent's half-life, the more it adversely affects daytime functioning (e.g., hangover) and the more delayed and attenuated its withdrawal symptoms.
- The shorter the half-life, the greater and sooner its withdrawal and anxiety between doses (interdose rebound).
- For the elderly and the hepatically impaired, shorter half-lives are safer.

**Lipophilic and Hydrophilic Properties**

- Single doses of more lipophilic drugs (e.g., diazepam, clorazepate)
  √ Enter the brain rapidly.
  √ Have a rapid onset of action.
  √ Wear off quickly.
  √ Distribute into body fat, where stored.
- Single doses of less lipophilic drugs (e.g., lorazepam)
  √ Produce clinical effects more slowly, but
  √ Provide more sustained effect.

**Duration of Effects**

- With acute doses, rates of absorption and distribution half-life are critical.
- With repeated doses, distribution is complete; the elimination half-life, which determines the drug's steady-state levels, becomes critical.
- Single doses of highly lipophilic drugs with long half-lives (e.g., diazepam) afford rapid relief but for shorter periods than would be expected by their elimination half-lives alone. Multiple doses of these drugs saturate body fat and then provide lasting relief. On the other hand, the less lipophilic lorazepam has a short half-life but sustains a longer action than diazepam, when each is given as a single dose, and has a shorter duration of action than diazepam with chronic multiple dosing.

**Potency**

- High-potency benzodiazepines (e.g., alprazolam) have a relatively high receptor affinity and more withdrawal symptoms than would be expected by just half-life alone.

## Pharmacology of Oral Antianxiety Agents

| Generic Names | Speed of Onset (Peak Plasma Levels in Hours) | Speed of Distribution (Lipophilicity: Diazepam =1.0) | Active Metabolites (Half-Life, Hours) | Mean Elimination Half-Life (Hours)* |
|---|---|---|---|---|
| *2-Keto* | | | | |
| Clorazepate | Rapid (1–2) | Rapid (0.79) | Desmethyldiazepam (30–200) Oxazepam (3–21) | 30–200 |
| Chlordiazepoxide | Intermediate (O.5–4) | Slow | Desmethylchlor-diazepoxide (18) Demoxepam (14–95) Desmethyldiazepam (30–200) Oxazepam (3–21) | 50–100 |
| Diazepam | Very rapid (0.5–2) | Rapid (1.00) | Desmethyldiazepam (30–200) Oxazepam (3–21) 3-Hydroxydiazepam (5–20) | 30–100 |
| Halazepam | Slow-intermediate (1–4) | Intermediate | Desmethylchlor-diazepoxide (18) Oxazepam (3–21) | 30–200 |
| Prazepam | Slowest (2.3–6) | Intermediate | Desmethyldiazepam (30–100) | 30–200 |
| *7-Nitro* | | | | |
| Clonazepam | Intermediate (1–2) | Intermediate (0.28) | None | 18–50 |

# Pharmacology of Oral Antianxiety Agents (Cont.)

| Generic Names | Speed of Onset (Peak Plasma Levels in Hours) | Speed of Distribution (Lipophilicity: Diazepam =1.0) | Active Metabolites (Half-Life, Hours) | Mean Elimination Half-Life (Hours)* |
|---|---|---|---|---|
| *3-Hydroxy-* | | | | |
| Lorazepam | Slow-intermediate (1–6) | Intermediate (0.48) | None | 10–20 |
| Oxazepam | Slow-intermediate (1–4) | Intermediate (0.45) | None | 3–21 |
| *Triazolo-* | | | | |
| Alprazolam | Intermediate (1–2) | Intermediate (0.54) | α-Hydroxy-alprazolam (6–10)** | 12–15 |
| *Other* | | | | |
| Buspirone | Rapid peak (0.6–15), very slow onset (> 7 days) | Rapid | 1-Pyrimidinyl piperazine (16) | 2–11 |
| Clonidine | Rapid (3–5) | Slow-intermediate | None | 12–16 |
| Hydroxyzine | Rapid (2–4) | Intermediate | None | < 4 |
| Meprobamate+ | Rapid (1–3) | Intermediate | None | 6–16 |
| Propranolol | Rapid (2–4) | Intermediate | None significant | 3–5 |

* Includes all active metabolites; longer in elderly; more important in chronic administration.
** Metabolite half as active as parent.
+ Included only for historical interest.

## DOSES

### General Antianxiety Doses

| Generic Names | Benzodia-zepine Dose Equivalents* | Usual Dose for Anxiety (mg/day) | Extreme Dose Range for Anxiety (mg/day) | Therapeutic Plasma Level (ng/ml) | Geriatric Dose (mg/day) |
|---|---|---|---|---|---|
| Alprazolam | 0.5 | 1.0–2.0 | 0.5–8 | > 48 ng/ml | 0.25–0.5 |
| Buspirone | N/A | 30–45 | 15–60 | 1–6 | 15–30 |
| Chlordiaze-poxide | 10.0 | 15–75 | 10–100 | > 0.7 | 5–30** |
| Clonazepam | 0.25 | 0.5–1.5 | 0.25–20 | 5–70 ng/ml | 0.25–1.0** |
| Clonidine | N/A | 0.2–0.6 | 0.1–2.0 | 500 | 0.2–0.4 |
| Clorazepate | 7.5 | 15–67.5 | 7.5–90 | — | 15–60** |
| Diazepam | 5.0 | 4–30 | 2–40 | 300–400 ng/ml | 1–10* |
| Halazepam | 20.0 | 40–80 | 20–100 | — | 20–40* |
| Hydroxyzine | 100.0*** | 200–400 | 100–600 | — | 10–50 |
| Lorazepam | 1.0 | 2–6 | 1–10 | — | 0.5–1.5 |
| Meprobamate | 800.0 | 400–1200 | 400–1600 | 5–20 | 200–600 |
| Oxazepam | 15.0 | 30–60 | 30–120 | — | 10–30 |
| Propranolol | N/A | 30–80 | 30–240 | 20 ng/ml | 30–60 |

*Not applicable.
**Because of exceedingly long half-lives, not generally recommended for use longer than 1 week in elderly or those with impaired hepatic function. Use lorazepam instead.
***Represents sedative equivalent.

## Antianxiety Drug Indications

| Generic Names | Anxiolytic | Panic Disorder | Obsessive-Compulsive Disorder | Hypnotic | Muscle Relaxant | Alcohol Withdrawal | Depression | EPS |
|---|---|---|---|---|---|---|---|---|
| Alprazolam | + | + | ± | + | + | + | ± | – |
| Buspirone | + | – | ± | – | – | – | – | – |
| Chlordiazepoxide | + | – | – | + | + | + | – | – |
| Clomipramine | – | – | + | – | – | – | + | – |
| Clonazepam | ± | + | ± | ± | + | + | – | ± |
| Clonidine | ± | ± | – | ± | – | – | – | – |
| Clorazepate | + | + | – | + | + | + | – | + |
| Diazepam | + | + | – | ± | + | + | – | – |
| Halazepam | + | – | – | ± | + | + | – | + |
| Hydroxyzine | + | – | – | + | + | – | – | – |
| Lorazepam | + | + | – | + | + | + | – | + |
| Meprobamate | + | – | – | + | + | – | – | + |
| Oxazepam | + | – | – | ± | + | + | – | – |
| Prazepam | + | – | – | – | + | + | – | – |
| Propranolol | + | ± | – | – | ? | – | – | + |

* This does not reflect FDA sanctioned indications but, rather, where it has been or can be reasonably used. This is even limited, e.g., all benzodiazepines have muscle-relaxant properties and ability to prevent alcohol withdrawal.

# General Information

## Barbiturates and Propranedols

Amobarbital, phenobarbital, pentobarbital, meprobamate, and related drugs should not be used to treat anxiety because

- They cause dangerous withdrawal symptoms.
- They are fatal in overdose.
- They have dangerous side effects.

## Benzodiazepines

Tolerance and physiological and/or psychological dependence can occur with benzodiazepines. Therefore, they should be

- Ideally, aimed at anxiety from identifiable stressors.
- Time limited: 1–2 weeks.
- Chronically used for specific, identifiable symptoms.

In general, risk of dependency is correlated with both dose and duration of use.

- Benzodiazepine dependency may occur on
  √ 3–4 times the normal daily dose over several weeks.
  √ Smaller therapeutic doses over months.
- Tolerance to daytime benzodiazepine sedative side effects often develops in
  √ 5–10 days, while tolerance to anxiolytic effect usually doesn't occur.
- Psychological dependency is also most likely if
  √ A fast onset agent is used (i.e., has a "buzz").
  √ It is prescribed in dosage intervals that are further apart than duration of action.
    □ Prn, "only when you feel really anxious."
    □ Tid in benzodiazepine that lasts only 5 h.
    □ May have interdose withdrawals several times a day that, combined with rapid relief and a "buzz," increase psychological dependency.
- Melatonin assists benzodiazepine discontinuation.
  √ All 30 patients elected to continue taking melatonin and 24 had discontinued benzodiazepines.
  √ After 6 months of melatonin therapy, 19 of 24 patients were benzodiazepine-free and 5 had resumed taking benzodiazepines.

Psychological dependency

- Can best be avoided by using a slower-onset agent with a long duration of action (e.g., clonazepam).

- If a shorter-acting agent is used, make sure it is given at appropriately short intervals.
  - √ Alprazolam and lorazepam often given 3 times a day.
    - ▫ Discontinue when patient is stable and confident in ability to manage the anxiety.
    - ▫ If possible, educate family and patient.
    - ▫ Use a slow taper of medication over 2–6 months.
- Consider prn only when the need is truly intermittent (e.g., 5 times a week and not twice a day).

Avoid meprobamate and barbiturates because they

- Have a higher risk of addiction and are more dangerous in withdrawal than benzodiazepines.
- Have a very low toxicity-to-therapeutic-effect ratio.
- Are more likely lethal as overdoses.
- Induce hepatic enzymes, causing a need for increased doses.

### Antidepressants

- HCAs, MAOIs, and SSRIs are helpful for a variety of anxiety disorders.
  - √ All are effective for panic disorder except perhaps bupropion.
- All may also be effective for generalized anxiety disorder (GAD).
  - √ This effect appears to be independent of nonspecific sedating effects.
- Because of low side effects and, in certain conditions, better efficacy, SSRIs are often preferred.
- SSRIs are effective for
  - ▫ Generalized anxiety disorder
  - ▫ Posttraumatic stress disorder (PTSD)
  - ▫ Obsessive-compulsive disorder and OC spectrum disorders
  - ▫ Social phobia
- MAOIs are effective for
  - √ Social phobia
- TCAs are effective for
  - √ School phobia
  - √ Separation anxiety

Treatment outcomes of panic disorder using serotonergic medications:

- In acute trials lasting 6–8 weeks, 50–80% became free of panic attacks with various medications (most were serotonergic).
- In large cross-national trial, after 8–12 months of treatment, 75% of patients were free of panic attacks.

ANTIANXIETY AGENTS

- In a recent large 12-month comparison of paroxetine and clomipramine, panic-free rates were 85% (paroxetine) and 72% (clomipramine).
  - √ At 3 months about 55% were panic-free.
- Recent trials suggest that a significant response to antidepressants may occur in the first 2–4 weeks, and benzodiazepines as early as the first or second week.

## Beta-Blockers

- Beta-blockers are most often used for performance anxiety or as adjuncts to other drugs.

*Propranolol*

- Nonselectively blocks $\beta_1$ (cardiac) and $\beta_2$ (pulmonary) receptors.
  - √ Increases pulmonary resistance.
    - □ Contraindicated in asthma.
- Complicates carbohydrate and fat metabolism.
  - √ Risks hypoglycemia in diabetes.
  - √ Relative contraindication in diabetes.
- Most useful against the "flight-or-fight" response—that is, the physical signs of anxiety:
  - √ Palpitations
  - √ Tachycardia
  - √ GI upset
  - √ Tremors
  - √ Sweating
- Only mild improvement in psychological symptoms.
- Before using propranolol, examine and interview patient for
  - √ Cardiovascular problems—r/o bradyarrhythmias, congestive heart failure, Reynaud's disease.
  - √ Pulmonary difficulties—r/o asthma.
  - √ Endocrine abnormalities—r/o diabetes.
  - √ Do not give propranolol if above specific conditions are present.
- Start at 10 mg bid and increase to 80–160 mg/day, if needed.
  - √ Most patients require small doses of propranolol (e.g., 10–20 mg tid–qid).
  - √ Minimal doses minimally drop BP.
  - √ Can use heart rate (HR) as guide to dosing.
    - □ Decreases HR at least 5–10 beats/min.
    - □ Can go down to 60 beats/min if needed.
    - □ Make sure patient able to increase HR to > 110 beat/min with exercise.

- Unlike benzodiazepines, propranolol does not dim consciousness, cause drowsiness, or produce drug dependency.
- Taper slowly in patients with preexisting hypertension, angina, or other coronary artery diseases to avoid rebound hypertension.

*Beta-blocker alternatives to propranolol for:*

Mainly peripheral sympathetic control.

- Propranolol has very high lipid solubility, so easily goes to the brain.
  √ May be associated with fatigue, depression.
  √ May exert some CNS anxiolytic effects.
- Atenolol and nadolol have very low lipid solubility and usually are low in CNS effects.
- Acebutolol, atenolol, metoprolol, and betaxolol are all cardioselective and mainly block $\beta_1$ (cardiac).

Pulmonary conditions

- $\beta_2$ (pulmonary) receptors pose a small risk of bronchospasm.

High dosage for aggression/agitation

- Propranolol most effectively gets to brain, but also can cause significant hypotension or bradycardia.
- Acebutolol and pindolol are relatively lipophilic and can affect brain in high doses but
  √ Also have intrinsic sympathomimetic activity.
    ▫ May decrease hypotension or bradycardia risk.

Long duration of action

- Propranolol has 4-h half-life.
- Propranolol LA (long acting) has 10-h half-life.
- Betaxolol has 10-h half-life.
- Nadolol has 22-h half-life.
- Atenolol has 7-h half-life.
- Propranolol LA, nadolol, betaxolol, and sometimes atenolol can be given only qd.

Liver impairment

- Kidney excreted beta-blockers (atenolol, carteolol, and nadolol) are preferred.
- Also consider these for geriatric patients.

Kidney impairment

- Liver excreted beta-blockers (propranolol, metoprolol, labetalol, and penbutalol) are preferred.

## Clonidine

- May be useful, but many side effects.
- Evaluate for medical complications (e.g., cardiac disorders, moderate-to-severe hypertension, metabolic or renal disease).
- For anxiety, start at 0.1 mg bid.
  - √ Increase by 0.1 mg every 1–2 days.
  - √ Reach a final dose of 0.4–0.6 mg/day.
  - √ Tolerance may develop quickly.
    - ▫ Consider only for short-term trials.
  - √ Taper slowly to avoid rebound hypertension.

## Neuroleptics

- Not generally recommended for nonpsychotic anxiety.
- Low neuroleptic doses (e.g., haloperidol 0.5 mg, chlorpromazine 50 mg, perphenazine 4 mg) tid quell anxiety. If not effective, higher doses may still be effective, but typicals provoke EPS, especially akathisia, which mimics anxiety.
- As an alternative, atypical antipsychotic medications can be more effective than typical agents.
  - √ May help near-psychotic anxiety (e.g., in borderline or schizotypal personality disorder or in hypomania/mania).
    - ▫ Risperidone doses can vary between 0.5 mg to 5 mg/day with a goal of low doses.
    - ▫ Olanzapine typically will require 10–20 mg/day.
    - ▫ Much lower EPS risk with atypicals.
    - ▫ May manifest as cognitive disorganization or overvalued ideas.
  - √ Neuroleptics do not generate drug dependency.
  - √ They may be quite sedating.
- Thus, usually better to give benzodiazepines than neuroleptics.
- If neuroleptics used, prescribe high or medium sedating ones, such as chlorpromazine or thioridazine, 25–50 mg qd–qid, or perphenazine 4–8 mg qd–qid.
  - √ Use only short trials to avoid EPS or TD.

## Antihistamines

- Sedating antihistamines reduce anxiety.
  - √ Their anticholinergic effects may be especially dangerous to the elderly or the cognitively impaired.
  - √ Their negative sedative effect may outweigh their therapeutic anxiolytic effect.

- Consider hydroxyzine for anxiety in some physical conditions.
  √ Pruritus due to allergic conditions.
- Examples
  √ Hydroxyzine 10–50 mg qd–qid.
  √ Diphenhydramine 10–25 mg bid–qid for daytime sedation.

## Trazodone

- Unlike other ADs, can be used acutely in low doses 25–50 mg qd–qid.
- Sedation, hypotension, and priapism (rarely) complicate use.
- Does not usually interfere with cognitive function.
- Doses into the antidepressant range are acceptable.
- Minimal tolerance develops.
- Best given on full stomach to avoid severe peak levels.

## Buspirone

- A nonbenzodiazepine antianxiety agent that differs from benzodiazepines.
- Although it has similar efficacy in treating anxiety, it is usually not preferred by those who have tried benzodiazepines.
- Its effect can best be described as "taking the edge off anxiety" rather than ablating it, as with benzodiazepines.
- More recent research suggests that, for a variety of anxiety-related conditions, the 45–60 mg/day dosage range may be optimally effective.
- Although former benzodiazepine users prefer benzodiazepines over buspirone, buspirone is still superior to placebo.
- Benzodiazepines affect buspirone response in GAD.
  √ Among those who continued buspirone, 62% of patients with no prior benzodiazepine treatment experienced a clinical response, compared with 46% of recent benzodiazepine users and 56% of remote users.
  √ Among recent benzodiazepine-treated patients there was a 42% rate of buspirone discontinuation, 23% for lack of efficacy and 19% for adverse events.
  √ Tell patients who recently discontinued benzodiazepine that buspirone lacks sedative effects, mild euphoria, and rapid onset of action frequently experienced with benzodiazepines.
- Effective in GAD, social phobia.
- May be good adjunct in OCD, PTSD.
- Not effective in panic disorder or acute anxiety.

## Comparing Buspirone and Benzodiazepines

| Areas | Buspirone | Benzodiazepines |
|---|---|---|
| Single dose effect | No | Yes |
| Full therapeutic effect | 2 weeks | Days |
| Sedating | No | Yes |
| Performance and motor coordination impaired | No | Yes |
| Interacts with other hypnosedatives | No | Yes |
| Alcohol potentiates | No | Yes |
| Tolerance developed | No | Yes |
| Drug dependency produced | No | Yes |
| Hypnosedative withdrawal suppressed | No | Yes |

# Adjustment Disorder with Anxious Mood

Acute situational anxiety outcomes

- Mild-to-moderate severity
  - √ Benzodiazepines, placebo, or supportive psychotherapy all have same good result: 70–80%.
- Marked severity
  - √ Benzodiazepines superior to placebo.
- If it is a single identifiable stressor, e.g., wedding, licensure exam, etc.
  - √ Use time-limited trial.
    - ▫ May try prn first.
    - ▫ Many find sufficient reassurance in knowing they can take something that will help; they may rarely or never use it.
  - √ If it is only for the event itself, it is performance anxiety, which is a subtype of social phobia.
    - ▫ Consider beta-blocker.
    - ▫ Benzodiazaepines may be useful.

Time-limited (less than one month) pervasive stressor with moderate-to-severe anxiety.

- Goal: To prevent anxiety that interferes with functioning.
  - √ Schedule benzodiazepines continuously to avoid breakthroughs and withdrawals.
  - √ Consider longer-acting benzodiazepines (e.g., clonazepam, clorazepate) for more sustained blood levels.
  - √ For elderly, prescribe 50% of the dose for younger patients; use intermediate half-life benzodiazepines without active metabolites (e.g., alprazolam, lorazepam, oxazepam) to prevent drug accumulation.

Time-limited intermittent stressor (if performance anxiety or social phobia, *see* pages 337–38).

- Prescribe benzodiazepine prn.
- If stressor onset is predictable, take 1–2 h before.
- If stressor duration is predictable, pick benzodiazepine with matching duration of action (e.g., 6-h stressor, try lorazepam).

Indefinite pervasive stressor

- Consider nonbenzodiazepine, which does not induce drug dependency (e.g., buspirone, TCA, trazodone, SSRI).

## Generalized Anxiety Disorder (GAD)

*Benzodiazepines*

- Because short-acting, high-potency benzodiazepines (e.g., alprazolam) produce more interdose withdrawal and require more frequent dosing, long-acting, low-potency ones (e.g., clonazepam 0.5–2 mg/day, chlordiazepoxide 25–75 mg/day) are preferred for GAD. Use approach described under adjustment disorder with anxious mood, time-limited pervasive stressor (page 326).
  √ High placebo rate can be expected (∼ 50–60%).
    ▫ Consider low initial dosing.
- Benzodiazepines may be more effective on specific GAD symptoms, particularly somatic autonomic symptoms in contrast to the psychic symptom cluster that includes apprehension and irritability.
  √ Although responding less well to benzodiazepines, psychic symptoms may be more responsive to another drug, e.g., buspirone, imipramine, or an SSRI.
  √ Information from several 6–8-month maintenance therapy trials have found continued efficacy over time; tolerance develops to sedation but not to the anxiolytic effect.
  √ Approximately one-third of patients with GAD have a remission of symptoms with adequate benzodiazepine treatment, and another one-third are improved but not well.
  √ Discontinuation of acute treatment should be slow (over months) because of the potential for rebound anxiety, withdrawal symptoms, and/or clinical relapse.
- Many with GAD have waxing and waning anxiety.
  √ Try to limit benzodiazepine use for exacerbations of GAD rather than continuous usage.
  √ Limit trials to 1–4 weeks.
  √ Some patients require chronic benzodiazepine dosing.
- Withdrawal syndromes when stopping are 5–10%.
  √ Withdrawal symptoms may persist up to a year after discontinuation of chronic benzodiazepine treatment at therapeutic doses.

- Relapse rate in first year after stopping medication is about 50–70%.
  √ Decreases to 38% after 40 months.

*Buspirone*

Since buspirone does not cause drug dependency, and since GAD is a long-term disorder, buspirone appears safer than benzodiazepines.

- Buspirone is effective when used for anxiety.
  √ Initial effects occur in 2–4 weeks.
  √ Full effect often requires 4–6 weeks.
- Buspirone must be taken regularly.
- GAD patients improve most if free of benzodiazepines for 1 month before starting buspirone.
- Buspirone does *not* prevent benzodiazepine withdrawal but also does not have a significant withdrawal effect when it (buspirone) is stopped.
- Dose for moderate anxiety:
  √ Start at 5 mg bid–tid for first week.
  √ Dose ranges from 15–30 mg/day, but may increase to 60 mg/day.
  √ Increase dose by 2.5–5 mg every 2–4 days.
    □ Assess at 2 weeks if this dose range is effective.
    □ If not, try 45–60 mg range.
- Dose for severe anxiety:
  √ If tolerated, go quickly to 45–60 mg range.
  √ If patient well stabilized on high dose, can very gradually decrease dose (5–10 mg q 10 days) to see if lower dose is equally effective.
    □ May cause fewer side effects and is cheaper.

*Other antidepressants*

- Antidepressants (e.g., TCAs, SSRIs, venlafaxine, and trazodone) have been used successfully in GAD without depression.
- Prescribe as for depression.
- Expect possible first-week activation effects (e.g., jitteriness, increased anxiety).
- Onset in 2–4 weeks.
- Tolerance does not usually develop.
- Venlafaxine XR at doses of 75 mg/day (N = 26), 150 mg/day (N = 29), and 225 mg/day (N = 28) was compared with placebo (N = 19).
  √ At 75 mg/day no statistical differences between drug and placebo except on anxiety subscale of Hamilton Anxiety and Depression scale.

√ At 150 mg and 225 mg statistically significant difference between these two doses and placebo.

◻ Hamilton anxiety scale, psychic anxiety factor, tension factor, clinical global impression (CGI), and improvement were all significantly better at these doses.

- All antidepressants except bupropion reduce anxiety in GAD.
  √ Very slow dosage escalation is better tolerated.

*Propranolol (and other beta-blockers)*

- Helps in GAD if there are predominant autonomic symptoms (e.g., palpitations, tremor, sweating).
  √ Betaxolol and pindolol may also be useful, with less sedation and dysphoria than propranolol.

## Panic Disorders

Choices for treating panic disorders include:

- Antidepressants (ADs), including TCAs, SSRIs, and MAOIs, but not bupropion.
- Benzodiazepines
  √ Diazepam vs. alprazolam for treatment of panic disorder.
  √ 8-week trial with 241 subjects with panic disorder or agoraphobia with panic attacks assigned to flexible doses of diazepam, alprazolam, or placebo.
  √ 60% of subjects taking either diazepam or alprazolam were at least moderately improved.
  √ Only 30% of those taking placebo responded.
  √ More severely ill subjects responded less well to either benzodiazepine.
    ◻ These patients need to be treated with antidepressants.
    ◻ Higher benzodiazepine doses (e.g., 4–6 mg/day alprazolam) may be necessary for remission of panic disorder.

*TCAs and SSRIs*

- ADs are preferred for treating panic disorder.
  √ Unlike benzodiazepines, ADs are not addicting.
  √ ADs decrease panic attacks, and to some extent, the anxiety and phobias associated with panic attacks.
  √ Reduced frequency is more likely than reduced severity of panic attacks.
  √ Antipanic effect of ADs may be related to suppression of locus coeruleus hyperactivity.
  √ Symptoms may continue to improve gradually for up to 3 yrs.

ANTIANXIETY AGENTS

- Patient does not need a depressed mood for ADs to prevent panic attacks.
- Beneficial effect requires 1–3 weeks of TCA treatment.
- Patient should remain on AD for at least 6 months.
  √ Taper drug only when patient is symptom-free.
  √ Unlike with depressive episode, patient probably needs to continue much longer.
  √ 83% relapse rate if discontinued in 6 months.
  √ 25% relapse rate if discontinued in 18 months.
- Because of greater safety and lower side effects, SSRIs, venlafaxine, or nefazodone are preferred.
  √ Fluvoxamine, paroxetine, sertraline, fluoxetine, and citalopram shown to be more effective than placebo.
  √ In one study, fluvoxamine, combined with exposure in vivo to situations that induce anxiety, demonstrated efficacy superior to other treatments.
    ▫ Twice as large effect size on self-reported agoraphobia and avoidance noted with fluvoxamine.
- Of TCAs, imipramine has been most widely studied in panic disorder.
  √ Other TCAs (e.g., nortriptyline) have also been reported to be effective.
- For imipramine, use same doses as in treating depression.
  √ Best total drug plasma level was 110–140 ng/ml of imipramine plus desipramine.
  √ Levels above 225 ng/ml are no more effective but are more toxic.
- Imipramine treatment extended for 24 weeks.
  √ Remission from panic attacks were 29% at week 8, 55% at week 16, and 80% at week 24.
  √ Phobias need higher levels to be effective.
    ▫ At 75 mg only about 50% of patients lost their phobia.
  √ The longer patients stay on medication the better they get; improvement often continues to the 3rd year.
- Nefazodone for comorbid major depression and panic disorder (N = 55)
  √ Patients had marked global improvement compared with placebo-treated patients, including relief of panic and phobic symptoms.
  √ Imipramine was not significantly better than placebo for improvement in depression and anxiety ratings.
- Venlafaxine for panic disorder (N = 9)
  √ 7 women and 2 men with an average of 2.2 panic attacks a week and average duration of illness 7.9 years.

√ Mean dose was 16 mg/day on week 1, and 78 mg/day by week 7.

√ All patients were panic-free by week 7.

- When patients with panic attacks are started on TCAs or SSRIs, they may initially experience "speediness," insomnia, jitters, tremor, diaphoressis, or even an increase in panic attacks. Therefore it is important to

  √ Start patient on a low dose (for imipramine, around 10 mg; fluoxetine, around 2.5–5 mg).

  √ Increase dose by 10 mg qod or slower for imipramine; 5 mg q 1–2 weeks for fluoxetine.

  √ Only if seen as essential, consider adding alprazolam 0.25 mg before beginning AD, and then gradually taper the alprazolam when the AD begins to work in 2–4 weeks.

    ▫ Full effect often takes 6 weeks.

    ▫ Patients usually are very reluctant to stop benzodiazepines.

- A 1-year trial of citalopram for panic disorder (N = 279)

  √ Of 475 patients 279 agreed to continue double-blind treatment at their assigned doses.

  √ Except in the lowest dose (10 or 15 mg/day), the treatment was generally better than placebo.

    ▫ 20 or 30 mg/day and 40 or 60 mg/day demonstrated the best response, with 70–75% of patients free from panic attacks up to the end of the 1-year treatment period.

- Paroxetine for panic disorder (N = 278)

  √ After a 2-week placebo washout, patients were randomly assigned to 10 weeks' treatment with either placebo or paroxetine at 10, 20, or 40 mg/day.

  √ 40 mg/day paroxetine was significantly more effective (p < 0.02) than placebo for panic-free status, reduction in full panic attacks, and improvement in CGI severity but not for 50% reduction in panic attacks.

  √ Lower dosages were not significantly better than placebo.

    ▫ 86% of patients taking 40 mg/day had been free of panic attacks for the prior 2 weeks.

    ▫ At 20 mg/day 65% or at 10 mg/day 67% were free of panic attacks for the prior 2 weeks.

    ▫ 50% were responders in the placebo group.

- Paroxetine and clonazepam for panic disorder (N = 67)

  √ Clonazepam 0.75 mg was given to 67 patients while still taking paroxetine 20 or 40 mg/day.

  √ In the first 3 weeks of treatment, patients who received both drugs improved significantly, but at 12 weeks of treatment there were no significant differences between the groups.

ANTIANXIETY AGENTS

  ▫ May be helpful in the first 3 to 4 weeks to have clonazepam available but after that, it is unclear if there is any more efficacy.
  √ Advise patient that benzodiazepine will not be necessary for more than 1–2 months.
- Sertraline for panic disorder (N = 176 patients)
  √ Patients were randomly assigned to 10 weeks of either placebo or sertraline beginning at 25 mg/day and eventually could reach maximum of 200 mg/day (avg. dose 130 mg).
  √ After 10 weeks, panic attacks were reduced by 80% in the sertraline group and 60% in the placebo group (p = 0.01).

Augmenting TCAs/SSRIs

- TCAs and SSRIs can augment each other in panic disorder.
  √ Consider if only partial response seen to one.
  √ Monitor TCA plasma level if SSRI inhibits CYP2D6.
  √ Augmentation with a beta-blocker (e.g., pindolol) or anticonvulsant (e.g., valproate) may be effective.

*Monoamine-oxidase inhibitors*

When depression is associated with panic attacks or anxiety is severe:

- MAOIs may be the drug of second choice (assuming patient follows diet).
- MAOIs (and possibly SSRIs) may be more effective than TCAs, benzodiazepines.
- MAOIs require 1–6 weeks for improvement.
- All MAOIs reduce panic attacks, but
  √ Phenelzine may be preferred, often up to 90 mg/day.
  √ May be the best drug for *severe* panic or phobic disorders.
  √ Unlike other ADs, they do not increase panic attacks and anxiety when started and may reduce symptoms more rapidly.

*Benzodiazepines*

- Response often seen in 1–2 weeks.
  √ May be superior to TCAs for phobic avoidance and anticipatory anxiety.
- Low-potency benzodiazepines can be effective (e.g., chlordiazepoxide) but at antipanic doses induce too much sedation, so high-potency benzodiazepines are recommended. These may be
  √ Short-acting (e.g., alprazolam) or
  √ Long-acting (e.g., clonazepam).
- In panic disorder a small number of patients may get depressed on high doses of benzodiazepines (e.g., > 1.5 mg clonazepam; 4–6 mg lorazepam).

- Clonazepam may be superior to alprazolam because clonazepam
  √ Exhibits little interdose rebound,
  √ Produces less severe withdrawal than alprazolam, and
  √ Can be taken bid, whereas alprazolam requires tid–qid dosage.
- One study showed that 86% of panic patients preferred clonazepam over alprazolam.

*Alprazolam*

- Start around 0.25 mg tid or qid and increase 0.25 mg every 1–3 days.
  √ Can try 0.5 mg in evening and, if no excess sedation, can begin with 0.5 mg tid or qid.
- Usually effective at 3–5 mg/day.
- Therapeutic dose may require 10 mg/day.
- Range is from 1–10 mg/day.
- Can cause manic symptoms.
- Withdrawal of alprazolam may trigger panic attacks and severe withdrawal symptoms, including seizures.
- Some patients only get 2–6 h duration of action, may have "mini withdrawals" before each dose, and need more than tid dosing.
- Patients withdrawing from alprazolam often have more clinical symptoms than when they first started.
  √ They have both the original panic symptoms along with new withdrawal symptoms.
  √ Adding AD for 6–12 weeks to prevent rebound panic attacks may aid subsequent benzodiazepine withdrawal.
- Some patients describe incipient withdrawal or rebound with alprazolam doses as a sense of "impending panic" after just 1–2 h of the previous dose.
  √ One option is to slowly discontinue alprazolam no faster than 0.125–0.5 mg every 7–14 days for doses above 2 mg/day, and 0.25 every 7–10 days for doses below 2 mg/day.
  √ Another popular option is to switch from the short-acting alprazolam to the longer-acting clonazepam over a week or more.
  √ Clonazepam takes about one week to approach steady state, so it cannot be immediately substituted for alprazolam.
  √ May need to start clonazepam at full equivalent dose and reduce alprazolam 15–25%/day, with prn alprazolam options available if withdrawal is too fast.
  √ 0.125 mg of clonazepam is equivalent to 0.25 mg of alprazolam.

*Clonazepam*

- Start at 0.25 mg bid for first 2 days; increase dose by 0.125–0.25 mg qd or qod.

- Antipanic effect usually around 1.5–2.5 mg/day.
- Range is from 0.5–4.5 mg/day.
- Because clonazepam is sedating, may prefer to dispense most of it at bedtime, with a smaller dose earlier in the day.
  - √ Some patients can have continuously effective serum levels with qd dosing.
- Clonazepam can induce depression in doses over 1.5 mg qd.
- Because of clonazepam's long half-life, normal liver function is essential to avoid toxicity.
  - √ Clonazepam does not cause liver damage.
  - √ Interdose rebound can occur.

When stopping alprazolam or clonazepam

- Titrate very slowly—about 5–10% every 1–2 weeks.
  - √ This is hard to do with clonazepam because its smallest dose form is 0.5 mg.

*Other agents*

- Verapamil
  - √ Moderately effective in controlled trial.
    - □ 160 mg qd first week.
    - □ Increase 160 mg qd/week until reach 480 mg.
- Nimodipine (a centrally active calcium channel-blocker)
  - √ 2 successful cases reported.
    - □ Dose 30 mg tid.
- Propranolol
  - √ Only one controlled trial found propranolol effective.
    - □ Average dose 183 mg/day.
    - □ 2 weeks until significant effect.
    - □ Bradycardia seen at 1 week but without antipanic effect.
  - √ Although propranolol does not have a proven antipanic effect, when lower doses of it (10–20 mg tid–qid) are added as an adjunct, there may be benefits, especially in patients who do not fully improve with TCAs, SSRIs, MAOIs, or benzodiazepines alone.
- Valproic acid
  - √ Possibly effective for panic in usual dose range.
  - √ Carbamazepine is ineffective.
- Bupropion
  - √ Not effective for panic.

## Anger Attacks

- Some may be a variant of panic attacks.
  - √ Symptoms are spontaneous and unprovoked.

√  Same physiological symptoms as panic attacks.
√  Anger instead of anxiety experienced.
√  Experienced as uncharacteristic and inappropriate.
• Case reports of successful use of TCAs and SSRIs.

## Phobic Disorders

Medications do not usually treat discrete simple phobias such as fear of bridges, elevators, heights.

*Agoraphobia*

- Persistent fears of open spaces, leaving home, or any place where it is difficult to escape or gain help.
- Arises with, or without, panic attacks.
  √  Some without panic attacks have social phobia, PTSD, or OCD.
- May occur in the elderly.

Agoraphobia can be treated by

- Alprazolam 3–6 mg/day
- Imipramine 150–300 mg/day
- Other drugs curtailing agoraphobia include
  √  Amitriptyline
  √  Clomipramine
  √  Trazodone
  √  MAOIs
  √  SSRIs

*Social phobia*

- It is the 3rd most common psychiatric illness, affecting as many as 13% of the general population.
- All treatments take 6–10 weeks for full effect.
- SSRIs are first choices because of low side-effect risk and lack of physical dependence, but
  √  Less proven than MAOIs.
  √  However, several SSRIs have been found superior to placebo for social phobia.
- Citalopram (N = 22 patients)
  √  All were able to tolerate the full dose (40 mg).
  √  7 patients were rated very much improved and 12 were rated much improved.
  √  Scales of fear and anxiety were also markedly better.
  √  Other SSRIs had similar outcomes.
     □ In open trials 67% responded to fluoxetine.

□ Had similar outcomes with fluvoxamine, sertraline, and paroxetine in controlled trials.

MAOIs

- Phenelzine (69% responders) seems more helpful than imipramine, amitriptyline, atenolol, or alprazolam.
  √ A clear, identifiable, predictable, and specific social phobia did equally well on phenelzine and atenolol, but a more generalized social phobia showed phenelzine superior.
  √ Phenelzine 45–90 mg/day works well in 6 weeks.
  √ Cognitive-behavioral group therapy (CBT) had a similar outcome to phenelzine at 12 weeks.
  √ Response rates for phenelzine 77% and for CBT 75%.
  √ When patient taken off of phenelzine, symptoms often reemerge.
  √ Can reverse the most severe, chronic form of social phobia: avoidant personality disorder.
    □ May take 3–12 months to reverse.
    □ 70% may no longer have avoidant personality disorder.

Other antidepressants

- Imipramine did not show efficacy for social phobia in one study in which there was no difference in outcome between imipramine (150 mg/day) and placebo.
- Nefazodone (N = 21)
  √ Patients completed 12-week trial.
  √ Dosing gradually increased from 300 to 600 mg qd, with mean dose 435 mg.
  √ 16 were considered responders, with moderate or marked improvement.
  √ 7 were considered to be nonresponders.
  √ Mean time to response was 9 weeks.
- Venlafaxine
  √ 12 patients (7 women, 5 men) with social phobia who had not responded to SSRIs.
  √ 6 of the patients had comorbid avoidant personality disorder (APD).
  √ Significant reduction of symptoms after 15 weeks on Liebowitz Social Anxiety Scale (LSAS).
    □ Average 18.2 baseline decreased to 3.7.
  √ For fear ($p < .05$), 5 patients had marked improvement, 6 moderate, and 1 slight.
  √ For avoidant behavior, 4 patients had marked improvement, 6 had moderate, and 2 had slight.
  √ Venlafaxine was more effective in women than men.

Antianxiety agents

- Alprazolam 1–7 mg (2.9 mg/day) improved by 3 weeks.
  - √ No sustained improvement after withdrawal.
- Buspirone
  - √ Works best for worry, apprehensive tension, and irritability.
  - √ Effective to some extent in social phobia.
  - √ Use 45–60 mg; under 45 mg often not effective.
  - √ May take 12 weeks.
- Clonazepam in doses 0.5–3 mg (mean 2.4 mg/day) effective sooner.
  - √ 78% improved in 6 weeks.
    - □ Only 20% responded in the placebo-treated patients.
    - □ Significant improvement seen in 1 week.
    - □ When maintained over 6 months, mean effective dose declined to 0.9 mg/day.

Anticonvulsants

- Gabapentin (N = 70)
  - √ Placebo-controlled trial shows it works significantly better than placebo.
  - √ After 2 weeks or more of treatment there was a 28-point decrease on social anxiety scale.

*Performance anxiety*

- Beta-blockers reduce
  - √ Heart rate
  - √ Tremor
  - √ Dry mouth
  - √ "Butterflies" in stomach
  - √ Anxiety (modestly)
- Beta-blockers include
  - √ Metoprolol 25–50 mg
  - √ Atenolol 30–100 mg
  - √ Propranolol 10–80 mg
    - □ A trial dose of 10 mg propranolol should be given 2 h before anxiety-provoking performance.
    - □ First take a trial dose at home and try to vividly imagine the stressful situation.
    - □ Raise dose if initial dose did not work and side effects are not a problem.
    - □ Then try dose in real-life situation.
    - □ If this works, administer propranolol 2 h before future stressful events.
    - □ If necessary, raise dose by increments of 10 mg.

ANTIANXIETY AGENTS

       ◻ Should not be used for an athletic performance—will decrease exercise tolerance.
- √ Benzodiazepines will decrease performance anxiety but also decrease performance ability.
- √ Maintenance for frequent occurrence of specific social phobias (e.g., walking into a classroom):
  - ◻ Try long-acting drug (e.g., atenolol or nadolol).
  - ◻ May be no better than placebo for this purpose.
- If the stressful situation is unpredictable, then chronic beta-blocker use or MAOIs are needed.
  - √ MAOIs are superior to beta-blockers for generalized social phobia.

*Selective mutism*

- May be a variant of social phobia.
  - √ Fluoxetine 10–30 mg/day for 12 weeks resulted in substantial improvement.
  - √ Benzodiazepines occasionally helpful.

## Separation Anxiety Disorder

- Follow TCA precaution procedures for children on pages 100–101.
- SSRIs may be as effective, but as yet less controlled data.
- For separation anxiety
  - √ May benefit from 25–50 mg/day of imipramine, but in conjunction with school avoidance, may need 75 mg/day.
  - √ When children recover completely, it is in 6–8 weeks.
  - √ TCAs are rarely continued for longer than 3 months.
  - √ For school phobia
    - ◻ Start children ages 6–8 on 10 mg of imipramine at bedtime.
    - ◻ Start older children on 25 mg at bedtime.
    - ◻ Raise dose 30–50 mg/week, depending on child's age.
    - ◻ Maximum dose is usually around 3.5 mg/kg/day of imipramine.

## Obsessive-Compulsive Disorder (OCD)

Serotonergic drugs are best.

- Drop-out rates are high for OCD patients.
  - √ 8–40% usual range.
- 10–15% full remission.
- Average response: 40% decrease in symptoms.
- 70% some response.
- Presence of depression not a predictor of OCD response.
- Presence of tics may predict a better response with augmentation with an antipsychotic drug.

√ In patients with onset of OCD symptoms before age of 10 (N = 7)
  □ "Tic-like" compulsions were present in 38%.
  □ 31% of early onset patients had a family history of OCD.
√ In the late-onset group (after the age of 18) only 13% had tic-like compulsions and none had a h/o OCD.
  □ Adding pimozide or low-dose haloperidol can significantly increase response.
- Other predictors of poor response include:
  √ Fixed belief in necessity of rituals.
  √ Absence of behavioral rituals (pure obsessional or mental rituals only).
  √ Severe depression.
  √ Hoarding and corresponding compulsions.
    □ Hoarders often have poor general functioning, limited insight, no resistance, secretiveness, denial concerning their collections, and a tendency to blame others for their hoarding. They frequently do not respond to usual OCD treatments (SSRI, clomipramine) and quit treatment.
- Non-serotonergic TCAs and trazodone have limited or no effect.
- Drug treatment best when accompanied by exposure and response prevention therapy.
  √ Behavior therapy produces more improvement (80%) without relapse when treatment is withdrawn; however, more patients drop out of treatment.
- Clomipramine was often favored in earlier studies of this disorder, but frequently has significantly higher drop-out rates than SSRIs because many patients can't tolerate clomipramine.
- Later studies show equivalent response rate with higher doses of all SRIs.
- Obsessions improve more than compulsions.
  √ Exposure and response prevention therapy is an important co-treatment.
- Dose 200–250 mg/day
  √ > 250 mg/day risks seizures.
  √ Should wait 10 weeks for a full response.
- Clomipramine may reduce trichotillomania.
  √ Poorer response than OCD.
- Many patients cannot tolerate clomipramine's side effects of
  √ Weight gain
  √ Excessive tremor
  √ Sweating, and
  √ Anticholinergic side effects.
- In a study of fluvoxamine vs. clomipramine in OCD (N = 217)

√ No statistically significant differences between them; both were equally clinically effective.
√ Clomipramine-treated patients had a higher incidence of adverse side effects (especially dry mouth, constipation, and tremor) and
▫ Premature withdrawals due to these side effects (18 vs. 9).

SSRIs

- May be first choice because of much lower side effects than clomipramine and efficacy equal to clomipramine.
- At 12 weeks 2/3–3/4 of patients receiving paroxetine 20–60 mg/day or clomipramine 50–250 mg/day considered themselves improved, as did nearly half of the placebo group.
- Dose often higher than antidepressant dose.
  √ Fluoxetine 50–120 mg/day
    ▫ A 60 mg dose compared to a 20 mg dose resulted in a greater drop on Yale-Brown Obsessive-Compulsive Scale and a greater drop in compulsion items.
    ▫ Steady-state plasma levels of fluoxetine and norfluoxetine are not related to clinical outcome in patients with OCD.
  √ Sertraline 100–200 mg/day
  √ Paroxetine 20–80 mg/day
    ▫ Efficacy 20 < 40 or 60 mg
  √ Fluvoxamine 200–300 mg/day
- Higher drop-out rates with higher doses.
- Sertraline treatment for pediatric OCD:
  √ 187 patients: 107 6–12-year-olds and 80 13–17-year-olds.
  √ Randomized to sertraline (N = 92) or placebo (N = 95).
  √ Sertraline produced significantly more improvement on Children's Yale-Brown scale (p = 0.005) and CGI (p = 0.002).
  √ 11% on sertraline and 2% on placebo discontinued due to adverse events.
  √ Insomnia, nausea, agitation, and tremor were significantly increased compared with placebo.
- Fluvoxamine has more studies supporting its efficacy than other SSRIs.
  √ However, all seem equally effective.
  √ Nausea rate is 40% and may be less well tolerated.

Overall, clomipramine and SSRIs give moderate or better improvement in up to 50% of cases.

- In treatment-resistant patients, clomipramine can be combined with fluoxetine, paroxetine, or sertraline if clomipramine dose is lowered to 25–75 mg.

- Later, clomipramine 100–150 mg with sertraline, fluvoxamine, or paroxetine may be more effective.
- Need to carefully monitor clomipramine side effects and interactions between the two drugs before and after adding SSRI.
- Adverse experiences in 28% of clomipramine patients, 16% of paroxetine patients, and 8% of the placebo group.
  √ Treatment withdrawals for adverse reactions occurred in 17% of clomipramine patients, 9% of paroxetine patients, and 6% of the placebo group.

Clomipramine and fluvoxamine were tested using 3 groups; group 1 (control group), no reduction; group 2, reduction of 33–40%; and group 3, reduction of 60–66%.

- Obsessive-compulsive patients did well at lower dosages of the antiobsessional drug(s) with clear advantages for tolerability and compliance.
- Surprisingly, several symptoms were predictive of good response: dry mouth, constipation, dizziness, insomnia, male impotence, nervousness, palpitations, and tremor.

Combining clomipramine 50–100 mg/day with nortriptyline in OCD:

- 30 outpatients with scores of at least 18 on Yale-Brown Obsessive-Compulsive Scale (Y-BOCS) and an illness of at least 1 year were included.
- After a 2-week washout, patients were randomized to 8 weeks of either clomipramine 150 mg/day plus nortriptyline 50 mg/day or clomipramine plus placebo.
- By week 4, Y-BOCS scores were significantly lower in the combined therapy group ($p < .007$); at week 8 $p < .0001$.
- At 8 weeks of treatment both groups showed significant improvement from baseline ($<.001$).

Long-term OCD treatment:

- Patients ($N = 281$) randomized to receive clomipramine 150 mg/day, fluoxetine 40 mg/day, or fluvoxamine 300 mg/day.
- 252 completed 6-month acute treatment phase, of which 130 responded to treatment.
  √ Probably because fluoxetine and norfluoxetine have much longer half-lives, e.g., 3–5 weeks.
    □ Takes up to 3 months to eliminate fluoxetine and norfluoxetine from the body.

Monoamine-oxidase inhibitors (phenelzine 45–90 mg/day, tranylcypromine 10–50 mg/day) may help OCD patients with panic attacks or severe anxiety, social phobia, or intractable depression.

ANTIANXIETY AGENTS

- Open studies suggest equivalent efficacy with clomipramine.
- Recommend trial if clomipramine and fluoxetine fail.
- Do not overlap MAOIs and SRIs.

In general, antianxiety agents do not improve OCD

- Once a successful treatment is found, the OCD patient will need to stay on the medication indefinitely.
  - √ 85% relapse rate seen within 2 months of quitting medication.

There are several possible augmenting agents for OCD.

Risperidone

- Addition to SSRI in double-blind placebo-controlled study of refractory OCD patients (N = 70).
  - √ 36 patients refractory to SSRI were randomized in a double-blind manner to 6 weeks of risperidone (N = 20) or placebo (N = 16).
  - √ 9 (50%) of 18 risperidone-treated patients were responders (mean daily dose 2.2 mg).
  - √ 7 (50%) of 14 patients who received open-label risperidone responded.
  - √ None of the 15 patients in the placebo group responded.
  - √ Risperidone addition was superior to placebo in OCD (p < .001), depression (p < .001), and anxiety (p < .003).
  - √ Tics or overvalued obsessions not necessary for improvement with addition of resperidone.
- In another study of refractory OCD patients, addition of risperidone, mean daily dose 3.6 mg, showed a mean decrease in Y-BOCS from 28 to 15.6.

Olanzapine

- 10 patients with OCD had residual symptoms following one adequate SSRI trial (12 weeks).
  - √ Open olanzapine augmentation for a minimum of 8 more weeks.
  - √ 9 of the 10 patients were treated with olanzapine and SSRI.
    - ◌ 4 demonstrated a complete remission or major improvement in OCD.
    - ◌ 3 had partial remission.
    - ◌ 2 had no benefit.
  - √ 9 patients experienced minimal adverse effects, primarily sedation.
  - √ Lack of placebo control limits interpretation of data.

Pindolol

- 11 refractory OCD patients treated for $18 \pm 2$ weeks with 60 mg/day paroxetine in an open manner.
- Patients were assigned to a double-blind placebo-controlled pindolol augmentation (2.5 mg Tid).
  - √ Pindolol augmentation demonstrated significant improvement on the compulsion scale ($p < .035$) and marginally significant on the obsession scale ($p < .08$).
  - √ Mean decrease in Y-BOCS was less than 25%.
  - √ 6 had significant improvement, but 5 had poor or no efficacy.
  - √ Depression and anxiety showed no significant change.

Lithium

- No better than placebo in one controlled study.
- Some positive case studies reported.
- Try if patient is still depressed.

Pimozide or haloperidol

- Especially for patients with tics or schizotypal or psychotic features.

Stimulants (methylphenidate or dextroamphetamine)

- Dextroamphetamine may be more effective than methylphenidate in augmenting responses.

Opiates

- May be helpful for refractory OCD patients.
- Naltrexone at 50 or 100 mg/day resulted in significant decreases in trichotillomania and compulsive picking.
- Morphine sulfate 10 mg was substituted for naltrexone with fast resolution of OCD symptoms.
  - √ However, patients also experienced rapid onset of euphoria.
  - √ Dose increased to 30 mg, with significant reduction of compulsive picking and dysphoria.

Tramadol

- Begin tramadol 50 mg bid.
  - √ Y-BOCS score of 26 decreased to 19 in 1 week.
- Fluoxetine increased to 40 mg/day after 3 weeks and tramadol increased up to 350 mg/day.
- Y-BOCS score decreased to 10.
- At one time, tramadol was thought to have a relatively low potential for abuse and physical dependence, but this has not proven to be the case. However, it is well tolerated.

Gabapentin

- Reported to be a beneficial augmenting agent in a small number of OCD patients.
- Obsessive thoughts and anxiety reduced after addition of gabapentin in patients poorly responsive to fluoxetine monotherapy.

Recurrent OCD with pediatric autoimmune neuropsychiatric disorder associated with streptococcal infection (PANDAS).

- Diagnosis must be based on two exacerbations of OCD triggered by Group A beta-hemolytic streptococcal (GABHS).
  √ Certainty requires positive cultures or rising antibody titers.
  √ A "possible PANDA" can rest on a single exacerbation of OCD associated with positive throat cultures or rising titers for GABHS.
- Approximately 25% of people who develop rheumatic heart disease from GABHS infection go on to develop Sydenham's chorea, characterized by awkward gait and diffuse choreiform movements.
  √ Unfortunately, many get misdiagnosed as having Tourette's disorder.
  √ As many as half of those with Sydenham's chorea may have OCD symptoms.
- Treatment (at least for life-threatening emergencies) consists of intravenous immunoglobulin G 3 times a week for 2 weeks.
- Plasmapheresis: 5 full volume exchanges over a period of 2 weeks.
  √ Tics declined 50% within 1 month in plasmapheresis patients.
  √ OCD symptoms reduced by 60% with plasmapheresis.
  √ Children showed significantly more improvement on global functioning measures, and overall improvement continued beyond a month following treatment.
  √ Brain structures (caudate nucleus, basal ganglia, and globus pallidus) enlarged during PANDAS flares normalized in children who received plasmapheresis.
- Intravenous immunoglobulin resulted in
  √ Tics declining 25%.
  √ OCD symptoms reduced by 45%.
  √ Treatment is effective but less so than plasmapheresis.

## Obsessive-Compulsive Spectrum Disorders

These disorders share many features of OCD.

- Those most closely resembling OCD have pervasive obsessional preoccupations.

√ Hypochondriasis
√ Pathological jealousy
√ Body dysmorphic disorder
√ Bulimia
  ▫ Has some impulsive component.
  ▫ See Antidepressants, page 132.
- Those that are like OCD but have a strong impulsive component, and may be better called impulsive-compulsive disorders, include:
  √ Trichotillomania
    ▫ Neuroleptics ineffective.
    ▫ Lower response to SSRIs than OCD patients.
  √ Anorexia nervosa
    ▫ May respond partially to fluoxetine 60 mg qd but improvement often not sustained after 3–6 months.
    ▫ *See* Antidepressants, page 131.
  √ Pathological gambling
  √ Paraphilias
  √ Sexual "addictions"
  √ Compulsive shopping
- Uncontrolled experience and a few small controlled trials suggest that both types (predominantly obsessive and predominantly impulsive) respond to serotonergic ADs after 8–12 weeks.
  √ Preliminary data suggest that the more compulsive types maintain a response while the impulsive types do not.

## Hypochondriasis

- May be a variant of OCD or a separate disorder.
- Open trial of 14 patients with high-dose fluoxetine (52 mg average) resulted in 10 responders after 12 weeks.
  √ Disease phobia and disease conviction decreased, but not bodily preoccupation.

## Paraphilias

- Open trials of fluoxetine suggest that the paraphilic behavior decreases while normal sexual behavior continues; however,
  √ Decrease in overall sexual drive may contribute to success.
- Controlled trials of antiandrogens (e.g., cyproterone acetate 50–200 mg/day) show suppressed sexual
  √ Arousal
  √ Fantasy
  √ Activity

## Body dysmorphic disorder (BDD)

- SSRIs may help if the belief is an overvalued idea but not fully delusional.

√ Open trials successful with clomipramine, fluoxetine, or fluvoxamine.
- If delusional, addition of pimozide or another antipsychotic (e.g.,
  haloperidol or olanzapine) is recommended.
- Patients who consider their body ugly because of their gender, but
  who do not appear to have sexual identity of the other gender,
  may better be treated as having BDD and not as transsexuals
  needing surgery.

*Compulsive shopping*

- 10 self-described compulsive shoppers (9 women, 1 man) with
  symptom duration of ≥ 10 years and very high scores on Compulsive Buying Scale.
- 9 had family history of psychiatric illness, mainly depression
  and/or substance abuse.
- 9 patients responded to fluvoxamine, judged as > 50% improvement on Y-BOC scale, shopping version.
- 3 subjects in 1 week.
- 3 in second week.
- 2 in third week.
- 1 in fifth week.

## Posttraumatic Stress Disorder (PTSD)

There is no clear drug treatment for PTSD.

- About 20% of women and 10% of men in general population have
  lifetime history of PTSD.
- Treatment is much less effective for combat veterans than victims
  of other types of trauma, e.g., sexual, physical, and/or emotional
  abuse/assault, or the witnessing of another's injury or death.

Try any drug trial for at least 6–8 weeks and possibly longer for chronic
illness.

- If efficacious, treat PTSD for 6–12+ months to limit relapse.

The positive symptoms of PTSD—reexperiencing the trauma and increased arousal and hypervigilance—respond better than the negative
symptoms—avoidance and withdrawal.

More positive findings stem from agents with serotonergic affects,
e.g., MAOIs, SSRIs, and nefazodone. All 3 drug categories work on
intrusive recall, numbing, and social withdrawal. MAOIs are used less
frequently for PTSD because of dietary restrictions and/or contraindicated drugs. Amitriptyline may also have similar effects. Specific reported treatments include:

- Sertraline (50–150 mg/day)
  - √ Compared to placebo, an average of 35% on sertraline had significant improvement of intrusive recall (53%) and avoidance behavior (47%).
  - √ At end point, sertraline-treated patients had a mean decrease in trauma scale ratings of 43% compared to 27% in the placebo group.
  - √ Women on sertraline had a significant improvement in intrusive reexperiencing, avoidance, numbness, and hyperarousal.
  - √ Men, all veterans, did not show any improvement on sertraline in this trial.
- Fluoxetine (20–80 mg/day)
  - √ One study showed 59% very much improved with fluoxetine vs. 9% on placebo.
  - √ Also diminishes rage reactions.
  - √ Better than imipramine for intrusive symptoms and avoidance.
- Nefazodone (200–600 mg/day)
  - √ Patients showed an increase in sleep hours, sexual functioning, and normalization of dreams.
    - ▫ Number of dreams that replicated trauma decreased, and normal fantasy distortions increased.
    - ▫ On clinician-administered PTSD scale, patients (all male) showed a 26% improvement for symptoms of intrusion, 33% for avoidance, and 28% for arousal.
    - ▫ Reduced the accompanying depression and anxiety in patients with chronic PTSD.
    - ▫ Anger ratings were greatly improved (up to 62%) over the course of study.
- Phenelzine (40–90 mg/day).
  - √ Older studies demonstrate improvement of hyperarousal, traumatic nightmares, and depression in PTSD patients.
  - √ Very effective in suppressing bad dreams.
- Amitriptyline (50–300 mg day).
  - √ Better than placebo for positive distress symptoms as well as for avoidance.
- Imipramine 200–300 mg/day.
  - √ Better than placebo for intrusive symptoms but not avoidance.

Try any drug trial for 6–8 weeks.

Promising new treatments for PTSD include:

- Carbamazepine 400–2000 mg/day
  - √ Reduces arousal and affective symptoms.

   √ Anti-kindling effect decreases recurrences.
- Topiramate was given to 19 outpatients with chronic PTSD at a mean dose of 150 mg/day (range 25–500 mg/day).
  - √ Target symptoms were intrusive memories (N = 19) and nightmares (N = 13).
  - √ 63% experienced suppression of nightmares.
  - √ 89% experienced suppression of flashbacks.
  - √ Efficacy occurred within 2–3 days.
  - √ In patients continuing treatment, topiramate remained effective without evidence of tolerance.
- Prazosin, an alpha-adrenergic antagonist, was given for nightmares.
  - √ 4 combat veterans with chronic PTSD and severe intractable combat trauma nightmares participated in an 8-week open trial of escalating-dose prazosin.
  - √ 2 patients who achieved a daily prazosin dose of at least 5 mg were markedly improved, with complete elimination of trauma nightmares and resumption of normal dreaming.
  - √ 2 patients limited to 2 mg of prazosin to avoid hypotension were moderately improved, with at least 50% reduction in nightmare severity.
- Lamotrigine given to 9 patients for treatment of PTSD.
  - √ 5 (55%) responded, compared to 1 of 4 (25%) who received placebo.
  - √ Lamotrigine patients showed improvement on reexperiencing and avoidance/numbing symptoms.
  - √ N too small for statistical comparison.
- Yohimbine *worsens* PTSD.
  - √ 4 middle-aged men had acute worsening of PTSD symptoms shortly after taking yohimbine.
  - √ It is an alpha-2-adrenergic receptor antagonist that increases release of endogenous norepinephrine and therefore increases arousal.

If trial drug does not work, the next approach depends on predominant symptoms.

Clonidine and buprenorphine may reduce self-mutilatory behavior.

Benzodiazepines risk dependence/abuse in this population, which is frequently comprised of alcohol and drug abusers.

- If used, long-acting medium-slow–onset drug preferred (e.g., clonazepam 1–5 mg).

## Drug Treatment of PTSD Symptoms

| Symptoms | Drug | Dose |
|---|---|---|
| **Behaviors** | | |
| Irritability, aggression, impulsiveness, flashbacks | Carbamazepine | 600–1800 mg/day |
| | Valproic acid | 750–1500 mg/day |
| Startle, hyperarousal, autonomic hyperexcitability | Benzodiazepines | usual dose range |
| | Propranolol | 40–1500 mg/day |
| | Buspirone | 40–80 mg/day |
| | Clonidine | 0.2–0.4 mg/day |
| | Carbamazepine, valproic acid | see above |
| Sleep disturbance, nightmares | Trazodone | 50–400 mg qhs |
| | Nefazodone | 300–600 mg qhs |
| | Zolpidem | 10–20 mg qhs |
| | Phenelzine | 30–90 mg/day |
| | Benzodiazepines, clonidine, carbamazepine | see above |
| | Propranolol | 40–160 mg/day |
| **Feelings** | | |
| Anger, anxiety | Buspirone | 40–90 mg |
| | Lithium* | 600–1800 mg |
| | Trazodone | 100–600 mg |

* Not for anxiety.

- Possible disinhibitory behavior can occur, particularly with initiation of treatment.
- Eventual withdrawal can be very difficult.

# Nicotine Abuse

Hypnosis, nicotine gum, and gradual substitution with lower nicotine-containing cigarettes help only a few smokers; behavioral treatments must be added for smoking cessation.

Nicotine gum and nicotine patches are preferred approaches to withdrawal symptoms in patients who have stopped smoking.

- Nicotine gum not well accepted.
  - √ Patient must chew but not swallow saliva.
  - √ If saliva is swallowed, more gastric discomfort and less efficacy.

Clonidine 0.2–0.4 mg may substantially decrease anxiety and craving—that is, the mental preoccupation with smoking. However, clonidine causes sedation and hypotension, which restrict its use to normotensive patients. Rate of nicotine cessation about the same as placebo.

ANTIANXIETY AGENTS

Alprazolam 1 mg relieves anxiety but risks benzodiazepine abuse.

Buspirone (started at 15–30 mg/day and increased to 40–50 mg/day) reduced, but did not stop, smoking in 7/8 subjects.

Bupropion 300 mg in 190 nondepressed treatment failures (e.g., nicotine patch, clonidine, support) yielded

- At 4 weeks 40% abstainers vs. 24% on placebo.
- At 23 weeks, 28% abstainers vs. 21% on placebo.

Treatment-failure nicotine abusers have high rates of prior major depressive episodes and depression relapses when attempting abstinence.

- SSRIs or bupropion recommended for this subgroup.
   √ Fluoxetine prevents smoking-cessation–associated carbohydrate cravings, weight gain, and dysphoric mood.
- Ondansetron (14–16 mg/day) reduces craving for all substances, including nicotine.
   √ Also has anxiolytic properties.

## Catatonia

Symptoms include:

- Immobility, mutism, withdrawal/refusal to eat, posturing, grimacing in ≥ 75% of cases.
- Staring, rigidity, and negativism in ≥ 50% of cases.
- Waxy flexibility, stereotypy, echolalia/echopraxia, and verbigeration in < 50% of cases.

Causes of catatonia, in order of frequency:

- CNS syndromes are the most common causes.
   √ *CNS* includes medication-induced (neuroleptic-induced).
- Mood disorders
   √ Most often bipolar or psychotic depression.
- Treatment with neuroleptics.
- Schizophrenia least common cause.

Acute treatment of catatonia

- ECT is the most effective treatment.
- Lorazepam 1–2 mg IM prn can eliminate symptoms.
   √ Allows patient to talk, eat, and move.
      □ Reduces risk of starvation, dehydration, pulmonary emboli.
      □ Ability to speak increases accuracy of diagnosis—e.g., grandiose thoughts (mania), nihilistic delusions (psychotic depression), confused thinking (delirium), etc.

Maintenance treatment of catatonia

- Benzodiazepine may be continued adjunctively with specific treatment of underlying disorder.
- Lorazepam can be continued orally 1–2 mg q 4–6 h.
- Clonazepam 0.5–1 mg bid can be substituted for lorazepam to provide more sustained effects.

## SIDE EFFECTS

## Cardiovascular Effects

*Bradycardia*

- Propranolol and other beta-blockers can cause bradycardia at modest doses.
  - √ Check pulse at rest and after brief exercise.
  - √ Consider decreased dose if resting pulse is under 60/min or exercise pulse is under 110/min.
- If doesn't develop at lower doses, rarely a difficulty after reaching 300–500 mg/day.

*Bronchospasm*

- Do not give propranolol to asthmatics.
  - √ Stop propranolol if patient starts wheezing.
  - √ Consider a more selective agent (e.g., acetabutalol, atenolol, metoprolol, or betaxolol) if a beta-blocker is necessary.

*Hypotension, dizziness, lightheadedness*

- Clonidine, propranolol, and sometimes trazodone can induce serious hypotension.
  - √ Hypotension milder with benzodiazepines, buspirone, fluoxetine, sertraline, paroxetine, and venlafaxine than with antipsychotics, TCAs, MAOIs, clonidine, or propranolol.
  - √ Hypotension becomes no worse after propranolol > 500 mg/day.
- Management
  - √ Measure BPs before and during the first few days of clonidine or propranolol, in both reclining and standing positions.
  - √ Increase dose more slowly.
  - √ Have patient deal with hypotension by
    - ▫ Sitting a full 60 seconds—or longer—if at all lightheaded,
    - ▫ Standing slowly while holding onto stable object (e.g., bed), and
    - ▫ Waiting at least 30 seconds before walking.
  - √ *See* pages 26–27, 139–42 for further management.

ANTIANXIETY AGENTS

*Raynaud's phenomena*

- Cold fingers and toes.
- Do not give beta-blocker if patient has history of Raynaud's.

## Central Nervous System Effects

*Amnesia*

- Anterograde amnesia especially with IV diazepam and lorazepam.
- Directly related to benzodiazepine's speed of onset.

*Confusion, disorientation, clouded sensorium*

- Occurs primarily in the elderly, cognitively impaired, or brain-damaged.
  - √ Caused by small doses of benzodiazepines.
  - √ Often reversible.
  - √ Misdiagnosed as dementia.
- On propranolol, not dose-related.
  - √ Can be due to chronic, relative hypotension (e.g., severe hypertensive corrected to low "normal").

*Depression*

- Occurs most often with
  - √ Propranolol (high doses)—only twice normal rate.
  - √ Symptoms often appear in days.
  - √ Patient usually doesn't report symptoms for weeks.
- Occurs more often with
  - √ Benzodiazepine doses, e.g., > 30 mg diazepam equivalent.
  - √ More common in high-potency benzodiazepines because it is easier to get "high" doses.
    - □ Clonazepam > 1.5 mg
    - □ Alprazolam > 3 mg
    - □ Lorazepam > 4–6 mg
  - √ At these doses there may be 25% rate of new depressions in panic disorder patients within 6 weeks.
  - √ Probably not unique to any particular benzodiazepine.
  - √ Also seen on equivalent quantities of alcohol (i.e., 5–6 drinks/ beers a day).
- Can escalate into
  - √ Neurovegetative signs of depression.
  - √ Catatonia.

*Excitement*

- Paradoxical reactions more often occur in children, the elderly, cognitively impaired, or brain-damaged.

- Disinhibition (as with alcohol) occurs more often below sedative doses.

*Incoordination, ataxia*

- Occurs with high doses of benzodiazepines.
  √ Arises in 25% of patients on ≥10 mg/day of clonazepam.
- In regular doses, only with meprobamate.

*Mania*

- Most often reported with alprazolam.

*Rage reactions, anger*

- Violent episodes with, or without, a h/o violence.
- Observed with alprazolam and diazepam.
  √ May be more common with fast-onset benzodiazepines that give a "buzz."
  √ May be secondary to acute disinhibition.
  √ Less with oxazepam.
- Treat instead with haloperidol 5 mg/IM, trazodone 25–200 mg, propranolol, or carbamazepine.

*Sedation*

- Common for benzodiazepines, clonidine, and propranolol.
  √ For instance, clonazepam produces drowsiness 50% of the time.
  √ Buspirone does not normally sedate, although a single 20–40 mg dose can exhaust people.
- Management
  √ Increase dose slowly.
  √ Reduce dose.
  √ With clonidine give 2/3 daily dose q hs and 1/3 q A.M.
  √ Sedation should be significantly less after 7–14 days on benzodiazepine and after 21 days on clonidine.

*Stuttering*

- Mainly with alprazolam.

## Endocrine and Sexual Effects

Endocrine and sexual effects include

- Sexual dysfunction common with propranolol and clonidine.
  √ Clonidine rarely causes gynecomastia.
- Buspirone a treatment for SSRI-induced sexual dysfunction.

## Eyes, Ears, Nose, and Throat

*Eyes, dry (see* pages 45–46)

Narrow-angle glaucoma worsening.

- Occurs on several benzodiazepines (e.g., clonazepam, alprazolam).

*Vision, blurred (see* page 45)

- Mild and rare with usual anxiolytics.
  √ Bethanechol 5–20 mg po tid or qid.

## Gastrointestinal Effects

*Constipation (see* page 47)

*Mouth, dry, nasal congestion (see* page 47)

- Most common with clonidine, benzodiazepines, and hydroxyzine.
- Nasal congestion alone occurs with trazodone.

## Renal Effects

*Urinary hesitancy or retention (see* page 52)

## PERCENTAGES OF SIDE EFFECTS

| Side Effects | Benzodiazepines | Buspirone | Clonidine | Propranolol |
|---|---|---|---|---|
| **CARDIOVASCULAR EFFECTS** | | | | |
| Bradycardia | < 1 | < 1 | 0.5 | 20.7 |
| Breath, short | < 1 | < 1 | — | 5.6 |
| Bronchospasm | 0 | 0 | 0 | + |
| Cardiac arrhythmias | 0 | 0 | 5.5 | 0 |
| Chest pain | — | 1.5 | 3.3 | 4 |
| Congestive heart failure | 0 | < 0.1 | + | + |
| Dizziness, lightheadedness | 13.4 (6.8–30) | 13.6 (10–30) | 18 (10–30) | 10.5 (1.5–30) |
| Edema | — | — | — | 9 (2–16) |
| Fainting, syncope | 3.1 | < 1 | — | 5 |
| Hands and feet, cold | — | — | — | 20 |
| Hypertension | 0 | < 1 | 0 | 0 |
| Hyperventilation | < 1 | — | — | |
| Hypotension | 4.7 | < 1 | 11.5 | 9.9 |
| Palpitations | 7.7 | 1 | 0.5 | — |
| Raynaud's phenomena | 0 | 0 | + | + |
| Tachycardia | 7.7 | 1.3* | 0.5 | — |

| Side Effects | Benzodiazepines | Buspirone | Clonidine | Propranolol |
|---|---|---|---|---|
| **CENTRAL NERVOUS SYSTEM EFFECTS** | | | | |
| Agitation, restlessness (motoric) | + | 20 | 3 | — |
| Anxiety, nervousness (mental) | 4.1 | 5 | 3 | — |
| Ataxia, clumsiness, incoordination | 17.6 (5–79) | 2.5 | — | — |
| Confusion, disorientation | 6.9 (1–10) | 2.0 | + | 4.5 |
| Depression | 8.3 (1–13.9) | 1.4* | 0.8 | 8.9 (0.1–50) |
| Dreams, weird | + | 5.5 | + | 4.3 (1–10) |
| Drowsiness, sedation | 35.1 (6.8–77) | 12.4 (1–24) | 30.8 (10–64) | 15 (1.5–30) |
| Excitement | + | 2 | — | — |
| Hallucinations | 5.5 | < 1 | — | 5.5 |
| Headache | 9.1 (5.3–12.9) | 10.6 (6–30) | 3.3 (1–30) | 8.4 (1–17.6) |
| Insomnia | 6.4 | 6.7* | 3 | 5.3 |
| Irritable, hostile, angry | 5.5 | 2 | — | 0 |
| Limb jerks, uncontrollable | — | < 1 | — | — |
| Mania, hypomania | + | < 1 | — | — |
| Memory loss | + | — | — | 11.8 |
| Muscle cramps | — | 1 | 0.6 | 2 |
| Numbness | — | 1.4 | — | 20 |
| Paresthesias | — | < 1 | — | 20 |
| Seizures | — | < 1 | — | — |
| Speech, slurred | + | < 1 | — | — |
| Stuttering | + | — | — | — |
| Tremor | 4 | 1 | — | — |
| Weakness, fatigue | 17.7 (7.7–42) | 7.6 (4–16) | 6.3 (4–10) | 17 (1.5–29.4) |
| **ENDOCRINE AND SEXUAL EFFECTS** | | | | |
| Breast swelling | — | — | 2.8 | — |
| Menstrual irregularities | 0 | < 1 | 0 | 0 |
| Sexual function, disturbed | 11 | < 1 | 4.3 | 8.7 |
| **EYES, EARS, NOSE, AND THROAT EFFECTS** | | | | |
| Diplopia | + | 0 | 0 | + |
| Eyes, burning, itching | + | < 1 | 6 | 0 |
| Eyes, dry | — | — | 5.5 | + |
| Nasal stuffiness | 7.3 | — | — | — |
| Neck glands, painful | — | — | + | + |
| Tinnitus | — | 5.5 | — | — |
| Vertigo | + | 0 | 0 | 0 |
| Vision, blurred | 10.6 (1–20.8) | 2 | 5 | 1.5 |
| **GASTROINTESTINAL EFFECTS** | | | | |
| Anorexia, lower appetite | + | < 1 | 5.5 | 16.6 (1.5–23.5) |
| Appetite, increased | — | < 1 | — | — |
| Constipation | 7.1 (1–10.4) | 1.3* | 7.8 (1–10) | 3.8 (1–10) |

| Side Effects | Benzodiazepines | Buspirone | Clonidine | Propranolol |
|---|---|---|---|---|
| Diarrhea | 7<br>(1–10.1) | 2.5 | — | 12.5 |
| Gas | — | < 1 | — | 4 |
| Hepatitis | 0 | 0 | 1 | 0 |
| Incontinence | + | 0 | 0 | 0 |
| Jaundice | < 1 | — | — | — |
| Mouth and<br>throat, dry | 12.6<br>(10.5–14.7) | 5.3*<br>(1–10) | 22.8<br>(1–40) | — |
| Nausea, vomiting | 7.4<br>(1–10) | 10.8<br>(6–30) | 5.4<br>(1–10) | 14.8<br>(1.5–23.5) |
| Salivation | 4.2 | < 1 | — | — |
| Weight gain | 2.7 | + | 3.3 | — |
| Weight loss | 2.3 | — | — | — |
| **HEMATOLOGIC EFFECTS** | | | | |
| Agranulocytosis | — | — | — | + |
| Bleeding, bruising<br>easily | — | < 1 | — | < 1 |
| **RENAL EFFECTS** | | | | |
| Nocturia | 0 | < 0.1 | 1 | 0 |
| Urinary frequency | — | < 1 | 0.2 | 1 |
| Urinary hesitancy<br>or retention | < 1 | < 1 | 0.1 | — |
| Urinary, pain | < 1 | < 1 | — | — |
| **SKIN, ALLERGIES, AND TEMPERATURE EFFECTS** | | | | |
| Allergies | 3.8 | — | + | 0.4 |
| Edema,<br>angioneurotic | 0 | 0 | + | 0 |
| Edema/facial edema | — | < 1 | — | — |
| Fever, hyperthermia | — | < 1 | — | < 1 |
| Hair loss | — | < 1 | + | + |
| Itch | 5.5 | < 1 | < 1 | — |
| Joint pain | — | — | — | 5.5 |
| Laryngospasm/<br>bronchospasm | 0 | 0 | 0 | + |
| Rashes | 5.5 | 1 | < 1 | 1.4 |
| Skin pigment,<br>abnormal | — | — | 0.2 | — |
| Sweating | — | 1 | — | — |
| Throat, sore | 0 | > 1 | 0 | + |

* Not greater than placebo; + Side effect occurs, but incidence not reported; — Data not available, presumed to be rare.

## PREGNANCY AND LACTATION

Teratogenicity
(1st trimester)

- Case-controlled studies with low-potency benzodiazepines (e.g., diazepam, chlordiazepoxide) do not show an increased rate of any congenital anomaly, including cleft palate.

- There are no data that higher-potency benzodiazepines cause congenital anomalies, but these agents have been insufficiently studied.

- Because of insufficient safety data with some preparations, patients should stop benzodiazepines at least 3–4 weeks before attempting to conceive and should remain off them until the first trimester ends.

- Buspirone does not appear to be teratogenic in animals, but its risk in pregnant humans has not been studied.

- The little data on behavioral teratogenicity in humans do not suggest long-term behavioral or cognitive effects from benzodiazepine exposure *in utero*.

- When possible, use behavioral techniques, psychotherapy, and caffeine abstinence to manage anxiety.

- If medication is necessary for panic attacks during the first trimester, imipramine or an SSRI may be slightly safer than high-potency benzodiazepines.

Direct Effect
on Newborn
(3rd trimester)

- Panic disorder typically continues during pregnancy.

  √ It is associated with higher rates of pre-eclampsia, preterm labor, prolonged labor, stillbirths, fetal hypoxia, and newborns with lower Apgar scores.

- Benzodiazepines with active metabolites (e.g., diazepam) are slowly eliminated by the fetus and neonate and are not recommended.
  √ With chronic diazepam administration, cord plasma concentrations are higher than maternal plasma concentrations.
  √ The shorter-acting benzodiazepine, lorazepam, develops lower concentrations in cord blood than in maternal blood and may be preferred.

ANTIANXIETY AGENTS

- Benzodiazepines can prolong labor.

- Benzodiazepines, especially in higher doses (e.g., over 25 mg diazepam equivalents), can cause "floppy infant syndrome" with lethargy, hypotonia, poor sucking, hyporeflexia, apnea, and/or cyanosis.
  - √ Combining benzodiazepines with narcotics may cause increased floppy infant symptoms.
  - √ For clonazepam, the hypotonia and lethargy typically resolve in 5 days; respiratory depression may persist for 10 days.

- Benzodiazepine withdrawal in newborn causes jitters, tremors, or jerking of extremities, hypertonia, hyperreflexia, vomiting, diarrhea, restlessness, irritability, abnormal sleep patterns, inconsolable crying, chewing movements, bradycardia, and cyanosis.
  - √ Withdrawal appears within a few days postpartum for lorazepam and up to 3 weeks for chlordiazepoxide and clonazepam and may continue up to several months.

- To avoid withdrawal, taper and discontinue benzodiazepines before delivery.

- If anxiety risks higher obstetrical complications (e.g., pre-eclampsia), use the best studied benzodiazepines—chlordiazepoxide, diazepam, or lorazepam.
  - √ Benzodiazepines with simpler metabolism, such as lorazepam and oxazepam, have a theoretical but unproven safety advantage for pre-eclampsia.
  - √ Don't use parenteral diazepam with sodium benzoate as a preservative. Sodium benzoate can prevent bilirubin binding to serum albumin and cause kernicterus.

- Propranolol (and other beta-blockers, e.g., atenolol) may foster intrauterine growth retardation, hypoglycemia, bradycardia, and respiratory depression at birth, and hyperbilirubinemia in neonates.
  √ If mother already on beta-blockers, closely monitor infant for 24–48 h.

- If indicated (e.g., panic attacks), use an SSRI or imipramine or other tricyclic antidepressant instead of benzodiazepines in the last month(s) before delivery.

Lactation

- Benzodiazepines enter breast milk and may induce withdrawal.

- Benzodiazepines can impair infant's alertness, appetite, and temperature regulation.

- With longer-acting benzodiazepines, effects persist 2–3 weeks in infants.

- Diazepam enters breast milk, causing sedation, weight loss, respiratory depression, and withdrawal in newborns. Women on diazepam should avoid breast-feeding.

- Clonazepam also enters breast milk. Its long half-life might encourage apnea. Check for CNS depression in any infant exposed to clonazepam.

- Meprobamate in milk is 2–4 times that of maternal plasma.

- Propranolol is excreted in breast milk; effects unclear.

- Infant oxazepam concentrations are lowest of the benzodiazepines, usually under < 10% of the maternal plasma concentrations.

- For maximum safety, if the mother continues benzodiazepines, assay the baby's plasma level after breast-feeding a week.
  □ Only zero or negligible levels are acceptable.

ANTIANXIETY AGENTS

## Drug Dosage in Mother's Milk

| Generic Names | Milk/ Plasma Ratio | Time of Peak Concentration in Milk (hours) | Infant Dose ($\mu$g/kg/day) | Maternal Dose (%) | Safety Rating* |
|---|---|---|---|---|---|
| Clonazepam | ? | ? | 2† | 1.3–3.0‡ | C |
| Clonidine | ? | ? | 0.41 | 7.8 | E |
| Clorazepate | ? | ? | 2.3 | ? | ? |
| Diazepam | 0.16 | ? | 3.3–11.7 | 2–2.3 | B |
| Hydralazine | ? | ? | 20 | 0.8 | A |
| Lorazepam | ? | ? | 1.3 | 2.2 | B |
| Oxazepam | ? | 1.5 | 4.5 | 0.9 | A |
| Prazepam | 0.11 | 22 | 13.4** | 3.2*** | B |
| Propranolol | 0.32–0.76 | 2–5 | 1.4–11.2 | 0.2–0.9 | A |

* A: Safe throughout infancy (probably safe = infant maximum plasma concentration <10% maternal plasma concentration); B: Reasonably unsafe before 34 weeks, but probably safer after 34 weeks; C: Reasonably unsafe before week 44, but safer after 44 weeks; E: Unsafe up to 34th week because infant plasma concentration approaches and may exceed the mother's, reasonably unsafe from weeks 34–68, and safest after 68th week.
† Infant therapeutic dose 20–200 $\mu$g/kg/day.
‡ Maternal dose not specified, but presumed to be 20–200 $\mu$g/kg/day.
** Metabolite N-desmethyldiazepam measured.
*** Assuming 100% conversion to metabolite.

# DRUG-DRUG INTERACTIONS*○

| Drugs (X) Interact with: | Benzo- diazepines (B) | Comments |
|---|---|---|
| *Alcohol | X↑B↑ | Alcohol escalates suicide risk from benzodiazepines. |
| *Aluminum hydroxide (see antacids) | | |
| Aminophylline (see bronchodilators) | | |
| *Amiodarone | B↑ | Increases clonazepam and probably other oxidatively metabolized benzodiazepines.** |
| *Antacids (aluminum hydroxide, magnesium hydroxide) | B↓ | Slows rate but not total amount of GI absorption. Probable clinical effect is to slow onset, perhaps peak magnitude of effect, and prolong duration of effect of single doses. In single but not repeated doses, interfered with transformation of clorazepate to desmethyldiazepam. |
| Anticholinergics (includes all drugs with anticholinergic properties) | B↓ | Slows time to peak absorption but not total amount absorbed. |
| Antifungal imidazoles (see ketoconazole) | | |
| Barbiturates (see also sedatives) | X↑ B↓↑ | Phenobarbital (and probably others) speed benzodiazepine metabolism and reduce levels. Potentiate each other's effects. |
| *Birth control pills | B↑↓ | Oral contraceptives may increase 2-keto and triazolo compounds while reducing 3-hydroxy agents.** |

| Drugs (X) Interact with: | Benzo-diazepines (B) | Comments |
|---|---|---|
| *Bronchodilators:*<br>Aminophylline<br>Theophylline | B↓ | Rapidly antagonize diazepam, lorazepam, and probably other benzodiazepine effects; increase benzodiazepine doses. |
| Caffeine | B↓ | Caffeine (250–500 mg) antagonizes benzodiazepines. |
| Carbamazepine | B↓ | Decreases alprazolam and clonazepam levels 20–50%. |
| *Cimetidine | B↑ | May increase most oxidatively metabolized benzodiazepines (*not* 3-hydroxy agents**) and increase benzodiazepine's side effects. Ranitidine and famotidine appear less apt to interact with benzodiazepines than cimetidine. |
| Digitalis | B↑ | Increases benzodiazepines, including diazepam, clonazepam, and alprazolam. |
| Digoxin | X↑ | Digoxin serum levels increased; monitor levels. |
| *Disulfiram | B↑↓ | Increases oxidatively metabolized benzodiazepine** levels (*not* 3-hydroxy agents) and sedation. May need to lower benzodiazepines or switch to 3-hydroxy agents.** |
| Erthromycin (*see* macrolide antibiotics) | | |
| Estrogen (*see* birth control pills) | | |
| Fluconazole (*see* ketoconazole) | | |
| Fluoxetine (and probably paroxetine and sertraline) | B↑ | Increases levels of diazepam and alprazolam and probably other oxidatively metabolized benzodiazepines except clonazepam or triazolam (and probably not lorazepam or oxazepam). |
| Food | B↓ | Slows absorption; for rapid effect, take on empty stomach. |
| Isoniazid (INH) | B↑ | INH increases effects of benzodiazepines that require oxidative metabolism**; lower benzodiazepine dose or switch to 3-hydroxy-benzodiazepines.** |
| *Ketoconazole:*<br>Fluconazole<br>Miconazole<br>Traconazole | B↑ | Increases oxidatively metabolized benzodiazepines** but not hydroxy.** |
| Levodopa (L-dopa) | X↓ | Benzodiazepines may reduce antiparkinson effect; seen with triazolam and temazepam. Oxazepam and flurazepam have not caused this problem. Carbidopa-levodopa agents may help. Monitor, and if parkinsonism worsens, stop benzodiazepines. |
| Magnesium hydroxide (*see* antacids) | | |
| MAOIs | B↑ | Greater intoxication with increased benzodiazepine levels. |
| *Macrolide antibiotics:*<br>Azithromycin<br>Clarithromycin<br>Erythromycin | B↑ | Decreases clearance of triazolo–benzodiazepines (alprazolam, triazolam, estazolam); increases benzodiazepine levels and toxicity. Spiramycin okay. Azithromycin possibly okay. |
| Metoprolol | B↑ | May slightly increase 3-keto compounds.** Minimal clinical changes noted; does not occur with atenolol. |
| Miconazole (*see* ketoconazole) | | |

ANTIANXIETY AGENTS

| Drugs (X) Interact with: | Benzo-diazepines (B) | Comments |
|---|---|---|
| Paroxetine (*see* fluoxetine) | | |
| Phenytoin (*see also* sedatives) | B↑↓ | Possibly increases benzodiazepine levels, including diazepam and clonazepam; may increase oxazepam clearance with decreased levels. |
| Physostigmine | B↓ | Reverses benzodiazepine effects; sometimes used after benzodiazepine OD. |
| Primidone (*see* sedatives) | | |
| Probenecid | B↑↓ | May increase lorazepam and its side effects. May affect other benzodiazepines, but more likely other 3-hydroxy compounds.** |
| Propoxyphene | B↑ | May increase oxidatively metabolized benzodiazepines (*not* 3-hydroxys).** |
| Propranolol | B↑ | May slightly increase 3-keto compounds.** Minimal clinical changes noted; does not occur with atenolol. |
| Rifampin | B↓ | Reduces diazepam's effects, and probably other oxidatively metabolized benzodiazepines (*not* 3-hydroxy agents).** May need to increase benzodiazepine. |
| Sedatives (alcohol, antihistamines, sedative-hypnotics, TCAs, low-potency antipsychotics) | X↑B↓ | Potentiate each other's sedative effects. Disinhibition increased with alcohol and barbiturates (including primidone). |
| Sertraline (*see* fluoxetine) | | |
| SSRIs (*see* fluoxetine) | | |
| Theophylline (*see* bronchodilators) | | |
| Tobacco smoking | B↓ | Decreases benzodiazepine levels; increase benzodiazepines or don't smoke. |
| Traconazole (*see* ketoconazole) | | |
| Valproic acid | B↑ | Increases unbound diazepam levels and may inhibit its metabolism while increasing its effects. May also increase levels of other oxidatively metabolized benzodiazepines.** |

| Drugs (X) Interact with: | Alprazolam (A) | Comments |
|---|---|---|
| TCAs | X↑ | Increases TCA levels 20–30%. |

| Drugs (X) Interact with: | Antihistamines (A) (e.g., diphen-hydramine/ hydroxyzine) | Comments |
|---|---|---|
| Alcohol | X↑A↑ | CNS depression. |
| Anticholinergics (*see also* pages 89–90 for list) | X↑A↑ | Increased anticholinergic effects. |
| Antipsychotics | X↓A↑ | Hydroxyzine may block antipsychotic actions. Increased CNS depression; increased anticholinergic effects. |
| Narcotics | X↑A↑ | CNS depression. |
| TCAs | X↑A↑ | CNS depression; increased anticholinergic effects. |
| Sedatives (benzodiazepines, barbiturates) | X↑A↑ | CNS depression. |

| Drugs (X) Interact with: | Buspirone (B) | Comments |
|---|---|---|
| Cimetidine | B↑ | May see more minor side effects (e.g., lightheadedness). |
| Food | B↓↑ | Decreases absorption speed but increases total amount in body. |
| Haloperidol | X↑ | Increased haloperidol levels. |
| MAOI | X↑ | Case reports of elevated BP; do not use together. |

| Drugs (X) Interact with: | Clonazepam (C) | Comments |
|---|---|---|
| Barbiturates | C↑↓ | Phenobarbital slightly decreases clonazepam level, but effect is unclear. |
| Carbamazepine | C↓ | In 5–15 days, carbamazepine may diminish clonazepam by 19–37%. Seizure effect unknown. Unclear if other benzodiazepines react to carbamazepine like clonazepam. Pure 3-hydroxy compounds (lorazepam, oxazepam, temazepam) are less apt to react similarly.** If combine drugs, check carbamazepine levels. |
| Phenytoin | C↓ | Lowers plasma clonazepam with reduced clonazepam effect. |
| Primidone | C↓ | May slightly decrease clonazepam level, but effect is not significant |

| Drugs (X) Interact with: | Clonidine (C) | Comments |
|---|---|---|
| Acebutolol | X↑C↑ | Potentiate each other. |
| Alcohol | X↑C↑ | Enhanced sedation and decreased BP. |
| Antipsychotics | X↑ C↑↓ | Isolated, severe hypotension or delirium, but usually not a problem. More common in patients with impaired cardiac function. May decrease hypotensive effect. |
| Beta-blockers (see acebutolol) | | |
| Caffeine | C↓ | Diminished clonidine effect. |
| Cocaine | X↑ C↓ | BP rise. |
| Diuretics | X↑C↑ | BP drop. |
| Enalapril | X↑ | May accelerate potassium loss. |
| Fenfluramine | C↑ | Possible increased clonidine effect. |
| Insulin | X↓ | Hyperglycemia; alert patient. |
| Labetalol | X↓ C↓ | Precipitous BP drop if both drugs are stopped together. |
| Levodopa | X↓ | Parkinsonian symptoms may emerge; combine carefully. |
| Lithium | X↓ | Can decrease hypotensive effect. |
| Marijuana | X↑C↑ | Weakness on standing. |
| Naloxone | C↓ | May reduce clonidine's antihypertensive action; if so, change clonidine to another antihypertensive or stop the narcotic antagonist. |
| Nicotinic acid (niacin) | X↓ | Clonidine may inhibit nicotinic flushing; no special precautions. |
| Nitrates | C↑ | BP drop. |
| Nitroprusside | C↑ | A few cases of severe hypotensive reactions; be alert to them. |

ANTIANXIETY AGENTS

| Drugs (X) Interact with: | Clonidine (C) | Comments |
|---|---|---|
| *Propranolol (*see also* clonidine entry under beta-blockers below, page 366) | X↑ | |
| *TCAs | C↑↓ | May lead to hypotension, especially imipramine and desipramine. More often may decrease clonidine's effects and may augment the hypertensive response to abrupt clonidine withdrawal. Maprotiline may interfere less with clonidine than might TCAs, although little clinical evidence. Consider alternative antihypertensive. Carefully monitor patients when clonidine is reduced; gradually tapering clonidine might lower risk. |

| Drugs (X) Interact with: | Clorazepate (C) | Comments |
|---|---|---|
| Primidone | X↑ | Combined use may cause depression, irritability, and aggressive behavior. |

| Drugs (X) Interact with: | Diazepam (D) | Comments |
|---|---|---|
| Ciprofloxacin | D↑ | Increased levels. |
| Digitalis, digoxin | X↑ | Diazepam may increase digoxin and digitalis. |
| Gallamine | X↑ | Prolonged neuromuscular blockade. |
| Isoniazid (INH) | D↑ | INH may increase diazepam; observe combination. |
| Succinylcholine | X↓ | Reduces neuromuscular blockade and its side effects (i.e., fasciculations, muscle pain, increased potassium, and CPK). |

| Drugs (X) Interact with: | Lorazepam (L) | Comments |
|---|---|---|
| Loxapine | X↑ L↑ | Isolated respiratory depression, stupor, and hypotension; switch one drug. |
| Scopolamine | X↑ L↑ | IM lorazepam may increase sedation, hallucinations, and irrational behavior. |

| Drugs (X) Interact with: | Meprobamate (M) | Comments |
|---|---|---|
| *Alcohol | X↑ M↑ | Meprobamate is an outdated and unneeded medication. Concurrent use induces CNS depression. More than 2 drinks (90–120 ml of 100-proof whiskey) and 200–400 mg of meprobamate usually cause problems. Long-term alcohol ingestion raises tolerance to meprobamate. |

| Drugs (X) Interact with: | Beta-Blockers Propranolol (P) | Comments |
|---|---|---|
| Acebutolol | X↑ P↑ | Increased antihypertensive effects of both drugs; adjust doses. |
| Albuterol | X↓ P↓ | Decreased albuterol and β-adrenergic blocking effects. Avoid propranolol in bronchospastic disease; cardioselective agents safer. |
| Alcohol | P↑↓ | May see variable changes in BP; no special precautions. Slows rate of propranolol absorption. |
| *Aluminum and magnesium hydroxides | P↓ | Decrease beta-blockers, such as propranolol (60%), atenolol hydroxides (35%), and metoprolol (25%). Clinical results unclear. Avoid combination; otherwise, ingest antacids and propranolol one hour apart. Calcium carbonates may be okay. |
| Amiodarone | P↑ | Bradycardia, arrhythmias. |
| *Anesthetics | X↑ | Beta-blockers and local anesthetics, particularly those containing epinephrine, can enhance sympathomimetic side effects. Acute discontinuation of blockers prior to local anesthesia may increase anesthetic's side effects. Do not stop chronic beta-blockers before using local anesthetics. Avoid local anesthetics containing epinephrine in patients on propranolol. |
| Anticholinergics | P↓ | ACAs can block beta-blockers' bradycardia. |
| †Antidiabetics | X↑ P↓ | Blunted recovery from both hypo- and hyperglycemia; decreased tachycardia. Cardioselective beta-blockers, such as metoprolol, acebutolol, and atenolol, are preferable in diabetics, especially if prone to hypoglycemia. |
| Antihistamines | X↓ | Decreased antihistaminic effect. |
| Antihypertensives | X↑ | Increased antihypertensive effect. |
| Anti-inflammatory agents | X↓ | Decreased anti-inflammatory effect. |
| *Antipsychotics (see also anticholinergic) | X↑ P↑ | Increased antipsychotic levels with chlorpromazine, thioridazine, thiothixene, resulting in increase of each other's effects, such as hypotension, toxicity, and seizures. Monitor serum levels or decrease dose. Propranolol level not affected. |
| Antipyrine | X↑ | Propranolol, and possibly metoprolol, may increase antipyrine. |
| *Barbiturates | P↓ | Barbiturates may lower propranolol. |
| Beta-blockers (see acebutolol) | | |
| Benzodiazepines (see propranolol entry under benzodiazepines above, page 362) | | |

| Drugs (X)<br>Interact with: | Beta-Blockers<br>Propranolol (P) | Comments |
|---|---|---|
| *Calcium channel-<br>blockers:*<br>*Bepridil<br>*Diltiazem<br>*Verapamil | X↑ | Bradycardia, heart block, increased left ventricular and diastolic pressure, particularly in those with conduction abnormalities or left-ventricular dysfunctioning. Calcium channel-blockers, such as diltiazem and verapamil, generally potentiate beta-blockers. Using nifedipine precludes increase of beta-blocker effects on atrioventricular node conduction. Beta-blockers not metabolized (e.g., atenolol) should also prevent this pharmacokinetic interaction. |
| Carbamazepine | P↓ | Might induce beta-blocker metabolism and decrease propranolol; combine with caution. |
| Chlorpromazine | X↑ P↑ | Levels of both increase. |
| *Cimetidine (*see* etinidine) | | |
| *Clonidine | X↑ | Beta-blockers can aggravate rebound hypertension in patients withdrawn from clonidine within 24–72 h. Symptoms include tremor, insomnia, nausea, flushing, and headaches. Patients receiving propranolol with clonidine should be withdrawn from propranolol *before* the clonidine to reduce danger of rebound hypertension. Noncardioselective beta-blockers more likely to cause this reaction than cardioselective beta-blockers. Metoprolol or another cardioselective beta-blocker may be preferable to propranolol. |
| Cocaine | X↑ | Irregular heartbeat. |
| Dicumarol | X↑ | Propranolol may produce small increases in dicumarol; effect on prothrombin times is unknown. |
| Digitalis | X↑ P↑ | Propranolol can potentiate bradycardia from digitalis; monitor heart rate. |
| Disopyramide | P↑ | Negative inotropic effects. |
| †Epinephrine | X↑ | Noncardioselective beta-blockers (e.g., propranolol, timolol) substantially raise systolic and diastolic BPs and drop heart rate, sometimes resulting in arrhythmias and stroke. Cardioselective beta-blockers (e.g., metoprolol) are safe. Whereas beta-agonist sympathomimetics (e.g., epinephrine) are dangerous, pure beta-agonist sympathomimetics (e.g., isoproterenol) are safer. Avoid combining noncardioselective beta-blockers and beta-agonist sympathomimetics; this includes injecting epinephrine as a local anesthetic. |
| Ergot alkaloids | X↑ | Propranolol may increase vasoconstriction. Using an ergotamine suppository, a patient on 30 mg/day of propranolol developed purple and painful feet. Adverse drug reactions (ADRs) more common with noncardioselective beta-blockers; use cardioselective beta-blockers. |
| Etinidine | P↑ | May substantially raise concentrations of propranolol and probably other beta-blockers that undergo hepatic metabolism (e.g., metoprolol, labetalol). Ranitidine, famotidine, or nizatidine may be safer than etintidine if an $H_2$ blocker is required. |

| Drugs (X) Interact with: | Beta-Blockers Propranolol (P) | Comments |
|---|---|---|
| Furosemide | P↑ | May increase propranolol levels. |
| Glucagon | X↓ | Propranolol may blunt glucagon's hyperglycemic action. |
| *Indomethacin | P↓ | Indomethacin, piroxicam, naproxen, and possibly other nonsteroidal anti-inflammatory drugs (NSAIDs) diminish propranolol's hypotensive effect. Sulindac and salicylates have minimal effect. NSAIDs and other beta-blockers can be unpredictable. If BP increases, may need to increase propranolol or decrease or stop indomethacin. |
| *Isoproterenol | P↑↓ | Noncardioselective beta-blockers (e.g., propranolol) are risky to combine with isoproterenol in asthmatic patients. Safer to use cardioselective beta-blockers (e.g., labetalol or metoprolol), but *no beta-blocker is absolutely safe for asthmatic patients.* |
| *Lidocaine | X↑ | Lidocaine may rise with propranolol, metoprolol, or nadolol. |
| Marijuana | X↓ | Propranolol delays the increase in heart rate and BP from marijuana and may prevent marijuana's impairment of learning tasks and eye-reddening effect. |
| *Methyldopa | X↓ | Patients taking a beta-blocker and methyldopa may develop hypertension; monitor. Hypertensive reactions may be helped by IV phentolamine. |
| MAOIs | X↓ P↓ | Depression occasionally worsens on beta-blockers. Anticholinergic MAOIs, such as phenelzine, may antagonize reduction of heart rate by beta-blockers. |
| Naproxen (*see* indomethacin) | | |
| Nonsteroidal anti-inflammatory drugs (NSAIDs; *see* indomethacin) | | |
| Nylidrin | X↓ | Propranolol may reduce nylidrin's greater gastric acid secretion and volume; no special precautions. |
| *Phenylephrine | X↑ | Phenylephrine added to propranolol may trigger hypertensive episode. A woman on chronic propranolol 160 mg/day developed a fatal intracerebral hemorrhage after dropping 10% phenylephrine in each eye. Phenylephrine 10% eye drops have also produced acute hypertensive episodes without propranolol. The risk therefore seems low. |
| Phenytoin | P↑ | Increased propranolol effect. |
| Piroxicam (*see* indomethacin) | | |
| Prazosin | X↑ | Beta-blockers may increase the "first-dose" hypotensive response to prazosin. Start prazosin cautiously in patients on beta-blockers. |

| Drugs (X) Interact with: | Beta-Blockers Propranolol (P) | Comments |
|---|---|---|
| Propoxyphene | P↑ | Increases highly metabolized beta-blockers (e.g., propranolol, metoprolol), but not beta-blockers excreted by kidneys (e.g., atenolol, nadolol). |
| Quinidine | X↑ P↑ | Propranolol may inflate quinidine level and foster lightheadedness, hypotension, slower heart rate, and fainting. |
| *Rifampin | P↓ | May decrease propranolol and metoprolol levels; consider increasing dose or changing to another beta-blocker when rifampin is added. |
| Reserpine | X↑ | Increased reserpine effect with excessive sedation, hypotension, fainting, vertigo, and depression. |
| Terbutaline | X↓↑ | Propranolol may antagonize terbutaline-induced bronchodilation, whereas cardioselective $\beta$-adrenergic blockers have little effect on terbutaline and are safer. |
| *Theophylline | X↑↓ | Propranolol raises theophylline levels but antagonizes bronchodilation; cardioselective agents are safer. |
| Tobacco smoking | P↓ | Decreases propranolol level and may produce arrhythmias. If smoking halted, propranolol level increases. Smoking patients need higher propranolol doses. Atenolol, and other beta-blockers not dependent on liver metabolism, are safer. |
| Tocainide | X↓ | May worsen congestive heart failure. |
| TCAs | X↓ P↓ | Depression occasionally increases on beta-blockers. Highly anticholinergic TCAs can antagonize cardiac slow by beta-blockers. Maprotiline toxicity may arise after propranolol added. |
| Tubocurarine | X↑ | Propranolol may prolong neuromuscular blockade. |
| Verapamil (*see* calcium channel-blockers) | | |
| Warfarin | X↑ | Propranolol may produce small increases in warfarin; effect on prothrombin times is unknown. |

---

* Moderately important interaction; †Extremely important interaction; ↑ Increases; ↓ Decreases; ↑↓ Increases and decreases.

** *Oxidatively metabolized* includes 2-keto compounds (clorazepate, chlordiazepoxide, diazepam, flurazepam, halazepam, prazepam) and triazolo-compounds (alprazolam, estazolam, triazolam). *Not oxidatively metabolized* are 3-hydroxy compounds (lorazepam, oxazepam, temazepam, and, partially, clonazepam).

° See also Appendix P450 111A3/4 for potential interactions (page 466 ).

## EFFECTS ON LABORATORY TESTS

| Generic Names | Blood/Serum Tests | Results* | Urine Tests | Results* |
|---|---|---|---|---|
| Benzodiazepines | WBC, RBC, LFT | ↓r↓r ↑ | None | |
| Buspirone | LFT, WBC | ↑ ↑↓ | None | |
| Clonazepam | LFT | ↑ | None | |
| Clonidine | Glucose (transient) | ↑ | Aldosterone | ↑ |
| | Plasma renin activity | ↓ | Catecholamines | ↑ |
| Hydroxyzine | None | | 17-Hydroxycor-ticosteroids | ↑f |
| Propranolol and atenolol | LFT | ↑ | None | |
| | $T_4$, $rT_3$, $T_3$ | ↑↑↓ | | |
| | BUN (with severe heart disease) | ↑ | | |
| | Antinuclear antibodies (ANA) | ↑ | | |

* ↑ Increases; ↓ Decreases; f = falsely; r = rarely; LFT = SGOT, SGPT, LDH, bilirubin, and alkaline phosphatase.

## WITHDRAWAL

Antianxiety agents, barbiturates, and nonbarbiturate hypnotics produce similar discontinuation syndromes and are discussed together in the next chapter on hypnotics.

### Clonidine

- Rapid withdrawal causes
  - √ Nervousness
  - √ Headache
  - √ Stomach pain
  - √ Tachycardia
  - √ Sweating
  - √ Other sympathetic overactivity
- Occurs in patients on 0.6 mg/day of clonidine.
  - √ Life-threatening withdrawal from higher doses.
- Starts 18–20 h after the last dose.
- Hypertension may persist 7–10 days.
- Management
  - √ *Do not*
    - □ Halt drug abruptly.
    - □ Use beta-blockers; may exaggerate hypertension.
  - √ *Do*
    - □ Readminister clonidine.

      ▫ Taper patient gradually (4–10 days).
      ▫ If severe, use IV vasodilators.
      ▫ Patients on clonidine and propranolol should halt propranolol before stopping clonidine to avoid rebound hypertension.
      ▫ Warn patients about abruptly stopping drug.

## Propranolol

* Usually safe to withdraw in psychiatric patients unless there are cardiac problems (e.g., hypertension, angina, or coronary artery disease).

## Buspirone

* No withdrawal symptoms from buspirone.
* Because buspirone has no cross-tolerance with benzodiazepines, withdrawal from benzodiazepines is not relieved by buspirone.

## OVERDOSE: TOXICITY, SUICIDE, AND TREATMENT

### Benzodiazepines

Benzodiazepine overdoses are relatively safe, but if benzodiazepines are consumed with alcohol, barbiturates, or other CNS depressants, they can be fatal. Benzodiazepine overdose by itself is only occasionally fatal.

More rapidly absorbed benzodiazepines (e.g., diazepam, clorazepate) may generate a "buzz," thereby encouraging abuse.

Severe sedation with benzodiazepine overdose is less common in patients who have developed tolerance to this effect.

*Chronic* benzodiazepine overdoses demonstrate

* Drowsiness
* Ataxia
* Slurred speech
* Vertigo
* Psychomotor impairment

*Acute* benzodiazepine overdoses manifest with chronic symptoms *and*

* Somnolence, confusion, lethargy, diminished reflexes
* Hypotension
* Hypotonia
* Coma

- Cardiac arrest (extremely rare)
- Death (rarer)

The general management of benzodiazepine overdoses includes the following (*see also* pages 65–67):

- Flumazenil (Mazicon), a specific benzodiazepine receptor antagonist, can reverse the effects of a benzodiazepine overdose when used IV. Can be used as adjunct to above general management.
  √ Only reverses benzodiazepine (not other sedative-hypnotic) effects.
  √ 75% of overdose patients respond to 1.0–3.0 mg.
  √ Takes 6–10 minutes for dose to have full effect.
  √ Re-sedation from most benzodiazepine overdoses occurs in 20–30 minutes after injection.
  √ Can precipitate benzodiazepine withdrawal.
  √ 1–3% of patients become agitated or anxious after flumazenil.
- 1.1% have seizures.
  √ Groups at high risk for seizure include OD with HCAs or benzodiazepine dependence.
  √ Avoid flumazenil in these risk groups or use extreme caution.
- 0.1 mg/min infusion may reduce risk of withdrawal.
- Monitor for re-sedation and respiratory depression.
- Many benzodiazepines (e.g., alprazolam, lorazepam, temazepam, triazolam) are not reported by urine tests.
  √ Low, possibly therapeutic, levels may not be reported by labs that use standardized cut-offs established for drugs of abuse.
  √ All are detected and reported in overdose situations.
- For hypotension
  √ Norepinephrine 4–8 mg in 1000 ml 5% D/S or D/W by infusion, or
  √ Metaraminol 10–20 mg SC/IM.
    ▫ 0.5–5 mg by IV, or
    ▫ 25–100 mg in 500 ml 5% D/W by infusion.
    ▫ Avoid caffeine and sodium benzoate because they are of questionable benefit.
- Hemodialysis does not alleviate benzodiazepine overdose.
- If normal kidney function, benzodiazepine elimination can be accelerated with forced diuresis, osmotic diuretics, IV fluids, and electrolytes.

# Buspirone

Unlike most antianxiety compounds, buspirone is not a controlled substance, and dysphoria at higher doses may discourage overuse.

Acute buspirone overdoses in humans have not been lethal. In animals the LD 50 is 160–550 times therapeutic doses. Overdoses can produce

- Nausea, vomiting, upset stomach
- Dizziness, drowsiness
- Miosis

Management

- *See* pages 65–67.
- Hemodialysis unnecessary.

## Clonidine

Acute clonidine overdoses can produce:

- Hypotension
- Bradycardia
- Lethargy, somnolence
- Irritability
- Weakness
- Absent or diminished reflexes
- Miosis
- Vomiting
- Hypoventilation

After large overdoses, may also see

- Reversible cardiac conduction defects or arrhythmias
- Apnea
- Seizures
- Transient hypertension

Management

- IV norepinephrine or metaraminol for hypertension.
- IV fluids, if indicated (e.g., hypotension).
  √ Can add dopamine infusion to treat hypotension.
- IV atropine 0.3–1.2 mg for bradycardia.
- IV furosemide 20–40 mg over 1–2 minutes for hypertension.
  √ If this fails, consider IV tolazoline 10 mg at 30-min intervals.
- Hemodialysis removes only 5% of clonidine and therefore is not useful.

## Hydroxyzine

Overdoses propagate side effects, especially drowsiness, GI hypo-motility, occasional hypotension, and confusion/delirium.

Management

- *See* pages 65–67.
- Hemodialysis of little help.

## Meprobamate

Even in low doses, meprobamate can be especially dangerous.

- A 7–10 day supply is often lethal,
- Particularly when mixed with alcohol or other CNS depressants.

Acute meprobamate overdose produces symptoms similar to barbiturate overdose.

- Drowsiness, lethargy, stupor
- Ataxia
- Coma
- Hypotension, shock, respiratory failure
- Death

Meprobamate can be eliminated by peritoneal dialysis, hemodialysis, or with an osmotic diuretic, such as mannitol.

## Propranolol

Acute propranolol overdose symptoms and their treatment include:

- Bradycardia
  - √ IV atropine 0.3–1.2 mg.
  - √ If no response to vagal blockade, cautiously administer isoproterenol 1 mg (maximum 2 mg) in 500 ml 5% D/S or D/W by infusion. Can have injection starting at 0.2 mg/ml or take 5 ml dossette ampul.
- Cardiac failure
  - √ Digitalis and diuretics.
- Hypotension
  - √ Epinephrine—drug of choice in anaphylactic shock.
    - □ 0.5 ml 1:1000 in 10 ml saline IV.
    - □ If no response, give 0.5 ml q 5–15 minutes.
  - √ Levarterenol 4–8 mg in 1000 ml 5% D/S or D/W by infusion.
- Bronchospasm
  - √ Isoproterenol and
  - √ Aminophylline 500 mg IV slowly.

## Toxicity and Suicide Data

| Generic Names | Toxicity Doses Average (Highest) (g) | Mortality Doses Average (Lowest) (g) | Toxic Levels % (ng/ml) | Fatal Levels % (ng/ml) |
|---|---|---|---|---|
| Alprazolam | — | — | — | — |
| Buspirone | — | — | — | — |
| Clonazepam | — | — | — | — |
| Clonidine | 100 | — | (370) | — |
| Chlordiazepoxide | 6.230 (17.00) | 0.6–1.0 | — | (30) |
| Clorazepate | 0.675 | — | — | — |
| Diazepam | 2 | 0.6–1.0 | (900) | (> 50) |
| Lorazepam | — | — | — | — |
| Meprobamate | 18.7 (40.0) | 20–40 (12) | 30–100 $\mu$g/ml | 100–200 $\mu$g/ml (> 200 mg/ml)* |
| Oxazepam | — | — | — | (> 25) |
| Prazepam | — | — | — | — |
| Propranolol | 2 | — | — | — |

* More than 50% fatalities.

# PRECAUTIONS

Benzodiazepines are contraindicated in hypersensitive patients. Give benzodiazepine medications cautiously to

- Elderly and debilitated people or patients with liver disease; avoid benzodiazepines with long or very short half-lives (except oxazepam and lorazepam).
- People who drink alcohol excessively.
- Patients who do not follow the time-limited restrictions on these medications.
- *Avoid* benzodiazepines for patients with
  √ Sleep apnea,
  √ Chronic obstructive pulmonary disease, $CO_2$ retainers,
  √ Dementia

Buspirone

- Sometimes triggers restlessness.
- Does not prevent benzodiazepine or barbiturate withdrawal.
- Less effective for patients recently treated with benzodiazepines.

Clonidine should be used cautiously for patients with

- Severe coronary insufficiency.
- Recent myocardial infarction.
- Hypotension.
- Chronic renal failure.
- Generalized rash.

Propranolol

- Contraindicated for patients with
  - √ Cardiogenic shock (systolic BP < 100 mm Hg)
  - √ Sinus bradycardia
  - √ Greater than first-degree AV block
  - √ Congestive heart failure
  - √ Bronchial asthma
    - □ Metoprolol, atenolol, and labetalol are less likely to produce bronchospasm.
  - √ Hypotension in MI.
- Give cautiously to patients with
  - √ Persistent angina, Wolff-Parkinson-White syndrome, or impaired myocardial functioning—all can become worse with propranolol.
    - □ Gradually withdraw propranolol from angina patients over a few weeks.
  - √ Glaucoma screen test.
    - □ Propranolol withdrawal can increase intraocular pressure.
  - √ Hyperthyroidism, thyrotoxicosis.
    - □ May mask (treat?) symptoms.
  - √ Diabetes mellitus.
  - √ Chronic obstructive pulmonary disease.
  - √ Hepatic failure.
    - □ Nadolol and atenolol are kidney-excreted.
  - √ Renal failure.
  - √ Depression.
    - □ May feel "washed out" or lethargic.
    - □ May intensify symptoms of depression.
    - □ Others (9%) develop neurovegetative signs of depression.
    - □ Probably less likely with low lipophilic beta-blockers atenolol and nadolol.

## NURSES' DATA

Most benzodiazepine antianxiety actions arise in 15–60 minutes and, thus, efficacy can be determined after 1 or 2 doses.

Avoid other CNS depressants (e.g., antihistamines, sedating TCAs, anticonvulsants, neuroleptics, or alcohol) without consulting physician.

- Tell patients that they may be unaware of their diminished skills when mixing benzodiazepines and alcohol.
  - √ Avoid alcohol 24–48 h after lorazepam injection. This is probably good advice after any benzodiazepine injection.

- Drinking caffeine counteracts anxiolytics.
  √ Patients with anxiety disorders tend to be hypersensitive to caffeine.
    □ Negative effects may occur with "normal" or "usual" amounts of caffeine (e.g., 2–3 cups of coffee).
    □ Caffeine is not a treatment for benzodiazepine overdose.

Tolerance, physical dependence, and withdrawal can occur from benzodiazepine agents. Inform patients about withdrawal symptoms (*see* pages 404–410).

- Inform patients about intoxication and overdose symptoms (*see* pages 370–74).
- Make sure patients realize that sudden benzodiazepine withdrawal can be more dangerous than narcotic withdrawal.
- It is generally not recommended to use benzodiazepines in high doses for longer than 3–4 weeks continuously.
- There is no easy way to extinguish a benzodiazepine habit.
  √ Withdrawal must be done slowly and under medical supervision.
  √ If there is an *acute* confusion during withdrawal between giving the patient too much or too little benzodiazepine, give too much; it's safer to avoid withdrawal.

Techniques of administration for benzodiazepines include

- IM injections
  √ Inject slowly into a single large muscle, especially the upper, outer, and deeper quadrant of the gluteus.
  √ Rotate sites.
  √ Insure the injection is for IM, not IV, use.
  √ Only lorazepam is absorbed better IM than po; for the rest, IM is worse than po.
- IV injections
  √ Differ with different agents, but generally inject slowly, such as IV diazepam 2.5–10 mg for anxiety.
    □ May repeat in 1–4 h, but
    □ IV diazepam should not exceed 30 mg in 8 h.
- Protect parenteral drugs from light.

## PATIENT AND FAMILY NOTES

Patients should be told that the treatment is unlikely to "cure" their problem, but should improve symptoms and overall functioning.

In many cases, particularly with panic disorder, social phobia, obsessive-compulsive disorder, and PTSD, improvement will take a while and adequate dosing is essential. Thinking that a little dose (other than with benzodiazepines) will help a little bit is inaccurate. Target symptoms should be selected and followed during treatments. Many of the anxiety symptoms may resemble side effects.

Before starting treatment, carefully list anxiety symptoms' frequency, duration, and severity so that this baseline can be compared with the time on medication.

Inform patient that buspirone will not eliminate anxiety, but will take the "edge" off of it and make it more manageable.

Inform patient about side effects. On all anxiolytics, dizziness and lightheadedness may occur.

Possible side effects of benzodiazepines

- Sedation, "fuzzy" thinking, fatigue, clumsiness, and blurred vision may be a problem at first, but tend to wear off a little more each day.
  √ If these do not improve, or if they worsen, call your doctor.
- Decreased mood or sexual interest might occur, and some patients get headaches or nausea.
- Impaired driving.

On buspirone

- The most common are headache, nausea, insomnia, and agitation.

Propranolol can cause

- Fatigue, depression, and decreased sexual interest.

Clonidine risks

- Dry mouth and sedation.
- Low blood pressure.

*Never* stop benzodiazepines, meprobamate, or barbiturates suddenly—induces seizures.

- Suddenly stopping these agents is riskier than suddenly stopping narcotics. Narcotic withdrawal can produce sickness; *benzodiazepine withdrawal can produce death.*

Hypertensive rebound occurs when

- Clonidine is suddenly stopped in any patient.
- Propranolol is suddenly stopped in cardiac patients.

Take antianxiety agent at prescribed time.

- If forget dose, can consume in 2 h.

ANTIANXIETY AGENTS

- Otherwise wait for next regular dose.
- Do not double dose.
- Some long-acting benzodiazepines (e.g., diazepam, clorazepate, clonazepam) can be taken once a day.

When starting benzodiazepines, patients should drive cars, work around machines, and cross streets very carefully. When first on antianxiety agents, drive briefly in a safe place, since reflexes might be impaired.

Benzodiazepines strongly potentiate alcohol: "One drink feels like 2–3 drinks." Buspirone, propranolol, and clonidine do not potentiate alcohol.

May take benzodiazepines, clonidine, and propranolol at any time; food does not interfere with final effect, but does slow onset of action. Buspirone's absorption is delayed by food, but this does not alter its efficacy.

Keep anxiety medications away from bedside or any readily accessible place, where they might be secured by "accident." Keep safely away from children.

Patients on beta-blockers (e.g., propranolol) should inform doctor if they are traveling to high altitudes or engaging in very strenuous exercise.

If doctor prescribes meprobamate or barbiturates, ask him/her if another agent would be superior, since benzodiazepines and other agents have largely superceded them.

# 8. Hypnotics

## INTRODUCTION

Hypnotics induce sleep. There are four main types:

- Benzodiazepines
- Barbiturates
- Barbiturate-like hypnotics
- Selective benzodiazepine-1 receptor agonists (imidazopyridine, i.e., zolpidem; or pyrazolopyramidine, i.e., zaleplon)

This chapter focuses on the benzodiazepine hypnotics, zaleplon, and zolpidem. It also addresses

- Insomnia (pages 383–84)
- Sleep movement disorders (pages 390–92)
- Amytal diagnostic interview (pages 392–94)
- Withdrawal from all anxiolytics (pages 404–410)
- Withdrawal from alcohol (pages 410–12)
- Carbamazepine-aided withdrawal of benzodiazepines and alcohol (pages 407–8)
- Pentobarbital-phenobarbital tolerance test (pages 409–410)
- Alcoholism prevention (pages 412–15)

Related topics detailed in other chapters are

- Cataplexy (Antidepressants, page 136)
- Narcolepsy (Stimulants, pages 435–36)
- Night terrors (Antidepressants, pages 137–38)
- Sleep apnea (Antidepressants, page 137)
- Sleepwalking (Antidepressants, pages 137–38)

## NAMES, CLASSES, MANUFACTURERS, DOSE FORMS, COLORS

| Generic Names | Brand Names | Manufacturers | Dose Forms (mg)** | Colors |
|---|---|---|---|---|
| **BENZODIAZEPINES** | | | | |
| Estazolam | Prosom | Abbott | t: 1/2 | t: white/coral |
| Flurazepam | Dalmane | Roche | c: 15/30 | c: orange-ivory/ red-ivory |
| Quazepam | Doral | Baker Cummins | t: 7.5/15 | t: all light orange-white speckled |
| Temazepam | Restoril | Sandoz | c: 15/30 | c: maroon-pink/ maroon-blue |
| Triazolam | Halcion | Upjohn | t: 0.125/0.25 | t: white/blue |
| **IMIDAZOPYRIDINE and PYRAZOLOPYRAMIDINE (Selective Benzodiazepine-1 Receptor Agonists)** | | | | |
| Zaleplon | Sonata | Wyeth-Ayerst | c: 5/10 | c: opaque green-opaque pale green/opaque green-opaque light green |
| Zolpidem | Ambien | Searle | c: 5/10 | c: pink/white |
| **BARBITURATES*** | | | | |
| Amobarbital | Amytal | Lilly | p: 50 mg/ml | |
| Butabarbital | Butisol | Wallace | t: 15/30/50/100 e: 30 mg/5 ml | t: lavender/green/ orange/pink e: green |
| Pentobarbital | Nembutal | Abbott | c: 50/100 su: 30 p: 50 mg/ml | c: orange/yellow |
| Phenobarbital | | | Many generic doses | |
| Secobarbital | Seconal | Lilly | c: 100 p: 50 mg/ml | c: orange |
| **BARBITURATE-LIKE COMPOUNDS*** | | | | |
| Chloral hydrate | | | c: 250/500 e: 500 mg/5 ml | c: red/red |
| Ethchlorvynol | Placidyl | Abbott | c: 200/500/750 | c: red/red/green |
| Paraldehyde | Paral | Forrest | e: 30 g/30 ml | |

\* Not recommended for general use.
\*\* c = capsules; e = elixir; p = parenteral; su = suppository; t = tablets.

## PHARMACOLOGY

The preceding chapter presented the pharmacology of benzodiazepines.

Benzodiazepine hypnotics all exert similar effects on sleep. They

- Extend total sleep time,
- Decrease stage 1,

- Increase stage 2, and
- Reduce stages 3 and 4.
  - √ Temazepam prolongs stage 3 in depressed patients.

Specific effects on REM sleep include:

- Decreased REM sleep, except for temazepam and low doses of flurazepam.
- Prolonged REM latency—the time to reach REM—except for flurazepam.
- Increased REM cycles, usually in the last part of sleep.

Zolpidem and zaleplon have minimal effects on sleep architecture.

- Stages 3 and 4 ("deep sleep") are preserved.
- Tolerance to zolpidem and zaleplon is unusual.
  - √ Zaleplon at 10 mg dose does not significantly impair cognitive or psychomotor skills.
  - √ At 20 mg showed effects similar to usual doses of zolpidem or triazolam.

## Pharmacology of Oral Hypnotic Benzodiazepines and Selective Benzodiazepine-1 Receptor Agonists*

| Generic Names | Speed of Onset (min) | Peak Plasma Level (hours) | Duration of: | | |
|---|---|---|---|---|---|
| | | | Half-Life (hours) | Action** (hours) | Active Metabolites |
| **SELECTIVE BENZODIAZEPINE-1 RECEPTOR AGONISTS** | | | | | |
| Zaleplon | 20–30 | 1 | 1–2 | SA 2–3 | None |
| Zolpidem | 20–30 | 1.6 | 2.5 | SA < 6 | None |
| **BENZODIAZEPINES** | | | | | |
| *2-Keto-* Flurazepam | 30 | 0.5–1 | 67 (47–100) | LA > 40 | N-Desalkylflurazepam |
| *3-Hydroxy* Temazepam | 20–60 | 2–4 | 12 (9.5–20) | IA 6–20 | None |
| *Triazolo-* Estazolam | 15–30 | 2 | 15 (10–24) | IA 6–8 | 4-Hydroxyestazolam, 1-Oxoestazolam |
| Triazolam | 20 | 0.5–1 | 2–4 (1.5–5.5) | SA < 6 | None |
| *Other* Quazepam | 30 | 0.5–2 | 25–40 (2–73) | LA 2–100 | 2-Oxoquazepam, N-Desalkylflurazepam |

\* For details on metabolism of benzodiazepine hypnotics, see Antianxiety agents, pages 313–15.
\*\* LA = long-acting; IA = intermediate-acting; SA = short-acting. The figures below represent the duration of action of the compound and its major active metabolites.

## Pharmacology of Oral Hypnotic Barbiturates and Barbiturate-like Compounds

| Generic Names | Speed of Onset (min) | Peak Plasma Level (hours) | Duration of: | | |
|---|---|---|---|---|---|
| | | | Half-Life (hours) | Action** (hours) | Active Metabolites |
| **BARBITURATES** | | | | | |
| Amobarbital | 45–60 | — | 25 (16–40) | IA 6–8 | None |
| Aprobarbital | 45–60 | 3 | 24 (14–34) | IA 6–8 | None |
| Butabarbital | 45–60 | 3–4 | 34–42 (34–140) | IA 6–8 | None |
| Pentobarbital | 15–60 | 30–60 | 22–50 (15–50) | SA 3–4 | None |
| Phenobarbital | 8–12 | 10–15 | 3–4 weeks | LA 80 | None |
| Secobarbital | 10–15 | 15–30 | 28–30 (15–40) | SA 3–4 | None |
| **BARBITURATE-LIKE COMPOUNDS** | | | | | |
| Chloral hydrate | 30–60 | — | 4–14† | — | Trichloroethanol |
| Ethchlorvynol | 15–60 | — | 10–25‡ | 5 | None |
| Paraldehyde | 10–15 | 0.5–1 | 3.4–9.8 | IA 8–12 | None |
| **SLEEP HORMONE** | | | | | |
| Melatonin | 30–120 | — | 0.5–1 | — | — |

** LA = long-acting; IA = intermediate-acting; SA = short-acting. The figures below represent the duration of action of the compound and its major active metabolites.
   † Half-life for trichloroethanol—chloral hydrate's principal metabolite—is 7–10 h.
   ‡ Half-lives for ethchlorvynol's free and conjugated forms of major metabolite are 10–20 h.

## DOSES

| Generic Names | Usual Doses (mg) | Dose Ranges (mg) | When to Take Before Bedtime (hours) | Geriatric Dose (mg) |
|---|---|---|---|---|
| **SELECTIVE BENZODIAZEPINE-1 RECEPTOR AGONISTS** | | | | |
| Zaleplon | 10 | 5–20 | 0.25 | 5–10 |
| Zolpidem | 10 | 5–20 | 0.5 | 5 |
| **BENZODIAZEPINES** | | | | |
| Estazolam | 1 | 1–2 | 0.5 | 0.5 |
| Flurazepam | 15–30 | 15–30 | 0.5 | 15 |
| Quazepam | 7.5–15 | 7.5–15 | 1.5 | 7.5 |
| Temazepam | 15–30 | 15–30 | 1–2 | 15 |
| Triazolam | 0.25 | 0.125–0.5 | 0.5 | 0.125 |
| **SLEEP HORMONE** | | | | |
| Melatonin | 1 | 0.5–3 | 0.5–1 | 0.5–1 |

| Generic Names | Usual Doses (mg) | Dose Ranges (mg) | When to Take Before Bedtime (hours) | Geriatric Dose (mg) |
|---|---|---|---|---|
| | | **BARBITURATES*** | | |
| Amobarbital | 150–200 | 65–200 | 0.5 | 65 |
| Butabarbital | 50–100 | 50–100 | 0.5 | 50 |
| Pentobarbital | 100 | 50–200 | 0.5 | 50 |
| Phenobarbital | 100–200 | 15–600 | 1 | 16 |
| Secobarbital | 100–200 | 100–200 | 0.25 | 50 |
| | | **BARBITURATE-LIKE COMPOUNDS** | | |
| Chloral hydrate | 500–1500 | 500–2000 | 0.5 | 500 |
| Ethchlorvynol | 500–750 | 500–1000 | 0.5 | 500 |
| Paraldehyde | 5000–10,000 | 2000–15,000 | 0.5 | 4000 |

\* Use of these agents for insomnia (or anxiety) is not recommended.

## CLINICAL INDICATIONS AND USE

Primary insomnia is defined as a difficulty sleeping that is *not* due to

- Drugs (e.g., prescription, over-the-counter, recreational, alcohol, caffeine)
- Sleep disorders (e.g., narcolepsy, sleep apnea)
- Medical ailments (e.g., pain)
- Mental disorders (e.g., depression, mania, panic attacks, obsessive-compulsive disorder)
- Circadian rhythm difficulties (e.g., jet lag, work shift changes)

These disorders should be addressed before insomnia is treated as an isolated symptom.

Sometimes the treatment effects of these primary disorders will be slow and treatment of the secondary insomnia may be needed. For example:

- All antidepressants can help insomnia if it is a symptom of depression, but this may take 3–6 weeks.
- Buspirone can improve anxiety-caused insomnia, but this takes 3–5 weeks.

Insomnia is defined as insufficient sleep that renders the person consistently tired the next day.

- A person sleeping 3 h a night who feels refreshed the next day is a brief sleeper (maybe manic) but not a poor sleeper.
- A person who must sleep 9–10 h a night to feel refreshed the next day is a healthy (albeit inefficient) sleeper.

Barbiturate and barbiturate-like hypnotics are not recommended for the treatment of anxiety or insomnia.

- These medications are poor sleep inducers, cause rapid development of tolerance, produce REM rebound, and are lethal in overdose.
- Brief inpatient use of chloral hydrate for insomnia may be acceptable.
- Amobarbital is indicated for "amytal interviews."

Nonprescription "sleeping pills" are not more effective than placebo and can produce tolerance and rebound insomnia. Most include pyrilamine or methapyriline, both antihistamines; some add an analgesic or anticholinergic agent. Commonly used ones include

- Compoz—methapyrilene (antihistamine), pyrilamine (antihistamine)
- Nytol—methapyrilene, salicylamide (salicylate)
- Sleep-Eze—methapyrilene, scopolamine (anticholinergic)
- Sominex—methapyrilene, scopolamine, salicylamide

Benzodiazepine hypnotics have largely replaced other hypnotics because benzodiazepines

- Are safer as overdoses,
- Do not suppress REM sleep to a significant extent,
- Cause less respiratory and CNS depression, and
- Induce less drug dependence.

Benzodiazepines marketed as anxiolytics can be as effective as benzodiazepines marketed for anxiety (see below).

Benzodiazepines are effective, but often for as little as 5–14 days.

- No hypnotic has been proven effective for more than 6 weeks.

Hypnotics have two clear indications: to treat

- Brief (1–7 day) episode of insomnia, and
- Transitory insomnia incited by acute stress or by a marked sleep phase change (e.g., jet lag).

Benzodiazepines are of most benefit for patients with shorter total sleep times.

Hypnotics create 4 common problems:

- Short half-life hypnotics (e.g., triazolam) can cause anterograde amnesia.
- If the hypnotic does not induce sleep, it can foster drowsiness, confusion, or agitation the next day.

- Longer-acting hypnotics (e.g., flurazepam, quazepam) may impair alertness and performance the following day. Can cause
  √ Higher risk of falling in geriatrics.
  √ Increased respiratory depression in those with respiratory problems.

- Hypnotics provoke
  √ Tolerance,
  √ Rebound insomnia, and
  √ Decreased memory.

Paroxetine (Paxil) effective for primary insomnia:

- 15 patients with primary insomnia were treated with paroxetine (median dose = 20 mg).
  √ 11 improved with treatment.
  √ 7 of these no longer met criteria for insomnia.

Adult night terrors

- Paroxetine was administered to 6 patients with disabling night terrors (from 2 per week to 3 per night).
  √ Dose 20–40 mg/day.
  √ 3 had complete recovery and 3 had reduction in symptoms.

Rebound insomnia has several causes:

- Rebound insomnia can be a part of the *general* abstinence syndrome, which arises after the abrupt withdrawal of any hypnotic taken over a *prolonged* period of time (*see* Precautions).
- Rebound insomnia can be a *specific* sleep disruption that occurs after the sudden halting of a *normal* dose of any *briefly* taken and *quickly* eliminated hypnotic. This may be secondary to tolerance developing rapidly and/or rebound of drug-suppressed sleep states. REM suppression may lead to REM rebound and many arousals from vivid dreams.
  √ Hypnotics with rapid (e.g., triazolam) elimination rates generate more rebound insomnia than do hypnotics with longer elimination rates (e.g., flurazepam, quazepam).
  √ After abruptly stopping hypnotics, shorter-acting drugs produce a more intense rebound insomnia the next night, whereas longer-acting hypnotics produce an attenuated version in 5–7 nights.
  √ Rebound insomnia is partly dose-dependent.
  √ Drugs causing rebound insomnia from the *greatest and fastest* to the *weakest and slowest:*
    ▫ Triazolam
    ▫ Temazepam

         □ Estazolam
         □ Flurazepam
         □ Quazepam
       √ Greater rebound insomnia may increase hypnotic dosage, which
         □ Aggravates tolerance and
         □ Fosters drug dependency.
- When rebound insomnia occurs, clinicians should either taper the dose or switch to a different hypnotic.
       √ Try to remove the patient from all hypnotics.
       √ If this is not possible,
         □ May prescribe trazodone 25–100 mg for a few nights.
         □ May prescribe a sedative antihistamine (e.g., diphenhydramine 50 mg) for a few nights.
         □ Employ another longer-acting benzodiazepine and gradually taper it.

Short-acting vs. long-acting benzodiazepine hypnotics differ according to these features:

| Characteristic | Short-Acting | Long-Acting |
| --- | --- | --- |
| Accumulation with more use | No | Marked |
| Hangover, sedation next day | Rare | Moderate |
| Tolerance | Moderate | Mild |
| Anterograde amnesia | Moderate | Mild |
| Rebound insomnia risk | Moderate | No |
| Early morning awakening risk | Mild | No |
| Daytime anxiety risk | Mild | No |
| Anxiolytic the next day | No | Moderate |
| Full benefit on first night | Moderate-marked | Moderate |
| Full benefit on 7th or 14th night | Low-moderate | Moderate-high |

## Qualities of Hypnotics

- Estazolam
       √ Rapid absorption rate
       √ Intermediate half-life
       √ Duration of action between triazolam and temazepam
         □ While estazolam's half-life is slightly longer than temazepam's, it is quickly taken up by adipose tissue.
- Flurazepam
       √ Rapid absorption rate
       √ Long half-life
       √ Sedates during the next day, which may, or may not, diminish with repeated doses.

√ In geratric patients, it may accumulate over 1 to 3 weeks and cause confusion and disorientation.

√ May work better on 2nd and 3rd nights.

- Quazepam
  - √ Marketed as a "selective" benzodiazepine receptor agent (like zaleplon and zolpidem), but N-desalkylflurazepam metabolite is a nonselective benzadiazepine.
  - √ Rapid absorption rate
  - √ Slower onset
  - √ Long half-life
    - □ The major metabolite, N-desalkylflurazepam (also called N-desalkyl-2-oxoquazepam), has a half-life of 73 h and a range of 47–100 h.
  - √ May work better on 2nd and 3rd nights.
    - □ Another key metabolite, 2-oxoquazepam, has a half-life of 2–3 h.
    - □ Quazepam and 2-oxoquazepam together have a half-life of 39 h.
    - □ Accumulation may be a particular risk in geriatric patients.
  - √ Manufacturer claims quazepam does not cause daytime sedation.
- Temazepam
  - √ Slow absorption rate
  - √ Intermediate half-life of 10–20 h
  - √ May take longer to induce sleep.
    - □ Less useful as a prn medication
  - √ Causes little or no daytime sedation.
- Trazodone
  - √ Rapid absorption rate; peaks in 20–30 minutes
  - √ Intermediate half-life
  - √ Large, potentially safe qhs dosage range, 25–500 mg
  - √ No respiratory depression
  - √ Sedates next A.M. or all day in 20% of people.
  - √ Orthostatic BP drop most common side effect
  - √ Tolerance mild to moderate
  - √ Rebound insomnia infrequent
  - √ Priapism ~ 1:6,000 males
  - √ No physical dependence
  - √ Short-term efficacy established in sleep labs.
    - □ Long-term efficacy not studied.
- Triazolam
  - √ Fast absorption rate
  - √ Very short half-life
  - √ No metabolites

√ May not treat early A.M. awakening.

√ May provoke early morning awakening and anxiety (e.g., same night rebound may be seen).

√ Daytime anxiety more common after 10 consecutive night's use.

√ No daytime sedation.

- Zaleplon and zolpidem (20 mg or less)

  √ Selectively bind to $BZ_1$ (also called omega$_1$) receptor of GABA complex in doses of 20 mg or less.

  □ Less selective and more nonselective at higher doses.

  √ No respiratory depression.

  √ Lacks myorelaxant, anticonvulsant effects, and ability to block benzodiazepine withdrawal.

  √ Rapid onset of action

  √ Usually minimal effect on memory, but memory impairment occasionally reported.

  √ May not treat early A.M. awakening.

  √ No daytime sedation

  √ Occasional, mild, first-night rebound insomnia

  √ May be less effective in very anxious patients

  □ Has no intrinsic anxiolytic effects.

  √ No tolerance seen after 5 weeks with 15 mg dose.

  □ However, company warning not to use zaleplon or zolpidem beyond 1 month.

Other benzodiazepines marketed for anxiety can also be used for sleep. There are no inherent differences between typical benzodiazepines for anxiety and those for sleep except how they are marketed.

- If a certain benzodiazepine is already being used for anxiety, it frequently can also be used for sleep.
- Clorazepate and diazepam resemble flurazepam and quazepam in pharmacodynamics and effects.
- Diazepam may have faster onset and, in single doses, may have shorter duration of action.
- Chlordiazepoxide and clonazepam resemble flurazepam and quazepam, but have intermediate absorption rates.
- Oxazepam resembles temazepam.
- Alprazolam and lorazepam resemble temazepam and estazolam but have intermediate absorption rates and, in some patients, longer durations of action (A.M. sedation risk).

Promising efficacious treatments for seasonal affective disorder (SAD), insomnia, and/or out-of-phase circadian clock include:

- Seasonal affective disorder responds to
  √ 10,000 lux light for 30 minutes at 5 : 30–7 : 00 A.M.
  √ Circadian clock moved earlier by taking melatonin ($\sim$ 0.5 mg) earlier ($\sim$ 3–6 P.M.) and later by taking melatonin at the end of the sleep phase ($\sim$ 4–7 A.M.).
    □ Doses of 0.5–0.75 mg replicate physiological amounts.
    □ When used for insomnia, a peak in the hypnotic effect of melatonin typically occurs about 2 hours after taking higher doses of melatonin (5 mg oral, 1.7 mg sublingual)
    □ Lower doses may be effective for many.
    ⊔ Overall efficacy $\sim$ 70%. Preliminary data suggests that tolerance to melatonin does not occur even after a year of daily melatonin intake.
- Melatonin at 3 mg at night in patients over 50 y.o. resulted in improved sleep efficiency in the insomnia group (N = 15) but with no effect on sleep in the controls (N = 15).
  √ Older patients, particularly those in the geriatric age range, frequently have decreased melatonin levels that often can be normalized by adding melatonin.
  √ Elderly patient (N = 10) with mild cognitive impairment, when given melatonin 6 mg/day 2 h before bedtime, had improved sleep quality, faster onset of sleep, decreased number of awakenings, and better memory recall.
- Abrupt melatonin withdrawal in patients who regularly take melatonin risks insomnia, agitation, and other side effects.
  √ Do not use melatonin for
    □ Women who are pregnant, lactating, or attempting to conceive
    □ Children
    □ Patients with immune system disorders, with cancer of immune systems, or taking steroids.

The following nonbenzodiazepines are indicated solely for patients who cannot tolerate the prior hypnotics.

- Antihistamines, which do not foster drug dependency, are weak hypnotics and are not generally recommended.
  √ Commonly prescribed are
    □ Diphenhydramine 50–100 mg (available over-the-counter in 25 mg capsules) and
    □ Hydroxyzine 25–100 mg.
  √ Tolerance develops in 1–3 nights.
  √ Antihistamines are anticholinergic.
    □ Increased nocturnal and daytime confusion, which particularly troubles the elderly.

          ▫ Urinary retention in elderly men.
    ✓ Cause REM suppression on the night(s) used, followed by nights of significant REM rebound and possible insomnia.
- Tryptophan is a fair hypnotic for mild to moderate insomnia in which there are multiple partial awakenings but not full awakening.
    ✓ Not addictive.
    ✓ Hypnotic dose is 1000–2000 mg.
        ▫ Minimal risk with pharmaceutical grade.

The choice of the "best" hypnotic for each patient depends on the patient's particular circumstances, in that *some*

- Hypnotics act more quickly (e.g., triazolam faster than temazepam).
- People wake up too early in the morning (e.g., on triazolam more than flurazepam).
- Hypnotics foster more drowsiness the next day (e.g., on flurazepam more than triazolam).
- Shorter-acting hypnotics create more dependence than longer-acting ones (e.g., triazolam more than flurazepam).
- Barbituate and related drugs are more lethal or toxic than others (e.g., secobarbital more than triazolam).
- Hypnotics cause withdrawal after a single dose (e.g., triazolam's traveler's amnesia).
- Short-acting hypnotics (e.g., triazolam) are more likely to cause rebound insomnia.

Historically, other medications have been prescribed for insomnia, but with modern choices, none of these medications holds much value.

### Sleep Movement Disorders

Restless legs syndrome (RLS) requires 4 basic elements to make the diagnosis:

- Restlessness in both legs and less often arms and other body parts.
- Urges to move extremities, usually associated with abnormal sensations (paresthesias) localized in same extremities. May have unpleasant sensory symptoms in calves.
- Motor restlessness, including one or both of 2 types:
    ✓ Voluntary movements to reduce symptoms;
    ✓ Smooth, short (0.5–10-second) bursts of involuntary, usually periodic, limb movements most often when patient is lying down. Often referred to as "dyskinesias while awake" (DWA). Periods between bursts vary between 20 and 90 seconds.

Symptoms become worse or begin when body is at rest and are temporarily relieved almost immediately after starting motor activity, especially walking.

Symptoms that have pronounced circadian patterns are significantly greater in the evening during sleep and much less in the morning. If symptoms are severe, may occur at any time with little or no circadian pattern.

- Additional RLS symptoms:
  - √ Any activity that serves to keep a sleepy person awake also appears to ameliorate RLS, and activities that induce sleepiness worsen RLS.
  - √ RLS occurs in about 2–6% of adults.
  - √ Persistent sleep loss is significant in RLS. A range of time awake while in bed varied from 12–67%, with a mean of 43%.
- Secondary RLS conditions:
  - √ Two studies on *iron deficiency* have shown that low serum ferritin levels correlate with RLS symptoms.
  - √ More severe symptoms can be avoided with 45–50 $\mu$g/l of ferritin.
  - √ In *end stage renal disease*, 20–40% have RLS.
    - □ Dialysis doesn't reduce RLS, but treatment with erythropoietin, which reduces the anemia in these patients, reduces the severity of RLS.
    - □ After kidney transplant, RLS largely resolves.
  - √ Pregnancy has high prevalence of iron deficiency and RLS.
    - □ RLS during pregnancy occurs in about 10–25% of patients.
    - □ RLS is most common in 3rd trimester and shortly after delivery.
- Restless Legs Syndrome treatment:
  - √ Pergolide, a dopamine agonist, has been shown in both open-label and double-blind studies to provide very effective treatment for RLS.
    - □ Pergolide can be started at one tablet of .05 mg taken once at dinner and one h before bedtime and increase by one tablet at each dosing time every 3 days until symptomatic relief is obtained.
    - □ Maximum dose is usually 0.5–0.75 mg/day.
    - □ Has advantage of positive effects on dopaminergic and noradrenergic systems.
  - √ Levodopa, carbidopa/levodopa (Sinemet), and the opiates (e.g., codeine, propoxyphene) significantly reduce RLS symptoms.

    ◻ Carbidopa/levodopa is effective in the 50–200 mg range.

    √ Classic opiates are less effective and appear to require larger doses (e.g., ≥ 200 mg propoxyphene).

    √ Tramadol (Ultram) may be more effective with lower side effects. Doses used 50–150 mg over 15 to 24 months.

        ◻ Of 12 patients, 10 reported clear improvement, 1 only slight improvement, and 1 no effect.

    √ Baclofen and benzodiazepines decrease arousal and awakenings and improve sleep, though not consistently.

- Periodic Limb Movement Syndrome (PLMS) may or may not coexist with RLS; 85–100% of patints with RLS have PLMS.

    √ PLMS, independent of RLS, increases dramatically with age.

    √ Bupropion sustained-release treatment significantly reduces PLMS from average of 178 pretreatment arousals/night to 86 posttreatment.

## Dubious Hypnotics

| Generic Names | Chemical Groups | Duration of: | |
|---|---|---|---|
| | | Efficacy | Side Effects |
| Amitriptyline | TCA | Strong | Significant |
| Chlorpromazine | Antipsychotic | Strong | Significant |
| Chlorprothixene | Antipsychotic | Strong | Significant |
| Clomipramine | TCA | Strong | Significant |
| Diphenhydramine* | Antihistamine | Minimal | Moderate |
| Doxepin | TCA | Strong | Significant |
| Hydroxyzine | Antihistamine | Minimal | Moderate |
| Meprobamate | Antianxiety | Moderate | Significant |
| Mesoridazine | Antipsychotic | Moderate | Significant |
| Paraldehyde | Hypnotic | Minimal-moderate | Moderate-significant |
| Thioridazine | Antipsychotic | Strong | Significant |
| Trimipramine | TCA | Strong | Significant |
| Tryptophan*‡ | Amino acid | Moderate | Minimal |

    * Can be sold over the counter.
    ‡ Now available again, but only pharmaceutical grade is recommended.

## Sodium Amytal Diagnostic Interview

IV amobarbital is used

- To determine if confusion is neurologically (tends to worsen with amytal) or psychologically (tends to improve with amytal) based.

- To facilitate the diagnosis of a conversion disorder or psychogenically-induced symptoms (e.g., pain).

    √ Frequently symptoms remit or improve with amytal, and sometimes psychological cause can be determined.

- To facilitate recall of repressed memories for diagnosis and treatment.
  √ Must carefully avoid any possibility of suggestion (e.g., "Is there another personality in there?").
  √ American Psychiatric Association guidelines caution against this use.

Amytal interviews are *not* recommended

- To detect malingering or lying.
  √ Liars and malingerers can easily continue their symptoms and statements during amytal interviews.
- For continuous use as a therapy tool.
  √ "New" memories may be suggested during therapy.

Administering an amytal interview:

- Interview in well-lighted room with patient's head elevated on a bed.
  √ Reduces risk of sleep.
- Be prepared to resuscitate patient if necessary.
- Mix 500 mg sodium amytal in 10 cc sterile water (not bacteriostatic).
  √ Will need more than 500 mg if patient has tolerance to alcohol or sedative hypnotics secondary to abuse.
  √ Inject into an intravenous line kept open with D5W.
- Using small butterfly needle, inject 50 mg a minute up to 150 mg and
  √ Wait 2–4 minutes.
- Attempt to interview, but avoid threatening material.
- After each increment in dose, assess whether there is definite, subtle, or no change.
- Add further increments of 50 mg over 1 minute and then wait 1 minute and reassess before injecting more.
- Increase to point of slurring of speech or lateral nystagmus.
  √ Test by having patient keep head still and following finger to extreme right and left sides.
- When desired point attained, conduct interview.
- If long interview (> 10 minutes), will need additional doses of amytal.
- If patient goes to sleep, try to awaken and interview.
  √ If fails to awaken or talk coherently, let patient sleep.
    ▫ Observe closely for respiratory depression
  √ Sometimes can have effective interview later when patient awakens.

## SIDE EFFECTS

The side effects caused by benzodiazepine hypnotics are basically the same as those discussed in the previous chapter for benzodiazepine antianxiety agents.

Long-acting benzodiazepine CNS effects follow a U-shaped time curve, with the most adverse consequences occurring in the first few days before tolerance develops and then reappearing a week or so later as the drug accumulates.

- This pattern of side effects is especially common in the elderly, who tend to accumulate the long-acting desalkylflurazepam after taking flurazepam or quazepam.
- These side effects are generally based on spontaneous reporting of subjective side effects.
  √ Memory, attention, and performance tests suggest greater impairment than the table below.
- The degree of CNS side effects varies with drug, dose, and age. To illustrate, the following percentages of CNS side effects arise from oral flurazepam.

| Factor | CNS Side Effect (%) |
|--------|---------------------|
| 15 mg/night | 1.9 |
| 30 mg/night | 12.3 |
| Patients under 60 | 1.9 |
| Patients over 80 | 7.1 |
| Patients over 70, 15 mg doses | 2.0 |
| Patients over 70, 30 mg doses | 39.0 |

Note the following side effects:

*Respiratory depression*

- Insomniacs with chronic obstructive pulmonary disease, asthma, or other respiratory disorders should *not* receive benzodiazepine or barbiturate-like sleeping pills. They might intensify effects of sleep apnea by increasing central sleep apnea or slowing respiration rate. High risk for obstructive apnea are people who
  √ Snore
  √ Have hypertension
  √ Are male
  √ Are obese

√ Are older (> 55 yrs.).
- For central sleep apnea, high risk for people who
  √ Are older
  √ Have dementia
  √ Have other general CNS disorders.
- If hypnotic needed, use trazodone, zolpidem, or zaleplon.

*Falls, fractures*

- Often from *ataxia* and *confusion*
- Can happen during night with any hypnotic.
- Happens more often during day on long-acting hypnotics (e.g., flurazepam).

*Hangover*

- Common
- Aggravated by
  √ Alcohol consumption and
  √ Restricted fluid intake.
- Management
  √ Reduce, halt, or switch hypnotic.
  √ Reduce risk with shorter-acting hypnotic.

*Anterograde amnesia*

- Due to withdrawal after a single dose.
- Particularly common with triazolam.
- Because of its ultra-short half-life, triazolam is often taken for jet lag.
- Symptoms present with
  √ A single dose, often just 0.5 mg.
  √ Are more common with alcohol.
  √ Normal behavior; nobody notices any abnormality.
  √ On awakening, the patient has no memory of events occurring 6–11 h after ingesting triazolam.
    ▫ Memory loss is longer than sleep duration.
  √ May swallow triazolam the following night without difficulty.
- May also be seen with zolpidem or zaleplon, particularly in higher (≥ 20 mg) doses (that effect all benzodiazepine receptors), when it more closely resembles triazolam.
  √ Occurs more in 1–3-h range.

Warn patients about this hazard.

# PERCENTAGES OF SIDE EFFECTS

## Part I

| Side Effects | Estazolam | Flurazepam | Quazepam | Temazepam | Triazolam | Zaleplon | Zolpidem |
|---|---|---|---|---|---|---|---|
| **CARDIOVASCULAR EFFECTS** | | | | | | | |
| Dizziness, lightheadedness | 7 | 23.9 | 1.5 | 13.3 | 11.4 | 7.5 | 5 |
| Fainting, syncope | <0.1 | — | — | <1 | — | <1 | — |
| Palpitations | <1 | — | — | <1 | — | <1 | 2 |
| Shortness of breath | <1 | — | — | <1 | — | <1 | 1 |
| Tachycardia | <1 | — | — | — | 0.7 | <1 | — |
| **CENTRAL NERVOUS SYSTEM EFFECTS** | | | | | | | |
| Anxiety, nervousness (i.e., mental) | 8* | — | — | — | 5.2 | >1 | 1* |
| Ataxia, incoordination, clumsiness | 4 | 23.9 | — | 20 | 12.8 (4.6–19.5) | <1 | >1 |
| Concentration, decreased | 1 | — | — | <1 | — | >1 | <1 |
| Confusion, disorientation | 2* | — | — | 4 (1–10) | 0.7 | <1 | >1 |
| Depression, malaise | 5* | — | — | 5.5 | 0.7 | 2 | 2 |
| Drowsiness, sedation | 42 | 29.5 (23.9–36) | 23 (12–34) | 18.5 (10–30) | 16.1 (14–19.5) | 5 | 8 |
| Drugged feeling/hangovers | 3 | — | — | 2.5 | 0.7 | <1 | 3 |
| Euphoria | <1 | — | — | 3 | — | — | >1 |
| Hallucinations | <0.1 | — | — | 3 (<0.5–10) | — | — | <1 |
| Headache | 16* | 4.6 | 4.5 | — | 5.9 (3.8–9.7) | 33 | 19* |
| Insomnia | <1 | 0.1 | — | — | 0.3 | — | 1 |
| Irritability | <1 | — | — | 5.5 | — | ??? | <1 |

**Part I (Cont.)**

| Side Effects | Estazolam | Flurazepam | Quazepam | Temazepam | Triazolam | Zaleplon | Zolpidem |
|---|---|---|---|---|---|---|---|
| Lethargy | 8 | 23.9 | — | 5 | 11.8 (<0.5–19.5) | 1.5 | 3 |
| Memory loss, amnesia | <1 | — | — | — | 0.7 (0.5–0.9) | <0.1 | 1 |
| Nightmares, abnormal dreams | 2* | 0.1 | — | — | 0.3 | <1 | 1 |
| Paradoxical excitement, agitation | <1 | 2.8 | — | 0.5 | 3.8 | — | <1 |
| Paresthesias | <1 | 4.6 | — | — | 2.9 | 3 | <1 |
| Weakness, fatigue | 11 | 23.9 | 1.9 | 1–2 | 11.4 (<0.5–4.4) 11.4 (<0.5–19.5) | 6.5 | 1 |
| **EYES, EARS, NOSE, AND THROAT EFFECTS** | | | | | | | |
| Ear pain | — | — | — | — | — | <1 | — |
| Eye pain | — | — | — | — | — | 4 | <1 |
| Hyperacusis | — | — | — | — | — | 1.5 | 3 |
| Mouth and throat, dry | >1 | 3.4 | 1.5 | — | — | >1 | — |
| Mouth or throat sores | <0.1 | — | — | <1 | — | <1 | — |
| Nystagmus | <0.1 | — | — | 0.5 | — | <1 | — |
| Sinusitis, pharyngitis | 1* | — | — | — | — | >1 | 3–4 |
| Tinnitus | <0.1 | 4.6 | — | — | 2.9 (<0.5–4.4) | <1 | <1 |
| Visual changes | <1 | 4.6 | — | 5.5 | 3 (0.5–4.4) | 1 | >1 |
| **GASTROINTESTINAL EFFECTS** | | | | | | | |
| Anorexia, lower appetite | <1 | — | — | 1.5 | — | 1.5 | 1* |
| Constipation | >1 | 0.7 | — | 5.5 | 1.4 (<0.5–2.2) | >1 | 2 |
| Diarrhea | — | — | — | 3.5 | <0.5 | >1 | 3 |
| Dyspepsia, upset stomach | 2* | 0.7 | 1.1 | — | 1.5 (0.5–2.2) | 5.5 | 5* |

## Part I (Cont.)

| Side Effects | Estazolam | Flurazepam | Quazepam | Temazepam | Triazolam | Zaleplon | Zolpidem |
|---|---|---|---|---|---|---|---|
| Jaundice | — | — | — | <1 | — | < 0.1 | — |
| Nausea, vomiting | 4* | 0.7 | — | 5.5 | 2.8 (1.6–4.6) | 7.5 | 6* |
| Taste changes | — | 3.4 | — | — | 0.6 | <1 | <1 |
| **RENAL EFFECTS** | | | | | | | |
| Dysmenorrhea | — | — | — | — | — | 3 | — |
| Urinary hesitancy or retention | <1 | — | — | 5.5 | — | <1 | < 0.1 |
| **SKIN, ALLERGIES, AND TEMPERATURE EFFECTS** | | | | | | | |
| Allergies | <1 | — | — | — | < 0.5 | — | 4 |
| Fever | — | — | — | — | — | 1.5 | — |
| Itching | 1 | — | — | 5.5 | 0.2 | > 1 | < 0.1 |
| Rashes | <1 | 0.6 | — | 5.5 | (< 0.5) | > 1 | 2 |

* Less than or equal to placebo.

## Part II

| Side Effects | Barbiturates | Chloral Hydrate | Disulfiram |
|---|---|---|---|
| **CARDIOVASCULAR EFFECTS** | | | |
| Apnea | < 1 | — | — |
| Breath, short | < 1 | — | — |
| Dizziness, lightheadedness | 10.5<br>(< 1–10) | 5.5 | — |
| Fainting, syncope | < 1 | — | — |
| Hypotension | < 1 | — | — |
| Hypoventilation | < 1 | — | — |
| **CENTRAL NERVOUS SYSTEM EFFECTS** | | | |
| Agitation, restlessness<br>(i.e., motoric) | < 1 | < 1 | — |
| Anxiety, nervousness<br>(i.e., mental) | < 1 | — | — |
| Ataxia, incoordination | < 1 | 5.5 | — |
| Clumsiness | — | 5.5 | — |
| Confusion, disorientation | 3.2 | < 1 | — |
| Depression | 5.5 | — | 5.5 |
| Drowsiness, sedation | 26.5<br>(10–33) | 5.5 | 20 |
| Hallucinations | < 1 | < 1 | — |
| Hangover | 20 | 5.5 | — |
| Headache | < 1 | — | 5.5 |
| Hyperkinesia | < 1 | — | — |
| Insomnia | < 1 | — | — |
| Muscle cramps | 5.5 | — | — |
| Nightmares | < 1 | — | — |
| Numbness of limbs | — | — | 5.5 |
| Speech, slurred | 5.5 | — | — |
| **ENDOCRINE AND SEXUAL EFFECTS** | | | |
| Sexual function, disturbed | — | — | 5.5 |
| **EYES, EARS, NOSE, AND THROAT EFFECTS** | | | |
| Eyes, painful or swollen | 5.5 | — | 5.5 |
| Throat, sore | 5.5 | — | — |
| Vision changes | — | — | 5.5 |
| **GASTROINTESTINAL EFFECTS** | | | |
| Bad taste | — | — | 5.5 |
| Constipation | < 1 | — | — |
| Diarrhea | 5.5 | — | — |
| Dyspepsia, upset stomach | — | 20 | 5.5 |
| Jaundice | < 1 | — | < 1 |
| Liver disease | < 1 | — | — |
| Nausea, vomiting | 3.2 | 20 | — |
| **HEMATOLOGIC EFFECTS** | | | |
| Anemia | < 1 | — | — |
| Bruising, easy | < 1 | — | — |
| **SKIN, ALLERGIES, AND TEMPERATURE EFFECTS** | | | |
| Allergies | < 1 | — | — |
| Fever, hyperthermia | 3.2 | — | — |
| Itching | 5.5 | < 1 | — |
| Rashes | 3.2 | < 1 | < 1 |

## PREGNANCY AND LACTATION

Overview
- See discussion of benzodiazepine use during pregnancy in Antianxiety chapter (pages 356–60).

- Flurazepam is officially contraindicated during pregnancy.

- With little reason for hypnotics during pregnancy, and given their potential risks, *avoid them*.

Teratogenicity
(1st trimester)
- Patients should stop benzodiazepines at least 2–4 weeks before attempting to conceive; they should remain off them until the first trimester ends.
  √ If menstrual cycle very regular, could take brief trial of short-acting benzodiazepine up to first missed period.
    □ Maternal-placental circulation not established until then.

- In a study of mothers taking amobarbital, 35% (95/273) of infants had congenital defects.

- Virtually no evidence that pentobarbital, secobarbital, or chloral hydrate are teratogenic.

- Ethchlorvynol may increase malformations.

- Ethchlorvynol (500 mg/day) may also induce infant withdrawal and/or mild hypotonia, poor suck, absent rooting, poor grasp, delayed-onset jitters, and CNS depression.

H
Y
P
N
O
T
I
C
S

Direct Effect on Newborn
(3rd trimester)

- Flurazepam linked to neonatal depression; mother who received 30 mg of flurazepam 10 days before delivery had sedated, inactive newborn during the first 4 days.

- No apparent harmful effects from secobarbital.
  √ Neonatal withdrawal could occur.

Lactation

- Benzodiazepines enter breast milk; may addict newborn and induce withdrawal.
  √ Check infant benzodiazepine blood level to determine if level may be harmful to newborn.

- Benzodiazepines can impair alertness, feeding, and temperature regulation.

- With longer-acting benzodiazepines, effects persist 2–3 weeks in infants.

## Drug Dosage in Mother's Milk

| Generic Names | Milk/ Plasma Ratio | Time of Peak Concentration in Milk (hours) | Infant Dose ($\mu$g/kg/day) | Maternal Dose (%) | Safety Rating* |
|---|---|---|---|---|---|
| Chloral hydrate | ? | ? | 0.47 mg† | 2 | B |
| Phenobarbital‡ | ? | ? | 1.56 | 23–156 | D |
| Quazepam | 4.13 | 3 | 14.4 | 5.8 | C |

*B: Reasonably unsafe before 34 weeks, but safer after 34 weeks; C: Unsafe before week 34, relatively safe from weeks 34–44, and safest after 44th week; D: Unsafe throughout infancy, largely because infant plasma concentrations may approach, and rarely exceed, those of mother.
†Infant dose 15–50 $\mu$g/kg/day with maternal dose administered as 1.3 g suppository.
‡Broad range in findings.

## DRUG-DRUG INTERACTIONS

After reviewing the benzodiazepine interactions on pages 360–64, examine these other interactions specific to hypnotics. All of these are potentiated by other sedatives and sedating drugs.

| Drugs (X) Interact with: | Chloral Hydrate (C) | Comments |
|---|---|---|
| *Alcohol | X↑ C↑ | This "Mickey Finn" combination yields CNS depression. Patients can have fainting, sedation, flushing, tachycardia, headache, hypotension, and amnesia. Avoid mixture, especially in cardiovascular problems. |
| *Dicumarol | X↑ | Chloral hydrate may briefly accelerate hypoprothrombinemic response to dicumarol, but effect quickly disappears. Adverse clinical responses are uncommon, but bleeding may occur. Benzodiazepine hypnotics are preferred. *Don't* give chloral hydrate to patients on anticoagulants. |
| Furosemide | X↑ | Diaphoresis, hot flashes, and hypertension occur with IV furosemide. Give IV furosemide with caution to any patient on chloral hydrate in past 24 h. |
| Sedatives and sedating drugs | X↑ C↑ | Increased sedation, confusion. |
| TCAs | X↓ | Decreased antidepressant effect. |
| *Warfarin (*see* dicumorol) | | |

| Drugs (X) Interact with: | Disulfiram (D) | Comments |
|---|---|---|
| †Alcohol | D↑ | (*See* pages 412–15.) |
| Amitriptyline | X↑ | Avoid combination until more information. When amitriptyline was added to disulfiram, 2 cases of a CNS cognitive disorder were reported with confusion, hallucinations, and memory loss in 1–4 weeks. Rapid improvement when one or both agents stopped. |
| Anticonvulsants | X↑ | Excessive sedation. |
| Barbiturates | X↑ | Excessive sedation. |
| *Benzodiazepines | X↑ | Disulfiram increases most benzodiazepine levels (not 3-hydroxy compounds, lorazepam, oxazepam, temazepam, and, partially, clonazepam); more sedation. Lower benzodiazepines or switch to 3-hydroxy compounds. |
| Cephalosporins | D↑ | Disulfiram reaction. |
| Cocaine | D↑ | Increased disulfiram effect. |
| †Dicumarol (*see* warfarin) | | |
| *Isoniazid | D↑ | Combination produces ataxia, irritability, disorientation, dizziness, and nausea. Frequency unclear, but combine cautiously. Reduce or stop disulfiram. |
| *Metronidazole | D↑ | Combination produces CNS toxicity, psychosis, and confusion. Avoid combination. |
| †MAOIs | D↑ | Severe CNS reactions. |
| Paraldehyde | X↑ | Disulfiram may inhibit paraldehyde's metabolism, leading to toxicity. |
| *Perphenazine | X↑ | Decreases perphenazine's metabolism, risking toxicity. |

| Drugs (X) Interact with: | Disulfiram (D) | Comments |
|---|---|---|
| † Phenytoin | X↑ | Disulfiram consistently increases phenytoin, inducing phenytoin toxicity (e.g., ataxia, mental impairment, nystagmus). Often occurs about 4 h after disulfiram's initial dose. After stopping disulfiram, symptoms may persist for 3 weeks. Avoid combination, but if must use together, observe carefully. Obtain serum phenytoin determinations. Monitor for reduced phenytoin response when disulfiram is stopped. |
| *Theophylline | X↑ | Disulfiram increases theophylline, which may prompt toxicity. Lower theophylline may be needed. If disulfiram is changed, monitor patient's theophylline level. |
| † Warfarin | X↑ | Disulfiram increases response to warfarin, which prompts bleeding. If disulfiram is started or stopped in patients taking oral anticoagulants, monitor carefully. Similar interaction with dicumarol likely but not reported. |

| Drugs (X) Interact with: | Ethchlorvynol (E) | Comments |
|---|---|---|
| Amitriptyline | X↑ E↑ | Transient delirium noted in patient taking 1 g of ethchlorvynol and amitriptyline. |
| *Anticoagulants | X↓ | Ethchlorvynol may inhibit response to dicumarol and possibly warfarin. May need to adjust oral anticoagulants or, preferably, replace ethchlorvynol with a benzodiazepine. |

* Moderately important interaction; †Extremely important interaction; ↑Increases; ↓Decreases.

## EFFECTS ON LABORATORY TESTS

| Generic Names | Blood/Serum Tests* | Results** | Urine Tests | Results** |
|---|---|---|---|---|
| Benzodiazepines | WBC, RBC | ↓r ↓r | None | |
| | LFT | ↑ | | |
| Chloral hydrate | WBC | ↓ | Ketonuria | ↑ |
| | | | Glucose*** | ↑ f |
| | | | Catecholamines**** | ↑↓ |
| | | | 17-hydroxycortico-steroids† | ↑ |
| Disulfiram | Cholesterol | ↑ | VMA | ↓ |

* ↑Increases, ↓Decreases; f = falsely; r = rarely.
** LFT = AST/SGOT, ALT/SGPT, LDH, bilirubin, and alkaline phosphatase.
*** Use oxidative test instead of copper sulfate.
**** Only flurimetric test.
† With Reddy, Jenkins, and Thorn procedure.

## WITHDRAWAL

Benzodiazepines, barbiturates, barbiturate-like hypnotics, and alcohol all produce

- Dependence
- Tolerance
- Addiction
- Withdrawal

Withdrawal can be fatal; *never* abruptly withdraw hypnosedatives after chronic use.

These agents are all cross-reactive, although high-potency benzodiazepines (i.e., alprazolam, triazolam, lorazepam, clonazepam) may not be predictably cross-reactive with lower-potency benzodiazepines such as diazepam and chlordiazepoxide.

In general, likelihood of significant withdrawal symptoms is correlated with dosage and duration of treatment.

- It is possible to have significant withdrawal symptoms in a person taking diazepam 5 mg bid for 2 years.
  - √ Increased risk of significant withdrawal from ordinary anxiolytic dose (not in panic disorder range) is more likely to occur after 6 months of treatment, not before.
- Dependence also is likely to occur if patient takes 3–4 times the normal therapeutic dose for anxiety for 4–6 weeks.
- The higher benzodiazepine doses used to treat panic attacks routinely risk significant withdrawal symptoms if doses are tapered too quickly.
- Patients with a h/o significant withdrawal symptoms and on the same dose as before are likely to have
  - √ Significant withdrawal symptoms again.
  - √ Same pattern of withdrawal as before.
- Withdrawal symptoms more common with
  - √ Short half-life benzodiazepines.
  - √ Last half of taper.

Compared to patients who *suddenly* withdraw, patients who *gradually* withdraw have fewer symptoms and no seizures.

Hypnoanxiolytic withdrawal can arise up to 10 days after the last dose. More typical presentations are

- 5–10 days from the last dose of diazepam, clorazepate, or clonazepam
- 1–3 days from alprazolam

- 12–16 h from barbiturates

Hypnoanxiolytics with shorter half-lives (e.g., amobarbital, lorazepam, alprazolam) present more severe withdrawal symptoms and earlier peaks (2–3 days). Because of more gradual declines in blood levels, hypnoanxiolytics with longer half-lives (e.g., chlordiazepoxide, diazepam, clorazepate, clonazepam) have less severe withdrawal symptoms, longer duration, and later peaks (5–10 days).

- Benzodiazepine half-lives are longer in older people because they metabolize them more slowly.
  - √ Benzodiazepines that are converted into active metabolites by the liver (chlordiazepoxide, diazepam, clorazepate, quazepam, flurazepam) are less likely to cause severe withdrawal symptoms.
  - √ Benzodiazepines that are conjugated by the liver and have no active metabolites (oxazepam, lorazepam, temazepam, triazolam, estazolam) are high-risk for a significant withdrawal.

Delayed withdrawal involuntary motor symptoms

- Seen occasionally days or weeks after all other signs and symptoms are gone.
- Usually muscle spasm and/or myoclonus.

## Signs and Symptoms of Hypnoanxiolytic Withdrawal*

| Stage | Signs and Symptoms | Timing for Alcohol Withdrawal | Untreated Patients (%) |
|---|---|---|---|
| "SHAKES" (Tremulousness) | Tremor, bad dreams, insomnia, morning sweats, apprehension, blepharospasm, agitation, ataxia, dilated pupils, labile BP, hypertension/hypotension, increased respiration and heart rate, nausea, vomiting, flushed; atypically have transient hallucinations and illusions; seizures—14%.† | 5–10 h after last dose; peaks at 24–48 h; usually lasts 3–5 days but may last 2 weeks; may occur on any substance. | 80 |
| HALLUCINATIONS | Auditory hallucinations both vague (e.g., buzzes, hums) and specific (e.g., accusatory voices); visual hallucinations or perceptual disturbances may also occur; clear consciousness; fear, apprehension, panic, tinnitus; other atypical hallucinations and some clouded consciousness may arise; rum fits—3%. | Onset may happen on agent or up to 12–48 h (and infrequently up to 7 days) after last dose; typically persists 1 week, but can extend over 2 months. | 5–25 |
| SEIZURES | Single or multiple grand malconvulsions; occasionally status epilepticus; muscle jerks. | Appears 6–48 h after last dose; peaks at 12–24 h; seizures usually erupt 16 h into withdrawal. | 10–25 |

## Signs and Symptoms of Hypnoanxiolytic Withdrawal* *(Cont.)*

| Stage | Signs and Symptoms | Timing for Alcohol Withdrawal | Untreated Patients (%) |
|---|---|---|---|
| DELIRIUM TREMENS (DTs) | Delirium with clouded and fluctuating consciousness, confusion, disorientation, loss of recent memory; illusions and hallucinations (of all types, often scary), autonomic hyperactivity, hyperthermia, agitation, emotional lability, persecutory delusions, severe ataxia, coarse tremor; REM rebound (up to 3–4 months); death from DTs very rare with current aggressive treatments. | Appears 48–96 h after last dose; persists 4–7 days without complications; convulsions appear 16 h into withdrawal and psychotic symptoms, 36 h into withdrawal. | 15 |

* This withdrawal pattern applies most to alcohol, barbiturates, and barbiturate-like hypnotics (e.g., ethchlorvynol); happens less often and less severely with benzodiazepines. Stages may evolve gradually or leap ahead. May pass through any stage without going through a previous stage.

†Seizures erupt during any stage. Stage III presents the most intense and frequent seizures. About 20% of patients with DTs have already had a seizure.

# Withdrawing Hypnoanxiolytics

## Benzodiazepine Taper

Outpatients do not usually require rapid tapers.

- In syndromes that have an effective nonhabit-forming alternative treatment (e.g., TCA or SSRI for panic disorder),
  √ May be better to begin alternative treatment before benzodiazepine taper is started.
  √ Avoids reemergence of symptoms that can exacerbate and complicate withdrawal.
- Frequently a long-acting drug (e.g., clonazepam) is substituted for a shorter-acting drug (e.g., alprazolam).
- If a slow taper is planned, switching to a long-acting drug is often unnecessary, unless shorter-acting drug is so short that interdose rebound is seen and can't be avoided by very small multiple doses.
- This substitution should not be made abruptly because the short-acting drug will already be at steady state, while the longer-acting drug may take 5 or more days to reach steady state.
- To allow for these different half-lives, the longer-acting drug can be started at the pharmacologically comparable dosage of the short-acting one and, at the same time, the shorter-acting drug can be decreased 25% of the original dose on the first day and 25% of the original dose on each subsequent day.
  √ Prn additions of the short-acting drug can be added, or
  √ For maximum speed, can "load" patient with twice the pharmacological equivalent dose of longer-acting drug for 2–5 days and then allow the drug to taper itself.

- The speed of the taper depends on the patient's preference.
  √ Reducing doses by a fixed percentage per unit of time rather than by a fixed dose per unit of time provides a more even and gradual taper.
  √ 10% reduction of the last dose every 3 days, or 25% per week, results in a longer but uncomfortable withdrawal.
  √ 25% reduction of the last dose every 3 days results in a shorter, more uncomfortable withdrawal, but without risk of seizures or serious symptoms.
  √ Sometimes patients delay the very end of the taper by halving or quartering the one remaining pill, more for psychological than pharmacologic reasons.

See also alcohol withdrawal (pages 410–12).

Very rapid benzodiazepine withdrawal can be done safely in an inpatient setting if daily benzodiazepine dose is under 30 mg diazepam equivalents. (*See* page 318 for dose equivalents of benzodiazepines.)

- Patients already on longer-acting benzodiazepines may get no benzodiazepine unless withdrawal symptoms are seen.
  √ Monitor heart rate, BP, temperature, tremulousness.
  √ Give previously used benzodiazepine prn for objective symptoms—not "I feel anxious."
    ▫ Make prn dose equal to 25% of original daily dose.
- If shorter-acting benzodiazepine has previously been used, switch to a longer-acting one.

### Diazepam and Chlordiazepoxide Dose Equivalents for Non-Benzodiazepine Sedatives (Oral Dose)

| | |
|---|---|
| Diazepam | 10 mg |
| Chlordiazepoxide | 25 mg |
| Alcohol | 1.5 oz |
| Chloral hydrate | 1000 mg |
| Ethchlorvynol | 750 mg |
| Meprobamate | 400 mg |
| Pentobarbital | 100 mg |
| Phenobarbital | 30 mg |
| Secobarbital | 100 mg |

### Carbamazepine-Aided Withdrawal

The addition of carbamazepine frequently accomplishes rapid (4–7 days) withdrawal from very high doses of benzodiazepines (or alcohol) with fewer withdrawal symptoms.

- Give 200 mg bid on first day. If tolerated, on second day increase to 200 mg q A.M. and 400 mg qhs. Beginning on 3rd or 4th day, reduce benzodiazepine dose by 25% of original dose a day.

- Maintain on carbamazepine for 4 or more weeks.
- Monitor vital signs daily.
- Anecdotal evidence suggests that valproic acid can accomplish same result.
  - √ May be preferred option for sedative-hypnotic withdrawal in patients with panic disorder because valproic acid may have antipanic effects while carbamazepine does not.
  - √ Valproate acts on GABA system, which is altered in CNS depressant withdrawal.
- Accelerated withdrawal may be risky if there are complicating conditions (e.g., seizure risk) being treated by other medications that might exacerbate withdrawal symptoms (e.g., MAOI).

### Attenuating Hypnoanxiolytic Withdrawal

- Neither clonidine nor propranolol have proven to be effective.

### Meprobamate Withdrawal

Withdrawal no faster than 10% every 2–3 days.

Immediate withdrawal of 3200 mg/day can induce convulsions, agitation, delirium, and death.

### Buspirone

Does not create tolerance, dependence, or withdrawal. It does *not* stop or prevent withdrawal from benzodiazepines.

- Can help alcohol withdrawal.
  - √ Best in highly anxious alcoholics.
  - √ Average dose 45–60 mg daily.
  - √ Longer time to relapse.
  - √ Fewer drinking days.
    - ▫ Only in patients whose only reason for drinking is to relieve anxiety.

### Hydroxyzine

May not produce physical dependence, but tolerance to sedative and anxiolytic effects usually develops.

- REM rebound can cause disturbed sleep on withdrawal.
- Cholinergic rebound can produce flu-like syndrome.

### Preventing Hypnoanxiolytic Relapse

- Non-benzodiazepine treatments for the original panic disorder, anxiety, depression, or insomnia can be instituted before withdrawal is started. These treatments have been discussed

previously and may include
- √ Buspirone for generalized anxiety.
- √ SSRIs, MAOIs, or TCAs for panic, OCD, depression, or general anxiety.
- √ Trazodone for insomnia, depression, or general anxiety.
- √ Melatonin for insomnia.

## Pentobarbital-Phenobarbital Tolerance Test

This test is seldom used but should be considered for inpatients whose history suggests a high risk for serious withdrawal—e.g., prior history of DTs, high dosages used, extensive mixtures of hypnoanxiolytics (alcohol, barbiturates, and benzodiazepines), or who are very unreliable historians about their drug intake. The pentobarbital-phenobarbital test can determine the degree of dependence before withdrawing people from hypnoanxiolytics.

*Step #1:* The patient should not be intoxicated before receiving any pentobarbital.

- If patient has been consuming shorter-acting hypnoanxiolytics, the hypnoanxiolytic test can be deferred 6–8 h.
- If a patient has been using longer-acting hypnoanxiolytics, the hypnoanxiolytic test can be deferred 1–2 days.

*Step #2:* Give the patient 200 mg of liquid pentobarbital, often the following morning.

*Step #3:* Examine the patient 50–60 minutes later. Signs of tolerance to a total daily dose of *pentobarbital-equivalents* are shown below.

### Possible Findings One Hour after Pentobarbital Challenge

| Patient's Condition One Hour after Test Dose | Degree of Tolerance | Estimated 24-Hour Pentobarbital Requirement after Test Dose (mg) |
|---|---|---|
| No signs of intoxication | Extreme | Over 850 |
| Fine nystagmus only | Marked | 700–850 |
| Slurred speech, mild ataxia, fine nystagmus | Definite | 450–700 |
| Coarse nystagmus, positive Romberg, gross ataxia, drowsy | Moderate | 300–450 |
| Asleep | None or minimal | < 300 |

*Step #4:* The patient's pentobarbital-equivalents can be altered by any of the following circumstances:

- The patient has not ingested the full test dose of pentobarbital or has secretly taken other hypnosedatives.
- Greater anxiety or agitation escalates tolerance.

- A 300 mg test dose is better for patients taking a confirmed pentobarbital-equivalent of over 1200 mg/day.
- For elderly patients, the test dose might be 100 mg.
- If the patient shows no intoxication to 200 mg of pentobarbital, the patient's tolerance is over 850 mg/day. If so,
  - √ Give patient pentobarbital 100 mg q 2 h until intoxication is manifested or total dose reaches 500 mg in 6 h (e.g., 200 + 100 + 100 + 100 = 500 mg).
  - √ The total dose given in the first 6 h (300–500 mg) is the patient's 6-hour requirement.

*Step #5:* Figure out the detoxification strategy.

- Establish the patient's phenobarbital-equivalent.
  - √ If the patient had nystagmus, mild ataxia, and some slurred speech, might go on 150 mg qid (600 mg/day) of pentobarbital.
- However, it is better to calculate the initial 24-h pentobarbital-equivalent.
  - √ Because phenobarbital has a longer half-life and greater anti-seizure activity than pentobarbital, this 24-h pentobarbital-equivalent (600 mg/day) is converted to phenobarbital requirements by substituting 30 mg of phenobarbital for 100 mg of pentobarbital. In this example, the phenobarbital-equivalent is 180 mg.

*Step #6:* Divide the daily phenobarbital dose into thirds (60 mg) and provide each dose every 8 h for the first 48 h.

- After 2 days, phenobarbital dose is diminished by 30 mg/day or by 10%/day (whichever is less) from the original dose. In this case, 10% is less and equals 6 mg.
- If patient is oversedated, reduce the dose slightly.
- If patient displays withdrawal signs, increase the dose slightly.
- If unsure whether patient has received too much or too little phenobarbital, dispense too much rather than too little, since seizing is a greater risk than sleeping.

## Alcohol

Although alcohol withdrawal resembles hypnoanxiolytic withdrawal, a somewhat different procedure might address certain aspects specific to alcohol.

Chlordiazepoxide provides an effective method because it

- Is long-acting,
- Offers less euphoria than diazepam, and
- Affords fewer side effects than other agents.

*But:*

- Chlordiazepoxide risks accumulation in geriatric patients and in those with renal/hepatic disease.
  √ Lorazepam better alternative in these situations.

Management of alcohol withdrawal involves the following:

- Treating or preventing Wernicke's syndrome with
  √ Thiamine 100 mg po or IM on admission, and
  √ Thiamine 50 mg/day po for one month.
- Managing the alcohol withdrawal per se:
  √ If patient not high risk for withdrawal, use symptom-triggered approach: Give chlordiazepoxide 25–50 mg prn based on objective symptoms, i.e., increased autonomic measurements (BP, HR, temperature), agitation, tremor, disorientation, perceptual (tactile, visual, auditory) disturbances, headache, nausea.
    ▫ Check vital signs hourly and repeat as often as needed.
    ▫ In many alcoholic patients one or two doses of chlordiazepoxide is enough to accomplish the withdrawal safely.
    ▫ This should not be used, or used only very cautiously, in patients who take medications that might mask symptoms (e.g., clonidine, propranolol) or illnesses that might mimic symptoms (e.g., febrile).
- Fixed approach
  √ Usually used in high-risk patients.
  √ Chlordiazepoxide 50 mg q 6 h for total of 4 doses.
  √ Chlordiazepoxide 25 mg q 6 h for 8 doses.
- 25–100 mg chlordiazepoxide prn
  √ Risks overmedicating, sedation, and longer hospital stays.
    ▫ Particular concern in geriatric patients or those with breathing or hepatic disorders.
  √ If patient is high risk for withdrawal,
    ▫ Initiate chlordiazepoxide 200 mg/day for first 2 days.
    ▫ Reduce total daily dose of chlordiazepoxide by 25% each day until reaching zero.
    ▫ Give extra doses of chlordiazepoxide as needed to prevent withdrawal symptoms.
- If there is adequate social support (or monitoring), low risk for severe withdrawal, and patient is well-motivated, outpatient withdrawal can be implemented.
  √ Start with chlordiazepoxide 25 mg taken q 4 h (or less often) for day one.
  √ Taper by 25% qd until no chlordiazepoxide remains.
  √ In very tremulous outpatient, use 100 mg/day of chlordiazepoxide.

- Patients with hepatic problems are best withdrawn using oxazepam or lorazepam, which are not metabolized in the liver.

## Alcoholism Prevention and Treatment of Comorbid Conditions

In bipolar alcoholic patients, lithium may reduce alcohol consumption but not depression. However,

- Moderate quantities of alcohol can trigger hypomania and large quantities can cause depression, leading to a misdiagnosis of bipolar disorder and unnecessary lithium use.

Some alcoholic patients have a primary mood disorder that should be treated with ADs. Higher chances of primary depression

- If depression present during times of sobriety and prior to onset of alcoholism.
- In women alcoholics and those with later onset (> 30 y.o.) alcoholism.
- If history of depression in family is independent of substance abuse.

SSRIs are probably preferred antidepressant in alcoholism because

- They have lower toxicity.
- They may help reduce impulsive drive to drink, even in those who are not depressed.
- Some open studies suggest that SSRIs can help prevent relapse in nondepressed alcoholics.

Treat alcohol-induced *aggression with hallucinosis* with high-potency antipsychotics, such as haloperidol 5 mg or risperidone 2–5 mg.

- Avoid low-potency neuroleptics (e.g., thioridazine) during alcohol withdrawal, since they are more likely to prompt seizures and severe hypotension.
- With aggression alone, consider trazodone 25–150 mg q 6 h.

The following drugs can be useful in reducing craving and impulse to drink.

### Disulfiram

If the goal is to *prevent* the resumption of impulsive alcohol consumption, disulfiram might help. All of these treatments work best as part of an overall monitored treatment program and not as the sole therapeutic agent.

Prior to disulfiram treatment, evaluation should include

- LFTs
- ECG
- Physical exam

If the disulfiram-taking patient drinks alcohol, he or she may experience the following within 5–10 minutes (usually in this order):

- Flushing
- Sweating
- Throbbing headache and neck pain
- Palpitations
- Dyspnea
- Hyperventilation
- Tachycardia
- Hypotension
- Nausea
- Vomiting

These symptoms should be described in gory detail to the patient new to disulfiram.

More serious reactions generate chest pain, difficulty breathing, more severe hypotension, confusion, and (especially in patients on > 500 mg/day) an occasional death. Reactions occur for 0.5–2 h, often followed by drowsiness and sleep.

- The reaction's dangers increase with higher amounts of disulfiram (> 500 mg/day) or ethanol.
- Reactions can occur up to 14 days after the last drink.

Disulfiram should be avoided in

- Masochistic or suicidal patients.
- Demented or confused patients who forget they ingest disulfiram.
- Patients with severe cardiac disease, moderate-to-severe liver disease, renal failure, peripheral neuropathies, or pregnancy.
- Patients using drugs metabolized by the liver, including TCAs, SSRIs, anticonvulsants, MAOIs, neuroleptics, vasodilators, alpha- or beta-adrenergic blockers, paraldehyde, or metronidazole.
- Patients extremely sensitive to thiuram derivatives in pesticides or rubber vulcanization.
- Patients who refuse to tell any relatives about their use of disulfiram.
- Patients who will not (or cannot) avoid alcohol in aftershave lotions, sauces, cough syrup.

Give disulfiram as follows:

- Wait until at least 12 h after last drink.
- Start on 250 mg hs for 1–2 weeks, and then
  - √ 250 mg to patients over 170 pounds and
  - √ 125 mg to patients under 170 pounds.
- For faster loading, a patient over 170 pounds who tolerates the initial 250 mg dose well, can be given 250 mg bid or 500 mg qd for the first 2 days; then return to 250 mg qd.

Side effects include

- Drowsiness, fatigue
- Body odor, halitosis (dose-related), foul taste in mouth
- Headache, tremor, impotence, dizziness
- Rarely hepatoxicity, neuropathy, psychosis

Management

- If there is a severe disulfiram reaction, give diphenhydramine 50 mg IM/IV.
- Treat hypotension, shock, and arrhythmias symptomatically.
- Oxygen is useful for respiratory distress.
- Vitamin C may reduce alcohol–disulfiram reaction.

*Naltrexone (ReVia)*

- Usual dose 50 mg po qd.
  - √ The serious side effects (e.g., LFT increase, lymphocytosis, GI disturbance) seen at 5-fold higher doses are not seen at this dose.
  - √ Patient must be opiate-free 7–10 days before starting.
  - √ Do not give to patient with hepatitis or liver failure.
- May help reduce
  - √ Alcohol craving
  - √ Number of drinking days
  - √ Percent of patients relapsing
  - √ Repetitive self-injurious behavior
    - ◻ In 7 female patients on 50 mg/day, 6 ceased repetitive self-injurious behavior.
- Side effects in 10% of patients include
  - √ Abdominal pain
  - √ Anxiety
  - √ Fatigue
  - √ Headache
  - √ Insomnia
  - √ Joint and muscle pain
  - √ Nausea

- Side effects in 1–9% of patients
  - √ Anorexia
  - √ Chills
  - √ Constipation
  - √ Decreased potency
  - √ Delayed ejaculation
  - √ Diarrhea
  - √ Dizziness
  - √ Feeling down
  - √ Increased energy
  - √ Increased thirst
  - √ Irritability
  - √ Skin rash
- FDA-approved for alcoholism prevention as well as opiate dependence.

*Odansetron (Zofran)*

- A selective serotonin 5-$HT_3$ receptor blocker
  - √ Study compared patients with early ($\leq$ 25 y.o.) vs. late onset (> 25 y.o.) problem drinking.
  - √ Average age of early onset was 37 y.o., and late onset was 44 y.o.
  - √ Patients were randomized to placebo or odansetron at 1, 4, or 16 $\mu$g/kg bid.
- Patients with early-onset alcoholism taking odansetron had less self-reported alcohol consumption than those taking placebo.
  - √ Abstinence rate, drinks per day, total days abstinent, and days abstinent per study were significant markers of improvement.
  - √ Plasma carbohydrate-deficient transferrin (CDT) levels confirmed reduced alcohol consumption in odansetron-treated early-onset patients.
  - √ Odansetron did not influence alcohol consumption in late-onset patients.

## OVERDOSE: TOXICITY, SUICIDE, AND TREATMENT

### Benzodiazepines

Benzodiazepine overdoses are discussed in the previous chapter.

### Barbiturates and Barbiturate-like Hypnotics

Barbiturates and barbiturate-like hypnotics present high suicide risks.

- About 10 times the daily dose of a barbiturate can be severely toxic.

- Death occurs in 0.5–12% of barbiturate overdoses. These fatalities may happen "on purpose" or from an "autonomous" state in which the patient falls asleep, awakes in a fog, cannot remember how many pills have already been taken, and overconsumes.
- Autonomous state as a reason for the overdose is usually an alibi and not true.
- The true autonomous state is believed to be quite rare because so many awakenings and ingestions are pharmacologically nearly impossible.
- Patient may truly not remember overdosing secondary to retrograde amnesia.

Barbiturates with shorter half-lives and high lipid solubility are more lethal.

## Chloral Hydrate

Chloral hydrate's lethal dose is 5–10 times its hypnotic dose of 1–2 g. Acute chloral hydrate overdoses display:

| Common | Less Common | Infrequent |
|---|---|---|
| Stomach distress | Miosis | Esophageal stricture |
| Hypotension | Vomiting | Gastric necrosis and perforation |
| Hypothermia | Areflexia | GI hemorrhage |
| Respiratory depression | Muscle flaccidity | Transient hepatic damage and jaundice |
| Cardiac arrhythmias | | |
| Coma | | |

Management of chloral hydrate overdose:

- General management, as listed in the previous chapter for benzodiazepines.
- Hemodialysis may eliminate the metabolite trichloroethanol.
  √ Peritoneal dialysis may assist.

## Ethchlorvynol

- Acute ethchlorvynol overdoses generate
  √ Hypotension
  √ Bradycardia
  √ Hypothermia
  √ Mydriasis
  √ Areflexia
- This may lead to
  √ Pulmonary edema
  √ Severe infections
  √ Peripheral neuropathy

√ Severe pancytopenia, hemolysis
√ Severe cardiorespiratory depression, apnea
√ Deep coma (lasting several weeks)

Management of ethchlorvynol overdoses involves (*see also* pages 65–67)

- Emphasis on pulmonary care and monitoring blood pressure gases.
- Value of hemodialysis is debated.
- Alkalinization of urine does not increase excretion.

## Toxicity and Suicide Data

| Generic Names | Toxic Doses Average (g) | Fatal Doses Average Lowest (g) | Toxic Levels* ($\mu$g/ml) | Fatal Levels* ($\mu$g/ml) |
|---|---|---|---|---|
| *Benzodiazepines* | — | — | — | — |
| Estazolam | — | — | — | — |
| Flurazepam | — | — | — | — |
| Quazepam | — | — | — | — |
| Temazepam | 2 | — | — | — |
| Triazolam | — | — | — | — |
| Zolpidem | | | | |
| *Barbiturates* | | | | |
| Amobarbital | 0.4 | 2–3 | 30–40 | > 50 |
| Butabarbital | — | — | 40–60 | > 50 |
| Pentobarbital | — | 2–3 | 10–15 | > 30 |
| Phenobarbital | — | 6–10 | 50–80 (30–134) | > 80 |
| Secobarbital | — | 2–3 | 10–15 | > 30 |
| *Miscellaneous* | | | | |
| Chloral hydrate | 30 | 10 (4) | — | — |
| Ethchlorvynol | 50 | 6 | — | — |

* *Toxic levels* produce coma, arousal difficulties, significant respiratory depression; *fatal levels* are usually lethal.

## PRECAUTIONS

All benzodiazepine, barbiturate, and barbiturate-like hypnotics contraindicated in patients with

- Hypersensitivity to hypnotics or antianxiety agents
- Pregnancy
  √ Benzodiazepines, except for flurazepam, are not contraindicated, but a careful assessment of risk-benefits must be done first.
- Sleep apnea
- Zolpidem and trazodone not contraindicated.

Barbiturates and barbiturate-like hypnotics should be avoided in patients with

- Liver impairment
- Alcoholism
- Renal conditions
- Porphyria
- Anticoagulant medication
- Suicidal ideation

## NURSES' DATA

Observe if patients have

- Trouble finding bed after taking hypnotic
- Trouble walking, falling
- Confusion
- Immediate sleepiness or overstimulation
- Skin rash
- Abdominal pain
- Muscle weakness

Note symptoms of withdrawal, intoxication, or overdose (*see* pages 370–71, 404–6, 415–17). Withdrawal symptoms may be difficult to distinguish from anxiety, and vice versa.

Ensure that patients do not take hypnotics for pain relief.

Also make sure patients understand the short-term value of hypnotics.

## PATIENT AND FAMILY NOTES

If taking a hypnotic, avoid

- Alcohol
  √ With a hypnotic, one drink feels and acts like 2–3 drinks.
  √ Worse for barbiturates and barbiturate-like hypnotics.
- Pregnancy
  √ If become pregnant, do not stop hypnotics until deciding on a withdrawal schedule with doctor.
- Long-term use
- Suddenly stopping hypnotics after long-term use!
  √ Abrupt hypnotic withdrawal is often more dangerous than abrupt opiate withdrawal—seizures, and worse.

If a doctor prescribes barbiturate or barbiturate-like hypnotic, ask if a benzodiazepine, which is safer, would be better short-term hypnotic.

If the elderly or debilitated are too confused to manage their hypnotics properly, the family may need to dispense them.

Store hypnotics away from the bedside or from any readily accessible location to avert accidental intake. Keep away from youngsters.

Within 6 h of taking a hypnotic, do not work around machines, drive a car, or cross the street.

- The next morning, check if reflexes are a "tad off" by, for example, stepping down on the car break in the driveway.
- There is a 5–10 times higher driving-accident rate in patients on benzodiazepines.
- People on hypnotics are more likely to ignore fire alarms, pain, a full bladder, a crying baby, or telephones.

Triazolam, zolpidem (to a lesser extent), and zaleplon can cause traveler's amnesia.

The doctor should suggest a specific time period to take a hypnotic (e.g., $1/2$ h, $1^1/2$ h before bedtime).

If patient forgets a dose

- Can consume it within 6 h of awakening.
  √ Zolpidem often can be taken within 4 h of awakening.
- Otherwise wait for next evening.
- Do not double dose.

May ingest with food, but this may slow onset of sleep.

# 9. Stimulants

## INTRODUCTION

Stimulants are used clinically to treat

- Attention-deficit/hyperactivity disorder (ADHD) (pages 426–31)
- Adult ADHD (pages 432–33)
- Conduct disorder (pages 433–34)
- Treatment-resistant depression (page 434; *see also* Antidepressants, pages 118–25).
- Narcolepsy (pages 435–36)
- Chronic, medically debilitating conditions (pages 436–37)
- Treatment-resistant obesity (pages 434–35)

Also discussed is management of

- Cocaine and stimulant withdrawal and abuse (pages 447–48).

## NAMES, DEA SCHEDULE NUMBER, MANUFACTURERS, DOSE FORMS, COLORS

| Generic Names (DEA Schedule #) | Brand Names | Manufacturers | Dose Forms (mg)* | Colors |
|---|---|---|---|---|
| Dextroamphetamine(II) | Dexedrine | SmithKline Beecham | t: 5<br>e: 5 mg/5 ml | t: orange†<br>e: orange |
| | Spansule | SmithKline Beecham | sr-sp: 5/10/15 | sr-sp: all brown—clear |
| Methylphenidate(II) | Ritalin | CIBA | t: 5/10/20 | t: yellow/pale green/pale yellow† |
| Methylphenidate SR | Ritalin-SR | CIBA | sr-t: 20 | sr-t: white |
| Pemoline(IV) | Cylert | Abbott | t: 18.75/ 37.5/75<br><br>ct: 37.5 | t: white/ orange/tan<br>ct: orange |
| Phendimetrazine(IV) | Plegine | Wyeth-Ayerst | t: 35 | t: beige |
| | Prelu-2 (timed release) | Boehringer Ingelheim | sr-c: 105 | sr-c: celery-green |

* c = capsule; ct = chewable tablet; e = elixir; sp = spansule; sr = sustained-release; t = tablets;
† = scored.

Similar drugs are marketed for appetite suppression and are occasionally used as alternative stimulants.

- Amphetamines (Schedule II)
  - √ Methamphetamine (Desoxyn)
  - √ Benzphetamine (Didrex)
  - √ Amphetamine plus dextroamphetamine (Obetrol)
- Non-amphetamines (Schedule IV)
  - √ Mazindol (Sanorex)
  - √ Diethylpropion (Tenuate, Tenuate Dospan)

## PHARMACOLOGY

Stimulants act by

- Directly releasing catecholamines into synaptic clefts and thus onto postsynaptic receptor sites.
- Efficiently blocking the reuptake of catecholamines, thereby prolonging their actions.
- Inhibiting MAO enzymes to slow down metabolism.

- Serving as false neurotransmitters.
- Methylphenidate and dextroamphetamine (and probably other stimulants) are more effective than behavioral treatment in reducing ADHD symptoms, but combined treatment is more effective at reducing comorbid conditions.

Dextroamphetamine

- Rapidly absorbed by GI tract; peak level in 2 h.
- Effects
  - √ Increased BP and increased pulse rate (mean 11/min), especially in African-Americans.
    - ▫ Usually not clinically significant.
  - √ Decreased appetite.
    - ▫ Reduces weight more than methylphenidate or pemoline.
  - √ Delayed sleep.

Methamphetamine

- Rapidly absorbed by GI tract.
- Provides 4–12-h duration of clinical action.
- Often taken once daily but is extremely expensive and can be quite habit-forming.

Methylphenidate

- Rapidly absorbed by GI tract.
- Effects persist 2–4 h from a single normal tablet and 3–5 h after sustained-release tablets.
  - √ Sustained-release tablets are absorbed more slowly and may yield a lower plasma level than regular tablets.
- Has less anorectic and cardiac effects than dextroamphetamine.
  - √ Often preferred for children.

Amphetamine mixed salts

- 25% levoamphetamine salts plus 75% dextroamphetamine.
- Of 53 children with ADHD treated with amphetamine mixed salts (Adderall), 61% had significant improvement on the Clinical Global Impressions.
- Adderall could be taken 2 times a day in 89% of patients, while Ritalin could be taken 2 or fewer times a day in only 25% of patients.
- Effective for adult ADHD.
- Not shown to be more effective than dextroamphetamine.

Pemoline

- Rapidly absorbed by GI tract.
- Chewable and may be better accepted by young children.

- May be smoother and better tolerated.
- 50% bound to plasma protein.
- Reaches a steady state in 2–3 days.
- Has less stimulant effect than dextroamphetamine and methylphenidate.
  √ No abuse potential in humans.
- Lower abuse potential may help
  √ Children with potentially drug-abusing parents.
  √ Adult and late adolescent ADHD with substance abuse risk.
- Using a predefined 30% or more reduction in symptoms as an indicator of improvement, 50% of pemoline-treated and 17% in placebo group were positive responders.
- Reduces appetite and delays sleep in 30% of children.
- Using usual dosing procedure of 18.75 mg q A.M. initially and increasing 18.75 mg q 5–7 days takes 2–4 weeks to establish effective dose.
- If started at 1–2 mg/kg, and if plasma level is > 2 ng/ml (3–4 h later), clinical effect seen in hours.
  √ Takes 2–3 days to achieve steady-state plasma level.
- In one study 41 of 43 patients, younger than 20 y.o., took daily doses of pemoline 100 mg.
  √ Clinical signs or symptoms of liver damage typically appeared 10–12 months after the start of treatment.
  √ Common complaints included nausea, vomiting, lethargy, and malaise.
  √ Patients had aspartate aminotransferase (AST) values of 100–4400 U/ml and alanine aminotransferase values of 100–3200 U/ml.
    □ Half of the patients in whom bilirubin levels were measured had jaundice.
  √ Hepatic failure was usually reversible after pemoline was discontinued.
  √ Because of risk of hepatic dysfunction, including hepatic failure, clinically significant hepatitis (3% of children), mild elevation in the activity of liver transaminases (up to 1000/l), and limited efficacy and tolerability, pemoline should be generally considered as second-line treatment for ADHD.
  √ Increases in liver enzyme levels have been reported several months after starting pemoline. Liver function tests should be performed prior to, and at least every 4–6 months during, pemoline therapy.
    □ Pemoline should not be administered to patients with impaired hepatic function or combined with drugs known to depress hepatic drug metabolism.

Bupropion

- In a group of 40 patients (7–10-year-olds) with ADHD symptoms, the medication group showed significantly reduced symptoms in 42% compared to 24% on placebo.
- On Clinical Global Impression scores, 52% of the bupropion group were rated as "much" or "very much" improved compared with 11% on placebo.
  √ Medication group did not separate from placebo until the final weeks.
- Bupropion, with its dopaminergic effects, is a poor choice for comorbid tic disorders.
  √ Induces a rash in about 17% of youths vs. 8% in placebo group.
  √ Rashes include maculopapular, urticarial, and pruritic.

Buspirone

- 12 children who met criteria for ADHD with hyperactivity and impulsivity, and unresponsive to combined TCA, cognitive therapy, and parental psychoeducation,
  √ Started on 0.5 mg/kg body weight per day.
    ▫ Actual doses ranged from 15 to 30 mg bid.
- Improvements were seen in both Connors Parent Abbreviated 10-item Index (CPAI) and Children's Global Assessment Scale (CGAS).
  √ Improvements seen after 1 week of treatment.
- Every child responded to buspirone with CPAI symptom score reduction of ≥ 50% by 4 weeks.
  √ Decreases occurred on all 4 subscales of CPAI measuring aggressive behavior, hyperactivity, impulsivity, inattention, and mood.

Heterocyclic antidepressants

- Clinically significant improvements with desipramine and nortriptyline.
- Effects of these agents are apparent within 2 or 3 days.
- Probably most effective for behavioral improvements and less effective on cognition and attention.
- Can be used to treat ADHD in children with Tourette's disorder without aggravating tics.
- Unlike adults who tend to have hypotensive reactions to heterocyclic agents, adolescents and probably children appear to have greater risk of developing hypertension.
- Desipramine is not preferred due to unexplained sudden deaths in 5 children (8–15 years old).
  √ Desipramine more likely to risk fatality from overdose than with other heterocyclic agents.

Venlafaxine

- Reduced inattention in an open trial in children with ADHD.

SSRIs

- SSRIs not very effective for inattention or hyperactivity.
- May improve impulsivity.

### Pharmacology of Stimulants in Children

| Generic Names | Peak Serum Levels (hours) | Serum Half-lives (hours) | Onset of Action (hours) | Duration of Action (hours) |
|---|---|---|---|---|
| Dextroamphetamine | 2–4 | 6–12 | 0.5–1 | 4–6 |
| Methylphenidate | 1–3 | 2–4 | 0.5–1 | 3–6 |
| Pemoline | 2–4 (5–12) | 2–12 (acute) 14–34 (chronic) | 3–4 | 4–12 |

## DOSES

### Attention-Deficit/Hyperactivity Stimulant Doses in Children

| Generic Names | Single Usual Starting Dose (mg) | Daily Dose Range (mg/kg/day) | Usual Dose Range (mg/kg/day) | Extreme Dose Range (mg/day) |
|---|---|---|---|---|
| Dextroamphetamine | 5–10 qd | 0.15–0.5 | 0.3–2.0 | 5–60 |
| Methylphenidate | 2.5–5 bid | 0.3–0.7 | 0.3–2.0 | 10–80 |
| Pemoline | 18.75–37.5 qd | 0.5–2.5 | 0.5–3.0 | 37.5–112.5 |
| Adderall | 5–10 mg bid | 0.15–0.5 | 0.3–0.9 | 1–1.5 |

### Other Stimulant Doses

| Generic Names | Adult ADHD (mg/day) | Adult Depression (mg/day) | Adult Narcolepsy (mg/day) | Geriatric Patients (mg/day) |
|---|---|---|---|---|
| Dextroamphetamine* | 10–60 qd or bid | 5–40 | 20–30 | 10–15 |
| Methylphenidate* | 10–80 qd or bid | 10–80 | 10–30 | 10–30 |
| Pemoline | 37.5–75 qd or bid | 18.75–150 | 37.5–75 | —— |
| Adderall | 10–30 mg bid | —— | —— | —— |

\* Usually in bid dosing.

## CLINICAL INDICATIONS AND USE

Stimulants are

- *Clearly* effective in
  √ Attention-deficit/hyperactivity disorder in children.
  √ Narcoleptic symptoms of daytime sleepiness and sleep attacks.

- *Probably* effective in
  - √ Attention-deficit/hyperactivity disorder in adults.
  - √ Adjunctive to antidepressants treatment-resistant depressions.
  - √ Apathy and withdrawal in medically ill and the elderly.
  - √ Chronic fatigue syndrome.
- *Possibly* effective in
  - √ Mood and motivation symptoms of AIDS and other chronic, debilitating diseases.

## Attention-Deficit/Hyperactivity Disorder (ADHD)

Children who exhibit symptoms in several settings (the narrower British definition of ADHD) may have more drug responsivity than those who exhibit symptoms in only one or two settings.

Roughly 85–90% of these children respond to stimulants if trials of 2 different stimulants are used.

Short-acting stimulants are the first choice.

- Dextroamphetamine or
- Methylphenidate
  - √ Patients (N = 144) receiving methylphenidate (Ritalin) treatment had greater improvement in specific ADHD symptoms, i.e., inattention and hyperactivity/impulsivity.
  - √ Medication treatment alone and combined meds plus therapy had very similar outcomes. However, combined therapy was superior for social adjustment.

If one of these drugs fails, there is a 25% chance the other drug will succeed.

- If a short-acting stimulant lasts only 3–4 h, with abrupt return of symptoms, consider sustained-release forms or pemoline.
- Dextroamphetamine spansules can have uneven effects, with early intense activity and a significant decline thereafter.
  - √ Anecdotal evidence suggests that sustained-release methamphetamines (Desoxyn Gradument tablets) have a longer and more even effect.

When a stimulant works, it

- Occurs quickly (often in 2 days),
- Persists, and
- Shows little or no tolerance over months to years.

Single stimulant trials superior to placebo in 70–80% of patients.

- 30% exhibit marked improvement,
- 40% display moderate benefit, and
- 10–30% are refractory.

Comparison trials of 2 stimulants, dextroamphetamine and methylphenidate, yield superiority of at least one agent over placebo in > 90% of patients.

- If child tolerates drug but shows only minimal or partial improvement, higher doses are likely to increase improvement.
- Methylphenidate appears to be safe and effective in ADHD and many mild to moderate tic disorders.

Academic performance and on-task (attention) behavior in classroom is directly related to dosage.

- Continued increases in performance occur up to 20 mg methylphenidate (single dose). Older uncontrolled studies reported doses above 0.6 mg/kg risked decrease in cognitive performance.
- Behavior ratings by teachers suggest maximum improvement at 10 mg (single dose).
- Different ADHD symptoms may respond at different doses.

Stimulants

- Decrease
  √ Motor activity
  √ Impulsiveness
  √ Emotional lability
- Increase
  √ Vigilance and attention
  √ Short-term memory
  √ More "normal" behavior
  √ In 122 children with ADHD combined with Tourette's disorder, 9% developed tics or dyskinesia during stimulant treatment.
    □ Most studies of children with ADHD and tic disorders show no increase in tics with stimulants.

Stimulants occasionally make some youngsters more active and others more withdrawn and despondent.

- Euphoria is a rare event.
- In "normals," stimulants do not induce euphoria before puberty.
- Methylphenidate treatment for cocaine abusers with ADHD appears to have positive results with both conditions.
  √ 50% had no cocaine-positive urine in last 2 weeks of treatment.
  √ Cocaine-positive urine samples still seen in last 2 weeks were fewer days/weeks.

**Adjunctive Treatments**

Clonidine

- Shows stronger effects on behavioral features of ADHD and weaker effects on cognition.

- Helped 95% of children with tic disorders and comorbid ADHD but only 53% of children with ADHD without tic disorders.
- Risks sedation and symptom rebound after 3–6-h clinical duration passes.

Guanfacine

- An alpha-2 agonist, longer-acting, more receptor-specific.
- Shows less trouble with sedation, changes in blood pressure, and altered heart rate.

### Dosing

- Dextroamphetamine uses bid-tid, and methylphenidate bid-qid, dosages.
    √ Typically taken 4 h apart.
    √ Increase individual doses prn every few days by 2.5–5 mg.
- Pemoline can be dispensed once every morning (*see* pages 423–24).
    √ Can increase stimulant doses q 2–4 days.
    √ Scored tablets useful.
    √ Children enjoy chewable pemoline.
- If possible, give after meals to reduce appetite-suppressing effects at mealtime.
    √ Absorption is not affected by full stomach.

### Initiating and Maintaining Therapy

- Methylphenidate may reduce WBC.
    √ Get baseline WBC and monitor every 3–6 months.
- Pemoline may increase LFTs.
    √ Get baseline LFT and monitor every 1–3 months.
    √ Half of patients in whom bilirubin levels were measured had jaundice.
- Get baseline HR and BP and monitor for possible increase.
    √ Especially if patient on dextroamphetamine and has African genetics.
- Inform family about most common transient side effects— anorexia, abdominal pain, headaches, irritability and moodiness—and that
    √ Tolerance to stimulants doesn't usually occur in ADHD.
    √ No cases of sustained or permanent growth suppression.
        □ Initial delay of growth eventually overridden.
        □ Get baseline height and weight.
        □ Monitor every 6 months.
    √ May see rebound growth with drug "holidays," but
        □ The social impairment that is frequently experienced on holidays and the overall effect on normal emotional maturation argue against them.

▫ Increased nutrition can offset growth problems.
- Inform patient and family of onset insomnia.
  ✓ May need to take last dose of day earlier.
- If possible, have assessment include teachers and parents.
  ✓ Use Connors or similar scales, if possible, to rate behavior changes.
  ✓ Compare with placebo, if possible.
    ▫ Pharmacy can prepare identical packets of stimulant and placebo. Give each for 1 week and compare ratings on each. If no different, patient does not require stimulant.
  ✓ If without full response, try another stimulant.

Therapeutic responses are not correlated with serum or saliva levels.

Safe to suddenly stop stimulants.

Safer to use sustained-release forms before TCAs.

TCAs, bupropion, or buspirone may help if

- Stimulants proved ineffective or were not tolerated.
- Single night dosing desirable for compliance.
- Child has a coexisting disorder requiring ADs (e.g., mood disorder).
- Strong family history of mood disorder.
- Drug-abusing children or parents.

Drawbacks of TCAs are

- Rare but serious cardiovascular side effects (especially in prepubertal children).
- Dangerous in overdose.

Alpha-adrenergic stimulants may help ADHD.

- May have some effects on behavior as monotherapy.
- Best used to augment other medications.

Clonidine nonselectively stimulates alpha $2_A$, $2_B$, and $2_C$ adrenergic receptors.

- Better than placebo in a few controlled trials.
  ✓ Can use doses up to 4–5 $\mu$g/kg.
    ▫ Most common side effect is sleepiness.
    ▫ Subsides in 2–4 weeks.

Guanfacine selectively stimulates alpha $2_A$ adrenergic receptors, mainly found in brain.

- May be better tolerated than clonidine.
- Has fewer side effects.
  - √ Lower frequency of sedation (21% guanfacine vs. 35% clonidine).
  - √ No significant effect on BP.
  - √ Rebound hypertension milder and less frequent.
  - √ 25% headache, stomachache, and tiredness, usually gone in 2 weeks.
- Guanfacine in 1 open trial
  - √ Significantly improved
    - □ Hyperactivity
    - □ Inattention
    - □ Immaturity
  - √ Did not significantly improve
    - □ Mood
    - □ Aggression
- Dosing guanfacine
  - √ Usual final daily dose 2–4 mg or 0.1 mg/kg given bid or tid.
  - √ Start 0.5 mg q A.M.
  - √ Add 0.5 mg q 3 days at other dosing times.
    - □ Typically noon, 4–5 P.M., qhs (1 mg).
    - □ Because drug has >12-h half-life, can give largest dose qhs to minimize daytime sedation.
- Iron supplementation in ADHD children (7–11 y.o.)
  - √ 30-day trial of iron supplementation (0.5 mg/kg/day)
  - √ At end of trial, 14 boys showed significant increases ($p < .005$) in mean serum ferretin levels from 26–45 ng/ml.
  - √ Parent scores on the Connors Rating Scale decreased from a mean 17.6 to 12.7 points.
  - √ There was no correlation between dose of iron supplementation and Connors Rating Scale score.

Other drugs have important limitations.

- *Avoid* benzodiazepines and barbiturates.
  - √ Can trigger "paradoxical" excitement.
- Diphenhydramine and chloral hydrate promote less agitation but may induce sleep.
- Neuroleptics (e.g., chlorpromazine 10–50 mg qid) nonspecifically calm but risk many side effects.
- Lithium only assists bipolar patients with impulsivity, short attention span, and hyperactivity.
  - √ Also helps conduct disorders.
  - √ May help child with "episodic" ADHD.
- Carbamazepine helps with aggressiveness, impulsivity.
  - √ Approved for use in children.

S
T
I
M
U
L
A
N
T
S

## Adult Attention-Deficit/Hyperactivity Disorder

Adults with attention-deficit disorder (with inattention, impulsiveness, concentration difficulty, anxiety, irritability, and excitability) who had onset of *DSM-IV* symptoms before age 7 may improve with stimulants.

- Often show poor work or academic performance, temper outburst, antisocial behavior, and/or alcohol abuse.
- Diagnosis in adults more difficult than in children.
  - √ Many diagnoses and conditions may resemble ADHD:
    - □ Substance abuse
    - □ Bipolar disorder
    - □ Personality disorder
    - □ Agitated depression
  - √ The majority of patients have comorbid mood, anxiety, substance use, and/or personality disorders.
  - √ Adults do not tend to have hyperactivity.
  - √ There is no neuropsychological or other test that confirms adult ADHD diagnosis.
  - √ Family members and those close to patient can help give corroborating information about diagnosis.
  - √ A history of having a paradoxical calming response to stimulants suggests a possible positive response to stimulants.
- Controlled studies in adults yield substantive improvement in attention, impulsivity, and hyperactivity.
  - √ Overall response rate 70%.
  - √ Includes methylphenidate, dextroamphetamine, methamphetamine, mixed amphetamine salt (Adderall).
- Adult ADHD doses are listed on page 426.
  - √ Adderall (a mixed amphetamine salt product) starting at 5 mg po bid, mean and dose 10.77 mg/day.
    - □ 24 outpatients (mean age = 33.3 years) started at 5 mg po bid.
    - □ Duration of treatment 16 weeks.
    - □ 13 patients (54%) responded positively, based on Clinical Global Impressions–Improvement scales.
    - □ Mean end dose for responders was 10.77 mg/day.
  - √ Decrease in the mean Copeland score from 99 to 63 (p < .001) and Brown score from 77 to 51 (.0001).

Bupropion

- In another study responders were defined as ≥ 30% reduction in symptoms: 76% of those on bupropion responded compared with 37% on placebo.
  - √ With Clinical Global Impression scores, 52% of bupropion group rated as "much" or "very much" improved, and only 11% on placebo responded as well.

Pemoline (magnesium permoline)

- In a 10-week double-blind placebo-controlled crossover design, target daily dose of 3 mg/kg/day in 35 adults with ADHD.
- In final week of the 4-week active phase, pemoline best tolerated at mean dose of 2.2 mg/kg/day.
  √ Adults preferred moderate 120–160 mg/day dosing.
- 30% reduction in symptoms used as indication of improvement.
  √ 50% of pemoline-treated subjects and 17% of placebo group were positive responders.

Desipramine

- 68% of 41 desipramine-treated patients, and no subjects in placebo group, were positive responders.
  √ Desipramine-treated patients had reduction of 12 of 14 ADHD symptoms.

Venlafaxine

- Improved attention and concentration in normal adult volunteers without ADHD at 12.5–50 mg/day.
- 80% of those treated with venlafaxine and 25% of the stimulant-treated adults showed a trend toward improvement in ADHD symptoms.

If risk of substance abuse
  √ Nonstimulant alternatives discussed earlier should be considered first, including
    ▫ Bupropion
    ▫ Low sedation TCAs, e.g., nortriptyline, desipramine
    ▫ Venlafaxine
    ▫ Clonidine or guanfacine

## Conduct Disorder

- Children with conduct disorder with or without ADHD can improve within 5 weeks on methylphenidate.
  √ Cruelty, property destruction, stealing, and use of obscene language significantly reduced on methylphenidate when compared to placebo.
  √ Mothers rated 78% of conduct-disordered children on methylphenidate globally improved vs. 27% on placebo.
  √ Professionals (teachers, psychiatrists, psychologists) similarly rated 50–55% more responders on methylphenidate than on placebo.

√ Level of ADHD symptoms at baseline not correlated with improvement in aggressive behavior.
√ Long-term data not available for this population.
√ Stimulant misuse common.

## Treatment-Resistant Depression

Stimulants are better than placebo in treatment of resistant depression, geriatric depression, and medically-induced depression.

- Hidden comorbidity of stimulant-responsive syndromes (e.g., sleep apnea, ADHD) might account for some of the responses in these groups.

Stimulants are not better than placebo as monotherapy of depression.

Stimulants dramatically aid a small, *select* group who

- Have failed on at least 2 other antidepressant classes (e.g., TCAs, SSRIs, MAOIs).
  √ Effective as adjunctive treatment.
- Have a serious, often life-threatening, ailment (e.g., AIDS, cancer) and who cannot tolerate antidepressants.
- Require a stimulant's boost until ADs work.

Stimulants can generate a true antidepressant effect.

- Effect may begin to outlive duration of action of stimulant.
- Mood on awakening in A.M. may still be improved.

Stimulants produce tolerance to antidepressant effect more often than conventional antidepressants.

- 20–40% tolerance seen with stimulants.

Childhood and adolescent depressions respond as well to placebo as to TCAs.

- Stimulants may be a reasonable alternative.

## Treatment-Resistant Obesity

Positive effects tend to be transient.

- By 6 months no difference between patients who used stimulant and those who did not.
- All appetite suppressants are stimulants except fenfluramine (Pondimin), which is primarily a serotonin releaser and is no longer on the market.
- Sometimes a good response is seen and maintained by adding adjunctive treatments, e.g.,

√ Metamucil or other noncaloric bulk product, used 3 times a day prior to eating, if possible.

√ Modest exercise on a daily basis if possible, but if not, can still have benefits doing it only 3 times a week.

## Narcolepsy

Established treatments include

- Methylphenidate and dextroamphetamine for sleep attacks and daytime sleepiness.
  √ Unlike ADHD, tolerance to stimulants occurs with higher doses.
- Phenelzine or tranylcyromine for sleep attacks
  √ Can completely suppress REM.
  √ Stopping MAOIs abruptly can cause extreme rebound due to increased REM.
  √ Takes 2–5 weeks for REM to return to normal.
- TCAs (e.g., imipramine) for cataplexy.

Modafinil (Provigil) is a new wakefulness-promoting medication.

- Modafinil is schedule IV, but it has only minimal dopaminergic and noradrenergic effects.
- Modafinil was effective in 2 trials.
  √ All volunteers had daytime sleepiness plus (1) recurrent daytime naps or lapses into sleep almost daily for at least 3 months, plus sudden bilateral loss of postural muscle tone in association with intense emotion (cataplexy); or (2) a complaint of excessive sleepiness or sudden muscle weakness with sleep paralysis, hypnogogic hallucinations, automatic behaviors, disrupted major sleep episode, and sleep latency < 10 minutes or REM latency < 20 minutes.
  √ Using Clinical Global Impression of Change, improvement on 200 mg was 64% and 58%; at 400 mg, 72% and 60%; vs. 37% and 38% on placebo.
  √ Modafinil has excellent safety profile for up to 40 weeks. Efficacy was maintained, and tolerance probably does not develop with long-term use.
- In addition to promoting wakefulness, modafinil produces psychoactive and euphoric effects and alterations in mood, perception, thinking, and feeling typical of other CNS stimulants.
- Pharmacologic profile
  √ Half-life after multiple doses ~ 15 h.
  √ Peak plasma concentrations occur at 2–4 h.
  √ Hepatic metabolism is major route of elimination (~ 90%) with subsequent renal elimination of the metabolites.
    □ 80% eliminated in urine and 1% in feces.

      □ With hepatic impairment, oral clearance decreased by ~ 60% and steady-state concentration is doubled.
- Modafinil induces CYP 1A2/2C/3A4, GT, and/or epoxide hydrolase.
  √ Carbamazepine, phenobarbital, and phenytoin at risk of too low blood levels.
- Modafinil inhibits 2C19 and 2C9.
  √ Felbamate, oxcarbazepine, topiramate, and valproate levels may be increased.
  √ 3 subjects with mitral valve prolapse or left ventricular hypertrophy, developed chest pain, palpitations, dyspnea, and transient ischemic T-wave changes.
      □ Recommend not using modafinil in patients with history of left ventricular hypertrophy, ischemic ECG changes, chest pain, arrhythmia, or mitral valve prolapse.
- Side effects
  √ Adverse reactions were significant for headache (50% on modafinil, 40% on placebo) and nausea (13% on modafinil, 4% on placebo).
  √ All other comparisons were 4% or less difference between modafinil and placebo.
- Modafinil may be effective for ADHD and major depression.
  √ May have less rebound than typical dopaminergic medications.
  √ May increase treatment efficacy as an adjunctive medication.
  √ If already on sympathomimetic medication, will need to taper off of this over 5–7 days.

## Chronic, Medically Debilitating Conditions (AIDS, Cancer, Chronic Fatigue Syndrome)

Antidepressants significantly help 50% of those treated, but

- Many could not tolerate side effects, particularly with TCAs, and
- Many had no response.

Stimulants should be considered as reasonable alternatives for those who are AD nonresponders or have intolerable side effects.

Methylphenidate or dextroamphetamine alone improved mood and cognitive impairment in patients with AIDS.

- In one small study of 7 patients with AIDS-related cognitive and emotional deficits, methylphenidate or dextroamphetamine was given to each patient.
  √ 3 patients had marked functional improvement.
  √ 5 of 7 became more spontaneous, reactive, and animated.
  √ Neuropsychologic testing showed improvement in a subset of tests.

□ Scores did not return to baseline after the treatment had been discontinued for 1–3 days.
- No common adverse effects except appetite suppression and feeling "hyper."
  √ Most patients actually ate more because they had energy to buy and fix food.
- No tolerance developed.
- Stimulants had moderate analgesic effects alone and as augmentation of opiates.

Chronic fatigue syndrome (CFS) has several treatments besides stimulants.

- Amitriptyline in low doses (25–75 mg) superior to placebo.
  √ Improvement noted in sleep, fatigue, and overall functioning.
- Imipramine (25–75 mg) did not show good response in one open study.
- Case reports suggest positive results with
  √ Nortriptyline 50 mg.
  √ Clomipramine 75 mg better for pain than depression.
- Cyclobenzaprine (Flexeril), a tricyclic norepinephrine uptake blocker, at 10–40 mg qd, better than placebo for
  √ Sleep
  √ Pain severity
  √ Fatigue
  √ Global improvement
- Fluoxetine 20 mg in open studies (N = 50) of CFS without depression improved nearly all patients in areas of
  √ Pain
  √ Fatigue
  √ Functioning
- Bupropion 300 mg qd improved nonresponders to fluoxetine in areas of
  √ Mood
  √ Energy
  √ Immune function

## Prolonged Amphetamine-Induced Psychosis

- Methamphetamine abuse, particularly in IV form, can cause prolonged psychoses.
  √ Development of chronic psychoses mimicking paranoid schizophrenia about 2 months after cessation of methamphetamine use, perhaps due to upregulation of dopamine receptors.

√ At the end of World War II methamphetamine used to keep soldiers alert was dumped on the Japanese market by both Japan and the Allied Forces.

- First year later the "schizophrenia" frequency in Japan doubled.
- In the following year, the "schizophrenia" frequency increased to 3 times baseline. At this point methamphetamine was barred from possession or use in Japan, and the psychosis frequency gradually returned to baseline.
- The greatest remission occurred in the first year, with fewer remissions each year later.
- Delayed spontaneous remission—almost 15% of postwar methamphetamine psychoses (in Japan) took ≥ 5 yrs. to recover in spite of continued abstinence.
- Good premorbid functioning and usually no family history of schizophrenia.
- Negative symptoms common between exacerbations.
- Theoretically, this syndrome can occur with other dopaminergic stimulants.

## SIDE EFFECTS

Stimulant side effects typically arise

- In 2–3 weeks after initiating drug, and
- From dose reduction, causing rebound symptoms.

Elderly develop more side effects.

From the greater to the lesser, stimulants cause:

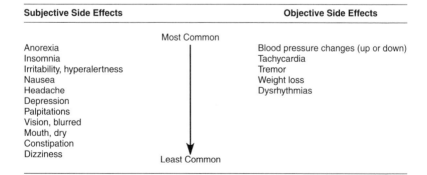

| Subjective Side Effects | Objective Side Effects |
|---|---|
| Most Common | |
| Anorexia | Blood pressure changes (up or down) |
| Insomnia | Tachycardia |
| Irritability, hyperalertness | Tremor |
| Nausea | Weight loss |
| Headache | Dysrhythmias |
| Depression | |
| Palpitations | |
| Vision, blurred | |
| Mouth, dry | |
| Constipation | |
| Dizziness | |
| Least Common | |

## Cardiovascular Effects

*Blood pressure changes*

- Highly variable.
  √ Greater risk in children of African descent.
- Unclear if taking stimulants with meals lowers BP.
- Reduce or stop drug if BP is too high or too low.

*Palpitations*

*Tachycardia*

## Central Nervous System Effects

*Choreoathetoid movements*

- Common with pemoline.

*Confusion, "dopey feeling"*

- Especially arises with > 1 mg/kg/day of methylphenidate.

*Dizziness*

*Dysphoria*

- Occurs with all stimulants but especially with methylphenidate, which causes
  √ Mild dysphoria
  √ Subtle social withdrawal
  √ Dulled affect, emotional blunting
  √ Cognitive "overfocusing"
  √ Perseveration
- Mild to moderate depression in children.

*Euphoria*

- Rare in prepubertal children; more common after puberty.

*Exacerbation of tics, exacerbation of Tourette's*

- Sometimes occurs in these patients.

*Headache*

*Insomnia*

- Usually initial insomnia.
- Affects 30% of children on moderately high stimulant doses.
- Often arises early, before optimal dose reached.
  √ May be transient with pemoline.

S
T
I
M
U
L
A
N
T
S

- Management
  √ Give more of the stimulant earlier in the day and/or
  √ Reduce dose.

*Overstimulation*

*Psychosis*

- Dextroamphetamine doses > 80 mg/day trigger psychosis with
  √ Agitation
  √ Tremor
  √ Toxicity
  √ Hallucinations
  √ Paranoia

*Restlessness*

- Give earlier in day and/or
- Reduce dose.

## Endocrine and Sexual Effects

*Changes in libido*

- Both increases and decreases reported.

*Impotence*

*Suppressed growth*

- Some stimulants suppress weight gain in some children; unlikely to suppress height gain.
  √ Incidence of suppressed growth is: dextroamphetamine > methylphenidate > pemoline.
  √ When methylphenidate is halted, compensatory growth occurs, which eliminates all growth difference between drug- and nondrug-treated patients.
- Growth rebound appears during drug-free holidays.

## Gastrointestinal Effects

*Anorexia*

- Reduced appetite occurs in 30% of children given moderately high stimulant doses.

*Mouth, dry*

- Mainly in adolescents

*Hepatotoxicity*

- Pemoline induces hepatotoxicity in 1–3% of children.

√ AST/SGOT and ALT/SGPT gradually increase over first 6 months of treatment with pemoline.
√ Enzymes return to normal after stopping pemoline.

*Weight loss*

- Usually begins early in treatment and
  √ May last up to 6 weeks.
  √ With pemoline, weight gain may follow in 3–6 months.

## PERCENTAGES OF SIDE EFFECTS*

| Side Effects | Dextroamphetamine | Methylphenidate | Pemoline |
|---|---|---|---|
| **CARDIOVASCULAR EFFECTS** | | | |
| Blood pressure, lower | —— | < 1 | < 1 |
| Blood pressure, higher | > 10 | 15.8 (1–26) | —— |
| Cardiac arrhythmias | < 1 | 5.5 | —— |
| Chest pain | < 1 | 4.4 (1–10) | —— |
| Dizziness, lightheadedness | 11.5 (1–23) | 7.7 (0–13) | 5.5 |
| Palpitations | 5.5 | 4.4 (1–10) | 5.5 |
| Tachycardia | 5.5 | 15 (1–20) | 5.5 |
| **CENTRAL NERVOUS SYSTEM EFFECTS** | | | |
| Agitation, restlessness (motoric) | > 10 | 6.7 (3.3–10) | —— |
| Awakening difficulty | —— | 15 (11–19) | —— |
| Confused, "dopey" | 10.3 (8–12) | 3.9 (2–10) | —— |
| Depression | 39 | 8.7 (0–16) | —— |
| Drowsiness, less alert | 5.5 | 5.7 (0–17) | 5.5 |
| Dyskinesias | < 1 | 3 | 5.5 |
| Headache | 18.3 (1–31) | 9.3 (0–15) | 13.8 (1–22) |
| Insomnia | 19 (5–43) | 16.9 (0–52) | 28.7 (< 10–42) |
| Irritability, overstimulation | 25 (17–29) | 17.3 (11–19.6) | 13.3 (1–21) |
| Mood changes | < 1 | > 10 | 5.5 |
| Psychosis (normal dose) | < 1 | < 1 | < 1 |
| Tics | < 1 | —— | —— |
| Tourette's syndrome | < 1 | < 1 | < 1 |
| Tremor | 5.5 | 6.5 | —— |
| **ENDOCRINE AND SEXUAL EFFECTS** | | | |
| Growth suppression | see text | see text | see text |
| Sexual function, disturbed | 5.5 | —— | —— |

| Side Effects | Dextroamphetamine | Methylphenidate | Pemoline |
|---|---|---|---|
| **EYES, EARS, NOSE, AND THROAT EFFECTS** | | | |
| Nystagmus | —— | —— | 5.5 |
| Vision, blurred | 5.5 | < 1 | —— |
| **GASTROINTESTINAL EFFECTS** | | | |
| Anorexia, lower appetite | 23.1 (1–56) | 26.9 (0–72) | 14.5 (1–34) |
| Bad taste | 5.5 | —— | —— |
| Constipation | 5.5 | 6.5 | —— |
| Diarrhea | 5.5 | —— | —— |
| Dyspepsia, upset stomach | 5.5 | 9.7 (1–28) | 5.5 |
| Hepatotoxicity | —— | —— | 2 |
| Mouth and throat, dry | > 10 | 8.7 (0–17.4) | —— |
| Nausea | 5.5 | 5.1 (1–10) | 5.5 |
| Vomiting | 5.5 | —— | —— |
| Weight loss | 29.5 (1–63) | 13.5 (3–27) | 5.5 |
| Weight gain | —— | 4.3 | —— |
| **HEMATOLOGIC EFFECTS** | | | |
| Bruising, easy | —— | 5.5 | —— |
| **RENAL EFFECTS** | | | |
| Enuresis | —— | 9 (3–20) | —— |
| **SKIN, ALLERGIES, AND TEMPERATURE EFFECTS** | | | |
| Dermatitis, exfoliative | —— | 5.5 | —— |
| Diaphoresis | 5.5 | —— | —— |
| Fever, unexplained | —— | 5.5 | —— |
| Hives | < 1 | 5.5 | —— |
| Joint pain | —— | 5.5 | —— |
| Rashes | < 1 | 5.5 | 5.5 |

* These figures are primarily based on reports of children and adolescents treated for ADHD.

# PREGNANCY AND LACTATION

Teratogenicity (1st trimester)

- There is usually no compelling reason for a mother to stay on stimulants; therefore they should be discontinued.

- Dextroamphetamine may cause congenital malformations, such as cardiac abnormalities and biliary atresia.

- Methylphenidate not linked with congenital defects.

| Direct Effect on Newborn (3rd trimester) | • One case of IV dextroamphetamine use reported in woman to produce withdrawal in newborn; experts strongly discourage dextroamphetamine use during pregnancy. |
| --- | --- |

• Stimulants can increase BP and worsen pre-eclampsia.

• Stimulants are associated with premature delivery and low birth weight.

| Lactation | • One of 3 studies revealed infants of amphetamine-using mothers were more irritable and poor sleepers; no figures given. |
| --- | --- |

• Methylphenidate: no data.

## Drug Dosage in Mother's Milk

| Generic Name | Milk/ Plasma Ratio | Time of Peak Concentration in Milk (hours) | Infant Dose ($\mu$g/kg/day) | Maternal Dose (%) | Safety Rating* |
| --- | --- | --- | --- | --- | --- |
| Amphetamine | 2.8–7.5 | ? | 20.7 | 6.2 | C |

* C: Unsafe before week 34, relatively safe from weeks 34–44, and safest after 44th week.

## DRUG-DRUG INTERACTIONS

| Drugs (X) Interact with: | Dextroamphetamine (D) | Comments |
| --- | --- | --- |
| Acidifying agents (e.g., ascorbic acid, fruit juice, glutamic acid) | D↓↓ | Decreases absorption of amphetamines. |
| *Acetazolamide (and some furosemides) | D↑ | Acetazolamide increases amphetamines. Monitor patients on acetazolamide or on other carbonic anhydrase inhibitors for excessive amphetamine levels. |
| Alkalinizing agents (see sodium bicarbonate) | | |
| Amantadine | X↑ | Increased amantadine effect with stimulation and agitation. |
| Antihistamines | X↓ | Amphetamines reduce antihistamines' sedation. |
| Antihypertensives | X↓ | Amphetamines may antagonize antihypertensives. |

S
T
I
M
U
L
A
N
T
S

| Drugs (X) Interact with: | Dextroamphetamine (D) | Comments |
|---|---|---|
| *Antipsychotics:*<br>Chlorpromazine<br>Haloperidol | X↓ D↓ | Amphetamines inhibit antipsychotic actions, while neuroleptics block amphetamines' anorectic and stimulating effect. Antipsychotics effectively treat amphetamine overdose, but amphetamines should never treat an antipsychotic overdose. |
| Citalopram (*see* SSRIs)<br>Ethosuximide | X↓ | Amphetamines delay absorption of anticonvulsant ethosuximide. |
| Fluoxetine (*see* SSRIs)<br>Fluvoxamine (*see* SSRIs)<br>†Furazolidone | D↑ | Amphetamines induce hypertensive crises in patients given furazolidone, especially after 5 days. *Avoid.* |
| *Guanethidine | X↓ D↑ | Amphetamines inhibit guanethidine's antihypertensive action. Does hypertensive patient need amphetamines? Use another agent. |
| Haloperidol (*see* antipsychotics)<br>Lithium | D↓ | Lithium slows weight reduction and stimulatory effects of amphetamines. No special precautions. |
| Meperidine | X↑ | Amphetamines potentiate analgesic action. |
| †MAOIs | X↑ | *Hypertensive crisis.* Tranylcypromine is the most dangerous MAOI. |
| Norepinephrine | X↑ | Amphetamine use may increase pressor response to norepinephrine. Combine with caution. |
| Phenobarbitol, phenytoin | X↓ | Amphetamines delay absorption. May also decrease seizure threshold. |
| Propoxyphene | X↑ D↑ | Can increase CNS symptoms in propoxyphene overdose, causing fatal convulsions. |
| Opiates | X↑ | Amphetamines potentiate the analgesic and anorectic effect of opiates. |
| Paroxetine (*see* SSRIs)<br>Sedative hypnotics | X↓ | Reverses sedative and anxiolytic effects. |

| Drugs (X) Interact with: | Dextroamphetamine (D) | Comments |
|---|---|---|
| Sertraline (*see* SSRIs) | | |
| *Sodium bicarbonate | D↑ | Hefty sodium bicarbonate can increase amphetamines' effect; preferred by abusers. |
| SSRIs | X↑ D↑ | Increased agitation; may augment antidepressant effect. |
| *TCAs | X↑ D↑ | Amphetamines may increase TCA effect; can also produce arrhythmias, agitation, and psychosis. TCAs (desipramine, protriptyline) increase amphetamine levels. |

| Drugs (X) Interact with: | Methylphenidate (M) | Comments |
|---|---|---|
| *Anticonvulsants:* Phenytoin Diphenylhydantoin Primidone | X↑ | Increases plasma levels; isolated cases of intoxication. |
| *Guanethidine | X↓ M↑ | Methylphenidate inhibits guanethidine's antihypertensive action. Try another antihypertensive. |
| *MAOIs | X↑ | Methylphenidate poses less risk than amphetamines for hypertensive crisis, but methylphenidate should still be avoided with MAOIs. |
| TCAs | X↑ | Methylphenidate may facilitate TCAs' antidepressant and toxic effects and increase TCA levels. |
| Warfarin | M↑ | Increases levels of methylphenidate; monitor closely. |

| Drugs (X) Interact with: | Pemoline (P) | Comments |
|---|---|---|
| Sedative hypnotics | X↓ | Pemoline can interfere with anxiolytic and sedative effects. |
| Anticonvulsants | X↓ | Pemoline may lower seizure threshold. |

* Moderately important interactions; † Extremely important interactions; ↑ Increases; ↓ Decreases.

STIMULANTS

## EFFECTS ON LABORATORY TESTS

| Generic Names | Blood/Serum Tests | Results* | Urine Tests | Results* |
|---|---|---|---|---|
| Dextroamphetamine | Corticosteroids | ↑ | Steroid determinations | Interferes |
| | Growth hormone | ? | | |
| | Prolactin | ? | | |
| Methylphenidate | RBC, WBC | ↓ r ↓ r | None | |
| | Growth hormone | ? | | |
| | Prolactin | ? | | |
| Pemoline | LFT | ↑ | None | |

* ↑ Increases; ↓ Decreases; ? Inconsistent; r = rarely; LFT are AST/SGOT, ALT/SGPT, LDH, alkaline phosphatase, and bilirubin.

## WITHDRAWAL

Stimulants can cause

- Psychological dependence
- Drug misuse

Stimulants less commonly cause

- Physical dependence
- Tolerance (more commonly in narcolepsy)
- Addiction
- Physical withdrawal

From the most to the least abused are

- Dextroamphetamine (Schedule II)
  √ At dosage of > 50 mg/day can often generate serious but not life-threatening withdrawal.
- Methylphenidate (Schedule II)
  √ Abused orally when mixed with other drugs.
  √ Addicts grind up tablets, inject, and develop emboli.
- Pemoline (Schedule IV)
  √ Rarely an addiction problem.

Dextroamphetamine and methylphenidate withdrawal symptoms include

- Increased appetite, weight gain
  √ Appetite may be huge for several days.
- Increased sleep
  √ Sleep may be excessive at first, and
  √ Often with vivid, disturbing dreams.

- Decreased energy, fatigue, psychomotor retardation, depression.
  - √ Rapid withdrawal, especially from high doses, can lead to profound inertia, depressed mood ("crashing"), and suicide.
- Paranoid symptoms may persist during withdrawal, but this is uncommon.

## Cocaine and Stimulant Withdrawal/Abuse

### Management

- Observe patient.
- Prevent suicide.
- Frequently reassure patient.
- About 30% of chronic heavy cocaine abusers have evidence of significant EKG abnormalities (N = 40).
  - √ 53% of subjects had ST-T wave abnormalities.
  - √ 37% had myocardial ischemia.
  - √ 31% had right bundle branch block (RBBB).
  - √ 29% had left ventricular hypertrophy (LVH).
  - √ 9% had evidence of old infarction.
  - √ 4.5% had premature ventricular contractions.
  - √ 4.5% had sinus arrhythmia.
- Give TCAs
  - √ If patient is depressed.
    - □ Since amphetamine and cocaine withdrawal involves noradrenergic activity, TCAs (e.g., desipramine) that increase noradrenergic (over serotonin) function are preferred.
  - √ If patient is not depressed
    - □ About half of studies did, and half did not, show desipramine helps in early abstinence.
    - □ Case reports suggest bupropion may help.
    - □ Case reports suggest SSRIs may lower craving, but depressed abusers still preferred TCAs (desipramine).
- Dopamine agonists
  - √ Generally have faster onset than desipramine.
  - √ Bromocriptine and amantadine in high doses sometimes decrease craving.
    - □ Amantadine better tolerated.
  - √ Open trial suggests pergolide decreases sleep and craving. Compared to bromocriptine it has
    - □ Longer duration of action and
    - □ More rapid onset of action.

Chronic amphetamine abuse may be treated best with desipramine or bupropion.

- Good short-term effect (1–6 weeks).
- Long-term outcome (3–6 months) only modestly improved.

Bupropion's seizure risk is of concern in ongoing stimulant user.

No medication specifically treats stimulant misuse.

## OVERDOSE: TOXICITY, SUICIDE, AND TREATMENT

Death rarely occurs from overdoses of prescribed stimulants, since there is a large difference between the therapeutic and toxic doses of the drug. Nevertheless, a 10-day supply taken at once can be very toxic, even lethal, especially in children.

Most amphetamine overdoses are from illegal, not clinically obtained, drugs.

Amphetamine overdoses produce

- Agitation (21%)
- Suicidal ideation (12%)
- Chest pain (9%)
- Hallucinations (auditory > visual) (7%)
- Confusion (6%)
- Dysphoria, weakness, lethargy (5%)
- Delusions (5%)

Other symptoms (< 5%) include

- Seizures, hyperreflexia, fever, tremor, rhabdomyolysis, hypertension or hypotension, stroke, aggression, headache, palpitations, abdominal pain, rashes, dyspnea, leg pain, and paresthesias.

For the general management of stimulant overdoses, *see* pages 65–67.

For specific symptoms of stimulant overdoses, other treatments include:

- For seizures
  √ Short-acting barbiturates (e.g., amobarbital) or
  √ IV diazepam.
- For agitation
  √ Haloperidol and diazepam are equally effective.
- For psychosis
  √ Isolate patient from environmental stimuli, which aggravate psychosis.

√ Haloperidol 2.5–5 mg IM prn q 2 h, or
√ Chlorpromazine 25–50 mg IM prn q 2 h.
- For high blood pressure
  √ Hasten excretion by acidifying urine with ammonium chloride.
  √ If hypertension is severe, may administer phentolamine 5 mg IV.
  √ May employ hypothermic measures if intracranial pressure rises.
  √ Combat cerebral edema and congestion.

**Toxicity and Suicide Data**

| Generic Names* | Toxicity Doses Average (Highest) (mg) | Mortality Doses Average (Lowest) (mg) | Fatal Supplies (days) | Toxic Levels (mg/ml) |
|---|---|---|---|---|
| Dextroamphetamine | 20 (1.5 mg/kg) | 400 | —— | —— |

* No data on methylphenidate or pemoline.

## PRECAUTIONS

Contraindications include

- Anxiety and agitation
- History of drug abuse (unless a solid clinical reason)
- Advanced arteriosclerosis, cardiovascular disease, hypertension
- Hyperthyroidism
- Allergy to stimulants
- Glaucoma
- Tics or Tourette's syndrome (in patients or family members)
- MAOIs
  √ Wait 14 days after MAOI discontinued.

Patients with seizure history or seizure risks are more likely to have seizures with stimulants.

If patient on pemoline has decreased appetite, fatigue, and stomach fullness, hepatotoxicity should be suspected and liver function tests ordered.

Decrements in predicted growth are reported after long-term use of stimulants; observe and chart.

## NURSES' DATA

Stress that stimulants have different medical and recreational uses.

- The medical stimulant alleviates specific symptoms, whereas the goal of recreational stimulant use is to get high.
- Patients given medical stimulants often do not develop a "high" or experience tolerance.

If a question exists about whether an adult or child is illegally trying (or selling) the drug, raise the issue tactfully but firmly.

Closely monitor the patient's

- Cardiovascular symptoms and vital signs,
- Blood glucose in diabetics (if appetite and food intake are affected),
- Signs of dextroamphetamine or methylphenidate withdrawal, intoxication, or overdose, and
- Slowing of growth.

## PATIENT AND FAMILY NOTES

A 10-day supply of stimulants can be lethal for children.

- Patients who take stimulants can sometimes become depressed.
  √ Patients who suddenly stop taking stimulants also become depressed.
  √ Monitor a youngster's use of the drug, just as one would any other drug.

Keep stimulants away from bedside or from any readily accessible place to deter accidental intake. For safety, protect other children by keeping pills in a safe place.

Family and patients should not make a "big deal" about taking stimulants: "It's a medication, like any medication."

Tell families that

- Most common temporary effects are anorexia, insomnia, abdominal pain, headaches, irritability, and moodiness.
- Temporary growth suppression may occur, but this usually is not permanent.

Tell families to *avoid*

- Excessive intake of sodium bicarbonate because it alkalinizes the urine, which reduces amphetamine excretion and prolongs its effects.

- Starvation and unprescribed dietary changes (e.g., increased vitamin C, citric acid intake) acidify the urine, which induces ketosis, accelerates amphetamine elimination, and lowers its effect.

Stimulants have no long-term effective role in weight-loss programs. Beware of a few weight-loss clinics touting the lifelong use of stimulants alone or with SSRIs in morbidly obese.

If anxiety erupts, excessive caffeine may be the culprit.

If patient neglects a dose

- Can take the medication up to 3 h later.
- Otherwise, wait for next dose.
- Never double the dose.

If patient forgets a long-acting (sustained-release) pill

- Take it the next morning.

## Dosage Times

- Dextroamphetamine
  - √ Give tablet or elixir early—possibly on awakening—or 30–60 minutes before breakfast.
  - √ Offer other doses at 4–6-h intervals.
    - ▫ Do not take within 6 h of bedtime, especially sustained-acting products.
    - ▫ Doses gobbled after breakfast or lunch are less likely to alter sleep or food intake.
  - √ If side effects (e.g., insomnia, anorexia) arise, try the once-a-day dextroamphetamine spansule.
- Methylphenidate
  - √ First dose with breakfast, which might reduce stomachaches.
  - √ Do not take within 6 h of sleep.
  - √ If insomnia or anorexia develop, consider the (8-h) methylphenidate-SR tablet.
  - √ Avoid the methylphenidate-SR tablet at first; try it later.
- Pemoline
  - √ Give as a single morning tablet and increase the morning strength.

# Appendices

## 1. DRUG IDENTIFICATION BY GENERIC NAME

| Generic | Brand Name | Chief Action |
|---------|-----------|--------------|
| acebutolol | Sectral | $\beta$-blocker (CS) |
| acetaminophen* | Tylenol | Analgesic |
| acetazolamide | Diamox | Carbonic anhydrase inhibitor |
| acetophenazine | Tindal | Neuroleptic |
| albuterol | Proventil | Sympathomimetic (DA) $\beta$ |
| alpha-methyldopa | Aldomet | Antihypertensive |
| alprazolam | Xanax | Antianxiety |
| aluminum hydroxide* | Gelusil | Antacid |
| amantadine | Symmetrel | Antiparkinsonian, antiviral |
| ambenonium chloride | Mytelase | Cholinomimetic |
| amiloride | Midamor | Potassium-sparing diuretic |
| aminophylline | Mudrane | Bronchodilator |
| amiodarone | Cordarone | Antiarrhythmic (III) |
| amitriptyline | Elavil | TCA |
| amobarbital | Amytal | Hypnotic |
| amoxapine | Asendin | HCA |
| ampicillin | Omnipen | Penicillin |
| anisotropine | Valpin | Anticholinergic |
| antipyrine | Auralgan | Analgesic (otic) |
| astemizole | Hismanal | Antihystamine (H1) |
| atenolol | Tenormin | $\beta$-blocker, antisocial phobia |
| atropine | Atropine Sulfate | Anticholinergic |
| azatadine | Optimine | Antihistamine |
| azithromycin dihydrate | Zithromax | Antibacterial (macrolide) |
| baclofen | Lioresal | Skeletal muscle relaxant |
| beclomethasone | Vanceril | Corticosteroid |
| benazepril hydrochloride | Lotensin | Antihypertensive (ACE) |
| benztropine | Cogentin | Antiparkinsonian |
| bepridil hydrochloride | Vascor | Calcium-channel blocker, antianginal |
| bethanechol | Urecholine | Cholinergic, anticholinesterase |
| biperiden | Akineton | Antiparkinsonian anticholinergic |
| bromocriptine | Parlodel | Prolactin inhibitor, antiparkinsonian, dopamine agonist |
| bupropion | Wellbutrin | Atypical antidepressant, HCA |
| buspirone | BuSpar | Antianxiety |
| butabarbital | Butisol | Antianxiety |
| caffeine | No Doz | CNS stimulant |
| calcium carbonate* | Tums | Antacid |

**453**

| Generic | Brand Name | Chief Action |
|---|---|---|
| captopril | Capoten | Antihypertensive (ACE) |
| carbamazepine | Tegretol | Anticonvulsant, anticycling |
| carbidopa-levodopa | Sinemet | Antiparkinsonian |
| carisoprodol | Soma | Muscle relaxant |
| casanthranol* | Peri-Colace | Laxative |
| cephalexin | Keflex | Antibiotic |
| chloral hydrate | Noctec | Hypnotic |
| chloramphenicol | Chloromycetin | Antibiotic |
| chlordiazepoxide | Librium | Antianxiety |
| chloroquine | Aralen | Antimalarial |
| chlorothiazide | Diuril | Thiazide diuretic |
| chlorpheniramine* | Chlortrimeton | Antihistamine |
| chlorpromazine | Thorazine | Neuroleptic |
| chlorprothixene | Taractan | Neuroleptic |
| cholestyramine | Questran | Hypolipidemic |
| cimetidine | Tagamet | $H_2$-receptor antagonist |
| ciprofloxacin hydrochloride | Cipro | Antibacterial |
| citalopram | Celexa | SSRI |
| clarithromycin | Biaxin | Antibacterial (macrolide) |
| clidinium bromide | Quarzan | Anticholingeric |
| clomipramine | Anafranil | TCA |
| clonazepam | Klonopin | Antianxiety, anticonvulsant |
| clonidine | Catapres | Antihypertensive, $\alpha_2$ agonist |
| clorazepate | Tranxene | Antianxiety |
| clozapine | Clozaril | Neuroleptic |
| cromolyn | Gastrocrom | Mast cell stabilizer |
| cyclobenzaprine | Flexeril | Muscle relaxant (tricyclic) |
| cyclosporine | Sandimmune | Immunosuppressant |
| cyproheptadine | Periactin | Antihistamine, serotonin antagonist |
| danazol | Danocrine | Androgen derivative, gonadotropin inhibitor |
| dantrolene | Dantrium | Skeletal muscle relaxant |
| desipramine | Norpramin | TCA |
| dextroamphetamine | Dexedrine | Stimulant |
| dextromethorphan* | "DM" products | Cough suppressor |
| diazepam | Valium | Antianxiety |
| dichloralphenazone | Midrin | Analgesic-sedative |
| diclofenac sodium | Voltaren | Anti-inflammatory (NSAID) |
| dicumarol | Dicumarol | Anticoagulant (oral) |
| dicyclomine hydrochloride | Bentyl | Anticholinergic |
| digoxin | Lanoxin | Cardiac glycoside |
| diltiazem | Cardizem | Calcium channel-blocker |
| diphenhydramine* | Benadryl | Antihistamine |
| disopyramide | Norpace | Antiarrhythmic (1) |
| disulfiram | Antabuse | Alcohol blockade |
| divalproex | Depakote | Anticonvulsant, mood stabilizer |
| dobutamine hydrochloride | Dobutrex | Sympathomimetic (DA) $\alpha\beta$ |
| docusate* | Colace | Stool softener |
| donepezil | Aricept | Enhances cholinergic function |
| dopamine | Intropin | Sympathomimetic (MA) $\alpha\beta$ |
| doxapram | Dopram | Respiratory stimulant |
| doxepin | Sinequan | TCA |
| doxycycline | Vibramycin | Tetracycline antibiotic |
| droperidol | Inapsine | Antiemetic, antianxiety, neuroleptic |
| edrophonium chloride | Tensilon | Cholinomimetic |
| enalapril | Vasotec | Antihypertensive (ACE) |
| enflurane | Ethrane | Anesthetic (general) |
| ephedrine* | Marax | Vasoconstrictor |
| epinephrine* | Primatene | Sympathomimetic (DA) $\alpha\beta$ |
| ergotamine tartrate | Ergostat | Ergot alkaloid |

| Generic | Brand Name | Chief Action |
|---|---|---|
| erythromycin ethylsuccinate | Pediazole | Antibacterial (macrolide) |
| estazolam | ProSom | Hypnotic |
| estrogens, conjugated | Premarin | Estrogen |
| ethacrynic acid | Edecrin | Loop diuretic |
| ethchlorvynol | Placidyl | Hypnotic |
| ethosuximide | Zarontin | Anticonvulsant |
| famotidine | Mylanta, Pepcid | $H_2$-receptor antagonist |
| felbamate | Felbatol | Anticonvulsant |
| fenfluramine | Pondimin | Serotonergic anorectic |
| flecainide acetate | Tambocor | Antiarrhythmic (1) |
| fludrocortisone | Florinef | Mineral corticoid |
| fluoxetine | Prozac | SSRI |
| fluphenazine | Permitil | Neuroleptic |
| fluphenazine | Prolixin | Neuroleptic |
| flurazepam | Dalmane | Hypnotic |
| fluvoxamine | Luvox | SSRI |
| fosinopril sodium | Monopril | Antihypertensive (ACE) |
| furazolidone | Furoxone | Antibiotic |
| furosemide | Lasix | Loop diuretic |
| gabapentin | Neurontin | Anticonvulsant |
| galantamine | Reminyl | Cholinergic function enhanced |
| gallium nitrate | Ganite | Hypocalcemic |
| gemfibrozil | Lopid | Hypolipidemic |
| glucagon | Glucagon | Antihypoglycemic |
| glutethimide | Doriden | Hypnotic |
| glyburide | Micronase | Hypoglycemic |
| glycopyrrolate | Robinal | Anticholinergic |
| griseofulvin | Fulvicin | Antibiotic |
| guanadrel | Hylorel | Antihypertensive |
| guanethidine | Ismelin | Antihypertensive |
| halazepam | Paxipam | Antianxiety |
| haloperidol | Haldol | Neuroleptic |
| halothane | Fluothane | Anesthetic |
| hydralazine | Apresoline | Antihypertensive |
| hydrochlorthiazide | Aldoril | Thiazide diuretic |
| hydroxyzine | Atarax, Vistaril | Antihistamine, antianxiety |
| hyoscyamine sulfate | Levsin | Anticholinergic, antispasmodic |
| ibuprofen* | Motrin | NSAID |
| imipramine | Janimine, Tofranil | TCA |
| indomethacin | Indocin | NSAID |
| ipratropium bromide | Bronkosol | Bronchodilator |
| isocarboxazid | Marplan | MAOI |
| isoniazid | Rifamate | Antibiotic |
| isoproterenol | Isuprel | Sympathomimetic (DA) $\beta$ |
| isosorbide | Isordil | Antianginal |
| itraconazole | Sporanox | Antifungal |
| ketamine | Ketalar | Anesthetic (general) |
| ketoconazole | Nizoral | Antifungal agent |
| ketoprofen | Orudis | NSAID |
| ketorolac tromethamine | Toradol | NSAID |
| labetalol | Normodyne | $\beta$-blocker (CS) |
| lamotrigine | Lamictal | Anticonvulsant |
| levodopa | Larodopa | Antiparkinsonian |
| lidocaine* | Xylocaine | Anesthetic (local), antiarrhythmic |
| liothyronine ($T_3$) | Cytomel | Thyroid hormone |
| lisinopril | Prinivil, Zestril | Antihypertensive |
| lithium | Eskalith, Lithane, Lithobid | Mood regulator, Anticycling |
| loperidide | Imodium | Antidiarrheal |
| lorazepam | Ativan | Antianxiety |

APPENDICES

| Generic | Brand Name | Chief Action |
|---|---|---|
| loxapine | Loxitane | Neuroleptic |
| magnesium hydroxide* | Maalox | Antacid |
| maprotiline | Ludiomil | HCA |
| mazindol | Sanorex | Anorectic agent |
| mebendazole | Vermox | Anthelmintic agent |
| mefenamic acid | Ponstel | NSAID |
| melatonin | Bevitamel | Enhances natural sleep process |
| meperidine | Demerol | Narcotic analgesic |
| meprobamate | Miltown, Equanil | Antianxiety |
| mesoridazine | Serentil | Neuroleptic |
| metaproterenol | Alupent | Sympathomimetic (DA) $\beta$ |
| metaraminol | Aramine | Sympathomimetic (MA) $\alpha\beta$ |
| methabarbital | Mebaral | Antianxiety |
| methadone | Dolophine | Narcotic analgesic |
| methimazole | Tapazole | Antithyroid drug |
| methotrimeprazine | Levoprome | CNS depressant |
| methyldopa | Aldomet | Antihypertensive |
| methylphenidate | Ritalin | Stimulant |
| methyltestosterone | Android | Androgen derivative |
| methyprylon | Noludar | Hypnotic |
| metoclopramide | Reglan | Dopamine blocking antiemetic |
| metoprolol | Lopressor | $\beta$-blocker (CS) |
| metronidazole | Flagyl | Antibiotic |
| mirtazapine | Remeron | Antidepressant |
| modafinil | Provigil | Anti-narcolepsy |
| molindone | Moban | Neuroleptic |
| morphine | Roxanol | Narcotic |
| nadolol | Corgard | $\beta$-blocker (CS) |
| naloxone | Narcan | Narcotic antagonist |
| naltrexone | ReVia | Narcotic antagonist |
| naproxen | Anaprox, Aleve | NSAID |
| nefazodone | Serzone | Antidepressant |
| neostigmine | Prostigmin | Anticholinesterase, cholinomimetic |
| nicotine | Habitrol | Smoking deterrent |
| nifedipine | Procardia | Calcium channel-blocker |
| nimodipine | Nimotop | Calcium channel-blocker |
| nitrofurantoin | Macrobid | Antibacterial agent |
| nitroprusside | Nipride | Antihypertensive |
| nizatidine | Axid | NSAID |
| norepinephrine | Levophed | Sympathomimetic (DA) $\alpha\beta$ |
| nortriptyline | Aventyl, Pamelor | TCA |
| olanzapine | Zyprexa | Antipsychotic |
| omeprazole | Prilosec | Gastric acid pump inhibitor |
| ondansetron hydrochloride | Zofran | Antiemetic |
| orphenadrine | Norflex | Analgesic, anticholinergic |
| oxazepam | Serax | Antianxiety |
| pancuronium | Pavulon | Neuromuscular blocker |
| paraldehyde | Paral | Hypnotic |
| pargyline | Eutonyl | MAOI |
| paroxetine | Paxil | SSRI |
| pemoline | Cylert | Stimulant |
| penbutalol | Levatol | $\beta$-blocker (NCS) |
| pentazocine | Talwin | Narcotic agonist-antagonist |
| pentobarbital | Nembutal | Hypnosedative |
| pentoxifylline | Trental | Hematologic agent |
| pergolide | Permax | Dopamine agonist |
| perphenazine | Trilafon | Neuroleptic |
| phendimetrazine | Bontril, Plegine, Prelu-2 | Sympathomimetic amine |
| phenelzine | Nardil | MAOI |
| phenmetrazine | Preludin | Anorectic agent |
| phenobarbital | Luminal | Anticonvulsant, sedative |

| Generic | Brand Name | Chief Action |
|---|---|---|
| phentermine | Fastin | Sympathomimetic anorectic |
| phentolamine | Regitine | Antihypertensive |
| phenylbutazone | Butazolidin | NSAID |
| phenylephrine* | Neo-Synephrine | Sympathomimetic (MA) $\alpha\beta$ |
| phenylpropanolamine* | Acutrim | Sympathomimetic (IA) $\alpha\beta$, anorectic |
| phenytoin | Dilantin | Anticonvulsant |
| physostigmine | Antilirium | Anticholinesterase |
| pimozide | Orap | Neuroleptic |
| pindolol | Visken | $\beta$-blocker (NCS) |
| piroxicam | Feldene | NSAID |
| prazepam | Centrax | Antianxiety |
| prazosin | Minipress | Antihypertensive |
| primidone | Mysoline | Anticonvulsant |
| probenecid | Benemid | Uricosuric agent, antigout |
| procainamide | Pronestyl | Antiarrhythmic (1A) |
| prochlorperazine | Compazine | Antiemetic, dopamine blocker |
| procyclidine | Kemadrin | Antiparkinsonian, anticholinergic |
| promethazine | Phenergan | Antihistamine, antiemetic |
| propantheline bromide | Pro-Banthine | Anticholinergic |
| propoxyphene | Darvon | Opioid analgesic |
| propranolol | Inderal | $\beta$-blocker (NCS) |
| protriptyline | Vivactil | TCA |
| pseudoephedrine* | Sudafed | Sympathomimetic (IA) $\alpha\beta$ |
| psyllium* | Metamucil | Bulk laxative |
| pyrimethamine | Daraprim | Antimalerial |
| quazepam | Doral | Hypnotic |
| quinapril | Accupril | Antihypertensive (ACE) |
| quetiapine | Seroquel | Antipsychotic |
| quinidine | Quinidine | Antiarrhythmic (1A) |
| quinine | Quinamm | Skeletal muscle relaxant |
| ramipril | Altace | Antihypertensive (ACE) |
| ranitidine | Zantac | $H_2$ blocker |
| reserpine | Serpasil | Antihypertensive |
| rifampin | Rifadin | Antibiotic |
| risperidone | Risperdal | Antipsychotic |
| rivastigmine | Exelon | Cholinesterase inhibitor |
| scopolamine | Transderm Scop | Anticholinergic, antiemetic |
| secobarbital | Seconal | Hypnotic |
| selegiline | Eldepryl | MAOI B |
| sertraline | Zoloft | SSRI |
| spectinomycin | Trobicin | Antibiotic (macrolide) |
| spironolactone | Aldactone | Potassium-sparing diuretic |
| succinylcholine | Anectine | Neuromuscular blocker |
| sulfadoxine | Fansidar | Antimalarial agent |
| sulfamethoxazole | Gantanol | Antibacterial |
| sulindac | Clinoril | NSAID |
| sumatriptan succinate | Imitrex | Antimigrane agent, $5HT_3$ agent |
| tacrine | Cognex | Cholinergic, antidementia |
| temazepam | Restoril | Hypnotic |
| terbutaline | Brethine | Sympathomimetic (DA) $\beta$ |
| terfenadine | Seldane | Antihistamine |
| tetrabenazine | ——— | Depletes & blocks dopamine |
| tetracycline* | Achromycin | Antibiotic |
| theophylline* | Bronkaid | Bronchodilator |
| thiopental | Pentothal | Anesthetic (general) |
| thioridazine | Mellaril | Neuroleptic |
| thiothixene | Navane | Neuroleptic |
| ticarcillin disodium | Ticar | Antibacterial |
| timolol maleate | Blocadren | $\beta$-blocker (NCS) |
| tocainide | Tonocard | Antiarrhythmic (1) |
| topiramate | Topamax | Antiseizure |

| Generic | Brand Name | Chief Action |
|---------|-----------|--------------|
| tranylcypromine | Parnate | MAOI |
| trazodone | Desyrel | Atypical antidepressant |
| triamterene | Dyrenium | Potassium-sparing diuretic |
| triazolam | Halcion | Hypnotic |
| trifluoperazine | Stelazine | Neuroleptic |
| trihexyphenidyl | Artane | Antiparkinsonian, anticholinergic |
| trimethobenzamide | Tigan | Antiemetic dopamine blocker |
| trimethobenzamide | Bactrim, Septra | Antibiotic |
| trimipramine | Surmontil | TCA |
| troleandomycin | Tao | Antibacterial (macrolide) |
| tubocurarine | Tubocurarine | Neuromuscular blocker |
| tyramine | | Sympathomimetic (IA) $\alpha\beta$ |
| urea* | Debrox | Earwax drops |
| valproic acid | Depakene | Anticonvulsant |
| vecuronium bromide | Norcuron | Neuromuscular blocker |
| venlafaxine | Effexor | Antidepressant |
| verapamil | Isoptin | Calcium channel-blocker |
| vinblastine | Velban | Antineoplastic |
| warfarin | Coumadin | Anticoagulant (oral) |
| yohimbine* | Yocon | Presynaptic $\alpha_2$ antagonist |
| zaleplon | Sonata | Hypnotic, anticonvulsant |
| zidovudine | Retrovir | Antiviral |
| ziprasidone | Geodon | Neuroleptic |
| zolpidem | Ambien | Hypnotic, anticonvulsant |

Codes:
* Can be sold in nonprescription drug.
NSAID = nonsteroidal anti-inflammatory agent. $\beta$ blockers: (CS) = cardioselective; (NCS) = noncardioselective
Sympathomimetics: (DA) = direct acting; (IA) = indirect acting; (MA) = mixed acting; $\alpha$ = alpha antagonist; $\beta$ = beta agonist.
ACE = angiotensin converting enzyme inhibitor.

# 2. DRUG IDENTIFICATION BY BRAND NAME

| Brand Name | Generic | Chief Action |
|-----------|---------|--------------|
| Accupril | quinapril | Antihypertensive (ACE) |
| Achromycin | tetracycline | Antibiotic |
| Akineton | biperiden | Antiparkinsonian anticholinergic |
| Aldactone | spironolactone | Potassium-sparing diuretic |
| Aldomet | methyldopa | Antihypertensive |
| Aldoril | hydrochlorthiazide | Thiazide diuretic |
| Altace | ramipril | Antihypertensive (ACE) |
| Alupent | metaproterenol | Sympathomimetic (DA) $\beta$ |
| Ambien | zolpidem | Hypnotic, anticonvulsant |
| Amytal | amobarbital | Hypnotic |
| Anafranil | clomipramine | TCA |
| Anaprox, Aleve | naproxen | NSAID |
| Android | methyltestosterone | Androgen derivative |
| Anectine | succinylcholine | Neuromuscular blocker |
| Antabuse | disulfiram | Alcohol blockade |
| Antilirium | physostigmine | Anticholinesterase |
| Apresoline | hydralazine | Antihypertensive |
| Aralen | chloroquine | Antimalarial |
| Aramine | metaraminol | Sympathomimetic (MA) $\alpha\beta$ |
| Aricept | donepezil | Enhances cholinergic function |
| Artane | trihexyphenidyl | Antiparkinsonian, anticholinergic |

| Brand Name | Generic | Chief Action |
|---|---|---|
| Asendin | amoxapine | HCA |
| Atarax, Vistaril | hydroxyzine | Antihistamine, antianxiety |
| Ativan | lorazepam | Antianxiety |
| Atropine Sulfate | atropine | Anticholinergic |
| Auralgan | antipyrine | Analgesic (otic) |
| Aventyl, Pamelor | nortriptyline | TCA |
| Axid | nizatidine | NSAID |
| Bactrim, Septra | trimethobenzamide | Antibiotic |
| Benadryl | diphenhydramine* | Antihistamine |
| Benemid | probenecid | Uricosuric agent, antigout |
| Bentyl | dicyclomine hydrochloride | Anticholinergic |
| Bevitamel | melatonin | Enhances natural sleep process |
| Biaxin | clarithromycin | Antibacterial (macrolide) |
| Blocadren | timolol maleate | $\beta$-blocker (NCS) |
| Bontril, Plegine, Prelu-2 | phendimetrazine | Sympathomimetic amine |
| Brethine | terbutaline | Sympathomimetic (DA) $\beta$ |
| Bronkaid | theophylline* | Bronchodilator |
| Bronkosol | ipratropium bromide | Bronchodilator |
| BuSpar | buspirone | Antianxiety |
| Butazolidin | phenylbutazone | NSAID |
| Butisol | butabarbital | Antianxiety |
| Capoten | captopril | Antihypertensive (ACE) |
| Cardizem | diltiazem | Calcium channel-blocker |
| Catapres | clonidine | Antihypertensive, $\alpha_2$ agonist |
| Celexa | citalopram | SSRI |
| Centrax | prazepam | Antianxiety |
| Chloromycetin | chloramphenicol | Antibiotic |
| Chlortrimeton | chlorpheniramine* | Antihistamine |
| Cipro | ciprofloxacin hydrochloride | Antibacterial |
| Clinoril | sulindac | NSAID |
| Clozaril | clozapine | Neuroleptic |
| Cogentin | benztropine | Antiparkinsonian |
| Cognex | tacrine | Cholinergic, antidementia |
| Colace | docusate* | Stool softener |
| Compazine | prochlorperazine | Antiemetic, dopamine blocker |
| Cordarone | amiodarone | Antiarrhythmic (III) |
| Corgard | nadolol | $\beta$-blocker (CS) |
| Coumadin | warfarin | Anticoagulant (oral) |
| Cylert | pemoline | Stimulant |
| Cytomel | liothyronine ($T_3$) | Thyroid hormone |
| Dalmane | flurazepam | Hypnotic |
| Danocrine | danazol | Androgen derivative, gonadotropin inhibitor |
| Dantrium | dantrolene | Skeletal muscle relaxant |
| Daraprim | pyrimethamine | Antimalerial |
| Darvon | propoxyphene | Opioid analgesic |
| Debrox | urea* | Earwax drops |
| Demerol | meperidine | Narcotic analgesic |
| Depakene | valproic acid | Anticonvulsant |
| Depakote | divalproex | Anticonvulsant, mood stabilizer |
| Desyrel | trazodone | Atypical antidepressant |
| Dexedrine | dextroamphetamine | Stimulant |
| Diamox | acetazolamide | Carbonic anhydrase inhibitor |
| Dicumarol | dicumarol | Anticoagulant (oral) |
| Dilantin | phenytoin | Anticonvulsant |
| Diuril | chlorothiazide | Thiazide diuretic |
| "DM" products (see pages 189–90) | dextromethorphan* | Cough suppressor |
| Dobutrex | dobutamine hydrochloride | Sympathomimetic (DA) $\alpha\beta$ |

| Brand Name | Generic | Chief Action |
| --- | --- | --- |
| Dolophine | methadone | Narcotic analgesic |
| Dopram | doxapram | Respiratory stimulant |
| Doral | quazepam | Hypnotic |
| Doriden | glutethimide | Hypnotic |
| Dyrenium | triamterene | Potassium-sparing diuretic |
| Edecrin | ethacrynic acid | Loop diuretic |
| Effexor | venlafaxine | Antidepressant |
| Elavil | amitriptyline | TCA |
| Eldepryl | selegiline | MAOI B |
| Ergostat | ergotamine tartrate | Ergot alkaloid |
| Eskalith, Lithane, Lithobid | lithium | Mood regulator, anticycling |
| Ethrane | enflurane | Anesthetic (general) |
| Eutonyl | pargyline | MAOI |
| Exelon | rivastigmine | Cholinergic function enhanced |
| Fansidar | sulfadoxine | Antimalarial agent |
| Fastin | phentermine | Sympathomimetic anorectic |
| Felbatol | felbamate | Anticonvulsant |
| Feldene | piroxicam | NSAID |
| Flagyl | metronidazole | Antibiotic |
| Flexeril | cyclobenzaprine | Muscle relaxant (tricyclic) |
| Florinef | fludrocortisone | Mineral corticoid |
| Fluothane | halothane | Anesthetic |
| Fulvicin | griseofulvin | Antibiotic |
| Furoxone | furazolidone | Antibiotic |
| Ganite | gallium nitrate | Hypocalcemic |
| Gantanol | sulfamethoxazole | Antibacterial |
| Gastrocrom | cromolyn | Mast cell stabilizer |
| Gelusil | aluminum hydroxide* | Antacid |
| Geodon | ziprasidone | Neuroleptic |
| Glucagon | glucagon | Antihypoglycemic |
| Habitrol | nicotine | Smoking deterrent |
| Halcion | triazolam | Hypnotic |
| Haldol | haloperidol | Neuroleptic |
| Hismanal | astemizole | Antihystamine (H1) |
| Hylorel | guanadrel | Antihypertensive |
| Imitrex | sumatriptan succinate | Antimigraine agent, $5HT_3$ agent |
| Imodium | loperidide | Antidiarrheal |
| Inapsine | droperidol | Antiemetic, antianxiety, neuroleptic |
| Inderal | propranolol | $\beta$-blocker (NCS) |
| Indocin | indomethacin | NSAID |
| Intropin | dopamine | Sympathomimetic (MA) $\alpha\beta$ |
| Ismelin | guanethidine | Antihypertensive |
| Isoptin | verapamil | Calcium channel-blocker |
| Isordil | isosorbide | Antianginal |
| Isuprel | isoproterenol | Sympathomimetic (DA) $\beta$ |
| Janimine, Tofranil | imipramine | TCA |
| Keflex | cephalexin | Antibiotic |
| Kemadrin | procyclidine | Antiparkinsonian, anticholinergic |
| Kerlone | betaxolol hydrochloride | $\beta$-blocker (CS) |
| Ketalar | ketamine | Anesthetic (general) |
| Klonopin | clonazepam | Antianxiety, Anticonvulsant |
| Lamictal | lamotrigine | Anticonvulsant |
| Lanoxin | digoxin | Cardiac glycoside |
| Larodopa | levodopa | Antiparkinsonian |
| Lasix | furosemide | Loop diuretic |
| Levatol | penbutalol | $\beta$-blocker (NCS) |
| Levophed | norepinephrine | Sympathomimetic (DA) $\alpha\beta$ |
| Levoprome | methotrimeprazine | CNS depressant |
| Levsin | hyoscyamine sulfate | Anticholinergic, antispasmodic |
| Librium | chlordiazepoxide | Antianxiety |

| Brand Name | Generic | Chief Action |
| --- | --- | --- |
| Lioresal | baclofen | Skeletal muscle relaxant |
| Lopid | gemfibrozil | Hypolipidemic |
| Lopressor | metoprolol | $\beta$-blocker (CS) |
| Lotensin | benazepril hydrochloride | Antihypertensive (ACE) |
| Loxitane | loxapine | Neuroleptic |
| Ludiomil | maprotiline | HCA |
| Luminal | phenobarbital | Anticonvulsant, sedative |
| Luvox | fluvoxamine | SSRI |
| Maalox | magnesium hydroxide* | Antacid |
| Macrobid | nitrofurantoin | Antibacterial agent |
| Marax | ephedrine* | Vasoconstrictor |
| Marplan | isocarboxazid | MAOI |
| Mebaral | methabarbital | Antianxiety |
| Mellaril | thioridazine | Neuroleptic |
| Metamucil | psyllium* | Bulk laxative |
| Micronase | glyburide | Hypoglycemic |
| Midamor | amiloride | Potassium-sparing diuretic |
| Midrin | dichloralphenazone | Analgesic-sedative |
| Miltown, Equanil | meprobamate | Antianxiety |
| Minipress | prazosin | Antihypertensive |
| Moban | molindone | Neuroleptic |
| Monopril | fosinopril sodium | Antihypertensive (ACE) |
| Motrin | ibuprofen* | NSAID |
| Mudrane | aminophylline | Bronchodilator |
| Mylanta, Pepcid | famotidine | $H_2$-receptor antagonist |
| Mysoline | primidone | Anticonvulsant |
| Mytelase | ambenonium chloride | Cholinomimetic |
| Narcan | naloxone | Narcotic antagonist |
| Nardil | phenelzine | MAOI |
| Navane | thiothixene | Neuroleptic |
| Nembutal | pentobarbital | Hypnosedative |
| Neo-Synephrine | phenylephrine* | Sympathomimetic (MA) $\alpha\beta$ |
| Neurontin | gabapentin | Anticonvulsant |
| Nimotop | nimodipine | Calcium channel-blocker |
| Nipride | nitroprusside | Antihypertensive |
| Nizoral | ketoconazole | Antifungal agent |
| No Doz | caffeine | CNS stimulant |
| Noctec | chloral hydrate | Hypnotic |
| Noludar | methyprylon | Hypnotic |
| Norcuron | vecuronium bromide | Neuromuscular blocker |
| Norflex | orphenadrine | Analgesic, anticholinergic |
| Normodyne | labetalol | $\beta$-blocker (CS) |
| Norpace | disopyramide | Antiarrhythmic (1) |
| Norpramin | desipramine | TCA |
| Omnipen | ampicillin | Penicillin |
| Optimine | azatadine | Antihistamine |
| Orap | pimozide | Neuroleptic |
| Orudis | ketoprofen | NSAID |
| Paral | paraldehyde | Hypnotic |
| Parlodel | bromocriptine | Prolactin inhibitor, antiparkinsonian, dopamine agonist |
| Parnate | tranylcypromine | MAOI |
| Pavulon | pancuronium | Neuromuscular blocker |
| Paxil | paroxetine | SSRI |
| Paxipam | halazepam | Antianxiety |
| Pediazole | erythromycin ethylsuccinate | Antibacterial (macrolide) |
| Pentothal | thiopental | Anesthetic (general) |
| Periactin | cyproheptadine | Antihistamine, serotonin antagonist |

APPENDICES

| Brand Name | Generic | Chief Action |
|---|---|---|
| Peri-Colace | casanthranol* | Laxative |
| Permax | pergolide | Dopamine agonist |
| Permitil | fluphenazine | Neuroleptic |
| Phenergan | promethazine | Antihistamine, antiemetic |
| Placidyl | ethchlorvynol | Hypnotic |
| Pondimin | fenfluramine | Serotonergic anorectic |
| Ponstel | mefenamic acid | NSAID |
| Preludin | phenmetrazine | Anorectic agent |
| Premarin | estrogens, conjugated | Estrogen |
| Prilosec | omeprazole | Gastric acid pump inhibitor |
| Primatene | epinephrine* | Sympathomimetic (DA) $\alpha$ |
| Prinivil, Zestril | lisinopril | Antihypertensive |
| Pro-Banthine | propantheline bromide | Anticholinergic |
| Procardia | nifedipine | Calcium channel-blocker |
| Prolixin | fluphenazine | Neuroleptic |
| Pronestyl | procainamide | Antiarrhythmic (1A) |
| ProSom | estazolam | Hypnotic |
| Prostigmin | neostigmine | Anticholinesterase, cholinomimetic |
| Proventil | albuterol | Sympathomimetic (DA) $\beta$ |
| Prozac | fluoxetine | SSRI |
| Quarzan | clidinium bromide | Anticholingeric |
| Questran | cholestyramine | Hypolipidemic |
| Quinamm | quinine | Skeletal muscle relaxant |
| Quinidine | quinidine | Antiarrhythmic (1A) |
| Regitine | phentolamine | Antihypertensive |
| Reglan | metoclopramide | Dopamine blocking antiemetic |
| Remeron | mirtazapine | Antidepressant |
| Reminyl | galantamine | Cholinergic function enhanced |
| Restoril | temazepam | Hypnotic |
| Retrovir | zidovudine | Antiviral |
| ReVia | naltrexone | Narcotic antagonist |
| Rifadin | rifampin | Antibiotic |
| Rifamate | isoniazid | Antibiotic |
| Risperdal | risperidone | Antipsychotic |
| Ritalin | methylphenidate | Stimulant |
| Robinal | glycopyrrolate | Anticholinergic |
| Roxanol | morphine | Narcotic |
| Sandimmune | cyclosporine | Immunosuppressant |
| Sanorex | mazindol | Anorectic agent |
| Seconal | secobarbital | Hypnotic |
| Sectral | acebutolol | $\beta$-blocker (CS) |
| Seldane | terfenadine | Antihistamine |
| Serax | oxazepam | Antianxiety |
| Serentil | mesoridazine | Neuroleptic |
| Seroquel | quetiapine | Antipsychotic |
| Serpasil | reserpine | Antihypertensive |
| Serzone | nefazodone | Antidepressant |
| Sinemet | carbidopa-levodopa | Antiparkinsonian |
| Sinequan | doxepin | TCA |
| Soma | carisoprodol | Muscle relaxant |
| Sonata | zaleplon | Hypnotic, anticonvulsant |
| Sporanox | itraconazole | Antifungal |
| Stelazine | trifluoperazine | Neuroleptic |
| Sudafed | pseudoephedrine* | Sympathomimetic (IA) $\alpha\beta$ |
| Surmontil | trimipramine | TCA |
| Symmetrel | amantadine | Antiparkinsonian, antiviral |
| Tagamet | cimetidine | $H_2$-receptor antagonist |
| Talwin | pentazocine | Narcotic agonist-antagonist |

| Brand Name | Generic | Chief Action |
|---|---|---|
| Tambocor | flecainide acetate | Antiarrhythmic (1) |
| Tao | troleandomycin | Antibacterial (macrolide) |
| Tapazole | methimazole | Antithyroid drug |
| Taractan | chlorprothixene | Neuroleptic |
| Tegretol | carbamazepine | Anticonvulsant, anticycling |
| Tenormin | atenolol | $\beta$-blocker, antisocial phobia |
| Tensilon | edrophonium chloride | Cholinomimetic |
| Thorazine | chlorpromazine | Neuroleptic |
| Ticar | ticarcillin disodium | Antibacterial |
| Tigan | trimethobenzamide | Antiemetic dopamine blocker |
| Tindal | acetophenazine | Neuroleptic |
| Tonocard | tocainide | Antiarrhythmic (1) |
| Topamax | topiramate | Antiseizure |
| Toradol | ketorolac tromethamine | NSAID |
| Transderm Scop | scopolamine | Anticholinergic, antiemetic |
| Tranxene | clorazepate | Antianxiety |
| Trental | pentoxifylline | Hematologic agent |
| Trilafon | perphenazine | Neuroleptic |
| Trobicin | spectinomycin | Antibiotic (macrolide) |
| Tubocurarine | tubocurarine | Neuromuscular blocker |
| Tums | calcium carbonate* | Antacid |
| Tylenol | acetaminophen* | Analgesic |
| Urecholine | bethanechol | Cholinergic, anticholinesterase |
| Valium | diazepam | Antianxiety |
| Valpin | anisotropine | Anticholinergic |
| Vanceril | beclomethasone | Corticosteroid |
| Vascor | bepridil hydrochloride | Calcium channel-blocker, antianginal |
| Vasotec | enalapril | Antihypertensive (ACE) |
| Velban | vinblastine | Antineoplastic |
| Vermox | mebendazole | Anthelmintic agent |
| Vibramycin | doxycycline | Tetracycline antibiotic |
| Visken | pindolol | $\beta$-blocker (NCS) |
| Vivactil | protriptyline | TCA |
| Voltaren | diclofenac sodium | Anti-inflammatory (NSAID) |
| Wellbutrin | bupropion | Atypical antidepressant, HCA |
| Xanax | alprazolam | Antianxiety |
| Xylocaine | lidocaine* | Anesthetic (local), antiarrhythmic |
| Yocon | yohimbine* | Presynaptic $\alpha_2$ antagonist |
| Zantac | ranitidine | $H_2$ blocker |
| Zarontin | ethosuximide | Anticonvulsant |
| Zithromax | azithromycin dihydrate | Antibacterial (macrolide) |
| Zofran | ondansetron hydrochloride | Antiemetic |
| Zoloft | sertraline | SSRI |
| Zyprexa | olanzapine | Antipsychotic |

Codes:
  * Can be sold as nonprescription drug.
  NSAID = nonsteroidal anti-inflammatory agent.
  $\beta$-blockers: (CS) = cardioselective; (NCS) = noncardioselective.
  Sympathomimetics: (DA) = direct acting; (IA) = indirect acting; (MA) = mixed acting; $\alpha$ = alpha antagonist; $\beta$ = beta agonist.
  ACE = angiotensin converting enzyme.

## 3. DRUG INTERACTIONS—CYTOCHROME P450 ENZYMES

## P450 Enzyme System

*Function:* Oxidation of substances (drugs) to make them more hydrophilic and easily eliminated.

*Coding Subtypes:* Each human P450 enzyme is the expression of a unique gene. Most 450 enzymes involved in drug metabolism belong to three distinct gene families (I, II, III). A special coding system is used. For example: P450 IID6 is a very specific subtype where II is first number, D is first letter, and 6 is second number.

- First number—expressed as I, II, III (or 1, 2, 3), represents families with > 40% amino acid sequence homology.
- First letter—represents subfamilies with > 55% amino acid homology.
- Second number—represents the single gene that controls the enzyme's expression.

There are four P450 enzymes (IA2, IID6, IIIA3, and IIIA4) that control a majority of the drug metabolism of psychiatric drugs. IIIA3 and IIIA4 are essentially the same enzymes, each controlled by a different gene, and are often descriptively condensed to IIIA3/4. Other P45O enzymes (e.g., 2C19) also play an important role.

## Definitions of Substrates, Inhibitors, and Inducers of P450 Enzymes

*Substrates:* Drugs metabolized by the specific enzyme.

*Inhibitors:* Drugs that interfere with the enzyme's oxidation of substrates and raise plasma levels of drugs that depend on that enzyme.

*Competitive inhibitors* are drugs that are substrates of the enzyme but compete with other substrates. All substrate drugs have the potential to be inhibitors if they compete with another substrate drug. *Noncompetitive inhibitors* are not metabolized by the particular enzyme that they inhibit.

*Inducers:* Drugs that increase a specific enzyme's activity and lower levels of substrates metabolized by that drug.

### P450 IID6 (hydroxylation)

No known inducers.

Populations deficient in this enzyme:

- 5–8% of Caucasians
- < 3% of Asians and Africans
- Nearly 0% of Japanese

## Drug Interactions–P450 IID6

| Substrates (drugs metabolized by IID6) | Inhibitors (substrates unless indicated) |
|---|---|
| **Antidepressants**<br>*TCAs:*<br>  amitriptyline<br>  clomipramine<br>  desipramine<br>  imipramine<br>  N-desmethyl-clomipramine<br>  nortriptyline<br>  trimipramine<br>*Atypical:*<br>  m-cpp (anxiogenic metabolite of<br>    nefazodone<br>**Neuroleptics**<br>*Phenothiazines:*<br>  e.g., trifluoperazine<br>*Other:*<br>  clozapine<br>  risperidone<br>**β-Blockers**<br>bufarol<br>labetolol<br>metoprolol<br>penbutolol<br>propranolol<br>timolol<br>**Antiarrhythmics**<br>encainide<br>flecainide<br>mexitiline<br>propafenone<br>**Other**<br>carbamazepine<br>methamphetamine<br>*Probable:*<br>  captopril<br>  dextroamphetamine<br>  papaverine<br>  phenacetin<br>  yohimbine | **SSRIs**<br>demethylsertraline<br>fluoxetine<br>norfluoxetine<br>paroxetine<br>sertraline<br>**TCAs**<br>desipramine<br>**Neuroleptics**<br>chlorpromazine<br>fluphenazine<br>perphenazine<br>thioridazine<br>**Opiates**<br>codeine (to form morphine)<br>dextromethorphan<br>ethylmorphine<br>**Other**<br>cimetidine<br>debrisoquine<br>diltiazem<br>diphenhydramine<br>labetolol<br>lobeline<br>nicardipine<br>propafenone<br>quinidine†<br>quinine<br>vincristine |

† Not metabolized by IID6.

## P450 IIIA3/4 (carboxylation, dealkylation, hydroxylation, N-demethylation)

No genetic polymorphism.

Higher activity in women.

### Drug Interactions–P450 IIIA3/4

| Substrates | Inhibitors | Inducers |
|---|---|---|
| **ANTIDEPRESSANTS** | **ANTIDEPRESSANTS** | carbamazepine |
| (*Demethylation*) | fluoxetine (weak) | dexamethasone |
| amitriptyline | fluvoxamine | estrogen |
| clomipramine | nefazodone | ethanol |
| imipramine | sertraline | ethinylestradiol (?) |
| **BENZODIAZEPINES** | *Calcium channel-blockers:* | glucocorticoids |
| *Triazolobenzodiazepines:* | diltiazem | isoniazid |
| alprazolam | felodipine | phenylbutazone |
| estazolam | nifedipine | phenytoin |
| midazolam | verapamil | rifampicin |
| triazolam | **ANTIMYCOTIC AZOLES*** | sulfinpyrazone |
| *2-keto benzodiazepines:* | fluconazole | tamoxifen (?) |
| clorazepate | itraconazole | |
| chlordiazepoxide | ketoconazole | |
| diazepam | miconazole | |
| flurazepam | **MACROLIDE ANTIBIOTICS*** | |
| halazepam | azithromycin | |
| prazepam | clarithromycin | |
| *Antiarrythmics:* | erythromycin | |
| lidocaine | troleandomycin | |
| propafenone | *Probable:* | |
| quinidine | flurithromycin | |
| *Calcium channel-blockers:* | josamycin | |
| nifedipine | ponsinomycin | |
| diltiazem | *Other:* | |
| felodipine | amiodarone | |
| verapamil | ciprofaxine (?) | |
| *H-1 blockers:* | grapefruit juice | |
| astemizole | | |
| terfenadine | | |
| *Other:* | | |
| aflatoxin B. | | |
| alfentanil | | |
| cocaine | | |
| cortisol | | |
| cyclosporine | | |
| debrisoquine | | |
| hexobarbital | | |
| lovastatin | | |
| methobarbitol | | |
| tamoxifen | | |
| testosterone | | |
| theophylline | | |
| warfarin | | |

* Spiramycin has no effect and azithromycin probably none.

## P450 1A2 (N-methylation, N-demethylation)

No genetic polymorphism; all have this gene.

### Drug Interactions–P450 1A2

| Substrates | Inhibitors | Inducers |
|---|---|---|
| acetaminophen | cimetidine | aminoglutethimide |
| caffeine | ciproflaxine | barbiturates |
| clozapine | disulfiram | carbamazepine |
| haloperidol | fluvoxamine | omeprazole |
| propranolol | **MACROLIDE** | phenytoin |
| tacrine | *Antibiotics:* | primidone |
| tertiary TCAs (minor pathway) | azithromycin | rifabutin |
| theophylline | clarithromycin | rifampin |
| | erythromycin | *Polyaromatic hydrocarbons:* |
| | troleandomycin | charcoal broiled foods |
| | pentoxifylline | cigarette smoking |
| | theophylline | smoked foods |
| | verapamil | |

## 4. SYMPTOM CHECKLIST

When patients gripe about side effects, do their complaints stem from the medication or from another problem, such as a psychiatric or a medical disorder?

The symptom checklist helps answer this question. Patients fill it out *before* they start on a medication so the clinician can detect symptoms unrelated to the medication. Subsequently, patients complete it every week or month to uncover symptoms that occurred only *after* the medication began. (I find that most "side effects" decline on medication).

For patients and doctors alike, the list saves office time for exploring more personal matters, while insuring that clinicians still know about any key side effects.

# Symptom Checklist

Patient's name _____ Date _____

| Do You Have Any of the Following Symptoms? | Yes | No | Does It Make You Uncomfortable? | |
|---|---|---|---|---|
| | | | Yes | No |
| Dizziness/lightheadedness | – | – | ◇ | ◇ |
| Faint | – | – | ◇ | ◇ |
| Rapid or pounding heart | – | – | ◇ | ◇ |
| Dry mouth, throat, or nose | – | – | ◇ | ◇ |
| Always hungry | – | – | ◇ | ◇ |
| Diminished appetite | – | – | ◇ | ◇ |
| Nausea or vomiting | – | – | ◇ | ◇ |
| Upset stomach | – | – | ◇ | ◇ |
| Diarrhea | – | – | ◇ | ◇ |
| Constipation | – | – | ◇ | ◇ |
| Jaundice | – | – | ◇ | ◇ |
| Weight gain | – | – | ◇ | ◇ |
| Edema (swelling ankles or hands) | – | – | ◇ | ◇ |
| Increased thirst | – | – | ◇ | ◇ |
| Different menstruation | – | – | ◇ | ◇ |
| Swollen breasts | – | – | ◇ | ◇ |
| Fluid discharge from breast | – | – | ◇ | ◇ |
| Decreased sexual interest | – | – | ◇ | ◇ |
| Lack of energy | – | – | ◇ | ◇ |
| Bruising easier | – | – | ◇ | ◇ |
| Sores in mouth | – | – | ◇ | ◇ |
| Blurred vision | – | – | ◇ | ◇ |
| Ringing in the ears | – | – | ◇ | ◇ |
| Skin rash | – | – | ◇ | ◇ |
| Increased sweating | – | – | ◇ | ◇ |
| Insomnia | – | – | ◇ | ◇ |
| Excessive sleeping | – | – | ◇ | ◇ |
| Weird dreams/nightmares | – | – | ◇ | ◇ |
| Stiff tongue | – | – | ◇ | ◇ |
| Body stiff or rigid | – | – | ◇ | ◇ |
| Difficulty in swallowing | – | – | ◇ | ◇ |
| Tremors, shakes, jitters | – | – | ◇ | ◇ |
| Unsteady gait | – | – | ◇ | ◇ |
| Slurred speech | – | – | ◇ | ◇ |
| Headache | – | – | ◇ | ◇ |
| Drowsiness | – | – | ◇ | ◇ |
| Poor memory | – | – | ◇ | ◇ |
| Nervousness | – | – | ◇ | ◇ |
| Other | | | | |

*CURRENT MEDICATION:* DRUG NAME AND DOSE

_____     _____

_____     _____

_____     _____

_____     _____

# Bibliography

## ANTIANXIETY AGENTS AND HYPNOTICS

Adler L, Angrist B, Peselow E, Corwin J and Rotrosen J. Noradrenergic mechanisms in akathisia: Treatment with propranolol and clonidine. *Psychopharmacol Bull* 23:21–25, 1987.

Albeck JH. Withdrawal and detoxification from benzodiazepine dependence: A potential role for clonazepam. *J Clin Psych* 49:43–48 (suppl.), 1987.

Altamura AC, Pioli R, Vitto M, Mannu P. Venlafaxine in social phobia: a study in selective serotonin reuptake inhibitor non-responders. *Int Clin Psychopharmacol* 14:239, 1999.

Ankier SI and Goa KL. Quazepam: A preliminary review of its pharmacodynamic and pharmacokinetic properties and therapeutic efficacy in insomnia. *Drugs* 35:42–62, 1988.

Baldwin D and others. Paroxetine in social phobia/social anxiety disorder. *Br J Psychiatry* 175:120, 1999.

Ballenger JC and others. Double-blind, fixed dose, placebo-controlled study of paroxetine in the treatment of panic disorder. *Am J Psychiatry* 155:36, 1998.

Black B and Uhde T. Treatment of elective mutism with fluoxetine: A double-blind, placebo-controlled study. *J Am Acad Child and Adolescent Psych* 33:1000–1006, 1994.

Bradford J, et al. Double-blind placebo crossover study of cyproterone acetate in the treatment of the paraphilias. *Arch Sex Behav* 22:383–402, 1993.

Bromberg FG, et al. (Eds.). Clomipramine vs phenelzine in OCD: Controlled trial. *Psychiatry Drug Alerts* 7:18, 1993.

Bruce M, Scott N, Shine P and Lader M. Anxiogenic effects of caffeine in patients with anxiety disorders. *Arch Gen Psych* 49:867–869, 1992.

Cassano GB, Perugi G and McNair DM. Panic disorder: Review of the empirical and rational basis of pharmacological treatment. *Pharmaco-psychiatry* 21:157–165, 1988.

Castaneda R and Cushman P. Alcohol withdrawal: A review of clinical management. *J Clin Psych* 50:278–284, 1989.

BIBLIOGRAPHY

**469**

Chouinard G, et al. Alprazolam in the treatment of generalized anxiety and panic disorders: A double-blind placebo-controlled study. *Psychopharmacology* 77:229–233, 1982.

Conant J, et al. Central nervous system side effects of $\beta$-adrenergic blocking agents with high and low lipid solubility. *Cardiovascular Pharm* 13:656–661, 1989.

Connor KM and others. Fluoxetine in posttraumatic stress disorder: randomized, double-blind study. *Br J Psychiatry* 175:17, 1999.

Cowley D, Roy Byrne P and Greenblatt D *Benzodiazepines: Pharmacokinetics and Pharmaco-dynamics in Benzodiazepines in Clinical Practice: Risks and Benefits,* Washington DC: APA Press, 1991.

Davidson JR and others. Response characteristics to antidepressants and placebo in posttraumatic stress disorder. *Int Clin Psychopharmacol* 12(6):291, 1997.

Elie R and others. Sleep latency is shortened during 4 weeks of treatment with zaleplon, a novel nonbenzodiazepine hypnotic. *J Clin Psychiatry* 60(8):536, 1999.

Folks DG, Burke WJ. Sedative hypnotics and sleep. *Clin Geriatr Med* 14(1):67, 1998.

Folks DG, Fuller WC. Anxiety disorders and insomnia in geriatric patients. *Psychiatr Clin North Am* 20(1):137, 1997.

Fones CSL, Manfro GG, Pollack MH. Social phobia: an update. *Harv Rev Psychiatry* 5:247, 1998.

Frishman W, et al. Clinical pharmacology of the new beta-adrenergic blocking drugs: Part 4. Adverse effects. Choosing a $\beta$-adrenoreceptor blocker. *Am Heart J* 98:256–262, 1979.

Garner SJ, Eldridge FL, Wagner PG and Dowell RT. Buspirone, an anxiolytic drug that stimulates respiration. *Am Rev Respir Dis* 139:945–950, 1989.

Gawin F, Compton M and Byck R. Buspirone reduces smoking. *Arch Gen Psych* 46:989–990, 1989.

Gillin JC and Byerley WF. The diagnosis and management of insomnia. *N Eng J Med* 322:239–248, 1990.

Greenblatt DJ and Koch-Weser J. Adverse reactions to propranolol in hospitalized medical patients: A report from the Boston Collaborative Drug Surveillance Program. *Am Heart J* 86:478–484, 1973.

Greist JH, Jefferson JW, Kobak KA, et al. Efficacy and tolerability of serotonin transport inhibitors in obsessive compulsive disorder: a meta-analysis. *Arch Gen Psychiatry* 52:53, 1995.

Herman JB, Brotman AW and Rosenbaum JF. Rebound anxiety in panic disorder patients treated with shorter-acting benzodiazepines. *J Clin Psych* 48:22–26, 1987.

Hewlett W, et al. Clomipramine, clonazepam, and clonidine treatment of obsessive-compulsive disorder. *J Clin Psychopharmacol* 12:420–430, 1992.

Kales A, et al. Quazepam and temazepam: Effects of short- and intermediate-term use and withdrawal. *Clinical Pharmacology and Therapeutics* 40:376–386, 1986.

Kales A, et al. Rebound insomnia and rebound anxiety: A review. *Pharmacology* 26:121–137, 1983.

Katzelnick DJ, Kobak KA, Greist JH, et al. Sertraline for social phobia: a double-blind placebo controlled crossover study. *Am J Psychiatry* 152:1368, 1995.

Keck PE, Jr, Taylor VE, Tugrul KC, McElroy SL and Bennett JA. Valproate treatment of panic disorder and lactate-induced panic attacks. *Biol Psychiatry* 33:542–546, 1993.

Knapp MJ, et al. A 30-week randomized controlled trial of high-dose tacrine in patients with Alzheimer's disease. *JAMA* 271:985–991, 1994.

Kranzler HR, Burleson JA, Del Boca FK, et al. Buspirone treatment of anxious alcoholics. *Arch Gen Psychiatry Gen Psychiatry* 51:720, 1994.

Kranzler HR, Burleson JA, Korner P, Del Boca FK, Bohn MJ, et al. Placebo-controlled trial of fluoxetine as an adjunct to relapse prevention in alcoholics. *Am J Psych* 152:391–397, 1995.

Kushner MJ, et al. You don't have to be a neuroscientist to forget everything with triazolam—but it helps. *JAMA* 259:350–352, 1988.

Liebowitz MR and others. Pharmacotherapy of social phobia. *Psychosomatics* 28:305, 1987.

Lion JR. Benzodiazepines in the treatment of aggressive patients. J Clin Psych 2:25–26, 1979.

McClusky HY, et al. Efficacy of behavioral versus triazolam treatment in persistent sleep-onset insomnia. *Am J Psych* 148:121–126, 1991.

McDougle CJ, Goodman WK, Leckman JF and Price LH. The psychopharmacology of obsessive compulsive disorder: Implications for treatment and pathogenesis. *Psych Clin N Am* 16:749–765, 1993.

Morris HH and Estes ML. Traveler's amnesia: Transient global amnesia secondary to triazolam. *JAMA* 258:945–946, 1987.

Mundo E, Bianchi L, Bellodi L. Efficacy of fluvoxamine, paroxetine, and citalopram in the treatment of obsessive-compulsive disorder: a single-blind study. *J Clin Psychopharmacol* 17(4):267, 1997.

Nagy LM, Morgan CA, Southwick SM and Charney DS. Open prospective trial of fluoxetine for posttraumatic stress disorder. *J Clin Psychopharmacol* 13:107– 113, 1993.

Nikaido AM and Elinwood EH. Comparison of the effects of quazepam and triazolam on cognitive-neuromotor performance. *Psychopharmacology* 92:459–464, 1987.

Nishino S, Dement WC. Neuropharmacology of sedative-hypnotics and central nervous system stimulants is sleep medicine. *Psychiatr Clin North Am Annu Drug Ther* 5:85, 1998.

Noyes R, et al. Diazepam and propranolol in panic disorder and agora phobia. *Arch Gen Psych* 41:287–292, 1984.

Oehrberg S, Christiansen PE, Behnke K, et al. Paroxetine in the treatment of panic disorder: a randomized, double-blind placebo-controlled study. *Br J Psychiatry* 167:374, 1995.

Ontiveros A and Fontaine R. Social phobia and clonazepam. *Can J Psych* 35:439–441, 1990.

Pande AC and others. Treatment of social phobia with gabapentin: a placebo-controlled study. *J Clin Psychopharmacol* 119:341, 1999.

Perse T. Obsessive-compulsive disorder: A treatment review. *J Clin Psych* 49:48–55, 1988.

Pinder RM, et al. Clonazepam: A review of its pharmacological properties and therapeutic efficacy in epilepsy. *Drugs* 12:321–361, 1976.

Ray WA, Griffin MR and Downey W. Benzodiazepines of long and short elimination half-life and the risk of hip fracture. *JAMA* 262:3303–3307, 1989.

Rickels K and others. Efficacy of extended-release venlafaxine in nondepressed outpatients with generalized anxiety disorder. *Am J Psychiatry* 157:968, 2000.

Rickels K, et al. Methylphenidate in mildly depressed outpatients. *Clinical Pharmacology and Therapeutics* 13:595–601, 1972.

Ries R, Roy-Byrne P, Ward NG and Neppe VM. Carbamazepine for benzodiazepine withdrawal. *Am J Psych* 145:536–537, 1989.

Rosebush PI, Hildebrand AM, Furlong BG and Mazurek MF. Catatonic syndrome in a general psychiatric inpatient population: Frequency, clinical presentation, and response to lorazepam. *J Clin Psych* 51:357–362, 1990.

Rosenbaum JF, Moroz G, Bowden CL. Clonazepam in the treatment of panic disorder with or without agoraphobia: a dose-response study of efficacy, safety, and discontinuance. *J Clin Psychopharmacol* 17:390, 1997.

Roy-Byrne P, Ward NG and Donnelly P. Valproate in anxiety and withdrawal syndromes. *J Clin Psych* 50:44–48, 1989.

Scharf M, et al. A multicenter, placebo-controlled study evaluating zolpidem in the treatment of chronic insomnia. *J Clin Psych* 55:192–199, 1994.

Scharf MB, Fletcher ACPK and Graham JP. Comparative amnestic effects of benzodiazepine hypnotic agents. *J Clin Psych* 49:134–137, 1988.

Schneider LS, Syapin PJ and Pawluczyk S. Seizures following triazolam withdrawal despite benzodiazepine treatment. *J Clin Psych* 48:418–419, 1987.

Silver JM, Sandberg DP and Hales RE. New approaches in the pharmacotherapy of post-traumatic stress disorder. *J Clin Psych* 51:33–38, 1990.

Stein MB and others. Paroxetine treatment of generalized social phobia (social anxiety disorder). *JAMA* 280(8):708, 1998.

Stein MB and others. Fluvoxamine in the treatment of social phobia: a double-blind, placebo-controlled study. *Am J Psychiatry* 156:756, 1999.

Sussman N. Treatment of anxiety with buspirone. *Psych Anls* 17:114–120, 1987.

Teboul E and Chouinard G. Principles of benzodiazepine selection. Part I: Pharmacological aspects. *Can J Psych* 35:700–710, 1990.

Teboul E and Chouinard G. A guide to benzodiazepine selection: Part II: Clinical aspects. *Can J Psych* 36:62–69, 1991.

Teoh SK, Mello NK, Mendelson JH, Kuehnle J, Gastfriend DR, Rhoades E and Sholar W. Buprenorphine effects on morphine- and cocaine-induced subjective responses by drug-dependent men. *J Clin Psychopharmacol* 14: 15–27, 1994.

Tesar GE, et al. Clonazepam versus alprazolam in the treatment of panic disorder: Interim analysis of data from a prospective, double-blind, placebo-controlled trial *J Clin Psych* 48:16–19, 1987.

Trimble MR. Worldwide use of clomipramine. *J Clin Psych* 51:51–54, 1990.

Van Ameringen M, Mancini C, Oakman J. Nefazodone in the treatment of social phobia. *J Clin Psychiatry* 60:96, 1999.

Van Ameringen M, Swinson R, Walker JR, Lane RM. A placebo-controlled study of sertraline in generalized social phobia. Presented at the 19th National

Conference of the Anxiety Disorders Association of America, March 25–28, 1999, San Diego, Calif.

van Vilet LM and others. Clinical effects of buspirone in social phobia: a double-blind placebo-controlled study. *J Clin Psychiatry* 58:164, 1997.

Watts VS and Neill JR. Buspirone in obsessive-compulsive disorder (letter). *Am J Psych* 145:1606, 1988.

## ANTIPSYCHOTICS, ANTIDEMENTIA, AND EXTRAPYRAMIDAL DRUGS

Addington DE and others. Reduction of hospital days in chronic schizophrenia patients treated with risperidone: a retrospective study, *Clin Ther* 15:917, 1993.

Adler LA, Angrist B, Weinreb H and Rotrosen J. Studies on the time course and efficacy of ß-blockers in neuroleptic-induced akathisia and the akathisia of idiopathic Parkinson's disease. *Psychopharmacol Bull* 27:107–111, 1991.

Allison DB, Mentore JL, Heo M, et al. Antipsychotic-induced weight gain: a comprehensive research synthesis. *Am J Psychiatry* 156:1686, 1999.

Alvir J and Lieberman J. A reevaluation of the clinical characteristics of clozapine-induced agranulocytosis in light of the United States experience (editorial). *J Clin Psychopharmacol* 14:87–89, 1994.

Alvir JM, Lieberman JA. Agranulocytosis: incidence and risk factors. *J Clin Psychiatry*, 55(suppl B): 137, 1994.

American Psychiatric Association. *Diagnostic and statistical manual of mental disorders-TR*, ed 4, Washington, DC, 2000, The Association.

American Psychiatric Association. Practice guidelines for the treatment of patients with schizophrenia. *Am J Psychiatry* 154 (4 suppl):1, 1997.

Applegate M. Cytochrome P450 isoenzymes: nursing considerations. *JAPNA* 5(1):15, 1999.

Arana GW, Goff DC, Baldessarini RJ and Keepers GA. Efficacy of anticholinergic prophylaxis for neuroleptic-induced acute dystonia. *Am J Psych* 145:993–996, 1988.

Arvantis LA, Miller BG. The Seroquel Trial 13 Study Group: Multiple fixed doses of "Seroquel" (quetiapine) in patients with acute exacerbation of schizophrenia: a comparison with haloperidol and placebo, *Biol Psychiatry* 42:233, 1997.

Barbee JG, Mancuso DM, Freed CR and Todorov AA. Alprazolam as a neuroleptic adjunct in the emergency treatment of schizophrenia. *Am J Psych* 149:506–510, 1992.

Barnes TR, Curson DA: Long-term depot antipsychotics: a risk-benefit assessment, *Drug Safety* 10(6):464, 1994.

Bartels M, et al. Treatment of akathisia with lorazepam: An open clinical trial. *Pharmaco-psychiatry* 20:51–53, 1987.

Barton A, Bowie J and Ebmeier K. Low plasma iron status and akathisia. *J Neurol Neurosurg Psychiatry* 53:671–674, 1990.

Bassitt DP, Louza Neto MR. Clozapine efficacy in tardive dyskinesia in schizophrenic patients. *Eur Arch Psychiatry Clin Neurosci* 248(4):209, 1998.

B
I
B
L
I
O
G
R
A
P
H
Y

Bauer M and Mackert A. Clozapine treatment after agranulocytosis induced by classic neuroleptics. *J Clin Psychopharmacol* 14:71–73, 1994.

Becker RE and others. Cholinesterase inhibitors as therapy in Alzheimer's disease: benefit to risk considerations in clinical application. In Becker R, Giacobini E, editors: *Alzheimer disease: from molecular biology to therapy*, Boston, 1997, Birkhauser.

Behl C, Davis J, Cole G, Shubert D. Vitamin E protects nerve cells from beta-amyloid protein toxicity. *Biochem Biophys Res Commun* 186:944, 1992.

Bever KA, Perry PJ. Olanzapine: a serotonin-dopamine receptor antagonist for antipsychotic therapy. *Am J Psychiatry Health-Sys Phar* 55(10):1003, 1998.

Binder RL and Jonelis F. Seborrheic dermatitis in neuroleptic-induced parkinsonism. *Arch Dermatol* 119:473–475, 1983.

Bitter I, Volavka J and Scheurer J. The concept of neuroleptic threshold: An update. *J Clin Psychopharmacol* 11:28–33, 1991.

Blair DT, Dauner A. Nonneuroleptic etiologies of extrapyramidal symptoms. *Clin Nurs Spec* 7(4):225, 1993.

Blin O. A comparative review of new antipsychotics. *Can J Psychiatry* 44:235, 1999.

Bodkin A, Cannon S, Cohen B, Alpert J, Zornberg G and Cole J. Selegiline treatment of negative symptoms of schizophrenia and schizo-affective disorder. Presented at the annual meeting of the American College of Neuropsychopharmacology, San Juan PR, December 1992.

Braude WM, Barnes TRE and Gore SM. Clinical characteristics of akathisia: A systematic investigation of acute psychiatric inpatient admissions. *Br J Psych* 143:139–150, 1983.

Breier A, et al. Effects of clozapine on positive and negative symptoms in outpatients with schizophrenia. *Am J Psych* 151:20–26, 1994.

Breier A, Hamilton S. Comparative efficacy of olanzapine and haloperidol for patients treatment-resistant schizophrenia. *Biol Psychiatry* 45:403, 1999.

Breier AF, Malhotra AK, Su T-P, et al. Clozapine and risperidone in chronic schizophrenia: effects on symptoms, parkinsonian side effects, and neuroendocrine response. *Am J Psychiatry* 156:294, 1999.

Brown KW, Glen SE and White T. Low serum iron status and akathisia. *Lancet* 1:1234–1236, 1987.

Burke WJ and others. The use of selective reuptake inhibitors for depression and psychosis complicating dementia. *Int J Geriatr Psychiatry* 12:519, 1997.

Carlsson A, Waters N, Carlsson ML. Neurotransmitter interactions in schizophrenia-therapeutic implications. *Biol Psychiatry* 46:1388, 1999.

Carpenter WT Jr, Buchanan RW, Kirkpatrick B, et al. Comparative effectiveness of fluphenazine decanoate injections every 2 weeks versus every 6 weeks. *Am J Psychiatry* 156:412, 1999.

Casey DE. Effects of clozapine therapy in schizophrenic individuals at risk for tardive dyskinesia. *J Clin Psychiatry* 59(suppl 3):31, 1998.

Chengappa KNR, Baker RW and Harty I. Seizures and clozapine dosing schedule (letter). *J Clin Psych.* 55:456, 1994.

Ciraulo D, Shader RI, Greenblatt DJ, et al. *Drug interactions in psychiatry*. Baltimore: Williams & Wilkins, 1995.

Cohen LS, Altshuler LL. Pharmacologic management of psychiatric illness during pregnancy and the postpartum period. *Psychiatr Clin North Am* 21:60, 1997.

Collins PJ, Larkin EP and Shubsachs APW. Lithium carbonate in chronic schizophrenia: A brief trial of lithium carbonate added to neuroleptics for treatment of resistant schizophrenic patients. *Acta Psychiatr Scand* 84:150–154, 1991.

Conley R and others. Olanzapine compared with chlorpromazine in treatment-resistant schizophrenia, *am J Psychiatry* 155:914, 1998.

Corey-Bloom J, Anand R, Beach J: A randomized trial evaluating the efficacy and safety of ENA 713 (rivastigmine tartrate), a new acetylcholinesterase inhibitor, in patients with mild to moderately severe Alzheimer's disease. *Int J Geriatr Psychopharm* 1:55, 1998.

Cummings JL. Cholinesterase inhibitors: a new class of psychotropic compounds. *Am J Psychiatry* 157:4, 2000.

Dabiri LM, Pasta D, Darby JK and Mosbacker D. Effectiveness of Vitamin E for treatment of long-term tardive dyskinesia. *Am J Psych* 151:925–926, 1994.

Davis JM, Matalon L, Watanabe MD and Blake Lesley. Depot anti psychotic drugs: Place in therapy. *Drugs* 47:741–773, 1994.

Devinsky O, et al. Clozapine-related seizures. *Neurology* 41:369–371, 1991.

Douyon R, Angrist B, Peselow E, Cooper T and Rotrosen J. Neuroleptic augmentation with alprazolam: Clinical effects and pharmacokinetic correlates. *Am J Psych* 146:231–234, 1989.

Dursun S, Oluboka OJ, Devarajan S, Kutcher SP. High-dose vitamin E plus vitamin $B_6$ treatment of risperidone-related neuroleptic malignant syndrome. *J Psychopharmacol* 12:220, 1998.

Easton MS and Janicak PG. Benzodiazepines (BZ) for the management of psychosis. *Psych Med* 9:25–36, 1991.

Ereshefsky L. Pharmacokinetics and drug interactions: update for newer antipsychotics. *J Clin Psychiatry* 57(suppl 11):12, 1996.

Ereshefsky L, Watanabe MD and Tran-Johnson TL. Clozapine: An atypical antipsychotic agent. *Clin Pharm* 8:691–709, 1989.

Factor SA, Friedman JH. The emerging role of clozapine in the treatment of movement disorders. *Mov Disord* 12(4):483, 1997.

Farlow M, Gracon SI, Hershey LA, Lewis KW, Sadowsky CH and Dolan-Ureno J. A controlled trial of tacrine in Alzheimer's disease. *JAMA* 268:2523–2565, 1992.

Feinberg SS, Kay SR, Elijovich LR, Fishbein A and Opler L. Pimozide treatment of the negative schizophrenic syndrome: An open trial. *J Clin Psych* 49:235–238, 1988.

Fenton W, et al. Risk factors for spontaneous dyskinesia in schizophrenia. *Arch Gen Psych* 1:643–650, 1994.

Fisch RZ. Trihexyphenidyl abuse: Therapeutic implications for negative symptoms of schizo-phrenia? *Acta Psychiatr Scand* 75:91–94, 1987.

Fleischhacker WW, Hummer M. Drug treatment of schizophrenia in the 1990s: achievements and future possibilities in optimizing outcomes. *Drugs* 53(6):915, 1997.

Fleishman SB, Lavin MR, Sattler M and Szarka H. Antiemetic-induced akathisia in cancer patients receiving chemotherapy. *Am J Psych* 151:763–765, 1994.

BIBLIOGRAPHY

Folks DG. Neuroleptics in the treatment of agitation in dementia. In Klein DL, Hay DG, editors: *Treatment of agitation in dementia*, Washington, DC, 2000, American Psychiatric Press.

Freedberg KA, et al. Antischizophrenic drugs: Differential plasma protein binding and therapeutic activity. *Life Sciences* 24:2467–2474, 1979.

Ganguli R. Newer antipsychotics versus older neuroleptics: is weight gain still a problem? *Ther Adv Psychoses* July 6, 1999.

Ganzini L, Heintz R, Hoffman WF, Keepers GA and Casey DE. Acute extrapyramidal syndromes in neuroleptic-treated elders: A pilot study. *J Geriatr Psych Neurol* 4:222–225, 1991.

Gardos G and Cole JO. Weight reduction in schizophrenics by molindone. *Am J Psych* 134:302–304, 1977.

Gardos G, Casey DE, Cole JO, et al. Ten-year outcome of tardive dyskinesia. *Am J Psych* 151:836, 1994.

Gelenberg AJ, Bellinghausen B, Wojcik JD, Falk WE and Farhadi AM. Patients with neuroleptic malignant syndrome histories: What happens when they are re-hospitalized? *J Clin Psych* 50:178–180, 1989.

Gelenberg AJ, Bellinghausen B, Wojcik JD, Falk WE and Sachs GS. A prospective survey of neuroleptic malignant syndrome in a short-term psychiatric hospital. *Am J Psych* 145:517–518, 1988.

Glazer WM, Morgenstern H and Doucette JT. Predicting the long-term risk of tardive dyskinesia in outpatients maintained on neuroleptic medications. *J Clin Psych* 54:133–139, 1993.

Goff D and Baldessarini RJ. Drug interactions with antipsychotic agents. *J Clin Psycho-pharmacol* 13:57–67, 1993.

Goff DC, Amico E, Dreyfuss D and Ciraulo D. A placebo-controlled trial of trihexyphenidyl in unmedicated patients with schizophrenia. *Am J Psych* 151:429–431, 1994.

Goff DC, et al. An open trial of buspirone added to neuroleptics in schizophrenic patients. *J Clin Psychopharmacol* 11:193–197, 1991.

Goff DC, et al. The effect of benztropine on haloperidol-induced dystonia, clinical efficacy and pharmacokinetics: A prospective, double-blind trial. *J Clin Psychopharmacol* 11:106–112, 1991.

Goldman D, Hien DA, Haas GL, Sweeney JA and Frances AJ. Bizarre delusions and DSM-III-R schizophrenia. *Am J Psych* 149:494–499, 1992.

Green B. Focus on quetiapine. *Curr Med Res Opin* 15(3):145, 1999.

Greenberg WM. Mechanism of neuroleptic-associated priapism (letter). *Am J Psych* 145:393–394, 1988.

Guzé BH and Baxter LR, Jr. Neuroleptic malignant syndrome. *N Eng J Med* 313:163–166, 1985.

Haller E and Binder RL. Clozapine and seizures. *Am J Psych* 147:1069–1071, 1990.

Haring C, et al. Influence of patient-related variables on clozapine plasma levels. *Am J Psych* 50:64–65, 1989.

Heikkinen H, Outakoski J, Meriläinen V, Tuomi A and Huttunen MO. Molindone and weight loss (letter). *J Clin Psych* 54:160–161, 1993.

Hemstrom CA, Evans RL and Lobeck FG. Haloperidol decanoate: A depot antipsychotic. *Drug Intelligence and Clinical Pharmacy* 22:290–295, 1988.

Horiguchi J. Low serum iron in patients with neuroleptic-induced akathisia and dystonia under antipsychotic drug treatment. *Acta Psychiatr Scand* 84:301–303, 1991.

Hustey FM. Acute quetiapine poisoning. *J Emerg Med* 17(6):995, 1999.

Hymowitz P, Frances A, Jacobsberg LB, Sickles M and Hoyt R. Neuroleptic treatment of schizotypal personality disorders. Comprehensive Psychiatry 27:267–271, 1986.

Ischikawa J, Meltzer H. Relationship between dopaminergic and serotonergic neuronal activity in the frontal cortex and the action of typical and atypical antipsychotic drugs. *Eur Arch Gen Psychiatry Clin Neurosci* 249(suppl 4):90, 1999.

Javitt DC, Zylberman I, Zukin SR, Heresco-Levy U and Lindenmayer JP. Amelioration of negative symptoms in schizophrenia with glycine. *Am J Psych* 151:1234–1236, 1994.

Jeste DV and others. Conventional vs newer antipsychotics in elderly patients. *Am J Psychiatry Geriatr Psychiatry* 7(1):70, 1999.

Jeste DV, Lacro JP, Bailey A, et al. Lower incidence of tardive dyskinesia with risperidone compared with haloperidol in older patients. J Am Geriatr Soc 47:716, 1999.

Kane J, Honigfeld G, Singer J, et al. Clozapine for the treatment-resistant schizophrenic: A double-blind comparison with chlorpromazine. *Arch Gen Psych* 45:780–796, 1988.

Kane JM. Pharmacologic treatment of schizophrenia. *Biol Psychiatry* 46:1396, 1999.

Kane JM. The current status of neuroleptic therapy. *J Clin Psych* 50:352–355, 1989.

Kapur S, Zipursky RB, Remington G. Clinical and theoretical implications of $5-HT_2$ and $D_2$ receptor occupancy of clozapine, risperidone, and olanzapine in schizophrenia. *Am J Psych* 156:286, 1999.

Keck P, Strakowski S, McElroy S. The efficacy of atypical antipsychotics in the treatment of depressive symptoms, hostility, and suicidality in patients with schizophrenia. *J Clin Psychiatry* 61(suppl 3):4, 2000.

Keepers GA and Casey DE. Use of neuroleptic-induced extrapyramidal symptoms to predict future vulnerability to side effects. *Am J Psych* 148:85–89, 1991.

Keltner NL. Neuroreceptor function and psychopharmacological response. *Iss Mental Health Nurs* 21:31, 2000.

Knapp MJ, Knopman DS, Solomon PR, Pendlebury WW, Davis CS, Gracon SI and the Tacrine Study Group. A 30-week randomized controlled trial of high-dose tacrine in patients with Alzheimer's disease. *JAMA* 271:985–991, 1994.

Kotin J, et al. Thioridazine and sexual dysfunction. *Am J Psych* 133:82–85, 1976.

Lam WFL. Clozapine and fluvoxamine. *Psychopharmacol Update* 10(2):2, 1999.

Lam WFL. Drug interaction potential of risperidone. *Psychopharmacol Update* 10(5):2, 1999.

Lederle Laboratories. (1985). *Loxitane*. Pearl River NY: J. Maxmen.

Levenson JL and Fisher JG. Long-term outcome after neuroleptic malignant syndrome. *J Clin Psych* 49:154–156, 1988.

Levi-Minzi S, Bermanzohn PC and Siris SG. Bromocriptine for "negative" schizophrenia. *Compr Psychiatry* 32:210–216, 1991.

Levinson DF and Simpson GM. Neuroleptic-induced extrapyramidal symptoms with fever. *Arch Gen Psych* 43:839–847, 1986.

Lieberman JA, Kane JM and Johns CA. Clozapine: Guidelines for clinical management. *J Clin Psych* 50:329–338, 1989.

Lieberman JA, Tasman A. *Psychiatric Drugs*. Philadelphia, 2000, WB Saunders.

Lindenmayer JP, Grochowski S and Mabugat L. Clozapine effects on positive and negative symptoms: A six-month trial in treatment-refractory schizophrenics. *J Clin Psychopharmacol* 14:201–204, 1994.

Lipinski JF, Zubenko GS, Barriera P, et al. Propranolol in the treatment of neuroleptic-induced akathisia. *Lancet* 2:685–686, 1983.

Marder SR and Meibach RC. Risperidone in the treatment of schizophrenia. *Am J Psych* 151:825–835, 1994.

Marder SR, Van Putten, T, Aravagiri M, Hawes EM, Hubbard JW, et al. Fluphenazine plasma levels and clinical response. *Psychopharmacol Bull* 26:256–259, 1990.

McEvoy JP. A double-blind crossover comparison of antiparkinson drug therapy: Amantadine versus anticholinergics in 90 normal volunteers, with an emphasis on differential effects on memory function. *J Clin Psych* 49:20–23, 1987.

McManus DQ and others. Quetiapine, a novel antipsychotic: experience in elderly patients with psychotic disorders. *J Clin Psychiatry* 60(5):292, 1999.

Medina A and others. Effects of central muscarinic-1 receptor stimulation on blood pressure regulation. *Hypertension* 29:828, 1997.

Mendez M, Younesi F, Perryman K. Use of donepezil for vascular dementia: preliminary clinical experience. *J Neuropsychiatry Clin Neurosci* 11:268, 1999.

Mulnard RA and others: Estrogen replacement therapy for treatment of mild to moderate Alzheimer disease: a randomized controlled trial. Alzheimer's disease cooperative study. *JAMA* 283:1007, 2000.

Nemes ZC, Rotrosen J, Angrist B, Peselow E and Schoentag R. Serum iron levels and akathisia. *Biol Psychiatry* 29:411–413, 1991.

Neppe VM and Ward NG. The management of neuroleptic-induced acute extrapyramidal syndromes. In Neppe VM (Ed.), *Innovative Psychopharmacotherapy* 152–176 , NY: Raven Press, 1989.

Nyberg S, Eriksson B, Oxenstierna G, et al. Suggested minimal effective dose of risperidone based on PET-measured $D_2$ and 5-$HT_{2A}$ receptor occupancy in schizophrenic patients. *Am J Psych* 156:869, 1999.

Ohmori T, Ito K, Abekawa T, Koyanna T. Psychotic relapse and maintenance therapy in paranoid schizophrenia: a 15 year follow up. *Eur Arch Gen Psychiatry Clin Neurosci* 249(2): 73, 1999.

O'Loughlin V, Dickie AC and Ebmeier KP. Serum iron and transferrin in acute neuroleptic-induced akathisia. *J Neurol Neurosurg Psychiatry* 54:363–364, 1991.

Opler LA and Feinberg SS. The role of pimozide in clinical psychiatry: A review. *J Clin Psych* 52:221–233, 1991.

Owen MW, Pickar D, Doran AR, Breier A, Tarell and Paul SM. Combination alprazolam-neuroleptic treatment of the positive and negative symptoms of schizophrenia. *Am J Psych* 143:85–87, 1986.

Owen RR, Jr and Cole JO. Molindone hydrochloride: A review of laboratory and clinical findings. *J Clin Psychopharmacol* 9:268–276, 1989.

Oyemumi LK. Does lithium have a role in the prevention and management of clozapine-induced granulocytopenia? *Pediatr Ann* 29(10):597, 1999.

Parsa MA, Bastani B. Quetiapine (Seroquel) in the treatment of psychosis in patients with Parkinson's disease. *J Neuropsychiatry Clin Neurosci* 10:216, 1998.

Pelonero AL, Levenson JL, Pandurangi AK. Neuroleptic malignant syndrome: a review. *Psychiatr Serv* 49(9):1163, 1998.

Pollock BG and others. An open pilot study of citalopram for behavioral disturbances of dementia: plasma levels and real-time observations. *Geriatric Psychiatry* 5:70, 1997.

Pope HG, Jr, et al. Frequency and presentation of neuroleptic malignant syndrome in a large psychiatric hospital. *Am J Psych* 143:1227–1233, 1986.

Rajiv T, Greden JF and Silk KR. Treatment of negative schizophrenic symptoms with trihexyphenidyl. *J Clin Psychopharmacol* 8:212–215, 1988.

Remington GJ, et al. Prevalence of neuroleptic-induced dystonia in mania and schizophrenia. *Am J Psych* 147:1231–1233, 1990.

Robinson D and others. Predictors of relapse following response from a first episode of schizophrenia or schizoaffective disorder. *Arch Gen Psychiatry* 56(3):241, 1999.

Robinson DG, Woerner MG, Alvir JMJ, et al. Predictors of treatment response from a first episode of schizophrenia or schizoaffective disorder. *Am J Psych* 156:544, 1999.

Rosebush PI and Stewart T. A prospective analysis of 24 episodes of neuroleptic malignant syndrome. *Am J Psych* 146:717–725, 1989.

Rosebush PI, Stewart T and Mazurek MF. The treatment of neuroleptic malignant syndrome: Are dantrolene and bromocriptine useful adjuncts to supportive care? *Br J Psych* 150:709–712, 1991.

Rosebush PI, Stewart TD and Gelenberg AJ. Twenty neuroleptic rechallenges after neuroleptic malignant syndrome in 15 patients. *J Clin Psych* 50:295–298, 1989.

Sachdev P and Loneragan C. The present status of akathisia. *J Nerv Ment Dis* 179:381–391, 1991.

Sachdev P and Loneragan C. The present status of akathisia. J Nerv Ment Dis 179:381–391, 1991.

Sanger TM, Lieberman JA, Tohen M, et al. Olanzapine versus haloperidol treatment in first-episode psychosis. *Am J Psychiatry* 156:79, 1999.

Sautter F, McDermott B and Garver D. Familial differences between rapid neuroleptic response psychosis and delayed neuroleptic response psychosis. *Biol Psychiatry* 33:15–21, 1993.

Sethi BB and Dube S. Propranolol in schizophrenia. *Neuropsychopharm Biol Psych* 7:88–89, 1983.

B
I
B
L
I
O
G
R
A
P
H
Y

Shalev A, Hermesh H and Munitz H. Mortality from neuroleptic malignant syndrome. *J Clin Psych* 50:18–25, 1989.

Sheehy LM and Maxmen JS. Phenelzine-induced psychosis. *Am J Psych* 135:1422–1423, 1978.

Shintani EY, Uchida KM. Donepezil: an anticholinesterase inhibitor for Alzheimer's disease. *Am J Psychiatry Health Syst Pharm* 54(2):2805, 1997.

Silver H and Nassar A. Fluvoxamine improves negative symptoms in treated chronic schizo-phrenia: An add-on double-blind, placebo-controlled study. *Biol Psychiatry* 31:698–704, 1992.

Silverstone T, Smith G and Goodall E. Prevalence of obesity in patients receiving depot antipsychotics. *Br J Psych* 153:214–217, 1988.

Sipahimalani A, Sime RM, Masand PS. Treatment of delirium with risperidone. *Int J Geriatr Psychopharmacol* 1:24, 1997.

Siris SG, et al. The use of antidepressants for negative symptoms in a subset of schizophrenic patients. *Psychopharmacol Bull* 27:331–335, 1991.

Small JG, Hirsch SR, Arvanitis LA, et al. Quetiapine in patients with schizophrenia: a high- and low-dose double-blind comparison with placebo. *Arch Gen Psychiatry* 1997; 54:549.

Spencer CM, Noble S. Rivastigmine: a review of its use in Alzheimer's disease. *Drugs Aging* 13:391, 1998

Spivak B and others. Clozapine treatment for neuroleptic-induced tardive dyskinesia, parkinsonism, and chronic akathisia in schizophrenic patients. *J Clin Psychiatry* 58(7):318, 1997.

Stahl SM. What makes an antipsychotic atypical? *J Clin Psychiatry* 59(8):403, 1998.

Sultzer DL and others. A double-blind comparison of trazodone and haloperidol for treatment of agitation in patients with dementia. *Am J Psychiatry Geriatr Psychiatry* 5:60, 1997.

Susman VL and Addonizio G. Reinduction of neuroleptic malignant syndrome by lithium. *J Clin Psychopharmacol* 7:339–341, 1987.

Szymanski S, Lieberman JA, Picou D, Masiar S and Cooper T. A case report of cimetidine-induced clozapine toxicity. *J Clin Psych* 52:21–22, 1991.

Tamminga CA. Principles of the pharmacotherapy of schizophrenia. In: Charney DS, Nestler EJ, Bunnery BS, eds. *Neurobiology of mental illness*. New York: Oxford University Press, 1999.

Tandon R, DeQuardo JR, Goodson J, Mann NA and Greden JF. Effect of anticholinergics on positive and negative symptoms in schizophrenia. *Psychopharmacol Bull* 28:292–295, 1992.

Tohen M, Sanger TM, McElroy SL, et al. Olanzapine versus placebo in the treatment of acute mania. *Am J Psychiatry* 156:702,1999

Tollefson GD, Beasley CM, Tran PV, et al. Olanzapine versus haloperidol in the treatment of schizophrenia and schizoaffective and schizophreniform disorders: results of an international collaborative trial. *Am J Psychiatry* 154:457, 1997.

Trzepacz PT, Wise Mg. Neuropsychiatric aspects of delirium. In Yudofsky SC, Hales RE, editors: *American Psychiatric Press textbook of neuropsychiatry*, Washington, DC, 1997, American Psychiatric Press.

Tsai G and others. D-serine added to antipsychotics for the treatment of schizophrenia. *Soc Biol Psychiatry* 44(11):1081, 1998.

Tune L, Carr S, Hoag E and Cooper T. Anticholinergic effects of drugs commonly prescribed for the elderly: Potential means for assessing risk of delirium. *Am J Psych* 149:1393–1394, 1992.

Van Putten T, Marder SR and Mintz J. Serum prolactin as a correlate of clinical response to haloperidol. *J Clin Psychopharmacol* 11:357–361, 1991.

Viguera AC, Baldessarini RJ, Hegarty JM, et al. Clinical risk following abrupt and gradual withdrawal of maintenance neuroleptic treatment. *Arch Gen Psychiatry* 54:49, 1997.

Wahlbeck K, Cheine M, Essali A, et al. Evidence of clozapine's effectiveness in schizophrenia: a systematic review and meta-analysis of randomized trials. *Am J Psychiatry* 156:990, 1999.

Walters VL and others. New strategies for old problems; tardive dyskinesia (TD). Review and report on severe TD cases treated with 12, 8, and 5 years of video follow-up. *Schizophr Res* 28(23):231, 1997.

Watkins PB, Zimmerman HJ, Knapp MJ, Gracon SI and Lewis KW. Hepatotoxic effects of tacrine administration in patients with Alzheimer's disease. *JAMA* 271:992–998, 1994.

Wells BG, Cold JA, Marken PA, Brown CS, Chu CC, et al. A placebo-controlled trial of nadolol in the treatment of neuroleptic-induced akathisia. *J Clin Psych* 52:255–260, 1991.

Wengel SP, Folks DG. Mood stabilizers. In Klein DL, Hay DG, editors: *Treatment of agitation in dementia*, Washington, DC, 2000, American Psychiatric Press.

Wilkins JN, Marder SR, Van Putten T, et al. Circulating prolactin predicts risk of exacerbation in patients on depot fluphenazine. *Psychopharmacol Bull* 23:522–525, 1987.

Wilson WH and Claussen AM. Seizures associated with clozapine treatment in a state hospital. *J Clin Psych* 55:184–188, 1994.

Winker A. Tacrine for Alzheimer's disease: Which patient, what dose? *JAMA* 271:1023–1024, 1994.

Wirshing DA and others. Novel antipsychotics: comparison of weight gain liabilities. *J Clin Psychiatry* 60(6):358, 1999.

Wirshing DA, Marshall BC, Green MF, et al. Risperidone in treatment-refractory schizophrenia. *Am J Psychiatry* 156:1374, 1999.

Woerner MG and others. Prospective study of tardive dyskinesia in the elderly: rates and risk factors. *Am J Psychiatry* 155(11):1521, 1998.

Woerner MG, Kane JM, Lieberman JA, et al. The prevalence of tardive dyskinesia. *J Clin Psychopharmacol* 11:34–42, 1991.

Woerner MG, Saltz BL, Kane JM, Lieberman JA and Alvir MJ. Diabetes and development of tardive dyskinesia. *Am J Psych* 150:966–968, 1993.

Wolf MA, et al. Low dose bromocriptine in neuroleptic-resistant schizophrenia: A pilot study. *Biol Psychiatry* 31:1166–1168, 1992.

Wolk SI and Douglas DJ. Clozapine treatment of psychosis in Parkinson's disease: A report of five consecutive cases. *J Clin Psych* 53:373–376, 1992.

Wolkowitz OM, Turetsky MA, Reus VI and Hargraves WA. Benzodiazepine augmentation of neuroleptics in treatment-resistant schizophrenia. *Psychopharmacol Bull* 28:291–295, 1992.

Yadalam KG and Simpson GM. Changing from oral to depot fluphenazine. *J Clin Psych* 49:346–348, 1988.

Zarate CA, Tohen M, Baldessarini RJ. Clozapine in severe mood disorders. *J Clin Psych* 56:411, 1995.

## ANTIDEPRESSANTS, MAOIs

Anton RF and Burch EA, Jr. Amoxapine versus amitriptyline combined with perphenazine in the treatment of psychotic depression. *Am J Psych* 147:1203–1208, 1990.

Artigas F, Perez V and Alvarez E. Pindolol induces a rapid improvement of depressed patients treated with serotonin reuptake inhibitors. *Arch Gen Psych* 51:248–251, 1994.

Barbey JT, Roose SP. SSRI safety in overdose. *J Clin Psychiatry* 59(suppl 15):45, 1998.

Bouckoms A and Mangini L. Pergolide: An antidepressant adjuvant for mood disorders? *Psychopharmacol Bull* 29:207–211, 1993.

Bresnahan DB, Pandey GN, Janicak PG, et al. MAO inhibition and clinical response in depressed patients treated with phenelzine. *J Clin Psych* 51:47–50, 1990.

Brinkley JR. Pharmacotherapy of borderline states. *Psych Clin N Am* 16:853–884, 1993.

Browne B and Linter S. Monoamine oxidase inhibitors and narcotic analgesics: A critical review of the implications for treatment. *Br J Psych* 151:210–212, 1987.

Charney DS, et al. Drug treatment of panic disorder: The comparative efficacy of imipramine, alprazolam, and trazodone. *J Clin Psych* 47:580–586, 1986.

Cohen LS, Altshuler LL. Pharmacological management of psychiatric illness during pregnancy and the postpartum period. *Psychiatr Clin North Am* 4:21, 1997.

Cooke RG, Joffe RT and Levitt A. $T_3$ augmentation of antidepressant treatment in $T_4$-replaced thyroid patients. *J Clin Psych* 53:16–18, 1992.

Cornelius JR, Soloff PH, George A, Ulrich RF and Perel JM. Haloperidol vs. phenelzine in continuation therapy of borderline disorder. *Psychopharmacol Bull* 29:333–337, 1993.

Cowdry RW and Gardner DL. Pharmacotherapy of borderline personality disorder. *Arch Gen Psych* 45:111–119, 45.

Davidson J. Seizures and bupropion: A review. J Clin Psych 50:256–261, 1989.

Davis JM, Janicak PG and Bruning AK. The efficacy of MAO inhibitors in depression: A meta-analysis. *Psych Anls* 17:825–831, 1987.

Dilsaver SC. Antidepressant withdrawal syndromes: Phenomenology and pathophysiology. *Acta Psychiatr Scand* 79:113–117, 1989.

Dunleavy DLF and Oswald I. Phenelzine, mood response, and sleep. *Arch Gen Psych* 28:353–356, 1973.

Gardner DL and Cowdry RW. Pharmacotherapy of borderline personality disorder: A review. *Psychopharmacol Bull* 25:515–522, 1989.

Gelenberg AJ. New perspectives on the use of tricyclic antidepressants. *J Clin Psych* 50:3, 1989.

Georgotas A, McCue RE, Friedman E and Cooper TB. A placebo-controlled comparison of the effect of nortriptyline and phenelzine on orthostatic hypotension in elderly depressed patients. *J Clin Psychopharmacol* 7: 413–416, 1987.

Gitlin MJ. Psychotropic medications and their effects on sexual dysfunction: diagnosis, biology, and treatment approaches. *J Clin Psychiatry* 55:406, 1994.

Glassman A, et al. The safety of tricyclic antidepressants in cardiac patients (commentary). *JAMA* 269:2673–2675, 1993.

Glassman AH and Roose SP. Cardiovascular effects of tricyclic antidepressants. *Psych Anls* 17:340–342, 1987.

Goodwin FK, et al. Potentiation of antidepressant effects by 1-triiodothyronine in tricyclic nonresponders. *Am J Psych* 139:34–38, 1982.

Greden JF. Introduction: Part III. New agents for the treatment of depression. *J Clin Psych* 55:32–33 (suppl.), 1994.

Gunderson JG. Pharmacotherapy for patients with borderline personality disorder. *Arch Gen Psych* 43:698–700, 1986.

Harrison WH, et al. MAOIs and hypertensive crisis: The role of OTC drugs. *J Clin Psych* 50:64–65, 1989.

Hellerstein DJ, Yanowitch P, Rosenthal J, Wallner-Samstag L, Maurer M, et al. A randomized double-blind study of fluoxetine versus placebo in the treatment of dysthymia. *Am J Psych* 150:1169–1175, 1993.

Himmelhoch JM, Thase ME, Mallinger AG and Houck P. Tranylcypromine verses imipramine in anergic bipolar depression. *Am J Psych* 148:910–916, 1991.

Höschl C. Do calcium antagonists have a place in the treatment of mood disorders? *Drugs* 42:721–729, 1991.

Howland RH. Pharmacotherapy of dysthymia: A review. *J Clin Psychopharmacol* 11:83–92, 1991.

Hudson JI and Pope HG, Jr. Affective spectrum disorder: Does antidepressant response identify a family of disorders with a common pathophysiology? *Am J Psych* 147:552–564, 1990.

Hunt KA and Resnick MP. Clomipramine-induced agranulocytosis and its treatment with G-CSF. *Am J Psych* 150:522–523, 1993.

Jacobson SJ, Jones K, Johnson K, Ceolin L, Kaur P, Sahn D, Donnenfeld AE, Rieder M, Santelli R, Smythe J, Pastuszak A, Einarson T and Koren G. Prospective multicentre study of pregnancy outcome after lithium exposure during the first trimester. *Lancet* 339:530–533, 1992.

Kahn D, Silver JM and Opler LA. The safety of switching rapidly from tricyclic antidepressants to monoamine oxidase inhibitors. *J Clin Psychopharmacol* 9:198–202, 1989.

Katz R and Rosenthal M. Adverse interaction of cyproheptadine with serotonergic antidepressant (letter). *J Clin Psych* 55:314–315, 1994.

Keck PE, et al. Frequency and presentation of neuroleptic malignant syndrome in a state psychiatric hospital. *J Clin Psych* 50:352–355, 1989.

Keck PE, Jr, Vuckovic A, Pope HG, Jr, et al. Acute cardiovascular response to monoamine oxidase inhibitors: A prospective assessment. *J Clin Psychopharmacol* 9:203–206, 1989.

Klaiber EL, Broverman DM, Vogel W and Kobayashi Y. Estrogen therapy for severe persistent depressions in women. *Arch Gen Psychiatry* 36:550–554, 1979.

B
I
B
L
I
O
G
R
A
P
H
Y

Lappin R and Achuincloss E. Treatment of the serotonin syndrome with cypro-heptadine (letter). *N Engl J Med* 331:1021–1022, 1994.

Lederle Laboratories. (1987). *Asendin.* Pearl River NY: J. Maxmen.

Levitt AJ, Joffe RT and Kennedy SH. Bright light augmentation in antidepressant nonresponders. *J Clin Psych* 52:336–337, 1991.

Liebowitz MR, et al. Phenelzine vs. imipramine in atypical depression: A preliminary report. *Arch Gen Psych* 41:669–677, 1984.

Liebowitz MR, Schneier F, Campeas R, Hollander E, Hatterer J, Fyer A, Gorman J, Papp L, Davies S, Gully R and Klein DF. Phenelzine vs atenolol in social phobia: A placebo-controlled comparison. *Arch Gen Psych* 49:290–300, 1992.

Lipinsky JF, et al. Fluoxetine-induced akathisia: Clinical and theoretical implications. *J Clin Psych* 50:339–342, 1989.

Maany I, et al. Increase in desipramine serum levels associated with methadone treatment. *Am J of Psych* 146:1611–1613, 1989.

Mann JJ. Loss of antidepressant effect with long-term monoamine oxidase inhibitor treatment without loss of monoamine oxidase inhibition. *J Clin Psychopharmacol* 3:363–366, 1983.

Marin DB, Kocsis JH, Frances AJ and Parides M. Desipramine for the treatment of "Pure" dysthymia versus "Double" depression. *Am J Psych* 151:1079–1080, 1994.

McGrath PJ, et al. A double-blind crossover trial of imipramine and phenelzine for outpatients with treatment-refractory depression. *Am J Psych* 150:118–123, 1993.

Murphy DL. The behavioral toxicity of monoamine oxidase-inhibiting antidepressants. In Garrattini S, et al. (Eds.), *Advances in Pharmacology and Chemotherapy* (vol 14), 71–103, New York: Academic Press, 1977.

Nelson JC, Mazure CM, Bowers MB, Jr and Jatlow PI. A preliminary, open study of the combination of fluoxetine and desipramine for rapid treatment of major depression. *Arch Gen Psych* 48:303–307, 1991.

Palladino A, Jr. Adverse reactions to abrupt discontinuation of phenelzine (letter). *J Clin Psychopharmacol* 3:206–207, 1983.

Pare CMB, Kline N, Hallstrom C and Cooper TB. Will amitriptyline prevent the "Cheese" reaction of monoamine oxidase inhibitors? *Lancet* July 24:183–186, 1982.

Pastuszak A, Schick-Boschetto B, Zuber C, et al. Pregnancy outcome following first-trimester exposure to fluoxetine (Prozac). *JAMA* 269:2246, 1993.

Peet M. Induction of mania with selective serotonin re-uptake inhibitors and tricyclic anti-depressants. *Br J Psych* 164:549–550, 1994.

Perry PJ, Zeilmann C and Arndt S. Tricyclic antidepressant concentrations in plasma: An estimate of their sensitivity and specificity as a predictor of response. *J Clin Psychopharmacol* 14:230–240, 1994.

Prien RF and Kupfer DJ. Continuation drug therapy for major depressive episodes: How long should it be maintained. *Am J Psych* 143:18–23, 1986.

Quitkin FM, McGrath PJ, Stewart JW, et al. Phenelzine and imipramine in mood reactive depressives. *Arch Gen Psych* 46:787–793, 1989.

Quitkin FM, Stewart JW, et al. Phenelzine versus imipramine in the treatment of probable atypical depression: Defining syndrome boundaries of selective MAOI responders. *Am J Psych* 45:306–311, 1988.

Razani J, et al. The safety and efficacy of combined amitriptyline and tranylcypromine anti-depressant treatment. *Arch Gen Psych* 40:657–661, 1983.

Remick RA, Jewesson P and Ford RWJ. Monoamine oxidase inhibitors in general anesthesia: A reevaluation. *Convulsive Therapy* 3:196–203, 1987.

Renaud J, Axelson D, Birmaher B. A risk-benefit assessment of pharmacotherapies for clinical depression in children and adolescents. *Drug Safety* 20:59, 1999.

Richelson E and Nelson A. Antagonism by antidepressants of neurotransmitter receptors of normal human brain in vitro. *J Pharmacol Experimental Therapeutics* 230:94–102, 1984.

Richelson E. The pharmacology of antidepressants at the synapse: Focus on newer compounds. *J Clin Psych* 55:34–39, 1994.

Rickels K, et al. Antidepressants for the treatment of generalized anxiety disorder: A placebo-controlled comparison of imipramine, trazodone, and diazepam. *Arch Gen Psych* 50:884–895, 1993.

Rickels K, Amsterdam JD, Clary C, Puzzuoli G and Schweizer E. Buspirone in major depression: A controlled study. *J Clin Psych* 52:34–38, 1991.

Robinson DS, Lerfald SC, Bennett B, Laux D, Devereaux E, et al. Continuation and maintenance treatment of major depression with the monoamine oxidase inhibitor phenelzine: A double-blind placebo-controlled discontinuation study. Presented at the 30th Annual Meeting of the New Clinical Drug Evaluation Unit (NCDEU), May 29-June 1, 1990, Key Biscayne, Florida.

Roose S, et al. Comparative efficacy of selective serotonin reuptake inhibitors and tricyclics in the treatment of melancholia. *Am J Psych* 151:1735–1739, 1994.

Roose SP, Glassman AH and Dalack GW. Depression, heart disease, and tricyclic antidepressants. *J Clin Psych* 50:12–16, 1989.

Sacchetti E, et al. Are SSRI antidepressants a clinically homogeneous class of compounds? (letter). *Lancet* 344:126–127, 1994.

Schlager D. Early-morning administration of short-acting $\beta$-blockers for treatment of winter depression. *Am J Psych* 151:1383–1385, 1994.

Shulman KI, Walker SE, MacKenzie S and Knowles S. Dietary restriction, tyramine, and the use of MAOIs. *J Clin Psychopharmacol* 9:397–402, 1989.

Sternbach H. The serotonin syndrome. *Am J Psych* 148:705–713, 1991.

Stewart JW, McGrath PJ and Quitkin FM. Can mildly depressed outpatients with atypical depression benefit from antidepressants? *Am J Psych* 149:615–619, 1992.

Stewart JW, McGrath PJ, Quitkin FM, et al. Chronic depression: Response to placebo, imipramine, and phenelzine. *J Clin Psychopharmacol* 13:391–396, 1993.

Stewart JW, McGrath PJ, Rabkin JG and Quitkin FM. Atypical depression: A valid clinical entity? *Psych Clin N Am* 16:479–495, 1993.

Sullivan EA and Shulman KI. Diet and monoamine oxidase inhibition: A reexamination. *Can J Psych* 29:707–711, 1984.

Tailor SAN, Shulman KI, Walker SE, Moss J and Gardner D. Hypertensive episode associated with phenelzine and tap beer: A reanalysis of the role of pressor amines in beer. *J Clin Psychopharmacol* 14:5–14, 1994.

BIBLIOGRAPHY

Teicher MH, et al. Severe daytime somnolence in patients treated with an MAOI. *Am J Psych* 145:1552–1556, 1988.

Thase ME, Mallinger AG, McKnight D and Himmelhoch JM. Treatment of imipramine-resistant recurrent depression, IV: A double-blind crossover study of tranylcypromine for anergic bipolar depression. *Am J Psych* 149:195–198, 1992.

Tingelstad J. The cardiotoxicity of the tricyclics. *J Am Acad Child and Adolescent Psych* 30:845–846, 1991.

Walsh BT. Use of antidepressants in bulimia. *Clin Pediatrics* 28:127–128, 1989.

Ward NG. Pain and Depression. In Bonica J (Ed.), *The Management of Pain* 2nd ed (vol 1), 310–319, Philadelphia: Lea & Fibiger, 1990.

Ward NG. Tricyclic antidepressants for chronic low back pain: Mechanisms of action and predictors of response. *Spine* 11:661–665, 1986.

Wesner RB and Noyes R, Jr. Tolerance to the therapeutic effect of phenelzine in patients with panic disorder. *J Clin Psych* 49:450–451, 1988.

Woods SW, et al. Psychostimulant treatment of depressive disorders secondary to medical illness. *J Clin Psych* 47:12–15, 1986.

Yonkers KA, Halbreich U, Freeman E, et al. Symptomatic improvement of premenstrual dysphoric disorder with sertraline. *JAMA* 278:983, 1997.

Young WF, Jr, et al. Human monoamine oxidase. *Arch Gen Psych* 43:604–609, 1986.

## LITHIUM, ANTICONVULSANTS, AND MOOD STABILIZERS

Alpert M, Allan ER, Citrome L, Laury G, Sison C and Sudilovsky A. A double-blind, placebo-controlled study of adjunctive nadolol in the management of violent psychiatric patients. *Psychopharm Bulletin* 26:367–371, 1990.

Altshuler LL, Cohen L, Szuba MP, et al. Pharmacologic management of psychiatric illness during pregnancy: dilemmas and guidelines. *Am J Psychiatry* 152:592, 1996.

American Psychiatric Association. Practice guideline for the treatment of patients with bipolar disorder (Suppl.). *Am J Psych* 151:1–36, 1994.

Amsterdam JD, Maislin G and Rybakowski J. A possible antiviral action of lithium carbonate in herpes simplex virus infections. *Biol Psychiatry* 27:447–453, 1990.

Ballenger JC. The clinical use of carbamazepine in affective disorders. *J Clin Psych* 49:13–19, 1988.

Bauer MS and Whybrow PC. The effect of changing thyroid function of cyclic affective illness in a human subject. *Am J Psych* 143:633–636, 1986.

Bauman P, Nil R, Souche A, et al. A double-blind, placebo-controlled study of citalopram with and without lithium in the treatment of therapy-resistant depressive patients: a clinical, pharmacokinetic, and pharmacogenetic investigation. *J Clin Psychopharmacol* 16:307, 1996.

Bendz H, Aurell M, Balldin J, et al. Kidney damage in long-term lithium patients: a cross-sectional study of patients with 15 years or more on lithium. *Nephrol Dialysis Transplant* 9:1250, 1994.

Bone S, et al. Incidence of side effects in patients on long-term lithium therapy. *Am J Psych* 137:103–104, 1980.

Bowden C, et al. Efficacy of divalproex vs lithium and placebo in the treatment of mania. *JAMA* 271:918–924, 1994.

Brewerton T and Jackson C. Prophylaxis of carbamazepine-induced hyponatremia by demeclocycline in six patients. *J Clin Psych* 55:249–251, 1994.

Brooks SC and Lessin BE. Treatment of resistant lithium-induced nephrogenic diabetes insipidus and schizoaffective psychosis with carbamazepine. *Am J Psych* 140:1077–1078, 1983.

Brown WT Side effects of lithium therapy and their treatment. *Can Psych Assoc J* 21:13–21, 1976.

Browne TR Clonazepam: A review of a new anticonvulsant drug. *Arch Neurol* 33:326–332, 1976.

Calabrese JR, Bowden CL, McElroy SL, et al. Spectrum of activity of lamotrigine in treatment-refractory bipolar disorder. *Am J Psychiatry* 156:1019, 1999.

Calabrese JR, Bowden CL, Sachs GS, et al. A double-blind placebo-controlled study of lamotrigine monotherapy in outpatients with bipolar I depression. Lamictal 602 Study Group. *J Clin Psychiatry* 60:79, 1999.

Calabrese JR, et al. Predictors of valproate response in bipolar rapid cycling. *J Clin Psychopharmacol* 13:280–283, 1993.

Cohen LS, Friedman JM, Jefferson JW, Johnson EM and Weiner ML. A reevaluation of risk of *in utero* exposure to lithium. *JAMA* 271:146–150, 1994.

Cummings MA, Haviland MG, Wareham JG and Fontana LA. A prospective clinical evaluation of an equation to predict daily lithium dose. *J Clin Psych* 54:55–58, 1993.

Dunner DL and Fieve RR. Clinical factors in lithium carbonate prophylaxis failure. *Arch Gen Psych* 30:229–233, 1974.

Faedda GL, et al. Outcome after rapid vs gradual discontinuation of lithium treatment in bipolar disorders. *Arch Gen Psych* 50:448–455, 1993.

Gelenberg AJ and Stone Hopkins H. Report on efficacy of treatments for bipolar disorder. *Psychopharmacol Bull* 29:447–456, 1993.

Ghaemi SN, Goodwin FK. Use of atypical agents in bipolar and schizoaffective disorders: review of the empirical literature. *J Clin Psychopharmacol* 12(suppl):57, 1999.

Ghaemi SN, Katzow JJ, Desai SP. Lamotrigine in bipolar disorder. *Int Drug Therapy Newslett* 34(4):25, 1999.

Gleason RP and Schneider LS. Carbamazepine treatment of agitation in Alzheimer's outpatients refractory to neuroleptics. *J Clin Psych* 51:115–118, 1990.

Goodnick P. Verapamil prophylaxis in pregnant women with bipolar disorder (letter). *Am J Psych* 150:1560, 1993.

Hetmar O, Brun C, Clemmesen L, Ladefoged J, Larsen S and Rafaelsen OJ. Lithium: Long-term effects on the kidney: II. Structural changes. *J Psychiatr Res* 21:279–288, 1987.

Himmelhoch JM, et al. Adjustment of lithium dose during lithium-chlorothiazide therapy. *Clin Pharmacology and Therapeutics* 22:225–227, 1977.

Hirschfield RM. Care of the sexually active depressed patient. *J Clin Psychiatry* 60(suppl 17):32, 1999.

Hudson JI and others. Fluvoxamine in the treatment of binge-eating disorder: a multicenter placebo-controlled, double-blind trial. *Am J Psychiatry* 155(12):1756, 1998.

Jefferson JW, et al. Lithium Encyclopedia for Clinical Practice (2nd ed.). Washington DC: *American Psychiatric Press*, 1987.

Jefferson JW. Cardiovascular effects and toxicity of anxiolytics and antidepressants. *J Clin Psych* 50:368–378, 1989.

Jefferson JW. Mood stabilizers: A review. In: Dunner D (Ed.), *Current Psychiatric Therapy*, 246–250, Philadelphia: WB Saunders, 1993.

Joffe RT and Singer W. A comparison of triiodothyronine and thyroxine in the potentiation of tricyclic antidepressants. *J Psychiatr Res* 32:241–251, 1990.

Kafantaris V, et al. Carbamazepine in hospitalized aggressive conduct disorder children: An open pilot study. *Psychopharmacol Bull* 28:193–199, 1992.

Kane J, et al. Extrapyramidal side effects with lithium treatment. *Am J Psych* 135:322–328, 1989.

Kastner T, Finesmith R and Walsh K. Long-term administration of valproic acid in the treatment of affective symptoms in people with mental retardation. *J Clin Psychopharmacol* 13:448–451, 1993.

Keck PE and others. Valproate oral loading in the treatment of acute mania. *J Clin Psychiatry* 54(8):305, 1993.

Keltner NL. Venlafaxine: a novel antidepressant. *J Psychosoc Nurs Ment Health Serv* 33(1):51, 1995.

Klein PS, Melton DA. A molecular mechanism for the effect of lithium on development. *Proc Natl Acad Sci U S A* 93:8455, 1996.

Lee H, et al. A trial of lithium citrate for the management of acute agitation of psychiatric inpatients: A pilot study (letter). *J Clin Psychopharmacol* 12:361–362, 1992.

Levy RH and Kerr BM. Clinical pharmacokinetics of carbamazepine. *J Clin Psych* 49:58–61, 1988.

Manji HK, Lenox RH. Lithium: a molecular transducer of mood-stabilization in the treatment of bipolar disorder. *Neuropsychopharmacology* 19:161, 1998.

Marcotte D. Use of topiramate, a new anti-epileptic as a mood stabilizer. *Affect Disord* 50:245, 1998.

Markoff RA and King M, Jr. Does lithium dose prediction improve treatment efficacy? Prospective evaluation of a mathematical method. *J Clin Psychopharmacol* 12:305–308, 1992.

Mattes J. Valproic acid for nonaffective aggression in the mentally retarded. *J Nerv Ment Dis* 180:601–602, 1992.

Mazure C, et al. Valproate treatment of older psychotic patients with organic mental syndromes and behavioral dyscontrol. *J Am Geriatric Soc* 40:914–916, 1993.

McElroy SL, et al. Valproate in psychiatric disorders: Literature review and clinical guidelines. *J Clin Psych* 50:23–29, 1989.

McElroy SL, Keck PE, Jr., Pope HG, Jr., Hudson JI and Morris D. Correlates of antimanic response to valproate. *Psychopharmacol Bull* 27:127–133, 1991.

McEvoy JP, Hogarty GE and Steingard S. Optimal dose of neuroleptic in acute schizophrenia: A controlled study of the neuroleptic threshold and higher haloperidol dose. *Arch Gen Psych* 48:739–745, 1991.

Nambudiri DE, Meyers BS and Young RC. Delayed recovery from lithium neurotoxicity. *J Geriatr Psych Neurol* 4:40–43, 1991.

Neppe VN, Tucker JG and Wilensky AJ. Introduction: Fundamentals of carbamazepine use in neuropsychiatry. *J Clin Psych* 49:4–6, 1988.

Pellock JM. Carbamazepine side effects in children and adults. Epilepsia 28:S64–S70, 1987.

Plenge P, Mellerup ET, Bolwig TG, Brun C, Hetmar O, Ladefoged J, Larsen S and Rafaelsen OJ. Lithium treatment: Does the kidney prefer one daily dose instead of two? *Acta Psychiatr Scand* 66:121–128, 1982.

Post RM, Trimble MR and Pippenger CE. *Clinical Use of Anticonvulsants in Psychiatric Disorders* New York: Demos, 1989.

Post RM. Time course of clinical effects of carbamazepine: Implications for mechanisms of action. *J Clin Psych* 49:35–46, 1988.

Preskorn SH, Magnus RD. Inhibition of hepatic P-450 isoenzymes by serotonin selective reuptake inhibitors: in vitro and in vivo findings and their implications for patient care. *Psychopharmacol Bull* 30:251, 1994.

Prien RF and Potter WZ. NIMH workshop report on treatment of bipolar disorder. *Psycho-pharmacol Bull* 26:409–427, 1990.

Ragheb M. The clinical significance of lithium-nonsteroidal anti-inflammatory drug interactions. *J Clin Psychopharmacol* 10:350–354, 1990.

Ratey JJ, Sorgi P, Gillian A, O'Driscoll MA, Sands S, et al. Nadolol to treat aggression and psychiatric symptomatology in chronic psychiatric inpatients: A double-blind, placebo-controlled study. *J Clin Psych* 53:41–46, 1992.

Ricketts R, et al. Fluoxetine treatment of severe self-injury in young adults with mental retardation. *J Am Acad Child and Adolescent Psych* 32:865–869, 1993.

Rosenbaum JF and others. Selective serotonin reuptake inhibitor discontinuation syndrome: a randomized clinical trial. *Biol Psychiatry* 44:77, 1998.

Ross DR, Coffey E, Ferren EL, Walker JI and Olanow CW. On-off syndrome treated with lithium carbonate: Case report. *Am J Psych* 138:1626–1627, 1981.

Sanborn K and Jefferson JW. Everyman's guide to the fluctuating lithium level: Obvious and obscure reasons why serum lithium levels change. *Anls Clin Psych* 3:251–258, 1991.

Schou M. Lithium treatment during pregnancy, delivery, and lactation: An update. *J Clin Psych* 51:410–413, 1990.

Segraves RT. Treatment-emergent sexual dysfunction in affective disorder: a review and management strategies. *J Clin Psychiatry* (Update Monogr) 1:1, 1994.

Sernyak MJ and Woods SW. Chronic neuroleptic use in manic-depressive illness. *Psycho-pharmacol Bull* 29:375–381, 1993.

Settle EC and others. Safety profile of sustained-release bupropion in depression: results of three clinical trials. *Clin Ther* 21:3454, 1999.

Sitsen JMA, Zivkov M. Mirtazapine: clinical profile. *CNS Drugs* 4 (suppl 1):39, 1995.

Souza FGM and Goodwin GM. Lithium treatment and prophylaxis in unipolar depression: A meta-analysis. *Br J Psych* 158:666–675, 1991.

Stahl S and others. Meta-analyses of randomized, double-blind, placebo-controlled efficacy and safety studies of mirtazapine versus amitriptyline in major depression. *Acta Psychiatr Scand* 96 (suppl 391):22, 1997.

Stanislav S, et al. Buspirone's efficacy in organic-induced aggression. *J Clin Psychopharmacol* 2:126–130, 1994.

Steiner M and others. Fluoxetine in the treatment of premenstrual dysphoria. *N Engl J Med* 332:1529, 1995.

Stoll AL, Severus WE, Freeman MP, et al. Omega 3 fatty acids in bipolar disorder: a preliminary double-blind, placebo-controlled trial. *Arch Gen Psychiatry* 56:407, 1999.

Suppes T, Webb A, Paul B, et al. Clinical outcome in a randomized 1-year trial of clozapine versus treatment as usual for patients with treatment-resistant illness and a history of mania. *Am J Psychiatry* 156:1164, 1999.

Swann AC, Bowden CL, Morris D, et al. Depression during mania. Treatment response to lithium or divalproex. *Arch Gen Psy*chiatry 54:37, 1997.

Tohen M, et al. Blood dyscrasias with carbamazepine and valproate: A pharmacoepidemiological study of 2,228 patients at risk. *Am J Ps*ych 152:413–418, 1995.

Tohen M, Sanger TM, McElroy SL, et al. Olanzapine versus placebo in the treatment of acute mania. *Am J Psychiatry* 156:702, 1999.

Tupin JP, et al. Long-term use of lithium in aggressive prisoners. *Compr Psych* 14:311–317, 1973.

Valles V, Guillamat R, Vilaplana C, Duno R, and Almenar C. Serum iron and akathisia. *Biol Psychiatry* 31:1172–1183, 1992.

Van Putten T, Marder SR, Mintz J and Poland RE. Haloperidol plasma levels and clinical response: A therapeutic window relationship. *Am J Psych* 149:500–505, 1992.

VanValkenburg C, Kluznik J, Merrill R and Erickson W. Therapeutic levels of valproate for psychosis. *Psychopharmacol Bull* 26:254–255, 1990.

Vestergaard P. Clinically important side effects of long-term lithium treatment: A review. *Acta Psychiatr Scand* 305:11–33, 1983.

Walton SA and others. Superiority of lithium over verapamil in mania: a randomized controlled single-blind trial. *J Clin Psychiatry* 57(11):543, 1996.

Wisner KL, Perel JM. Serum levels of valproate and carbamazepine in breast-feeding mother-infant pairs. *J Clin Psychopharmacol* 18:167, 1998.

Yassa R, et al. Lithium-induced thyroid disorders: A prevalence study. *J Clin Psych* 49:14–16, 1988.

Yonkers KA: Treatment of premenstrual dysphoric disorder. *Curr Rev Mood Anxiety Disord* 1:215, 1997.

Young LT, Robb JC, Hasey GM, et al. Gabapentin as an adjunctive treatment in bipolar disorder. *J Affect Disord* 55:73, 1999.

Yudofsky SC, Silver JM and Hales RE. Pharmacologic management of aggression in the elderly. *J Clin Psych* 51:22–28, 1990.

## STIMULANTS

Angrist B, D'Hollosy M, Sanfilipo M, Satriano J, Diamond G, Simberkoff M and Weinreb H. Central nervous system stimulants as symptomatic treatments for AIDS-related neuropsychiatric impairment. *J Clin Psychopharmacol* 12:268–272, 1992.

Ayd FJ, Zohar J. Psychostimulant (amphetamine or methylphenidate) therapy for chronic and treatment-resistant depression. In Zohar J, Belmaker RH, editors: *Treating resistant depression*, New York, 1987, PMA.

Chiarello RJ, Cole JO. The use of psychostimulants in general psychiatry. *Arch Gen Psychiatry Gen Psychiatry* 44:286, 1987.

Derlet RW, et al. Amphetamine toxicity: Experience with 127 cases. *J Emerg Med* 7:157–161, 1989.

Elia J, Borcherding BG, Rapoport JL and Keysor CS. Methylphenidate and dextroamphetamine treatments of hyperactivity: Are there true non responders? *Psychiatr Res* 36:141–155, 1990.

Fernandez F, et al. Methylphenidate for depressive disorders in cancer patients. *Psychosomatics* 28:455–461, 1987.

Flitman SS. Tranquilizers, stimulants, and enhancers of cognition. *Phys Med Rehab Clin North Am* 10(2):463, 1999.

Glass RM. Caffeine dependence syndrome. *JAMA* 273:1419, 1995.

Hirschfield RM. Management of sexual side effects of antidepressant therapy. *J Clin Psychiatry* 60 (suppl 14):27, 1999.

Holmes VF, Fernandez F and Levy JK. Psychostimulant response in AIDS-related complex patients. *J Clin Psych* 50:5–8, 1989.

Hunt R, et al. An open trial of guanfacine in the treatment of attention-deficit hyperactivity disorder. *J Am Acad Child and Adolescent Psych* 34:50–54, 1995.

Johnson M, et al. Methylphenidate in stroke patients with depression. *Am J Physical Med Rehab* 71:239–241, 1992.

Klein RG, et al. Methylphenidate and growth in hyperactive children: A controlled withdrawal study. *Arch Gen Psych* 45:1127–1130, 1988.

Klein RG and Mannuzza S. Hyperactive boys almost grown up: III. Methylphenidate effects on ultimate height. *Arch Gen Psych* 45:1131–1134, 1988.

Kosten TR and others. Depression and stimulant dependence: neurobiology and pharmacotherapy. *J Nerv Ment Dis* 186(12):737, 1998.

Lazarus A. Neuroleptic malignant syndrome: Detection and management. *Psych Anls* 15:706–711, 1985.

Lazarus LW, Winemiller DR, Lingam VR, Neyman I, Hartman C, Abassian M, Kartan U, Groves L and Fawcett J. Efficacy and side effects of methylphenidate for poststroke depression. *J Clin Psych* 53:447–449, 1992.

Leibowitz SF, Alexander JT. Hypothalamic serotonin in control of eating behavior, meal size, and body weight. *Biol Psychiatry* 44(9):851, 1998.

Little KY, Gay TL. Acute stimulant response prediction of chronic trazodone effects. *Prog Neuropsychopharm Biol Psychiatry* 20(5):815, 1996.

Rapport MD, Denney C, DuPaul GJ and Gardner MJ. Attention deficit disorder and methyl-phenidate: Normalization rates, clinical effectiveness, and response prediction in 76 children. *J Am Acad Child and Adolescent Psych* 33:882–893, 1994.

Rosenberg PB, Ahmed I and Hurwitz S. Methylphenidate in depressed medically ill patients. *J Clin Ps*ych 52:263–267, 1991.

Satel SL and Nelson JC. Stimulants in the treatment of depression: A critical overview. *J Clin Ps*ych 50:241–249.

Spencer T, Biederman J, Wilens TE, et al. Is attention deficit hyperactivity disorder in adults a valid diagnosis? *Harvard Rev Psychiatry* 1:326, 1994.

Spencer T, Wilens TE, Biederman J, et al. A double-blind, cross-over comparison of methylphenidate and placebo in adults with childhood onset attention deficit hyperactivity disorder. *Arch Gen Psychiatry* 52:434, 1995

Sylvester C. Psychopharmacology of disorders in children. *Psych Clin N Am* 16:779–791, 1993.

Tinsley JA, Watkins DD. Over-the-counter stimulants: abuse and addiction. *Mayo Clin Proc* 73(10):977, 1998.

Wilens T, et al. Nortriptyline in the treatment of ADHD: A chart review of 58 cases. *J Am Acad Child and Adolescent Psych* 32:343–349, 1993.

Wilens TE, Biederman J, Spencer TJ, et al. Controlled trial of high doses of pemoline for adults with attention-deficit/hyperactivity disorder. *J Clin Psychopharmacol* 19:257, 1999.

## GENERAL

American Psychiatric Association. Treatment of Psychiatric Disorders. Washington DC: A Task Force Report of the American Psychiatric Association, 1989.

American Psychiatric Association. Diagnostic and Statistical Manual of Mental Disorder (4th ed.) Washington DC: Author, 1994.

Arana GW and Hyman SE. *Handbook of Psychiatric Drug Therapy* (2nd ed.). Boston: Little, Brown, 1991.

Baastrup PC, et al. Adverse reactions in treatment with lithium carbonate and haloperidol. *JAMA* 236:2645–2646, 1976.

Bernstein JG. Psychotropic drug induced weight gain: Mechanisms and management. *Clin Neuropharmacol* 11:194–296, 1988.

Bezchlibnyk-Butler KZ and Jeffries JJ (Eds.). *Clinical Handbook of Psychotropic Drugs* (2nd ed.). Lewiston NY: Hogrefe & Huber, 1990.

Brophy JJ. Suicide attempts with psychotherapeutic drugs. *Arch Gen Psych* 17:652–657, 1967.

Cohen LS, Heller VL and Rosenbaum JF. Treatment guidelines for psychotropic drug use in pregnancy. Psychosomatics 30:25–33, 1989.

Coplan JE and Gorman JM. Treatment of anxiety disorder in patients with mood disorders. J *Clin Psych* 51:9–13, 1990.

Gelenberg AJ, Bassuk EL and Schoonover SC (Eds.). *The Practitioner's Guide to Psychoactive Drugs* (3rd ed.). New York: Plenum, 1991.

Griffith HW. *Complete Guide to Prescription and Non-prescription Drugs* (5th ed.). Los Angeles: Body Press, 1988.

Hansten PD and Horn JR. *Drug Interactions: Clinical Significance of Drug-Drug Interactions*. Philadelphia: Lea & Febiger, 1994.

Klein DF and Davis JM. *Diagnosis and Drug Treatment of Psychiatric Disorders* (2nd ed.). Baltimore: Williams & Wilkins, 1969.

Kranzler HR and Cardoni A. Sodium chloride treatment of antidepressant-induced orthostatic hypotension. *J Clin Psych* 49:366–368, 1988.

Kunik ME, Yudofsky SC, Silver JM and Hales RE. Pharmacologic approach to management of agitation associated with dementia (2, Suppl). *J Clin Psych* 55:13–17, 1994.

Mammen GJ (Ed.). *Clinical Pharmacokinetics in Drug Data Handbook* (2nd ed.). Auckland, New Zealand: AIDS Press, 1990.

Maxmen JS and Ward NG. *Essential Psychopathology and Its Treatment.* New York: Norton, 1995.

Pelham WE, Aronoff HR, Midlam JK, et al. A comparison of ritalin and Adderall: efficacy and time course in children with attention-deficit/hyperactivity disorder. *Pediatrics* 103:43, 1999.

Pliszka SR. The use of psychostimulants in the pediatric patient. *Pediatr Clin North Am* 45:1085, 1998.

Roger SL, Friedhoff LT. The efficacy and safety of donepezil in patients with Alzheimer's disease: result of a multicentre, randomized, double-blind, placebo-controlled trial. The Donepezil Study Group. *Dementia* 7:293, 1996.

Shinn AF and Hogan MF (Eds.). *Evaluations of Drug Interactions.* New York: Macmillan, 1988.

Shlafer M and Marieb EN (Eds.). *The Nurse, Pharmacology, and Drug Therapy.* Redwood City CA: Addison-Wesley, 1989.

Stoudemire A, Moran MG and Fogel BS. Psychotropic drug use in the medically ill: Part I. *Psychosomatics* 31:377–391, 1990.

Swanson J, Wigal S, Greenhill L, et al. Objective and subjective measures of the pharmacodynamic effects of Adderall in the treatment of children with ADHD in a controlled laboratory classroom setting. *Psychopharmacol Bull* 34:55, 1998.

Talbott JA, Hales RE and Yudofsky SC (Eds.). *Textbook of Psychiatry.* Washington DC: American Psychiatric Press, 1988.

Thompson JW, Ware MR and Blashfield RK. Psychotropic medication and priapism: A comprehensive review. *J Clin Psych* 51:430–433, 1990.

Wender PH and Klein DF. *Mind, Mood and Medicine: A Guide to the New Biopsychiatry.* New York: Meridian, 1981.

B
I
B
L
I
O
G
R
A
P
H
Y

# Index